BISON
BOOKS

MAP I

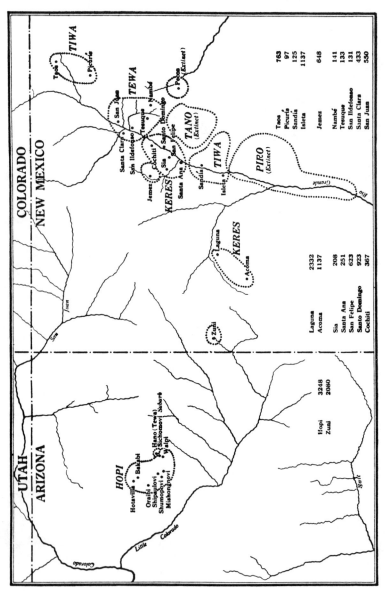

PUEBLOS, 1937

PUEBLO INDIAN RELIGION

Volume I

ELSIE CLEWS PARSONS

Introduction to the Bison Books Edition
by Pauline Turner Strong

University of Nebraska Press
Lincoln and London

⊚ The paper in this book meets the minimum requirements of American
National Standard for Information Sciences—Permanence of Paper for
Printed Library Materials, ANSI Z39.48-1984.

First Bison Books printing: 1996
Most recent printing indicated by the last digit below:
10   9   8   7   6   5   4   3   2   1

Library of Congress Cataloging-in-Publication Data
Parsons, Elsie Worthington Clews, 1875–1941.
Pueblo Indian religion / Elsie Clews Parsons; introduction to the Bison
Books edition by Pauline Turner Strong.—Bison Books ed.
p.   cm.
Vol. 2: Introd. to the Bison Books ed. by Ramón A. Gutiérrez.
Includes bibliographical references and index.
ISBN 0-8032-8735-6 (v. 1: pbk.: alk. paper).—ISBN 0-8032-8736-4 (v. 2:
pbk.: alk. paper)
1. Pueblo Indians—Religion.   2. Pueblo mythology.   3. Pueblo Indi-
ans—Rites and ceremonies.   I. Title.
E99.P9P32   1996
299′.784—dc20
95-47046   CIP

INTRODUCTION TO THE BISON BOOKS EDITION

Pauline Turner Strong

Pueblo Indian Religion, the culmination of over two decades of research and writing on the Pueblos, was hailed soon after its publication in 1939 as "a cornerstone and monumental contribution to American ethnology" (Spier 1943:246). Today, nearly six decades and several theoretical and methodological revolutions later, Elsie Clews Parsons's encyclopedic volumes remain a monumental contribution to scholarship on the Pueblos. *Pueblo Indian Religion* ranks with Eggan's *Social Organization of the Western Pueblos* (1950), Dozier's *The Pueblo Indians of North America* (1970), Ortiz's *New Perspectives on the Pueblos* (1972b) and *Southwest* (1979), and Sando's *The Pueblo Indians* (1976) and *Pueblo Nations* (1992) as indispensable syntheses of scholarly knowledge of Pueblo culture, society, and history.

This is not to say that *Pueblo Indian Religion* and its author are uncontroversial, for the life and work of Elsie Clews Parsons have never been free of controversy. As a modernist, as a feminist, as a pacifist, as an ethnographer, and as an interpreter, Parsons challenged conventions, took liberties, and pushed limits—living and thinking in a way that has brought admiration from the like-minded and disapproval from those who found their conventions violated, be they scholars, pillars of society, or ethnographic subjects.[1]

Born in 1874 into upper-class New York society, Elsie Worthington Clews rebelled at an early age against the expectations and restrictions of her social class—refusing, as her friend and protégée Gladys Reichard noted, "to observe such conventions as she felt were based upon traditional unreason" (1943:45). As an undergraduate at the newly established Barnard College, Elsie found in sociology the basis for a critique of the cultural beliefs underlying women's subordination. Within three years of receiving her B.A. (in 1896), she obtained an M.A. in sociology and a Ph.D. in education at Columbia, after which she assumed a position at Barnard supervising the fieldwork of sociology students. In 1900 she married Herbert Parsons, a lawyer and fellow social reformer, and two years later became a lecturer in sociology at Barnard, teaching on the organization of the family. She gave up the position in 1905 when she accompanied Herbert, a newly elected Republican congressman, to Washington. There she completed a controversial textbook, *The Family* (1906), the first of six books that employed comparative ethnological material to critique contemporary social classifications based on sex, age, race, and nationality.[2]

In 1910 Parsons took a trip to the Southwest that turned her interest from sociology to anthropology. Like many nonconformists of her generation, Parsons found freedom, adventure, solace, and romance in the Southwest. Above all, she relished the intellectual challenge of understanding an unfamiliar set of cultural beliefs and practices. An unpublished memoir, "In the Southwest,"[3] tells of her curiosity being aroused during an exploration of Pueblo ruins whenever her guide, Pedro Baca of Santa Clara Pueblo, became "conspicuously incommunicative." For example, when Baca answered "Don't know" to her request that he explain the purpose of feathers planted at a spring, she was intrigued by "an indifference in the manner of that answer that suggested that he *did* know." Confronted with the wall of silence that surrounds privileged knowledge in the Pueblos, Parsons became all the more interested in the meanings behind that wall. As the memoir puts it, "One thing at least I have learned on this trip, I thought as we rode back to the ranch—what interests me most. Not the artifacts we've dug up or the construction of that chamber or even the impressions of a woman's hand on the plaster of that northern wall, none of these, but the comment of Santiago [Pedro Baca], more particularly his unspoken comment." It was less the "ancient town builders" that interested Parsons than the "minds and ways of their descendants" (Hare 1985:128–29), less the northern wall of the ruin than traversing the wall of silence that separated her from the Tewa guide.

While seemingly a radical departure from her sociological work, Parsons's new interest in Pueblo culture, like her feminism, involved a foray into realms from which she was excluded. Her interest in breaking through Baca's wall of silence, like her modernism, involved a challenge to social classifications she deemed unreasonable. To someone of Baca's upbringing, however, Parsons's questions regarding religious practices would be profoundly threatening. He had learned to respect the power of sacred knowledge, beings, objects, and practices; to approach the sacred only when ritually prepared to do so; and to surround the sacred with protective walls of silence. Unlike Parsons's modernist and rationalist world of rebellion against tradition for the sake of self-expression and freedom of association, Baca's cultural world was one that respected the ancestors and their ways, one that had seen its traditions censored and repressed by colonial powers, one that had protected and sustained itself through erecting walls, both literal and figurative. To be sure, these walls were permeable—and this, in fact, would become Parsons's special interest. But that the walls Parsons most wished to breach were the very walls to which the Pueblos attributed their survival and their well-being: this is the crucial colonial situation of unequal power and disparate meanings within which Parsons's studies of the Pueblos must be evaluated.[4]

Upon returning to the East Parsons soon moved back to New York, where she immersed herself in the ethnological literature on the Southwest and acquainted herself with both the Native American collections and the curators of the American Museum of Natural History. Among the curators were Pliny Goddard and Robert Lowie, both of whom "shared Parsons's mixture of skepticism of received wisdom and concern for social change" and led her to embrace the inductive empiricism of Ernst Mach and Franz Boas (Deacon 1992:25). She soon came into contact with Boas himself and with Alfred Kroeber—both of whom became close friends and colleagues. In 1915, after two additional short trips to the Southwest, Parsons plunged into fieldwork in Zuni, presenting a paper on "Zuñi Pregnancy and Conception Beliefs" (Parsons 1917) that same year. The following year she published the first half-dozen of some ninety professional articles on the Pueblos as well as her last sociological book, *Social Rule* (1916). The book concluded that science offered an escape from the restrictions and intolerance of conventional social classifications—an escape route upon which Parsons had already embarked with uncommon energy, confidence, and absorption.

The centrality of Zuni to the Boasian ethnology of the time is suggested in a letter of 1915 in which Kroeber told Parsons, "You were missed this summer. We were eight of the profession here, Goddard and then Lowie being the last" (Deacon 1992:25). If Zuni was inundated by contentious anthropologists, other pueblos were considerably less well "known," a situation that spurred the "indefatigable" Parsons to visit most of the Pueblos between 1916 and 1932, including Zuni, Acoma, Laguna, Hopi, Jemez, Sandia, Isleta, Cochiti, Santo Domingo, Tesuque, Nambé, Santa Clara, San Ildefonso, San Juan, and Taos.[5] That most of her field trips were brief is acknowledged by Parsons in the introduction to *Pueblo Indian Religion*, where she characterizes her knowledge as based upon a "visiting acquaintance of many years among all the Pueblos" (p. xxxv).

While at Zuni, Parsons stayed at the home of Margaret Lewis, as Kroeber had before her. Mrs. Lewis, a Cherokee ("of three races at least," according to Parsons), originally came to Zuni as a schoolteacher, and married a prominent Zuni man who served as Governor of the Pueblo from 1912 to 1917. Much of Parsons's understanding of the Zunis was mediated through Margaret Lewis, an intelligent woman whose "half White, half Zuni" ways fascinated Parsons, always keenly interested in cultural mixture (Zumwalt 1993:153). In the 1960s Mrs. Lewis remembered Parsons as "a real friend of my husband and me. We always wrote to each other. She had four children, as I have, and they were born at the same times when mine were. We joked about it. Although she was very talkative, we enjoyed having her with us and she was also glad for that. She used to pay us well and we did whatever she wanted us to do. You see, she did not have many friends in Zuni. We were her best friends and we worked hard for her. I am not a Zuni and I don't know everything about the Zunis. So if there was something which Mrs. Parsons wanted to know about them and I didn't know, I asked the people and they told me everything. My husband was an important Zuni and he helped her a lot. One year she asked me to maintain a diary of whatever took place in Zuni and I did that. I guess she got that published as a book" (Pandey 1972:329).

That Margaret Lewis may not have seen *Notes on Zuñi* (1917), which includes her diary of events, is illustrative of Parsons's mode of collaboration—which involved the anthropologist soliciting and interpreting information rather than a mutually produced text—as well as her sense of the audience for ethnographies, which excluded the subjects themselves (but not their descendants). Although not an example of full co-authorship, *Notes on Zuñi* is, indeed, one of the works in which Parsons, like Paul Radin (1913, 1963 [1920]), pioneered in the creation and interpretation of personal documents in order to provide a view of culture "from within" (Parsons 1925b:6). *Pueblo Indian Religion* is enriched by excerpts from several personal journals (pp. 514–31, passim): Margaret Lewis's diary; a remarkable record of an annual round of events in the Hopi town of Sichomovi that Parsons solicited from her Tewa host, Crow-wing (Parsons 1925b); and Parsons's extensively annotated edition of the *Hopi Journal* of Alexander M. Stephen, a Scotsman who married a Hopi and lived in his wife's village from 1880 or 1881 through his death in 1884 (Parsons 1936).

Parsons's lifelong interest in the relationship between cultural conventions and individual experience—which she, like other modernists, construed as mainly antagonistic[6]—together with her desire to influence public opinion, led to a second innovation in ethnographic form: a fictional biography that traces the life of a typical Zuni woman, "Waiyautitsa," from cradleboard to grave (Parsons 1991 [1919]). A piece that, in Parsons's words, derived "the differentiation of sexes at Zuñi" from "the division of labor" rather than "intrinsic differences" (Parsons 1991 [1919]:89, 104), "Wauyautitsa" is one of her most enduring ethnological works—and among those that shows the most obvious continuity with her feminist sociology. After its publication Parsons persuaded Boas, Kroeber, Lowie, Spier, Radin, Sapir, and other anthropologists to write similar fictional pieces, which she gathered together with a revised "Waiyautitsa" into a popular collection, *American Indian Life*, illustrated by her friend Grant LaFarge (Parsons 1922b). In the introduction to the collection Parsons identifies herself as a "Member of the Hopi Tribe," basing this designation upon the formal hair-washing and name-bestowing ceremony given her by a Hopi host in the hope that clan membership would mitigate others' opposition to her presence. By all accounts the adoption meant a lot to Parsons, although she, like her host, thought of the ceremony instrumentally, hoping (in vain, it turned out) that it would help her obtain entrance to ceremonies closed to non-Hopis (Hare 1985:

143–45). Perhaps she used her adoption in an equally instrumental way in *American Indian Life*, seeking to appeal to an audience that, as she wrote in her preface, usually got their ideas about Indians from romantic novels.

Partly because of restrictions on her movements and observations, partly because of her concern for individual expression and variation, and partly because of her thoroughgoing empiricism, Parsons's ethnographic studies are polyphonic and situated, meshing together her own observations, those of other scholars, and native texts (in English); generalizations, speculations, and examples of individual "deviations and rebellions"; and assessments of both informants' accuracy and the limitations of her own knowledge (Boyer 1971:21; cf. Babcock 1987, 1991a). As a comparative survey and summation of a life's work, *Pueblo Indian Religion* is inevitably couched in a more impersonal and authoritative voice than many of Parsons's writings. Even here, however, she is by no means an invisible or omniscient narrator. She draws widely on the work of others, makes frequent use of anecdotes, admits the incompleteness of her knowledge, and ties her own material to particular informants, indicating through the latter practice that even this broad-sweeping synthesis is dependent upon a research method that typically relied, in each town, upon one or two key informants—often, like Margaret Lewis and Crowwing, some kind of outsider.[7]

In contrast to the Western Pueblos, where she lived in the governor's house at Zuni and was adopted into a Hopi clan, Parsons's research in the more secretive Rio Grande Pueblos was generally clandestine.[8] Even at Zuni she sometimes resorted to deceit, as she reveals in introducing the revised "Waiyautitsa" with a reference to seeking "the shrines of the War Leaders and the Song Youth and the Earth Woman as we ostensibly hunted rabbits" (1967 [1922a]:157). In the Eastern Pueblos she routinely "imitat[ed] the secretiveness observed in all the Rio Grande Pueblos," meeting with informants alone or in pairs outside the pueblos, usually on a ranch (Parsons 1929:7, quoted in Babcock 1994:xi). Employing an interpreter related to the informant, she would persuade both to reveal sensitive or privileged religious knowledge through payments or exchange of information.

Parsons called this her "secretive method," and was not unaware of its questionable ethics or its potential for personal and social devastation. She knew that trespassing in the area of shrines, except by those ritually empowered to do so, leads to their desecration (p. 311), and at Taos was told, "*Our ways would lose their power if they were known,* just as Zuñi ways and the ways of other places have lost their power" (Parsons 1936a:14, quoted in Zumwalt 1993:240). She knew that "story telling is not always a harmless pastime in the Southwest" (Parsons 1994 [1926]:6), and that religious objects and knowledge are dangerous and surrounded with restrictions to protect initiates and non-initiates alike (pp. 167, 491). Informants told her they would be jailed or killed for revealing privileged knowledge, that they feared bringing illness or a difficult pregnancy upon themselves, or that they felt compelled to confess their betrayal before dying (p. 83). Joe B. Lente, an Isleta painter who offered to sell paintings of social and ceremonial life to Parsons in order to support himself—eventually producing over 140 paintings—did so fearing he would be killed if discovered, and wrote Parsons of his deep sense of shame (Goldfrank 1967).[9] Parsons herself wrote in letters of having "kidnapped" an Isleta informant and "cleaned out" a woman from San Juan, and upon another occasion called herself "the most ruthless of detectives" (Zumwalt 1993:244–45; Babcock 1994:xi; Hare 1985:146).[10]

At Taos, Jemez, San Juan, and elsewhere, the publication of Parsons's monographs (Parsons 1925a, 1926, 1936a) prompted animosity toward and reprisals against those believed to have betrayed their people. Trying to prevent this—and viewing her work as primarily for the consumption of other anthropologists—Parsons attempted to conceal the identity of many of her informants in publications, and to keep all her works, including *Pueblo Indian Religion*, from being distributed outside of scholarly circles in the Southwest.[11] While she voiced regret over the consequences of the dissemination of her manuscripts in the Pueblos—particularly at Taos, where her friends Tony and Mabel Dodge Luhan were targets of hostility—she continued to justify her scholarship in terms of her scientific commitment to documenting a way of life and thought she saw as disintegrating. In the end, Parsons's "secretive method"—which was adopted by her protégé Leslie White and others—exacerbated factionalism in the Pueblos, reinforced their self-protective secrecy, and increased their suspicion of anthropologists and other outsiders. Parsons's sense of Western science's entitlement to Pueblo religious knowledge continues to this day to cast a shadow upon her oeuvre on the Pueblos.[12]

As exploitative as were her relationships with many of her informants, Parsons was dedicated to egalitarian collaboration among scholars. In 1918, soon after initiating her own research in the Southwest, Parsons founded the Southwest Society, an organization that, until her death in 1941, supported and coordinated ethnological fieldwork and the publication of research results—including dozens of volumes with expensive color plates. Under the auspices of the Southwest Society, Parsons supported the work of Franz Boas, Ruth Benedict, Ruth Bunzel, Esther Goldfrank, and Leslie White on the Pueblos, as well as, among others, Gladys Reichard, Ruth Underhill, Berard Haile, and Morris Opler. In addition to serving as a benefactor, Parsons was a mentor to many younger anthropologists, particularly Gladys Reichard and Leslie White. She also underwrote the *Journal of American Folklore*, and served for many years as assistant editor.

According to Reichard, Parsons was "herself an institution" (1943:45)—a characterization that, given her aversion to all things institutional (Friedlander 1988:284), she would likely not have appreciated. Although her classroom teaching of anthropology amounted to one term at the New School in 1919 (when she introduced Benedict to anthropology), between her financial support, her mentoring, her prolific publications, and her service to the American Folklore Society, the American Ethnological Society, and the American Anthropological Association (over which she presided in 1918–20, 1923–25, and 1940–41 respectively), Parsons was central to the development of American anthropology between the world wars (cf. Stocking 1992a).

Upon at least two occasions Parsons's social and institutional prominence allowed her to be of genuine service to the Pueblos. When the U.S. Senate's passage of the Bursum bill in 1922 threatened Pueblo land tenure and water rights, Parsons contacted friends in Congress and the press; organized resolutions on behalf of the Pueblos from the Peabody Musuem, the American Ethnological Society, and the American Anthropological Association; helped to form the Eastern

Association of Indian Affairs, a non-Indian advocacy group; and organized public gatherings with and publicity for a Pueblo delegation to Washington. When this threat passed, Parsons turned her attention to opposing an executive order of Indian Commissioner Charles H. Burke that prohibited summer religious ceremonies in the Pueblos on the grounds that they took time better spent in agricultural labor. The opposition to Burke, like that to Bursum, was successful, and ultimately led to the appointment of John Collier, a reformer active in both struggles, to head the Bureau of Indian Affairs under Franklin Roosevelt (Zumwalt 1993: 257–67). It would seem that these experiences in the political arena might have led Parsons to reevaluate her assessment of the future of Pueblo religion, and to consider the disintegration she and her colleagues had witnessed as at least partly reversible through more extensive political reform. However, at the time she wrote *Pueblo Indian Religion* Parsons was convinced that Pueblo religious life was not only changing but disintegrating under the twin assaults of Protestantism and capitalism (see vol. 2, pp. 1127–65). She advocated urgent research efforts on that basis— without, however, acknowledging that intense research by outsiders might, in fact, actively contribute to religious disintegration through heightening factionalism and secrecy.[13]

Pueblo Indian Religion, published just two years before Parsons's death, was conceived as early as 1918, and is the product of over two decades of intermittent research on the Pueblos. (During that time Parsons completed other research projects as well, including her acclaimed *Mitla: Town of the Souls* (1936b), an acculturation study of the Zapotecs of Oaxaca that grew out of her interest in Spanish influence upon the Pueblos.) The theoretical framework for *Pueblo Indian Religion* was largely established by 1924, when in two landmark articles (1924a, 1924b), Parsons began to address systematic variations in social organization and religious ceremonialism between the eastern and the western Pueblos. *Pueblo Indian Religion* builds upon these articles, incorporating not only her own research but the entire corpus of Pueblo ethnology, Boasian and pre-Boasian, into a discussion of continuities, variations, and innovations in religious belief and practice across the Pueblos. Despite its broad scope and detailed exposition, Parsons considered her *magnum opus* far from complete, and concluded with an ambitious program for future research (vol. 2, pp. 1211–13). "We have much to learn," she stressed, "in a shortening period" (p. xxxvi).

In classic Boasian fashion Parsons begins by defining "religion" as an external classification for a domain that is not differentiated in Pueblo experience. "Obviously," she writes in the Preface, "from both native and scientific points of view this book should be concerned with the entire life of the Pueblos and not merely with the aspect we are pleased to call their religion" (p. xxxiv). Despite this caution, however, she brings a modernist, rationalistic bias to her study in describing religion as "less antithesis to science" than "science gone astray," a realm based on analagous thought that "precludes fruitful observation" and involves "causation pondered falsely" (pp. xxxiii, 1154, 97).

The meticulous detail of *Pueblo Indian Religion* is perhaps best understood through Reichard's recollection that Parsons "thought of her work as a mosaic," and "hated to omit any detail, even if at the time it might seem irrelevant, for she believed, and often had had proved to her satisfaction, that the record of an apparently trivial detail might after many years furnish an invaluable clue to someone with a different point of view" (Reichard 1943: 47). In her attachment to empirical detail and awareness of the significance of the interpreter's perspective, as well as in her attention to historical processes, Parsons was a consummate modernist and Boasian. Similarly modernist, as well as feminist, is her disenchantment with the patriarchal individualism of her own society. Although her approach to the Pueblos pioneered the "repressive" or coercive interpretation that Bennett (1946) opposes to Benedict's "organic" or idealistic interpretation (cf. Stocking 1992b), Parsons does strike an idealistic note in her preface and introduction, which offer praise for the Pueblos' "social cohesion and integrity" and close with appreciation for their "co-operative spirit" and "way of identifying the good of the individual with the common good." Crow-Wing has nearly the last word in the introduction: "So everybody is very busy, everybody is helping. Because at any time anyone may need help, therefore all help one another" (pp. xxix–xxxvi, 109–11).

While in these passages Parsons suggests that much could be learned *from* the Pueblos, her writings are primarily concerned with what could be learned *about* them. As the telegraphic, somewhat undigested prose of some portions of *Pueblo Indian Religion* suggests, Parsons worked with a sense of great urgency, attempting to locate and fill in "gaps" in knowledge "before the Pueblo cultures disappear, in a few generations" (p. xxxvi). Fortunately, Parsons and her contemporaries have been proven wrong in their estimation that the Pueblos and their ceremonial life would soon become extinct. Quite to the contrary, in the five decades between the publication of the original edition of *Pueblo Indian Religion* and this reprint, there has been a renaissance in Pueblo religion that has included both a revitalization of ceremonial life and a renewed control over sacred knowledge, sites, and objects (Vecsey 1991; Merrill, Ladd, and Ferguson 1993; Ortiz, n.d.). Taos Pueblo, for example, succeeded in 1970 in regaining control over its sacred Blue Lake after a struggle that dates to Parsons's earliest years in the Southwest (Bodine 1973, 1988; Hecht 1989). Equally dramatic is the success of the Zuni Tribe in regaining, between 1978 and 1992, sixty-nine *Ahayu:da*—sacred images of the brothers Uyuyewi and Ma'a'sewi, the powerful protectors known in English as "war gods"—that had been removed from shrines by anthropologists and others, and held in museum and private collections throughout the U.S. (Robert E. Lewis, the son of the governor during Parsons's fieldwork at Zuni, was instrumental in negotiating the repatriation during his own service as governor.)

While Parsons did not remove *Ahayu:da* from Zuni, she did visit their shrines, and both *Pueblo Indian Religion* (fig. 2, passim) and an earlier article include a detailed drawing and discussion of the *Ahayu:da*. In the article Parsons reports turning down the opportunity to "bargain" for objects found at a shrine "since not only the [pieces for the] altar games but an image of the war god were, I knew, accessible for study elsewhere" (in the American Museum of Natural History). She attributed her guide's willingness to bargain to what she called "religious formalism," claiming that "fear of being found out and fear lest something will happen, i.e., magically, is all he [the generic Zuni] appears to know of reverence" (1918:397). In contrast, Zuni anthropologist Edmund J. Ladd attributes the sales of sacred objects to hunger, and has found contemporary Zunis quite saddened that "the Zunis had not thought about the consequences of 'selling their life' and perhaps not being able to enter the afterworld because they were trying to feed themselves"—a reference to the belief that the spirit invested in a sacred object is trapped if the object is preserved rather than allowed to disintegrate (Merrill, Ladd, and Ferguson 1993:547).

Both the continuing significance of Parsons's work and the stunning transformation of ethnographic practice between her time and ours is indicated in a recent article describing the negotiations among Zuni leaders, museum curators, and anthropologists over repatriation. While the article reprints the sketch of the *Ahayu:da* found in Parsons's works, it does so with the explicit permission of the Zuni Tribe, and identifies it not as a "war god image" (an erroneous designation) from the "altar-shrine on Corn Mountain" (a sacred site) but more intimately as the "image of the younger brother Ahayu:da created by the Bear clan" (Merrill, Ladd, and Ferguson 1993:523).

This reprint of *Pueblo Indian Religion* appears at a time of continued or renewed interest in Parsons's work among at least four groups of potential readers. In the first place, some contemporary readers will be Pueblo Indians themselves, an eventuality that Parsons foresaw, although she did not predict that such readers might actively practice their native religion, nor that they might extend or challenge her interpretations in scholarly works, as have Edward Dozier, a Hopi-Tewa, Alfonso Ortiz of San Juan, Joe Sando of Jemez, Edmund Ladd of Zuni, and others.

Undoubtedly the volumes remain of interest to students of Pueblo belief and ritual—who, as Parsons hoped, continue to mine her "massive marshalling of data" (White 1973:582), aided by the detailed index, while employing newer interpretive frameworks and working under quite different conditions. Contemporary scholars tend to study much more localized and specialized religious phenomena than Parsons, conducting intensive, long-term studies of one Pueblo in the native language; collaborating closely with or working within limits set by religious leaders; attending primarily to relatively public knowledge and events; and analyzing closely the local meanings and uses of symbolic forms such as cosmologies and landscapes, rituals and art forms, narratives and songs. Interest in historical processes such as innovation and syncretism (now hybridity) and polyphonic and dialogical forms of ethnographic representation have reemerged after a period of structuralist studies.[14] Perhaps most significantly, religious themes are now explored as much, or more, in the writings of Pueblo writers and artists than in the works of anthropologists.

Scholars in the fields of feminist and gender studies have recently turned their attention to Parsons's studies of reproduction, socialization, gender roles, and institutionalized gender-crossing in the Pueblos. Mythological and ceremonial expressions of gender and sexuality are scattered throughout the volumes, while the introduction—praised in its time as the "first rounded discriminating general account of Pueblo life" (Spier 1943:246)—generalizes upon Parsons's pathbreaking articles on marriage, childbearing, childrearing, rites of passage, and gender roles (see Babcock 1991b). While Parsons wrote one of her first and one of her last ethnological publications on the Zuni *lhamana* or "transvestite" (Parsons 1916b, 1939), relatively little is included in these volumes (but see vol. 2, p. 1268).

Ethnohistorians, colonial historians, and others will continue to turn to *Pueblo Indian Religion* in the context of ongoing debates on the course of Pueblo history.[15] While many of Parsons's interpretations have been challenged in or superseded by subsequent works, when used judiciously *Pueblo Indian Religion* continues to be a valuable source for students of historical processes among the Pueblos, between the Pueblos and other indigenous peoples, and between the Pueblos and their Spanish and Anglo-American colonizers.

In a recent assessment of Parsons's life and work Louis Hieb writes that "most of us today find Parsons' work a source of frustration. We go to her for answers to our questions only to find that her answers—for all their scientific rigor and concern for accuracy—were shaped by very different questions" (1993:73). Some would disagree: Lurie, for example, has pointed to Parsons's concern for historical process as as an indication of the place of her work "in the modern tradition of anthropology" (1966:74). Others would point more specifically to Parsons's interest in "heterogeneity within a culture" (p. xxxi) and in processes of syncretism, resistance, and innovation (chapters 8 and 9); still others, such as Babcock (1991a) and Roscoe (1991), to her anticipation of recent work on the cultural construction of gender. Hieb, for his part, is particularly frustrated by what he sees as a lack of concern with meaning in Parsons's work. Because of its scope this is more true of *Pueblo Indian Religion* than of some of her other works, but even in these two volumes a concern for meaning underlies Parsons's accumulation of detail and analysis of their complex interrelationships—but hers is a meaning that resides more in particular modes of thought, speech, and action than in underlying themes or coherent patterns, a meaning that is fragmentary, pluralistic, particularistic, and open-ended.

As she writes in the Preface, Parsons preferred thinking in terms of "habits of life and mind" over Kroeber's "cultural core" or Benedict's "configurations." When she ventures to offer an "impressionistic" preliminary cultural analysis in the introduction, analyzing such "mental traits" or "attitudes" as avoidance of conflict, reciprocity, concentration and self-control, metaphorical thought processes, and cooperation, she does so in a tentative fashion. To her credit, Parsons carefully qualifies these as traits evident in texts and rituals, stressing that "in what degree these traits characterize the individual Pueblo [person] I do not know" (pp. xxxii–xxxiv, 76–111). Her nonsystematizing, nonessentializing, anti-reductionist approach bears obvious resemblances to both the modernist and Boasian empiricism in which it is rooted and the postmodern ethnography to which it points (cf. Lamphere 1989; Babcock 1987, 1991a). If ultimately unsatisfying to the contemporary reader, one suspects it was so also for Parsons, who wished to convey how "religion is felt by the insider as an integral part of his life" (p. xxxiii). This is conveyed to some extent in the many native statements sprinkled (in translation) throughout the text, but for a better sense of how particular beliefs and practices fit together to form meaningful experience one must turn to her fictional biography and edited journals.

In approaching *Pueblo Indian Religion* today it is useful to remember the reply of T. N. Pandey's astute Zuni hostess (who had also hosted Benedict and Bunzel) when he remarked that Zuni had changed a lot. "So have anthropologists," she shot back. "You are not asking me what Mr. Kroeber used to ask" (Pandey 1972:333). Both Pueblo religion and anthropological scholarship have changed profoundly since these volumes were originally published, and both are complex, internally differentiated, and contested domains. We may bring different questions to the text and find different meanings embedded therein than did Parsons or her contemporaries—but this, as Reichard has written, is precisely what Parsons expected. Regarding this, if not the resiliency of Pueblo religion, she was prescient.

1. Babcock (1987) uses the phrase "taking liberties." My approach is consistent with Lamphere's (1989, 1992) and Gordon's (1993) in its attention to how Parsons is implicated in neocolonial power relations, which Gordon has called the "complex underside of white women's ethnographic practice" (1993:130). I am grateful to Desley Deacon for allowing me to read a draft of her forthcoming biography of Parsons (Deacon, n.d.), which is especially illuminating with regard to her modernism. I am also indebted to Desley Deacon, Alfonso Ortiz, and Kamala Visweswaran for insights and suggestions, and to Raymond D. Fogelson for stimulating and encouraging my interest in Parsons's contributions to psychological anthropology (Strong n.d.).

2. The sociological critiques were published between 1906 and 1916, along with many popular articles. For Parsons's bibliography, see Reichard (1943), to which Hare (1985:169) adds several titles.

3. Zumwalt (1992:229–79) quotes extensively from "In the Southwest," a yet-unpublished three-hundred-page memoir written for a popular audience that contains many valuable discussions of Parsons's fieldwork (Babcock, n.d.).

4. My discussion of privileged knowledge and Parsons's modernism derives primarily from discussions with Alfonso Ortiz and Desley Deacon, respectively; written sources include Merrill, Ladd, and Ferguson (1993), Deacon (1992, n.d.), and Manganaro (1990b). For analyses of ethnography in "colonial situations," see Stocking (1991); for silence as resistance, Visweswaran (1994:60–72).

5. Both White (1932:5) and Reichard (1943:45) characterize Parsons as an indefatigable worker. Zumwalt (1992:274, n. 2) gives dates for Parsons's fieldwork, which also took her to the Caddo, Kiowa, Navajo, and Pima reservations for comparative research.

6. Leslie Spier wrote in Parsons's obituary that her work consistently stemmed from "a desire to understand others, the trammels of their conventions, and a positive credo—by which she lived rigorously—to allow the utmost freedom of self-expression to every individual, herself included" (Spier 1943:245). Handler (1990) discusses the modernist tension between convention and self-expression in the work of Benedict, whose resolution differed markedly from that of both Sapir and Parsons.

7. In addition to Margaret Lewis (p. 4) and Crow-Wing (p. 20), early on in *Pueblo Indian Religion* Parsons refers to her informant at Jemez, originally from Santa Clara (p. 7); her friend at Laguna, an Isleta woman married into the Pueblo (p. 11); and Nick [Tomaka], the "outstanding intellectual" who opposed the authority of the Bow Priests by calling in Anglo-American authorities when he was being tried for witchcraft as a young man, subsequently established himself as a religious authority, and served as a "courageous informant" for anthropologists at Zuni from Stevenson's to Bunzel's time (p. 64, passim). On Tomaka [Tumaka, Dumaka], see Pandey (1972), Eggan and Pandey (1979:477) and Roscoe (1991:243 n44 and passim).

8. Commentators who write of Parsons's close relationships with her Pueblo hosts and collaborators are generally referring to her research at Zuni and Hopi (e.g. Friedlander 1988:287; Babcock 1994:ix). An accurate appraisal of her ethnographic relationships must also take into account those she established in the Eastern Pueblos with collaborators who did not also serve as hosts.

9. The Isleta paintings were published posthumously by Esther Goldfrank with an introduction by Parsons (Parsons 1962).

10. In his obituary Kroeber also applied the term "ruthless" to Parsons, writing that not only as an intellectual but "as a person, she was dominated by a similar uncompromisingness, which at times took on the appearance of ruthlessness. She was ruthless toward sentimentality, weakness, and sham, yet never needlessly unkind. . . . She valued control preeminently: first in herself, next in others." He also noted that she was "spiritually close kin to Boas" in the tenacity with which she maintained her point of view (1943:255). Babcock (1991a:x) praises similar qualities—that she was "intrepid" and "indomitable"—from a feminist perspective, but it should be noted that these qualities in the ethnographic setting can only be called colonialist. Recent reappraisals of Parsons's work, in their enthusiasm for her feminism, have generally neglected the ethical issues involved when a scorn for conventions—including those of others—structures ethnographic research.

11. According to Zumwalt (1992:248), Robert Redfield agreed to Parsons's request to restrict distribution of *Pueblo Indian Religion* by the University of Chicago Press.

12. Zumwalt (1992:227–57) contains the fullest treatment of Parsons's research methods although, as Handler (1993:1127) notes, its consideration of the ethical issues involved remains inadequate. For brief discussions, see Simmons (1979:219), Bodine (1979:267), Hare (1985:147, 162), Deacon (1992:29–30), Hieb (1993:71–73), and Pandey, who discusses the Zu-

nis' realization early in this century that "they had been betrayed by anthropologists; that is, some of them had written about aspects of Zuni life that had been told in confidence" (1972:322). For an insightful and disturbing meditation on "betrayal" in contemporary feminist ethnography, see Visweswaran (1994:40–59).

13. Clifford (1981) has expressed suspicion at the "persistent and repetitious 'disappearance' of social forms at the moment of their ethnographic representation," and concludes that preservation of the disappearing ethnographic object is a central legitimating allegory of modernist anthropology (Clifford 1981:112–13; Manganaro 1990a:29–30).

14. Relatively contemporary works on Pueblo religion include Ortiz (1969), B. Tedlock (1992), and M. J. Young (1988) on cosmology and world view; Ortiz (1972a), Hieb (1972), and Rodríguez (1991) on ritual; D. Tedlock (1972, 1983) and Frisbie (1989 [1980]) on narrative and song; and R. Gutiérrez (1991) and B. Tedlock (1992) on syncretism and hybridity.

15. For the debate surrounding Gutiérrez's history, see Rodríguez (1994). Other interpretations of Pueblo history, excluding works on individual Pueblos, include Dozier (1961), Spicer (1962), Ortiz (1979), Cordell (1984), Cordell and Gumerman (1989), Sando (1992), and Weber (1992).

BIBLIOGRAPHY

Babcock, Barbara A.
1987 Taking Liberties, Writing from the Margins, and Doing It with a Difference. *Journal of American Folklore* 100:390–411.
1991a Elsie Clews Parsons and the Pueblo Construction of Gender. In *Pueblo Mothers and Children*, ed. Babcock, pp. 1–27. Santa Fe: Ancient City Press.
1991b (ed.) *Pueblo Mothers and Children: Essays by Elsie Clews Parsons, 1915–1924*. Santa Fe: Ancient City Press.
1994 Foreward to *Tewa Tales* by Elsie Clews Parsons, pp. vii–xix. Reprint. Tucson and London: University of Arizona Press.
n.d. (ed.) *In The Southwest*. Albuquerque: University of New Mexico Press, forthcoming.
Bennett, John
1946 The Interpretation of Pueblo Culture: A Question of Values. *Southwestern Journal of Anthropology* 2:361–74.
Bodine, John J.
1973 Blue Lake: A Struggle for Indian Rights. *American Indian Law Review*, vol. 1, no. 1.

1979 Taos Pueblo. In *Southwest*, ed. Alfonso Ortiz. Volume 9, *Handbook of North American Indians*, pp. 255–67. William C. Sturtevant, general ed. Washington DC: Smithsonian Institution.

1988 The Taos Blue Lake Ceremony. *American Indian Quarterly* 12(2):91–126.

Boyer, Paul S.

1971 Elsie Clews Parsons. In *Notable American Women, 1601–1950*, vol. 3, ed. Edward T. James, Janet Wilson James, and Paul S. Boyer, pp. 20–22. Cambridge: Belknap Press of Harvard University Press.

Clifford, James

1986 On Ethnographic Allegory. In *Writing Culture: The Poetics and Politics of Ethnography*, ed. James Clifford and George Marcus, pp. 98–121. Berkeley: University of California Press.

Cordell, Linda S.

1984 *Prehistory of the Southwest*. Orlando FL: Academic Press.

——— and George J. Gumerman, eds.

1989 *Dynamics of Southwest Prehistory*. Washington DC: Smithsonian Institution Press.

Deacon, Desley

1992 "The Republic of the Spirit": Fieldwork in Elsie Clews Parson's Turn to Anthropology. *Frontiers* 12:13–38.

n.d. *Elsie Clews Parsons: Constructing Sex and Culture in Modernist America*. Chicago: University of Chicago Press, forthcoming.

Dozier, Edward P.

1961 Rio Grande Pueblos. In *Perspectives in American Indian Culture Change*, ed. Edward H. Spicer, pp. 94–186. Chicago and London: University of Chicago Press.

1970 *The Pueblo Indians of North America*. New York: Holt, Rinehart and Winston, Inc.

Eggan, Fred

1950 *Social Organization of the Western Pueblos*. Chicago: University of Chicago Press.

——— and T. N. Pandey

1979 Zuni History, 1850–1970. In *Southwest*, ed. Alfonso Ortiz. Volume 9, *Handbook of North American Indians*, pp. 474–81. William C. Sturtevant, general ed. Washington DC: Smithsonian Institution.

Friedlander, Judith

1988 Elsie Clews Parsons. In *Women Anthropologists: Selected Biographies*, ed. Ute Gacs, Jerrie McIntyre, and Ruth Weinberg, pp. 282–90. Urbana: University of Illinois Press.

Frisbie, Charlotte S.
1989 [1980] *Southwestern Indian Ritual Drama*. Prospect Heights IL: Waveland Press.

Goldfrank, Esther S.
1967 *The Artist of "Isleta Paintings" in Pueblo Society*. Smithsonian Contributions to Anthropology, vol. 5. Washington: Smithsonian Press.

Gordon, Deborah
1993 Among Women: Gender and Ethnographic Authority of the Southwest, 1930–1980. In *Hidden Scholars: Women Anthropologists and the Native American Southwest*, pp. 129–45. Albuquerque: University of New Mexico Press.

Gutiérrez, Ramón
1991 *When Jesus Came, the Corn Mothers Went Away: Marriage, Sexuality, and Power in New Mexico, 1500–1846*. Stanford: Stanford University Press.

Handler, Richard
1990 Ruth Benedict and the Modernist Sensibility. In *Modernist Anthropology; From Fieldwork to Text*, ed. Marc Manganaro, pp. 163–80. Princeton NJ: Princeton University Press.
1993 Review of *Wealth and Rebellion* by Rosemary Zumwalt. *Journal of American History* 80:1126–27.

Hare, Peter
1985 *A Woman's Quest for Science: Portrait of Anthropologist Elsie Clews Parsons*. Buffalo NY: Prometheus Books.

Hecht, Robert A.
1989 Taos Pueblo and the Struggle for Blue Lake. *American Indian Culture and Research Journal* 13(1):53–77.

Hieb, Louis A.
1972 Meaning and Mismeaning: Toward an Understanding of the Ritual Clown. In *New Perspectives on the Pueblos*, ed. Alfonso Ortiz, pp. 163–95. Albuquerque: University of New Mexico Press.
1993 Elsie Clews Parsons in the Southwest. In *Hidden Scholars: Women Anthropologists and the Native American Southwest*, pp. 63–75. Albuquerque: University of New Mexico Press.

Kroeber, A. L.
1943 Elsie Clews Parsons. *American Anthropologist* 45:252–55.

Lamphere, Louise
1989 Feminist Anthropology: The Legacy of Elsie Clews Parsons. *American Ethnologist* 16:518–33.
1992 Women, Anthropology, Tourism, and the Southwest. *Frontiers* 12:5–11.

Lurie, Nancy
    1966 Women in Early American Anthropology. In *Pioneers of Ameri-
        can Anthropology*, ed. June Helm, pp. 29–82. Seattle: University
        of Washington Press.
Manganaro, Marc
    1990a Textual Play, Power, and Cultural Critique: An Orientation to
        Modernist Anthropology. In *Modernist Anthropology: From Field-
        work to Text*, ed. Manganaro, pp. 3–47. Princeton NJ: Princeton
        University Press.
    1990b (ed.) *Modernist Anthropology: From Fieldwork to Text*. Princeton
        NJ: Princeton University Press.
Merrill, William L., Edmund J. Ladd, and T. J. Ferguson
    1993 The Return of the Ahayu:da. *Current Anthropology* 34:523–67.
Ortiz, Alfonso
    1969 *The Tewa World*. Chicago: University of Chicago Press.
    1972a "Ritual Drama and the Pueblo World View." In *New Perspec-
        tives on the Pueblos*, ed. Ortiz, pp. 135–61. Albuquerque: Uni-
        versity of New Mexico Press.
    1972b (ed.) *New Perspectives on the Pueblos*. Albuquerque: University
        of New Mexico Press.
    1979 (ed.) *Southwest*. Volume 9, *Handbook of North American Indi-
        ans*. William C. Sturtevant, general ed. Washington DC:
        Smithsonian Institution.
    n.d. Special Issue on Native American Religious Freedom. *Cultural
        Survival Quarterly*. Forthcoming.
Pandey, Triloki Nath
    1972 Anthropologists at Zuni. *Proceedings of the American Philosophi-
        cal Society* 116:321–37.
Parsons, Elsie Clews
    1906 *The Family: An Ethnographical and Historical Outline*. New York:
        G. P. Putnam's Sons.
    1916a *Social Rule: A Study of the Will to Power*. New York: G. P.
        Putnam's Sons.
    1916b The Zuñi La'mana. *American Anthropologist* 18:521–28. Re-
        printed in *Pueblo Mothers and Children*, ed. Barbara A. Babcock,
        pp. 39–47. Santa Fe: Ancient City Press.
    1917 *Notes on Zuñi*. Memoirs of the American Anthropological Asso-
        ciation, no. 4.
    1918 War God Shrines of the Laguna and Zuñi. *American Anthropolo-
        gist* 20:381–404.
    1919 Waiyautitea of Zuñi, New Mexico. *Scientific Monthly* 9:443–57.

Reprinted in *Pueblo Mothers and Children*, ed. Barbara A. Babcock, pp. 89–105. Santa Fe: Ancient City Press.

1922a [1967] Waiyautitea of Zuñi, New Mexico. In *American Indian Life*, ed. Parsons, pp. 157–73. Lincoln: University of Nebraska Press.

1922b (ed.) *American Indian Life*. New York: B. W. Huebsch.

1924a Tewa Kin, Clan, and Moiety. *American Anthropologist* 26:333–39.

1924b The Religion of the Pueblo Indians. *Proceedings of the 21st International Congress of Americanists*, pp. 140–48. The Hague: E. J. Brill.

1925a *The Pueblo of Jemez*. Papers of the Southwestern Expedition, no. 3. New Haven: Yale University Press.

1925b (ed.) *A Pueblo Indian Journal, 1920–21*. Memoirs of the American Anthropological Association, no. 32.

1929 *The Social Organization of the Tewa in New Mexico*. Memoirs of the American Anthropological Association, no. 36.

1936a *Taos Pueblo*. General Series in Anthropology, no. 2. Menasha WI: American Anthropological Association.

1936b (ed.) *Hopi Journal of Alexander M. Stephen*. Columbia University Contributions in Anthropology, no. 23.

1939 The Last Zuñi Transvestite. *American Anthropologist* 41:338–40.

1962 *Isleta Paintings*. Ed. Esther S. Goldfrank. Bureau of American Ethnology Bulletin, no. 181. Washington: Smithsonian Institution.

1991 *Pueblo Mothers and Children: Essays by Elsie Clews Parsons, 1915–1924*, ed. Barbara C. Babcock. Santa Fe: Ancient City Press.

1994 [1926] *Tewa Tales*. Memoirs of the American Folklore Society, no. 19. Reprint with new foreword by Barbara A. Babcock. Tucson: University of Arizona Press.

Radin, Paul

1913 Personal Reminiscences of a Winnebago Indian. *Journal of American Folklore* 26:293–318.

1963 [1920] *The Autobiography of a Winnebago Indian*. University of California Publications in American Archaeology and Ethnology, no. 16. Reprint. New York: Dover Publications.

Reichard, Gladys

1943 Elsie Clews Parsons. *Journal of American Folklore* 56:45–56.

Rodríguez, Sylvia

1991 The Taos Pueblo Matachines: Ritual Symbolism and Interethnic Relations. *American Ethnologist* 18:234–57.

1994 Subaltern Historiography on the Rio Grande: On Gutiérrez's *When Jesus Came, The Corn Mothers Went Away*. *American Ethnologist* 21:892–99.

Roscoe, Will

    1991 *The Zuni Man-Woman*. Albuquerque: University of New Mexico Press.

Sando, Joe S.

    1976 *The Pueblo Indians*. [San Francisco]: Indian Historian Press.

    1992 *Pueblo Nations: Eight Centuries of Pueblo Indian History*. Santa Fe NM: Clear Light.

Simmons, Marc

    1979 History of the Pueblos since 1921. In *Southwest*, ed. Alfonso Ortiz. Volume 9, *Handbook of North American Indians*, pp. 206–23. William C. Sturtevant, general ed. Washington DC: Smithsonian Institution.

Spicer, Edward H.

    1962 *Cycles of Conquest*. Tucson: University of Arizona Press.

Spier, Leslie

    1943 Elsie Clews Parsons. *American Anthropologist* 45:244–51.

Stocking, George W., Jr.

    1991 (ed.) *Colonial Situations: Essays on the Contextualization of Ethnographic Knowledge*. History of Anthropology, vol. 7. Madison: University of Wisconsin Press.

    1992a Ideas and Institutions in American Anthropology Thoughts Toward a History of the Interwar Years. In Stocking, *The Ethnographer's Magic and Other Essays in the History of Anthropology*, 114–77. Madison: University of Wisconsin Press.

    1992b The Ethnographic Sensibility of the 1920s and the Dualism of the Anthropological Tradition. In Stocking, *The Ethnographer's Magic and Other Essays in the History of Anthropology*, pp. 276–341. Madison: University of Wisconsin Press.

Strong, Pauline Turner

    n.d. Culture from Within: Experimental Ethnographic Writing on the Pueblos, 1919–1929. In History of Anthropology, vol. 10. Madison: University of Wisconsin Press, forthcoming.

Tedlock, Barbara

    1992 *The Beautiful and the Dangerous: Dialogues with the Zuni Indians*. New York: Viking.

Tedlock, Dennis

    1972 *Finding the Center: Narrative Poetry of the Zuni Indians*. New York: Dial.

    1983 *The Spoken Word and the Work of Interpretation*. Philadelphia: University of Pennsylvania Press.

Vecsey, Christopher, ed.

    1991 *Handbook of American Indian Religious Freedom*. New York: Crossroad.

Visweswaran, Kamala
  1994 *Fictions of Feminist Ethnography*. Minneapolis: University of Minnesota Press.
Weber, David J.
  1992 *The Spanish Frontier in North America*. New Haven: Yale University Press.
White, Leslie
  1932 *The Pueblo of San Felipe*. Memoirs of the American Anthropological Association, no. 38.
  1973 Elsie Worthington Clews Parsons. *Dictionary of American Biography, Supplement 3, 1941–45*, ed. Edward T. James, pp. 581–82. New York: Charles Scribner's Sons.
Young, M. Jane
  1988 *Signs from the Ancestors: Zuni Cultural Symbolism and Perceptions of Rock Art*. Albuquerque: University of New Mexico Press.
Zumwalt, Rosemary Levy
  1992 *Wealth and Rebellion: Elsie Clews Parsons, Anthropologist and Folklorist*. Urbana: University of Illinois Press.

PREFACE

There is much about the Pueblo Indians of New Mexico and Arizona that has impressed observers as bearing upon major problems in the general study of culture. Despite sporadic controversy and division, Pueblo society appears remarkably unified, whether compared with our own life or with the life of many Indian peoples. Pueblo habits of mind harmonize with Pueblo behavior or ritual. Art, morality, and philosophy are one. What is it that makes for such cultural sincerity or that results in social cohesion and integrity, among Pueblos or in any community?

Looked at from without, Pueblos appear as a marginal people, on the fringe of that highland culture area of America which is distinguished economically by maize and cotton, by fine pottery and cloth and great buildings, and in social structure by elaborate priesthoods, calendar, and rituals.[1] Here is presented a special archeological problem. Did Pueblo culture originate or rather develop distinctively in the area it once occupied, a far more extensive area than the one it covers today, or did the culture of the south spread northward to people in the Pueblo area? Pottery, weaving, and building show all stages of local development, but corn kernels and possibly cotton seeds are not indigenous. It seems improbable that the intricate and elaborate ceremonial life of the Pueblos developed before a full development of town life, yet the big towns were built comparatively late, in the eleventh and twelfth centuries, and abandoned surprisingly soon. What cultural seeds blossomed so quickly into something not so unlike Aztec ceremonial? Were some of the cultural seeds of Middle America, say the proto-Nahuan languages (and whatever sticks with language), carried down from the Southwest? On the other hand, given the Basket Maker–Mogollon–Pueblo development as peripheral to a southern nucleus,[2] did cultural traits spread from group to group in various fortuitous ways or was there actual immigration by the culture-carriers? Probably diffusion occurred in both ways; nor let us forget in studying Pueblo migration that when a group migrates it establishes contact lines between those left behind and those joined—lines good for centuries of travel.

From their most conspicuous culture-carriers in historic times, from Franciscan friars and Mexican colonists, what did Pueblos borrow and how did they fit their borrowings into their own culture? Has part of their amazing ceremonialism been a sort of gigantism stimulated by the fungus of Catholicism? Here we have a historical inquiry which is restricted, to be sure, by the paucity of observation of Pueblo life by the early Spanish chroniclers, but which stands out, nevertheless, as a fruitful study in acculturation. Pueblos are or were Spanish Indians, although we rarely think of them as such, and their history should be compared with that of Hispanicized Indians elsewhere, the better to analyze out the Spanish and the Indian, and understand early cultural changes. Although foreign influences are different nowadays, the analysis may enable us also to foresee changes in contemporary Pueblo society.

Contacts with Mexico, with both White and Indian Mexico, produced changes in Pueblo society, in historic or prehistoric periods. The nomadic tribes of the Southwest also affected the town-dwellers with whom they fought, traded, and now and again mated. In the eighteenth century there was a great deal of circulation not only between Pueblos and Southern Plains tribes, Athapascan Apache and Navaho, Shoshonean Ute and Paiute, but among Pueblo tribes themselves, rendering a discussion of borrowed traits rather difficult. During the last hundred years and particularly during the recent decades further changes have taken place as a result of contact with Americans of all kinds, of late especially with Americans of good will. To all of us, whether we are with or without faith in that development toward our own values which we call progress, social change is of the greatest interest.

Change in Pueblo life has not taken place equally, for one reason the degree of foreign contact in the historic period has varied from town to town. And there were certainly prehistoric differentiations to start with, in the social classifications of kinship and population, in ceremonial groups, in language, in handicraft. How did these differences come about? From early tribal contacts? From early composition with non-Pueblo peoples? Or from differences in exposure to attack?

Uniformity in pottery or building does not prove uniformity in other cultural particulars, as archeologists are at last beginning to realize; but probably they are right when they tell us that there was at one time a more uniform culture in the Pueblo area. That hundreds of towns were abandoned before the advent of the Spaniards in 1540 and that then there was a Pueblo population of twenty thousand in seventy towns against about two-thirds of that population today in twenty-five towns are facts of untold significance. With the disappearance of towns (e.g., the towns between Acoma and Zuni), the towns which survived were left in greater isolation and would develop distinctive traits. Consolidation of towns went on as well as destruction, and this led to adjustment or invention. Possibly, indeed most certainly, the obscure processes we call invention were ever active, and familiar traits were sporadically combined into something novel. At any rate, there is today not only a large measure of homogeneity among Pueblos but a large measure of differentiation, from tribe to tribe and even from town to town. This condition of heterogeneity within a culture is, of course, not peculiar to Pueblos and is of general interest.

Once it was the fashion to collect cultural facts to string on some favored theme or fancy, by what might be called the introverted anthropological method; but today, outside of journalistic or psychoanalytic circles, it is realized that, although this method may be admirable to express personal predilections and the creative spirit, it is misleading in science, for cultural facts removed from their setting may be snare and delusion.* They may show how a single mind is functioning, the mind of the

---

* I am not referring to the correlation of intertribal data or to distributional study, as I believe that "accurate information on distributions raises problems of a basic character and helps toward their solution" (Lowie 6:307). See chap. viii.

theorist, but not how society functions. To describe even a part
of a culture is a dangerous enterprise, so interwoven is one part
with another that the fabric tears when we begin to separate,
leaving meaningless shreds in our hands. This is particularly
true of those values and forms we call religion, which is far more
a dispersal of phenomena than, according to its etymological
sense, a binding of them together; for religious facts get their
values or weighting from the general life. Religion is an instrument of life.

Of Pueblo religion in particular one may say that it is a form
of instrumentalism controlling the natural through the supernatural, usually, of course, as a flow of interest, not as planned
enterprise. The technique of control is largely magical, that is,
ritual acts are automatically effectual: prayer or song or dance,
color or line are formulistic or compulsive; but there is more here
than magic—there is conceptual control. Weather phenomena—
rain, snow, hail, lightning, wind—are conceived of as anthropomorphic Spirits accessible in various familiar ways. A sun being
who needs clothes is sympathetic to the needs of man. Flood
can serve as punishment for the antisocial among Pueblos as
among Semites, if it is associated with an invocable Spirit.
Failure of crops can be endured with greater patience if the crops
are fleeing Corn Maidens whose return the chiefs can compel by
abstinence and concentration. Disease and sickness can be cured
or prevented when understood as the result of malevolence in
man or beast or insect that can be countered by benevolent men
or beasts or insects. The dead, friends or foes, are less disturbing
to the mind when identified as propitious cloud beings. Similarly, wild animals can be converted into friendly doctors or guards
or hunters if they are taken into the pantheon of the Spirits.
Hunting becomes less arduous when Sun or Earth participates
and after the game animals have been rendered willing victims.
Plants, clay, salt, turquoise—the "flesh" of all these may remain
unimpaired if their spirits are graciously inclined to their despoil-
ers. Acomans made prayer-sticks for the first American locomotive they saw, just as, if he knew how, any Pueblo might do for
whatever he conceived to have power or to be of value. Pueblos

have classified and interpreted their world the better to control it. Other peoples have done likewise. Religion is less antithesis to science than it is science gone astray.

Pueblo arts are also the servants of this undeliberate kind of utilitarianism—words, rhythms, motions, color, and line all contribute to the control of the Spirits. Poetry and song, dance music and steps, mask, figurine, fresco and ground painting, beautiful feather-work, weaving and embroidery, whatever else they are, also are measures to invoke and coerce, to gratify or pay, the Spirits. A very remarkable insight into early art as ritual is afforded in Pueblo religion.

Thus in all aspects Pueblo religion is far from being a system external to the rest of life. What the outsider from another age or culture calls religion is felt by the insider as an integral part of his life. Description of religious complexes or particulars as borrowed or disintegrated or marginal is also the outsider's classification. To those concerned, a religious fragment, indeed any social fragment, may be as vital and significant, be it loan or survival, as any self-developed or intact unit. In the pueblos, a dance horse is as sacred as a dance deer, and dancing in honor of their saint seems to the townspeople quite as much their own *costumbre* as dancing kachina. Of the kachina or mask cult so penetrating in the other pueblos there is at Taos merely a tradition that the Black Eyes society was once in possession of a mask, but this tradition led a member of that society to search eagerly for the lost mask in a New York museum. This Taos mask, to us the meager expression of a merely marginal trait, was to our Black Eyes visitor inestimably precious as having been brought to his society by its original chief.

This feeling of cultural integrity I have tried to recognize, convinced historian though I am. Also I have implicitly evaluated not only the instrumentalism or utilitarianism of the people which is quite generally Indian—resigned materialism Kroeber has called it—but various habits of life and of mind which others, if they like, may call the cultural core or configuration of the Pueblos. Some such analysis is inevitable in considering cultural change, although without more knowledge of the occurrence of these traits in individuals than is now available among Pueblos the analysis is highly speculative, we must admit, and offers little more than conveniently descriptive categories. It must also be understood by the reader that no trait is uniquely or even distinctively Pueblo merely because parallels in other Indian tribes are not mentioned, not to speak of culture at large. For the most part comparative analysis is confined to a final section and to tribes of the Southwest and Mexico.

Obviously from both native and scientific points of view this book should be concerned with the entire life of the Pueblos and not merely with the segment we are pleased to call their religion. Once a White woman, it is said, asked a Taos man what the Indian religion was, and he answered, "Life," meaning that religion was a means to life, that it covered life as a whole, and, thorough animist as he was, that everything significant was alive and a part of religion. Life, in Zuni terms *tekohana*, light, life, well-being, and, we must add, how to ask for it—that is indeed Pueblo religion.

In the Introduction I have attempted a brief general survey, emphasizing habits of life and mind close in one way or another to religion; but this is necessarily an impressionistic, not a systematic, discussion. There are still too many gaps in our knowledge to write a general book: certain pueblos have been barely described at all; only two of the four stock languages have been published, and language as a key to history has been completely ignored; there is little comparative study of handicrafts and arts, little comparative physical data, and studies of the individual in relation to culture are meager. Of Pueblo social organization we have learned but recently that there is a far wider range of variation than we had supposed, and variation in material culture or in social psychology may be expected. Pueblo archaeology is still at loose ends.

However differentiated, all the Pueblos have a well-developed ceremonial life. The Pueblo genius tends strongly toward group rather than individual experience, and this tendency makes for ritual rather than for mysticism.[3] Pueblos outchurch the most rigid churchmen. Consequently, of all aspects of their life, their ceremonialism has attracted most attention and inspired most interest in most observers, myself included. A large amount of observation has been recorded, but data are scattering and publications often not accessible. And there has been little comparative analysis of Pueblo ceremonialism as a whole. "The history of the cults and institutions of any of these pueblos cannot be understood without a knowledge of the customs of the others: the problem is in its very nature a comparative one."[4] Yet few observers have had comparative experience, so arresting and absorbing is each Pueblo region or tribe, and so difficult and time-consuming is the acquiring of ceremonial information from people severely trained to keep such information secret.

To assemble and compare our ceremonial data is my primary purpose. After a visiting acquaintance of many years among all the Pueblos, as well as among other peoples who might contribute to a comparative point of view, I would try to draw the threads together, for myself and, I hope, for others, both for students of the Southwest and for students of cultural problems at large. For most statements of fact I have cited sources either to validate the statement or to direct the reader to a fuller account. For statements without references I am responsible, although I fear that now and again information from some source not my own may have slipped in unaccredited.

A word about localizing traits. Localization does not necessarily mean that the trait does not occur elsewhere, only that it has not been recorded. Frequently statement may seem over-localized, but so many problems of distribution are involved and so uncertain is the early history of the Pueblo tribes to which our survey may contribute, once Southwestern archeologists acquire an interest in relating contemporary and prehistoric culture, that I feel certain localized treatment will be more serviceable to students than more generalized descriptions.

Information has been tabulated whenever possible, and I recommend the Index, made with an eye not only on finding the facts but on relating them. But the reader who is not satisfied with bald outlines[5] must do some work for himself, re-reading early chapters after he has read later ones, and reading with patience discursive reports of ceremonies that become lifeless in table or summary. The reader must also bear with a measure of repetitiousness, for in any culture as well integrated as Pueblo culture the same fact must be considered in different connections. Indeed to understand Pueblo religion or religionists there is no short cut, however the trail meander or double back. And the trail must be followed, the details mastered, before generalizations can be properly enjoyed.

In the back of my own mind, salting the labor of description, has lain the theme of cultural change, the problems of variability. The problems, no doubt, will change or present themselves differently to others, yet the survey will be of service as showing the gaps to be filled in before the Pueblo cultures disappear, in a few generations.

Those gaps have been listed in an appendix, one of the many helpful suggestions made by my friend, Robert H. Lowie, in reading the manuscript. Dr. Lowie, Dr. Leslie A. White, Dr. Boas (to all I am grateful for criticizing manuscript) and indeed every student of the Pueblos or of the Southwest will have something to add to this appendix—something the rest of us would be glad to be shown. We have much to learn, in a shortening period.

Indian ideology is frequently inconsistent with our science, but the Pueblo Indian's sense of town solidarity and his general way of identifying the good of the individual with the common good may appeal to us. Also we may admire his kindly live-and-let-live attitudes, which in a more comprehensive social survey would appear more pronounced. Social responsibility combined with individual tolerance—here perhaps is an American lead to that working substitute for the glorification of God or of State or of Mankind other Americans are seeking.

TABLE OF CONTENTS
VOLUMES I AND II

LIST OF ILLUSTRATIONS

PLATES

VOLUME I

VOLUME II

LIST OF ILLUSTRATIONS

TEXT FIGURES

MAPS

INTRODUCTION*

HOUSE, HOUSEHOLD, AND TOWN

As their Hispanic name indicates, the Pueblo Indians of New Mexico and Arizona are town-dwellers, twenty-five towns and their colonies shelter a population enumerated in 1937 as 15,287:† 3,248 Hopi in seven towns and two or three colonies; 2,080 persons at Zuni and four colonies; 5,781 Keres in seven towns and several colonies; 2,122 Tiwa (Tanoan) in four towns; 648 persons at Jemez (early Tanoan, sometimes called Towa); 1,388 Tewa (Tanoan) in five towns.‡ The town life of this population may be broken into by household visits to outlying farms or orchards or sheep camps or to the mesas and mountains to gather wild fruits or nuts, and men go on hunting and trading trips, on trips for timber or plants, for salt or mineral pigments; they leave town to herd sheep or round up cattle; but attachment to town or house life on the part of both men and women, more particularly on the part of women, is very marked. The house is more than a shelter; it is a place of manifold and binding associations, to the Pueblo, as to many other peoples, an outstanding part of existence.

When the paternal grandmother or aunt is called in to look after a newborn Hopi infant, one of the first things she does is to rub on each wall four short parallel lines of corn meal, the "house." "Now thus I have made a house for you," she says. "Now thus you shall stay here."[1] When the Zuni potter paints a deer, she gives him a "house."[2] "Come into your house!" sings the Hopi eagle-snarer from his pit to the eagles.[3] "Stay in your

* References to sources are indicated by numerals and given on pp. 1167–94; additional information or comment is given as footnote.

† This census total includes twenty persons recently settled at Pojoaque, an abandoned Tewa town.

‡ See map (Vol. I, frontispiece) for more detailed figures and for the names and tribal affiliations of the towns.

house!" Wind is begged, the hateful old woman who destroys young crops or drives away rain. To houses all creatures, natural and supernatural, are assigned, the dead, the clouds, the sun, even butterflies, even dogs, for there is a bluff northeast of Oraibi called Butterfly house,[4] and, in Hopi tradition, the dogs once had a distinctive dwelling, an opening in the side of the mesa, Pohki, Dog house.[5] It was because Coyote Old Man could not build a house that the father of the Santa Clara girl said he did not want her to marry Coyote, adding characteristically, "But if you want to marry him, marry him!" and then letting Coyote and his wife live with him, until the couple fell out.[6]

Even sometime enemies are given shelter. Navaho, the hereditary enemy, will be taken into a house with which they have some association, however slight; and, once received, at some festival season, they know they may return here year after year. Twice at Zuni I have been joint guest with an old Navaho woman and some of her descendants in a house her son married into half a century ago. He is long since dead, but to this house there has been a yearly trickle of Navaho visitors. That "they always come here" is ample reason to expect them to keep on coming.[7] Any Pueblo Indian, too, is accustomed to resort to a particular house when he is visiting another town. It is the house, as well as the household, with which he feels acquainted and at home.

Recently built houses are of one story;* the older houses are of two or three stories, terraced back. The house clusters of Taos and the highest house in Zuni pinnacle to a fifth story. Houses are usually contiguous, in clusters. In the older houses ground rooms may be entered only by ladder from the second story, and Zuni still refer to themselves in ritual phrase as the "ladder-descending children of the Corn chiefs." In these ground or cellar-like rooms or in the windowless back rooms of more modern houses, in "the fourth inner room" (Zuni), ritual paraphernalia are generally kept (and removed only with great reluctance), or

---

* As were houses of a remote period. Here we are concerned only with the houses of historic times.

here ceremonial is performed.* Openings between such rooms are low and narrow. Ordinarily, even in modern houses, there is but one house door.† Large windows, with wooden frame and window glass, are now in general use; formerly, in all pueblos until about 1864, openings were small and placed high in the wall, and selenite was used as windowpane.

Houses are built of adobe brick or, in some towns, of stone chinked with clay, and walls outside and inside are muddied or plastered. Large beams are used in roofing, with a mat of sticks of varying size, muddied over. Upper stories are of wood and mud, so well plastered as to give the impression of a much more solid construction. Many of these upper rooms are used as storerooms (possibly this was their original object). In the rear ground rooms stuck into the timbers or hanging from them are other stores: roots, dried plants or seed corn, the ritual feather box, pieces of dance costume. The corn ears are very carefully stacked in one corner or in a separate room. There are bins for grain, and wall niches for what cannot be hung up. Most Pueblo rooms are very orderly: everything in its place, and a place for everything.

In some back rooms there is a large, oblong, hooded fireplace, where the characteristic wafer-bread is baked;‡ the most common kind of fireplace is an oval opening in the flue which runs down at right angles to the house wall, extending into a low wall on top of which is sometimes available a small bowl of prayer-meal. Except among Hopi, who bake in pits, the Mexican outdoor clay oven is common. American stoves are in quite general use.§ The house floor is of clay, well smoothed down. (Is a smooth floor part of a pottery complex? I have lived among Indian nonpotters where the floor was anything but smooth.)

---

* At Zuni the societies meet in front rooms, on the streets.

† In the modern outlying houses of Zuni it is notable that the house door opens toward the town (Kroeber 2:198), as do distant stone shrines. For both spirits and men the road to the "middle place" should be direct.

‡ At Walpi there are also detached bakehouses (Stephen 4:Appen. 11).

§ Stoves were introduced into Hopi kivas in the nineties, curiously enough for a ritual reason, to hasten the growth of the omen beans of the Powamu ceremony (Stephen 4:178, 179).

Now and again in a recently built or remodeled house, there is a plank floor. Plank ceilings are also to be seen, and in the eastern pueblos, not uncommonly, tin roofs. Recently the "courthouse" at Isleta remained unfinished for several months because the town was divided about roofing it; the tin roofers won out. Everywhere there is a tendency to enlarge the size of rooms; new rooms are several times the size of old. There is likewise a tendency to build new houses either detached or in blocks, on the edges of town—a tendency which may interfere with ritual as, for example, in the roof-to-roof dance-song of the Koyemshi clowns of Zuni.[8] Planking furnishes another illustration of novel building methods interfering with ritual, since it precludes placing prayer-sticks underfoot or overhead.

In these new and larger houses, rooms are enlarged rather than multiplied. Rarely are there in old houses or new more than three or four rooms: one or two storerooms, perhaps a grinding- or baking-room and the general living- and sleeping-room. Sometimes a newly married couple withdraws into the back room, but ordinarily the whole household sleeps in the same room, and at that more or less alongside, although the older boys and girls will be separate from the others, and boys from girls. The pelts and blankets for the sleeping pallets are taken down from the roof poles or the wall seats and spread out all at the same time, and commonly all are occupied at the same time, the household going to sleep together and arising together. But household mates may sit up late into the night talking with visitors while others in the house are or would be asleep. A woman of mixed blood and culture married into Zuni told me that, no matter what hour her husband might return from dance practice or visiting around, he would wake her to talk. She was enough of a White woman to grumble, "They are all like that."

Of individual privacy there is little or none, but household privacy is well provided for. Between households where there are no familial links or other ties there is scant visiting—"We do not visit them" (Zuni). Except in the family circle, visitors will stand at the door until invited in, and Indian visitors would venture into a back room even less freely than our visitors into our kitchen. Looking into windows is not done, and lurking about window or door at night would expose one to being suspected of witchcraft. This insistence on household privacy has a bearing, I think, on the rules of secretiveness of the societies,* just as the lack of personal privacy may have been a factor in making the individual Pueblo, like many other Indians, secretive or reticent. Pueblo disposition or etiquette must be considered from the point of view of manners as affected by life in close quarters. Small-town manners!

In the West,† houses belong to women of the family and are passed down from one generation of women to the next. In the East, men as well as women are householders; there is a tendency indeed toward male proprietorship which at Isleta and among Tewa is marked and at Taos still more marked.[9] It was natural to ascribe this difference of proprietorship to Spanish influence, more potent in the East than in the West, until we learned more about the distribution of clan and moiety organization, and it became clear that, wherever the matrilineal clan prevailed, women owned houses, and where the patrilineal moiety occurred, men were equally or predominantly houseowners. Of course the example of the patriarchal Mexican houseowner may have contributed in the northeastern pueblos to a pre-existing tendency to male proprietorship. At any rate, houseownership and descent appear to be closely related.[10]

The household rather than the clan or any consanguinous group is the economic unit; we might even say the social unit. The household is a co-operative group, each member having a certain status and more or less fixed duties. The actual composition of the group may be diversified and quite unstable, but the

---

* But I would not infer with Kroeber that Zuni societies were not secretive because they met in front rooms (Kroeber 2:198). Rules of privacy such as not looking in or listening in may be quite as protective as back rooms. Initiation by trespass is another protective device (see pp. 113, 130).

† By which I mean the Hopi towns, Hano which is the Tewan town on First Mesa, and Zuni. Correspondingly, the East refers to the Keresan- and Tanoan-speaking towns, including Jemez, Tiwan towns, and the Tewan towns of New Mexico. Acoma and Laguna will be referred to as western Keres and generally accounted in the West, as in this matter of houseownership.

feeling of household unity is strong. As an adoptive child you may pass from one household to another; in marital adventure, in the West, you may join first one woman's household and then another's, or, as an interval celibate, return to the household of your mother or sister; but, whatever your household, you are, for the time being, an integral and responsible part of it. That is, economically, in its ceremonial connections the household may be considerably differentiated.

Joint households are common in the West, i.e., a married daughter or kinswoman may occupy an adjacent room which is thought of as her own house, and both West and East there are clusters of houses belonging to the same kin. The distribution of houses has been shown[11] definitely to be a matter of affiliation by kin rather than by clan. The house groups are a kind of reproduction by budding. There is less of this in the East, where a youth when he marries is often given an old house belonging to one of his parents, or with the help of his relatives builds himself a new house, necessarily in some cases in another part of town. But even in the East there is a marked inclination toward the family house cluster. I recall one conspicuous case at Taos where in the northwest corner of town eight houses are lived in by one family connection.

Here the tendency to grouping by kin had an opportunity for expression on a piece of town land not yet built upon. There is little such unoccupied land left at Taos, which is a walled town, where the concept of town solidarity is expressed by living within the walls, "in one nest." Within the walls there are rules to be followed: no window glass allowed; men must wear their hair in braids and keep to their blanket; women must wear their great boot moccasins, and men, heel-less shoes;* at certain seasons ritualistic conduct is prescribed for all. Here town walls, once a protection as elsewhere against raiders, are but a visible sign of that sense of town solidarity which is strong in all the pueblos.

Permission to leave town for a considerable period or at all

---

* "Sneakers," being heel-less, are allowed in Santo Domingo but not boots (White 4:23). The Isletan who wears boots inserts a bit of *native* cotton and feels all right about it.

must be got from Governor* or from Town chief (Isleta, Santo Domingo, First Mesa), permission which is often withheld, especially from those who have ceremonial connections. It was withheld from Juan Rey of the Laguna colony in Isleta, a medicine man of distinction, who in 1923 wished to remove to Sandía and did so, only to die within the year. ("He did not last long because he broke his promise to do his ceremony at Isleta." After his death his daughter returned to Isleta to claim house and land; but the Governor had already reassigned them.)[12] The sister of the Hano War chief was married to an Oraibi man, an obstreperous fellow, who after making trouble at Hano started with his wife and children for Oraibi. The Hano War chief is in charge of a war kachina mask which his sister should look after, so the mesa hierarchy did not wish her to leave the mesa. Three Walpi chiefs went after the family to talk them into coming back; after the proper interval of quarantine,[13] they came back.

Even when no ceremonial ties are involved, there is opposition to people moving away. A single family, one person even, is a loss and, besides, may start a migratory trickle. Town endogamy is one expression of this feeling. Girls in particular are made to feel that they should not marry out. A Sia girl wanted to marry a Jemez man and live at Jemez. "If she marries him, some day she may not be found," said the girl's father, "just as it happened once when a Santa Clara girl left to marry a San Juan man. That Santa Clara girl went into the hills and never came back."[14] No doubt this was an extreme attitude, for Santa Clara girls have married out and survived.[15] My own hostess at Jemez was from Santa Clara, sprightly old Juanita, still in love with the man she had followed forty years before to a town speaking a strange tongue and having different *costumbres*.

The sense of town solidarity expresses itself again and again in attitudes of conceit or superiority. The Hopi term for "bad" is *kahopi*, "not Hopi." Descendants of Pecos immigrants to Jemez are still saying that Jemez people "know nothing." An Isletan friend writes: "This pueblo has all different ceremonials;

* Just as Spaniards had to get permission to leave the Colony.

other pueblos or any other tribe have not much." Santo Domingo will refer to the people of neighboring towns as "no good" or "crazy." They laugh at the way other Keres speak Keresan. They assume that pueblos with customs similar to theirs have borrowed them, never admitting that they themselves have been the borrowers[16]—a common Pueblo attitude. Pottery designs are borrowed from town to town, but borrowing is seldom if ever acknowledged. Zuni potters laugh at the bird designs of Sia and Laguna.[17] In Laguna it is asserted that Hopi and Zuni did not know how to get salt from Zuni Salt Lake until Laguna people showed them what to do. When Tsiwema, the sole surviving doctor of Laguna, manipulated my badly sprained ankle, he remarked complacently that he could heal it,* but a White doctor would cut it off. A gun may be more powerful than a bow, but lightning, which is shaman-controlled, is more powerful than either.[18] White people, not to speak of Mexicans, Navaho, Ute, who were nicknamed Snotty Noses, or other tribes, even the enemy who destroyed whole towns, all seem inferior or ridiculous to the Pueblo patriot.

Town solidarity shows in ritual or myth. Prayer-sticks or prayer-feathers are buried in the middle of the court or immured in walls, to represent "the roots of the town."[19] To this spot, in Laguna terms, the people are "tied."[20] The shrine is "fixed so there will always be people here."[21] Nambé people say also that at their "earth navel," where lie the magic roots of the town, "if we keep up feeding the stones there, our pueblo will live forever."[22] Jemez people "wanted to put up the pueblo solid as a rock, so they deposited a reddened eagle feather to be the root toward the north to Wawanatutu (whence the first people emerged and whither the dead return), and another eagle feather to be the root toward the west to Wawanatutu, and another eagle feather to be the root toward the south to Wawanatutu, and another eagle feather to be the root toward the east to Wawanatutu, and another eagle feather to be the root up to

---

* To be sure, this was not only racial conceit but professional self-confidence, which is probably strong among Pueblo doctors as among Navaho doctors (Newcomb and Reichard, 15).

Wawanatutu, and another eagle feather to be the root down to Wawanatutu. This will be the place for us to live forever, they said." Zuni story-tellers have a like formulistic conclusion, and Zuni itself is called Itiwana, "the middle place," the middle of the world. Did not Water Skate, after laying himself down and finding he could stretch his arms out fully in every direction, decide for the chiefs that here indeed, at his heart, was the Middle Place?[23] Here was the center of the court of early Zuni.

In several towns houses stand in parallel rows,* but mostly the houses outline one or more courts, with kivas placed within the courts. Kivas are subterranean or partly subterranean buildings or buildings above ground, round or rectangular: at Zuni and Acoma and in some instances in Tewa towns kivas are part of the ordinary rectangular house construction;† elsewhere kivas are detached structures. Kivas‡ are communal or partly communal buildings, clubhouses used by the men as meeting-place, workshop, or as a place to dance or hold ceremonials; women visit the kivas merely for dance practice or as audience.§ The particular group with which a kiva is associated varies: among Hopi it is primarily the maternal family or clan that built or

---

* Acoma, Santo Domingo, Santa Ana, San Juan. Courts are barely defined, if at all, at Taos, Isleta, or Walpi.

† A safer because less conspicuous type of building. Similarly back rooms are safer than the "small prayer-houses" noted by Luxán at Hawikuh, "where they speak to the devil and give him offerings of ollas and earthen bowls containing *pinole* (prayer-meal) and other vegetables," ceremonial bowls which servants in Espejo's party went in to get (Hodge 3:67).
No "small prayer-houses" have been excavated at Hawikuh (Hodge, personal communication). The square kiva in the court was pre-Conquest but built by a later people than the builders of the round kivas.
Acoma was a mesa-top town on the arrival of the Spaniards, but before that in Acoma tradition people lived in the round kiva ruin below the mesa (Stirling).

‡ Spanish, *estufa;* Hopi, *kiva;* Zuni, *kiwitsine;* Keres, *chi''kya (chita),* also *k'a''ach',* Acoma, Laguna; Jemez, *owa;* Tewa, *te'e';* Isleta, *tuthlai;* Taos, *töata;* Sandía, *tuthla* (? stick-house, note that Oraibi kivas have inner walls of wattled canes thickly plastered (Cushing, Fewkes, Parsons, 257; Stephen 4:1177, 1178). The southern Tiwa sojourned in Hopiland after the Great Rebellion.

§ Among Hopi, kivas are loaned to women's societies just as to men's societies, and in Oraibi until 1901 one of the thirteen kivas was used exclusively by the women's Marau society.

rebuilt the kiva, but neighbors or societies habitually use it, and in each town the number of kivas varies; at Zuni and at Taos it is the society organization into which every boy is initiated, and in both towns there are six kivas; at Jemez and Isleta, among Keres and Tewa, it is one of the ceremonial moieties into which the townspeople divide. In this two-kiva system, Isleta excepted, offspring are associated with the kiva their father belongs to, also their mother, since a girl at marriage shifts to the kiva group of her husband. The use of kivas supplies a capital illustration of how the towns are both alike and unlike: kivas in all, but kiva organization and use varying considerably.*

The town is the collective unit, not the tribe which may be defined as composed of towns speaking the same language, possessed of the same kinship principles and by and large of the same ceremonial system. With so much in common, a considerable degree of solidarity might be supposed to exist within each of the five tribes. Actually there is but little. Kachina dancers visit other towns, bestowing the blessings of rainfall and abundance; societies may send delegates to a neighboring town to participate in an initiation or installation;[24] and intertown foot or horse races, intertown games, and even intertown working-parties occur among Hopi: otherwise I know of no formal intertown co-operation.† But visitors or sojourners will be expected to dance or sing[25] for their hosts,‡ or take part in dances performed by their hosts; and there is considerable intertown visiting and trading, particularly in the East, at the fiesta of the

* Given this differentiation, we see how mistaken were some of the earlier writers in assuming a clan organization wherever they found a kiva. *The kiva neither presupposes nor determines any type of organization.* It is used by the prevailing units of organization, and in the same town it may be used by groups differing in type. In the archeological period called Pueblo II and dated from about 875 to 1000 the room clusters to a kiva are smaller than in the big-town period Pueblo III (1000–1250), 6:1 as against 6.5–25.1:1 (Steward 3:97–98), which indicates some difference in usage, *but not what difference.*

† But see p. 111 and Index, "Interpueblo."

‡ Just as they would farm or herd for them, for dancing or singing *is* an economic service.

In migration tales newcomers will be asked to show efficiency in rain-making by performing their ceremony.

patron saint. Spanish fiesta and in intertribal relations the Spanish language have contributed a good deal to amicable intertown and intertribal relations. Today English is taking the place of Spanish.

In the less Hispanized or Anglicized western pueblos the clanship system contributes somewhat to intertown or even intertribe intimacy. Visitors usually seek a house of their clan, expecting more hospitality from clanspeople. Even a visiting Navaho may be correlated through his clan and called brother or uncle. Hopi or western Keres will adopt clanless visitors into a clan "to make them feel at home."[26] At Acoma a foreign spouse will have his or her head washed by clanswomen,[27] the usual rite in adoption or initiation. Said my friend Lucinda, an Isletan married into the Laguna colony at Isleta, "When you go to old Laguna, first thing they ask you is what *hano* (people, i.e., clan) you belong to. If you belong to theirs, they want to wash you; but," added Lucinda, "we don't tell them." Being from a pueblo without true clans, Lucinda thought she was being questioned about the esoteric societies, and so went dumb and missed out on forming a satisfactory tie with her Laguna acquaintances.

Despite connections through clanship or from trade, a good deal of controversy or fighting between towns has been recorded or is legendary. Acoma and Laguna have always been reputed to be very quarrelsome neighbors, for two centuries over water rights[28] and once over the picture of a saint.* In 1813 San Felipe appropriated Santa Ana lands and sold them to Spaniards; the ensuing controversy lasted over a decade.[29] Hopi of First Mesa and Hopi of Second Mesa have been disputing for many years about grazing land, First Mesa contending that land belonging to Second Mesa but not used because Second Mesa people are poor in stock should be opened to the stockowners of First Mesa, a move toward tribal unity opposed by the conservative chief of Shipaulovi.† In 1700 Awatobi and at an earlier period Awatobi's

---

* Lummis 2:262 ff. Although San José is the patron of Laguna, the American judge awarded the picture to Acoma. This in 1857.

† And perhaps other boundary questions are involved (see Parsons 40:79).

colony Sikyatki* are said† to have been destroyed by other towns. Because of the hostility of Pecos, Tano towns were abandoned.[30] Taos refers secretly‡ to Tewa as Wolf Dung, and Tewa call the people of Taos Rats. "They call us Rats; like rats we will chew them up, if we fight them," blusters Taos. In the seventeenth century[31] Taos together with Pecos and some Keres did fight the Tewa.

Today intertown antagonism or suspicion often takes the form of imputing witchcraft. A keen trader of Isleta told me she would not go to Sandía to trade because there were so many witches in Sandía. One year Laguna would not buy women's dresses from Zuni because of a rumor that Zuni witches were trading in dresses they stole from corpses. A grasshopper plague at San Ildefonso I heard laid to Santa Clara witches. A Nambé woman sees a suspicious light one night at Santa Fé; since a vanishing light generally means a witch, María of Nambé thinks it is a Tesuque witch spying on her. Once a strange black dog was seen near Taos and shot; a little later in the bush a San Juan man was found pierced by an arrow. "He had come to steal a Taos girl."[32] Almost the same story is told of an Acoma man who stole a Laguna girl.[33] Witches may "trade lives": a witch may bring a fellow-townsman to another town to add to the life of a witch there who will reciprocate with the life of one of his own townsmen (Taos). At fiestas, strangers mean witches, and a Taos acquaintance with trachoma he believes to be caused by

* Dated 1504–1550 by "tree time" (Brew, 126–27).

† Voth 5:241–56; Parsons 42:227–33. The motivation is given in such fictitious terms of personal revenge or outrage or of desire to capture young women and children that it seems quite probable the towns were destroyed not by Hopi but by nomadic tribesmen. The invitation to the Tewa (see below) makes better sense if Awatobi was destroyed by Utes than if it was destroyed by Hopi. But see p. 862, n.†.

Punishing the town or expressing personal despair by sending for the enemy is a Pueblo tale pattern which has been interpreted as a daydream of suicide (Benedict 3:I, XVIII–XIX). For a recent use of this pattern by the Mishongnovi narrator of an actual Navaho attack made about seventy years ago see Nequatewa, 52 ff., and compare Stephen 4:1002, 1019. Again the pattern is used on Second Mesa in describing a great famine caused by a jealous woman, the sister of the Town chief of Shipaulovi (Beaglehole 3:71). See p. 108, n.*.

‡ Possibly a secret war name, Navaho way.

witchcraft always finds his eyes in a worse state at fiestas, unless he uses his antiwitch prophylaxis, peyote. No wonder that fiesta visitors from different pueblos are sometimes averse to sleeping in the same room!

Given this picture of the lack of neighborly feeling between towns both within and without the tribe, it is a little surprising to find records of intertribal co-operation. In 1650, Isleta, Alameda, San Felipe, Cochiti, and Jemez valley towns "conspired" against the Spaniards, and this was followed by the very remarkable concert of all the towns or tribes under the leadership of Pope' of San Juan, when on the same day of the year 1680 over four hundred Spaniards, including twenty-one Franciscan friars, were killed throughout Pueblo territory.* General massacre may not be a difficult type of co-operation, but the conspiracy implied with few exceptions† common understanding and sympathy. Besides, the eastern Pueblos joined subsequently in the siege of Santa Fé, forcing the withdrawal of all the Spaniards from the Colony; and several years later a town was built near Cochiti to harbor rebel refugees from several towns. But it was Spanish policy to separate the towns just as in the next century they were to play the nomadic tribes one against the other. During the reconquest, in 1694, Vargas led Sia and Santa Ana men against Jemez, and in the revolt two years later Sia, Santa Ana, and San Felipe sided with the Spaniards against Jemez, Cochiti, Santo Domingo, Acoma, and Zuni. The immigrations of Tiwa and Tewa (including Tano) to Hopiland‡ during the reconquest or early in the eighteenth century were undoubtedly due in part to trouble at home with Spaniards or through them with Indian neighbors, rather than wholly to the desire, as postulated in Hano tradition, to help the Hopi against their enemy, the Utes.[34] In recent years there has been a movement to build up intertown

---

* There were about 2,800 Spaniards in the Province, of whom from 80 to 90 per cent were born in New Mexico. Most lived in or near Santa Fé or southward on the lower river (Hackett, 99). Scholes estimates 2,300–2,400.

† Isleta, some Piro towns, and some Tano chiefs who betrayed the plot to the inert Spanish governor.

‡ To Second Mesa (cf. Stephen 4:1180–81) or to First Mesa (see pp. 913 ff).

co-operation through the All-Pueblos Council against "Washington." Without their ardent and crusading leader, a white man, one wonders what the co-operation would amount to.* However, Pueblo historians should make a record of this modern movement† in political confederation.

Although attached to their houses or town, the Pueblos are far from being absolutely sedentary peoples. They have the house or town living habit, but they are assiduous builders³⁵ and will move from house to house, new or old, quite freely; many move annually into the country, and many are ready-enough colonists, when need be. This is true today and must have been so in the past, according to historical and archeological records.‡ The very great number of ruins in the Pueblo territory, once much larger than it is today, can only be accounted for as the result of seminomadism. The early Pueblos were nomads in terms not of days or seasons but of decades or centuries.

War or dread of war was one factor in such migrations. Mesa

---

* Since this was written, some time ago, co-operation against "Washington" became for a period co-operation with "Washington," the White leader having become Indian Commissioner. Now the pueblos have fallen apart on a fresh Washington issue, a woman Agent. Antonio Mirabal of Taos is the present-day Pope' inciting to rebellion. In an open letter to the Commissioner, dated May 9, 1936, Mirabal writes: "I am going to use all my power to put her out," and to this end Mirabal has gone from pueblo to pueblo asking, "How are we going to manage our own affairs by keeping our mouth shut?" One pueblo at least, Santa Clara, did not join the rebellion.

† Also of the All-Hopi Council formed under Government pressure in 1936.

‡ At Pecos six distinct towns are indicated, and Pecos was not settled until after the eleventh century. The population kept shifting about from one part of the mesa to another, building and rebuilding. A still earlier population had moved from across the Arroyo de Pecos to the Pecos ridge (Kidder 1:30–32; Kidder 3:143), much as did Walpi people who moved from the foot of the mesa to the top, or the early Zuni population which shifted from one side of the river to the other (Kroeber 2:200–202), not to speak of the major migrations from Hawikuh or other towns of Cibola. There was "a sort of milling around" in the Zuni Valley. "It is certainly startling to come on ruin after ruin with long rows of rooms stretching away in straight lines or graceful curves, but with hardly a sign of ashes and broken pottery—in short, every jot of evidence pointing to a flitting occupation" (Spier 1:300). The town in Red Paint Canyon, near Zuni farmers at Nutria, the nameless "village of the great kivas," built about A.D. 1000, was occupied only two decades or less (Roberts 1:169).

tops were safer than valley sites. Walpi people and all the Second Mesa townspeople moved higher up for such reasons, and so, we may surmise, did the peoples of Acoma and Pecos. The abandonment of whole regions such as were occupied by southeastern Piro or Tano or Tiwa has been put down to enemy attacks, likewise at an earlier period the concentration of population into large towns or into inaccessible cliff dwellings.[36] In the poetic terms of an Oraibi commentator, "The people warred with one another until it became necessary whenever they ceased their journeyings that they should build their houses on high mountains with but one road leading up or in caves with but one path down, or in the sides of deep canyons."[37] Contrariwise, with apprehension lessened, a move to a nearer and more abundant water supply or to more fertile land would be in order, just as San Felipe or Cochiti moved down to the edge of the river and just as Acoma has almost entirely removed into the fertile valley of Acomita.

Internal feud has also been a factor in migration. There is a Taos tradition that during the building of the first Catholic church the people quarreled and some left Taos, going eastward.* Even the abandonment of Pecos has been cast into a tradition of feud, plus witchcraft.† The very old feud of Santa Clara is said to be healing without exodus, but the more recent one of San Ildefonso appears to be ripening for a split if it has not already taken place, across the plaza. At Laguna about fifty years ago religious conservatives moved to Mesita and thence to Isleta, carrying with them their altars and other sacred things, and leaving the progressive, Americanized townspeople to a state of irreligion from which they have never fully recovered. The kivas were torn down, and, although the kachina cult now flourishes at Laguna, the kivas were never rebuilt, and Laguna is the sole pueblo which is not still controlled by its "old men"

* See p. 1057, n.†, for another version.

† Lummis 3:137 ff. Actually, factions developed at Pecos after the Great Rebellion. In 1700 the chief called by the Spaniards Don Felipe executed five "rebels" and had others imprisoned at Santa Fé, whence they escaped to the Jicarilla Apache (Bancroft, 223).

(at least it was not when Dr. Boas and I lived there in 1920).[38] Shipaulovi and Oraibi were similarly disrupted. Because of quarrels over sending the children to school or living below the mesa, Shipaulovi and Oraibi conservatives also moved away, to Shumopovi in 1899 or to found the town of Hotavila, in 1906. Since then Shipaulovi and Oraibi have been without some of their major ceremonies.[39] When Shalïko, the Snake clan mother of Walpi, became a convert to Protestantism, about 1907, and moved off the mesa, the Snake-Antelope societies of First Mesa must have been gravely disturbed, but all of Shalïko's family did not follow her, and the organization survived; Marau, the women's society of which Shalïko was chief, did not survive.

"Famine" has contributed to Pueblo migration, since individuals or families move away to seek sustenance in another town. There are many stories of individuals or families going from Zuni to Acoma, Jemez, or Hopiland, or from one Hopi mesa to another, during the crop failures of the last hundred years. In the Hopi famine of 1862, due to three successive crop failures, people scattered to Zuni and to the eastern pueblos.[40] The abandonment of northern Arizona pueblos at the close of the thirteenth century has been imputed to the drought of 1276–1299 as established by tree-ring chronology.[41]

Immigrants are culture-carriers.[42] In large groups they may introduce a new language, like Tewa on First Mesa, or novel building or handicraft techniques, like Pueblos in the Gila River drainage, or even major forms of social organization; in small groups, like the Keres on First Mesa,[43] the Pecos at Jemez, or the Laguna at Isleta,[44] they may introduce minor changes in organization such as new clans,* new rituals, or new ceremonies to complicate the calendar. Also long-term visits have much significance in the study of cultural interpenetration, sojourns such as those of the Isletans to Hopiland after the Great Rebellion or,

---

* Which is quite a different thing from migration by clan, as the earlier ethnologists were prone to describe all movements of population. One immigrant woman or family may introduce a new clan; but any sizable group of travelers is bound to be composed of two or more clans, the fathers not belonging to the clan or clans of the mothers. Even if a man's clan was not straightway established, it might contribute a name, among Hopi, to an existing clan.

about the same period, of Jemez people among Navaho or Hopi. Thus connections of hospitality and trade are established, and these may be continued after the visitors have returned home.

Lack of copious water or of fertile land has caused not only migratory trickles or streams to other groups but colonization. Many of the towns have budded into colonies. Moenkopi, fifty miles or so distant, is a colony of Oraibi, and will continue to be so thought of, in spite of its larger population, until it institutes its own winter solstice ceremony, the criterion of separate township. Nutria, Pescado, Ojo Caliente, and Tekapo are colonies* of Zuni; Acomita and McCarty's, of Acoma; and Laguna has seven or more colonies which duplicate some of the ceremonial organization but are all theoretically dependent upon the organization of old Laguna, meager as that is. Analogously, long after the complete abandonment of a town, its ruin will be visited as a shrine.

Given the large number of ruined towns that are usually within reach of the inhabited town, given the varied record of social mobility, it is not surprising that to the Pueblo "history" is so largely a tradition of migrations, not of actual migrations but of migrations according to a traditional pattern. The Pueblo localizes his folk tales in the neighboring ruins, and his general origin story is one of emergence from the underworld or worlds† and of subsequent wandering. Particular social organizations have each its own migration story, which is recited at group meetings either as society ritual or, among Hopi, as an expression of clan solidarity.[45] Individual life the Pueblo also thinks of or expresses, particularly in ritual, as a journey. Life is a road; important spirits are, in Zuni, *a·'wona·wi'lona*,‡ "keepers of the

---

* Started from the desire to grow wheat on irrigable land. After irrigation was introduced at Zuni through the construction of the dam at Black Rock, many colonists returned to Zuni (Bunzel 6:1–2).

† Beliefs of Emergence and of an Earth composed of several levels are held by tribes of Middle America and of the Southeast, and probably throw back, among them and in the Southwest, to a very ancient source, which may have nothing to do with migrating habits.

‡ Stevenson applied this term to a remote high god of whom later students found no trace. But now from the Apache neighbors of Zuni, the White Moun-

roads," the life-roads. All spirits or sacrosanct persons have a road of corn meal or pollen sprinkled for them when their presence is requested.

FARMING AND COMESTIBLES

One of the few rites recorded by the gold-seeking Conquistadores was the sprinkling of corn meal, which "sign of peace," as Espejo described it, after his party had been besprinkled outside Walpi, made them look "like clowns in carnival time."* For many centuries maize has been grown in the Southwest, and long before the advent of the Spaniards the Pueblos practiced dry farming or flood farming or even irrigated by ditch. In pre-European days corn, beans, squash, and gourds were the crops, also tobacco (questionable)† and cotton.‡ All these are grown today; cotton is confined to Jemez, Santa Ana (White), Isleta, possibly Moenkopi and generally to ritual use. The Spaniards introduced wheat, oats, and barley, peaches, apricots, apples, grapes, and melons, chili and other vegetables, also the plowshare.

Preparing the ground by digging-stick, however, is still a practice in the West. In several towns wheat is threshed in the old Hispanic fashion, on circular floors of stone or earth around which horses or mules are driven or ridden, women winnowing in baskets. How long these archaic methods of farming will hold their own against modern machinery, in particular the machinery supplied by United States government agents, is an interest-

---

tain Apache, a similar high god is reported, In-Charge-of-Life, sometimes identified with the Sun (Goodwin 2:26). In both tribes one may surmise Christian dogma, unless one is an indefatigable searcher after high gods.

* Luxán, 99. In Zapoteca, Mexico, once in carnival time I was strewn solemnly with confetti after acting the benevolent stranger.

† Hopi do not cultivate tobacco but gather wild tobacco (Nicotiana attenuata), which is used also at Zuni and by Tewa who formerly cultivated it (Robbins, Harrington, Freire-Marreco, 103). At Santa Ana today tobacco identified as Nicotiana rustica is cultivated for ritual use. This is the plant that was cultivated in the Southeast and by Iroquois and Algonquin (White). Did it get into the Southwest by way of Southern Caddoans?

‡ Basket Maker predecessors of Pueblos grew corn, beans, squashes, not cotton (Kidder 1:78; Roberts 1:3), which grows wild in Arizona mountains.

ing question. As long ago as 1891 the introduction of American agricultural machinery was opposed at Oraibi.[46] In 1922 I found the harrow still forbidden at Jemez* and plowing by oxen instead of by American machinery was obligatory in plowing the field of the Town chief; but ten years earlier the threshing floor had begun to yield to the government threshing machine, and in 1921 a Jemez man of Pecos descent bought his own thresher. A machine harvester is forbidden in Jemez (1937), but there may be little demand for it as the plots are small. A Taos man owns a thresher and rents it out, getting one sack of grain in ten. At Zuni the government thresher was little used (1918),† whereas a harvester was coming into use. I saw the same field of wheat, a large field, being cut one day by sickle by a row of six or seven men, and the next day finished off by a horse-drawn machine.

The six or seven men were kinsmen of the owner of the field, even the driver of the machine was of the family connection. (But the driver was also the only man available who understood the machine. Probably the day came when his services were called for outside his particular family connection, a change in economic methods affecting, as so often happens, a change in social relations.) As yet not the skilled laborer but kinsmen or clansmen or some ceremonial group with which the owner of the field is associated are those called upon to help farm it.

Before Tewa began to use a thresher, in 1912 at Santa Clara, a group of relatives would make a threshing floor and use it together.[47] Hopi do not grow wheat, since they do not irrigate, but for their corn fields "working-parties" are organized among neighbors‡ as well as kindred. Here as elsewhere a meal is served

* It is reported (1936) that a man cultivating by machine was ordered from his field and whipped.

† In 1937 another thresher is reported to be owned by a townsman.

‡ Up to 1880, before the helpful burros were numerous, the Crier called out in the evening for all to go to a group of fields the next day. On returning, men and women alternating carried their baskets in procession to a certain point where they were met by the less vigorous home-stayers who deployed, men and women alternating, from the field-owner's house to the meeting-point on the trail. Then the baskets were speedily transferred from back to back (Stephen 4: 953–54; cf. Beaglehole 3:43).
Wheat harvest parties are held in Santo Domingo (White 4:117).

to all the workers before the close of the afternoon (field work is always over early), and what is left of the food the home-staying women have been all day preparing is taken home by the servant-guests, who are thus paid in accordance with the general Pueblo principle of feeding persons who work for you. From such a supper circle I can recall seeing Crow-Wing, who was to be my First Mesa host, standing up and stepping to the door to see what I wanted. Eight or nine men had been harvesting with him that day in his wife's field, a field she had inherited from her uncle, her mother's brother, and that her children, a boy and three girls, would inherit from her. The boy's share would go eventually to one of his sisters or her children.

Thus the Hopi fields descend within the maternal family or clan, the clan mother having the duty to settle disputes.[48] A similar land system seems to have existed formerly in Zuni, perhaps also among western Keres:* individual ownership with inheritance in the maternal family, on the dying-out of the family mere clanspeople being preferred to paternal descendants. In the East, and at Zuni† too, paternal as well as maternal relatives inherit, i.e., a man will leave his land to his own children, not to his sister's children, although it may eventually revert to them or their descendants.‡ In the East unused agricultural land reverts to the town, to be reallotted by Town chief or Governor. Title to a newly cleared field or to a new building site may also be granted by the Governor.[49] The attitude toward unused agri-

---

* Today at Acoma land descends from mother to daughter, but clanspeople have no claim; a man who got land because he had no sister or through an allotment would leave it to his children (White 7). Dispute about a house would be settled at Laguna by the clan head (Parsons 33:249). Land disputes are and were (Cushing 6:142) settled at Zuni by the Governor.

† Parsons 33:197-98; Forde 3:383; Bunzel 2:477. Dr. Bunzel states that the maternal household owns fields that may not be alienated. (See p. 149.) Cf. Cushing 6:131 ff. Today, title to land is based on many different principles (Bunzel).

‡ Actually, the same practices occur among the Hopi (Forde 3:377-78). Where a family depends on fields from the father's clan, the mother would make regular presents of food to the man's family.

Ceremonial offices may also go over to the paternal side and then revert to the maternal side.

cultural land is held in a measure toward an unused house or old building site. After a time, if an absentee owner has not disposed of site or house, it reverts to the town. Grazing and timber lands are always communal. Theoretically no town land may be disposed of to strangers. The Spanish Crown gave the towns titles to land, to each town, *5,000 varas, measured from the central cross in the cemetery in the four directions:* a Spanish act in Pueblo style.

Maize is the staple crop. "Do we not live on corn," says a Hopi, and, expressing a concept central to much of the ceremonial life, he adds, "just as the child draws life from the mother?"[50] The corn is ground with a stone muller on a stone slab sloping up to the grinder, who kneels to the fixed slab. There are three slabs set side by side in frames of wood or stone, one for the first coarse grinding, and two for the successively finer ones. Pueblo cookery is or was a varied craft, but among several ways of cooking corn meal, the most distinctive are overnight baking in a pit oven, boiling sweetened blue corn meal in corn husk, and wafer-bread baking, in which the batter is spread very quickly on the stone griddle, a large rectangular slab, smooth and well greased, raised from the hearth a few inches, over a hot fire.[51] In the West, wafer-bread is made frequently, in large quantities, particularly by Hopi; in the East, wafer-bread is going out except as a ritual food. Even twenty years ago at Santa Clara there were only a half-dozen houses with the special hooded fireplace used in making wafer-bread.[52] Recently, the foremost ceremonialist of Isleta removed the hooded fireplace from his house. Grinding at home is also rapidly passing out (Isleta, Tewa, Taos); grain is taken to the near-by White town to be ground or to an Indian millowner. Such an innovation in the West, particularly in Hopi pueblos, would disrupt many customary ways.

Squash and beans are other Pueblo staples. Squash designs are used extensively in ritual art, and in the West beans figure in ritual roles. Beans like corn fit into the Zuni scheme of color-directions, and the order of kachina initiation is determined by the color order of the beans the families of initiates are to cook for the kachina. In the Hopi wedding procession while the bride carries a bowl of corn meal and her kinswomen, wafer-bread, the bride's mother carries a bowl of beans.[53] So important is the growing of beans in the kivas in the Hopi Powamu ceremony that the Hopi refer to the celebration in speaking to Whites as Bean festival.

Formerly, Hopi considered beans as filling as meat. In those premutton or prebeef days boiling meats were deer, antelope, mountain sheep, elk, and rabbit (cottontail or jack); baked meats were squirrel, prairie dog, porcupine, and other small game.[54] In scarcity Hopi (also Jemez) would eat dog, coyote, or horse.

Buffalo was hunted from Taos* and, of course, eaten; and bear and wild turkey, not eaten elsewhere,† are said to be eaten there. I have my doubts about bear, but domestic turkey I have seen Taos men eat, much to my surprise, for south of Taos turkey is a ritual bird, kept that its feathers may be used in prayer offerings; and it would not be eaten, people say, even in time of famine.‡

Formerly wild potatoes, wild onions, and cacti were gathered for food,[55] and also wild seeds, some of which still figure in ritual, for example, the amaranthus seeds in the most sacred bundles of Zuni,[56] or peritoma, which is mentioned in Hano songs.[57] Rocky Mountain bee plant is another common wild-plant food, a spinach which is taboo to certain societies in Laguna, Cochiti, Santa Ana (White) and Zuni, thereby helping, by the way, to identify them. Jackrabbit is taboo to the same societies.[58]

Today coffee is the common drink, taking the place of what in Mexico is called *atole*, a light corn-meal gruel. This *toshküyi*,[59] to use the Hopi term, is still used on ritual or fast days. Mescal,

* Buffalo-hunting parties went out from Jemez and other pueblos also. They had to be licensed by Spanish authority.

† Bear meat is eaten at Acoma (White 6); wild turkey is eaten at Isleta, also at Laguna (Boas) and Santa Ana (White).

‡ No turkey bones were found in early Pueblo settlements in the San Francisco Mountains, where turkeys abound, indicating that the taboo in Hopiland is an ancient one (Bartlett 1:68).

Turkey is not eaten by Navaho (Reichard) and Apache (Mescalero, Opler), to whom inferably the taboo spread from the Pueblos.

the fermented juice of agave, is known to Hopi, but it is little used. Formerly Zuni got it from White Mountain Apache. Whiskey or "white mule" has been procured through Mexican or Navaho bootleggers, and at one time worked havoc in the East, and even at Zuni. Shalako night in 1915 I went around with the Governor and the Government Farmer while they confiscated whiskey from visiting Navaho, about one hundred bottles. The Acoma Governor used to arrest whiskey-selling Mexicans.[60] Pueblos themselves decided to put an end to this drinking as uncongenial to their life. The success of their prohibition movement* together with the lack of native intoxicants has been cited as indicative of the nonorgiastic spirit of Pueblo character, sober and moderate in all ways[61] and, let me add, predisposed toward an utilitarian attitude, as may be seen from an old Zuni woman's account of the whiskey trade: "Whoever had whiskey sold it for sheep, blankets, headbands, money, bracelets, for all kinds of property. When those who drank came to their senses, they were poor. They had no more sheep. They had no blankets. They had no headbands. They had no shirts. It was very bad. In order to drink a little, the young men would waste all their property. They had no sense. They fought together. They tore their clothing; they wasted their flocks. It was not good."[62] Today "white mule" is back, not in Zuni, but in Taos and the Rio Grande towns.

Pueblos are light eaters. A tortilla or fragments of wafer-bread, or a little wheat bread, sometimes a meat stew with hominy, beans, and coffee, make a meal, and formerly there were only two meals a day, a late breakfast after several hours of work and an early supper. (Nowadays there is also a cooked midday meal.) Nevertheless, a great deal of attention is given food or food supplies. Household prestige is affected by the character of the meal that is served, for at mealtime there is considerable visiting about in the family connection. There is literally a family meal circle—and generally a lively circle it is, full of chat and jokes and good humor. The meal begins and

* Other tribes also learned from experience not to endure the sight of whiskey, e.g. the Cree (Kurz, 178).

concludes for all together, although I have seen guests after saying thanks shove back from the circle.* At the meal for a working-party it is polite for the workers to taste each dish four times
only and then to finish eating, a rule which applies, in fact, to
guests at large (Mishongnovi).[63]

Food is a medium of exchange. With food "they pay each
other" (Hano).[64] Among Hopi, in particular, there is a constant
interchange of service and food. Whoever is in charge of or heads
any enterprise, not only field parties for planting or harvesting
or kiva parties for spinning or weaving but a dance, an initiation,
a wedding, has to supply food, usually with the help of the
family connection, kinswomen coming in to grind or bake, kinsmen slaughtering sheep or steer. If your "aunt" is having a
working-party, you contribute a basket tray of corn meal, just
as at your marriage or funeral she, in her turn, will contribute
meal or wafer-bread. The kinsmen of your bridegroom who
weave your bridal outfit of belt and blankets are paid in food,
and for months afterward, when any of these men are performing
a dance, you don your bridal blanket and carry them a bowl of
food.[65] For food needed at an Acoma ceremony the ten "little
chiefs" summon the unmarried girls and boys to the War
chiefs' house to shell corn from the communal farm; then the
"little chiefs" carry the shelled corn to the houses and fill the
basket, large or small, which the woman brings out; the women
carry their meal to the War chiefs' house, and the War chiefs'
"cooks" give each woman a little meal as pay when they return
her basket; now the "little chiefs" take the meal to the houses of
skilful wafer-bread makers, giving each woman that day at noon
a little rabbit stew as pay.[66] In Pueblo society, in general, the
households of men engaged in any ceremonial are kept very busy
preparing food; at the conclusion of any celebration there is a
feast, with leftovers usually carried home.

Gambling debts or forfeits are paid in food (Hopi). Losers in
the game of hidden ball or, rather, the women of their households

* In earlier days etiquette at Zuni was stricter. It was considered shameful
for anyone to cease eating while any other remained obviously unsatisfied; or for
anyone not to cease eating very soon after even one of the others, if a respected
or elderly one, had done so (Cushing 6:581).

contribute the supper for the entire party. When women play against men, if the women lose, the following afternoon they take food to the kiva; if the men lose, they bring the women firewood.[67]

Marriage proposals may be made with food. On the "walk" Hopi young people take the day following ceremony or dance, a girl may give a boy a loaf of bread made of sweet corn meal. This is a matrimonial offer, and the boy must tell his parents. The same kind of offer may be made at the Powamu dance, when women give bread to the dancers as they file out of kiva; the girl suitor substitutes a loaf of *gomi* for the usual "tied bread"; unless the young man pass the loaf on to the dance leader, the family must be told.

Formerly on First Mesa wood was sometimes fetched by a large party. As the men returned with their wood packs, each would be met by a girl, bringing food. "Rest!" said the girl, and the man sat down and ate. Then she led the man to her house, where he left his load and was given more food. The following day he in turn took a bowl of meat to the girl's house.[68]

The same kind of interchange between men and girls may take place on the communal rabbit drives among Hopi, at Santo Domingo, San Juan, and elsewhere when the younger women go out* and the woman first to reach the hunter after he captures an animal receives it. The day following, the Hopi girl takes the boy's household a bowl of food. The Santo Domingo girl gives the hunter his lunch, and the San Juan girl takes the boy to her house to give him a basket of meal, which is subsequently returned filled with meat. Today at Zuni, when there are no hunters in the family, girls will go out to meet the returning hunters and be given a rabbit or two. "This rabbit is worth a good squash or so much meal," says the girl's mother, and that evening the girl takes the pay to the boy's house.[69]

Expressive of all this preoccupation with food[70] are certain

* What determines or motivates a hunt with the girls is obscure, except that in the East the kachina dancers have a say. Possibly it is to *pay* the girls for something. On Second Mesa the girls go out with the hunters after an adolescence ceremony at which they have been grinding, or after the Home-going kachina ceremony where the "clan mothers" are important (Beaglehole 2:13).

moral standards and a considerable amount of etiquette. Any food gift or exchange is accepted with a chorus of thanks (Hopi); the men of the household thank the women who have fed them (Zuni) as the women thank the men returning from the fields (Hopi).[71] Hospitality is identified as everywhere else with food. For the near-by caller, a watermelon will be cut, or piñon nuts, peaches, or grapes will be offered, and it is proper to eat before announcing the object, if any, of your visit. To a visitor from a distance, whatever time he arrives, a regular meal will be served. When the Hopi boy visited the Snake people, "they gave the boy something to eat right away." Similarly in a San Juan tale when Flower-Bird finds his lost wife in her parents' house, her mother urges food upon him. "Do not be ashamed, Flower-Bird, you are in a new house, eat well!"[72] Again in the Hopi-Tewa story of the poor boy who is transformed by Spider Grandmother into a good-looking boy, when he goes to the dance at Awatobi, he is offered food by one man after another, "Let us go to my house and have something to eat!" Just as, actually, visiting kachina impersonators are taken home by their hosts and given food. In no circumstances may you refuse food or, asking for it, be refused. To be stingy with food is greatly reprehended, and anyone denied food would feel very resentful. Because the War Brothers were thus neglected when they visited a certain town, did they not turn the townspeople into stone, and their children into birds? The Awatobi boy, while he was still dirty and unattractive, had been denied food, much to the indignation of Spider Grandmother, who said, "My grandchild, people have been treating you very badly, giving you nothing to eat." A notorious witchcraft case at Zuni was said to have started from the failure of a woman baking bread in an outdoor oven to give a piece to a man standing near by.[73] Feeling injured, the man planned to send a centipede into the body of the niggardly woman.

Meat might be given away by the Zuni hunter to anyone he met on his way home. After the return of Cochiti hunters, the whole town was invited to a feast. At Acoma paternal relatives were invited to eat boiled deer head, the paternal grandmother or senior "aunt" getting eyes or tongue.* Second Mesa deer hunters† also had a party to which "aunts" and sometimes other guests contributed wafer-bread, the "aunts" being served tongue or other meat before the others. A rabbit-hunter will present a rabbit to his senior "aunt"; formerly he also gave a rabbit to the hunt leader. The Isleta deer-hunter gives a piece of venison to Town chief and Hunt chief and to all his relatives, "in order to have luck and get more deer." In the San Juan tale of how the young hunter escapes the witches he is described as freehanded as the Zuni hunter, "a good boy, he gave meat to everybody, he left out nobody."[74]

HUNTING, WAR, AND TRADE

Formerly game was more abundant in the country‡ and formed a much more important part of the supply alike of food, as noted, and of clothing. Buckskin is still used for moccasins and for dance mantles, coats, or kilts, but the rabbit-fur blanket is no longer made, and buffalo hides no longer bartered. Quivers were made of mountain lion or wildcat hide. These animals are scarce today, and antelope, elk, and mountain sheep have disappeared, except in personal name[75] or in dance impersonation. Fox and coyote are trapped for their fur, which is needed in dance costume.

Deer and antelope were run down on foot. Antelope were also driven into a stockade through a brush chute extending several miles, the band started running by lads who built fires by fire

---

* Taboo to hunter: eyes would make his own eyes water, dimming them, and tongue would make him thirsty (Stirling). It is prescriptive for the Zuni hunter to eat the liver (Cushing 1:37).

† In Mishongnovi and Cochiti deer drives the quarry was partitioned according to the order in which the hunters came up; and the killer also received the head and hide (Goldfrank 3:87; Beaglehole 2:7). The third man to come up was given the internal organs and the blood which he might drink on the spot (Hopi), probably, as at Isleta, to become strong.

‡ Benavides, 37–38. Note the surrounds in the hills described as engaged in by four or five thousand hunters, big parties although the numbers were undoubtedly exaggerated, for there is no suggestion of the hunt being interpueblo. But Hopi did conduct interpueblo deer or antelope surrounds (Beaglehole 2:6–7).

drill and yelled like wolves (Hopi).* Such yells in hunting (and in war) were also given at Isleta as signals, a "coyote tele-graph."[76] Zuni hunters would give the cry of the mountain lion, hunter par excellence, to intimidate and paralyze deer.[77] Zuni deer-hunters painted their face and arms yellow and white to look like deer; and, in stalking, they put the hide and antlers over their back and head (as did Acoma hunters)† and took to a stooping posture, probably bending over a stick or sticks as do impersonators in the animal dances of the East. The exhausted animal was thrown down and choked to death (Zuni, Hopi). Deadfalls were also used. Bow and arrow were used and also, in hunting rabbits, a throwing-stick, straight or curved, the curved "false boomerang" being a very early type. Rabbits are drawn out of holes by twisting a spiny stick in their fur (Zuni,[78] Hopi, Tewa).‡ Nowadays the gun is used, in the East almost exclusively, except at Taos, where it is taboo in the rabbit drive and bow and arrow only are used. The wolflike dogs of the country are used in hunting, although these ever yelping curs serve mainly as watch dogs, against all strangers§ but primarily against night-prowling witches.

Small birds are trapped for their feathers in ritual. Eagles are taken from the nest, as at Zuni, among Keres, and today among

* Stephen 4:278. Never a practice on Second Mesa, where this chute-and-pound method of First Mesa was said to be borrowed from Navaho (Beaglehole 2:8). But the hunt pound is Northern Paiute, also the hunt fire (Lowie).

† White 6. (In 1887, seventy-four Acoma hunters killed 744 antelopes in one day, an almost incredible report in view of Pueblo conservation theory [see p. 95], but, as Dr. White suggests, Indian theory might have been given up owing to the pressure of Whites.)
Havasupai hunters wear a disguise in stalking (Spier 2:110). This method is said on Second Mesa to be Navaho (Beaglehole 2:8). It is also Apache (Mescalero and Chiricahua, Opler), Papago (Underhill), and Northern Paiute (Lowie, Steward).

‡ Havasupai also (Spier 2:113), also Northern Paiute (Lowie); probably quite general.

§ Let Bourke be our spokesman: "I was beset by a horde of snapping mangy Zuni dogs, half a million more or less" (Bourke 2:120).

Hopi, or lured into pits as formerly among Hopi and at Taos*
and as today at Jemez. The captive birds are kept tethered on
the housetop (Hopi) or in a wooden cage on roof or ground
(Zuni,† Jemez, eastern Keres); they are fed rabbit or, if need be,
dog (Hopi); after plucking, they are choked (Hopi).[79] Parrots
also are kept caged. A few years ago pigeon cotes were introduced into Jemez. A few ducks are kept at Zuni, and chickens
in several towns. There are flocks of turkeys in several towns.
The wild turkey was domesticated long before the Conquest, and
cloaks were made of turkey feathers. Today both turkey and
eagle feathers are in great demand in ritual.‡ So are parrot and
duck feathers. Chicken feathers are dyed and used in dance
headdress.

Chicken eggs are sold to the stores; they are not eaten. Nor is
poultry of any kind eaten, excepting turkey, as noted, at Taos.
The important idea of domesticating or breeding for food was
not conceived by the early Pueblos. (Otherwise, would they not
readily have bred rabbits?) The nearest they came to it was in
praying to the game animals to reproduce themselves, to send
"their children" to be captured. (Here, as on the Northwest
Coast, a striking illustration of coming near an invention and
because of conceptual block not making it!)

Domestication§ for food was introduced by the Spaniards

* Also among Northern Paiute (Lowie) and Jicarilla Apache, who cage the
birds, pluck them twice, and then set them free (Opler 2:207). The pit snare
was typical of the Plains tribes (see Kurz, 182–83).

† The day Bourke arrived in Zuni, May 18, 1881, a large number of eagles
were plucked. Their wicker cages stood upon the ground "in the corners of
buildings" (Bourke 2:114, 115). Mrs. Stevenson saw an eagle plucked inside a
Rain chief's house during the winter solstice ceremony (1891) (Stevenson 2:114).

‡ Possibly turkey was once a sacrificial bird, as it is in Mexico. In four Chaco
Canyon kivas, dated 850–1000, a turkey skeleton has been found behind the
fire screen (Brand, Hawley, Hibben, 74); and in one recorded Zuni prayer an
offering of the whole bird is indicated (Bunzel 4:677). Turkey feathers are the
commonest of all feathers used on prayer-sticks or as prayer-feathers (see pp.
275, 290–91).

§ A woolly animal was reported from Cibola which Cushing opined was llama-
like (Bourke 1:475), perhaps because of the llama-like figurines he found in
Arizona (see p. 317, n.†).

together with sheep and goats, cattle and pigs. Pigs did not "take" very generally.* Today they are kept at Isleta and at Taos. I do not recall seeing them elsewhere, although Stephen describes them at Hano, ridden by the children. Mutton in stew and dried beef are quite generally important foods, particularly in ceremonial feasting.

Cattle, sheep, and goats, as well as horses, mules, and burros, the other domestic animals of the Spaniards, are variously distributed. Hopi and western Keres are particularly well off in cattle and horses; Zuni and Sia, in sheep. Isleta, once rich in sheep, today has but two flocks. At Jemez there is a flock of goats, no sheep. No sheep at Taos, but lots of horses. Generally, horses have displaced mules or burros, which held their own longest among the mesa-dwelling Hopi. In the valley country over fifty years ago the ox cart with its spokeless solid wheels gave way to the horse-drawn wagon, as it and the buggy have begun to give way nowadays to the automobile. There are sixty-five Indian-owned automobiles today in Zuni against one in 1917, which was owned by Leopold, son of the Yaqui who somehow or other by way of raid or barter was adopted into a Zuni household.

Formerly, raiding or war must have figured very importantly, directly and indirectly in so far as dread of war determined the town site. The position of ruins on inaccessible mesa tops where both soil and water were scant is evidence of a deep-felt need of security against attack. Listen to the reproachful speech of an Oraibi townsman to Apache and Yavapai visitors, erstwhile enemies: "We walk down into that valley to plant our corn. 'Perhaps an enemy will come and kill me while I am working in the valley,' I think. So while I am working I look all around. I do not work very long; I come right back; then I sally down again. That is what I have to do all the time."[80]

For the most part, in historic times at any rate, it was defensive warfare, although, as noted, there was some intertown fight-

---

* A Santa Ana man said: "They ruin your gardens unless you pen them up, and if you do that you have to feed them. It is too much trouble and it doesn't pay" (White).

ing, and counterraids or attacks were sometimes undertaken against aggressive peoples. Also the Spaniards organized joint punitive campaigns against Comanche or Apache. The buffalo-hunt parties from Taos frequently became war parties in encounter with parties of Plains Indians. The downfall of Pecos* is ascribed not only to long-continuing attacks made on the town by their neighbors, the Comanche, but to an aggressive attack made on Comanche, in which all but one of the Pecos warriors were killed.[81] An Isletan told me how his father, one of the three surviving scalp-takers, went on a party against Apache who had carried off thirty head of cattle. The Isletan scouts found the Apache asleep, the others closed in and killed "lots of them."[82] Retaliatory motivation is indicated in Zuni war prayers.

> We cannot see him of whom we think.
> Because it is thus,
> To be avenged
> We have made up our minds.[83]

Zuni have even described themselves as the aggressors just as they were described in the earliest of historical accounts (see p. 878, n.*). "Because our ancestors were very poor, they wished for the flocks of the Navaho. Sometimes late at night they went about stealing the Navaho sheep and horses."† The War chief reminds his warriors that with "the enemies' flocks, their clothing, their precious stones, their good shell beads, our houses may obtain hearts."[84] Navaho scalps, being potent rain-makers, were in themselves sources of wealth.

The now extinct Piro once accounted a population of nine thousand were raided by Apache. The Tano of Galisteo as well as the people of Pecos were scattered or greatly reduced by Comanche. In the north, against Hopi and people of Taos, Ute, Paiute, and Apache were the hereditary enemies; against Zuni and Isleta, against Keres and Tewa, Apache and Navaho. Chama River towns may have been abandoned because of Navaho.

---

* In the eighteenth century: 1707, population 1,000; 1765, 344; 1782, 84, reduced by 1840, the date of removal to Jemez, to 20 men, women, and children.

† Bunzel 6:30; also 31, 34–35, 42. An Athapascan or Plains-like distinction between raid and war is suggested. For Hopi aggressiveness against Navaho see Nequatewa, 51.

Navaho were great raiders of stock and sheep. "When I was a boy," related old Tsiwema or José of Laguna (Pl. I), "the country was full of enemies, Navaho and Apache, always stealing cattle, sheep, and horses. This fight was in the north corner. The Navaho took some sheep from the corral of Tsitosh. So all the men went out to fight. They tied bread around their waist and took their bows and arrows. The Navaho went toward Paguate. One Laguna man was shot through the big toe, another in the left hand, another through the chest. By this time all the Laguna men had come up, and the Navaho fled. One Navaho wearing a cap of wildcat fur with ears,[85] they shot through his forehead and back. He was the bravest of the Navaho, so the others fled. The Laguna men brought back the sheep."[86] And presumably one scalp.

About this time Hopi of First Mesa had gone on a foray against Navaho, killing many and bringing back sheep. This was after four Hopi had been killed by Navaho as they were returning, a party of ten, from Fort Defiance to receive print goods from their Agent. One Hopi lay close to the ground and, holding a saddle over his head, heard bullets and arrows pelting against it. A bullet cut his leg. Another man, Moccasin, ran for the Hopi mesa and reached Sun Spring at sunrise. He yelled, and the people ran down to the spring, and he told them of the disaster. The women sat in groups wailing on the housetops; men sat huddled in their blankets; and no food was prepared or eaten.*

In escaping from the enemy or overtaking him as in stalking game, fast running was necessary; even when horses were available, war parties went on foot. Except at Oraibi† no massed

---

* Stephen 4:1002. Compare Hani's dramatic story (Nequatewa, 52–59). Oraibi had at least one big fight against Navaho raiders. The buckskin pad armor worn by Hopi (and by Navaho) was said to be very effectual against the poisoned arrows of the Navaho (Voth 5:258–66). Hopi may have used arrows similarly poisoned with rattlesnake venom (Voth 5:126; cf. Parsons 42:250). Rattlesnakes were kept penned at Hawikuh for arrow-poisoning (Hodge 3:81, Pl. XVII).

† Snake, Coyote, and Burrowing Owl clansmen engaged the enemy in front with war clubs, the others following with bows and arrows. The clubber clansmen were supposed to organize parties of revenge (Voth 3:344).

PLATE I

From painting by W. Langdon Kihn

JOSÉ, SHIWANNA CHEANI OF LAGUNA

fighting is reported—only a quick attack and a quick getaway. The early association of running with war still appears in the races characteristic of Pueblo ceremonials and possibly in the pace sometimes required of prayer-stick depositors or of dance couriers (Hopi).

Raiding also survives, as trespass on grazing lands, by Navaho, Mexicans, or "Americans," or stealing cattle, not to speak of land theft and "stealing water," forms of "peaceful penetration" established on the arrival of the White man. The Governor and his officers deal with this kind of encroachment as best they can; encroachment on the customs, *los costumbres*, another form of peaceful penetration, it is the function of the War chiefs to counter. As a rule neither War chiefs nor Governors concern themselves with the encroachments or innovations that come through trade, being oblivious of the axiom, "new goods, new customs."

Trade itself is not novel. The Pueblos have ever been traders: travelers or middlemen, mostly middlemen, since they were the more settled people to whom traders came. Shells alone would indicate old trade connections to the Gulf of California.* No turquoise mine with Indian workings has been uncovered as yet anywhere in Mexico, but Sahagún reports turquoise mines and Saville opines that the turquoise used as inlay on Middle American masks, ritual shields, and other objects was not necessarily traded from New Mexico.[87] However, turquoise (and white and pink shell) necklaces found recently in graves in Oaxaca are like those to be had today in the Southwest, where from earliest times turquoise has been accounted a jewel for personal adornment. Cibola (Zuni or Ashiwi tribe) traded turquoise and buffalo hides into southern Arizona and northern Mexico[88] probably long before the arrival of Fray Marcos, who was told about it. For a long time Hopi going to the Colorado for salt or pigments made

* Abalone has been found in Basket Maker II sites as well as in later Basket Maker and early Pueblo sites (Roberts 1:160). Also shell rim bracelets from the Gulf of California. Trade routes were established by the Arizona Pueblos of the San Francisco Mountains to southern Arizona and the west coast of Mexico by the ninth century (Bartlett 1:64). Cushing told Bourke that Zuni made trips every four years to the ocean! (Bourke 2:94).

side trading trips to the Havasupai for buckskin, baskets, or red ocher; and Havasupai have visited the Hopi mesas, and particularly Oraibi.[89] Through a Havasupai-Walapai-Mohave trade route to the Yumans of the Lower Colorado the Pueblos got their abalone and haliotis shells,[90] also some of the parrot feathers now become so scarce. Formerly White Mountain Apache and Paiute came to the Mesas to trade, Apache bringing in mescal cakes, high buckskin moccasins, and green (blue) bows, stronger than Hopi bows, and the Paiute, wood and piñon gum, bows and arrows, horses and meat—all these in barter for textiles or yarn, for wafer-bread or corn mush. Paiute also traded children for food as did Navaho.[91]

Navaho and Pueblos barter continuously: sheep and horses, blankets and buckskin, firewood and house beams for corn and wafer-bread, melons, chili or peaches; silver and turquoise jewelry for turquoise matrix. One dressed sheep is worth one forty-eight-pound sack of unhusked corn, or one smaller sack of corn together with a bowl of sweet corn meal, or one small bag of dried peaches and a large basket placque of wafer-bread (Hopi).[92] But at one time Navaho would give a sheep for four pounds of corn meal or two sheep for two handfuls of dried peaches (Zuni). "They had to pay high because Zuni and Navaho had been enemies."[93]

Lina Zuni tells how her father and Jesús the Yaqui "Mexican" and another man went on a trading trip to the East, Lina's father trading his slave, a little Navaho boy taken in a raid, for sheep, robes, and saddle blankets, thereby on his return home making his family very happy.[94] Trading trips were made by Tewa to the Apache; Apache baskets and mutton are in demand in the eastern pueblos. Formerly Comanche traders came to Santa Clara to barter buffalo hides for bread and meal, and Santa Clara men went into Comanche country where a sack of hard-baked wheat bread would buy a pony.[95] In 1853 Lieutenant Whipple encountered in western Oklahoma a party of eight men from Santo Domingo who on their burros were packing bread and flour to trade for horses and buffalo robes with

Comanche or Kaiowa.* Taos Indians also traded with Comanche and other tribes of the southern plains, and within the last few decades visiting parties between Taos and Oklahoma have carried on an interchange of "presents," including peyote. Horses, sheep, and corn are bartered with White traders for wheat, flour, coffee, sugar, canned goods and dress goods, and household furnishings.

Between the pueblos barter is general; no doubt it has always been practiced. Single merchants or more commonly small parties† make trading trips. In his journal for 1892 Stephen notes:

December 8, a party of four men arrive from Jemez. They are seeking to trade indigo for the women's blue woolen gown. They offer two five-pound boxes, about ten dollars in value at the trading-post, and ten yards of prints, for one gown, but they stipulate for new ones only. They display their ware in the main court, two boxes at a time, and sit around it chattering and talking with a group of Hopi, one of whom talks very good Spanish, in which their intercourse is wholly carried on.[96]

The pottery of First Mesa is bartered for the baskets of Second and Third Mesas. All the pottery-making pueblos have a pueblo trade. For slipping pottery and painting masks kaolin is traded by Acoma to Zuni.[97] At Jemez there is a special trade in the slabs for baking wafer-bread,[98] a stone slab,‡ laboriously made and polished, being worth a dress.§ Women's belts and men's hair "belts," woven at Zuni, and women's dark woolen

---

* White 4:19. Trade with Comanche was reported again in 1864. Buffalo robes and dried meat, horses and mules, were sought (*Report of the Commissioner of Indian Affairs*). See Bourke 1:530.

† The Hopi party to the Havasupai in 1890 consisted of four men (Stephen 4:996), and the above-mentioned Santo Domingo and Zuni parties of eight and three. As Espejo's party journeyed from Zuni to Hopiland in 1583, they passed a party of Zuni returning home, a man, three women, and three boys, inferably a trading party (Hodge 3:68).

‡ In the West the making of a bake slab is ritualized, not commercialized, although in the end, as Cushing puts it, the slab may be well paid for. At Oraibi a man will volunteer to lead a quarrying party, and prayer-feathers are offered at the quarry (Titiev 3). For Zuni see Cushing 6:327 ff. See pp. 90, 433.

§ A dress or piece of cloth is near-currency in the West as it was in early days in the Province (Scholes 1:33, 109) or as it was among Aztecs.

dresses and men's cotton dance kilts, woven by the Hopi, are traded to the eastern Pueblos. Probably kilts and dresses were the stock in trade carried by the Hano husband of whom his wife says in prayer, after sprinkling prayer-meal to the eastward at daybreak:

> Buffalo hides he shall find for me,
> Costly things* he shall find for me.[99]

Paper money has not always been acceptable, but silver circulates and, somewhat like turquoise, is sometimes a medium of exchange, sometimes jewelry. With silver dollars a Jemez trader will buy Navaho blankets to barter for turquoise, in matrix or as jewelry, at Santo Domingo, the turquoise center, at the Saint's-day dance. At Cochiti a Navaho blanket may be bought with shell beads much more cheaply than with American money.[100] Formerly shell may have circulated even more freely as wampum, for shell is "paid" today to the Spirits. Likewise turquoise.

At Saint's-day dances traders—Pueblo, Navaho, Mexican—go about from house to house or make a deal with a passerby.† Except for a few comestibles, there is no open market. Probably most of the trade within the town, too, is from house to house, or among Hopi spinners from kiva to kiva,[101] but little markets are held too. Crow-Wing of First Mesa writes on January 2, 1921, "The women are having a trading party. They have lots of things to trade."[102] What they had to trade in 1892, and how they did it, is described by Stephen:

In the court are set out five trays of dried peaches, two trays of salt, one tray of white beans and half a dozen trays from Oraibi, Middle Mesa, and Kohonino (Havasupai). In a little house with the door opening on the court there is about half as much again. No one remains specially with the stuff.

* Among them beads, no doubt, since there are few if any beadmakers today in the Arizona pueblos (Curtis, 29). Turquoise from New Mexico was traded in from early times (Bartlett 1:61, 73). See White 4:178 for a version of trade between beadmakers and textile workers after the Emergence.

† Hopi and Navaho visitors trade during the summer Home-going kachina ceremony (Beaglehole 3:79).

Later:

Eight, sometimes a dozen or more women are seated in an irregular circle in the court; before them are numerous small basket trays of sweet corn meal, peach stew, agave; a large basket tray of blue meal; mealing stones; baking powder, a few spoonfuls in slips of corn husks. Some women come from their houses and make exchanges for articles displayed, without sitting down. Generally, when a woman brings any article to be exchanged for something else, she first sits down and enters into the conversation which is constantly and volubly maintained. News, gossip and scandal are exchanged as well as commodities. Two or three women at the passage leading into Chief kiva court have beans, jerked mutton, and chili before them. They seem to enjoy each other's society, but talk very little and that very quietly. I noted yesterday a basin of beans and a handful of salt in a rag in the middle of the dance court. The woman who owned these things set them down and told another woman what she wished to barter for and left. The exchange was made during the owner's absence, some jerked mutton and baking powder were laid on her tray. She came back after an hour's absence and took up these exchanges and went home.*

MEN AND WOMEN

The home market, where there is one, carried on by the women,† or house-to-house trading, in which the women of the house have assuredly an important voice, and trading trips, by the men—that is a division of functions between the sexes which is as characteristic for Pueblos as for many other peoples, home work for women, work abroad‡ for men. But the division

* Stephen 4:245–46. Surely this is a picture of the aboriginal market, not the grandiose Aztec type, rather what I surmise was an earlier village type (Parsons 62:287). Also the Inca type (Means, 314–16). For Mishongnovi, see Beaglehole 3:81–82.

† At the Zuni market described by Stevenson an old man acted as go-between (Stevenson 2:378–79).

‡ Weaving excepted. Hopi women contribute nothing to this handicraft, although once they wove rabbit-fur rugs. Zuni men no longer weave (Stevenson 2:372–73); the women weave belts; and in 1881 they were weaving blankets (Bourke 2:198). Among the Pueblos living in east-central Arizona in the fourteenth century women were weavers, or at least spinners. In a woman's burial under a house floor were found spindle and cotton in a twilled basket, just as the deceased had left them, the cotton fiber around the spindle under the whorl, in her work basket. (On the deceased were a cord skirt [cf. p. 337] and sandals,

of labor is not rigid,* up to a certain point.† I have seen a man
shelling corn (this perhaps for his horse) (Hopi), or drawing a
water-jar design for the woman potter in his household (Hopi,
Zuni),‡ like that early Basket Maker who may have proposed to
some woman to transfer to a bowl the pattern of inclosed cross on
his sandal.§ Men are the beadmakers, but at Zuni now and
again a woman makes beads. Hopi women weave the basket
plaques, but winnowing trays are woven by men. Women are
the oven-builders, the house masons and plasterers, but men will
carry the mud and help the women mix; and the men transport

---

and she was wrapped in a plain cotton blanket. Over the grave was a large twilled
mat weighted down with rocks [Haury, 89, 146, Pls. XL, LVIII]).

In 1925 there were four women belt-weavers at cotton-growing Isleta, and
two women blanket-weavers. One of the oldest men of the town once wove
blankets, and the men are said to weave their dance kilts or clouts of white cloth
embroidered with the terrace design, an art learned undoubtedly from Hopi
weavers, possibly when the Isletans sojourned in Hopiland after the Rebellion
of 1680.

At Cochiti men are the belt-weavers.

* Not even in trading, for women traders will come from other mesa towns
to the women's market. Also, when women go to dances at other towns, they
may trade from headquarters at a friend's house (Beaglehole 3:81–82; cf.
Parsons 40:18).

Today it is, of course, easier and safer than formerly for women to visit
other towns; but I have known First Mesa women who had never been to Second
Mesa towns, six miles away.

† If beyond this, should a man take to women's work, he is expected to wear
women's clothes and conform in general to women's ways. Mannish women do
not become transvestites. I have known only two: Nancy of Zuni, who like a
male transvestite is an expert builder of fireplaces and dances kachina, and
Mrs. Chavez of Isleta, who is an independent traveler and trader and a member
of the War society.

‡ See the account of Julián Martinez of San Ildefonso as a designer given in
Bunzel 1:88.

§ See Morris, 197; but mine is the rash guess on the particular instance of the
use of a sandal pattern. Sandal patterns were not *as a rule* transferred to the new
art of pottery. Basket patterns were transferred, of course, because mud bowls
developed from lining baskets with mud; and inferably women made baskets.
Inferably men made sandals, upon which there was a "profusion of colored orna-
mentation, constituting, regardless of the medium of expression, the most
elaborate and artistic decoration ever produced in the San Juan country."

The inclosed cross is a design on early Hohokam pottery (Snaketown.)

stone or timbers and place the heavy beams.[103] Modern carpentry, making doors and window frames, is done by men.

Supplying wood for his wife's cook fire is a man's responsibility. The care and use of the domestic animals pertain wholly to men. Pueblo women, the women of Taos excepted,* unlike, Apache and Navaho women, do not ride horseback.† Nor do Pueblo women, again unlike the Navaho, herd sheep. Men slaughter and butcher sheep or steers; the women dress the meat. The heavy agricultural work, clearing the ground and plowing, is done by the men only, but women may help to plant, cultivate, harvest, or winnow.[104] At Zuni‡ and at Hotavila, the archaic town of the Hopi of Third Mesa, at Jemez and at Taos, women keep small vegetable gardens on the outskirts of the town or near the springs. All the crops are thought of as belonging to the women of the household. "Crops once housed belong to the mistress of the house, who has to store and care for them, so as to feed the family during the year. She uses, gives, and sells the corn at her discretion, making a daily allowance for her husband's horses, and, at his request, for those of guests. A man always speaks of the stored corn and other food as his wife's and does not dispose of it without her leave. Sometimes he speaks of it as hers while still in the fields" [Tewa].[105] Once I asked Nick of Zuni to sell me some of the colored ears of corn he had just brought home from *his own field*. "They are my wife's," said he, "I will ask her for you." A Zuni plants the seed corn his wife has prepared;[106] seed corn given away at ceremonials is usually given to the women. At Hopi planting parties, ceremonially organized, a girl will follow each man as he digs a hole with his stick, dropping in the seed. Possibly this was once the general planting practice.

When parties of men were about to set forth to the plains to trade with Comanche, women ground the loads of meal they were to carry at parties held at night when the men sang the

---

* Zuni girls going to a rabbit hunt would ride double (see p. 759).

† It is believed at Jemez that it would stretch their vagina (Harper).

‡ Bunzel 6:10. Chili and onions are grown, and gourds for water dippers.

grinding songs to drumbeat (Santa Clara).[107] In the West men
still come to sing at the grinding parties women hold sometimes
before ceremonial events. Prayer-meal is used on every ceremonial occasion, and it is always ground, of course, by the
women.

Thus in most economic activity men and women are engaged
on one part or another of the same general process, in "indus-
trial union." Even in connection with hunting and war, the most
distinctively male activities, the home-staying women have certain responsibilities and duties. This holds, in general, for the
ceremonial life, although women's roles are minor; and the most
precious things, fetishes, songs, prayers, and myths are usually
possessed by men.

The need of co-operation, at least for women, is amusingly
told in the widespread story of the sex lockout as incorporated
in the Hopi tale of the Emergence. "We do not need to be
married to live," said the women. "We can do our work and get
along without men." So the men departed across the river. The
first year the women raised good crops. The second year they
raised only about half as much. The third year they raised about
a third, and the fourth year they raised nothing. They were tired
out. The men were raising corn, peaches, and everything. They
got along without the women. They cooked for themselves and
did everything for themselves. About that time the women said,
"Let us erect a tower! We have sense enough to build a tower
and go up to the world above." They began to build, but they
never reached the sky; the tower fell down. The women grew
tired and needed the men. They needed children. They had to
have children. They could not get along without men.[108] And so
they begged the men to allow them to swim the river. The chief
gave permission, and the men received them gladly. The men
had built fine houses, and these they gave to the women. They
had also woven many fine gowns and girdles, and these they
also gave to the women; and there was abundance of corn and of
the flesh of elk, deer, antelope, and bear.[109] Houses, clothes,
food, and children, all by the grace of men! A far cry from
matriarchy. Unless someone insists that, as told in the most

maternally organized society of all the Pueblos, the tale is merely a man's wish fulfilment.

Actually Hopi women can be forward. On the only occasion when it is conventional for Hopi youths and girls to be seen together, on the loitering or walking parties following the conclusion of a ceremony, on plant-gathering parties, and formerly on wood-gathering or in rabbit hunts the girls appear to make the advances, each girl selecting a man to give food to. We noted that if she gives a sweet corn loaf it is tantamount to a proposal of marriage.[110] Carrying a basket of meal to the house of a boy's mother is another way of proposing. The young men go courting only by night, according to hints in the folk tales and to recent reports from Oraibi and Mishongnovi,[111] slipping in to a girl's house to talk or even to sleep with her. Night-prowling seems to be on the increase, but possibly it derives from an old practice akin to early Zuni (and Papago and Northern Paiute) courtship. "Formerly at Zuni a young man would patiently wait, standing silently of nights in the neighborhood of the girl's house, sometimes playing on a flute or singing a love song, not to her, but in her hearing. Favor granted, the youth visited the girl's house. If the mother and father approved of him, they reminded the girl of the duties of hospitality. She brought him a vase of fresh water, and offered him a tray of wafer-bread, and if still favorably inclined sat down and tasted the food and drink with him. The lover was required to make a bundle, that is supply the adornments and make the costume and moccasins of the girl, also to show his ability in tilling the soil and in hunting deer. With the acceptance of the bundle the young man himself was accepted."[112]

Of flute-serenading, a Papago, Yuma, Shoshone, and Plains practice, one also hears at Taos; but, except at Acoma corn-grinding parties and in ritual, flute-playing has gone out. Presents to the girl are still made, still consisting in the West of dress and blanket, belt and moccasins—wedding bundles which figure vividly in folk tales[113] as in daily life. In tales the good hunter is ever the chosen or favored man; no other qualifications are mentioned. Before or after they have slept together, the girl will go to the youth's house to grind corn or to get corn to grind at home. She will also grind her own corn to pay for her dress (Zuni).* Among Hopi there is head-washing ritual for the couple; the bride's hair is dressed in the style of the married woman, a mud-incased twist on either side; and during the making of the trousseau by the groom's relatives there is an elaborate series of visits and of food exchanges and feasts.[114] Wedding festivity occurs also in the East,[115] in a European setting.

Monogamy prevails with casual intercourse licensed on occasion† and with remating not infrequent.‡ In the West the marriage tie is brittle, a man has not only to please his wife§ but the seniors of the household. Whether he is turned out or leaves of his own accord, he is welcomed back to the house of his mother or sister, from which he has really never separated. In the East, where Catholic influence counts against formal remarriage, there are probably a larger number of clandestine relations, both in and out of marriage. Adultery was punished by public whipping at Taos and Acoma,[116] and in other eastern pueblos the Governor has supported the Church in regulating sex conduct.‖ At Zuni any such interference by the Governor would be out of the question; adultery is not punished, but some years ago when the Agent, a determined Catholic, imprisoned couples for adultery, the people did not criticize him; they only laughed, once particularly when he imprisoned together, thinking them man and wife, the very couple he wished to come between. At Oraibi crop failure may be attributed to adultery.[117] Throughout the folk tales, although adultery may have grave consequences or be punished, particularly adultery with a chief's

---

* Bunzel. In return she is given food and wheat. Cf. Benedict 3:I, 146–47.

† See pp. 624–25. "Laughter" (*waha*) is the reference (Benedict 3:I, 33, n. 1) for the promiscuity of Zuni "big dances" (Wood and War societies' ceremony, Owinahaiye, Shalako, Scalp dance, Saint's dance).

‡ One separation to three marriages has been estimated for Oraibi (Titiev 3).

§ To divorce him, she has but to pile his belongings outside at the ladder: his box of valuable feathers and willow sticks cut for prayer-sticks, his mask, rattle, dance kilt, and moccasins (Zuni; Benedict 3:II, 81).

‖ Dumarest, 148, 150–51; Parsons 49:36. White men were tried for adultery or concubinage under Spanish administration.

wife, incontinence during ceremonial or in emergent or critical situation is the major offense.

From an economic point of view clandestine relations are not approved,* since the woman's household may have to forego a worker, besides, in case of offspring certain obligations, ceremonial as well as economic, between the two family connections are foregone. The unfathered child is "stolen" from his father's people. Nevertheless, gossip and genealogical records indicate that in every town there are many "stolen" children; not uncommonly in the East the eldest child in the household has his mother's surname, which generally indicates illegitimacy. Yet a bastard is cared for by his maternal grandparents or other relatives, or brought up in whatever household his mother becomes part of, in just the same way as children born in marriage.† Pregnancy or childbirth often leads to marriage. In the Oraibi bridal outfit a present will be included for the little bastard: a miniature wedding robe for a girl, the boy's little black and white blanket for a boy.[118]

Girls marry as young as fourteen or fifteen; but the usual age is from sixteen to eighteen, and the age for youths is a few years later. Seldom is a woman older than her husband. I recall two

* Except at Sia, where a girl's mother will bargain for her, a near form of prostitution (White 5).

† The only discrimination of any kind I ever heard of occurs at Taos in the rule that a bastard may not hold any secular office.

From the severity of its sanctions, the Church appears to have had special difficulty in enforcing its marriage rules at Taos in early days, when it reports the existence of plural marriages, also a miracle against them. "It went hard with them to give up having many wives as they used to have before they were baptized; and each day the Religious preached to them the truth of the holy sacrament of marriage. . . . . The one that most contradicted this was an old Indian woman, a sorceress," until "the heavens being clear and serene, a thunderbolt fell and slew that infernal mistress of the Demon, right between the good Christians (four women out wood-gathering with her) who were resisting her evil doctrine. . . . . Directly all the pueblo flocked thither, and seeing that rap from heaven, all those who were living in secret concubinage got married, and believed very sincerely all which the Father taught them. He promptly made them a sermon there, upon the event" (Benavides, 26), and, of course, he remained unaware that his listeners believed the old lady had gone to the gods. (See p. 171.) In fact, what he said may well have confirmed that belief. Inferences from miracles are rarely identical.

instances of a widow remarried to a man some years her junior, one at Laguna, one at Picurís, and in both instances comment was similar: "I don't know why he married her." On the other hand, the marriage of a widower to a girl is not uncommon in the East; at Jemez, in particular, I noted several instances. Among Hopi such a marriage is uncommon; it is believed that if the once-mated remate with a virgin both are doomed to carry burden baskets after death.[119]

The widowed may remarry at Zuni after six months;* if sooner, his or her stomach would swell, and he or she would die.† After Lina Zuni had observed the proper time for the husband who had been killed by Americans, her father and uncle desired her to marry again. "Do not think of where you have come from, but rather look forward to where you are to go," counseled Lina's wise old uncle. "If you are lucky, this good man [her then suitor] will be kind to you. He will be the one to provide food for us properly; furthermore, he may have some sheep."[120]

In the West clan exogamy is strict, and marriage into the father's clan is also disapproved of. In the East restriction in choice is based primarily on kinship which can be traced within the family in both maternal and paternal lines. The restrictions extend beyond what might be imputed to Catholic influence; but the idea that cousin marriage would entail sickly offspring, cripples or albinos (Taos), may be European. Clan exogamy is established among Keres, but among Tewa the clan seems barely to be considered in marriage. Marriage into another town is always disapproved of, if not forbidden, particularly for girls; and interracial marriage is thoroughly condemned. An Isletan girl who would marry a Mexican has to face the possibility of turning into stone.[121] After death, if you have married Mexican, you will become a mule; American, a horse; Navaho, a deer (Zuni, Acoma).‡ The grandfather of María of Taos used to tell her

---

* A year (Bunzel); six months are sometimes called a year in Zuni.

† Parsons 1:247. A sickness from the dead.

‡ A Huichol mating with a Mexican woman will encounter her after death as a mare and have to ride her. She will trample him unless he have buried with

that, if she consorted with White men, "on the last day" she would turn into a red ant. Even in life you have to make a lot of adjustments if you are married to a foreigner whom the townspeople are unwilling to adopt. In Taos a man would have to sever his kiva associations, and here and elsewhere Mexican or American spouse would not be allowed to live in town.

FAMILY AND EDUCATION

Large families are uncommon. Child mortality is high, nor is it offset by a high birth-rate.[122] Emmenagogues or contraceptives are referred to,[123] but probably they are little used, and abortion is condemned. Children are much desired, and, if need be, there is always someone glad to adopt, within the family connection.[124] In familial as in ceremonial life adoption is an important adjustment. Girls are prized more than boys (western towns), since girls remain in the household and, descent in the clan being matrilineal, contribute to the importance of family or clan. In the comparatively man-made society of Taos boys are more desired than girls. "Girls are the meanest things," echoed a Taos girl, "our parents say they are more troublesome than boys."

Infants born at the waxing or full moon will live well and long. The days of the waning moon are inauspicious. This belief affects the ceremonial calendar very importantly. Initiations are thought of as rebirth, and so initiatory ceremonies will be timed for a waxing moon.[125]

Except at Sia, there are no professional midwives; the paternal grandmother generally takes charge. The confinement lasts twenty or forty days among Hopi, ten days at Sia, four days at Zuni, and various periods at other towns. Every fifth day the Hopi woman is given a steam or sweat bath under a blanket. At Zuni, Acoma, and Sia the infant is delivered on a heated sand

---

him a nail for a spear, a machete to beat her with, a hank of horsehair for a rope, and a cactus spine for a spur (Zingg).

The Southern Ute who married a first cousin would be compared with the mythical trickster (Lowie).

bed,* in Zuni phrase, "it is cooked." The unborn beings of Zuni, the supernaturals, are always referred to as the raw people.

Usually the child is presented to the Sun, is blessed with corn-ear ritual, and receives a name, four days after birth. Among Hopi the naming ritual is performed on the twentieth day; each "aunt" or paternal kinswoman bestows a name associated in some way with her clan,† but one name only "sticks."[126] The Acoma baby like the Hopi gets his name from his father's clan.[127] At Zuni head-washing and presentation are performed by paternal grandmother or aunt on the eighth day (Bunzel). In other accounts the woman who has been present at the birth, who is the first to pick up the baby, gives the name in presenting the infant, her husband or son becoming the ceremonial or kiva father of the child; or a woman whose own children have thriven may become the name-giver. In the East a doctor may conduct the naming ritual of presenting the newborn to the Sun. The Acoman doctor paints bird or animal tracks under the eyes of a boy baby and smears the face of a girl baby with corn pollen and meal, singing the song Iyatiku, the Corn Mother, sang when she first saw the sun.[128] A child born at the time of kachina dancing may receive a name from the kachina (Cochiti, Laguna,‡ Nambé),[129] somewhat as a Catholic child is named for the saint of the day he is born. At Taos a chief of the kiva or kiva society to whom the newborn is given becomes the name-giver. At Isleta infants are given their group names at the ceremonials of the groups they are to belong to, moiety or Corn group. In general, at any initiation into a ceremonial group a name is given; nick-naming is also in vogue, so that names accumulate, and a person

* Cf. Havasupai (Spier 2:300), Papago (Underhill 3), Southern California, Northern Paiute (Kelly, Steward). See pp. 986, 990.

† See p. 60, n.†.

‡ Kisuwetsa told me that one day, say in 1852, at a kachina dance her mother heard the name Kisuwetsa in a song and asked the dancers for it for her little girl who was still without a name liked by the family. The child was led out into the dance court to breathe in from a dancer (*katsena guputstani*) and subsequently taken to the house of the dance leader to have her hair washed by his people. See p. 454.

may have three or four "Indian names" besides his Spanish church name and American school name.

Although there is little understanding of child hygiene, all members of a household are solicitous about the welfare and growth of the children, whether through food or through magic.[130] Education proceeds very largely through imitation or apprenticeship. Little girls at Cochiti, for example, are given small baskets to fill with ground meal, and an especially light grinding stone, the size of the basket and the weight of the stone being increased as the girl grows up. Boys are given hoe and spade to help their father in the fields.[131] Almost as soon as a Hopi boy can walk, he accompanies his father to field or sheep corral. As he grows older, his father sets aside a few sheep as the boy's special property or, having taught him about soils and dams and boundaries, gives him a small plot to farm.[132] From his father a boy may learn beadmaking or moccasin-making.[133] Presumably, his first lessons in hunting are given by his father or by an older boy in the household, but, when he kills his first jackrabbit, his father or uncle invites a good hunter to become his "hunt father" and instructor; his ceremonial father has already been selected by his mother (Second Mesa)[134] or by both parents. This "father" sponsors the little boy when the children are whipped at the Powamu kachina ceremony, and later the boy joins the Men's society his "father" belongs to and possibly any other society of which his "father" is a member. At any time even before initiation the "father" of a boy or man may call upon him for assistance, in salt expeditions, in sheep-herding, or in any working-party (Mishongnovi, probably elsewhere).[135] Throughout Pueblo life the functioning of sponsor or ceremonial father (in Spanish or English, *padrino* or godfather) is of the utmost importance to the individual, to the family, and, in maintaining ceremonial organization and social standards, to the whole community. Only "good men" should be chosen by parents as godfathers.

A limited amount of direct moral instruction goes on in the family. If a Zuni child whimpers from hunger or impatience from having to wait for the meal all are supposed to eat together, grandfather or somebody else will say, "There now, never lie around longing for food; never whine for it—dogs do that!"[136] The Jemez child is instructed: "You must not carry tales or lie about people. You must be industrious."[137] A Hopi will impress on his son the need of being thrifty, energetic, and hardy against inclement weather.[138] Crow-Wing notes in his journal of January 25 that, it having been decided by the old men of Hano to talk this day about old ways, "in nearly every house grandmothers and grandfathers and our old uncles are talking of these old ways and whence the people came, words to be kept always and never forgotten."* When old Tsatiselu of Zuni, a Ne'wekwe doctor, told me folk tales, little Jim Lewis, his favorite grandson, always sat by to listen, and the old man saw to it that at the end of the tale both Jim and I stretched our arms up or out, saying "May our corn be *so* high!† Our melons *so* big!" As the night wore on and little Jim grew sleepy, his grandfather would tell him that if he did not sit up straight during a story his back would grow crooked.

Races and dances are planned for the children. First Mesa kick-ball races begin with a children's race, as do relay races at Isleta, and formerly at Zuni there were kick-stick races for the little boys. After mint-grass-gathering parties on Second Mesa the little boys are made to race with the kachina who have given them tasty bread.[139] Formerly on First Mesa there was a "zig-zag," throw-away dance for the children.[140] On the first day of the Hopi Buffalo dance it is the children who dance or perform the first round of the dance, and in the Butterfly dance little girls come out.[141] Little girls dance with the Marau society, and very little boys as young as four or six may come out with the clowns[142] or with the Snake and Antelope societies. After telling how the men had spun all day in kiva, Crow-Wing mentions in his journal for January 26 that some children danced there in the evening, "so everybody enjoyed it." At Jemez, at the conclusion of dances boys are allowed to tail on and dance, and from earliest years children are taught by parents or by older

* Parsons 40:38. Compare the pedagogic speeches or sermons of the Aztecs.

† Compare Hopi (Shumopovi), Wallis 1:58.

children to dance and sing and drum.* Little boys dance Buffalo
and Deer at Taos, and the children have a Christmas vespers
dance in which the girls pretend to grind corn on the backs of
the kneeling boys, a pretty little play. Christmas night at Taos
or the night of Kings' Day celebration at Acoma groups of children go about from house to house to dance in foreign style, Ute,
Apache, Navaho, or Plains, a Pueblo rendering of Las Posadas.

A good deal of trouble is taken to make the children believe
in the masked dancers, the kachina, who are to administer a
ritual whipping at a tender age (an exciting and dreadful occasion), whose dances have been watched from infancy, whose
masks are sometimes fed by a child (Zuni),† and who like our
Santa Claus ever bestow upon children, *good children*,‡ a variety
of presents—sweet corn and fancifully baked breads, moccasins,
and toys: small rattles, bows and arrows, "dolls" and miniature
cradles. These things will be made by the child's father or uncle
and conveyed secretly to some masked dancer who will step out
of the ranks to give the child the present.§ A little Walpi boy of
five or six had been begging his father for a bow and arrows,
relates Stephen, so the father gave the little fellow a pinch of
prayer-meal and told him to go with his little sister to the
kachina shrine, sprinkle the meal, and ask (pray) for what he

* Harper; Parsons 41:89. Boys of six or seven, several years before kachina
initiation, are taken in a group to their father's kiva and given some instruction
(Harper). Inferably this corresponds to what is called elsewhere the first initiation, and it is after this that little boys are allowed to tail on to their kiva's
maskless dancers.

† For good luck the youngest child will be sent to throw a handful of crumbs
toward the mask recess and to say this prayer: "Grandfathers, here, eat! May I
become a woman, and may my older brothers and older sisters reach young man-
hood and young womanhood!" (Bunzel 5:854).

‡ Mishongnovi children are told that kachina bring gifts only to those whose
footprints the kachina have observed about the mesa at dawn, to those who rise
early and are industrious (Beaglehole 3:20).

§ Stephen 4:194, 212, 220, 224, 351, 373, 574, 575. Sweet corn is given Jemez
children. One day a little girl came home from the dance carrying some spruce-
set ears which, as soon as she saw me, she hid behind her back, demonstrating
an Eastern feature of kachina training, never to let a white person learn anything
about the kachina. In the West it is quite different. During a Zuni Shalako celebration a girl of seventeen and I were alone in the house when we heard the
kachina hoot. Waiyautitsa ran into my room asking me to come and sit with her;
the Salimobia were bringing a present of bow and arrows, and she was afraid!

wanted. Meanwhile the father retired to Stephen's house and
made a bow and five arrows which he took to the dance court;
and, returning home, he gave them to the little boy, saying the
kachina had brought them. Another time a maiden who was
boiling some eggs for Stephen arranged to have a dancer give
them to him together with some red and yellow wafer-bread in a
basket. Knowing about this, the mother of a boy of six took him
to the shrine and had him cast prayer-meal and pray the kachina
to bring Stephen something. When the gift of eggs and wafer-
bread was made by the dancer, the mother of the little boy took
care to have him see it. A speedy response to prayer! The boy
marveled, and everybody was gratified.[143]

Formerly at the afternoon Zuni Shalako dances the masked
clowns gave children toy bows and arrows or kachina dolls hung
with bread in the shape of turkeys or game animals or babies.
The clown would go searching cautiously and grotesquely as
though afraid of the person he sought. (Mock fear is a regular
clowning trait.) The child half-frightened would be induced by
its mother to reach for the gift. Then the clown would suddenly
straighten up, become grave, and deliver a long, loud-toned
harangue, a sermon on hunting or housekeeping.[144]

But the most elaborate religious or moral training given the
children is through the bogeys who are advertised as carrying
children away in their basket or sack. Any naughty or unruly
child will be threatened with one of these bugaboos—"I am
going to send Su'ukyi to eat you up," says a Zuni mother.[145]
Sings the Tewa mother:

> Stop crying! Go to sleep, my little boy Primrose.
> That Saveyo Sendo (old man) will take you if you cry.
> Over there he will eat you, if you do not stop crying
> Right now he will eat you, if you do not stop crying.
> That Saveyo Sendo in his bag he will put you,
> Stop crying! Go to sleep, my little boy Primrose.
> Over there he will take you, then I will be crying!
>
> . . . .
>
> That Saveyo Sendo whose teeth we all fear.
> Over there now, if you do not stop crying,
> Over there now, on the crest of the mountains,
> Those Saveyo walk and they hear every sound.[146]

The bogeys are supposed to guard the peach orchards against child pilferers (Zuni, Santo Domingo); also they go around town or make house-to-house visits to lecture or frighten the children. "Go into that rock crevice over there!"* said Lina's mother when they were camping at their peach orchard and Atoshle came down off the top of Corn Mountain. "Where are the children who live here?" asked Atoshle. "They are very naughty. Therefore I have come down."¹⁴⁷ When the masked "grandfather" came into our house at Zuni, the little girl of four or five† ran whimpering to hide her eyes in her mother's lap, whereas her younger brother made brave responses, "Yes, yes," to the terrifying "grandfather" who bade him wash his face every morning, mind his parents, or help his father, and who punctuated his harangue with thrusts of his knife. As soon as Atoshle had been sprinkled with prayer-meal and given bread, the little boy was taken outside to wash his face in the snow. Sometimes Atoshle and his attendant clown mask will take a little boy down to the river and duck him. If the boy has rebelled against delousing, the old woman Atoshle will brush his hair, and the old man will pretend to eat the lice. The old woman will catch a little girl around the ankle with her crook and, to show what is going to be required of her, pull her over to the grinding stones.

Outdoors the children are free to run away from Atoshle, and as he goes through town, hooting and pushing back his long wild locks with his knife, supposedly a gesture of wiping off the blood, all the children rush away, and even young women take refuge in corral or doorway.¹⁴⁸ How rigidly respect for Atoshle was inculcated in earlier days comes out in a story told by old Lina Zuni: Atoshle came out of the kiva. The children were all frightened. Two little boys ran into an oven. One of them began to

* When Isletan mothers heard the jingles of Chapiude, they would hide their children between the walls of the houses because in those days, said my naïve Lucinda, the cannibal monsters or giants really did range for prey. Zuni bogeys are also associated with the early monsters who were killed by the War Brothers, one of whom is regularly called by Navaho and Apache, Slayer-of-Monsters.

† Children under six appear very much afraid of the Powamu bogeys, reports Stephen; older children assume a bold front (Stephen 4:183, 187).

cry. "Don't cry!" said the other. "It's not really Atoshle. Somebody is just pretending. Atoshle is not dangerous." These comforting words were repeated at home. "That boy has no sense, and you have no sense," said the boy's mother. "It is a wonder that Atoshle did not kill you! Some dangerous creature, some angry gods will cut your throat!" The woman was angry because the boy had mocked the kachina, and that was very dangerous, and she knew the boy would be punished. When the angry kachina did come to cut the boy's throat, his father raised his gun and threatened to shoot. Another kachina, Father Koyemshi, intervened and suggested that they merely cleanse the boy. "Don't cut off his head! Just cleanse him, to frighten our friends. Whip him with yucca!" And so this little boy escaped the fate of K'aiyuani, who, after he was initiated, mocked the kachina and was beheaded,* his head thrown into the lake of the kachina.[149] This dire example is related at the initiation of the boys into the Kachina society; but long before that a boy's mother has said to him, "Don't mock at the kachina! Blue Horn and Homachi will cut off your head. It is very dangerous. The kachina chief will hear of it somehow. He will summon the dangerous kachina, the Blue Horns, and they will whip us."[150]

On First Mesa, in the winter of 1921, people were complaining that the initiated children were betraying secrets to their juniors, and it was decided to send out a bogey kachina to give the children a lesson. After the kachina made his threatening round, the Town chief met him and begged him not to carry any of the children away. A beheading may even be staged to the terror of the children (and women) who shout and scream when they recognize their kinsmen in the victims.[151] Mere infants or toddlers may be frightened at dances by the "angry kachina." Once during a masked dance at Santo Domingo a little boy ran across the dance court. The whipper kachina chased him and had not a War captain picked up the child the kachina might have whipped him to death, at least so the Acoman who was looking on was told.[152] Jemez children are warned that if they

* In Santo Domingo tradition it was a woman who was beheaded for not believing in the kachina (White 4:175). See p. 341.

stray too far from home the "dancers" will get them, and a mother will say to a misbehaving child, "I'll tell the dancers."[153] There are still other appeals to infantile fear. The owl will pick out the eyes of a naughty child or will carry him off. Once at Cochiti I saw a three-year-old child bury his head in his mother's lap, terror-stricken by the hoot of the owl she was imitating. When a Zuni child strays from home, he may be told that the Navaho will get him or that he will come back with snakes hanging to his legs or he will be beset by witches. The twelve-year-old girl who used to sleep out with me on the house-top would never climb the ladder first; she was too much afraid of witches. One night we heard some young men singing as they drove their horses to pasture. "They are singing to keep off the witches," said little Margaret.[154] Young people who would have premature sexual relations may be threatened with earthquake which releases wild animals from underground, a sanction also against clan incest.[155]

In such ways the young are frightened into conformity or obedience, frightened rather than punished. Lina Zuni's father whipped her when from some contrary impulse she threw a new jar down the hatchway and it broke;[156] and the girl who abandoned her baby to Red Deer Woman is struck by her uncles when they hear her story. "You big fool!" each says and strikes her.* We hear of an Acoman whipping her son because in play with a slip noose he almost strangled his younger brother.[157] When Corn Tassel's father heard that together with her lover and Laguna's transvestite she had killed her husband, he took off his belt and beat her, although she was playing sick.[158] But abandoning an infant or strangling a brother or being party to a murder is strong and very unusual provocation; beating or whipping in a Pueblo family is infrequent. The Hopi say they do not whip because once after a little girl would not stop crying and was struck by her mother, with her brother she ran away to

---

* Bunzel 6:110. In a variant it is the girl's brother who whips her. He also takes away her turquoise earrings and necklace, putting them on his nephew (*ibid.*, 123).

one of the shrines of the War Twins, who turned both children to stone.[159]

There are several tales about children or young people running away after a scolding. "We do not scold our children," Isletans* say, "because of the girl who turned into an eagle and flew away after she was scolded for delay in filling her water jar," or, in another version, "for doing everything her mother did and getting in her way."[160] In Zuni tale the youngest of the Rain chief's four daughters never did any work. "You are a good-for-nothing girl," say her sisters, "if you don't feel like cooking, go down to the field and help father with the hoeing! For what purpose are you alive?" The girl feels sorry for herself and cries and, barefoot and without a blanket, runs away to the south. She says to the Cloud boy she meets, "When I got angry at my house, I left it." The Cloud people hide the girl because her sisters should not have scolded† "even though they saw the girl doing wrong" by shirking household obligations.‡ My little Zuni friend, Jim Lewis, ran away one late afternoon after his mother had scolded him for prying into my purse. His "fathers" searched for him on foot and on horseback, his grandmother wept, and it was not until Jim was found playing unconcernedly in the streets late that night that any other one of us was again at peace.

Being talked or sung at or about is quite as unpleasant to a Pueblo as it is to us, perhaps more so, particularly in terms of ridicule,§ and I have the impression that one source of this

* Lummis, who lived five years in Isleta, remarks that excepting one case he never saw a child impudent to parents or seniors or a child chastised (Benavides, 40 n.).

† Sensitiveness to scolding has been noted among Papago (Underhill) and Northern Paiute (Kelly). Is it a widespread Indian trait?

‡ Bunzel 6:185 ff. For household friction caused by shirkers cf. Beaglehole 3:6.

§ A thief is jeered at in pointed allusion by the clowns (Mishongnovi, Beaglehole 3:12). Even witches may be punished by being made ridiculous. After Star-Lightning exchanges the bodily parts of some Oraibi witches, giving a young wife the wrinkled leg of an old man or a man the head of a woman, the god says, "You are bad, and this shall be your punishment; you shall be ridiculed by people" (Voth 2:130).

sensibility is reproving children by laughing at them. When little Lina reached for the salt and fell into the bean pot and her father exclaimed, "You big salt-eater!" that stuck in her memory for life.[161]

In general, the young are assumed not to entertain, still less to obtrude, contrary individual interests. "Manners" express this point of view. Titbits are fed a child at family meals, but the child may not ask for them, and, as remarked, a hungry child must learn to wait patiently (Zuni). A child on visiting may not touch anything in the house, nor is a child allowed to pass in front of an older person (Cochiti).[162] On bringing something to a senior and waiting to have it returned, a child should stand with folded arms (Cochiti, Laguna),* an old, old posture of submission.[163] Children are expected to pause in their play when an elder passes by (Isleta).[164] Elders are always greeted respectfully, by some kinship term, never by name.

KIN, CLAN, AND MOIETY

Children grow up learning to call everybody in the household and most visitors by a kinship term, not by the same term their mother uses, but by a corollary term, for example, anyone she calls child, her own child will usually call brother or sister, anyone she calls mother will be called grandmother, and so on. Kin and clan terms are the same, and kin-clan terms are applied in all sorts of fictitious ways. Lusteti of Zuni was once found unconscious on the roadside. The man who found and revived him became his "father" and might have initiated him, had he wished, into his society just as the Walpi man who saved Hani from the Navaho became his "father."[165] Oraibi warriors become the "fathers" of wounded men whom they carry home and take care of or bury.[166] In San Juan tale the man who finds the deer-boy claims him for his own family, for his "uncle," instead of returning the boy to his mother. To the family or household or, among Hopi, to the entire clan of such adoptive or ceremonial father or initiator you apply kinship terms, as well as, at Zuni,

---

* Goldfrank 3:80; Parsons 16:38. "May you grow tall!" says the senior. "Good (thanks)!" says the child.

to the family of your ceremonially established friend. The animals are commonly spoken of or to as kindred, often as if they were the children of men. For example, in the Zuni version of the dog tattler the cur says, "Father! last night my mother (meaning the man's wife) slept with another man," and when the man refers to the affair, he says that it was his child who told him about it. "Which child?" asks his family. "The one that watches over me, my little dog." When a hunter speaks to the deer, he may say, "Which of you will let me take him home to your mother?" meaning his own wife. Spider is invariably "grandmother," and Coyote, "grandfather" or "uncle." Birds, plants, anything in nature, may be thought of in the familiar and warm bonds of kinship. Thus Hopi clans "got their names."* For example, as the Mustard clan was traveling along in the early migratory days, a child on its mother's back began to cry. They pulled some mustard weeds to quiet the child. "These weeds we will have in our clan," they said. In turn they come across an oak tree, a chaparral cock, a magpie, and each is taken into the clan. They went on and met Chakwena, a warrior kachina woman. "We will have her in our clan," they said, "our eldest mother, our grandmother."[167]

In kin-clan nomenclature the classificatory system prevails, but each tribe has different nomenclature practices. Emphasis on seniority within the same generation is a common principle, except among Keres; there are different terms for elder brother or sister and younger brother or sister, and among Tewa brother-sister terms do not express sex, only seniority. The nomenclature appears to be affected by clanship, at least it is characterized by the forked merging type of classification which is associated with

* But relations to the eponymous beings are very slight. To some of them prayer-sticks are addressed at the winter solstice ceremony by the clan chief, and the eponymous animals are frequently referred to as uncle, indicating clan relationship (Oraibi; Eggan). On the other Hopi mesas no similar observations have been made, and it has been held that "the relationship of a clan to the eponymous animal is so irregular as hardly to merit the term 'totemic' " (Lowie 4:337). The relationship is the common animistic one, now and again a little intensified, as when Hani of the Tobacco-Rabbit clan refrains from killing a rabbit which later causes Hani's tracks to mislead the pursuing Navaho (Nequatewa, 57).

clanship; maternal and paternal lines are distinguished, and direct and collateral kin are classified together. But there are some notable exceptions. The much beclanned Hopi have the same term for maternal and paternal grandmother, whereas Jemez, where the clan counts for little, has distinctive terms. Keres do not distinguish between mother, mother's sister, and father's sister; Zuni distinguishes between mother and mother's sister. On the whole, clanship partially excepted, the social variations which occur from tribe to tribe appear not to be expressed in the nomenclature.[168]

You are the "child" of your father's kin or clan, and between you and them there are definite obligations. Your father's brother you call "father," and you aid him more or less as you would your own father. Like your father he contributes sheep at your marriage and works on your bride's outfit (Hopi). Father and father's brother may be provided for in old age by their "child."[169] A child of the clan may be called upon for various ritual services (Zuni, Hopi), and ceremonial and economic rights may go to a child of the clan to revert eventually to the proper lineage or clan. Your father's mother makes your hooded wicker cradle* and, as noted, takes care of you as soon as you are born, for which she is well regaled.† In ritual head-washing, which occurs when a name is given whether after birth or upon joining a ceremonial group, in connection with dances, or at death, it is the father's or godfather's sister or next kinswoman,‡ perhaps merely his clanswoman, who takes charge, particularly among Hopi. To the Hopi baptism with which the confinement of twenty days concludes, all the paternal kinswomen bring gifts for the infant, and with invited guests contribute corn meal to the feast they help prepare, all being given meal or leftovers to take home,

---

* Nowadays made by father (Mishongnovi, Beaglehole 3:73).

† Voth 7:53 and Fig. 8, showing the grandmother carrying home the huge bundle of food she has been paid. Cf. Zuni (Benedict 3:I, 81).

‡ Hopi (and Hano, Zuni, Laguna) have the so-called Crow system of reckoning cross-cousins, father's sister's daughter is "aunt" and father's sister's son is "father." Hano and Laguna have borrowed from Hopi, since Keres and eastern Tewa (also Tiwa) are without this system. Evidence here, if wanted, for relating the system to clanship!

especially the paternal grandmother.[170] It is the Hopi girl's
"aunt" who takes her to be whipped at the Powamu ceremony,
afterward washing her head, and at every Powamu subsequently
giving her a placque basket, each year a little larger.[171] In this
aunt's house the little girl grinds corn for a day and has her hair
dressed in a bunch on each side (Mishongnovi),[172] and here the
more elaborate four-day grinding ritual and headdressing for the
adolescent girl is or was held (Mishongnovi, Walpi);* and, if this
aunt belongs to a women's society, the girl is expected to join it
(Oraibi).[173] A girl will help her aunt in special chores, in fetching
water, or in plastering. In fact, niece or nephew may be called
upon by their aunts whenever extra help is needed (Mishongnovi).[174] If an Acoma boy were asked to work for his father's
sister and his mother's brother at the same time, he would favor
his aunt, "because she is a woman and needs it more."[175] As
noted, hunters give their "aunts" a party (Acoma, Mishongnovi). "Aunts" contribute food on many ceremonial occasions,
especially to clowning "nephews."† The "aunts" of First Mesa
sometimes run a race for the benefit of the children of the clan.
When the god Masauwü engages in a planting rite, his father's
sister's daughter, his "aunt" is expected to drop the seeds in his
holes.[176] In telling about a harvesting party organized "in the
old way" by a Bear clan family, Crow-Wing says that the Bear
clan woman went the night before to her brother's son and told
him to announce the working-party from house to house. In the
evening when they came home, the boy's aunt gave him some

---

* Stephen 4:139 ff.; Beaglehole 1:44–45. At her first menstruation a Taos
or Zuni girl will grind for a little family feast, and her hairdressing is altered
(Parsons 58:47; Bunzel, personal communication). The Hopi girl's adolescence
ritual with fasting from meat and salt, self-scratcher, and shade is more like that
which is deep-rooted among California peoples and among Northern and Southern Paiute. See pp. 989, 1039.

† The joking relationship between "aunt" or father's sister's daughter and
"nephew" or mother's brother's son (Hopi) is to such an extent of a sexual
character as to suggest, if not sometime cross-cousin marriage (Titiev 3), a
clash or incongruity at some time in marriage rules, such as a rule against marriage within bilateral kinship and a rule or conception that any marriage outside
the maternal lineage or clan was permissible. Hence the sex jokes about "aunts"
or the formalized licence. Here as in many other connections Pueblo humor is
based on the incongruous.

wafer-bread "to show that they loved their child."[177] The next day the boy returned the basket, filled with meat or rabbit. The "aunt," among Hopi and elsewhere, comes in to wash the corpse. In telling about the suicide of Albert Naha, Crow-Wing mentions that Albert's "aunt" contributed the funerary bowl as well as wafer-bread.

Only the father's sister is referred to in English as aunt, and similarly only the mother's brother as uncle, an interesting illustration of how custom may adapt to itself a borrowed language. "Uncle" is an important relative. He is a quasi-member of the household in any Western town, since his sister's house is also his house.* Here he keeps his most sacred things, and among his sister's sons he looks for his apprentice or assistant, for his successor. Uncle or "our old uncle," as great-uncle is called, is sent for and advised with on all important family occasions, in connection with a marriage, when giving a dance, when initiation into a society is under consideration, or a long journey such as in tale the Hopi boy plans in order to see whither the river runs. When his father and mother have washed his head and begun to make his prayer-sticks, his mother says, "We have forgotten our uncle," and she sends her daughter to summon him. After they explain what the boy wants to do, their uncle says it is all right, and he joins in the prayer-stick-making and helps the boy's father to launch the box which is the boat.[178] It was her uncle who sent Po'haha, the Tewa tomboy, to war, since as a girl she would not obey him, who gave her bow and arrows and hung the bandoleer around her, and it was her "eldest uncle" who decided after Po'haha's victorious return that she was to be War chief, "watching for the people."[179] In one of the early Zuni school rows it was the Governor's uncle who blustered that the Governor would no longer consent to serve such irate people. Taking the cane of office from the wall, he said, "I won't let him go on being Governor. I am taking away the cane. Nor can you do anything about it. I am his uncle!"[180]

* The tie between brother and sister is unusually close, Dr. Titiev has pointed out, and through it develop the close and affectionate relationships with "uncle" and with "aunt." An Acoma woman and her children call her brother "our head"; he is the family head (White 7).

Uncles, old uncles, and old, old uncles, together with mothers and "our old mother" form a group which as midway between the family and the matrilineal clan has been called the maternal family. The maternal family or lineage is notable among Hopi, where it appears to have led through various processes to the development of the clan.[181] However, a clan group usually consists of several irreducible lineages and has several names (clan names are drawn from plants or animals, from sun, earth, or water, or from kachina associated with the clan), which perplexing traits have led some students to hypothecate the existence of phratries, unwisely, I think, since outside the multiple names there are no facts to warrant anything but classification by clan. Multiple naming may be due to assimilating clans in different towns, to merging reduced clans or lineages, to splitting a lineage, or it may be merely a trait borrowed without special significance. At Zuni the maternal lineage figures in the importance attaching to the house you come out of and in the limitation of certain ceremonial functions to special families within the clan; some of these families or lineages are referred to as "name-having,"* but they do not take on particular names, just as multiple birth names do not occur at Zuni or anywhere except among Hopi.

Among Hopi, clanship organization is all-important. The clan functions throughout the personal and public life, in naming,† in

---

* Kroeber 2:133-34. There are also traces of subdivision with distinctive names among Zuni clans (*ibid.*, 100–103). This obsolete naming practice strongly suggests Hopi practice.

† The father's kinswomen bestow names from a stock of personal names belonging to their clan, so that your name indicates not your own clan but your father's clan of which you are the child. I would note that in southern Arizona women of the Maricopa-Halchidhoma tribes have personal names of totemic, i.e., clan import, the clan being patrilineal (Spier 3:186–87). So that Maricopa-Halchidhoma women and Hopi women actually are named in the same way.

Both Hopi and Maricopa (Spier 4:5) are referred to by their clan name, the Hopi adding a term (*wungwa*) which indicates that one person, not the group, is referred to. Giving "totemic" names from the father's clan and calling women by the clan name are widespread practices, from Miwok to Pima (Spier).

Note, too, that plurality of names for the clan itself based on the indefinite number of "totemic" associations of the clan is characteristic of Yuman tribes (Spier) as well as of the Hopi.

marriage choices, at marriage and at death, in ownership of land, springs and reservoirs, of eagle eeries and eagle feathers, of houses and kivas, more or less informally through working-parties, in hospitality, in sporadic emotional attitudes toward beings associated with the clan, and throughout the ceremonial system with which the clan system interweaves. Zuni clan organization affects marriage choices; otherwise except in certain ceremonial connections which are ever important it figures comparatively little in the personal life, that is as far as actual functioning is concerned; conceptually, in popular estimate, the fifteen clans are certainly important as a way of classifying or placing people. Among Keres clan exogamy prevails, but ceremonial associations weaken, and in the eastern towns they disappear. Even clan exogamy lapses among Tewa. Clan membership means nothing but a name, and the name may be carried through the father. In fact, this tendency is marked enough for Tewan clans to have been considered patrilineal. Evidence for the principle of descent is very confused. Being marginal among Tewa, the clan has been affected probably by the moiety system in which descent is patrilineal.[182] Tiwa are without clans.

The predominant social category of Tewa is the moiety; they have Winter people and Summer people. Membership is patrilineal, but at marriage a woman usually transfers to her husband's moiety, if she belongs to the other moiety. If anything, the moieties are or were endogamous. The moieties have ceremonial associations, notably a double Town chieftaincy and a two-kiva system.

The two-kiva system with patrilineal descent prevails among eastern Keres, with influence upon dance presentation, upon kick-stick races, and upon the selection of the secular offices. At Isleta there is again a moiety kiva system. Also two all-inclusive groups associated with clowning, racing, playing shinny, and in irrigation, the Black Eyes and the so-called Red Eyes. To these kiva-moiety groups the children in a family are given alternately, if the parents belong to different groups, the firstborn being given, theoretically, to the father's group. Only the Black Eve group appears today at Taos, and as a society rather than as a moiety classification; but there are expressions of moiety in the six-kiva organization and in racing. These expressions are disconnected from descent, since parents may give a child to any kiva. At Picurís there are North side and South side moieties which figure in the relay race, in shinny, and in kiva affiliations; offspring belong to the father's moiety, but a woman may join her husband's moiety if she belongs to the other moiety. In the West there are a few slight and obscure traces of moieties in calendrical distributions, for example, the Zuni Ne'wekwe come out to clown in the winter, whereas the Koyemshi clown primarily in the summer, or again at Oraibi where half the year Sun is in charge of one group and half the year in charge of another.

SICKNESS AND WITCHCRAFT

A sick Tewa may change moiety, as at Cochiti, Santa Ana, and Laguna a person may change clan; it appears to be more important to be cured than to remain even in a hereditary group. Consistently, the curing society of Keres is the dominant town group, and the practices and beliefs of the doctors or shamans* receive great attention. Specific aspects spread to Zuni and to Tewa and were carried by Keresan or Tewan immigrants to First Mesa, although some of the curing and jugglery societies failed to endure.† The curing society is established at Isleta, but at Taos it is asserted that the "bear medicine" of the southern pueblos is not practiced.

The foundation of Keresan doctoring or shamanism is belief that the doctors are possessed of the powers of animals associated with disease,‡ and that doctors, having the powers of

---

* Throughout I use this term as more general or inclusive than "doctor," but merely as a short term for society member, without necessary connotation of special powers, including guardian spirit, and so in a somewhat different sense from the way the term is used in California, on the Northwest Coast, or in northern Asia.

† But see p. 1127 for another perspective.

‡ You may provoke anger and reprisal in an animal, e.g., if you urinate on an ant hill, the angry ants will enter your body. Or you may be frightened by an animal and sicken. However, sickness is caused by witches rather than by animals.

witches, can overcome witches. Witches can transform into animals, so can doctors. Transformation into animals and getting power from animals—these are the double aspects of the concept of nagualism or spirit familiar or guardian spirit held by many Indian peoples. Among the Pueblos this concept is rendered collective through the societies; even witches do not always operate on their own; there is a witch society, and a witch gets power from the animal that belongs to his ceremonial father (Oraibi).[183] However, the witches are far more individualistic than the shamans whose techniques they use outside of their proper setting, even to possessing a medicine bundle.[184] Shamans themselves misusing their power, for nefarious, private ends, are considered to be witches. Witchcraft is power used improperly.

A witch* may injure individuals or the entire community. He can cause landslide or flood; he may send an epidemic upon the town or he may sicken or kill a person by stealing his heart which is his life or by sending (blowing, Taos) into his body injurious things: insects, a piece of flesh from a corpse or a shred of funeral cloth or a splinter or bone, thorns, cactus spines, glass, anything sharp. A witch destroys crops through sending caterpillars or grasshoppers into the fields; he checks rain or causes wind. He is a potential murderer, a grave-robber, and a perpetual menace.

To the Pueblo, witchcraft and immorality or crime are almost synonymous. A witch has all the traits people consider antisocial. He is envious, jealous, retaliatory or revengeful, quarrelsome, self-assertive, and non-co-operative, entirely too unconventional or from the Pueblo point of view too much of an individualist. Anybody who has such traits is exposed to the charge of being a witch. Besides, special forms of behavior arouse suspicion, as roaming about at night, looking into a window† or lurking about a house, particularly if anyone within is sick, being well off without any visible source of wealth, thieving, talking

---

* Hopi, *powaka;* Zuni, *hathlikwi;* Keres, *k'a'nadyaiya* (*kanadia*); Tewa, *chuge;* Jemez, *sawah;* Isleta, *shaxo;* Taos, *chahöna* (*tsa'hena*).

† Compare Navaho belief about the witch-wolf looking down through the smoke hole into the hogan (Morgan, 14, 16).

boldly or recklessly about others or about one's self, particularly boasting of having power, magic power. Unhappiness or disappointment may arouse suspicion. A disappointed suitor, no matter how he behave, is more than suspect when anything untoward befalls his rival or the desired one. In 1917 at Zuni there died a girl who had been courted by two youths. One gave her a dress, the other a pair of shoes which her father in disapproval threw into the fire. Both suitors were suspected of witchcraft, particularly the shoe-giver, since he was the son of a member of the Ne'wekwe society which is versed in black magic. Once at a communal cure at Isleta the doctor took out from a girl's body a bit of cloth and a burning candle sent into her by a boy she refused to marry; in a few days, said the doctor, she would have died.[185] In Tewa tale, after a light snowfall Yellow Boy goes out rabbit-hunting, chases a jackrabbit, falls into the rabbit's snow-covered hole, and breaks his leg. Someone wearing rabbit ears and painted white all over is sitting in the rear of the hole. Yellow Boy sees him turn into a fly and fly away. "Who was it?" asks Badger who comes along to cure Yellow Boy. "A Corn clan boy who wanted me to marry his sister, but I did not want to marry her."—"Yes," says Badger, "I heard about it. The girl wanted to marry you but you did not want to marry the girl and that is the reason he wanted to kill you. I know all about it."[186] In other witch tales a rival is transformed into a coyote, a snivelling wretched little coyote, hounded from home by the dogs.[187]

Thus as evildoers or potential evildoers, witches are ever dreaded and hated. Nick of Zuni was a young man when in 1893[188] he was charged with witchcraft; as an old man "the people still hate him," said a townswoman, "nobody likes him."[189] Nick* was the witch I mentioned as being charged with the intent of sending a centipede into a woman who begrudged

* Every anthropologist who visited Zuni knew Nick or Tomaka and liked him. He spoke English and Spanish. He was a courageous informant, "the outstanding intellectual of Zuni" (Kroeber). Nick may have achieved his intellectual independence through the persecution he suffered, or, as the story of his witch trial indicates, he may have been persecuted because of his independence. He died in 1932.

him food. This was the story told me of what was undoubtedly the most famous witch case ever known at Zuni. Twenty years later another version was given Dr. Bunzel by a woman of an older generation, a contemporary of Nick's, and this no doubt was the true version of the affair. Nick got fighting drunk and was beaten up. When he came to, he boasted, being still drunk, that he would not die because his heart was in his toenails and he was wise, that is, a witch. The War chiefs ordered Nick to confess and reveal his power. Nick did not remember what he said when he was drunk; he had nothing to confess. The War chiefs hung Nick in the usual way, by his arms behind his back over the church beam. Still he would not talk, so they took him down and beat him with their clubs. Meanwhile Nick had defied the War chiefs by sending his brother to Fort Wingate for the American soldiers. Three "soldiers" came to investigate and were beaten up when they tried to arrest the man who had given Nick whiskey. A regiment followed; the townspeople were terrified and gave up the two War chiefs and Wewha, the transvestite who was related to the whiskey-giver and had resisted the military. Wewha* and the War chiefs were imprisoned for a year. Because of this, "they no longer strip witches of their power" by making them tell, concluded the old woman.[190] Power confessed is power lost. It is true that witch-hanging has gone out at Zuni, but confession is still forced. The War chiefs visit a suspect in his house and nag him into talking, a kind of third degree that any townsman and his family would find exceedingly trying. "Tell them something to get rid of them," would beg the family.

The War captains of Laguna used also to take drastic antiwitch measures. One day, some time in 1906, coming into Laguna from Paguate, Naiuri started to call on Tsatsi. He entered her house by a back door, and in the dark rear room he saw a wolfskin hanging on the wall, tie strings in front and the paws arranged as moccasins. Naiuri was frightened. He went and

---

* "The strongest character and the most intelligent" person in Zuni (Stevenson 2:20, Pl. XCIV). Gossip goes that Mrs. Stevenson took Wewha to Washington without knowing "she" was a man.

told the War captains. People had long been suspicious of Tsatsi. She was quarrelsome and a reckless talker. Besides, she and her husband, although they were known to be poor, always seemed to have plenty. They were supposed to pilfer corn by night, like an Aztec nagual.[191] So after Naiuri's report on the wolfskin,* the War captains shot Tsatsi.

The right of the War captain to kill a witch would not be questioned, I surmise, in any Keresan or Tewan town, in Jemez or in Isleta.† Nor is it questioned at Zuni. But actual executions are probably quite rare, and a person may live under suspicion of being a witch for a long time without anything happening. One dark night the old man who owned more turquoise and peach trees than anybody in Zuni, who had been calling on us and telling me folk tales, said goodbye, "I am going," and left the house, but presently we saw him back, looking through the window. When we opened the door, he asked for a lantern. "He may be a witch," said my Zuni hostess. "They say he is; but they have never done anything about it." However, reputed witches are more or less shunned. At a night dance at Zuni I saw a woman move deliberately away from two women, mother and daughter, sitting down next to her. The two women were said to be witches and nobody wanted to sit next to them. If social ostracism becomes extreme, a suspected person or family may leave town, going into exile.‡ No wonder that "when people

---

* Animal transformation is effected through putting on the animal pelt or through "turning over," that is, passing through a hoop or ring. A Shumopovi Hopi says, "A Hopi witch merely turns over and becomes a coyote or a crow. If you look at a witch carefully, you can see the snout or beak pressing under the skin of the witch's forehead" (Wallis 1:12). "Their mother" of the Town chieftaincy at Shipaulovi was going around as a wolf; when they killed the wolf, famine and disease ended (Beaglehole 3:71).

† Witch effigies are "killed" in annual curing ceremonies, and townspeople refer to these "witches" as living beings (see pp. 729-30).

In 1888 in Sandía a woman was shot by arrow, from left side to right, the conventional way of shooting a witch (Lummis 3:145). Compare reference to a witch execution in Sandía in 1797 (Twitchell II, 384). For Tewa see Aitken, 383.

‡ Exile for "bad people" is not novel; the Spaniards banished Indians (also Whites), e.g., in 1731 Melchor, an Indian of Isleta charged with drowning his wife, was banished for two months, and Antonio Yuba of Tesuque and Ascen-

quarrel they call one another witch,"[192] the most abusive and insulting term in Pueblo vocabularies!

Witchcraft is bound up with morals; it also affects manners. You offer a visitor food or anything he may admire lest he take offense or begrudge you some thing and work black magic against you. You keep your affairs as much as possible to yourself, and you do not meddle in the affairs of others. You avoid quarrels. The Pueblos are rarely surly or unmannerly, even to persons far from welcome. At hostile Hotavila people did not look at you as you passed by, but even there, after my manners to a rather fresh Navaho had been approved by the woman looking out of her doorway, I was invited in and given a slice of watermelon. She did not think me a witch, of course, but she did not want me to think of her as offensive like the Navaho. "The thing that a Zuni will avoid above anything else is giving offense," writes Bunzel.[193] "Why are the people so pacific?" queries Father Dumarest. "Why do they not defend themselves in quarrels? Because from their youth their elders have taught them that nobody can know the hearts of men. There are witches everywhere."[194] Bad people everywhere!

Tomás of Taos told me that after he came home from boarding school he fell sick—there was something in his chest. He was bewitched, said his mother, and she sent for a Ute doctor. The doctor sucked out "something" from his chest and told him that he would make the witch come to the house. "Shoot him! He wanted to kill you, you kill him!" But the patient, being, not a Ute, but a Pueblo disinclined to dangerous reprisals, refused. "I was afraid. All I wanted was to get well." Fear of witchcraft, fear of ridicule, fear of public opinion! Apprehensiveness is a noticeable Pueblo trait. After Chi'pai'u had made a "dangerous" trip with me to a Shalako shrine and I had paid him the stipulated sum for his mules, he asked for more: "What are you paying me for my fear?" I never regretted paying extra for an insight so valuable in future dealings with those I asked to incur danger—

---

sion Pobia of Nambé, accused of "abominable transgressions," were banished, Yuba to San Felipe, and Pobia to Zuni, for four months (Twitchell, II, 197).

the very great danger of visiting forbidden places or of imparting forbidden information. "If I die from telling you this, at least I shall have a new dress," said a friend who had suffered anxiety dreams every night during her week's visit to my ranch.

DEATH AND BURIAL

Fear lest something may happen, as they say at Zuni, is more general than any explicit fear of dying. "If our road is cut, we cannot resist,"* said Keres to Father Dumarest, who opined that people had a fatalistic attitude toward death,† confirmed, he might have added, by a sense of assurance about life after death much greater than that afforded by the Church. A Zuni girl "dreamed" when she was ill that she visited the town of the dead and saw her grandfather and other relatives. "Since then I've never worried about dying," she said, "because I saw all these dead people and saw that they were still living the way we do."[195] The dead are described as carrying on in familiar circumstances in many tales, and rarely if ever does a Pueblo question this common continuity theory of life after death.

Nevertheless, there are specific fears about death and about the dead who may pull or draw to themselves the living. A Zuni witch may bury a prayer-stick for a deceased member of a family and, calling the deceased by name, ask him to draw to himself his living relative.‡ In offering prayer-sticks to the deceased, he or she is asked to "drag down" none but the one who caused death.

> One, perhaps even a valuable man,
> Who, his heart becoming angry because of something,
> Injured you with his power,
> That one only you will think to drag down.[196]

* Compare the attitude of the Western Apache, who believes in the allotted *road* of life (Goodwin 2:36).

† Dumarest, 153, n. 3. On Second Mesa this seems to hold only for the old and entails a sort of "he has lived his life, what matter" attitude toward them (Kennard).

‡ Parsons 45:107; cf. Benedict 3:II, 184–85. In this tale a Rain chief acts like a witch or is the witch, asking a man's ancestors to draw him to Kachina town.

Through pining for the dead, through dreaming of them, or through some kind of death scare, sickness may come. Wild mustard is given at Laguna as medicine against pining away.[197] Quite generally the dead are not recalled by name, for a season, and, except among those I knew at Taos, not spoken of. Hopi or Zuni will say,[198] "He who has gone away."* At Zuni one who recalls the dead or dreams or falls sick soon after assisting at a burial inhales smoke from piñon gum (copal), and any frightened member of a household will inhale smoke from a lock of hair cut from the head of the deceased (Zuni, Isleta).[199] "This is the last time we are going to give him food," says a man's widow in a San Juan tale, "so he won't come back again, even when we sleep, and we won't dream of him." A San Juan man, telling me of a sick kinswoman, observed, "Maybe she sick because she got scared." A day or two before, a girl of whom she was fond had died. Death scare is a Zuni explanation of rheumatism,† the risk of which is ever run by those who bury the dead or dig up their bones.‡ At San Juan they say that San Ildefonso people have been dying off because they took out skeletons at Puye′ for White people. Once the foot of a workman was held fast, and the dead spoke, "Do not take me from this ground!" The man was greatly scared, "I do not know who is talking to me underground," he said, and he got sick and died.

Neglect of burial or death ritual will cause death scare or sickness, since the ghost returns. "Put the food out for him," said a Nambé woman of her uncle who died in California; "we can't have him running about here." In a San Juan tale the camp of some hunters is visited by a ghost-girl from whom they escape in terror. "You have to make four days," says the old man. "When the girl died, we did not make four days; so she came." So they cooked and called in their relatives. "By making those

* Our idiom "passed on" they will certainly adopt as soon as they learn it.

† Rheumatism is called "fear sickness." The War god drinks water and sweet corn meal and blood from the scalps he has taken as a prophylactic against fear sickness (Bunzel 6:34).

‡ Parsons 18. Hopi too believe that rheumatism is from the dead (see p. 1101, n.*).

four days they took all the scare away from those boys."[200] The
actual touch of a ghost is fatal (Zuni).

The dead are buried the day or even, among Hopi, the night
of the death, just as soon as the "breath," or, as we would say,
the soul, leaves the body and the body has been prepared for
burial. Talahongsi's father died about dawn, writes Stephen,
and he was buried before eight in the morning. His hair was
washed in yucca suds by his "aunt" who, moving the ritual corn
ear before his face in the usual way, gave him a new name, as she
would after an initiation. The body was washed lightly and
dried with prayer-meal which was also rubbed on the face. His
father blackened the chin, to represent the clouds, the black
clouds of the Nadir. A fillet of pendent prayer-feathers made by
kinsmen was put around the head and lay over a cotton mat or
mask which covered the face. (Feathers and cotton render the
breath-body light for travel.) The dead man's best apparel, his
dance kilt, was put on, and a string of beads, all being slashed or
impaired. Two or three rolls of wafer-bread, some cooked or
dried meat, mescal cake, and prayer-meal were laid on the belly
as journey food. The body was wrapped in a rabbit-skin rug and
carried on a man's back to the grave in the rocky foothills.[201]

At Zuni a single prayer-feather is tied to the scalp lock; the
chin is painted black, and cotton placed on the face or head, only
of chiefs.[202] For Rain chiefs, pollen is used as well as the iridescent
black paint, *tsuhapa*, of kachina impersonators (see p. 733). A
morsel of food is placed in the mouth of the moribund, and a
morsel is cast on the fire, a cooked or burnt offering being ever
proper for a ghost.[203] Certain personal belongings, including
dance mask and corn fetish, are buried not in the grave but in or
near the river bank at "wide river" whence the dead go to
Kachina town. Here, too, prayer-sticks made by relatives are
buried.

The Hopi corpse is placed in a sitting posture, facing east. On
First Mesa formerly the circular pit was walled up and timbered
over,* with as much care as was given a house;[204] but on Third
Mesa the grave was merely a pit filled up with earth and sand

* Compare roofed-over Papago grave for the *seated* corpse (Underhill 3).

and covered with rocks.[205] At Zuni and in the East, the burial is in the churchyard, and orientation is regulated obviously by the position of the church, the deceased in the Catholic way facing the altar, also, at Zuni, facing Kachina town, which is westward.* "Do not sit facing the west," says the dead wife to her living husband, "You are not dead yet."[206]

A stillborn or premature infant is buried under the floor of the house, just inside the threshold (Santo Domingo, Cochiti).† The Cochiti baby dying before baptism is also buried in the house, as was any Zuni infant "because it would have no place to go to."[207] The spirit of the uninitiated Hopi child lingers about the house until it is reborn to its mother or until she dies,[208] a belief in child reincarnation as held at Cochiti and Jemez. Food offerings are made to Hopi children, in their special cemetery in cliff or cave,[209] to the stillborn of Isleta in a "cave," and possibly to the stillborn of Sia or of Taos (also unbaptized infants) who are buried apart, north of the town[210] or in the mountains.

The paternal Zuni grandmother carries her deceased grandchild to the churchyard;[211] the only time Zuni women go there. Nor do Keresan women attend burials; Hopi, Tewa, and Taos women do attend. Kinsmen generally carry through the burial, a fearsome function which may be performed in eastern towns by church officers, the Fiscales. The Hopi who buries his father inherits a double share of personal property.

Into the Hopi grave are thrust a planting-stick said to represent the projecting end of the ladder into the house of Masau-wü, god of death,‡ and a single long black prayer-stick with a cornhusk tied on. "The corpse is like a cornhusk after the corn has been gathered." Across the trail back from the grave four

---

* Burials in the refuse heaps of Kiatuthlanna (Pueblo III), 40 miles southwest of Zuni, were all head to the east (Roberts 1:170).

† White 4:80; Goldfrank 3:77. Formerly at Jemez, premature births, still-births, and infants dying before weaning were buried indoors, female near the grinding stones, male near the door (because boys leave home), because of the belief, still current, that all these are reborn to their mother (Harper).

Infant house burial dates back to the earliest Pueblo period (Roberts 1:170).

‡ Stephen 4:825; but see p. 92.

parallel lines are marked with cedar charcoal, in four places, to close the way against Masauwü. Burial attendants wash their hair in the water from washing the corpse, and the bowl is taken to the grave. A jar of water was buried at the feet of the corpse, and for four days food from the family meals is taken to the grave.* Meanwhile an ear of red corn is left lying where the deceased died. The ear will be stuck in the rafters, and at the next planting he "who has the bravest heart" will use it for seed corn.[212]

Zuni burial attendants take an emetic, and after four days all mourners have their hair washed by a paternal kinswoman who comes in, or, in case of widower, by his mother or sister in their own house. During these days funerary washbowl and burial implements are left on the rooftop, the household neither buys nor sells, and the house door is left ajar, but not for living visitors. Everyone in the household makes prayer-sticks or has them made, and the bundle is deposited for the deceased at "wide river" where the bank is honeycombed with offerings.[213]

At Acoma prayer-sticks are made by the family, but they are taken out to the hills by the shaman who has been invited to paint the face of the deceased, with two short diagonals on each cheek like hunter or warrior or, according to another account, with the same design the deceased was painted as an infant on being presented to the Sun.[214] A woman's face is smeared with pollen, with a disk of red on each cheek, as if for a dance. With the prayer-sticks the shaman deposits the fire stick or poker that for four days has lain where the deceased died, also an offering of food—the food that has been offered each day. The pottery bowl of water is broken over the grave to give the deceased "his last drink."[215] In all other Keresan towns and in Jemez the chief of a curing society has similar but wider funerary functions; on

---

* At Oraibi on the third day after burial (about the fourth day after death) a bowl of cooked food is placed on the grave; also by a kinsman a double green-blue prayer-stick with black butts, a single black prayer-stick called "seat," and a "road" prayer-feather. The following morning the breath body will partake of the breath [odor] of the food, will mount the "seat," and travel along the "road" to the house of Masauwü, taking the double prayer-stick as offering (Voth 9:102–3) or, in modern Acoma terms, as letter.

the fourth day the society holds a singing and praying service in the house of the deceased, "driving out the spirit with their eagle plumes" (Sia). At Cochiti pollen is placed in the mouth of the corpse.[216] Miniature clothes and moccasins, bits from the family meals during the four days of mourning, and the prayer-sticks from the corners of the deathroom are taken out to the hills. At Laguna bits of food eaten on the fourth day are cast into the fire, and beverages are poured in; prayer-sticks and a bowl of meal and of wafer-bread are deposited on the hill north of town. Food is placed under the left arm of the corpse (Sia, Santo Domingo)[217] or in both armpits (Santa Ana). An ear of corn is placed Hopi-like in the place of death (Cochiti, San Felipe, Santa Ana, Santo Domingo), also the poker. They are the heart of the deceased and the heart's protector. (At Acoma the "heart" is an arrowpoint.) The corn will be used as seed corn. Again Hopi-like, pottery and clothes taken to the hills are "killed." As the Jemez corpse is being carried out, it is sprinkled with water, with corn meal and pollen. Two loose feathers, turkey and eagle, are put in each hand. After their ceremony the medicine men deposit beautifully made prayer-sticks and prayer-feathers.[218]

At Isleta not the curing Fathers but the Fathers of the Corn group of the deceased conduct the funeral, making a road of meal from the door to the altar for the ghost to come in by and leave by. Before this fourth-night ceremonial the mourners have washed their hair, bathed in the river, and cast prayer-meal on its waters. After the Corn Fathers have taken out the bowl of food and the prayer-feathers and "chased" the ghost from town, the Fathers return and pass their arrowpoints over the walls of the room, and the chief tells those present to forget it all, saying in chiefly language, "It is now four *years* since he is dead."[219] Taos mourners stay indoors for the usual four days (were the house left empty, the ghost would come and make a noise) and then take out to the north a bowl of cooked food, the moccasins of the deceased, and the tools he used in making moccasins, and some loose prayer-feathers. After the burial the women were fumigated with smoke from burning some of the hair of the deceased, while men washed hands and face in the river, also the grave shovel. Santa Clara kinspeople bathe in the river, and all the washable things of the deceased are washed (San Juan also). After the funerary meal on the fourth night at San Juan, a bowl of cooked food is taken out to a field by kinsmen (no feathers except for a society member), and the dead is addressed: "Here is food for you! Do not be mean to people here, do not come around! If you do come, do not let us hear you!" On the road between cemetery and town four lines are drawn to represent a mountain not to be crossed by the ghost.[220]

Details of behavior during the four days the ghost lingers vary from town to town, details of exorcism vary, according to the prevailing pattern of purification, and whether kinsfolk or society perform the rites; but separating the dead from the living and preparing the deceased for the journey he has to make, whatever his destination, are the general and outstanding funerary traits of all the Pueblos, since all fear sickness or death through the dead by whom they would be well quit. When I visited Acoma with the Governor of Zuni, the day after our arrival the daughter of our hosts died in childbed. It was Lusteti's first visit to Acoma, and he was enjoying it, cutting a figure,* but he was afraid to stay in that house of death and, after contributing a blanket to the burial, departed for home, a shaken man. "Death or approaching death strikes such terror to the Hopi heart," writes Voth, "that he shuns or flees the sickbed and deathchamber as much as possible,"[221] and grave-digging is too much for his nerves. Recently a Shipaulovi man was digging a grave for his brother, but, when he got a little below the surface, he became so frightened that he stopped work and went home, letting another man show his bravery by completing the burial.[222]

The first prayer said for an infant is addressed to the Sun, the source of longevity: "Your beautiful rays may they color our faces; being dyed in them, somewhere at an old age we shall fall

---

* Actually he was no longer Governor, but he did not feel called upon to inform his hosts of the change of officers, and I was cautioned not to mention it.

asleep old men."* To fall asleep of old age is one of the fondest hopes not only of every Hopi[223] but of every Pueblo. Suicide is almost unheard of. In 1922 Albert Naha, a Hopi rich in children and in cattle, killed himself; he had tuberculosis. This was said to be the first Hopi suicide on record, although recently Dr. Titiev reports that at Oraibi suicide by sulky girls is not unfamiliar,† and from Second Mesa Nequatewa works the idea of a suicide pact into a "true story." I heard at Taos of a woman suicide who had failed to recover her health after childbirth,‡ at Isleta of a man suicide jealous of his wife, and at Laguna of the suicide of a man implicated in murder, an act almost as rare as suicide. A story went around Zuni about an addict to Jamestown weed (Datura) who took an overdose, deliberately;§ but even this story has been forgotten, for Dr. Bunzel writes that suicide is absolutely unknown; the very idea is so remote from their habits of thought that it arouses only laughter.[224]

---

* Or old women, for a girl baby (Voth 7:53). The Acoma shaman lifts up the infant so that the rising sun shines on him, and prays for a long life (Stirling).

† Possibly the suicide is only an imputed act. On Second Mesa it is held that young and middle-aged people will not die if they try not to; if they do die, it may be from lack of will or from spite (Kennard). From perversity, Governor Anza wrote in describing how the Cacique of Oraibi refused his offer of mediation with Utes and Navahos "because he was firmly resolved to die at the hands of his enemies" (Thomas, 234-35). Something of a Plains Indian or Apache flavor here. From grief or desperation the Jicarilla Apache warrior, after tearing off everything, even his loincloth, to signify that he had broken completely with all ordinary conventions, would throw himself into the thick of the fight until he received a death wound (Opler 2:213). Saddened and angered by death, a Plains tribesman would organize a war party, whether the deceased was killed by the enemy *or not* (Smith, 453). The reaction of the angry or depressed Pueblo who in tales and possibly in life sends for the enemy to destroy him and his people seems to be related to this Plains Indian reaction.

‡ In folk tale a jealous wife, Yellow Corn Girl, goes under Blue Lake to join the Grandfathers, the kachina.

§ Parsons 4:169-70. Although the use of this narcotic may be an aberrant trait, or, say, a marginal trait (see p. 414), it should not be overlooked at Zuni and among Hopi (Stephen 4:557, n. 3; Voth 5:114 ff.) in estimating the ineluctably moderate spirit of the people.

HABITS OF MIND

In the foregoing survey certain mental traits of the Pueblos have been mentioned or suggested: susceptibility to ridicule or criticism and to fear, the urge to separate one's self from whatever may seem offensive or dangerous, and that very widespread way of mistaking an attribute for an independent object.[225] I would like to indicate several other habits of mind or attitudes which are fostered in Pueblo life and which in turn support this ever systematizing culture, more particularly in its religious aspects. These traits I find expressed in ritual, in folk tales, and now and again in the talk or conduct of individuals, but *in what degree these traits characterize the individual Pueblo I do not know.* Nor is the list of traits even from the point of view of cultural survey at all complete. No doubt, many other traits might be described. I am giving the traits that have become conspicuous to me; to another, other traits might be conspicuous. The field is defined more or less subjectively, much as national or racial traits are described in any travel book. For the social psychologist able to develop a superior field theory and technique it is a virgin field. Thus tentatively I would note as Pueblo characteristics (but not exclusively Pueblo, by any means) the feeling that whatever is received must be acknowledged, most suitably by a return gift or payment, and the corollary feeling that a gift once accepted is compulsive—it has to be returned; the feeling that concentration or keeping your mind on what you want, including self-control and self-discipline, assures or compels the end desired; belief in foresights, through omen and dream; thinking by analogy; acceptance of the sanction of automatic self-harm; the sense of order as expressed in orientation, in symmetry, in familiar number or sequence; amusement from the incongruous or break in the orderly or conventional, but in other circumstances fear of the unconventional or of infraction of habit or of rules; further exorcising attitudes, and desire to merge in the group and to co-operate, all in self-protection.

GIFT EXCHANGE

The view that service should be compensated, that a gift necessitates a return gift, is deeply held. When Anza offered the Cacique of starving Oraibi a horse loaded with supplies, the Cacique "refused on the pretext that he had nothing with which to return the gift, for without such his customs would not allow it"*—pretext to the Spaniard but gospel truth to the Indian, even if he did suspect ulterior design. Old Juanita of Jemez suspected me of nothing and accepted my gift of a warm nightrobe, but she had the padre mail me back some of the wafer-bread I liked. The idea of free or spontaneous giving is certainly not entertained. "How can a man expect much without paying something?" says Coyote to the Zuni hunter.[226] The Pueblo "pays," as he says, the shaman who cures him or contributes to the growth of his crops; he "pays" the witch-sent grasshopper to forego these crops; he "pays" the animals he hunts or the animal that helps him hunt, the eagle he keeps in captivity, the enemy he has killed, whom, as well as his own dead, he expects to serve him; and he "pays" all those beings he associates with his natural sources of supply—salt and clay, herb, shrub or tree. The woodchopper is paid for the load he gives a girl; the hunter for the rabbit he gives her. Girls in the Hopi Butterfly dance or in the Buffalo dance receive presents from their partners. "So now† those girls," writes Crow-Wing, "are going to make a return to those boys. And all the women are helping. They will bake wafer-bread all day and in the afternoon, late, take it to the boy's houses. . . . . Some of the women are boiling meat to send to the houses of the girls who took wafer-bread yesterday to the boy's houses. It is called out for the women who helped the girls to go to the houses of the girls to eat."[227] In the Buffalo dance as in other women's dances

* Thomas, 235. Compare Kurz's comment on the need of returning a gift made by a Crow chief: "Indians are never generous toward a White person; they expect always a gift in return, sooner or later. Even among his own people an Indian is liberal with gifts (*meat excepted*) only to win friends or partisans (Kurz, 269).

† The dance was in November; the payment, in January. Characteristically of Pueblo circles, payment is not pushed.

and the Howina war dance the women are generally paternal relatives or "aunts" in connection with whom gifts and services as noted are remarkably prescriptive. The salt-gatherer, on returning from his dangerous journey, made his first present of salt to his "aunts," perhaps as a return for baskets or food given him at a dance (Oraibi) or at his arrival (Zuni, Mishongnovi, Laguna, Acoma) after his head and body have been washed by his "aunts."[228] The rabbits the clowns get in the drive after the harvest dance of Isleta they give to their aunts in return for bread in the shape of a rabbit given them by their aunts.[229] "The rabbit hunt held today," writes Crow-Wing, "is for the little boys to pay their aunts for the pottery their aunts gave them last spring."

Young and old are expected to make a practical return, in so far as they can, to the household that supports them; if a girl does not want to cook, she should at least help her father in the field;[230] sons help their father or godfathers; brothers co-operate; suitor or husband works for a woman and her people. In the Zuni tale of witches who would destroy the young man's crop, his father says to the newly wed youth, "Do not come back to us! You must work, that is why the daughter of the Rain chief married you." When the youth planted his corn for his parents and not for his wife, that was ample reason to the woman and her people, they being witches, to raid his field.[231]

VOW OR PROMISE

Ordinarily, in marriage or in any trade, people are willing to pay; they have no wish or intent to cheat; barter or gift exchange is too well regulated, too ingrained a habit. Besides, a defrauded person might feel revengeful. Saiyap' of Laguna believed that the epilepsy of his daughter was caused by a Navaho who was displeased by the outcome of a deal in turquoise. In Zuni tale a Rain chief who was cheated of his pay, two pairs of moccasins, two women's dresses, and two women's belts, pay for showing a man how to cause an epidemic, offers prayer-sticks and tobacco to the cheat's forefathers to draw their living kinsman to themselves. To justify this ritual murder, the chief says merely, "You said you would pay, but you did not."[232] The Zuni who fails to carry out his pledge to entertain the masked dancers at Shalako, entertainment which is very costly, knows that "something will happen." Something did happen to José of Isleta, who did not return in time to perform the ceremony due his patron Lightning; he was struck by lightning.[233] And there was that Juan Rey, the stick-swallowing shaman who died within the year when he moved to Sandía, failing to keep his promise to perform his ritual at Isleta. Formal vows to fill an office or join a society are rarely broken (except in such irreligious towns as Laguna or Cochiti); it would be too "dangerous."

Pueblos, like many Indian peoples, keep their word or fulfil obligations from fear of consequences, frequently supernatural consequences; but there may well be other motives. Once a Zuni kachina impersonator dropped dead on a ceremonial circuit. After a while they pulled off the mask and with it the skin, for it was stuck to the dead man's face. When the society chief said it was imperative to have the circuit completed, "because misfortune will surely come to our people if we do not go through with everything," the deceased man's son put on the mask and went on to all the houses, undeterred by the idea that the mask was dangerous and might kill him also.[234] When the Tewan hero, Olivella Flower, is told by the kachina guard that his journey will take so long he will grow old on the way, he rejoins, "I have to do what I said I would. I do not care if I die on the way." Later, one of Olivella Flower's helpers says to him, "You are still traveling because you wanted to do what you said you would do. That is the way men should do. Whatever they say they will do, they should do."[235]

COMPULSIVE BEHAVIOR OR CONCENTRATION

Gifts are compulsive. If a girl accepts a man's "bundle," she thereby agrees to marry him; if she carried a basket of meal to his mother's house, in theory at least he had to marry her. The Zuni receiving presents from a would-be *kihe'* or friend at a kachina dance is bound to make return presents and to become

a lifelong friend.* A trading "friend" brings a present, perhaps
a bit of turquoise or shell to his host who does as much trading
with his guest as possible† (Acoma, Hopi).‡ With a gift of meal
or tobacco, a Cochiti man will apply for adoption into a clan or
will secure assistance in harvesting.²³⁶ Once some Navaho
wanted to get a dance from the people of Zuni. They could be
refused, I was told, because they had not asked in the *right* way,
with a gift of tobacco.§

Other forms of behavior are compulsive, trying hard or concentrating through continence or some kind of abstinence,
through prayer and song, drawing and painting, or through
freedom from temper, anger, or grief; opposite behavior or feeling, incompetency, or lack of concentration mean failure, even
death. Misplacing or forgetting words invalidates prayer or
song. If paint runs, somebody has been incontinent. A hidden-
ball player jeers at his opponent, "Your thought has gone away
(you are distracted); you won't beat us" (Hano).²³⁷ Were a Zuni
trader among the Navaho to let his attention wander to a woman, bargaining power would fail him automatically, particularly
if he be under an obligation of continence from having planted
a prayer-stick before leaving home. In Zuni tales of the youth
who brings his wife back from Spirit town or from the home of
Water Serpent he is instructed to remain continent on the way.
In the first tale he approaches the sleeping girl, who awakes and
declares that he has not cared for her enough and, turning into
an owl, flies westward.²³⁸ In the second tale the youth observes

* Parsons 7:94. You can make a *kihe'* of an animal by giving it something. If
you have a sore, you tie a thread from your clothing around its neck to pay for
taking away the sore.

† As in Zapotecan Mexico (Parsons 62:60, 375-76, 443). Such trade friendship or hospitality is widespread and ancient.

‡ Beaglehole 3:84. The Keresan term for friend (*kwa·'ɒzi*) is used by the
Hopi. The two men embrace (Mexican fashion) and breathe each from the hand
of the other. The hostess provides food for the return journey.
Formal trade apart, food gifts are interchanged between a woman and her
hostess in another town (Beaglehole 3:80).

§ They knew better, too, for Navaho as well as Apache make requests with a
cigarette, placing it on the foot of the recipient.

the injunction of continence, but he lets his attention wander by pursuing a deer. So Water Serpent, seeing the woman alone, stretches himself and reaches her, saying, "Your husband does not love you; he did not do as he was told; I have come after you."[239]

In curing, where continence is exacted of both patient and doctor, the desire to recover has to be paramount. "I cannot do it all," remarked a Ne'wekwe doctor of his patient, "she must help herself." Because this woman had intercourse with her husband during the cure, she had a relapse after the surgical operation, her doctor believed, and died. She should have been continent until all signs of the wound had disappeared.

On the other hand, conjugal indifference and infidelity may be a kind of vicarious failure of concentration or, more simply stated, the rule of continence involves a couple. When Olivella Flower sets forth from San Juan on his quest for parrot feathers, his father and others go into ceremonial retreat to help him on his journey, and Yellow Corn Girl, his wife, is expected to provide for their comfort, to sweep their room, to bring them water and food, to look after them until his return; instead, Yellow Corn Girl makes an assignation in the irrigation ditch, and in consequence the journey of Olivella Flower is immeasurably prolonged. Kachinas, the Water Serpent ferryman, Snake chief, the Ants, and Parrot chief all tell him he is having a hard time because his wife has failed him.[240]

Similarly, if a Cochiti hunter gets no game, it is because during his absence his wife has been unfaithful. A Taos hunter shot himself by accident, but his mother declared the fatality was because his wife had a lover. Hunters themselves must remain continent during the period of the hunt; and hunters are expected to concentrate all their attention upon the game and not recall home or other affairs.[241] If the Mishongnovi mountain-sheep hunter thought about women, he would surely have an accident.[242] Before an antelope hunt at Isleta the War captains had to remain continent for four days. Once, the night before the hunt a War captain broke this rule, and during the hunt, as he chased an antelope (a spirit antelope since it ran in the ritual

directions),* his horse threw him, and he became a stone image.[243] The Isletan tale of the Sun's kick-stick shows even more
pointedly how failure results from incontinence or the mere
thought of it. Blue Corn Girl and Yellow Corn Girl have heard
the song of the kick-stick runner, their hearts are happy, and
they would marry him. The next day, "because of the wishes
and hopes of the girls," the youth's kick-stick falls short of its
goal, the sunrise, and reaches only the middle of the sky.[244]

Fasting from food or drink, from sleep or from speech, are
mainly ritualistic practices, but there are instances in daily life
of such abstinence. Mishongnovi children are taught to dip into
the food bowl only four times at the first meal of the day, and
party manners for a bridegroom or a guest prescribe tasting only
four times of a dish.[245] It is mannerly not to drink until the end
of the meal (First Mesa, Acoma, Laguna).[246] A woman in labor
is warned not to drop asleep lest she die (Taos), or lest the sex of
the child be changed (Zuni). Should the Sia woman fail to concentrate upon the birth, "the child would not care to be born
and would lie still and die."[247] The Hopi bride and her women
connections have to stay up all night making wafer-bread the
night before the marriage is consummated, an effort that possibly may signify more than just providing for a feast. In the
San Juan tale of the Yellow Snake Girls who send the man back
to his people to become a shaman, the girls lay a taboo of silence
upon him, saying, "If no words come from your mouth for
twelve days, you will prove yourself a good man."[248] In something of the same spirit Crow-Wing refers to a search by the
Hopi Snake clan for "a good woman," a close-mouthed woman
"who will not tell anybody," to take the position of medicine-
maker.[249] During their ritual hunt the snake-hunters have to
observe a taboo on speech, as did, in general, salt-gatherers.
Speechlessness is required almost always of kachina impersonators, and not merely to conceal identity. Secretiveness about the
kachina may be a remotely related rule. Various factors enter
into the secretiveness of the Pueblos in regard to their cere-

* But compare Mishongnovi, Beaglehole 2:9, for the danger to hunter and
horse from an antelope running, *in a circle*, an albino antelope.

monial life, but one which is certainly strong with them is the belief that their ceremonies, their *costumbres* or *ofisi*, will lose their potency if told, a common Indian attitude. Even as in witchcraft, power talked about is power lost.

Personal potency or efficacy is enhanced through tranquillity. When the paternal grandmother or kinswoman is summoned to take charge of a newborn Hopi infant and its mother, she is supposed to be in a happy frame of mind, so anything at all disturbing is removed from the house.[250] If parents quarrel, a nursing infant may become sick (it may indeed), since its mother is not "all right inside." The parents should confess to the doctor who is called in or to the woman's uncle.* In announcing a Hopi ceremony, the Crier exhorts people to live in kindness, to be good to one another. "Until that many days [sixteen], we, all the people, without having any contentions, must live."[251] As Voth discernedly comments: "Any worry, sorrow, or anger disqualifies a Hopi, as a rule, to participate in a ceremony, and contentions and quarrels in the village are supposed to interfere with the efficacy of a ceremony." The Antelope chief of Shipaulovi tells Stephen that Cloud has come to Shipaulovi and heavy rain has fallen during his ceremony because peace and love prevail at Shipaulovi, whereas Cloud does not care for the ceremony at Walpi where there is no unison.[252] "Our grandfathers used to love one another," comments a Zuni critic, and, ignoring many a tale of drought she might have heard from grandfather or greatgrandfather, she adds, "therefore the rain never failed them."[253] Here is as close an approximation to the sense of virtue or its opposite, the sense of sin, as was ever achieved in Pueblo circles.

Hunters and their families are expected to remain in amiable

---

* Eggan. A remarkable parallel to modern Mayan (Quiché) practice (Bunzel, Lothrop) and to early Salvador confession in protracted labor (Strong), and suggestive of the early Aztec-Mayan practice of confession. Confession also occurs among Papago (as exorcism) (Underhill) and among northern Athapascans, Eskimo, and Iroquois (Lowie 1:106). The Athapascan Carriers hold that you must confess to get well (Bourke 1:465, n. 8).

Yellow Corn of Isleta told me that, if she fell sick from giving me information, she would have to confess it. Lucinda also remarked: "What I am telling you I am going to confess it before I die. I am not going to carry it away with me."

mood. Mishongnovi hunters may not be un-co-operative or entertain bad thoughts toward one another, an obligation falling
also on their wives.[254] If a Jemez child is "mean" while his
father is off hunting, the deer will be "mean." A Cochiti hunter
should not quarrel,[255] and a hunter on setting forth may caution
the women of his household not to quarrel with neighbors. One
time a Laguna man went hunting, and, although the deer were
plentiful, he got none. On his return he was told that his wife
had been quarreling. "It is not surprising I did not kill anything," he said to her. "You have been quarreling all the time."
From his relatives a hunter must have "the best of thoughts."
They must not "think anything bad." Indeed, at no time should
people think anything bad.

Among bad thoughts are thoughts of death. Another unsuccessful Laguna hunter found on his return that his father had
been dead eight days. "I knew from the way the deer was acting," he said, "that something had happened." Bereaved of wife
or child, the Hopi does not take part in his ceremony—"his
heart is not good."[256] Generally, a death in the family precludes
participating in ceremonial during the set period of mourning.
When the great-niece of my Acoma hostess died in childbirth,
none of the permanent household attended the dance which
began the fourth day after the death. But on the day following,
after the hair wash which closed their mourning, several from
the household were out in street or court, and the great-aunt of
the deceased was among the women who threw bread to the
dancers.[257] The death of a ceremonialist while his ceremony is in
progress or imminent is always very disturbing, and the assemblage is usually transferred to a distance. After the head
War captain of Laguna was killed by lightning while rabbit-
hunting in connection with the winter solstice ceremony, the
town was so upset that it resolved to observe the ceremony at
the colony of Paguate, an extraordinary procedure.

FOREKNOWLEDGE

Proper circumstances or conduct are essential, but, would you
control conditions or events, you should also know about them

as or before they occur, through clairvoyance or divination. The farmer wants to know in advance about rainfall or frost, the hunter whether the deer are near, the runner how he is to bet on his race, the warrior what his chances are against the enemy or whether or not an enemy is approaching. Clairvoyance is mainly a technique for detecting witchcraft or witches, but it may be resorted to in other circumstances. In a Cochiti folk tale a woman is ordered by her husband to stay home and grind while he and her younger sister who is "stealing" him go on the rabbit hunt. The jealous wife peers into a bowl of water, as would a shaman, and sees her sister sitting in the lap of her husband under a cedar tree.[258] At Isleta a white arrowpoint serves for second sight, and with one in his hand a hunter describes vividly to his camp companion a flirtation going on at home: "Your sister has gone to the river to get water. A young man has come to talk to her. She is throwing water on him (a courtship stereotype). He leaves her. She has filled her jar and is going back. She sees the young man under some trees. She sets down the jar and goes over to speak to him. They see a woman coming along. The girl says she does not want the woman to see her. She has picked up her jar and is going home."[259]

The comfort or assurance that derives from divination or foresight is often expressed in the folk tales,* particularly in forecasting the coming of the Whites and their ways. A Taos prophet foretells flood or enemy attack; he is "a good man." Poseyemu, the Tewan prophet, even dresses himself up as he says the coming conquerors are to be dressed, in trousers and shoes and hat, and hitches elk to a buggy.† Why worry because your town does not grow, since Poseyemu predicted that Indians would not increase! Why worry about anything that has been foretold or foreordained and thus explained by a chief knowing how to relate the new to the old. "I had to do it; I was born to do it,"

---

* Or in clan tradition (Hopi; Nequatewa, 107).

† This was actually done about seventy years ago by a White man in Colorado named Michael Studien. Possibly the story spread to New Mexico. But there is an older source. About 1629 a certain captain, *maesse* (*maestre*) *de campo*, "for pomp had his coach drawn by two deer of this kind (? elk), which they tamed when little" (Benavides, 37).

says he (Isleta, Hopi); and when people weep for the girl who is to be sacrificed by drowning, to comfort them, the chief has but to say, "She was born into this world to go back alive into the other world" (Isleta).

Omen-seeking occurs most commonly as ritual, but belief in nonritualized signs is also common and usually not reassuring. At Zuni a light appearing and disappearing is a sign of fatality.* One evening, on returning to our empty house, we saw a light which went out. There was considerable perturbation and months later, on the death of a relative, the incident was recalled as an omen of her death. A sound at night at the water jar is another sign of imminent death: a ghost is drinking and may be coming for someone in the household. At Cochiti a chick getting wet in a puddle and cheeping is a sign that one's child is going to fall sick or die. Breaking a gun or bow is another sign of sickness or death, likewise twitching of the eyelid,[260] the left one, the left always being associated with death. When the eye of my Isletan visitor began to twitch, the right eye I guess, he predicted a letter from his daughter. The next day the letter arrived, and Juan's satisfaction was twofold. To Lucinda of Isleta a big fly in the house meant company and she would say, "Let's clean up!" Was Big Fly a messenger, as in Navaho lore?

When the sun or moon "dies," in eclipse, it is ominous. In 1919, a year of influenza, many girl babies died at Zuni; that was what it meant, people said, when the preceding summer the moon had died.† The lunar eclipse of 1921 occurred the eve of the day the school children were to return to Taos. The Governor of Taos telegraphed to Santa Fé to postpone the journey, inferably lest something happen on the way. At Mishongnovi a solar eclipse about this time had been followed by an epidemic of measles very fatal to the children.[261]

On that notorious and now legendary first trip to Fort Defiance made by First Mesa men, the boy Hani shot at an eagle which turned out to be a buzzard. This was witchcraft or an

---

* In the East, witches are supposed to move at night as lights, a borrowed Mexican belief.

† A landslide was the omen of the influenza of 1918.

omen, and the boy felt like turning back.[262] Any unusual personal experience such as this may be taken as sign or omen, often so disturbing that it will be reported to some chief or shaman, just as in Zuni tale the hunter who sees a human boy running with the deer and who feels very unhappy lest it be an omen, instead of telling his father about it, has his father summon the War chief.[263] To this Zuni as to Hani of Walpi the unusual personal experience was harassing or depressing, not the exciting adventure it might be to Apache or Plains Indian, let us say, a seeker of power or visions.

Dreams are frequently, not always, bad signs to the Pueblo. While old trachoma-blinded Kawi'ts'irăi' of Laguna was telling me of her "bad dream," her son arrived home minus his horse and saddle, and Kawi'ts'irăi''s anxiety turned to tears and lament, and she was convinced of her dream come true. At Isleta dreaming of grapes means something is going to happen to your relatives; dreaming of somebody in a canyon means a grave (pointing to early cliff burial?), a relative is going to die. Shaking hands or talking close up to somebody is a good dream and so is a dream about a medicine man.[264] Some of my Taos acquaintances were constantly dreaming true. A dream of blood meant to them a death in the family; a dream of water or fish meant rain.[265] In the deer-hunting days of Cochiti a hunter might have dreamed of deer, and the following day he would kill the same number he had dreamed of.[266] Similarly, on First Mesa after the hunt announcement it is a good omen to dream of game; the dreamer will surely be fortunate in the hunt.[267] On Second Mesa to dream of your sweetheart was a good hunt omen, but continence being required of hunters, to dream of intercourse was unpropitious.[268] A Hano man told me that, if you dreamed of cow, bear, or snake chasing or fighting or biting you, "you might get into trouble with somebody," and a dream of flood was a sign of wind, "sure windstorm next day." Stephen was told it was well to dream of the clowns dancing, for rain would follow; to dream of clowns being flogged, as they are in ritual, meant cold.[269] Good dreams on First Mesa are of getting goods or victuals and of raising big crops; bad dreams are of falling off the cliffs, as is actually not unheard of, or of being sick. For a bad dream you would chew a bit of wafer-bread at night and somewhere in the dark spit it out, saying, "I must not dream of bad things again." Stepping on dung in your dream is fatal (Cochiti);[270] in waking life it causes sickness (see p. 439). An Isletan would not touch the scalps lest he dream of them. Dreams of the dead are visitations of the dead, bad dreams, portents of death; at Zuni and probably elsewhere the dreamers are exorcized by ritual flagellation.

THINKING BY ANALOGY

In interpreting most of these dreams or omens, people are thinking by analogy, taking resemblance of a kind as an explanation of relationship. This use of resemblance as a principle of cause and effect or a means of determining effects is a conspicuous habit of the Pueblos,* controlling and fundamental in their ceremonial life. In such ideology, which is quite familiar, since it is far from being confined to the Pueblos,† like causes or produces like, or like follows like; like may also preclude or cure like.

Like causes like: Illustrations abound in Pueblo agricultural and weather theory. At Zuni, to make the wheat crop white, seed wheat may be sprinkled with white clay,[271] and, to make melons sweet, melon seeds may be sprinkled with sweetened water. That insects may not attack the crop, little children, who are like little insects, are told not to play about the seed corn. Seed corn will be sprinkled with water that the crop may be

* It was conspicuous to Cushing, who remarks that to Zuni the whole world is related on a basis of resemblance (Cushing 11:9), a habit of mind that leads to reversing causes and effects, e.g., summer birds are supposed to bring summer instead of summer bringing summer birds, or willows explain the presence of water instead of being explained by water (Cushing 6:634).

† The average individual does not carry to completion the attempt at causal explanation of phenomena "but carries it only so far as to amalgamate it with other previously known facts" (Boas 1:204). In dreaming, we see this process in reverse and in its crudest expression, one thing suggesting another in what is questionably called "free association," an irrational process and yet the beginning of reasoning or mental activity comparatively independent of response to immediate stimuli. Is this a tenable explantion of sleep or mental activity in sleep?

rained on;* that rain may fall on the newly planted fields, the women of the house dash water on the back of the man who is starting forth to plant, a practice quite general in all the towns. Tewa farmers believe, like farmers all over the world, that grain should be sown under a waxing moon to grow with the moon.[272] While planting, Hopi do not throw anything to one another, "a hailstorm would come," just as is believed that heavy mud-making rains will follow a rite of throwing mud. After a day of planting, the farmers may run a race, "to have the corn get ripe quickly."[273] Isletans believe that the ear of corn in which grains are missing not at the tip but in the body of the cob was planted by a hungry man, and the ear is called "our mother hungry old woman." Wild mustard is mixed with seed corn in order that, like mustard, the corn may come up vigorously (Laguna). To this end beans grown rapidly in kiva hothouse are placed by Hopi in their corn stores.[274] Some corn meal is buried under the grinding stones that in them the corn may be ground rapidly (Cochiti); nor would yucca root be kept near wheat or corn store lest the grain disappear rapidly like the foam from yucca root.[275] A corn ear impregnated with salt or a lump of salt is kept in the Zuni granary that, as the hole from which salt is taken refills, so may the hole left by removing ears of corn. When Coyote put up boundary stones for the people of Second Mesa, leaving restricted strips between clan or town lands, he buried prayer-feathers and with them a blind beetle and a poisonous spider, saying that, if anyone cultivated the restricted pieces, he would go blind or die of poison.[276]

After finishing the fireplace of a new Zuni house, before they make a fire, "they will tie dog dung to a hair and pull it up straight so that the smoke will go out straight."† In firing pottery, bones of sheep, cattle, or deer may be laid in the fuel of dung cakes; as the bones turn white in burning, they make the

* Hopi practice also. Lest rain fail in summer, cobs of seed corn may not be burned as fuel until they have been moistened by rain or by snow water that has been preserved for such use (Beaglehole 3:39)—Hopi "holy water!"

† Bunzel 6:3. This seems to me like a secondary explanation. Elsewhere dog dung, any dung, causes or cures sickness; so this particular fireplace practice ought to be one of exorcism or cleansing.

pottery white (First Mesa).[277] The quarryman of bakestones should wear no turquoise with markings lest his sandstone slabs split or be scored (Mishongnovi).[278] The Keresan hunter may not put his hand into the round cook pot, lest he walk in a circle and get lost. If the hunter's wife move about much, the game will roam. The hunter who blows on his food blows the game away.[279] Zuni hunter or traveler or courier will put a straw of redtop or lighttop grass on his pack to make it light. "Straw," he prays, "make me walk easily and travel fast!"[280]

Is not the Zuni who adopts woman's dress, the transvestite, thought of as thereby taking on woman's nature? Sympathetic magic does operate through clothes. In making a dress at Zuni, no scraps would be thrown out indifferently lest an enemy, a witch, find them and through them inflict harm; the scraps are burned. To avenge himself on a jilt, a man will get a thread or two of her belt and fasten it to a tree in a high windy place; as the winds wear away the thread, the woman wastes away. Analogously, to keep a man, a woman will immure a lock of his hair in her house wall or wear the lock over her heart. She may take soil from the man's footprints and place the soil where she sleeps; at night the wanderer will think of her and return, even if the other woman is better-looking.

In connection with the conception, carrying, birth, and rearing of children, the idea that like causes like is very common. At Cochiti a newborn child, more particularly of a prolific family, may be taken by a barren woman into her house and cared for there four days, in order that the foster-mother whom the child will afterward call "mother" may become a mother indeed. To determine the sex of her child, a woman would conceal under her clothes some implement associated with the sex desired and visit the house of an industrious woman or man or of a family with many daughters or with many sons.[281] If an Isletan who is the mother of twins give away her dress, the recipient will bear twins. The Zuni woman who eats the bread brought back by a deer hunter will conceive twins—the doe drops two fawns. Eating the inner whitish leaf of the cornhusk will cause offspring to be albino. Albinism is said by Hopi to be caused by making white prayer-sticks during a wife's pregnancy.[282] A Hopi woman of child-bearing age would not eat the meat of a fetal calf, lest her offspring be born blind; nor, in painting a bowl, would she close the top circle, lest labor be prolonged and the child be stillborn (Mishongnovi).[283] A pregnant Acoma woman would not eat rabbit lest the child's belly be large and the skin taut like the thin skin on the belly of a rabbit.[284] Deformity in offspring or blindness may be caused by the prospective father disabling game (Zuni).* The father of a boy blind in one eye had shot a rabbit in the eye, I was told, and the father of a man with a crooked jaw had slaughtered a sheep. The Jemez husband who kills any animal during the pregnancy may expect a stillbirth.[285] A skin eruption in a Zuni child may be explained as due to his mother sprinkling bran on her oven floor before his birth. During pregnancy a Sia woman should not use a sewing machine lest the umbilical cord tangle;† an Isletan should not go to a moving-picture show, lest the child twitch like the film, and have no sense. Old wine in new bottles!

To hasten delivery at Zuni, a bean may be swallowed—it slips down quickly; or a badger's paw may be worn in the belt (left near by on the ground [Isleta])—the badger digs itself out quickly. So does the weasel, and among the Hopi the meat, fat, or skin of a weasel are medicine for protracted labor, also a herb called weasel medicine.[286] A pregnant woman, you are told at San Juan, should sweep her dust out without dallying about the door, otherwise at birth her child will start out and then draw back or take a long time to come out. Similarly, at Isleta and elsewhere a woman should not start out of the door and then return,‡ she should not even stand in the doorway (Sia) or peek out, lest the delivery be retarded. An Isletan woman should be

* Compare Papago (Underhill 2:41).

† The Hopi taboo against a pregnant woman coming near tanning or dyeing processes lest she injure them (Beaglehole 3:19) has obviously a different source, but it is obscure.

‡ Kiva regulation at Acoma because the underground Corn Mothers did not turn back at the Emergence. The Acoman's life would be shortened unless his family made a gift of food to the kiva inmates (Stirling).

generous to children passing the house; were she stingy and tena-
cious, the afterbirth would stick.[287] The presence of a man in the
house at the birth will cause the child to be a boy (Zuni).

The cord of a girl baby is buried deep near the grinding stones
so that when she grows up she will not be lazy; the boy's cord is
buried in the field he will work in (San Juan, Laguna). Hopi cut
the cord on an arrow shaft, for a boy, or on a stirring stick, for a
girl; and, when the cord drops off, it is attached to shaft or stick
to be thrust behind a joist, "because the boy will become a hunter and the girl, a cook."[288] The ear of corn completely or perfectly kerneled is the characteristic sacrosanct or ritual ear used
in many circumstances, but at San Juan it is left alongside the
newborn infant[289] in order that he too may grow up perfect.

To make her child's hair fluffy, a Cochiti woman will wear a
bunch of turkey feathers in her belt.[290] For retarded dentition a
person who has been bitten by a snake will rub the infant's
gums; a snake has teeth (Zuni). I was told at Isleta that José
María Lucero was born with teeth because his mother had been
lashed by a whip snake. That the Zuni child may talk well and
with tongues, a mockingbird's tongue will be cut out and held
to the child's lips.[291] The bird is released and, as the tongue
grows in, the child's tongue will wag. The Acoma child is given
corn that has been placed in a mockingbird's nest.[292] That the
Zuni child may keep well and walk early, hairs from a deer are
burned, and the child held over the smoke; deer are never sick
and their gait is rapid. Their hearing, too, is acute, so wax from
a deer is put into the baby's ear. A feather of that sleepy bird,
the owl, is placed near a wakeful baby. A baby's garments are
not hung up to dry because, if they fell down, the baby would
tumble and be as hurt as if it fell from a height.

Funerary practices express the feeling about like causing like.
The planting-stick on the Hopi grave aids resurrection. "They
plant a dead person for another world" (Acoma idea also).[293]
Cotton is placed over the face of the dead Hopi, "so the dead
may become a white cloud"; and a cotton string is bound around
the head with four downy feathers pendant over the face, "so
the dead will go with them to the clouds, and not be heavy."[294]

Just so the courier in Zuni tale asks for a downy feather, so he "may run easily."[295] The Zuni potter who closes the circle or "road" around her pot feels that her own life road will end, and she will die.*

Like causes like in the principle of a whole following a part and perhaps in the common Pueblo feeling against wastefulness. At Zuni, corn is sold out of the house with reluctance; the rest of the corn may follow what is sold, just as the stored corn once followed the fleeing Corn Maidens.† On the other hand, a few grains from corn that is sold may be retained so that the rest of the corn may return to the seller. Compare the idea we noted about the dead drawing the living or that, if two relatives are buried in near-by graves, others in the family will die. In a Sia tale about the dead returning to town overnight, husbands and wives do not sleep together lest the living follow the dead or, as in the Tewan Orpheus tale, be pursued by the dead.[296]

The principle of the whole following a part may be expressed in general terms of much from little. When the abandoned little boy takes Wolf's advice and puts a single grain of corn in each deserted house, straightway the houses fill up with grain (Zuni, San Juan). Again, from the storeroom where a nut is thrown the piñon packs up so close that they cannot open the door, "the piñon has known how to make lots of itself" (Tewa). The small food offerings to the dead thrown into house fire or into river are thought of as increasing unto the dead. When bits from his possessions are thrown on the fire, the deceased is informed definitely that the rest will follow (Laguna). The miniature funerary garments of Cochiti[297] are contributed surely from an analogous point of view just as is the thread a Zuni patient puts with the prayer-meal he gives his doctor. (The thread is from the blanket

* Bunzel 1:69. "This is a true symbol, the only one in Zuni art," writes Dr. Bunzel. I would not make this exception. See p. 489.

This pottery feature is characteristic of Pueblo III and of the Chaco range of culture (Roberts 1:131). For Hopi see above.

† That is, in modernizing language, the corn store was used up quickly, for there was no life in it (Benedict 3:I, 20, 25). Compare the Navaho story of the gambler who takes away with him from the corn pits an ear of each of the five colors. Four days later the corn was all gone, and famine set in (Goddard 1:161).

he will pay the doctor, and the doctor will offer thread and meal to the curing animals.)

Scant or diminutive offerings among Pueblos are not, as is often said, symbolic, rather are they supposed to increase to the recipient; they are a kind of magical seed. When Dark Star's sons visit Blue Cloud and Yellow Cloud on the mountain summit, the boys are given rinds of melon, scraps of deer and buffalo meat, and a bit of black cloth. Opening their bundles at home in San Juan, the boys see lots of clothes, lots of meat, lots of melons.[298] There is a single turkey feather on Hopi and Keresan prayer-sticks which is called the mantle or blanket, for it is destined to become actually a feather mantle, as did the single feathers in the tale of the Hopi girl ordered to sleep on a cake of ice. She weeps and says to herself, "I shall be frozen to death." But Spider Grandmother unties her bundle of medicine in which there are two turkey feathers. "Put this turkey feather on top of the ice," says Spider to her grandchild, "and you will be able to sleep on it, and this other feather put on your chest for your blanket." The feathers keep the girl warm all night. Compare the Jemez rule that a woman on weaning her infant has to squeeze a few drops of her milk into a little pit in the floor in order to have enough milk for her next child.[299]

The recurrent tale incident of the tiny cup that never empties or the scrap of food that never lessens is another expression of "much from little," the so-called motif of the inexhaustible found throughout America. In the Cochiti tale of Kotona, the fully kerneled ear of corn, Shrew gives the thirsty child water to drink in an acorn cup. She drinks and her sister drinks, and the cup remains full. In Isleta or Tewa tale Canyon Wren or Chipmunk brings water in an acorn cup or a piñon shell to the parched boy or the boy in the owl's nest. "Don't drink it all," says Chipmunk, "it will last you two days." Spider Woman is a notorious possessor of inexhaustible things. When she gives the Hopi youth a speck of meat and of mush and half a nut, it becomes a large mouthful.[300] Her handful of flour feeds all the starving families of Zuni.[301] Flour-hanging Mesa, where there is a Zuni War god shrine, is so called because two girls, invited thither by the god, saw his grandmother Spider Woman make bread from flour in a sack hanging to a tree. The sack was diminutive, but the old woman made a great basket of bread.[302]

Magical increase obtains also in the recurrent legend of creation from epidermis. In the first Zuni curing society there were but two old men and one old woman. The sons of Sun said to them, "It is too bad you are alone. Take rubbings from your skin and make a little figure. Cover it up and sing over it." This they did, and a little boy came up, the first Ne'wekwe, a restless, reckless chatterbox, saying the opposite of what he meant and saying anything.[303] In the same way originated the first funmakers of Laguna. Iyatik said to her sisters, "I wish we had something to make us laugh. We sit here so quiet without anything to make us laugh." So she rubbed her skin and covered the ball of epidermis (corn meal) with a cloth. Out came the Kashare,* to make fun, to make people forget their troubles.[304]

This principle of much from little Father Dumarest sees expressed in Pueblo hospitality. "An Indian treats the stranger kindly and makes him presents from the same feeling that he plants his seeds in the soil, that is, in the hope of a return, sooner or later, at least tenfold."[305] Or, the Franciscan might have added, with the same hope that he makes offerings of meal or feathers to the Spirits.

Aside from hope of gain there is here a predisposition toward thrift. Wastefulness is very offensive to the Pueblo and is found penalized in tale or current belief. The Jemez woman who lets her breasts drip will not have milk for her next infant.[306] Natural supplies of all kinds fail when they are wasted. Salt Woman and Turquoise Man deserted the neighborhood of Zuni because their valuable flesh was being wasted.[307]

Like cures like: A Laguna woman who thinks she is carrying twins will eat a piece of fruit, say a peach, growing double in order to keep from having them. In the Zuni tale of White Bison a sour or salty plant family give balls of their skin to the seeking

* The anthropomorphic fetish of the Tewa clowns was of corn-meal dough (see p. 1025, n.†).

husband to rub on himself against snakes and knives. The Zuni deer-hunter who sees a buck mount his doe knows that the deer are "telling" him of what is happening at home. His faithless wife is far from "staying still" in the house she should leave only at noontime to fetch water while her husband is off hunting. It becomes his business, therefore, to shoot the deer and take out their hearts. On his return home he will find his wife and her lover sick. To cure them, if he pity them, he will have to rub them with deer heart made up into a ball with meal, rubbing the woman with the heart of the doe, and the man with the heart of the buck.* In Pueblo medicine heart and life are ever identified.

Should a Zuni be struck or shocked by lightning, he or she must be given some rain water of that same storm to drink (plus black beetle and suet); otherwise the person will "dry up" and die. About 1913 three women in a house struck by lightning neglected to take the prescribed drink; within a short period all three women were dead. A lock of hair from the corpse may be burned and survivors fumigated in the smoke, lest they be frightened or upset by the death (Zuni, Jemez, Taos).

Persons who have been through an experience or have caused it are qualified to deal with it. The lightning-shocked are qualified at Zuni, Acoma, and Laguna to treat lightning-shock. A sore navel in a baby is thought to be caused by the presence of one who has been a victim of snake bite, and the snake-bitten is therefore summoned to breathe upon the child or wave ashes around its head (Laguna, Zuni). To cure a Zuni infant of diarrhea caused by throwing water, either parent having been sprinkled in play or having had his or her head washed ritually during the pregnancy, the water-thrower or godfather must make a present of a new bowl and give infant or parent a drink.[308] If a Zuni infant has been born with a mark caused by his father having danced kachina before the birth, the father has to put on the same mask and dance for the child, rubbing him with his sweat. The Jemez father will wash a crybaby with water he has

---

* Parsons 4:168. The incident is consistent with the general belief that sickness is caused and cured by animals. That deer cause sickness is White Mountain Apache belief (Goodwin).

used on his own leg and on the leg of the horse he maltreated before the infant was born. When Lucinda of Isleta was pregnant, her husband went deer-hunting, and her baby was born gasping for breath; so her husband had to run as if chasing a deer and then pass his hands over the baby. As soon as he did this the baby began to breathe normally.

ARBITRARY SANCTION

In thinking by analogy reasoning is involved, for causation is pondered, if falsely; but now and again we see another attitude toward cause and effect in which the relationship is unconsidered, acceptance of the kind of magical sanction familiar to us in the nursery, for example, telling a child that if she eats oatmeal her hair will curl or that his tongue will blister if he tells a lie. The Hopi believes and apparently does not know why he believes that to pit-trap for eagles would cause him to break out in virulent or fatal sores on his back[309] or that, after leaving town in disgrace if he return before his four days of quarantine are concluded, he will die, or that he will die if he call a woman married into his clan by her personal name.[310] Keres believe that looking upon an unmasked kachina causes sores and itch (Acoma)[311] and that in gathering salt, if they speak or laugh or make fun, they will "die on the spot" (Cochiti).[312] "If I tell you the story of how we came up," said Lucinda of Isleta, "before I reach home I shall be dead." The famine, pestilence, and war decimating them in 1777-1779 Hopi believed to be consequences of their treatment of Father Garcés in 1776, as predicted by the friar.* Many folk tales conclude with an equally arbitrary interpretation of sequences. Because Tarantula once stole a Zuni boy's clothes, Tarantula has ever been hated and stepped on by everybody. Because Spider Woman enlarged the genitals of Lazy Bones, enabling her to win the youth all the nicer girls wanted, despised persons marry the nicest people in town and

* Thomas, 237. Probably the friar threatened them with descent of the wrath of God for their haughty behavior; but even this simulacre of causation dropped out for the Indian, since he had little or no conception of a god of punishment. But see Stephen 2:66, where Sun is a punitive god, and p. 185 for Water Serpent as punitive.

get to be nice too. Because a poor old man recovered the youth who married the eagle girl, "we always honor old men."[313]

Obviously, like our own religious or even scientific folk, the Pueblo is quick to entertain explanations, however arbitrary, that make him feel at home in his world. But the Pueblo also arranges things in more categorical or orderly ways, not to speak of his linguistic categories* he has spatial or temporal categories of orientation and symmetry, of number and sequence, all aids to spiritual comfort.

ORIENTATION

Although there is no general rule of orientation for Pueblo buildings, we have noted the central court or Middle,† and that the town itself is thought of as the Middle Place for which the wandering ancestors were searching.[314] Even the now scattered Tewa lived together after their Emergence in a midmost town.[315] When Water Skate found the middle of the world for his Zuni people, he said, "My people shall live here always. They will never be overthrown, for their hearts will not be to one side of the world."[316]

Streets as such rarely have names; but parts of the town or house clusters are given directional names in accordance with situation.‡ At Laguna the visitor is told formally to "come in from the south" or from whatever direction the door faces.[317] The Zuni visitor is seated near the door, by the fireplace, away from "the valuable place," which is on the side of the room away from the door, where the altar is placed.[318] The Taos visitor is directed, in folk tales, to sit down "on the right side of the fireplace or on the left side." Prayer-stick-making in the Hopi kiva goes on conventionally in the southwest corner, but the War Chief will sit in the northwest corner.[319]

There are rules for placing the sleeping pallets. Nobody in Zuni, Acoma, or Laguna and not everybody in San Juan would

---

* Once the Pueblo languages are fully recorded, the student of language as a psychological or cultural determinant should find the Pueblo field very interesting.

† Keresan, *kakati;* Hopi, *kisombi;* Tanoan, *pałpinthla;* Spanish, *el centro.*

‡ A comparative study of town plans and nomenclature would be of interest.

sleep head to the east. It is the position of burial, facing the direction you are to go in, they say at Zuni; and to sleep so would be fatal. Similarly at Isleta and at Taos, where burial is head to the south, people would not sleep head to the south. The idea of orientation in sleep is unfamiliar to Hopi. As noted, a corpse is seated with legs flexed facing the east,[320] although usually Hopi associate life with the east[321] and death with the west.

In ritual and folk tale the Pueblo sense of direction is very conspicuous;* the cardinal directions are often a frame for the conduct of ceremonial or for securing repetition in song or narrative. The six directions are associated with color: yellow, with the north; blue, west; red, south; white, east; variegated or black, zenith; black or variegated, nadir.† Other colors are recognized and named, but the direction-colors are paramount in thought. They would be named first, and you might even be told by somebody that there were no other color terms.

Plants and trees, animals and birds, are associated with color-direction. The Corn Girls are all named by color excepting Dwarf Corn or Sweet Corn. The animals who come by night to guard the Zuni youth in search of his lost wife appear from the directions they belong in, Mountain Lion from the north, Bear from the west, Badger from the south, Wolf from the east, Eagle from the sky, Mole from underground.[322] When the mother of Yellow Corn girl asks the girl's suitor where he lives, since he is Wolf Boy he answers as was to be expected, "I am living in the east."[323] Dr. Kroeber's Zuni name is Onothlikia, Oriole, the bird of the north. Did he not reach Zuni from the north, wearing yellow (khaki) clothes?

The order of the cardinal directions establishes the conventional circuit which is countersunwise or sinistral, whether in coiling baskets (Hopi Second Mesa) or in pottery design‡ or in

---

* On how marked it may be in individuals no systematic observations have been made. Ritual is not adequate evidence, for ritual may be borrowed. It is very puzzling to find few if any terms for direction and little sense of direction among peoples who have a ritual of direction in common with the Pueblos: Huicholes, Zapotec, and Maya.

† Thus in the West; for variants among Tewa and Tiwa see p. 365.

‡ From Pueblo I (Roberts 1: Pls. XXII, XXIII).

dancing, although now and again the sunwise circuit is followed. A striking illustration of how the circuit may be read into life is the view, held at Zuni, that eagles nest successively in four places and then repeat their nesting round. Again, one of the few pathetic incidents in Pueblo tales is constructed in this rigidly familiar way. White Corn girl has been ordered to cast her un-fathered infant into the lake. In her reluctance to drown the child, she sits down to suckle him, on the north side. Then she stands up, but again sits down to suckle him, this time on the west side. Only after she has suckled him again, on the south side, and again on the east side, can she bring herself to obey the order.

FIXED NUMBER AND SEQUENCE

As among many Indian peoples, four is the favored numeral, although it is so much used, especially in folk tales and ritual where freedom of repetition is unrestricted, that often it means no more than "some" or "several." Coyote calls to the sleeping lynx four times before lynx wakes up (Sia). The Zuni Governor is entitled to hit a recalcitrant four times to enforce an order.[324] The confinement period is four days (in some Zuni families, Laguna, Tewa); when ceremonialists "count their days," the count is usually four; spirit exorcism is performed on the fourth day after death.

A person might ask the truth of another three times before expecting to get it (Zuni); the fourth request compels candor. Just so when the Earth Mothers Utsét and Nowûtsět are com-peting in sagacity, each asks her question four times before getting an answer (Sia); and when the malicious War gods are asked by their mother if they have injured the people of Oraibi for refusing them food, they withhold confession until asked four times. Once an Oraibi boy gave away kachina secrets, goes the legend, and the society chiefs consulted the War chief on what to do about it; they had to ask the chief four times before he would give advice.[325] Requests may be made four times before being taken seriously, for example, the Acoma War chief asks permission of the Town chief four times before he convoys a foreign spouse into the town, and four times the Town chief welcomes the newcomer—"asking four times makes it more complete."[326] In the San Juan Emergence myth the man chosen to be the first leader has to be asked four times before he consents.[327] In the Hopi-Tewa tradition that the Tewa ancestors of the people of Hano were invited by Walpi to give aid against raiding Utes, three invitations were declined, the fourth was accepted. After the Tewa arrived, to their disgust they were not allowed up on the mesa, but when the Utes were about to attack, the Tewa were promised a mesa-top site. "If you drive them back, there from the Gap east, all this land we will let you have." The Tewa made the Hopi chiefs say this four times. The Tewa killed all but one Ute who said, "I will never fight against you again." This he said four times.[328]

Six as well as four is a numeral of direction, the zenith and nadir being included, and six is a common ritualistic number. Cushing asserts that at Zuni the center is added, making of seven a favored numeral. The concept of the middle is familiar, but Zuni do not place any emphasis on seven either in daily or in ceremonial life. Nor did Stephen find seven to be identified with the center in Hopi ceremonials.[329] Twelve is also a favored numeral, figuring particularly in war myth or cult. At Isleta, Picurís, and Taos three, or more often five, takes the place of four as favored numeral: star designs are given five points instead of four, in folk tale a race will be run five times around a certain point, and the ritual circuit will begin in the east and end in the east, thereby preserving the association between cardinal directions and favored numeral. The Isletans combine up, down, and middle into one direction, the fifth. This deviation from Pueblo pattern, the preference for five, is one among other striking anomalies presented by the culture of Tiwan towns.

The pair, whether of the same or opposite sex, carries an assurance of companionship rather than of number. This is conspicuous wherever the two War gods figure, in ritual or in tale. The Corn Girls figure by pairs in Tewa tales, and there are Cloud Boys and Cloud Girls, Blue Cloud Boy and Blue Cloud Girl, etc. Kachina Girl or Yellow Woman is the associate of the male kachina. Society impersonations are frequently paired, Snake

Boy and Girl, Flute Boy and Girl, or Hawk Boy and Girl (Hopi). This pairing is usually without sexual significance, but there are a few married couples—Wind Old Man and Wind Old Woman, Kachina Old Woman and her incestuous brother, Father Koyemshi. The Hopi Maize god is mated; Spider Old Woman is generally solitary except for her grandsons, but sometimes she is mated with Spider Old Man.

With the supernatural pair of male and female is associated color—turquoise* and yellow. Alternation of these two colors, as well as alternation in the use of other colors and of white and black, is a constant principle in almost all uses of pigments.

A feeling for seasonal or calendrical sequence is marked among the Pueblos as among all peoples who live on periodic yields of nature. The solstices are watched to determine the ceremonial calendar, and, among Hopi, planting dates are established by the progress of the sun toward the summer solstice, after which there may be no further planting. At Zuni there is no such organized planting, but the summer solstice is observed and determines the beginning of the dance series for the summer rainfall. Desire for rainfall determines the summer ceremonies throughout the pueblos. Harvesting starts another season for ceremonial. Hunting is somewhat of a seasonal activity, after harvesting, in the autumn and early winter. Formerly raids were organized at this season. Nowadays it is a time, at Zuni, for house-building or repair. Winter is the season for getting married, for playing games, and for story-telling; racing goes on in winter and early spring.

Of yearly sequence or chronology in our sense there is little or no expression. Nor apart from the migration and Emergence patterns is there any sense of historic continuity or origin. "They brought it up with them," or "it was that way when they came up," you are told when you ask the origin of, let us say, the Zuni War chief cane or any of the fetishes, or why Shulawitsi, the kachina, is impersonated by a little boy. A formula such as "it came up with them" or "thus it was from the time they came

---

* I am using the term "turquoise" to describe the blue-green which is called sometimes blue, sometimes green.

up" gives authenticity to precious things as well as a starting-point back of which there is no call to search. Thus it serves also as a guaranty for novelties, obscuring any recent, foreign source.

The very ruins of the country are little more than sites for mythical occurrences. Awatobi, left a ruin as recently as 1700, is said to have been destroyed because its chief was angered by the accidental death of his daughter or by the slights the girls put on his son. Sikyatki was burned and some of the women taken to Oraibi because a girl rebuffed two youths who then shot her through the window where she was grinding; her brother visited Sikyatki as the hair-cutting kachina and cut off the head of the sister of one of the murderers.[330] Not even this much explanation is advanced for the post-Spanish abandonment of Hawikuh and other Zuni towns. Instead we are told that when they were living at Heshokta all the people of the seven towns went there to gamble, or that at Kyakima lived a girl who had never married or that the son of the Town chief of Halona married the daughter of the Town chief of Pinawa, or that the people who were seeking the Middle came to Matsakya, and heard the snow-making society people coming from Nutria and went out to meet them, which is why Nutria is cold and the wind is from the east.[331] In other words, the ruins are brought into the standardized patterns of the tales, into lines of thought as familiar and orderly as to us is the story of the destruction of Sodom and Gomorrah or the story of the Garden of Eden.

CONVENTIONAL AND UNCONVENTIONAL BREAKS

Yet breaks in the established order, as caricature or burlesque, delight the Pueblo. The more formal burlesque is performed by the clown societies,* but backward speech, as used by some

* Clowns who are said to act like children (Zuni) probably set an example for children. Jemez children will imitate cripples, "shaky people," pregnant women, the deaf and dumb, the blind, the drunk, and white people (Harper). I used to catch Jemez children mimicking my gait behind my back. Mimicry of white people would not be protested by parents, but mimicry of defectives is "too dangerous" (Harper), no doubt because of the persuasion that like causes like, the mimic will become blind, for example, or give birth to a blind child (cf. Isleta, Parsons 52:213).

Jemez children, like clowns, play guessing games: "Guess what I have in my hand," or "guess what hand it is in" (Harper).

clown societies, saying in joke the opposite of what you mean, is not uncommon in daily intercourse. In fact I would say that it is the commonest form of Pueblo humor. There is also a love of punning or of double meanings, at least at Zuni, where language lends itself to such verbal play. Love of metaphor is general. Father Dumarest noted it at Cochiti: "They call a man whose horses are always thin from hard riding by the name of an insect which dries up melons when it gets on top of them and stings them." They would say to the padre, "Father, do not try so hard to change us; a poplar will never be a fruit tree."[332] Enemies or strangers call forth analogies. A Navaho may be referred to as a coyote and his scalp as "sacred bark," and boys were told they might not smoke until they had killed a "coyote" (Zuni, Laguna) or brought in some "oak bark" (Isleta).[333] Isletans will warn of the presence of an alien by referring to the hawk. If the stranger understands Tanoan, they may say, "The beam is broken," meaning, "Beware lest the roof fall" (upon our house of secrecy). From such verbal play much of the ritual language may be derived and, as Bunzel has pointed out, ritual imagery may be built up.

Unconventional breaks in ritual are envisaged quite differently. Any ritual infraction is believed to involve one in disaster or in some untoward accident, or, putting it the other way around, an accident points to ritual infraction. If a Zuni Shalako impersonator falls in his running ritual, it indicates that he has been incontinent. Any kachina impersonator who after dancing fails to plant his prayer-stick will die. In 1917 one of the Zuni kivas instead of presenting the prescriptive kachina dance in the winter dance series danced Hilili, a very popular but modern dance. This "caused someone to have a bad dream,"* so the kiva members had to dance again, a proper old kachina dance. During a dance at Laguna, when instead of raining it blew a dry gale, the feathers were blown off the headdress of one of the dancers, and the paint on his mask ran, signs that the windstorm was due to incontinence during the ceremonial period of the

* Bad dreams," including hallucinations, are caused by the kachina and the dead, who also cause rheumatism.

dance. Crow-Wing writes that the windstorm at Second Mesa when they were dancing kachina one spring day was ascribed to carelessness on the part of the youths sent to gather spruce for the dancers; on their trip they had indulged in tossing pebbles instead of keeping their minds on their mission. When antelopes refused to go into their "house" or stockade, it was because the Hunt chief had been remiss in his hunt rituals.[334] I am reminded of that time when Chi'pai'u was driving me behind his mules to the Shalako shrine. The mules kept balking. They had been worked hard all morning at the plow, and the road to the shrine was hard going; but their driver believed that the mules could not or would not keep up because he was guiding me to the shrine. Either the mules had been enfeebled or they were giving him a warning.

During the Zuni Molawia ceremonial of 1915, when the house-tops were crowded, the roof of one of the houses enlarged that season caved in. The accident occurred, people began to say, because turquoise had not been deposited under the floor of the new chamber. Zuni accidents are not infrequently attributed to improprieties toward the Koyemshi, one of the clown groups. An old man blind in one eye had lost his sight, his family believed, because he criticized a Koyemshi, and in 1912 a towns-man was kicked in the eye by a horse because, people said, he complained of a kinsman consenting to impersonate a Koyemshi and so involving his relatives in expense. In 1917 I heard of three similar mishaps. In one family both father and son were kicked by horses because they refused to cut prayer-sticks in connection with the Koyemshi; and a man's hand was crushed because his wife refused to give some cloth to the wife of the Koyemshi manager. To refuse or begrudge the Koyemshi anything is ever disastrous. A story goes that on one of their domicili-ary food-begging trips a woman refused them the bread or meat they expected. Her house was on the outskirts, and before the Koyemshi got back into town the woman's child was burned to death. Once I overheard a woman married into Zuni protest against having to contribute a bag of meal to the Koyemshi. "Hush!" said her young daughter, more of a Zuni than her mother, "Something will happen to you or to us children if you say anything against the Koyemshi." In 1927 Flora's mother received a present of a box of apples about the time when people were preparing presents, "pay," for the Koyemshi. "She was thinking it would be nice to keep that box of apples. While she was whitewashing the house, she fell off the ladder and bruised her leg. Then she knew that she must give that box of apples to the Koyemshi."[335] Ritual impropriety together with witchcraft, having a bad heart, are the Pueblo's characteristic explanations of untoward happenings or misfortunes.

SAFEGUARDING AGAINST DANGER

A careful observance of the proprieties and a spirit of conformity are safeguards. Against witchcraft you may use ashes or an arrowpoint. Like the woman who stepped out on her house terrace in 1590 and threw ashes at the Spanish lieutenant,[336] a Laguna woman who is alone at night in her house will throw some ashes toward her window or door. The forehead of a Laguna infant is ash-besmeared. Gum is put on an infant's forehead, on First Mesa, during "the dangerous moon"; but any adult going abroad at night in this December moon will smear ashes on his forehead against the witches "around everywhere." Women tie an arrowpoint into their belt, or a point may be held under the tongue on venturing forth at night (Laguna, Isleta). The grave is protected by marking around it with an arrowpoint, protected against witches who prowl as dogs or coyotes or wolves (Isleta).* The idea in using ashes is obscure; to be sure, witches smear themselves with ashes, so it may be an instance of like curing like: arrowpoints have power because they have been shot by a powerful spirit, by Lightning.

Both ashes and arrowpoint are used in separating a person from a dangerous influence. Any supernatural relation may be dangerous, and so in every ceremony the Hopi cast ashes off a feather as a final rite of exorcism or discharming or breaking the supernatural tie. There are several other rites to this end, waving

---

* It is indicated in the folk tales that witches habitually transform into animals to rob graves or retrieve a corpse (Hopi, Voth 5:126–27; Laguna, Boas 2:57; Laguna-Acoma, Gunn, 190–91; Isleta, Parsons 52:438).

ashes or cedar bark around the head and casting away, spitting, emesis, fumigating, or whipping. All appear to be expressive of the concept of cleansing from the supernatural which has encroached or might encroach upon the body, or upon the house or town, causing sickness or other misfortune.

To keep clear of pernicious influences, whether from witch or Spirit, is fundamental in Pueblo motivation. It appears most plainly in ritual, but it controls other forms of conduct in social relations at large, whether of manners or morals. It enters into Pueblo ideas or feelings of discretion, prudence, and caution, producing a code of live and let live, of taking no responsibility apart from what is conventional, of suppressing or ignoring grief or distress, and of remaining indifferent to the strange or unknown—indifferent if not afraid.

SENSE OF CO-OPERATION

In such a social code or theory of conduct innovation is discouraged, and any show of individualism condemned. Individual distinction is shunned rather than sought. A certain amount of individual selection does occur among the Pueblos, but the individual is selected for his social quality. For example, the Hopi chief, who will choose his successor among his younger brothers or nephews, is not bound strictly by the theory of choosing the eldest son of his eldest sister, he will choose the youth whose memory is good for prayer and song and who has the proper interest. In 1921 the Snake society of Walpi had to fill the place of their woman medicine-maker. Two women were eligible and willing to take office; but they were passed over because they were not discreet enough and another woman chosen who was close-mouthed and would not "tell anybody."[337]

In the hunt and in war individual prowess counted, but the hunter was esteemed because he provided well for his family or was freehanded, and the warrior or scalp-taker was obligated to join a group that would perform ritual for the general welfare. The warrior may have bragged a little privately[338] or backstage in kiva shown a little vanity,[339] but he was not spurred on to boast publicly of his exploits as among other tribes nor was he ambitious for warrior status. In the Zuni scalp ceremony, to be

sure, certain individuals are mentioned by name—the man first
to hear the returning war party, the makers of the War god
images, the impersonator of a prominent kachina[340]—but I cannot help thinking that such unusual personal distinction has
slipped in somehow from another culture. Usually, distinction
or power is achieved through social solidarity rather than
through personal experience. A man would change his group to
better himself in health or other matters when he would not feel
able to improve himself on his own.

Submissiveness is naturally a corollary of this attitude of
social dependence. Rebellion is rare. The town may be divided
within itself, as was Oraibi or Laguna or as are Santa Clara and
San Ildefonso, or, over peyote, Taos, but that is a question of
group against group, not of individual rebellion. Even rebel leaders assert they are acting in accordance with traditions, just as
Yukioma asserted that his great-uncles taught him he was to
destroy Oraibi or be destroyed himself.[341] Self-assertion or even
self-expression is not a Pueblo trait. Racer or lover who has
asked for the power of swiftness or seduction after he has won
race or woman has to have the power removed; it is dangerous
(Isleta). Dreaming does not give power as among many tribes;
it is dangerous, and dreamers ask to be whipped or exorcised.
As has been said of the Zuni, the man "who thirsts for power or
knowledge, who wishes to be, as they scornfully phrase it, 'a
leader of his people,' receives nothing but censure and will very
likely be persecuted for sorcery,"[342] just as would be the planner
of earthquake or epidemic; innovators, reformers, braggarts, unhappy men who would make others unhappy,* all are dangerous,
all are potential witches.†

---

* Cf. Benedict 3:II, 82. This tale supplies a very striking illustration of the
sense of solidarity perverted. The cuckold does nothing to his wife or his successor, but seeks a way to hurt other people as he has been hurt. Personal
revenge becomes communal revenge. In several Zuni-Hopi tales the Town chief
who feels injured or disappointed brings on flood or earthquake or summons the
enemy to destroy his town (cf. Voth 5:256), a Jehovah-like reversal of good will.
    This tale incident, "sending for the Apache," Benedict considers daydreaming

[Footnote (*) continued on following page]

† Hopi, *nukpana;* Zuni, *at'ani.*

On the other hand, the chief or group in authority for the time being, that is, while conducting a ceremony, are highly respected by the townspeople. They are "valuable men," using their knowledge, i.e., supernatural power,* for the good of all. Individual power should be socialized.

The co-operative person, in general, is highly esteemed. There is a great deal of co-operative spirit or enterprise among the Pueblos, from the household to the hierarchy, from the young woman who wet-nurses without compensation (Jemez)† to the Town chief who shares his corn store with his "children," from the brothers who take turns herding their sheep to the large intervillage working-parties of Second Mesa.[343] We have mentioned the communal hunts, the parties for grinding and spinning, the firewood and field parties. Women plant their bean fields co-operatively, and early sweet corn is harvested and roasted by a working-party when anybody met on the way home will be invited to take a few ears of corn, after the manner of hunters (Mishongnovi).‡ There are wild-food-gathering parties at which the girls and youths trade for plants and food or as in the rabbit hunt the girls race to the youth holding up what he, has gathered.[344] Then there are parties for basket-making or for sheep-dipping or shearing or house-building. Crow-Wing tells about a working-party to build up a wall that had fallen into the dance court in Walpi. The bugaboo kachina "went around from house to house gathering up the men for the work. Everybody

and compensatory for suicide technique; but Second Mesa informants assert that plotting with the enemy is an actual suicide technique; the miserable man agrees to wear his turquoise beads so that, on killing him, the enemy can get them as pay (Nequatewa, 107). Convincing touch!

Compare the story about the Zuni witch who, after putting on crow and owl feathers to see quickly like the crow and by night like the owl, summoned the Apache and then when he was discovered by a woodcutter promised to expose himself to the Apache when they came (Stevenson 2:394).

* Zuni, *sauwanikya* or *pinane* (breath); Acoma, *tsisha'ats*; Laguna, Cochiti, *k'o''k'imunᵛⁱ* Tewa, *pinan*; Isleta, *nathlöide* (*nathörde*); Taos, *tuwaiega* (?).

† Were she stingy, she would have no milk for her next infant (Harper).

‡ Beaglehole 3:28, 44–45. Formerly to arrange a large mixed party a sheep's carcass would be hung up outside the house as a sign of "help wanted." Nowadays the senior woman of the household will spread the news from house to house, as is or was done at Zuni (Cushing 6:195).

went to help. The women cooked for the people that worked.[345] Kiva work repairing and plastering is done collectively, by the men and women associated with the kiva; and work on the church is also collective.

The men of Laguna take turns, night by night, in tending the horse corral, the service passing from household to household.* Similarly, the War captain of Sia would name the six households which were to contribute each a herder for the weekly roundup of horses. During this roundup the men would catch wood rats and string them around their horses' necks, and, in rabbit-hunt fashion, the women first to come up with the returning horsemen got the rats. The eight San Felipe War captains themselves take turns tending the horses and cattle on the range, two by two, two weeks at a time.[346] These officers, ten of them, at Santo Domingo are helped in their herding by men and boys drawn each week from one of the five sections the town is divided into for this work.†

At ceremony or fiesta each woman is responsible for the space in front of her house. Out they come, each woman with her broom, to clean up during the hour or so before the dance begins. Orders for removing snow are called out from the housetops at Taos. After a snowfall at Zuni the Governor himself used to drive the snowplow. At Cochiti, manning the river boat is a communal job.[347]

Of all the communal undertakings, work on the irrigation ditches is the most important. Throughout the farming season work on the ditch is called for, literally, by town officers, and there is the annual spring cleaning. The procedure at San Juan is fairly typical. Toward the close of February, the chiefs meet at the Governor's house "to talk about the day for cleaning the ditch." Late in the afternoon before the appointed day the crier goes about town calling out the order. Food is supplied the workers on the first day by women of the south-side houses; on

* The year one man tended the corral for several months, the other townsmen built him a house, furnishing materials.

† White 4:41. In 1864 the Indian Agent is reporting that throughout the pueblos the War captains have charge of the horse herd, appointing the herders from week to week (*Report of the Commissioner of Indian Affairs* [1854]). A like system still prevails at Taos for burros, if not for cattle or horses.

the second day by women on the north side. The women are counted, and if anyone delays, a Fiscal goes after her.

Hopi do not irrigate, but in time of drought springs must be cleaned out, and this may be done co-operatively by the clan associated with the spring or by the whole community. One July day in 1893 all the men of Hano went down to Amüba, a large deep spring unused for years, and cut and dug away all the vegetation and scraped out the mud. Stretching in double file from bottom to brim the men passed up their vessels from hand to hand, while the girls in their white festive mantles sat around the brink watching them work. Then the chiefs deposited prayer-feathers where the water was oozing in, with prayer for the clouds to hasten with rain.[348] Just as irrigating or cleaning a spring is work for all, so are rain dances and ceremonies. It is not surprising therefore that men are expected to dance at least once a year (Zuni) or that "valuable men" are expected to do their "work" for rainfall or snowfall.

Why do people co-operate? There may be now and again a magical or automatic sanction, but there is a more general motivation. After describing preparations for a First Mesa dance, Crow-Wing expresses it: "Some men and boys are going for wood, some are killing steers and sheep. Wagons are being driven down for water. Some women are baking wafer-bread and some baking bread. And women go to the house of the man who is head of the dance to bake wafer-bread and bread for the dance. So everybody is very busy, everybody is helping. *Because at any time anyone may need help, therefore all help one another.*"

This theory of mutual aid may be expressed in interpueblo terms. When famine refugees are about to arrive, the Town chief of Acoma calls out: "The people of Zuni are coming. They have no crops. They are coming to work for us.* Some day we might have to go to them when our own crops are small. We shall treat them as we wish to be treated when our crops fail."[349] Asked to help by "earthquake"-stricken Zuni, Hopi chiefs say, "Yes, we should go, because if we ever have trouble and need them, then they will come and help us."[350]

---

* As did Zuni refugees at Jemez, the women grinding and the boys herding (Bunzel 5:60). Long-term guests should be paying-guests.

CHAPTER I

CEREMONIAL ORGANIZATION

In Zuni definition, poor people are people without ceremonial property or connection, belonging in no rain or curing society—people who are not "valuable." In this sense the poor of Zuni are about half the population. The proportion of poor would be very much larger in the East, but I doubt if the distinction between ceremonially poor and rich would be made at all there;* the society membership lists are too small.[1] As against membership of from thirty to sixty in the West, a society membership in the East generally numbers under ten or twelve (in lapsing societies, of course, there may be only three or four members, even two or one) and in Eastern towns there are comparatively few societies.†

Corresponding more nearly in size to the society in the East are the rain-making societies or so-called priesthoods of Zuni which are organized through maternal descent, and the maternal family group in control of the Hopi society. The constituency of

* Among Keres there is a term, *sishti*, denoting any person not actually engaged in ceremonial work (Santo Domingo) or any common person without ceremonial (or governmental) affiliation (Acoma; White 4:167; White 7), or anyone who knows all about the kachina (San Felipe; White 3:27). Compare Laguna and Cochiti, *shuts, shŭrdze* (Dumarest, 198). The kachina dance cult is everywhere that of the "poor man" or commoner. This may be why the Hopi Kachina Father repeats, "I am poor, I am poor" (Stephen 4:371). Distinctive terms or references are applied or made by Hopi of Second Mesa to chiefs, neophytes, or members merely (*pavunshinum* ? small mound caused by corn just starting to come up out of ground [Nequatewa, 103, Stephen 4:Glossary]) and to nonmembers or commoners.

† In this discussion I am following the Hopi distinction between belonging to a ceremony (or society with ceremony) and belonging to a dance group (or society without ceremony). Dance groups or societies are large in all the towns, since they are generally inclusive of all the males. Kiva memberships are similarly inclusive, and, of course, moiety membership. The memberships of the clown societies at Cochiti and Jemez are strikingly large, showing moiety influence.

the Hopi society is formed in part of members of a given clan, in part of godchildren who join the society their sponsors belong to, and in part, like Zuni curing society, of persons treated for snake-bite or other untoward accident, or for disease. The principle of initiation into Eastern societies is not hereditary, nor is initiation, as systematically as in the West, the outcome of convalescence. In all the towns doctors may be paid down in goods, but in the West the pay consists more characteristically of the patient himself; he is "given" to the doctor as "his child," personally or to be initiated by the doctor into his society. In the West trespass is also a common cause of initiation. By trespass is meant not only straying into a place where ritual is being conducted* but touching any society member who happens to be taboo or any object associated with a society. I knew two little boys who had to be initiated into the Zuni Wood society for inadvertently touching the society swallowing-sticks hanging on the wall. If a man is struck by flying bits of cactus during the ceremony of the Cactus society, he is caught, if possible, and straightway painted and arrayed to come out in the dance. Later, he will be fully initiated.†

In the East trespass or "trapping" as well as cure are familiar reasons for initiation, and cure is probably the most common reason, but the reason commonly given is personal bias—you want to belong, or you have made a promise or vow, or your

* This idea extends even to encountering the society people abroad if they are bent on ritual business. Any Hopi falling in with Snake society men on their snake hunt must join the society. Acoma shamans make nocturnal visits to shrines during initiations. If a shaman met anyone, he would take hold of him, stroke his hair, and call him "son"; the man would have to be initiated (White 7). Not only straying into the ash or meal "house" or into the dressing-room of the clowns entails joining them but, at the Hano war ceremony, by what seems to us an excess of logic, you must join them if you laugh at their jokes (Parsons 44:217, 218).

† Stevenson 2:570, 575a. Meddling with anything the society has title to may necessitate initiation. Acoma shamans wear dyed owl feathers in their hair. Any townsman who dyes owl feathers may be compelled to join a society; likewise any townsman who paints a snake on a rattle. The Laguna Kapina society chief owned moccasin dyes and had to be called upon to dab pigment on buckskin before it was dyed. I surmise that the sanction was having to join the society.

father or mother has wanted you to belong and has "given" you. (At Zuni none would ever suggest joining a society in these ways—"something would happen to you or to your child," perhaps the very misfortune because of which you would be ordinarily initiated. It is very "dangerous" to join a society except as the result of sickness or mischance.)[2]

Because of these differences of composition, the ceremonial organizations in the West bulk larger in the general life than they do in the East. No household in Zuni, it is safe to say, is without some society affiliation; quite commonly several societies are represented. Besides, in the lay membership, so to speak, or the nonmanagerial part of the society, there are many women (among Hopi there are also three women's societies); whereas in the East, as a rule, comparatively few women belong to societies, and the duties of those who do belong are mostly economic. Also the principle of plural society membership prevails in the West as against that of exclusive membership in the East. It is not at all uncommon for a Zuni townsman to belong to two or three societies, whereas no Keres or Tewa would belong, say, to both Flint society and Fire society.

In brief, the societal picture consists in the East of comparatively small groups which are recruited through vow or dedication, and in the West of large groups recruited after cure or peculiar experience or, in certain weather-control groups, through matrilineal descent.

From a functional point of view the ceremonial organization, although kaleidoscopic, is somewhat more homogeneous, as may be seen from study of Table 1, where by tribe or town the ceremonial homologues are presented. By and large, chieftaincies are affected by the idea of inheritance or descent, and general membership by the idea of sponsorship or godfatherhood, a distinction due to the possession or trusteeship of permanent sacrosanct property which is to be handed on like other property. In general, there are village or town chief, House chief or chiefs they are called in the West, and in the East, to outsiders, Cazique; a War chief or War society, including Scalp women; a Hunt chief as among Tewa and at Isleta or a Hunt society, as at

Zuni or among Keres; clown societies with fertility or phallic traits, likewise war traits; clown-related Women's societies among Hopi and at Jemez; weather-control and curing societies, more or less differentiated; a masked dance society or societies, except among Tiwa and Tewa; and a council of the chiefs.

The functions of these groups are, broadly speaking, directing the sun and keeping the calendar of moons or seasons; weather control and control of terrestrial waters; care of the crops; control of game animals; control of the slain enemy, and, formerly, war; control of witches; curing; and control or direction of the dead. For each distinctive function there is in the main a separate organization or group; for sun and calendar, Sun Speaker or Pekwin of Zuni, Hopi Sun chief or watcher, Town chiefs of Keres, Tewa, and Tiwa; for weather control, the rain societies and on occasion the curing societies of Zuni, certain familial groups and societies of the Hopi, both Zuni and Hopi war societies, most of the societies in the Eastern pueblos, kachina dance groups; for care of crops, kachina groups, Women's societies and Clown societies; for control of enemies, including witches, War society of Zuni and Scalp chiefs, male and female, and, of course, the societies that cure bewitchment, War chief and society of Hopi, War or Under chief and society of scalp-takers of Keres, Jemez, and Hopi, Scalp chief of Tewa (San Juan) and women assistants or War society, War chief of the Cane and Scalp chief with men and women helpers of Isleta, and throughout the East and at Acoma and Laguna the annual War captains; for control of game, Hunters' and Cactus societies of Zuni, Mountain Lion and Eagle-watchers societies of Jemez, Hunt chief or society of Keres, Hunt chief of Tewa and of Isleta; and, for curing, the several societies of all the tribes. Although the dead at large are addressed, deceased predecessors are more potent and the control of the dead is vested more particularly in the groups to which they belonged in life: society or kiva or clan groups.

However, to any one of these functions no group is limited specifically. The rain societies of Zuni and the Hopi War chief promote fertility in women; the Hopi War chief conducts ritual for disease of the lungs;[3] the Big Shell people of Zuni, a war and rain society, cures for bloating;[4] Zuni kachina perform ritual against venereal disease[5] or for offspring;[6] San Felipe and Sia kachina will call on an invalid and stroke him with their whip,[7] and Hopi kachina whip for rheumatism; Santo Domingo Rainbow kachina come out for epidemics, and with them comes Bear kachina to hold the heads and hands of the sick and cure;[8] Acoma kachina touch the sick with their lightning-stick, and the clown kachina medicate initiates after their whipping;[9] many clowning groups medicate for a sick stomach; the Tesuque Hunt chief performs a curing rite with a buffalo head;[10] the Hano War chief is bound to drive away any epidemic,[11] and Laguna war dance leaders performed a ritual against witch-sent grasshoppers.* Only curing societies have diagnostic medicine giving a vision of disease-causing witches, but Zuni rain societies have narcotics for finding the lost, strayed, or stolen. One of the rain societies is in charge of clown masks and sets them out on its altar on the fourth day of its eight-day retreat; another rain society cures for lightning shock and broken bones.[12] Most of the Zuni curing societies hold rain ceremonials, and one of them is organized and accounted a rain society.[13] Another Zuni curing society, the Ant society, takes an active part in war ceremonial,[14] functioning indeed as an understudy to the War society. Among Keres and at Isleta the same society may cure disease, make rain, and allay winds, and the Town chief can be called upon to cure and, although a man of peace, to look after the Scalps (San Felipe, Isleta). Lightning shamans cure stomach trouble (Acoma, Laguna). Hopi groups appear also as undifferentiated weather-control and curing (or disease-making) groups. For example, on First Mesa the night running of Agave and Horn society members is a rain- or snow-making rite, but should anyone encounter the runners or even look at them—everyone stays indoors, with windows shaded—not only would he impair the efficacy of the rite but his knees would become stiff.[15] Probably the patrol is also against night-roaming ghosts or witches. The Flute ceremony is for rain, but the racers, as in other Hopi races,

* Parsons 33:257, n. 4. At Acoma grasshoppers are Scalp-sent (p. 350).

perform a rite for longevity, and the society doctors cure for lightning shock and probably for arrow or gun wounds. Again, the dancers in a ceremony of one of the Hopi Women's societies are called rain-water girls—"should it rain while they are dancing they would drink the rain"—but the society treats venereal disease, caused in Hopi opinion, by an insect which eats away wood.*

As to details of organization, there is in every ceremonial group the head or chief;† one assistant, as in all the offices of Sia or Isleta, in the clown societies of Cochiti, in the Santo Domingo Town chieftaincy, in some Hopi societies, and as in all but the rain societies of Zuni,‡ or two or more assistants, as in the Town chieftaincy of Zuni, Cochiti, and Jemez, in the "war captaincy" of Laguna and Acoma, or in all Tewa (N.M.) groups. To the chief or chiefs are added what we would call executives who carry out directions or counsel or see to it that they are carried out by others. These messengers or mouthpieces, administrators or police, may form a distinctive group like the war societies or war captains and be loaned, so to speak, to the groups needing their services. (Errand men, gatherers of ritual wood or plants, may be drawn too from the class of recent initiates [Hano, Isleta, Taos].) A chief, his speaker or assistant, and executives or mes-

---

* On Third Mesa this society (Lakon) causes and cures "a peculiar eczema on the upper part of the body." Similarly, caused and cured is swelling of the abdomen, by the Snake society; sore ears, by the Soyal society; a hornlike swelling on the top of the head, by the Oaqöl society; deafness, by the Mamsrau society; twisting and twitching of face and neck, by the Horn society; swelling of kneepan and contraction of knee tendons, by Popwamu society (Voth 3:109 n.; Voth 4:44).

† Zuni, *shiwanni* or *mosona*; Hopi, *mongwi*; Keresan, *hocheni*; Isleta, *k'abede*; Jemez, *whi*; Tewa, *toyo*; Taos, *t'unena*.

Mosona, mosi (? Sp. *mozo*, servant) should be translated as director or manager but it is customary to translate Pamosona or Komosona, Scalp chief or Kachina (society) chief. *Wo'le* is another Zuni term for servant-manager, a subordinate to *mosona. Cheani* in Keresan, shaman, doctor, ceremonialist, refers to any society member; I know no equivalent in the other languages or any proper word in English; Stevenson used "theurgist." Throughout, headship or leadership, is usually expressed in parental terms: their Father or Mother, our Father.

‡ The Zuni assistant is called *pekwin*, "speaking place," speaker. The Zuni Pekwin par excellence, the Crier chief, is speaker to the Sun, but he serves also as speaker to the Council of the paramount Rain chiefs.

sengers—that is the general pattern of organization, although where the hereditary principle is more to the fore, as among Hopi and the rain societies of Zuni, the group is less fixed and may be enlarged to include special functionaries, among them a woman whose services in brewing medicine or in feeding the ceremonial group or the fetishes are accounted indispensable.

Zuni curing societies have a medicine chief, the head of the medicine order, and, inferably, chiefs or directors for their other orders. Hopi assign particular functions to particular persons: the medicine chief who ranks next the chief is in charge of the medicine bowl (Pl. II), whirls medicine-dipped whizzers, and in general asperses; a tobacco chief looks after the pipe and blows smoke clouds over fetishes and medicine bowl; a fire chief looks after the fire; a sand chief fetches the sand necessary for the altar. Altar parts do not all belong to the chief to whom the paramount fetish belongs; other fetishes, slabs or tiles, netted water gourds, sacrosanct stones, all may be contributed by participants in altar ritual who inherit objects and functions. Depositing prayer-sticks or prayer-feathers and impersonating Spirits associated with the ceremony are functions usually delegated to a son or nephew.

In all ceremonial groups there is an initiation ceremony on joining the group or an installation ceremony at which ceremonial paraphernalia are handed on. Initiation is commonly thought of as a saving kind of rebirth, and various details of the ceremony may be thus interpreted, particularly the indispensable rite of head-washing and naming. As at childbirth, a sister or kinswoman of the sponsor or "father" performs the baptism, and clothes, prayer-feathers, or ritual paraphernalia are given the initiate or godchild. Between godchild and godfather an intimate, lifelong relationship of reciprocal aid or service is established together with a rule against marrying into the godfather's family. Initiations and installations alike may be deferred for long periods. In case of deferred installation an assistant will serve as chief. At Acoma and among Tewa the installation of Town chief is regularly deferred, for a year of preparation.

At Zuni the Town chief is associated with male kindred,

PLATE II

ORAIBI ANTELOPE SOCIETY CHIEFS
Society *tiponi*, rattle, medicine-water bowl (Voth 3: Pl. CXCVIII)

formerly there was a woman in the group. The group is of the Dogwood clan, the largest Zuni clan, but clan affiliation is not rigid. The Hopi Town chief is associated with male and female kindred, particularly with the senior woman, his mother or sister, of his maternal house; she it is who on certain occasions supplies corn meal or seed corn or marks a ceremonial chamber with corn meal.* (The Town chief of Walpi watches the sun, i.e., sets the date, for the planting of sweet corn for the kachina.) In all Hopi towns the clanship of the chief is of significance, and in all the towns but Walpi the Town chief is theoretically† of the Bear clan. At Walpi the passing of the chieftaincy from the Bear clan to the Horn clan is dramatized in the Flute ceremony, the Horn clan's ceremony. The Bear clan is almost extinct. In spite of the hereditary factor, the actual selection of the Walpi Town chief rests with the Council of Chiefs.‡

The office of Town chief is nonhereditary at Jemez and among Keres except at Acoma, where the office belongs definitely to the Antelope clan. Possibly there is or was elsewhere a predilection for filling the office from certain clans. Stevenson was told that the Sia office alternated between two clans, Coyote and Corn, the only clans of numerical importance, and at Santo Domingo I was told that the office was filled through the Coyote clan; now, some years later, Dr. White is told that between the office and clanship there is no relationship either at Sia or at Santo Domingo.[16] At Jemez the Town chief in 1921 was of the Young Corn clan. So was his predecessor. The office, it is said, may be filled within this clan or the Sun clan; it would not be filled from the Coyote clan, the third of the three numerically predominant clans of Jemez. On the whole, both at Jemez and among all but

* The woman in the Zuni Town chieftaincy may have had some such functions. Stevenson does not name them, but she always refers to her as the "priestess of fecundity." The Council met in her house, and here installations into office were made. There is a woman, "their sister," in the other Rain chieftaincies of Zuni.

† On Second Mesa rotation by clan was once in vogue (Cushing, Fewkes, Parsons, 297; Nequatewa, 48).

‡ For the selection of Tü′ïnoa, the present Town chief, and of his predecessor, Simo, see Stephen 4: 59, 139, 203, 951, 952, 1020, 1045-48.

the Acoma Keres, the relation between Town chieftaincy and clanship is, I think, merely loosely conceptual, if not based outright on the idea of having the office circulate among the clans; there is certainly no such hereditary principle as in the West.

On the other hand, between Town chieftaincy and organization by medicine society there is a definite relationship not at Jemez but among Keres. The Town chief is the chief of the Flint society (Cochiti, Santo Domingo, San Felipe), or the Town chief is or was installed by the chief of the Flint society (Laguna).[17] The Town chief is also chief of the Koshare clowns (San Felipe, Santo Domingo). The office is appointive, by the Council of society chiefs or by the War chief (or annual War captain) (Santo Domingo, San Felipe, Sia, formerly Cochiti), or at Acoma, by the Antelope clan. At Taos there is a tendency for chiefly office to pass from father to son. The chief of the three northern kivas who is Town chief and the chief of the three southern kivas incline to giving a son to their own kiva and training him to succeed in office, subject to the approval of the kiva chiefs. There is no *theory* of paternal inheritance, except in the office of Cacique, which is regarded as a Spanish office.

Among Tewa of First Mesa one man is referred to as Town chief, but the fact that there are two chiefs for the winter solstice ceremonial points to the double chieftaincy of the eastern Tewa and of Taos. Eastern Tewa in accordance with their moiety system have a chief from their Summer people and a chief from their Winter people, but Summer chief is in charge of all the people as paramount chief from March to November, Winter chief, from November to March. Each chief has two assistants, a right-hand man who literally sits to the right of the chief and a left-hand man who sits to the left. At the death of the chief his right-hand man succeeds, the left-hand man becoming right-hand man. In native theory neither clanship nor kinship is an essential for office, but kinship is a circumstance that is considered. "When there is a relative, they put him in, so they won't have to come out from their house," a comment significant of the importance attaching here as elsewhere in ceremonial to associations with a given house. The power to appoint the left-hand man may lie within the group, but this appointment like that of any chief has to be approved by the War chiefs (Hunt chief also Scalp chief, San Juan, and Red Bow Youth, the woman War chief). At Santa Clara and probably San Ildefonso the Town chieftaincy group may be recruited through sickness,[18] and at Santa Clara women are included.

At Taos the chief of the Big (or Abalone) Earring people's kiva is chief of the three kivas of the north side of town. He is Town chief and president of the Council. He conducts an early winter ceremony; and he alternates with the Water Man in being in charge of the ceremonial camp or the pilgrimage to Blue Lake in August. Water Man is chief of Water people's kiva and of the three kivas of the south side of town. Water Man may also be the Cacique, but the two offices are distinguishable. The Spanish caciqueship is considered to be hereditary in the male line, and the Cacique may belong to any kiva group. According to one account, the Cacique watches the sun for the winter solstice and for the beginning of the series of winter ceremonies; according to another and more probable account, each chief of ceremony watches the sun for his own ceremony, and the Cacique is only the head of the Catholic religion. Big Earring Man and Water Man correspond to Winter people's chief and Summer people's chief among Tewa, but they are not thought of in seasonal terms.

Quite generally the Town chief is thought of as presiding, barely as paramount, chief. "If the Hopi Town chief gets on the wrong road, the War chief tells him, 'You are on the wrong road; get back on the right road!' Then he will get back" (Shumopovi).[19] In the West and probably at Taos the chief of any ceremony is chief of all the people during the ceremony.[20] "Not one boss at Zuni," said Nick, "many bosses"; each in his own realm. After the Kachina society chief has decided on a kachina dance, the high Rain chiefs have nothing to say, "not even the Town chief."[21] Among Keres and at Isleta the Town chief has comparatively more power or greater control; but even among them he shared or shares some of his functions with the War chief (Nahia, Kapina society chief, or Kumpawithlawe, the

Snake society chief) or with the Steward chief (Chraik'ats[i] or Kabew'iride) or with the chiefs of the societies, e.g., appointments of the annual secular officers. In these appointments as in other matters the Zuni Town chiefs are associated with the chiefs of the other major rain societies, the ranking Ashiwanni. In their Council, however, the entire Town chieftaincy of three men takes part, whereas the other major rain societies are represented each by its chief only. Among Keres the Town chief is considered the host or "father" of visiting kachina; the Acoma Town chief appoints the kiva-kachina officials in charge of masks; Tewa Town chiefs are themselves custodians of the masks. The chief of the three Taos kivas on the south side of town, Water Man, is custodian of the Black Eyes or clown masks, the only masks known to Taos. The Oraibi Town chief is in charge of the mask of Eototo, the chief of the kachina, and the Town chief must impersonate the kachina chief; permission to give a kachina dance must be got from the Town chief.[22]

The Keresan Town chief represents the Mother, the Underground Corn Mother of Shipap, source of Keresan custom and welfare. Logically, at Acoma, title to all the land vests in the Town chief. Something of this landholding theory has been noted also on Third Mesa, where the Town chief may assign fields to certain maternal families in return for performing ceremonies (see p. 863).[23] In most towns the shrine par excellence which is or represents the Middle Place or place of the Emergence is in the care of the Town chief.[24] As the general welfare of the townspeople is in the hands of the Town chief, he is expected not to leave town, except on pilgrimage.

The office of Sun-watcher and Crier chief is at Zuni peculiarly distinctive. The appointment is made by the Council from the Dogwood clan, and usually from the Rain society or chieftaincy of the West. It is for life or good behavior* which includes not only periods of ritual abstinence but continuous moderation. Pekwin determines the solstices by watching the sunrise in win-

---

* For the Zuni standard of ritual morality see p. 153. For his more technical "rules" the new Pekwin may choose between the rules of the Town chieftaincy and the rules of the Rain society or chieftaincy of the East (Pathltok).

ter from a petrified stump on the east edge of town, and the sunset in summer, from a hill below Corn Mesa. Pekwin has no sacred bundle; the sun is his sacred possession.* The solstices date other ceremonies, so Pekwin is virtually the keeper of the calendar. He announces the solstice ceremonies from the housetop; other announcements he makes privately. Pekwin represents the zenith among the high Rain chiefs, and so goes in fifth at the rain retreats; but Pekwin is the officiating priest at all ceremonies at which the high Rain chiefs function jointly, setting up his meal altar of terrace cloud design. Pekwin welcomes or "makes the road" for the kachina chiefs; he installs new Rain chiefs, including the War chiefs, and formally he appoints to office the impersonators of the kachina. Pekwin is the most revered and most holy man in Zuni, or, in Zuni terms, the most valuable man in a community that "lives by the thoughts of those who are good people."[25]

The Crier chief of the Hopi is also a conspicuous personage, for he takes part in the meeting or smoke-talk preliminary to almost every ceremony, and he announces ceremonies from the housetop, from the roof of his maternal house (Walpi), the house of the lineage in which the office descends. Ceremonial dates are determined not by Crier chief but, for the solstices, on First Mesa, by a special functionary, the Sun-watcher,† and for the various ceremonies by the chief of the ceremony which impends. Among Keres (Acoma and Sia) and Tewa and at Jemez, solstice determination is a function of the Town chief. There is no crying from the housetop, and in general announcements are made in a circuit about town by the War captains. At Taos we find announcement again from the housetop, and more of it than in any other town, by all the secular officers, and for the solstices, some say, by the Cacique. At Isleta there is housetop announcement, from the Black Eyes housetop, by the Crier who is, as at San Juan, a lifelong but secular officer.

* See p. 219.

† There is no Sun-watcher at Mishongnovi; horizon or solar observation is made by Town chief, Crier, or other chiefs. The summer solstice is observed by Crier chief (Beaglehole 3:23).

The officials in the East who are called in English "war captains" are appointed or elected annually, together with the
secular officials, Governor, Lieutenant-Governor, and Fiscal;
but the War captains have ritual functions of prayer and offering,
of guarding against witches or intruders, of maintaining the
customs, of appointing to office and installing, and of serving as
executive messengers, functions which are performed in the
West by the War chiefs; and among Keres and Tewa the War
captains or Outside chiefs, like Zuni War chiefs, are representatives or proxies for the War gods and go by their names. In
other words, the War captains are both secular and ceremonial
officials, which dual character we shall be explaining later on
in historical terms.

Among Hopi there are no War captains, nor do the War gods
figure as prototypes for organization, except in the winter war
ceremony and in the cult of Masauwü; instead, for the war
society there is a single chief whose office and ceremony descend
within his maternal family, likewise the chief of the Masauwü
cult or society who impersonates Masauwü and at one time was
chief of the Agave (nadir) society (Walpi), a sometime war
society. Formerly there was an affiliated stick-swallowing group.
Horn society and Snake-Antelope societies are also sometime
war societies. The Snakes took to the warpath, and the Antelopes made war magic at home. The War chief (Po'tali) of Hano
impersonates a kachina warrior girl, and there is war ritual at
the winter solstice ceremony, but the Kabena war society is
extinct. Nor is there today a war society among eastern Tewa
excepting a women's group called Tse'oke (? Bear Face or Hard
Metate [? Stone] Face or Apienu, Red Bow Youth, also called
Blue Corn Girls) of whom the woman chief has a voice in appointment to chiefly office and at long intervals presents an
initiation dance (Santa Clara). Recruiting is through dedication
in childhood, through trapping any woman stepping into the
rabbit-hunt circle, or through self-dedication in sickness. Reyes
Archuleita of San Juan, who was initiated in 1928, gave herself
after a series of accidents; she fell off the roof and hurt her arm,
was kicked by a horse, and bitten by a pig. In the initiation

chamber the Scalps are hung up to watch and take care of the novice, and later, on special occasions, the women feed the Scalps. In Taos and Tewa tale the Corn Girls bring in on a pole the heads of the Redheads killed by Morning Star or the scalps taken by the girls themselves.*

Zuni War chiefs are heads of a war society into which scalp-takers are initiated. The chiefs, Elder Brother Bow chief and Younger Brother, are said by Stevenson to be appointed from the membership by the Town chief. She also reports that once when Naiuchi, Elder Brother, and Meshe, Younger Brother, were demoted, they ceased to attend society meetings. There are also Scalp chiefs, a man and his assistant, also a woman (office lapsed), in charge of the Scalps. It is not known how they are selected. Four girls are vowed to dance in the Scalp ceremony for four presentations. Among Keres there were scalp-taker Opi societies into which, except at Acoma, killers of prey animals were also taken. At Cochiti, possibly in other Keresan towns, the War chief (Nahia) was drawn from the scalp-takers; he was not necessarily their chief; but the two offices might be filled by one man. The War chief installed (perhaps appointed) the Town chief. At Isleta there are scalp-takers and a War chief who is called from-the-beginning or permanent war chief, Pą'ide, in contrast to the annually appointed War chief of the Cane, i.e., War captain. Pą'ide is Scalp chief and chief of the war Snake society recruited by vow in sickness and consisting of several men and two women who carry the Scalps in the victory dance, make medicine by chewing and spewing bits from the Scalps, and feed the Scalps in kiva. The society are witch-baiters, and through their annual ceremony of bringing in Rattlesnake they cleanse the town. Scalp-taking is associated with the Jemez War society; their Nadir chief, Opi'soma, keeps a scalp. This Scalp or War chief is appointed by the Town chief and, like him, he may summon the Council. Scalps are kept at Taos, probably in charge of the War chief who is chief of the Bear People society. This chief, like the Pą'ide war chief at Isleta and the War chiefs

* This may be the myth for the Isletan Scalp Mothers. (See below.)

of Zuni, is associated with ritual racing; fast running was a function of war.

War societies are also associated with weather control, control of wind and of cold or winter. The Zuni War society conducts an early spring ceremony against wind and cold. The Hopi War society never dances outside lest it cause wind and cold; their chief is possessed of a "hail headdress" so he must have some control over this destructive form of precipitation. Hopi Agaves are associated with hail and snow, and they are associated conceptually with fertility. The Kapina-Kahbena society controlled wind (Laguna, ? Hano). At Jemez the War society observes rain retreats, and the chief co-operates in a ceremony to control windstorm. Since the Zuni Scalps are rain-makers, the Scalp chiefs belong in the weather-control groups. Zuni War chiefs are counted among the paramount Rain chiefs, being the sixth group "to count their days" after the summer solstice, although they do not go into retreat. Other functions of the War society are: serving as executive messengers to the Council with the right to attend all ceremonies; scouting or trail-opening, i.e., ceremonial trail-opening and guarding on salt trips (Mishongnovi, Acoma) or pilgrimage; conducting ceremonial games and races; leading out dancers, war or kachina dancers; protecting supernatural power that is used properly and destroying it when used improperly, that is, guarding against witchcraft; in general, policing public morals and preserving the customs.

A Zuni war chief represents the Nadir, *manilama shiwanni*, Below chief. The War chief of Cochiti was referred to as Nahia, Below. Members of the Jemez War society are called Under (Below) chiefs. The chief of the Hopi Agave society is a Nadir chief because of his association with the god of death, and Agaves guard the trails of the underworld. In the other tribes the association between the Below and the War chief or society is probably derived also from death or next-world concepts.

Among Hopi there is no permanent hunt chief; any man may organize and become hunt leader or chief, but the Rabbit clan chief (Walpi) or Badger clan chief (Mishongnovi)* an-

* "Because the Badger clan owns all the animals" (Beaglehole 2:4, 10, 12).

nounces the hunt and offers prayer-sticks, made by the hunt leader (Mishongnovi). The hunt leader or Rabbit clan chief builds the ceremonial fire on which an offering is made to the rabbits and through which, as elsewhere, the hunters pass their rabbit sticks (to make them throw straight [Mishongnovi]). There is or was a permanent Hunt chief or society among the other Pueblos. Men would go to the Hunt chief or to a society member to get him to make them prey animal fetishes (Zuni, Acoma)[26] and prayer-feathers or prayer-sticks, to sing for them, or to teach them hunting songs (Keres, Isleta).[27] To the Zuni Hunt society belong hunting songs which if used by one not a member of the society would entail misfortune, and only members of the society may deposit the skull of a prey animal in the cave shrine of the prey animals. Communal hunts may be conducted by the War chiefs or captains or by the Clown societies (Zuni, Isleta, some Keres), but among Keres (Santo Domingo, San Felipe, Acoma, Sia), also at Zuni, the Hunt society takes an important ritual part in the rabbit hunt,* Acoma and Sia Hunt societies holding a ceremony the night before the hunt.[28] The Jemez Hunt society provides game for the Town chief (probably to feed fetishes or, as at Acoma, the kachina). Game animal dances are usually in charge of the Hunt chief (Keres, Tewa); but at Taos they belong to the Town chief.

Associated with the hunt in Keresan towns is or was an official called Chraik'ats[i] (Chaik'atse), also Bow, in charge of game or of the wild-food supply.[29] He co-operated with the Town chief in planning for rabbit hunts to provide food for his fetishes or in announcing the time to harvest (Santo Domingo). The office appears to be paralleled at Isleta (Kabew'iride, Bow chief). The Tewa Hunt chief (Pįkę or Samaiyo) keeps the Scalps in his house and, together with the woman Scalp chief, makes or approves appointments to chiefly office. He instals chiefs.[30] According to his functions he is War chief rather than Hunt chief.

Of the four Hopi Men's societies, tribal societies into one of which every youth has to be initiated, Singers, Wüwüchim,

* Among Keres always under the general direction of Ma'sewi, the head War captain (White).

Agave, and Horn, the last two have warrior functions,[31] guarding* and scouting for other groups, and the Agave chief instals all chiefs in office. Agaves are associated with the underworld; they are guards or arbiters on the trail taken by the dead. On Second Mesa they are recognized as the most powerful of all societies.† In organization, however, Singers society controls, Singers chief being chief of Wüwüchim (Walpi), the joint ceremony of all four societies. Wüwüchim is an annual ceremony, but Singers chief decides on celebrating it in its long form as an initiation ceremony, which used to be when there were enough boys. A boy is pledged or given in infancy to a "father" who breathes into his mouth and, later, will sponsor him; first, when he is whipped by the kachina at Powamu and, later, when he is initiated into the Men's society of his "father." At Mishongnovi, before this Wüwüchim initiation, a boy is also initiated into any other society his "father" may belong to (Kennard).‡ Parents like to see their firstborn son in the Men's society of his own father, and other sons distributed in the other three societies (Walpi).[32]

Two of the Men's societies, Singers society and Wüwüchim society, have clowning traits and form into temporary clown groups, of whom Singers chief is theoretically chief; and the Singers are in charge of burlesque masks. Hano has or had a permanent clown society, with a chief, altar properties, and medicine, called Paiyakyamu or Koyala or Kossa. Masked clowns also appear on First Mesa in the dance ceremonials borrowed from Zuni which have these kachina clowns, the Koyem-

---

* Agaves and Horns (also members of the Snake society), one man or several, guard by night the kiva in which society ceremonial is in progress (Voth 4:30; Stephen 4:11, 969–70, 977, 981). Horns are especially on guard during the daytime dances of the Wüwüchim ceremony, and Horns and Agaves patrol by night.

† They seem to be less outstanding on First Mesa; but Anawita, the Agave chief at Walpi in Stephen's day, was a dominating personage; he went to Washington with Simo, the Town chief, in the Hopi party escorted by Tom Keam early in the eighties (Nequatewa, 109).

‡ Besides this "father" or sponsor, a person may have a "doctor father," one who has cured him and whose society he also joins (Mishongnovi, Kennard; and possibly in the other Hopi towns).

shi. Once the Walpi Koyemshi masks were kept at Chief kiva, but in Stephen's day they had been removed to Horn or Goat kiva or to the house of Wikyatïwa, a guesthouse for Zuni traders or for kachina impersonators from Zuni, and Wikyatïwa of the Agaves, of Horn kiva and Goat kiva, was recognized as the Koyemshi chief.

Koyemshi impersonators at Zuni are appointed annually from the membership of one of the curing societies or, latterly, of one of the kivas. Actually this rule applies strictly only to the chief, Koyemshi their father. The clans have to be well represented by the ten impersonators. There are several sets of impersonators in town. The Rain society of the West keep the Koyemshi masks. The other clown group of Zuni is an order of one of the curing societies, the Ne'wekwe. The clowning "grandfathers" of Isleta belong four to one moiety and four to the other, and the Town chief is at their head. Twelve temporary clowns (K'apio) are appointed, six by each moiety chief, for a harvest dance by maskless kachina, just as in Emergence myth twelve K'apio (K'apiunin), six from each moiety, were appointed (by the War chief) to make an exit and lead the people up. (The Gopher [Shure'] or Red Eye Younger Brothers with hair in poke make the gap after the failure of the Black Eye Elder Brothers with hair bunched on the sides.) For another maskless kachina dance, for spring vegetation, moiety representatives are appointed to fetch spruce, sing teasing or jeering songs, burlesque foreigners, duck shirkers, set out food in the court for themselves or Indian guests, get out and valet the dancers, and announce and take charge of a subsequent rabbit hunt—all clown society functions.

There is a clowning group at Taos called Black Eyes which is the name of one of the Isletan moieties. The complementary group, Red Paint people, which had war associations, getting out dancers, is extinct. There are two clown societies, Tabö'sh and Ts'un'tatabö'sh or Ice society, at Jemez, and most townsmen belong to one or the other. Among Keres and Tewa there are or were two clown groups, Kurena (Qwirana) and Koshare (Kashale) or Kossa. Seasonal and kiva associations are to be found in some of these groups, somewhat confused or obscure; but it is

inferable that each Tewa moiety had its own Kossa;* as for
Keres, sheer clownishness is so confined to the Koshare that
were not the Kurena possessed of other traits in the general
clown complex and did they not complement the Koshare in
managerial or war or kachina functions they would not be considered a clown society, just as their historically connected
society at Zuni, the Shi'wanakwe, is not a clown society. At
Acoma there is no Kurena society, and the Kashale show dichot-
omous influence. Kashale dedicated their own sons, an extreme
expression of the patrilineal character of moiety and in the East
of kiva membership. (But compare Walpi dedication.)

San Juan Kwirana (and Taos Black Eyes) have been recruited
through the practice of vowing infants; the Kossa, through
trespass. A peculiar form of trespass is found among all the
clown groups, Koyemshi excepted. The clowns make a circle of
ashes or meal on the ground at any public celebration and capture child or adult straying into the circle which they call their
house.[33] At their initiations the clown societies may make the
circle or arc at their chamber entrance. On the first and fifth
days of the Oraibi Snake-Antelope ceremony a meal circle is
made around the two society kivas to keep out intruders. All
the societies do likewise at Acoma and at Sia, where the circle
is made larger each day of their four-day ceremony.

Clowning consists of gluttony or eating or drinking filth; of
drenching or being drenched with urine or water; simulating
lust, fear, or anger; playing games together or with lookers-on;
begging from house to house; distributing prizes or in general
distributing corn or melons; burlesquing ceremonial, satirizing
individuals and other peoples, scouting and valeting for the
kachina, getting out dancers, and acting or speaking by op-
posites. Inverse or backward behavior or speech is, of all, the
most characteristic trait, as it subsumes a good many particulars
of behavior and appearance and almost all clown humor. Among

* Parsons 42:14; Parsons 49:125 ff. Probably these were distinguished by
headdress, like the Isletan K'apiunin, or as Santo Domingo Kurena with hair
on top in poke are distinguished from Koshare with hair bunched over ears
(Twitchell, I, 474).

Pueblos, as among us, clowning is a release from ordinary, conventional conduct. It entertains, but it is also dangerous or rather the clowning society is dangerous and fear-inspiring. The clowns are licensed to do what they choose; they are punitive and have express police or warrior functions, particularly getting out dancers or racers or workers on town enterprises like repairing a bridge or getting in a harvest; they are warlike scouts, if not fighters;[34] at Acoma and Taos they had charge of the Scalp ceremony; they are hunt managers, particularly for hunts with the girls asked for by the kachina; they are generally supposed to practice black magic,[35] having as well exorcising power;[36] they use excreta as medicine against sickness from contact with excreta, which is a partial explanation of their filth-eating or filth-smearing ways.

With the clown societies of Jemez and with two of the Hopi Men's societies, two Women's societies are affiliated, in tradition or ritual, and there is a Women's society at Cochiti which functions like the Jemez societies, in connection with harvesting for the Town chief.[37] The organized corn-grinding women of Acoma* use Koshare songs, and the musical grinding parties of First and Second Mesas are called Kashailĭlalauwu, Koshare-doing.† The outstanding feature of the Pu'węre dance given by the Tewa women's war society (Tse'oke or Apienu) is burlesque,‡ women and men exchanging clothes together with economic roles; but with the clown organization, the Kossa, there is no connection. In the Ne'wekwe clown society of Zuni, women are members, al-

---

* In one of these three groups—the one introduced by a Laguna woman married into Acoma—there are the makings of a Women's society. The chief is called mother. She sets a date for grinding four days in advance, and all members are obliged to attend the midnight assemblage. Once a woman joins the group, she may not withdraw (White 7).

The grinding songs of Laguna women are clan songs (Parsons 33:215–16). Grinding songs are known to certain Zuni women (Bunzel 2:495). Zuni curing societies invite girls in to grind pigments (Bunzel 5:859).

† Stephen 4:153; Beaglehole 3:31–32. The idea of the party is borrowed from Zuni, and Kashaili is Zuni for Koshare. At the Isleta party to grind meal for the Fathers, maskless kachina and women impersonations dance "kachina basket dance" (Parsons 52:314).

‡ Hopi Marau women burlesque, impersonate warriors, and carry weapons.

though they never "come out to play," nor do they doctor.* The Ne'wekwe chief has an important role in the Molawia ceremonial dramatizing the recovery of the Corn Maidens; but the women's growth ceremony, the Thla·hewe, Zuni's Tablita or Corn dance, is not related to the clown organization; it is Pekwin's ceremony.[38]

One of the clown societies of the Keres, Kurena or Quirana, is affiliated with another society, the Shikani (Shikame) or, more properly speaking, the Shikani is differentiated into a curing and rain-making society, with the Kurena limited to the function of weather control. Koshare have a like relationship with the Flint society (Santo Domingo, Santa Ana, San Felipe, Cochiti). At Zuni, societies are so much differentiated in their weather-control and curing functions as to necessitate a classification by rain society.† Included in the classification, however, are the Town chieftaincy group, the scalp-taking War society, Pekwin, one of the curing societies, and possibly the Big Shell war society. One of the paramount rain societies has charge of the masks of the kachina clowns, the Koyemshi; another can call lightning and cure lightning shock. A group is classified in native opinion, as well as in Table 1, as a rain society if it takes part in the series of retreats for rain beginning at the summer solstice.

---

* Women members of curing societies sometimes doctor at Zuni; among Keres they never doctor; they brew medicines and they make yucca suds to simulate clouds (San Felipe, Santo Domingo) or to wash the head ritually, all functions close to their ordinary economic ones. Even in the Hopi Women's societies, in which there are male members and chiefs, the men take the lead in placing the altar and conducting altar ritual.

† There is indeed such a marked differentiation, at Zuni, of the rain society from other societies that observers have called these weather-control groups "priesthoods," and their members, "priests." The distinguishing terminology is justifiable, since in these groups there is no lay membership; but for comparative purpose the terminology is misleading. The usual Hopi society terminology is even more misleading, lay members as well as chiefs have been called priests. Observers of Keres have also confused the terms "priest" and "chief." It seems to me more in accord with the native point of view and historically more accurate to use but three terms: the generic term "society," which can be qualified; "chief," meaning a society head; and "society member" or, according to what he is doing, "doctor" or "shaman."

Everybody who functions in these retreats is called a *shiwanni*.*
Elsewhere, except among Hopi and at Isleta, a like series of rain
retreats is observed, and these retreats are followed by kachina
dances (Keres, Jemez).

Flint, Shikame, Giant, and Fire are the outstanding societies
of Keres, all organized primarily to control weather and secondarily to cure for witchcraft. There are also Snake, Ant, and
Lightning doctors, curing, respectively, for snakebite, for ail-
ments caused by ants in the body such as skin disease or sore
throat, and for lightning shock and broken bones; but these
doctors are less well organized; they may be grouped in some
other society or may even practice on their own. The Kapina or
Spider society, being a war society, has been lapsing, although at
Acoma it functioned importantly for the Town chieftaincy up to
a few years ago, when the last member died, and in Sia lore it was
the original society. It existed at Hano. At Sia it assembled with
the Snake society. The Sia Snake society fits into the regular
organization and has its own ceremony and ceremonial house.[39]
This is true also of the Jemez Snake society.[40] The only other
curing societies of Jemez are Flint and Fire.[41] Flint and Fire are
the "Bear medicine" societies among Tewa; and there is an
Eagle society which presents the Eagle dance and also doctors
(San Juan, probably elsewhere). At Zuni the Ant society, which
is also called Knife (Flint) society, functions intimately with the
War society. (Keresan Flint societies also have war associations.) The Ant society also removes ants and cures skin diseases. There are two Zuni fire societies, Big Firebrand and Little
Firebrand. Besides there are Bedbug, which is a split-off from
Little Firebrand; Cactus which cures wounds and to which anyone was eligible after killing but not scalping an enemy; Thle'-
wekwe or Wood society which conducts two annual winter ceremonies for snow or cold rains, and cures or discharms for sore
throat; Uhuhukwe or Eagle-Down which was curing for small-

---

* The term is also applied to the Spirits, to the Animal Spirits, the Stars, the
Chiefs of the Directions, to anyone endowed with the means of securing or bestowing blessings, regardless of whether he is human or supernatural (Bunzel
4:808, n. 68). To the doctors the term is not applied.

pox* when the Stevensons attended one of its ceremonies, but which habitually cures pulmonary maladies; Rattlesnake Medicine which is a split-off from Uhuhukwe; Shuma'kwe which treats for twisting of the body or convulsions; Ne'wekwe, the clowning society which also cures, and Shi'wanakwe, a Rain chieftaincy or society as well as a curing society, accounted the oldest of the curing societies and Zuni-born. There is also the Coyote or Hunters' society. This society has "medicine" for trading with Navaho or for acquiring goods. A Hunter would not be afraid to kill a Navaho.[42] Among all Pueblos there is a close conceptual relationship between killing men and killing prey animals, between hunting and warring organizations.

The curing societies of Zuni and several societies of Cochiti, Sia, and Jemez are subdivided into what properly enough has been called orders, curing or medicine order, fire order, stick-swallowing or jugglery order; and passing from one order into another requires additional initiation ritual. The medicine order is the superior order; but even in it only certain individuals, more particularly the chief, conduct cures.† Analogously, in the undifferentiated Hopi societies the chiefs only are doctors. The society chief, possibly the medicine chief, will be called upon to cure whatever disease is associated with the society. Zuni and Keresan societies also specialize more or less in diseases, and encroachment is dangerous since only the initiated are immune. Tsatiselu of Zuni, a Ne'wekwe, not an Ant society, doctor, used to remove ants with his own medicine, so he had sensations of ants under his skin, and on it appeared antlike rings.

Communal cures are conducted by societies (Keres, Isleta, Zuni) at which anyone present is treated gratis, sucked, brushed, or given a drink of medicine water. At Zuni, probably elsewhere, there is no charge for treatment given at any regular assemblage of a society.[43]

---

* Note that the Winds of the Directions were appealed to through the Animals of the Directions to be present and heal (Stevenson 2:528). At Taos a wind spirit causes smallpox.

† At Zuni initiations, however, as described by Stevenson, every member of the curing order, including women, appears to suck.

An invalid may wish to be treated privately by a single doctor or, if the sickness is grave, by the whole order. Father or kinsman will carry a handful of prayer-meal to the doctor or society chief.[44] At Zuni a bit of the pay for the doctor, a thread from the blanket or shawl, is placed with the prayer-meal in a cornhusk. This is "clothing" for the Animals or "beast gods," patrons of the societies. The patient is not initiated, but at the winter solstice he goes to the house of his doctor's society, his head is washed, and he becomes the society's "child." Each year at the winter solstice his doctor, his "father," will make him a prayer-stick to plant.[45] The single doctor smokes, sings, mixes his medicines in a bowl, massages with ashes, locates the seat of pain with his crystal, sends his animal helper into the body by exhalation, and sucks out the witch-sent object.[46] When the one to be "saved" is very ill or wishes to become a member of the society,* the society will come in a body to his house, for four nights (Zuni, from midnight to dawn), holding their most elaborate ritual, initiatory ritual, on the conclusive night, or on the fourth night the patient may be taken to the room of the society for the treatment or initiation that all have been four days preparing for. At this time the doctors impersonate the bears from whom they get their power, "they become bears," chewing the bear root which gives them second sight against witches, and pawing and clawing the patient like a wild animal. At this time too as well as at initiation as part of a periodic ceremony appears the masked impersonation or kachina of any society possessed of kachina, as the Big Firebrand, Ne'wekwe, and Shuma'kwe societies of Zuni or the Giant society of Cochiti.

At kachina initiation among Keres a shaman impersonates the whipper kachina.[47] Leading in the kachina or "making the road" for them, at a dance, and supplying choirs or altars are also functions of the medicine societies. In the East the societies go into retreat for rain during the late spring or summer or early

---

* At Zuni it is understood that if the whole society is summoned the patient will be given to the society. "It is always a last resort, since the expense of initiation is very great" (Bunzel 4:791). The expense of joining another order within the society is also considerable. Hopi initiation is costly (Kennard).

autumn (Keres, Jemez). During their rain retreats it is supposed that they visit the Mother at Shipap and ask her to send the kachina to dance. "They bring the kachina back with them," so that a kachina dance follows the conclusion of the retreat. In the West, kachina dances follow upon the retreat of the Zuni rain society of the North or upon the short winter assemblages of the Hopi societies, but without the Keresan interpretation.

Keres also hold a rain ceremony one night during the winter solstice ceremony. The medicine societies of Zuni hold a like synchronous ceremony, and the Big Firebrand society performs a new fire ritual. At the winter solstice ceremony Keresan societies make offerings to the Sun, among them rabbit sticks and miniature clothes (Acoma); the burden of the solstice ceremonies which are initiated by the Town chief is carried by medicine societies.[48] Infant-naming ritual and funerary ritual, presenting the child to the Sun, and speeding the deceased on his journey— functions confined to kinsfolk or marriage connections in the West—are performed in the East, as we have noted, by medicine societies.

The organization of medicine societies is imitated by the witches they thwart or, at times, fight in searching for a stolen heart.[49] Witches are believed to have a supernatural patron,* a chief, and other officers; they hold assemblages, in cave or kiva; they initiate, sometimes bringing the dead to life; like curers they transform into animals or birds by putting on animal or bird skins; and they use prayer-feathers, the feathers of owl and crow because, they say at Zuni, those birds drive away other birds and so keep away the rain.[50] Thus witches control weather, keeping the rain off or causing wind.† Most witch practices are

---

* The Mother was afraid people would forget her in the upper world, so Witch chief came up with the people. Through him people get sick and then remember the Mother who will cure them (Parsons 52:360–61). So goes Isletan tradition; in Cochiti tradition Witch chief slips by the Mother in order to be born into this world (Dumarest, 161, 163).

† A Cochiti man once confessed to the War captain that he had been burying human bones in the corners of the town to keep the rain from falling beyond in the fields (Goldfrank 3:98). The wind may be raised by pulling up a Jamestown weed by the roots (Laguna); until the deep hole is filled, the winds will blow. A

curing society practices perverted, and that may be why black magic is so often attributed to the Clown societies who habitually do things backward or why, vice versa, witches or witch images are described as looking like these society people, like Ne'wekwe or Koshare.* But all society people are particularly open to the charge of witchcraft.

The organization of the Kachina cult and of its masked dances is curiously varied and cross-classificatory. At Zuni the Kachina society is organized somewhat like a curing society, with official and lay membership, the chief (Komosona) and his "speaker" (Kopekwin) being, respectively, from the Antelope (Deer) and Badger clans,† each having a guard or warrior or dance leader theoretically from his own clan (Stevenson) and from the War society; and the lay membership consisting of all the adult males with a few females—four in 1902,[51] today but three. These women members, in dances impersonating kachina maidens, were initiated into the Kachina society because they were subject to bad dreams or hallucinations which are sent by the kachina. This aspect of the Zuni Kachina society, having patrons who both cause and cure disease, links it with the curing society. However, the male membership of the Zuni Kachina society is constituted quite otherwise, by kiva, that is, a person dances kachina with his kiva mates, ordinarily, but not necessarily.‡ This is so also among Hopi, although here kiva dance mates are those who live in the neighborhood of the kiva and use it informally as a secular clubhouse. The Zuni boy joins automatical-

person with a grievance, perhaps a jealous grievance, against a kachina rain dancer might uproot the plant, unless he preferred to sprinkle red pigment as an offering to Wind.

* Dumarest, 164, Pl. VII, Fig. 1; Parsons 42:46; Parsons 6:270. There are two Zuni versions of the story of the bears who in revenge eat down a man's standing corn. In one version the bears are witches, in the other the bears are medicine men, "life-giving society priests" (Parsons 6:307–13; Bunzel 6:235–48).

† Kachina chief and speaker will train a successor within their lineage, the selection having to be ratified by the high Rain chiefs (Bunzel 5:875).

‡ So the dance group may be composed of men from various kivas, although it is imputed to one kiva, that of its dance director.

ly the kiva of his ceremonial father: husband or kinsman of the woman who picked him up at birth; the Hopi boy may join the various societies of his ceremonial father, the man to whom he has been given by his parents or by his mother, but kiva membership, strictly speaking, goes by clan.

The Hopi Kachina society is, like every Hopi society, in charge of a maternal family,* with a wider membership, into which at the society's ceremony of Powamu there is an initiation. There are kachina dance series, and an open season, so to speak, for exchanging dances with other towns: a group from Second Mesa, let us say, will give a dance on First Mesa one year which will be reciprocated the year following by a First Mesa group. But particular dances in the annual series or as intertown amenities are arranged for by individuals, often as a form of vow in sickness. For example, Hokya Anakchina danced in Hano on April 2, 1921, was proposed by Tsulu of Hano because he had been having sore eyes, notes Crow-Wing, and the Anakchina danced on April 9 in Walpi was proposed by Posumi of Hano for his sick daughter. Tsulu or Posumi would lead the kachina in together with the man chosen to head the dance, in both these cases Walpi men, and would supply food to the dancers. Permanent society proxies for the Kachina society chief called Kachina Fathers also lead dance files. Between Kachina Fathers who conduct ceremony and Kachina impersonators who merely dance there is a marked distinction (Oraibi). As noted, the kachina sponsors of children are also their sponsors in the Men's or Women's societies or in other societies, a feature traceable at Acoma and Isleta in kachina dramatization or dance.

There are kachina dance series at Zuni, three series: the winter series for three months after the winter solstice, the summer

* Or families; for, besides the Parrot-Kachina lineage, a lineage of the Badger clan is prominent at Walpi and at Oraibi. The Oraibi Badgers are in charge of the kachina for two months (Titiev 3). They conduct the initiation into the Powamu society (Powamuwïmkya) at which there is no whipping ritual and which supplies the Kachina Fathers. Children who go into this group are not whipped in the whipping ritual of Powamu ceremony conducted by the Parrot-Kachina-Crow chief of the Kachina society (Kachinawïmkya) (Kennard and Titiev).

series for three months after the summer solstice, and the series for five days after Shalako. Each kiva is expected to present a group dance in each of these series; also to take part in the winter dances of the other kivas either by presenting a group dance of its own or by sending representatives to dance with another group.[52] The entire kiva membership does not have to turn out in all the dance series, for a man need not dance kachina more than once a year. No sanction attaches to not dancing. A man merely takes for granted that he is to dance because he belongs to the Kachina society. The Kachina society chief leads in or "shepherds" the dancers in the first dance of the summer series; in other dances a Kachina society warrior, a Ne'wekwe, or a curing society member will serve as "their father," making the road or sprinkling meal to the Sun, "praying in his heart" throughout the dance. "When it rains hard, he has tried hard." (Pl. X.)

The most important and the most dramatic kachina associated with Zuni kiva groups are the Shalako. The two annual impersonators in each kiva have a complicated dramatization to perform and long prayers to memorize. They are taught by managers in each kiva. The two annual Salimobia impersonators in each kiva also have a manager. Other dramatic kachina, kachina chiefs, are in charge of a cult group who may nor may not be in charge of the mask, who themselves impersonate or teach prayers and ritual to annual impersonators, and who fill their own vacancies, usually with consideration of clan or lineage affiliations.[53] One plan is to have a clansman and a child of the clan alternate as impersonator. The function of arraying an impersonator may belong in a different clan (Zuni, Hopi).

For some of their chiefly and dramatic impersonations* Hopi also have cult groups, although, here as ever among Hopi, clan or lineage considerations are more to the fore. Clanship plays as much of a part in kachina organization at Acoma as farther west; there is some dramatization, but no out-and-out cult groups; inferably the same men always play the more dramatic roles,

---

* Ahul, Ahulani, Eototo, Masauwü (Stephen 4: Appen. 4).

like the Gumeyoish scouts in the Kachina Attack or the roles of Kimash°, the Kachina chief, or of the kachina with Shuracha. Kachina cult groups are organized at Santo Domingo but probably not elsewhere in the East, where there is comparatively little dramatization, and the chiefly kachina roles are much less significant. Heruta, Kachina grandfather, is a dramatic personage, carrying on a lively pantomime,[54] but other kachina chiefs merely dance or caper on the sidelines or in front of the dance line, playing distinctive parts but, excepting the whipper or policing kachina, parts not very pronounced.

At Cochiti there is, as among Hopi, a restricted kachina society which is organized, however, not by maternal family or with clan affiliations but like any other Keresan society. This society has charge of the masks and appoints kachina dancers from the males who have been initiated to dance kachina; formerly all males were thus initiated. Formerly, at Sia and Laguna, the Quirana chief appointed the kachina dancers. Then the medicine societies took control at Sia (as at Santa Ana), and the Zuni system of Deer (Antelope) clan and Badger clan control prevailed at Laguna, where there are three dance societies. At San Felipe there are also three kachina dance societies, of which only two are kiva groups. A few women are qualified to serve these groups but not to dance. Santa Ana women do dance kachina, impersonating female kachina.[55]

At Jemez there are two kachina dance groups into one of which every youth is initiated. These dance groups are associated with the two kivas. Kachina dances may be performed also by the two Men's societies,* in fact, by any of the societies, all of whom are possessed of masks. (On First Mesa, society memberships have also functioned as dance groups.)† The Town chief appoints a "kachina father" to be in charge of the initiatory whipping ritual and of the corn-ear "mother," but there is no

---

* Until a youth is initiated into one of the Men's societies, he may not dance kachina. The same rule holds among Hopi: Wüwüchim initiation is a prerequisite to dancing kachina.

† For example, in July, 1893, the Singers presented the Navaho kachina, and the Wüwüchimtü sent out a clown group (Stephen 4: 500, 504).

kachina society. As among Keres, kachina dances may be performed at Eastertide and on the day following the retreats or ceremonies of societies.

Nor is there among Tewa any kachina society. The masks are in the keeping of the Town chiefs, who decide (Santa Clara) "when they want them," i.e., the chiefs decide on kachina dances, which are infrequent. At San Juan there is only one mask dance a year. At Isleta and Taos there is no mask dancing, although there is a kachina cult which at Isleta is served through Corn groups and moiety organization and for the Spruce dance by a permanent dance chief, Chakabede. The Turtle dance at Taos, as at San Juan, is a maskless kachina dance, like the Spruce dance at Isleta or the Hopi dance at Jemez. The Taos Turtle dance is presented by the Water people's kiva.

The Kachina cult is associated conceptually and economically with a great deal of Pueblo activity, at least in the West. There is a rabbit hunt with the kachina (Zuni), and there are kachina races (Hopi, Jemez). Kachina dance groups become working-parties, planting or harvesting or house-building for the people who are to entertain them (Zuni, Hopi). When a Hopi has several fleeces, he arranges with kiva chiefs for a spinning party at which as many as fifty men will spin and sing kachina songs, the elders and good singers correcting errors of words or tune. The host will have killed a sheep, and his wife and his kinswomen carry a dinner of mutton stew and breads to the kiva. After the little feast work and songs go on until near sunset.[56]

As already suggested, kiva organization also varies, with membership based on clan or maternal descent among Hopi (other principles of loan and neighborhood operating also in use of kivas) and on paternal descent or marital connection among Keres and Tewa, and at Jemez. At Zuni a man in the household of his father's sister is generally chosen to be the boy's initiator into the Kachina society, which means into one of the six kivas,* so that the Zuni system of kiva membership is thus loosely con-

* Corn people's kiva excepted, for this kiva is associated, Hopi way, with the Corn clan which again, Hopi way, is in charge of a ceremony (Ky'anakwe) and a chiefly mask (Kiaklo).

nected with the Eastern system; with the Hopi clan kiva system
it has no connection at all. At Taos even the Zuni form of connection between kiva and family is lacking; every boy is given
by his father to one of the six kiva societies, irrespective of kinship ties. In practice, kiva groups dance kachina, but, except at
Zuni, Acoma, and perhaps Santo Domingo, the connection between kachina cult and kiva is more or less fortuitous.

The Zuni kiva chief is the kachina dance chief. He has one or
two assistants, and there are two kiva managers who have charge
of paraphernalia, and special kachina managers. It is not known
how any of these men are selected. Inferably the Kachina society chief and speaker have a say, and function in arranging the
comprehensive kachina calendar, but in details the kiva dance
chief and the others decide on dances and set certain dates, call
rehearsals, compose and teach the songs, superintend the preparation of the masks which are kept at home, paint the masks or
consecrate or animate new masks, and make and plant the
kachina prayer-sticks. The dance chief stands as song leader in
the center of the dance line.[57]

Of the Chief kiva of Acoma the Town chief, Antelope man,
father of the kachina, is head. Each of the other five kivas has
four officers, appointed for life, by the Town chief. They feed
and paint the masks which medicine men animate; and they
function in organizing the kachina celebrations of which the
Town chief is the head[58] and in ratifying his secular appointments which are apportioned among the kivas. The kachina
Shuracha bonfire ceremony is in charge of Corn clan chief.

At Santo Domingo the kivas are in charge of cult societies,
although there are the makings of a kiva kachina society.
Turquoise and Squash kivas have each a chief who organizes kachina dances, is in charge of rehearsals, is custodian of
the masks and paints them. He has as helpers self-dedicated
persons or boys and girls dedicated by father or father's father.
Elements of initiation are observed, for meal in a cornhusk is
carried to the kiva chief, and the new helper is given paraphernalia: rabbit sticks, arrows, rattles, *and a new name*. A
dance follows, and the family of the novice feeds the dancers.

The female helpers fetch water, clean, or carry out ashes. There are from three to eight helpers in each kiva group, male or female. Each kiva has a fire chief, Poker boy, with one or two helpers, whose functions are to attend to the fire and to announce dances. The offices of kiva chief and of fire chief are lifelong and are filled by the person who was initiated after the deceased chief.

Between double kiva and double clown society systems there is a connection (Cochiti, Jemez). The Turquoise kiva is associated with the Summer clown society and the Squash kiva with the Winter clown society.* Among Tewa this association does not occur or has become confused. Tewa kivas are associated with the patrilineal moiety system, one kiva belonging to Winter People, the other to Summer People, although in nonmoiety dances both kivas may be used indifferently. Of the six Zuni kivas, three are elder brothers to the other younger brother kivas. Each pair co-operates in dances, the affiliated kiva supplying the women impersonations to the group giving the dance.

Between kivas and secular offices a relationship may be made. At Cochiti the Governor and his assistant must belong to different kivas; so must the War captain and his assistant, and the Fiscal and his; and so must Governor and War captain.[59] A like rule applies at San Felipe to the two War captains and their aides,[60] and at Acoma all the secular officers are equably distributed among the five dance kivas. Again, at Isleta there is association between kiva and moiety, two kivas belonging to the Black Eyes, two to the Gophers or Red Eyes. At Taos the Town chief functions somewhat indeterminately as head of the north side kivas, and chief of Water People kiva functions as head of the south side kivas.

Dwellings as well as kivas are used ceremonially. Among Hopi of First Mesa the maternal house of the chief of the society is ceremonial headquarters (Winter solstice, War, Flute). In the East the society chief may use the house he is living in, his own

---

* Actually, at Cochiti, the clown societies alternate in functioning at ceremonial planting and harvesting, rabbit-hunting, and kachina road-making, by year, not by half-year or season (Goldfrank 3:45).

or his wife's; but generally the society has a special house.* At Zuni, that meeting-ground of Eastern and Western ceremonial traits, there is a mixed system: the rain societies assemble in the maternal house of the chief, and the curing societies in the house the chief or some member lives in or once lived in.⁶¹ The use of dwelling-houses by ceremonial groups is an important aspect of the somewhat surprising failure of the Pueblos, ceremonialists and stylists as they are, to develop to any extent† the temple idea, or, having once developed it, if they did, say on Mesa Verde,⁶² to preserve it. Chief kiva in Hopi towns is more council-house than temple. In Acoma, Chief kiva does in a way suggest a temple, as does the upper chamber near He'iwa kiva used by the high Rain chiefs of Zuni, and He'iwa itself.‡

Although the general Pueblo attitude is that the chief of the ceremony being performed is paramount or general chief for the time being, in every town there is something of a hierarchy, the society chiefs forming a council that is referred to as the "fathers" (Jemez, San Ildefonso) or "grandfathers" (Taos) or "mothers" (Keres) or "chiefs" (Hopi) or at Zuni, the Ashiwanni, meaning not all the Ashiwanni but only the chiefs of the rain societies identified with the six cardinal directions.§ These nine men at Zuni appear as a veritable hierarchic council, with all the affairs of the town, sacred and secular, ultimately in their con-

---

* San Felipe and Santo Domingo societies (including Town chief) have distinct ceremonial houses (White 3:13; White 4:64). At Acoma the kivas are used by the societies and Town chief (White 2:44, 107). The Acoma Fire society has a ceremonial house, and so together have the Town chief and high Rain chiefs of Zuni. The Town chief and the two curing societies of Isleta have ceremonial houses.

† In so far as masks or images are kept in kivas they are temples or shrines. The presence of a *sipapu* or sunken altar (Acoma) contributes to sanctity, also wall or beam paintings or even those handprints in the plaster which express a desire to grasp at the clouds and bring rain (Stephen 4:198).

‡ Fetishes are not kept here, as far as I know, but ritual is performed.

§ These may be referred to at Zuni as the *tekohanakwe* or daylight people. *Tekohana* means not only day or sunlight but, figuratively, good fortune, welfare, life. "Night people" the other rain societies are called because, it is variously said, they have no Pekwin (Crier chief or Sun chief), or because they are less public, "people do not know what they are doing."

trol. They make all appointments to office or to kachina impersonation, either directly or by appointing the head of a group who in turn appoints the members. They determine the variable parts of the year's calendar, and upon them would fall the responsibility of making any major calendrical change. There are stated ceremonial occasions for the Ashiwanni to meet, but they meet also as affairs demand. Their decisions and behavior are under constant popular discussion, and, if they disagree, controversy rends the town. The homologous council among Hopi appears to meet far less frequently and to be possessed of less power or control. Through the Ashiwanni, Zuni church and state are centralized, and the whole ceremonial system is closely integrated. The Hopi system is looser. And yet Hopi chiefs seem nearer the people to whom they will preach at meetings called by the War chief (First Mesa). The chiefs "talk" each in turn to the people, telling them how to live, repeating in Hopi stereotype: "You must watch over your girls and over your boys. Let us live well and have good rains and good crops, and so live to be old." Account of a meeting occasioned by the misconduct of an Oraibi married into Hano is more particularized. This man had broken the "rules," both White and Pueblo, talking in Third Mesa style against sending the children to school as well as against "old Tewa ways," asserting that the chiefs were "driving the people." After being reprimanded by the Agent, he betook himself and his family off the mesa. As his wife was the sister of the Tewa War chief, the people did not want her to leave the mesa. So Horn society chief went after the man; "others were afraid to go after him, he was always fighting." He told Horn chief that the Tewa people had driven him away. So Horn chief told all the Tewa men to go to Walpi to the house of the Town chief's wife. "Down we all came there," writes Crow-Wing. "They talked to us about the ways of the Hopi, and how the people came to this place. Every chief talked; they said we must not break government law, and we must also mind our own rules," such as asking permission to remove from the mesa. (Dance groups have to ask permission of the council to dance abroad.)[63] The order in which the chiefs preached repetitiously* was: Town chief who is Flute society chief, Bear clan chief, Crier chief who is Snake clan chief, Coyote clan chief who is the kachina Eototo chief, Horn society chief, Agave society chief, Singers' society chief, Wüwüchim society chief, Winter solstice chief, Powamu society chief, Sunwatcher, and War chief.†

The "old men" of Tewa and of Jemez approximate in power the Ashiwanni of Zuni, with a similar control over the calendar and over certain appointments to office, and to their meetings likewise are brought all the affairs of the town. We know little about the Keresan council,‡ perhaps there is little to know except that the Town chief consults with the chiefs of the societies. At Laguna and Cochiti, at Isleta and Taos, the council has been secularized or partly secularized through the inclusion of *principales*, i.e., former Governors and other secular officers§ or even, at Isleta, of young men with American education, appointed by the Governor. Formerly the Taos council consisted of only the chiefs of the kiva societies and was probably less conspicuous. Today it is a self-assertive group, conducting affairs far more publicly than does the council in any other town.

* Compare Papago, where Dr. Underhill shows very clearly that oratorical repetition, whether in political assemblage or in the household at break of day, is conditioning for complete agreement, action being ineffective unless the group acts as a whole with complete conviction.

† Parsons 40:26, n. 38; Antelope society chief and Snake society chief were omitted inadvertently.

In 1893 the order of precedence was slightly different: Town chief (Flute chief) or chiefs, Bear clan chief, Wüwüchim society chief, Singers chief, Horn society chief, Agave society chief, Eototo chief, Winter solstice chief or chiefs, Powamu society chief, Antelope society chief, Snake society chief, Speech (Crier) chief, War chief who travels in the rear in peacetime and is the last to speak (Stephen 4:956).

‡ Neither Stevenson nor Dumarest give data: Bandelier refers in general terms to the "Mothers," although in *The Delight Makers* he draws vivid pictures of the influence of the council in the town life. That he did not draw from Cushing's reports of the Ashiwanni of Zuni and of the Oraibi feud of which Cushing got a lively impression I would not be sure.

§ *Principales* is a loosely applied Spanish term among Spanish Indians. In Pueblo circles it generally refers to men who have held secular offices (Spanish), but it may be applied to ceremonial chiefs (Parsons 41:56), and in Acoma it refers to ten men (Parsons, White) of the ruling Antelope clan (Parsons, *not* White).

In all the towns, Hopi towns and Laguna excepted, it is the Town chief and the Fathers who appoint the Governor* and his officers, their go-betweens with foreigners (representatives of the Indian Bureau, traders, missionaries, or tourists), and their agents in merely secular matters of co-operation or dispute. By royal edict of 1621 the Spanish system of town government was decreed or recognized for the Pueblos, just as it prevailed in other parts of Spanish America. Town officers were to be elected annually at the New Year independently of Spanish officials or priests; they were to receive canes of office. These provisions went into effect in New Mexico, all except the provision for election which was too alien to existing hierarchic control to be acceptable.† And so the "government" appointments are made by the chiefs of the curing societies including the Town chief or at Zuni by the high Rain chiefs in consultation with the curing-society chiefs. At Acoma the Town chief appoints, and the kiva chiefs and chiefs of the societies meet as a council to ratify.[64] In Taos the Council votes on two or three appointees for Governor and War captains made by Big Earring Man, Water Man, War chief, and perhaps by Cacique. In Isleta a general assemblage (Sp., *junta*) votes on two or three appointees made by the Town chief for Governor and head War captain‡ who appoints assistant War captains by moiety. As noted, in Isleta and else-

* Zuni, Keres, Tapup, Dapop; Isleta and Sandía, Tabude, Dabuide; Taos, Ta'abuna; Tewa, To'yo', chief.

† Possibly the earlier system of the friars was merely being favored as more compatible with Indian attitude. Before 1621 the friars had given the Indians to understand that their authority was superior to that of the Spanish Governor (Scholes 1 : 154). The Pueblo priest-chiefs were modeling on the Catholic priests.

‡ Then the elected Governor asks the Town chief to appoint the Lieutenant-Governor; but the Town chief will say, "No, you have to choose him yourself." The Governor chooses but tells the meeting if they do not like this choice to choose for themselves. But the meeting will accept the appointment. Now the appointee will say to the Town chief that he does not want to be Lieutenant-Governor; but the Town chief says he must be. This little farce in self-government is due to the circumstance, I am guessing, that the Lieutenant-Governor at Isleta, as at Taos, is a penal officer. Punishing a fellow townsman is a most unwelcome task.

Nominees are not objected to in a general meeting because the objector runs the risk of being asked to take the office himself (Acoma, probably elsewhere).

where, the secular offices are carefully distributed by ceremonial groups.

The provision for annual change of officers held everywhere except at Zuni, and here it probably held as long as the Franciscans remained in town and supplied calendrical information, but the Mission was discontinued in 1821, and now for some time Governor and lieutenants, *tenientes*, have been replaced* only when something happened that made people want a different set of officers, as, for example, in 1891, when the Governor was accused of being a horse thief† or when one of the high Rain chiefs was threatened with jail, or the War chief was actually jailed, for not sending a child to school. For such "an awful thing" as imprisonment of Shiwanni or War chief the go-between officers were held responsible.[65]

The Town chief instals the officers, at Zuni moving the cane before the mouth of the incoming officer to breathe from.[66] Prayer-meal is sprinkled on the canes, or they are blessed in the church with holy water. At Acoma the medicine men (Fire and Flint) breathe on them, handing them on.[67] The canes have power; without them the officers would not be acknowledged, just as without his fetish bundle a chief were not a chief.

The Governor hears and settles disputes over land or water rights or trespass, over livestock or other property, and he may punish by fining or confiscating, by whipping, and in the East by jailing, formerly using the stocks.‡ The lawsuit over some peach trees which Cushing describes as occurring when he was Lieutenant-Governor ("Mexican chief")§ of Zuni is a matchless

* Very recently through pressure by the Indian Office in enforcing "self-government" annual "elections" have been held.

† Stevenson 2; 290. Jesús, the Yaqui (see p. 635, n.†), was the accuser. The court or *junta* of about 100 men met in Big plaza. Elder Brother Bow priest (the War chief) supported Jesús. There was much argument, but after decision was rendered by the high Rain chiefs, the deposed Governor and his officers left the plaza, without a word.

‡ Keresan War chiefs or captains put an offender into stocks, so to speak, by sprinkling around him a circle of meal that he had to stand or sit in, until exhausted (Dumarest, 201; White 4:23). At Oraibi the scalp-taker had to sit four days within the circle (Titiev 3).

§ The Lieutenant-Governor of Taos is also called Mexican chief.

picture of a courtroom. Cushing was living in the Governor's house, and the meeting was held there, just as the Taos Council today meets in the Governor's house. "How be ye these many days?" everybody says on entering. "Happy; gather and sit!" Everybody rolls his preliminary cornhusk cigarette, as in the smoke-talk of a ceremony. Follow witty jokes, coarse jokes, none-too-gentle pranks, and any quantity of sarcasm. The Lieutenant-Governor, who is sergeant-at-arms, thumps for order with his cane of office. The formal opening words of the Governor and his final decision are listened to in silence and respect, but in between there are "hours of vituperant recrimination and violent personal abuse, which scorns not to rake up from the traditional tribal annals every scandal, calumny, and other vicious bit of backbite" of at least two generations past,* and all this through the mouths of from five to fifteen persons speaking at the same time! Witnesses are summoned from the Cactus society the deceased orchard owner belonged to, since, at a night meeting, in accordance with custom, he gave them his verbal testament.[68]

Zuni public meetings are just as turbulent today if I may infer from one I attended, called to discuss whether taking pictures was to be allowed at Shalako. War chief Ts'awele and the minority "Catholic group" including visitors from Isleta and the Catholic Agent were against it. Everybody spoke at once. The chief exhibit was a large blank piece of drawing paper said to have been given somebody by Mr. Hodge, who was then excavating at Hawikuh. It was damning evidence and quite as stirring to everybody as that Hopi's report of seeing altar pictures in notebooks, which Stephen characterized as "a damn lie" but which kept him out of the Flute society assemblage.†

The Governor makes admonitory or hortatory speeches inside the church or at the portal; he has his orders for work called out

---

* Among Tiwa, as at Zuni, inheritance of property is the prime source of family feud. Are Tiwa and other Easterners more quarrelsome over property than less Hispanicized or Americanized Westerners?

† Stephen 4:12. All the Zuni hierarchy excepting Ts'awele had agreed to the cinema, also at long last the Agent; nevertheless, Zuni and Isletan youths posted themselves before the camera and ruined most of Mr. Cattell's film.

from court or housetop, or he himself may call them out. The officers are in charge of co-operative work like irrigation or herding horses or sheep-dipping or cleaning up town. Fiscales* look after the church and after collections for the priest, in some towns taking a hand in burials and at Sia conducting a bridal couple to the church. Formerly Fiscales were responsible for church attendance and were empowered to whip. Their stick of office is a cross, if not a whip. At the celebration of the patron-saint's day all the officers figure prominently. There is no pay for the officers, and no emolument except exemption from other forms of communal service, like working on the ditches or dancing kachina.[69] No non-Catholic ritual functions attach to the officers, War captains excepted.† War captains may be in charge of ritual hunts. They make important prayer-stick offerings (Acoma, Laguna). They make (Laguna) or made (Acoma) solar observations. The War captains of Cochiti instal the Town chief; in San Felipe and Santo Domingo they appoint him. Quite generally War captains appoint to temporary offices. War captains guard not only against intrusive Whites but during society assemblages against witches. War captains or chiefs handle witchcraft situation of all kinds, also reprisal for naturalistic murder which is very rare.‡ In general, War chiefs or captains safeguard the customs.

In the complex ceremonies of the West there are many minor offices to be filled. These are filled sometimes by a "child of the clan," including the chief's son by blood, sometimes by invitation, that is, the chief or director "gathers up," in Indian English, the dancers, or others and sometimes by order of chief or council. Such appointments are usually for the year only or for a single ceremony, but in some cases the office must be held for a

* The Spanish form is kept because the English term "fiscal" is not an equivalent for this church term, widespread among Spanish Indians.

† At Zuni no officers are called *capitanes*, or war captains. The *tenientes* or lieutenants are strictly secular officers.

‡ Few homicides came to the attention of the Spanish Alcaldes, and of these some were committed against foreigners; for example the case of Juan Miguel Martin and José Guadalupe of Picurís, on trial for murdering a Pawnee in 1808 (Twitchell, II, 529).

stated number of successive performances, usually for four ceremonies, almost as if for a vow.

So much for the dry bones of the ceremonial organization which I would now vivify with a more discursive or pictorial account of the performers.

The "old men," the chiefs, "our fathers and mothers," are not distinguished from the other townspeople by attribution of personal powers, by dress or badge, by their daily occupations, or by behavior in general. At Jemez I lived in the house of the chief of the Fire society, and but for outside information never would I have learned of his office. The kindly old man spent a good deal of time at home, looking after his two-year-old grandson, mending moccasins, chopping wood, feeding his horses, chatting with visitors. He worked in his field; he drove the family out to the hills to gather piñon nuts, or he drove out with a son for a load of wood. I slept in the back room, where hung his box or rather splints for prayer-feathers and the white cotton bag in which he kept his corn-ear fetish, and only once during my visit of two months were these objects removed from the wall. It was not a season of ceremonial activity for his society. I recall my first meeting with gentle old Waihu'siwa of Zuni, chief of the Rain society of the East. He was chopping wood before his house, and he dropped the ax to shake hands and say something about his visit with Cushing to Washington. So inconspicuous are these high chiefs of Zuni that a storekeeper who had lived in the town thirty years did not know of their offices. There is an element of design in being inconspicuous to White people, of course, since the whole ceremonial system, in the East at least, is supposed to be hidden from these intruders, and the annual, secular officers are the only proper go-betweens; but even in the less secretive western towns it may take the newcomer some time to know by sight the high command.

By the townspeople themselves the chiefs are far from being unnoticed. Close-mouthed as are the Pueblos toward strangers, among themselves they are prime gossips, and much of their gossip is over those who are their priests, politicians, comedians, and clubmen, turn by turn. In gossipy interest the only rivals are American trade and "Washington." As Mrs. Stevenson says plaintively, in discussing modernization at Zuni, sometimes people prefer to talk about the Agent and the storekeepers rather than about their "theurgists."

Gossip, as well as the more formal satire of clowns or clowning kachina, is largely concerned with the way ceremonial duties are performed, including observance of the taboos that fall upon all engaged in ceremonial. A society woman gives a drink of water to an initiate who should be abstaining, and she is twitted about it in a kachina song (Zuni).[70] In a recent drought at Zuni during the retreat of the Rain chiefs of the West a critic observed, "I think one of those who are now in (retreat) has traded; therefore it does not rain."[71] After announcing the Wüwüchim ceremony in 1921, the Crier chief of Walpi left the mesa to go to a Navaho dance. "That is not the way chiefs do," commented Crow-Wing. "He did not do right; he should have stayed until the ceremony was over; he had to make prayer-sticks with the other chiefs. So everybody is talking about it. The people are very sorry about it. They want to replace him with a good man." There was so much talk that Honi, the man's uncle, whom he had succeeded as Crier chief, had to call a meeting, in fact, three meetings, to discuss the situation, and in the end Honi, old and blind and full of service though he was, had to take back his office, for the rest of his life, because he was "the only good man."[72] One year at Zuni a Koyemshi impersonator was much criticized for leaving town. He was married to Edith, the half-wit Laguna woman, who used to persuade him into trips to Gallup, forty miles away.

Absenteeism on the part of any Town chief would be talked about. In the Isletan tale of the Town chief who flies away on his eagle, there is a vivid expression of the rule or feeling against the Town chief not leaving town. As soon as the Town chief begins to talk about going away, the animals, all of them, begin to sicken. Drought and famine follow on his going; everything is parched by the sun; the people are dying. But once he is recovered and starts for home, it rains daily as he whistles; and he and the clouds approach town together. The springs start and the river runs; the animals begin to revive; and from the grains Town chief gives his people, just like a kachina, the houses fill up with corn. The Town chief does indeed represent, as at Acoma, the Corn god.

Incontinence during ceremonial is an even more scandalous offense than absenteeism. Crow-Wing refers to a former Powamu society chief as not a good chief. "He got into trouble with a woman." This meant that the people would be crippled with rheumatism (Powamu being a ceremony against rheumatism), and "they got very mad about it."[73] Sexual trouble or immoderation is not infrequently alleged as cause for not appointing to office (or even to society membership) or for not retaining in office. Once a Zuni Pekwin "lasted" only half a year because of immoderation. "And so when the crops were burned by the sun, they changed Pekwin."* During those months there must have been no end to the scandal, for the behavior of Pekwin, a veritable high priest, should be beyond reproach.

Quarrel invalidates ceremonial; a peaceable and peaceful spirit is essential to religious concentration. "You chiefs are not good," old Lina of Zuni upbraids her brother, one of the major Rain chiefs, "You scold one another; your hearts are bad; no wonder it does not rain!"[74] Because of a conjugal quarrel the chief of the Oraibi Antelopes was not allowed to preside at the society's ceremony, in 1902.[75] The Antelope society chief of Shipaulovi asked Stephen if the Flute chief of Walpi had brought rain by his ceremony. "No," said Stephen. "No. There is no unison at Walpi," said the old chief, "but at Shipaulovi there is harmony; me, the Clouds desire and love, and bring rain."[76] In Walpi they were interpreting the drought in much the same way. "Some hearts and heads must be bad," lamented the assembled chiefs with a degree of emotion not unusual at Hopi assemblages.†

---

* Bunzel 6:32. This informant refers to the discredited Pekwin merely as being "without understanding."

† Stephen 4:794, 796. The Oraibi factional row was, of course, a cause of drought. "Cloud has no ear for the Oraibi, he hates discord" (Stephen 4:337, n. 1).

Such an outcry elsewhere, in very witch-fearing towns, would indicate suspicion of witchcraft, possibly in someone of high position, for the chiefs are peculiarly open to the charge of witchcraft. "The best men of the pueblo may be witches" (Laguna). Giwire of Laguna was blind, and his sister believed that his blindness had been caused by another shaman, from envy.[77] When Tsatiselu of Zuni was dying of tuberculosis, a member of his own society, the Ne'wekwe, would visit him. The next day Tsatiselu would be worse, and so his family believed that the visitor, an envious man, was bewitching his old colleague. One of the Rain societies of Zuni is said to have supplied "medicine" against peach trees and to have brought on a grasshopper plague. Ts'awele himself, War chief and therefore lord high prosecutor of witches, for many years the most commanding personality in Zuni, was charged while conducting a witch case with keeping owl feathers inside his moccasins and was demoted from his high office.[78]

Since the character of the chiefs should be above suspicion and a man's behavior affects the validity of his ceremony, town gossip, or much of it, is not idle or barren; it is public opinion bringing pressure upon those whose behavior or character is believed to be vital to the efficacy of ritual and so of supreme interest to all the townspeople, to their health and to their crops.

Obviously the selection and education of those who may become chiefs is an important matter. The selection does not go strictly by birth or seniority or other form of automatic succession even when these are prevailing principles of choice. Character, interest, and mentality, particularly memory, are taken into account. To be a good chief, a man must be self-controlled, patient, enduring, and devoted; to have "power," he must know long and difficult prayers or chants. In council and sometimes before the people he must be skilled in the art of oratory. A Hopi chief has to choose his successor within his maternal lineage, theoretically his successor is his younger brother or the eldest son of his eldest sister, but practically the chief may choose a junior nephew if he think the youth is better qualified. He will take the nephew with him when he goes to the fields or off wood-gathering or herding in order to teach him songs and prayers, the whole ritual of his office; instruction may not be given indoors or near town. Crow-Wing is guardian of the ancestral mask of the Tewa Bear clan and more besides, and he was chosen in preference to his elder brothers by his uncle, who thought he had a better memory for the songs and prayers. When the dying uncle named Crow-Wing and somebody objected that Crow-Wing was young and uninformed, the old man said, "I have taught him everything; he has got it all in his head, right now." Simo, Town chief and Flute society chief of Walpi, died suddenly while working in his field one October day in 1892, without having selected his successor. Simo had several nephews, and there was much troubled talk about the succession. One nephew was married into Mishongnovi; another was quite young; and Tü'ínoa, who was the proper successor since he was the eldest son of Simo's eldest sister, was very reluctant to accept office. A Snake clansman was suggested as Town chief, but, as he belonged to the Agave society, he was not acceptable. Finally Tü'ínoa was prevailed upon to accept both offices. Tü'ínoa was a mild young man, and Stephen opines that the choice was wise; not being forceful, Tü'ínoa was for that very reason in sympathy with the people—"a reforming chief would be an evil."[79] Tü'ínoa is still Town chief.

The Town chief is prescriptively a man of peace. At Zuni and Isleta and among Keres the Town chief (and at Zuni any Rain chief) is not free to hunt or fight. Fighting and hunting and derivatively herding* are conceptually precluded because Town chief or rain chief has to attract peace-loving Spirits. In Isletan tale a young Town chief is whipped to death by an invisible being because he used an ax and went rabbit-hunting.[80] The rule he

---

* Formerly the Oraibi Town chief was not allowed to own sheep; the men killed sheep for him and made clothes for his wife (Forde 1:376, quoting Freire-Marreco). During the last half-century the Town chiefs of Third Mesa and Second Mesa have not only become owners of flocks and herds but they have been full of fight. For a picture of one of these notorious chiefs, Lololoma of Oraibi, coming in from his field, hoe in hand, see Voth 4: Pl. IV. Lololoma was once imprisoned in a kiva where he believed he would have been left by the hostile faction to starve to death had he not been rescued by the Agent.

had been given was "not to chop wood, nor kill anything, not even an insect, nor hurt anybody's feelings." The people of Sia were critical of their young Town chief, Stevenson noted, because he would go ahunting. No Zuni Rain chief may belong to the Hunters' society or to the Cactus society, and the fact that the high Rain chiefs, particularly Pekwin, get a large share of the trophies of ceremonial hunts is probably due in part to the idea that they are not to go hunting on their own account. "Give your largest deer to the Town chief!" says the tale hero Poshaiyanne to the hunters of Sia. In the contemporaneous words of a San Felipe man, "We must hunt for the Cacique. He works hard for everybody, for White people, too. The Mexicans tell us we lose time hunting for the Cacique; but it is *very important* to hunt for him,"[81] because, Miguel might have added, he needs rabbit meat for his fetishes.*

One day Stephen was in the Corner kiva of Hano when a young Tewa brought in a chaparral cock. The feathers were divided among the kiva inmates; they were highly prized for winter solstice prayer-feathers, since, tied to a horse's tail, they rendered him, like the cock, tireless and swift; but the body was to be eaten by one of the Tewa chiefs, to render him also tireless and swift.[82] Similarly, in the early days of war or raid, booty was distributed to the chiefs. When Zuni raided a Navaho camp and the sheep and goats were driven home, after each member of the war party was given three animals, they would give animals "to the houses where sacred possessions are kept," including the houses of the war fetishes, Big Shell and Navaho fetish. Then they gave some of the loot to the two Scalp chiefs, and the men who were to be initiated into the War society, the two Scalpers, would get the most.[83]

Since contact with the foreigner tends to be productive of war or quarrel,† the Town chief and his peace associates have been

---

* At Sia he also uses it to entertain kachina impersonators (White 5).

† Even home contacts may be upsetting. "That our hearts may be always good and gentle, that our prayers be answered of the beloved, we may not too often speak to the foolish among our children," said the Town chief of Hawikuh (Cushing 6: 122–23). War chiefs and Governor, the mouthpieces, must bear the brunt of dissension. At Laguna shamans might not become War chiefs

precluded from being representatives of either Spanish or American government, at least this is a factor in the rule against having them hold office as Governor or indeed come into any direct relationship with foreign authority (Zuni). No Rain chief of Zuni may serve on the Governor's staff. For many years on First Mesa, Hani, chief of Singers' society and a noted warrior, and not Tü'ïnoa, the Town chief, was the "American chief." "Our Town chief *could* not be American chief!"* Nor could a Keresan Town chief; American matters or intruders are a concern of the secular officers or of those fitly called chiefs of the outside,† i.e., War chiefs or captains. I doubt if the Winter and Summer chiefs of Tewa or the Big Earring Man (Town chief), Water Man, or Cacique of Taos would serve as Governor.

In several towns people work for the Town chief and in Acoma for the War chiefs.[84] At Zuni the field work of Pekwin as well as of the Town chief was done for them, and the embryonic temple ceremonially associated with the Town chieftaincy or the major Rain chiefs—the second-story house in the northwest corner of the central court—was kept in repair. Wood was brought in for the Town chief of Sia, and his fields worked for him. The Town chief of Acoma once had his fields harvested for him, but not planted. Planting, as well as harvesting, is done by the townspeople for the Town chiefs of Cochiti, San Felipe, Santo Domingo,[85] and Jemez, and seed corn would be distributed by the Town chief in time of stress (Cochiti, Zuni).[86] The people of Isleta worked for their Town chief, the men bringing in wood and

---

(Parsons 20:122), and in general there is division of functions between warriors and medicine men, but I think Aitken and Benavides before her have exaggerated this division as "seeds of disruption." Writes Benavides in 1630: All in their gentilism (before conversion) were "divided into two factions, warriors and sorcerers" (medicine men) "wherefore there were continuous civil wars, so great that they killed each other and laid waste whole pueblos" (Memorial, 30–31). The alignments of the feuds we know about in detail are far more complicated.

* On the other mesas the Town chiefs have often been belligerent, heading the "hostiles" against American encroachment.

† Compare the Spanish term used in New Mexico, *maestre de campo*, field master, adjutant.

planting and harvesting for him, and the women going to his house to grind. Probably such services were once rendered systematically in Hopi towns,[87] and even now at Mishongnovi the first corn planting is done by a general working-party for the Town chief; they "plant for the Father,"[88] and the men of First Mesa plant and harvest the Town chief's fields not every year but when anyone proposes it. The women plaster his house or go there to cook for the men workers, although these do not enjoy a real meal, since they taste but five times of each dish, a form of ceremonial eating which leaves the bulk of the food to the household.

Such a working-party on First Mesa was described by Crow-Wing in his journal for 1921.

On October 18 the War chief gathers the people and tells them he wants to have them work for our Father [Town chief of Hano]. Everyone says he is glad to do some work for our Father and Mother. October 19. Tewa boys go out to get wood for the Town chief, and the women and girls go to the Town chief's house to grind corn. We like our Father, this is the reason everyone wants to help. One woman or girl goes from every house. They want to show themselves; otherwise people would think that they did not like our Father. October 21. The women have to go to the Town chief's house to cook for tomorrow. Some carry water. Everybody is happy. October 22. All the Tewa people have their wagons and burros ready early this morning to go to the field of the Town chief. All the people work. The old men and the chiefs stay and smoke.* Everybody is busy all day. When they get through, the boys have a foot race. [Both smoking and racing are services for rain and crops.] October 23. The Town chief puts down a road [of meal] on the east side of town. The people pray to the Sun and come back on the road, to have a long life.

After the working-party for the Walpi Town chief, he and the Bear clan chief stay up all night to smoke and ask for snow and rain, "to have more crops next year."[89] Thus the chiefs work for the people at large, and the people work gratefully to pay them.

It is not uncommon for ceremonial groups to co-operate in secular work. At Zuni the kiva or kachina dance group to which

---

* Near the corn fetish that has been unwrapped and set out. On it the people cast meal when they return from the fields (Forde 1:376, quoting Freire-Marreco).

a man belongs may be called upon to help farm. A kiva group will cut wheat for the people of the house in which the kiva's Shalako mask "lives,"[90] and the impersonating groups that are going to be entertained in new houses help the houseowners to build or rebuild. Mishongnovi Wüwüchim societies—all the men—are obligated to plant for the impersonator of Soyalmana.[91] A Hopi women's society may help to bring in a person's harvest, just as the Oaqöl women did one year for Crow-Wing, or as the Lakon women will do at Mishongnovi, dancing in the field and after the harvest-home in the court.[92] Nya'hü wanted a field cleared, relates Stephen, so he sent half a beef to a society possessed of power for fertility and sweetness, the Agave society, and the other half to his own society, the Wüwüchim, and next day enough men went to the field to have it cleared by two o'clock. Women relatives cooked the meat which the men ate later in the afternoon in kiva.[93] Similarly at Cochiti any kiva or society membership may be invited to form a working-party.[94] There is a story at San Juan that a townsman, old man Cata who was chief of the Catholic Penitentes, an organization the Indians observe with interest as comparable to their own esoteric groups, that Cata would call upon his Penitentes, Mexicans though they were, to help him get in his harvest.[95]

Kinship terms are regularly applied to the chiefs or used between members of the same ceremonial group. The Town chief at Zuni and among Hopi, Keres, and Tewa is referred to as "Father," or, among the last three tribes, as "Father and Mother." On First Mesa this form of address is meant to include the chieftaincy group or family, the women in the group, mother or sister of the Town chief. "We are all their children," says a Hopi. The Keresan and Tewan reference is merely nominal and may be linked in Tewan thought with the curious recurrent phrase in folk tale of "being man-and-woman" in circumstances of special personal potency; Town chiefs and even the Governor are exhorted to be man-and-woman. At Jemez the society chiefs are referred to as "the Fathers"; at Isleta the general name for the society member or shaman is "Father," Town Fathers or Laguna Fathers, the chiefs being called Elder Sister

or Younger Sister, references possibly to the Underground
Mothers. The chiefs of the Isleta Corn groups are referred to as
Mother and so are or were Laguna shamans, "mothers of everyone, mothers chiefs."* Any chief at Taos will be referred to as
"our father, our mother," and boys initiated together are "Corn
brothers." *Tiupare*, younger-elder (brother or sister), is the regular term of address in Tewa societies. The Zuni family that
keeps a Shalako mask refers to the kiva group associated with
the mask as "our children," and hosts during the ceremony are
referred to by impersonators as "our fathers." Two impersonators, Shulawitsi and Bitsitsi, are assigned year-long "fathers."
Then, too, a feeling of kinship is indicated by the rule against
sexual relations between members of the same curing society or
with the wife of a kiva or society mate (Zuni).[96] Besides, adultery with the wife of a Rain chief is dangerous. One season I arrived in Zuni when the town was excited over a landslide in the
mesa to the north, and an old story was going the rounds of how
a Rain chief, angry about the adultery of his wife, had caused
landslide by prayer-stick ritual.[97]

As already noted, Hopi and Zuni Rain society chieftaincy is
organized along kin-clan lines, and membership in the Hopi
Snake society is in part a clan membership. At Zuni, society
censuses have shown that relatives or connections are likely to
join the same society;[98] but between clan and curing society
there is, in the matter of the membership as a whole, no formal
relationship. Between society office and clan membership there
are cases of relationship. The fetish of the Ne'wekwe society is
kept in a Crane clan house, and the chief of the society must be
a Crane clansman. The two fetishes of the Thle'wekwe or Wood
society are kept, respectively, in Crane clan and in Corn clan
houses; and the offices of society chief and speaker are, or were,
filled by a Crane clansman and a Corn clansman. Formerly the
chief of the Shuma'kwe society had to be a Chaparral cock
clansman.[99] In 1919 at Zuni two Bear clansmen were initiated
into the Thle'wekwe society because it is necessary for the sand-

* Boas 2:64, 65, 66. All represent the Corn Mother.

painting to be made by a Bear clansman. The chief of the Kachina society should belong to Antelope (Deer) clan and his crier to Badger clan. The high office of Pekwin is not vested in a maternal family like the offices of the other paramount Rain chiefs, but the incumbent has to be chosen from the Dogwood clan. In both Zuni and Hopi societies, certain ritual functions are to be performed, for conceptual reasons, by a society member belonging to a certain clan. A Tobacco clansman should have charge of the smoking ritual; a Sand clansman should fetch sand for the sand altar; a Bow clansman should make ritual arrows and wrist guards;[100] a Badger clansman should have charge of the medicine water; a Coyote-Cedarwood-Fire clansman should be fire-tender.* The drawer of water for the Antelope race should belong to the Water-Corn clan, and the starter should be of the Horn clan or a child of the clan that he may properly tell the youths to run fast like an antelope.[101] The function of fire-making at Zuni is associated with the Badger clan, and so the new-fire maker in the winter solstice ceremonial is a Badger clansman or a child of the clan. The medicine water for the altar of the Big Firebrand society in the ceremonial of "whipping the children" was fetched by a Frog clansman.[102]

From similar analogies other clan functions are derived. For example, before a turtle shell may be used by a Hopi dancer, it has to be smoked over by the chief of the Water-Corn clan, since turtles are water creatures. As a Hopi would say, the turtle belongs in that clan. Hopi names, personal and clan names, are products of a like habit of thought; also the occasional practice by clan chief or head or member of addressing prayer-sticks or feathers to the beings associated with the clan (Hopi, Laguna).[103] Possibly the selection of the Jemez War or Under chief from the Badger clan and of the Town chief from the Young Corn or Sun clan is motivated by similar conceptualism. "They would not take a Coyote man for Cacique," says the Jemez townsman; the coyote is not a peace-loving animal.

* In Acoma tradition the first chief of the Fire society was appointed from the Oak clan because oak makes good firewood (Stirling).

Seniority within clan or society* is a factor sometimes considered in ritual or organization, particularly among Hopi. The kiva "old man" is the senior man of the clan or lineage owners, at least theoretically.[104] When women race by clan, the oldest woman of the clan assembles the clanswomen in her house.[105] When the clan meets to hear its traditions, it is the oldest member who tells them. In general, in story-telling, whether in a clan assembly or in kiva, the oldest man present appears to take the initiative. In filling the office of "Father to the kachina," Powamu chief first offers the position to the oldest member of the society. At Cochiti also in several societies the chief and his assistant or prospective successor are the two senior members of the society.[106] In Acoma tradition when the Mother instituted the chieftaincies she selected the oldest man of the clan.[107] In the East, particularly among Tewa, the chiefs are constantly referred to as the old men, whatever their actual age. It is an honorific address, applied also to the Spirits. Tewa of Hano still refer to their Town chief as "our old man," and to his sister as "our old woman." In the winter solstice ceremony of Hano the prayer-stick distributing clansmen are led in single file by their oldest man. The Isletan tale of the rebellious Town chief brings out very clearly the point of view about qualifications through age. "Young men have too many ideas; they will not mind the rules like an old man. On that account the War chiefs never make a young man Town chief." In general, chiefs, both male and female, are middle-aged to old. In the Oraibi Marau ceremony as observed by Voth all the women who participated in altar ritual and slept in kiva were from fifty to seventy years old.

At the death of ceremonialists various distinctions are observed. The face of the deceased shaman is painted red (Cochiti),[108] or streaked red and black (Laguna),[109] or banded black and white (Acoma)† with two short stripes on the chin made by

---

* At Santo Domingo seniority refers not to actual age but to the time of joining the group. A Pueblo does not keep count of his years, so I think it will be found that, where the principle of seniority is considered, the reference is to priority of initiation.

† Stirling. This is the face-painting of the Hopi Snake society.

scraping off the white pigment, or his chin is blackened (Zuni), or his hair parting is painted red, and white zigzags are painted on arms and legs (Isleta). The food offering is set out in the hills a day later, the conclusive rite of exorcism occurring on the fifth day instead of the fourth (Laguna),[110] or the mourning period of four days is even lengthened to twelve days (Nambé) with a taboo on noise or dancing. Cotton is put over the face of deceased members of the Zuni War society; cotton represents clouds and deceased War chiefs become storm-cloud beings. A stick of office, chief's stick, is placed on the grave of any Hopi society man who carried a stick, and a society prayer-stick on the grave of a member of the Marau women's society.[111] Deceased society members are represented on Marau, Snake, and Antelope altars by prayer-sticks or crooks. The crooks represent the wise old men bent with age; the long prayer-sticks, the younger unbent members.[112] On the Hano winter solstice altar, the "strong old men" of the past are represented by long prayer-sticks, the dead at large merely by eagle feathers. At Zuni, Pekwin keeps days and makes prayer-sticks for his fathers, the Sun chiefs long since passed away.[113]

From these funerary and memorial distinctions it may be inferred that, after death, people continue to exist in groups similar to those they belonged to in life, and this has been stated directly. It is believed that, if one who has been "given" or vowed to a society dies before initiation, he will be initiated after death, under Sand Lake (Nambé).[114] The deceased Sia chief remains a society chief. The Zuni Rain chief prays:

> Our fathers,
> Our ancestors,
> Yonder, you who were priests when you were alive,
> We have reached your appointed time [ceremony].

All the deceased priests (chiefs) are invoked by name as far back as names are remembered; from their home with the Uwanami rain-makers they are invoked and they come.[115]

The ceremonialist joins the community of his spirit patron. The Zuni Bow or War chief joins Lightning; Hopi Agaves may join Masauwü underground, working for him as Tokonaka

scouts, or as warriors they may be thought of as Lightnings*
since they are associated with black storm clouds; Keresan clown
society members go to the springs their spirit patrons live in,
east, northeast, or north;[116] medicine society people go to Shipap
or Shipapolima to join their Mother or their Beast gods; members of the Zuni Kachina society go to Kachina town under the
Lake of Whispering Waters. Death journey's end is as varied for
the Pueblo as is his ceremonial organization.

Various attitudes considered in our introductory survey have
an application in chiefly circles. How compensation is or was
made to the Town chief through working for him and to the
shaman through paying down or through the establishment of a
lifelong ceremonial relationship of implicit obligations, we have
noted; likewise the gifts or perquisites that go to chiefs from the
hunt, such as rabbits or buckskin. Furthermore, ears of corn
brought into the dance court by the kachina are perquisites of
the rain societies. Water from a sacrosanct spring is poured on
the field of the society chief. The girls initiated into the Hopi
Lakon society grind corn two days for their "mothers," the two
head women of the society; the more they grind, the more
abundant the rainfall and the crops. At Isleta, households are
expected to contribute wood or food to those performing ceremony in which the household has an interest, so for example,
when the whole town is exorcised by the medicine societies,
thlaide—beans, apples, peaches, meats of all kinds—will be collected from house to house by the War captains.[117] Collecting
food on domiciliary rounds is generally done at Zuni by kachina,
a practice definitely thought of as a return to the impersonator
for his work for the people, as was plainly expressed one year in
gossip over the food collected after the kachina rabbit hunt and
the confinement of Chakwena Woman.[118] The morning collections went as usual to the Salimobia impersonators and the afternoon offerings to the other impersonators. On this occasion a

* This is merely inference. At Oraibi it is said that deceased Agaves go to
Agave peak (Kwanwi); that Horns go to a lake called Alosaka; Singers, to
Duwanasavi; Wüwüchimtü, to any of the mountain homes of the kachina
(Titiev 3).

Salimobia impersonator had only six pieces of bread to take home after the kiva meal, whereas the other impersonators, although unlike the Salimobia they had not gone into retreat, had each a blanketful of food. Since the Salimobia impersonators rendered more service and got less, Salimobia positions, it was grumbled, would be hard to fill another time.

But it is perhaps in the return made to Koyemshi at Shalako that the idea of compensation at Zuni is most conspicuous. Clan by clan the women and men parade into the court, loaded down with the pay they feel called upon to make their "children" for their year-long services in procuring rain and in amusing the people. As the ten stacks of goods pile up around the house walls of the court, each Koyemshi keeps an eye on his heap of presents, like a child at a Christmas tree.

At times during the year Koyemshi (or Ne'wekwe) have come out "to play" at the bidding of another ceremonial group, through the compulsive gift of a cigarette. Similarly, one Zuni kiva will ask another kiva to dance. Formerly the Cochiti War chief was asked for a kachina dance with a package of meal and tobacco. Taking the package, the War chief would say, "It is well, it is well. I will lead in to you the Shiwanna so that all the people will have long life and abundant harvests."[119] The Jemez woman who receives a handful of meal from the dance chief feels called upon to dance, and Jemez youths who accept the feather proffered by a society have to join the society. The doctor who receives a package or handful of meal has to answer his call. In San Juan tale a woman bereft of her husband has her relatives take the "old men" meal and pollen and "black dirt," and *of course* the "old men" say, "Yes, we will help you." Even the Isletan runner who with a ritual cigarette asks the shaman for power against another runner may not be denied, although it is against rules to aid one townsman against another.[120]

Vow. There are many scattering instances of a man taking on a ceremonial office because he had promised to or because his parent had promised. Ben Dixon of Cochiti joined the Kachina society because his mother dedicated him when he was sick in boyhood; and the Antelope clansman of Laguna who is now kachina chief undertook during a sickness to fill the office. After Masauwü's society had lapsed, nobody at Walpi wanted to undertake the dreadful, bloody impersonation; but, when Chaka of the Snake clan almost died in 1924, he volunteered and came out as Masauwü to frighten the wild-mint-gatherers.[121] At Santo Domingo certain kiva offices are regularly filled through self-dedication or dedication by father or father's father; if a man drops his office, he will die.[122] Special functions are performed at Santa Ana as a result of a vow, some for life, some for the single occasion. If you have been ill, or one of your children, if several children have died or you have suffered unusual misfortune, you may take a vow to take part in some ceremony, perform some special ritual, or join a society.[123] The present Winter chief at Santa Clara was given to the Winter People's ceremonial group when he was sick in boyhood; both Town chieftaincy groups may be recruited through dedication or vow. The Kossa of Santa Clara are recruited by dedication in sickness or even before birth; and formerly at San Juan boy babies were vowed by their mothers to the Kwirana. The War society of Isleta is recruited through vow in sickness, and the most unusual Pueblo woman of my acquaintance who dramatized herself as a little Tousle-head, outspoken, tough-minded, and fearless, was "given to them" by her mother when she was a sick little girl.

At Zuni, initiation into a society as a result of convalescence is the most common kind of initiation, and this may be thought of as a standardized form of vow, more particularly as the initiation does not have to take place at once, sometimes years intervene during which the pledged one will act like a godchild to his prospective godfather, sharing some windfall or rendering him a service, an earnest of the large expenditure for the benefit of the society he will be put to at his initiation. Nina of Zuni,[124] daughter of Halian', granddaughter of Naiuchi, was not initiated into the society she was promised to for twenty-five years, and this not because she was the one and only convert of the Moravian Mission, but because society taboos were not to Nina's liking.

Taboos of personal conduct must be observed by society

PLATE III

ZUNI SOCIETY MEMBER

Navaho blanket, blue jeans, white cotton shirt, turquoise and white bead necklace, inlay tu quoise earrings, leather wrist guard, red silk *banda*, red-dyed buckskin moccasins.

people: concentration on the work in hand, continence, fasting, silence, or vigil. Withdrawal from household life to staying in kiva or society room, i.e., ceremonial retreat, is in part to conform to such standards of ritual behavior. During retreats continence is always required, and as a rule some degree of fasting— either one meal only is eaten, generally after the day's work of prayer-stick-making or other ritual tasks, or certain foods, particularly meat, grease, or food cooked with salt, are cut out. An early morning emetic is used by Keresan ceremonialists during those days of their "retreat" in which they may sleep at home. The duration of withdrawal or the degree of restriction varies according to importance of position, that is, the chief or chiefs of a society are longer in retreat or undergo taboos not incumbent upon the members at large. The chiefs are in closest contact with sacrosanct and *dangerous* things, so they must be most careful and meticulous. They must safeguard themselves lest they or their relatives sicken and die[125] or, more rarely, lest they be killed, like the Isletan shaman who postponed holding his ceremony and was struck by lightning, the source of his power.*

Ceremonial restrictions, taboos, and obligations are heaviest on the chiefs, but they fall also on persons in minor positions as well as in one way or another on all the townspeople, particularly in the West. Zuni Rain chiefs and their households must refrain from barter during rain retreats and for the ten days of the winter solstice ceremony; but there is a four-day taboo on barter for everybody at the solstice, and everybody must fast from meat and salt. Zuni society members (Pl. III) and kachina impersonators must be continent and peaceable[126] for four days after planting or offering prayer-sticks, every month or after a dance, and, the kachina cult being the "poor" man's cult, every man is expected to dance kachina at least once a year. Any Keres dancing kachina must observe preliminary taboos. Generally, whenever any of the family connection are engaged in conducting or performing ceremonial, personal ornaments or costume have to be

* Parsons 52:455. This destruction by one's own offended "power" is Apache-like; the automatic sanction is more Pueblo-like.

loaned, all kinds of personal assistance is called for, and lavish contributions of food are expected. Even those who are merely present at ceremonials, including kachina dances, are expected to help, concentrating their attention.* "My children," said the War chief of Cochiti to the spectators of a kachina performance, "think of nothing but our Mothers, the kachina. Take care to think of nothing else!"[127] That "all our prayers converge upon the same object at the same time"[128] is a requisite of magical compulsion.

Ceremonial organization is ever tinctured with the concept of like causing or curing like. Rain societies acting like storm clouds cause storm clouds; curing societies acting like the animals that cause sickness cure sickness. Diseases cured by societies are caused by breaking society regulations. The doctors thwart witches because they themselves have witch power and can turn witch at option. According to a Zuni tale, even witches are subject to this principle; forced to act like warriors and to take Apache scalps, they had to go into retreat and be purified, becoming warrior or bow priests.[129] ("That is why there is no witch kiva any more; they were all made into bow priests.") The Big Shell Rain chieftaincy were deprived of their shell fetish, it is said, because like witches they were using it to kill people.[130] We shall see that the War gods themselves, prototypes of the War chiefs, first killed wantonly like witches before they learned to kill in the right way and were "saved" through initiation. Again, the kachina that brings or announces misfortune is the kachina to exorcise misfortune, or the old, old kachina brings people longevity.

Although now and again clashes occur between chiefs† or

---

* This, if no other, were a good reason for excluding outsiders.

† See pp. 514, 597. In distribution of functions between Keresan Town chief and War or Under chief there are hints of clash both in Acoma tradition (Stirling) and in the Cochiti record. In Cochiti war dances the Town chief had the appointment of the women dancers. Once the War chief appointed a woman, and the woman was already dressed for the dance, when the Town chief ordered the War chief to have her take off her array and give it to another woman. "The episode made considerable noise" (Dumarest, 200).

TABLE 1

	Zuni
Town chief- taincy	*akyakwemosi* (*klashi*), houses chief (old) *kyakweamosi tsana*, house chiefs, little (2) *shiwano"kia*, chief, woman (lapsed) (constituting rain chieftaincy of the North)
Sun-watcher	*pekwin*, speaker (Dogwood clan)
Crier	*pekwin*, speaker (Dogwood clan)
War chief- taincy and society	*pithlashiwanni an papa* and *an suwe*, bow *shiwanni* elder brother and younger brother, War chiefs *apithlashiwanni*, bow *ashiwanni*, War society *pamosona*, Navaho (scalp) chief *pamosona okya*, Scalp chief woman Coyote clan war ritualists *ts'u'thlanna*, Big Shell society *k'oshikwe*, Cactus society *thle'wekwe* (Wood society, stick-swallowers)
Hunt chief- taincy and society	*suskikwe*, Coyote society, or *tsaniakwe*, Hunter society *na'etone* (deer fetish) custodian
Clown society	*ne'wekwe* society *koyemshi* kachina, 10 annual impersonators
Women's society	Scalp chiefs and *hashiya*, Shake girls

Other societies	major rain chieftaincies
	   kyakweamosi (house chiefs, north)
	   pathltokwe (west), *onakwe* (road, south), *koyemshi*
	   (east)
	minor rain chieftaincies
	   Eagle, *upts'anawa*, Corn (2 sets), *kolowisi* (Water
	   Serpent), Step or Red Door
	   Big Firebrand, Little Firebrand, Bedbug, *shi'wanakwe*,
	   shuma'kwe, *uhuhukwe*, Rattlesnake Medicine, *chi-*
	   kyalikwe (Knife or Ant)

Kachina organiza- tion	*kotikyane*, *koko* (kachina) society

TABLE 1 (cont.)

	Hopi
Town chief-taincy	*gigmongwi*, house chief (Bear clan; Walpi, Horn clan) 　　his uncles (lineage) *gigyawuxti*, house, ?, woman, his mother or sister
Sun-watcher	*tawa otaiwa*, sun-watcher (First Mesa, Patki clan)
Crier	*chaakmongwi*, crier chief
War chief-taincy and society	*kaletaka*, War chief, *kaletakwĭmkya* or *momchit* War 　　society Antelope society: Snake society, woman medicine-maker Agave society Horn society *tataukyamu*, Singers society *wüwüchim* society *maswĭmpkya* or Masauwü society scalp-takers (Coyote clan) (Oraibi) *nasosotan*, stick-swallowers (extinct)
Hunt chief-taincy and society	*maakmongwi*, hunt chief (temporary)
Clown society	*chüküwĭmkya*, squatting society, not a society, per- 　　formers drawn from Singers and *wüwüchim* societies *paiyakyamu* or *kossa* (Hano)
Women's society	*marau* *lakon* *oaqöl*
Other societies	Flute (Blue and Drab) *poboshwĭmkya* (extinct) *yayatü* (extinct) *shumaikoli* (F.M.)
Kachina organiza-tion	*powamuwĭmkya* *kachinawĭmkya* (Oraibi)

TABLE 1 (cont.)

	Keres
Town chief-taincy	*tiamuni* (*sht'eamunyi*) *hocheni* (chief) or *ha'askichani*, pueblo person, no clan affiliation (excepting Acoma, Antelope clan) 1 or 2 assistants
Sun-watcher	no office, function of Town chieftaincy
Crier	no office, function of war captains
War chief-taincy and society	*nahia*, Under (chief) (Cochiti) *opi* (*ompi*), scalp-takers (extinct) *tsatio hocheni*, Outside chief, "war captain"; 1 or 2 assistants: representing war gods (annual offices by appointment) *kaʙina* society Snake society (Sia) *kaowata* (stick-swallowers, extinct) (Santa Ana)
Hunt chief-taincy and society	*shaiyaik* (*sha'ak*) chief *sha'akia* society (Acoma) Mountain Lion society (Sia)
Clown society	*koshare* (*kashale*) *kwirana* (*kurena*)
Women's society	*k'oyakwe*, old women (Cochiti)
Other societies	*kaʙina* (Spider) (A., L., S.) *hakani* (Fire) *hishtean* (Flint) *shikame* (*shikani*) Giant Ant *boyaka* (S.D.) *shahaiye* (L.) *saiyap* (L.)
Kachina organiza-tion	Town chief or kiva chiefs in charge Cochiti, Kachina society Sia, society chiefs in charge

TABLE 1 (cont.)

	Jemez
Town chief- taincy	*wabu'naw'i*, ?, chief or *w'ivela*, chief, old man 2 assistants: *dyę wu*, right side; *tsa wu*, left side
Sun-watcher	no office, function of Town chieftaincy
Crier	no office, function of war captains or *Fiscal*
War chief- taincy and society	*nunusomaw'i* (Under chief) and *opi'soma* *nunusombashi*, Under chiefs (society); (no *opi*) 2 "war captains," *dahesoma*, petrified wood chief *haiyakish*, Rattlesnake society Cactus society 2 *shochun* men's societies: *dyakish*, Arrow society, *seykish*, Eagle society
Hunt chief- taincy and society	Mountain Lion society Eagle hunt societies (Pecos and Jemez)
Clown society	*tabö'sh* (Flute-Flower society) *ts'un'tatabö'sh* (Ice society)
Women's society	*owish* (women) societies, Jemez and Foreigner
Other societies	*fuakish* (Fire) *dyikish* (Flint) *sh'obawuhush* (Morning-star) *bat'aash* (Paste-together) *pekish* (Sun) *towahe'sh*
Kachina organiza- tion	Kiva chiefs in charge

TABLE 1 (cont.)

	Tewa
Town chief-taincy	*po'ętoyo* (*payoke*), water run chief, chief of Summer people moiety 2 assistants, right-hand man, left-hand man, who succeed *oyike*, ice hard, chief of Winter people moiety 2 assistants, etc.
Sun-watcher	no office, function of Town chieftaincy
Crier	*tokędi* (San Juan) for secular affairs only
War chief-taincy and society	*tse'oke* (*po'se'e*, San Juan), (society recruited through scalp-takers, extinct) *apienu*, red bow youth, women's society (San Juan, San Ildefonso) *tse'oke kwiyo*, women scalp custodians (Santa Clara) 6 *akono'toyo*, outside chief or *towa'e'* representing war gods (*towa'e'*, little person) appointed annually
Hunt chief-taincy and society	*pikę* (San Juan; extinct, Santa Clara, San Ildefonso), chief in charge of rabbit hunts and of Deer dancers
Clown society	*kossa* (Santa Clara: Oke' or San Juan *kossa* and Nambé *kossa*) *kwirana* (San Juan); extinct, Santa Clara, San Ildefonso
Women's society	*tse'oke* (Santa Clara)
Other societies	*pahpuſona* (Fire) *tsihpuſona* (Flint)
Kachina organiza-tion	Town chiefs in charge of masks and dances

TABLE 1 (cont.)

	Isleta
Town chief-taincy	*t'aikabede*, people chief chief of *shifunin* (Black Eye) moiety chief of *shure'* (Gopher) moiety
Sun-watcher	
Crier	
War chief-taincy and society	*pq'ide*, permanent War chief, Scalp chief, chief of Snake society Kumpawithlawe *mafornin*, 2 scalp women or Snake society women *a'uku'wem*, scalp-takers *tuwithlawe*, cane war chief and annual war captains appointed by moiety
Hunt chief-taincy and society	*humaxu*, hunt chief 1 assistant
Clown society	*k'apio shifunin*, clowns of Black Eye moiety *k'apio shuren*, clowns of Red Eye (Gopher) moiety *te'en*, grandfathers, 4 from each moiety, with Town chief (Black Eye) as head
Women's society	

Other societies	Corn societies (*wakuakaben*)
	    White corn (East): *tö'tainin*, Day people
	    Black corn (North): *narnin*, Poplars, *kǫaraɴ*, Shrikes
	    Yellow corn (West): *namtainin*, Earth people
	    Blue corn (South): *pachirnin*, Water-bubbling, *tutenehu'*, Blowing-through-cane
	    All color corn (Up, Down, Middle): *ietaide*, Corn person; *shyu*, Eagle; *kǫi*, Goose; *shichu*
	curing societies
	    Town Fathers
	    Laguna Fathers

Kachina organization	*chakabede*, Kachina chief 1 male assistant, 1 female

TABLE 1 (cont.)

	Taos
Town chief- taincy	*töbiana t'unena*, house rule chief, chief of 3 kivas of north side, including Big Earring, *fialuthla*, hence called Big Earring Man, Council chief *p'ataina*, Water (People) Man, chief of 3 kivas of south side, including Water People kiva *kasikei'na*, Cacique, Spanish-Catholic office, may combine with office of Water Man, hereditary in family
Sun-watcher	no office, functions of Cacique (winter solstice), of Old Ax People chief, or of all chiefs
Crier	no office, function of secular officers
War chief- taincy and society	*talat'unena*, war chief or scalp chief, chief of Bear People (with woman associate) *talana*, temporary scalp-takers 2 "war captains," annually appointed by Town chief and other chiefs; 8 assistants; all 10 "chiefs" attached to Governor, annually appointed
Hunt chief- taincy and society	chief of Day or Sun People, hunt chief Day People and Old Ax People in charge of buffalo
Clown society	Black Eyes, in Dripping Water People kiva Red Paint People (extinct)
Women's society	
Other societies	White Mountain (in House or Sun People kiva) cures against Bear Corn Mother (*kuyu kana*) (in Knife People kiva and Dripping Water People kiva) *papta* (in Feather People kiva and Big Parrot People kiva)
Kachina organiza- tion	Water People in charge of clown masks and of Turtle dance

ceremonial groups, co-operation prevails. Kiva groups combine to present a dance (Zuni) or a kiva supplies the clowns for another kiva's dance (Hopi); shamans function with kiva groups or with war chiefs; war chiefs or captains protect all groups. Office means work rather than power so that encroachment on others is not a temptation. Ceremonial government looks more hierarchical than it is, even in Zuni. Nick said and was fully warranted in saying, "Not one boss at Zuni, many bosses." And he might well have added, "Not one god for us Indians, many gods."

CHAPTER II

THE SPIRITS

"They act like Shiwanna," Cloud people, Keres say of the society chiefs performing their winter solstice ceremony. Hopi Antelope society chiefs are each a chief of one of the cardinal directions, that is, he represents the chief of the Northwest or the Northeast or the Southeast or the Southwest, the Cloud chiefs. The paramount Rain chiefs of Zuni are similarly orientated, with Pekwin, chief of the Zenith, and the War chiefs, chiefs of the Nadir. The War chiefs also impersonate the War God Brothers as do the War captains of Keres or as Hopi warriors impersonate Masauwü, god of various attributes. Isletan shamans are called Elder Sister or Younger Sister and the Keresan Town chief, our Father and Mother, since all represent the underground Mothers. When the dancers put on their masks, they not only impersonate the kachina but they *are* kachina, just as when Keresan doctors draw on their bear paws, Bear comes into them, and they become bears, with the curing power of Bear. When the clowns paint at Zuni with mud from their sacred spring, they identify themselves with their patron or prototype, Paiyatemu, the Youth, the first of the Ne'wekwe or Koshare, son of Sun Father or of underground Mother, a powerful person who travels along the Galaxy, who is funny and so senseless that his father has to let him do just as he pleases.[1] Through their chiefs, their doctors, and their sacred clowns and dancers Pueblos are in close contact or accord with their Spirits. "Me Cloud loves!" exclaims Hümimüïnwa, the old Antelope society chief.

When Hümi dies, he will join Cloud. The Rain society chiefs of Zuni probably are thought of as joining the Uwanami, the water spirits whose houses are the cumulus clouds. War chiefs become Lightnings, most potent of rain spirits. When Giwire died, the Shikani-Kurena shaman of Laguna, a thunderstorm was raging. "The Shiwanna, the storm spirits, have taken him," said his glad people.[2] Similarly at Cochiti if it rain after a death people will say of the deceased, "He is already a Shiwanna; he brings us rain."[3] At Taos "those who always believe," the upright and good chiefs, men who perish in the mountains,* and suicides become Lightnings or Cloud beings.

A special class of deceased rain-makers are the enemy dead who through scalp ceremonial are taken into the tribe and by prayer converted into rain-makers (Zuni). "Though in his life the enemy [Navaho] was a worthless lot, now through the Corn priests' [Rain chiefs'] rain prayers and seed prayers, he has become a rain person."[4]

But the dead at large may be associated with the Cloud beings. The Hopi say in haranguing the dead, "You are no longer a Hopi, you are Cloud. When you get yonder you will tell the chiefs to hasten the rain clouds hither."[5] The exorcising speech of San Juan is very similar. "Now you do not belong here; you belong to Oxuwah, to Cloud, whether you become warrior or storm spirit, blue cloud spirit or yellow cloud spirit or red cloud spirit or white cloud spirit or dark cloud spirit or speckled cloud spirit, from the mountains and hills you must help your people."[6] The Uwanami of Zuni are not to be identified with all the dead, yet these Cloud people are described as "our ancestors, the ones who have died," and when a heavy cloud looms up anyone might turn to a child and say, "There comes your grandmother!"† "The Clouds are people, just as we are people. They are our ancestors, the ones who have died. These are the rain. These become Uwanami, raw [supernatural] people. When they put on their beautiful garments, they are just like the clouds. Therefore they just impersonate clouds with their breath, but they are people,"[7] and the curving cumulus clouds painted on Acoma and Sia altar frames are given eyes and mouth like people. An Oraibi visitor to the underworld of

* This may be a reference to dead warriors, to whom in the Scalp dance a food offering was made, in order to give power to living warriors.

† A courtesy term of relationship. Except in ceremonial groups, and in them rarely, a deceased individual would not be addressed or represented.

the dead is told: "You must wrap up the women when they die, in the wedding mantle, and tie the big belt around them; these mantles are not tightly woven and when the skeletons move along on them through the sky as clouds the thin rain drops through these mantles; the big rain drops fall from the fringes of the big belt,"[8] and the dead add, "We shall send you rain and crops." Because of the mask of cotton covering the face of the deceased and the prayer-feathers, because the dead eat only of the odor or essence of food,[9] the dead and the clouds are light. "The dead have to go up to become clouds."[10]

The Cloud beings are always described by the cardinal colors, the colors associated with the cardinal directions, as are those dim, perhaps obsolescent spirits, the Chiefs of the Directions.[11] At Acoma, Laguna, and probably in other Keresan towns these chiefs who live on mountaintops, on the four sacred mountains of the color-directions (Acoma), are identified with the seasons and have personal names; but they may be identified merely with the Shiwanna or Clouds (Cochiti),[12] as the Hopi identify them: "At the north sits a chief wearing a yellow cloud as a mask,* covering his head and resting upon his shoulders. Yellow butterflies flutter before him, and yellow corn grows unfailingly. At the west sits a chief wearing a blue-green cloud mask. Blue butterflies flutter, and blue corn grows. At the south sits a chief with a red cloud, red butterflies, and red corn. At the east sits a chief with a white cloud, white butterflies, and white corn. Above sits a black chief wearing a black cloud, with black butterflies and black corn. Below sits Müy'ingwa wearing a mask of clouds of all five colors, with butterflies and birds of all the colors, with speckled corn and sweet corn, with melons, squash, cotton, and beans."[13] Here the corn of the directions is referred to naturalistically; frequently it is personified as Corn Maidens, Yellow, White, Red, Blue, Black, or Speckled who are associated with the Cloud Youths.

The Cloud beings live in the six or four regions of the universe, in towns on the shores of the encircling ocean (Zuni), or in the

---

* For the cloud masks of the Zuni Uwanami see Stevenson 2:21.

mountains, below spring or lake. Mountains or lakes* are the general habitat of the kachina, too, and the members of certain group kachina such as the Shalako or Salimobia of Zuni or the Shui'yana of Cochiti are individually localized by cardinal direc tion. Cloud may appear as a kachina impersonation in mask.[14] The dead or some of them† become kachina,‡ and the kachina bring rain. Nevertheless, the Uwanami or Cloud beings of Zuni are not identical with the Koko (kachina) nor the Shiwanna or Storm Clouds of Keres, with the K'atsena (kachina);§ and Hopi Chiefs of the Directions are addressed by societies without kachina connections.

With few exceptions all Spirits, except among the Tiwa, may be represented as kachina, i.e., impersonated by mask, even the War Twins, the Stars, the Sun. Only the Earth spirits are never so represented, Müy'ingwa, the male maize spirit of the Hopi underworld, or Iyatiku, the Keresan Corn Mother, who lives

* Mountains or lakes are themselves quasi-spirits,being represented on altars through clay effigies, stones, or water bowl and referred to in tales as animate beings: Blue Water old man (Tewa) (compare Water Grandfather, Zuni, Cushing 6:19), White Mountain (Taos), San Mateo Mountain (Isleta). In collecting mountain woods for prayer-sticks, the Acoma War chiefs sprinkle meal before ascending as if going in to a sacred place, and they pray to the Mountain for per-mission to cut wood and not to be blamed for anything (Stirling).

† Like all the dead, members of the Kachina society go underground, back to the world before the Emergence, but boys who have been whipped by the kachina are privileged to visit after death the kachina dance house under the lake (Stevenson 2:20, 66). For comparative note see White 4:198–99; also Benedict 3:I, 175, for the Zuni boy who dies and becomes Atoshle kachina. "That is why we know that when people die they become kachina." Says the Hopi of First Mesa to the defunct, "You are changed into a kachina; you are Cloud" (Stephen 4:826).

‡ One identifying concept should not be overlooked: dreaming of the dead is treated by the kachina, by whipping. On the other hand, the prayer-stick for the kachina is plainly differentiated from the prayer-stick for the dead, by reversely tied duck feather. An analogous ritualistic differentiation is followed at Isleta: food for the dead is held in the left hand; food for the wenin or thliwan, in the right hand.

§ Terminology indicates some distinction among Tanoans: Thlatsi or thliwa (Taos); wenin (?) or thliwa (Isleta); k'ats'ana or dyasa (Jemez); but the Tewa have the same term or very similar terms for kachina and cloud—oxuhwa or, according to Harrington (p. 54), 'ok'uwa, cloud, 'ōk'uwa, kachina.

below at Shipapu. In other words, the kachina are not a special class of spirits like the Cloud chiefs. The term "kachina" refers to whatever spirit is being impersonated by mask * and by whatever ceremonial group, Kachina society of Zuni, the curing society with whom one or more kachina may be associated, Hopi or Keresan kiva membership, or the Winter or Summer moiety of Tewa.

Together with this generalized theory that the clouds and the dead as Clouds are kachina, there is a specific kachina ideology which is fuller and clearer at Zuni than anywhere else. Here the first kachina were the children who were transformed into water creatures and slipped off their mothers' backs as the people were fording a river in their early search for the middle of the world. These water children went down river to the Lake of Whispering Waters, eighty-three miles west of Zuni,† where underwater they became kachina and established Kachina town whence in answer to prayer they would come to dance for their people at Zuni. After these dance visits, women followed them back to their underlake town or, in another version, they took some one with them, i.e., someone died, so they said they would not come any more to Zuni in person, only in spirit would they invest the representations or masks the people were to make. Then after the dance, at "wide river" they would turn into ducks[15] and fly back to their town. Whenever they came, they would bring rain, and on the care and attention paid to them the crops of all would depend. Not to treat their masks or impersonators properly, with proper gifts of prayer-meal or food and of prayer-sticks or feathers would be very dangerous; drought or sickness would result. At death the mask of an impersonator was to be buried, and he was to journey to their town and live under their chief, Pa'utiwa, a magnificent personage, possessed of beauty, dignity, and kindliness,[16] also of a par-

---

* Excepting the K'oʙishtaiya of Acoma, who, although they are impersonated in mask, are not called kachina. What the conceptual distinction may be to the Acoman is not clear.

† See Stevenson 2: Pl. IV. It is the junction of Zuni River and the Little Colorado.

ticular power of turning to duck; and in company with Kiaklo, Pa'utiwa's speaker, an exacting "grandfather" who has to be carried into town; with war chief Sayatasha or Long Horn, who sends the deer, and his warrior companions of whom two represent trees: with Sayathlia or the Blue Horns, the four terrible flagellators; with the twelve wind-makers or Salimobia who whip, too, but gaily, to prancing steps; with Shulawitsi, the boy god of fire and maize and hunting; and with many other kachina chiefs, not to speak of hosts of kachina who appear together under one name in a dance group and about whom there is a multitude of legends. The twelve Shalako war chiefs live not at Kothluwela but apart, under the springs near ancient Hawikuh; nor does the Koyemshi family live under the river-lake created by their incestuous father but on top of the mountain he also created. A few Zuni kachina live on Sandía Mountains.

Hopi kachina live mostly on San Francisco Mountains to the westward or on Black Mountain or Kishyuba (Ki'shiwuu) from forty to sixty miles north or northeast. Eototo is their chief, their father, and there are several kachina mothers. There is no kachina town. The spirits of the masks that are kept in the maternal houses of certain lineages, the kachina chiefs, are thought of as clan ancestors, not progenitors, but as beings encountered in the early clan migrations just as plants or animals were encountered and "taken into the clan."* The Kachina-Parrot clan chief of Oraibi prays over his Powamu prayer-feathers: "From there east, at Ki'shiwuu do I call my ancestors."[17] Apart from clan legends there is less lore about Hopi kachina than about Zuni kachina. In the tales Cloud youths figure rather than kachina. What we may call kachina anecdotage or hagiology is scantier. Much the same is true of Keresan kachina, who are not even associated with clan legends except in a few instances at Acoma, Zuni's nearest Keresan neighbor. Possibly lore about the kachina associated with the Keresan societies has not been fully recorded. Keresan kachina,

* At Oraibi (and Laguna) these clan plants or animals may be addressed in prayer (Voth 4:17, n. 1; Parsons 33:212-13).

who have not always been identified with the Dead,* live at Wenima or Wenimats, a beautiful mountain region in the west, where the spirits gamble, dance, hunt, or farm.[18] From Wenima the kachina used to come in person, to White House, the early home of Keres. Then the kachina had a fight with the people and refused to return, except in spirit to invest their masks (Acoma).† But some day they will come back, a belief about the kachina not restricted to Keres. At the close of Shalako, all the kachina depart on a visit to the east. The winter kachina of Acoma all live in the east. There are no kachina masks at Isleta, and, when the mountain being Thliwale comes in from Welima before daybreak, he appears as an actual spirit (at least to some Isletans).[19]

Everywhere the kachina are associated with rainfall, with crops, and with game. When the people of Cochiti asked their War chief to lead in the kachina, they would say, "We hope they will bring to us good life and plentiful harvests of corn, wheat, watermelons, and melons and of all other things which our people need to live on." When Water-pouring Woman and other kachina take their new daughter-in-law back to her parents, they bring presents of corn and melons (Hano). "And the houses of all in the town they filled up with watermelons and muskmelons, while the people slept."‡ Actually at a dance the kachina will throw to the onlookers corn or fruit, their raiment (Acoma), as well as pretty much everything, at Zuni, that can be bought in the store. More ceremonially the kachina may bring packages of seeds or ears of corn to bestow after the dance upon chiefs or special persons who help themselves to spruce

* It is significant that Keresan masks are not buried with the dead, nor are Hopi masks.

† White 2:149. This is Oraibi tradition also. In their early wanderings the Hopi were accompanied by the kachina. In an encounter with Mexicans the kachina were killed and returned underground. The Hopi kept and used the masks of the slain (Titiev 3).

‡ Similarly, in the Hopi tale about T'aiowa stealing Yellow Cloud Boy's wife, when the Cloud people travel on their rainbow and arrive in the rain at the bride's house, they fill up all the houses with their presents of corn and melons. "We must be kind to that boy," say the worldly wise townspeople.

twigs from kachina array. Or "to make the children happy" the kachina bring presents of bows and arrows, "dolls," moccasins, and good things to eat, like sweet corn. Bee kachina brings honey on the top of his mask (Zuni). All the game animals who "give themselves" are represented as kachina, and the kachina associated with the directions seem to be associated also with the hunt.*

The Dead, the Clouds, the Kachina—these are the outstandingly collective Spirits among anthropomorphic Spirits; but even individual spirits or gods like the underground Mother or the War Brothers or Sun are given companions: Iyatiku has a sister or sisters, all Corn Mothers together; warrior couples are assigned to each of the cardinal points; Sun has sons to carry his shield across the sky. Paiyatemu, Sun Youth, I had always supposed was a single personage and now in a recently recorded Zuni tale I find the Paiyatamu referred to as a group, their chief sending forth their butterflies to find a lost girl.[20] At dawn not only the Dawn Youths are addressed but Dawn Old Man, Dawn Boys, Dawn Old Women, Dawn Matrons, Dawn Maidens, Dawn Girls (Zuni).[21] Pueblo Spirits are readily collectivized.

Conspicuously individualized† supernaturals are Sun, Moon, some of the Stars; Dawn Youths of the Tewa or Dawn Mothers of Zuni[22] or Dawn Woman of the Hopi who lives underwater‡ and possibly is to be identified with Hürü′ingwühti, Hard Substance Woman, the owner of shells, coral, and turquoise;§

---

* Zuni, Shalako, Shulawitsi, Salimobia, and see Stevenson 2:440; Isleta (Parsons 52:337); Cochiti (Goldfrank 3:89).

† Yet sometimes collectivized as in the Keresan term for the cosmic beings, k'oвishtaiya. Another Keresan collective term is maiyanyi, spirits, "anything that we don't know," and airplanes are included (White), as was formerly the railway locomotive (see p. 293).

Note wahtainin, all the (spirit) people, used at Isleta.

‡ She is the Mother of the Agaves. She was also associated with the Poboshwĭmkya, a medicine society of Keresan type. Before Iyatiku, lived Thought Woman, whose every thought became a creation, in the bottommost white world, surrounded by water (White 7). This describes the Woman of Hard Substances of Oraibi (Voth 4:1 ff.).

§ At Zuni, White Shell Woman and Turquoise Boy. The "flesh" of Turquoise Boy was wasted, so he deserted to Santo Domingo (Stevenson, Parsons) and

Sho'tokününgwa who lives in the sky and is both Star and Lightning, the god who kills and renders fertile and who initiated
the practice of scalping;[23] Kwatoko, the killer bird, or Knife-
Wing, also patron of scalpers (Zuni, Oraibi), who in Zuni and
Acoma myth is a woman-stealer and in Sia myth flaps his wings
to frighten Lightning and the Cloud people into working harder;
Iyatiku, the great underground mother or maize goddess of
Keres, and Müy'ingwa of Hopi who is a male maize spirit,
god of vegetation, chief of the Nadir, father of the underworld;*
the sister of Müy'ingwa and wife of Masauwü, Child-Medicine
Woman or Sand-Altar Woman who bestows infants and guards
the game animals, who is related genetically to the kachina
Chakwena Woman (Hopi, Zuni)[24] and conceptually to the Deer
Mother of Taos or to one of the Corn Mothers of Keres or to
Fire Old Woman of Cochiti (Nambé, Zuni, Isleta), the one asked
for animals; Whirlwind† and Hükyangkwü, the Hopi spirit of
high winds‡ and sandstorms, a malevolent old woman except
in war when as Scalp Woman she goes ahead and bewilders the
enemy, "taking their mind away"; Echo, a restless little boy

---

beyond to the White man's country. That is why White people have better
turquoise. Turquoise Boy left only his outer clothes near Santo Domingo (Benedict 3:I, 44-45).

* He is covered with grains of corn—body, face, head, and hands. As his
feet are ears of corn, he could not move very fast when he came up with the
people (Voth 5:39).

† Jemez people say that stepping into a whirlwind causes miscarriage
(Harper), and at Mishongnovi, where it is believed that Whirlwind is abroad at
noon, a child might say, "I'll be back before Whirlwind gets me" (Beaglehole
1:42). In Laguna tale Whirlwind Man does carry away a girl (Boas 2:118 ff.).
Among Keres and Tewa, wind is often witch-sent. Zuni witches travel by whirlwind (Stevenson 2:394). Papago believe Whirlwind causes a dizzy sickness, and
sing:

> A little gray whirlwind
> Is trying to catch me.
> Across my path it keeps whirling (Underhill 4).

‡ Cold winds from the north driving away rain clouds are referred to at Zuni
as giant chiefs, Suni *ashiwanni*, frost chiefs. The first pair were outcasts from
the Wood society (Stevenson 2:21, 445; Cushing 6:98). At Taos there are wind
beings of disease (Parsons 58:110). The winds of the four directions may be
asked at Zuni to carry away disease (Stevenson 2:528, 552).

(Taos) who may be identified with one of the War Brothers,* bringing cold and ominous of misfortune;[25] Poshaiyanki (Zuni) or P'ashaya''n^y'i (Keres) or Poseyemu (Tewa) or Puspiyama (Isleta), the somewhat Christlike culture hero, brother and deputy of Iyatiku at Sia, father of curing societies (Zuni), giver of raiment and riches (Zuni), a despised little boy, a miracle worker or nothing more than a juggler and deceiver who has finally to be killed (Laguna),† assimilated by Catholic Acoma with the Serpent in the Garden of Eden; the patron saints of all the towns but Hopi; Wẹide, whom an Isletan may correlate with Dios or God but who is virtually chief of kachina-like beings, perhaps Lightning; the patrons or prototypes of the clown or curing societies—scouts, leaders, curers, often living under springs like the kachina, but not kachina, in particular T'aiowa (Hopi) or Paiyatemu (Keres, Zuni), the handsome seductive flute player associated with the Sun, who allures or frightens away and then recovers the Corn Maidens, prototype of lovers; the Twins, sons of the Sun or of Sun and Waterfall, war gods and at Zuni associated with lightning,[26] culture heroes, patrons of gamesters and arrant mischief-makers, all in one; and, finally, Masauwü, the first denizen of Hopiland, a towering personage of Death and War and Fire and Night.

Our Sun Father, Sun Old Man, makes his daily journey across the sky, at sundown reaching his house in the west which is also the house of Hard Substance Woman or White Shell. As he comes forth in the east, Sun should be greeted and prayed to. It seems probable that anciently every Pueblo sprinkled corn meal or pollen at sunrise and said a prayer. Elders and cere- monialists still do so, sometimes not to Sun but to his people, the Dawn People (Zuni, Hopi, Tewa). Benina's father on awak- ening would sing, "Dawn Youths are waiting for you to feed them, to bring you health and food," and then he would name

---

* At Zuni. He is also obscurely identified with a star spirit (Laguna, Hopi, Zuni) who makes and closes fissures in the earth (Parsons 20:95; Bunzel 5:1036– 40).

† Apparently the Moctezuma necromancer story reported from Pimería (Velarde, 130). See pp. 965, 1090.

one of the household to go out and sprinkle meal (Nambé).[27] At noon Sun stands still for a little and in Isleta belief may be brought down to the altars of his children who, wherever they are, say a midday prayer.*

Sun's diurnal journey varies a trifle from day to day so that at the winter solstice the farthermost point toward the south is reached and at the summer solstice the farthermost point toward the north. These most distant points Sun visits for four days before turning back, and this is the proper time for him to receive the prayer-sticks of his children. Being a man and unstable, he must be helped on his journey; he must be "turned" or "pulled back." When Sun was first placed in the sky, he came too close to the earth and scorched it (Keres, Hopi), just as did, in Tewa mythology, the younger son of Sun to whom he intrusted his shield. And then Sun can "die," in eclipse, a terrifying experienec boding so much ill to men that purifying ceremonial is called for (Taos). If the eclipse occurs immediately after the sun rises, people to the east (Zuni and Rio Grande people) will die; if in the middle of the morning, Hopi will die; if at noon, people to the southwest will die (Mishongnovi).[28]

Infants are presented by name to the rising sun, with a prayer for longevity, and throughout life Sun is prayed to for longevity. Sun is supremely "the holder of the roads of men." Sun is also a hunt deity. Keresan hunters pray to Sun; rabbit throwing-sticks are offered him.† The antelope hunters of Mishongnovi offered him prayer-sticks.‡ In Taos myth Sun gives his questing sons a hunt bundle just as in Zuni myth he gives them a turquoise rabbit stick or amulet. Sun, who is himself a head-taker

---

* Noon, as noted above, is also a supernatural moment on Second Mesa. It is dangerous for anyone to be out at noon, especially children who are told not to leave the house. To look into a spring at noon is fatal: the water spirit(?) looks out at you and that kills you (Beaglehole 1 : 42).

† Probably a very ancient practice. In the crater shrine of Laguna-Acoma, a solstice shrine still visited, there are grooved Basket Maker rabbit sticks (Parsons 13:384, Fig. 39).

‡ Beaglehole 2:6. Sun is addressed by hunters, also at dawn, among the Havasupai neighbors of the Hopi (Spier 2:109–10, 285).

(Isleta, Picurís),[29] gives power in war as well as in hunting. Sun fertilizes the fields.[30] The phallic clown societies are ever associated with Sun. (Sometimes with Moon.)

Among Hopi and Tewa, at Taos, Jemez, and Sia, Moon is a male being, and probably more important in the pantheon than among the Pueblos where Moon is a female being. At Zuni, Moon is the younger sister of Sun and except at the winter solstice when women put down a prayer-stick for her* she is rarely addressed, although her phases set the time for a large part of the ceremonial calendar. When Moon dies, in eclipse, it bodes ill for women, more particularly for female infants.†

Morning star has associations with war and with the War Brothers.[31] Falling stars, comets, all the stars are associated with war. Sho'tokününgwa of the Hopi is Lightning shooting arrow-points from his fingertips, but he is also a starry war god. Dark Star Man (Morning star) used to be addressed in war by Tewa; the Evening star they call an old woman, Faded Yellow Old Woman, an old woman whose gray locks hang over her face. Hano Tewa pray to Ponu'chona, whom they identify with Morning star, for animals, game and domestic. "They say he has lots of animals, so we ask him for rabbits, deer, antelope, and mountain sheep, also (as at Mishongnovi)[32] for cows, horses, and sheep." Hunters sprinkle meal for Ponu'chona. The star effigy Mother of the Walpi War chief is Mother of the domestic animals.[33] In San Juan tale the sons of Morning Star set his animals free from the sky corral and distribute them on earth.[34] Arrow Youth of Laguna was a good hunter "because Great Star [Morning star] was his friend."[35] Morning Star kills seven enemies, seven Redheads, for the Taos Corn Girls ordered not to come home without those heads.[36] Scalps were called Morning Star

---

* Oraibi Marau women address prayer-feathers to Moon (Voth 8:43).

† Witnessing an eclipse, lunar or solar, may cause miscarriage (Jemez, Harper). A pregnant woman should stay indoors or, if she has to go out, carry a key (or arrowpoint) in her belt lest the moon eat the unborn infant, causing some malformation such as hairlip. This Spanish belief is widespread among Spanish Indians (Parsons 62:72). In pre-Columbian Middle America also there was the belief that if a pregnant woman went outdoors during an eclipse the child would be born a monster.

at Hano, and at Pojoaque as the Blue Corn Girls return with
their scalps they sing the song given them by Spider Grandmother:

> Once Blue Corn Girls
> Now Dark Star Man.[37]

Orion and the Pleiades are the two constellations known best
to the Pueblos. They time night ceremonies. With their usual
dichotomizing bent Tewa call "the three stars in a line," Orion's
Belt, winter stars, and the Pleiades, summer stars.* They are
watched by the Town chiefs, and, as at Jemez, are thought of
as supernaturals.[38] The Galaxy is represented by a formal design
on masks and altars (Zuni, Acoma), and its meal painting on the
Shi'wanakwe altar is given eyes and mouth,[39] like Sun or Moon.
Probably all the stars, the Galaxy and the entire starry heaven,
have an anthropomorphic divine character to the Pueblos. Zuni
refer to "all the little sparkling stars" as *ashiwanni*, priests or
chiefs, "our night fathers, our night mothers," says the Scalp
chief in prayer;[40] the Night People, they say at Taos.

Among Keres, Iyatiku, the maize mother, has the paramount
position Sun or the War Brothers have at Zuni or Masauwü
among Hopi. From her underground house at Shipap mankind
emerged; from there infants today are born and thither go the
dead, with the prayer-feather they carry to their Mother.
Iyatiku created the kachina. Of the rubbings from their skin
Iyatiku and her sister made the Koshare, to entertain them in
sadness. The Mothers sent their son Ma'sewi into the universe
to place the sun properly in the sky. All the societies get title
from Iyatiku; her corn-ear fetish, the fully kerneled ear of white
corn, they place on their altar and cherish as their most valuable
possession. "Corn is my heart," says Utsĕt, the Mother of Sia,
after planting bits of her heart, "and it shall be to my people
as milk from my breasts."[41] Iyatiku has the attributes of an
earth mother, but Earth is referred to in prayer as a separable
supernatural (Acoma,† Sia, Zuni), and, among Hopi and Tiwa,

---

* Compare Zuni, Seed stars; and for Orion, Row (Bunzel 2:487).

† White 7; White 5. The turtle or horned-toad sand-painting called Earth
is laid by a shaman at infant-naming.

Earth is the Mother of game.[42] Hopi also call her Sand-Altar Woman or Childbirth or Child-Water Woman.*

At Zuni and Sia not the Maize or Earth Mother but the War Brothers established the curing societies. Zuni gets all its "rules" from the Twins, an idea readily entertained, since the Twins are impersonated by the War or Bow chiefs, elder brother and younger brother, who make or enforce the "rules" of the town. The Twins figure in a great number of Zuni myths and folk tales, often as naughty or bad little boys who disobey or plague their grandmother, play ball, free the world from monsters, turn the inhospitable into stone, and steal salt from the animals or masks from the kachina; the Twins live inside the mountain or visit their "house" on hill or mesa top, guarding the town as the Ones Who Hold-the-High-Places. To their shrines are carried miniature bows and arrows, war clubs and netted shields, and to their cedar-girt ground altar on Corn Mountain, miniature implements of their games and, annually, new images, made from a lightning-riven tree, by specially intrusted members of their clans, Bear and Deer.

On First Mesa there are three sets of War Brother images— stone images kept by a Tewa chief, by the Kachina society chief of Walpi, and by the War society chief—and the Brothers are impersonated at the War society ceremony and as kachina; but the Brothers have a rival in Masauwü, who has his own warrior clan†, his own society, dramatic war or fertility rituals and distinctive culture hero attributes. Masauwü was the first housebuilder, and to his underground house journey the dead. Masauwü gave the first people squash and other vegetables; he is summoned by farmers. In some obscure way he is the god of

---

* The name, Tihküyi wühti, Child-Water Woman, may refer to the incident of the misdelivery of her child, "woman with the protruding child." This happened when she was wandering with the Snake Clan Woman. She still wanders and wails (Voth 3:352–53). It is Child-Water Woman who sends women their children by projecting into them infant images, Dr. Eggan was told at Oraibi.

† Coyote-Firewood (*Kokop*). Yukioma of the Coyote clan of Oraibi who led the anti-American faction to Hotavila always said that having Masauwü in his clan he could arrest enemies by blowing a handful of ashes against them, the usual discharming rite. Masauwü can paralyze with fear, "hypnotize" says the Hopi modernist (Nequatewa, 65).

fire, perhaps because he walks only at night by firelight,[43] perhaps because offerings to the dead are cast into fire and Masauwü is the god of death. He is the protector of travelers, and the traveler who places a bit from his burden on a cairn near the trail and the tuft of grass he has rubbed himself with says a prayer to Masauwü.[44] When the early people emerged into this world, the War Brothers sat one on each side of the *sipapu* and gave a hand, but Masauwü also welcomed everybody coming up, since he had been caught without his mask on by Shrike, the emissary from the underworld, and could not frighten him away.

With spirit birds or animals we are back to collective concepts, often conflicting and obscure. To what extent are the animals independent spirits, to what extent are they helpers, intercessors (Stevenson's recurrent reference), or spirit companions and "pets" (Stephen's term)? Among Hopi the prey animals, Lion, Bear, Wildcat, and Wolf, are associated with the War gods; and the Hawks as war chiefs, with the sky god Sho'tokününgwa;[45] the game animals that are always asked "to give themselves" are mentioned as pets of the Somaikoli society (in Zuni the term means dragonfly; see p. 191 n.†): deer, mountain sheep, antelope, elk, jackrabbit, cottontail; the horned or plumed Water Serpents who live in springs and all the water creatures are pets of the Clouds.[46]

But Water Serpent who figures everywhere except among Tiwa is also a separable and important personage.* In Zuni he has his own cult group or Rain chieftaincy, and his image appears conspicuously at the kachina initiation. On First Mesa he has his own distinctive celebration, an elaborate fertility dramatization, and at Jemez his image is also brought in from a spring at each of the annual rain retreats. Water Serpent is a collective being living in springs sometimes associated with the color-directions (Sia, Jemez); but he is also referred to as a single personage, a god of terrestial waters. He came, say Hopi, from the Red Land of the south and he is a patron of the Water-

---

* Hopi, Palülükong; Zuni, Kolowisi; Keres, Tsitsshrue, water snake, but Gatoya for mythical serpent (see below); Tewa, Avanyo; Jemez, Wanakyudy'a.

Corn clan who also came from that Red Land; in Zuni tale he lives in the ocean, although near Zuni he frequents a mesa point.* Zuni women never immerse themselves in spring or pool lest Water Serpent impregnate them;[47] in tale, maidens do mate with Water Serpent, going into his spring. In Zuni-Hopi tale, sacrifice of the young is made to Water Serpent; the children are told to go down into the water to meet their "uncle," to check the flood that Water Serpent has caused. In general, Water Serpent controls flood (also earthquake or landslide), which is destructive, an expression of revenge or punishment, particularly in connection with sexual misconduct,† whether

* Between Horned Water Serpent and the mountain, cave-dwelling, double-headed snake (K'a''Dowi of Santo Domingo [White 4:202], Skatowe of Sia [Stevenson 1:125-26], Gatoya of Acoma, Ka'toya of the Hopi Antelope society, Ikaina, probably Rattlesnake, of Isleta) there have been some confusing identifications. In spite of his name, Skatowe of Sia is referred to as the plumed (horned) serpent of the North. The patron of the Antelope society is certainly Rattlesnake, yet he is referred to not only as Ka'toya but by a hybrid Hopi-Tewa term as Hish'avanyu, "ancient water serpent" (Parsons 59:555; Stephen 4:675, 697,718; cf. the horned rattler of Acoma, White 2: Pl. IIa). The snake swallowed in Aztec ceremony is a water snake (see p. 1020). In the Mishongnovi Snake-Antelope ceremony the snake-hunters perform ritual at a spring for Horned Water Serpent, praying to get snakes and not to be seen or bitten by them (Dorsey and Voth 2:188-89). Of course, between bringing in the live snakes of the desert and bringing in images of Horned Water Serpent from their springs there is some conceptual identity.

Like the horned or double or plural-headed serpents of the Aztec and Maya (Sahagún [b] Book XI, chap. v; Chilam Balam, 179), the Isleta or Sia serpent draws or with his breath sucks things to himself (cf. Hopi belief, Voth 5:217). Ikaina of Isleta and Huwaka of Sia, serpent of the zenith, are both closely related to the Sun.

The serpent painted on Acoma kiva walls is double-headed (Stirling), and so is Water Serpent of Shipaulovi (Wallis 1:12). Navaho refer to a double-headed serpent, a head at each end (Newcomb and Reichard, 53). On the Northwest Coast a double-headed or rather triple-headed serpent is referred to, a head at each end with a human head in the middle. When it moves, it causes earthquake (Boas).

† In September, 1918, a few days before I reached Zuni, there was a landslide in the mesa to the north. People were not running away to Corn Mountain (see Benedict 3:I, 11), but they were concerned. They were telling the story about the Mustard clan Rain chief who was angry over the adultery of his wife, and with prayer-sticks asked somebody, inferably Horned Water Serpent, to cause an earthquake. Rain chiefs from the Hopi were sent for, and they put down prayer-sticks in the flood caused by the earthquake (Parsons 53:47-48; and cf. Benedict 3:I, 10-11). Curtis reports a First Mesa incident that may be historic

promiscuous or, like that of the Tewa girls at the river, un-
yielding. Water Serpent is a punitive and fearsome personage.*

At Zuni the birds are referred to as "little servants"; they are
messengers or scouts, as elsewhere,† and they are sent to find
the lost Corn Maidens or any stray girl; but the prey animals,
including the eagle Knife-Wing, appear as quite independent
Spirits and as supernatural patrons of the societies. The home
of the "beast gods" is Shipap or, in Zuni, Shipapolima, in the
East; but the animals are also orientated and associated with
the colors of the cardinal directions, Lion with the north and
with yellow, the color of the north; Bear with the west and with
blue; Badger with the south and with red;‡ Wolf with the east
and with white; Eagle with the zenith; and Gopher or Shrew
with the nadir. In Hopi war cults Wildcat is associated with
the south, Kwatoko (see below) with the zenith, and Snake with
the nadir.[48]

The prey animals are associated with war, particularly in the
West and at Jemez. Mountain Lion is sand-painted on the
Hopi Snake society altar, lion paws lie on the altar, lion muzzle
hairs are tied to the warrior's bandoleer, also the muzzle hairs
of Wildcat and Bear. The claws of Bear, Badger, and Porcupine
were worn by Snake men or by warriors,§ and bone from the

or only a version of the Zuni tale. Once the Mustard lineage people in charge of
Water Serpent at Sichomovi were departing from the mesa as a result of feud—
a Mustard man had taken the wife of Crier chief—but they were persuaded into
returning, the Hopi being afraid lest Water Serpent cause an earthquake (Curtis,
18; cf. Parsons 42:181 ff.; and for a winged water serpent at Cochiti that de-
voured unmarried mothers and their infants, Dumarest, 229). Shipaulovi people
say, "If we baptize or go to school or if we fail to behead witches, Water Serpent
will shake the world and we shall be turned upside down" (Wallis 1:12).

* When Crow-Wing drew me a picture of the Tewa winter solstice altar, he
left out Water Serpent, whose clay image belongs on the altar, as being "too
dangerous to draw"; designs in themselves may be potent. The black pigment
for the cotton serpent effigies is taboo to young men lest it cause fatal swelling
(Stephen 4:309, 311). Black pigment is sprinkled over the clay image also.

† Hummingbird is Acoma's special messenger, but war captains or clowns
are called canyon wren or mocking-bird, see pp. 883, 885.

‡ See p. 365 for variations.

§ Stephen 4:98, 643, 699–700, 709. The Acoma War chief wore a necklace
of bear claws (Stirling).

scapulaṣ of a bear (or slain enemy) is put into the wristguard
of a warrior impersonation.* At the Snake initiation, Bear and
Lion are impersonated. A slain bear at Jemez is treated as a
slain enemy (see p. 909). Like scalps, the heads of slain bears
and mountain lions and of live eagles are washed, that is, the
creatures are taken into the tribe. Hopi too wash captive eagles.
Hopi eagles are killed on a set ceremonial day, offerings of miniature bows, arrows, and "dolls," and of food are made to them
and they are buried or cast away in a special place, an eagle
cemetery.† On a Walpi rock next to a tally of victims is a
pictograph of Kwatoko,⁴⁹ the giant eagle the Zuni and Acomans
call Knife-Wing.⁵⁰ Women are stolen by Knife-Wing, and scalps
are said to be taken by Kwatoko⁵¹ or Knife-Wing‡ or, as is said
at Zuni, "Our fathers the Beast Bow priests [animal war chiefs],
with their claws, tear from the enemy his water-filled covering
(scalp)."⁵²

From the beasts and birds of prey the Hunt shamans get
their powers, from mountain lion, wolf, wildcat, the blackfooted
ferret,⁵³ and an unidentified, perhaps a mythic, animal called in
Keresan *shuhu'na* (*shroho'na*),§ from eagle and several species
of hawks. The boomerang stick is said by Hopi to be modeled
after the wing of Sparrow-Hawk, a great hunter; he was the
first possessor of the stick which he carried under his wing; it is

* Voth 8:58. By their Sun father the Twins were given wrist guards of buffalo
hide, to be their "heart" (Acoma, Stirling).

† In a very small chamber in the Tano ruin of San Cristobal were found the
bones of three eagles (Nelson, 63).

‡ On the meal road to the sand-painting of Knife-Wing on the Wood society
altar are placed hairs taken from the heads of Knife-Wing's victims (Stevenson
2:462).

§ The same term is used by Hopi: *ʋzo''hona'*, Beaglehole 2:9; Stephen 4:
Glossary, *zroho'na*, associated with southeast, an animal in size between coyote
and fox that kills an animal by penetrating its ear (Cochiti; Goldfrank 3:85). A
Zuni who had lived at Laguna equated the Zuni Hunters or Coyote society with
Laguna Shuhuna (Kroeber 2:145, n.1). Boas and Goldfrank incline to identify
the creature with weasel (cf. Parsons 20:127, n. 3), chief of the underground
(burrowing) animals (Acoma, Stirling). Weasel is a prey animal, and weasel
pelts are used on the Mishongnovi Snake-Antelope standards, but weasel in Hopi
is *pivani*. White suggests the jaguar which formerly ranged into New Mexico,
and that the penetrating animal is shrew operating by anus as at Santo Domingo.

referred to as his wing. A Hopi youth got the stick from him.* Coyote may teach hunting ritual (Zuni)† as the hunter god of the West, or bring in buffalo (Taos), but Eagle and Mountain Lion are the particular patrons of the hunt society. The Hunt chief (Acoma) or custodian of hunt fetishes (Zuni) was an Eagle clansman. The lion figurines of the Zuni Hunters society are fed when members of the society go deer-hunting, and a bit of venison is rubbed on their mouths; also the fetish in the hunter's pouch is buried in the deer's heart (Zuni, Acoma, Santa Ana)[54] or dipped in the blood (Cochiti, Laguna).[55] In Hopi-Tewa tale after Handmark Boy has killed a witch mountain sheep, the mountain lion in his pouch says to him, "That is not a real mountain sheep. It was a man to kill you. We had better look for a real sheep." Handmark Boy's figurine turns into a big lion and chases a real mountain sheep and kills it. Again, on a bear hunt, his mountain lion says to Handmark Boy, "My father, stop here! That bear is asleep. Soon he will wake up and attack you. Take me out!" Handmark Boy takes him out. "I will stay here," says Mountain Lion. "Shoot the bear in his paw when he wakes and stands up and raises his arms. If he is strong enough to kill you, run to me!" Handmark Boy cuts out the bear's heart and drags him to Mountain Lion, who puts him on his back and carries him until they come near town where Mountain Lion turns into a "little lion" and goes back into the pouch. The hunt society of Jemez is called Mountain Lion society; and on the hunt Laguna War captains are addressed as Mountain Lion or as Shuhuna.

In connections other than hunting, Lion and the other animals are guardians or protectors.‡ Their stone images are always prominent on altars; and a like guardian is kept in the family

* Stephen 4:100. A near guardian spirit episode.

† Cushing 1:26; Cushing 6:414 ff.; Bunzel 5:1045. The Zuni Hunters society is referred to as Suskikwe, Coyote people. Their chief impersonates Coyote in the Scalp dance (see pp. 629, 634–35).

‡ As eponymous clan associates, though hardly totemic, they were formerly offered prayer-sticks or addressed in prayer (Zuni, eponymous prey animals at the full moon [Cushing 1:19]; Hopi [Parsons 55:38]; Laguna [Parsons 33:212–13]).

(Hopi, Laguna, Acoma, San Juan).⁵⁶ A Hopi traveler will carry a "watcher" with him which he places inside his pillow to give him dream warning of danger. Keresan and Tewan doctors may give animal images to their patient to protect him against the witch who has been making him sick. The prey animals have been considered mediators between man and Poshaiyanki of the Zuni curing societies.⁵⁷ The animals are the givers of medicinal plants which are named for them, as, for example, the root which is called lion medicine or the root of aster (ericæ folius. Rothrock) famous as "bear medicine."*

Of all the curing societies, Keresan, Zuni, or Tewan, Bear is the particular patron. The doctors or shamans are called bears;† by drawing on the bear paws which lie on the altar the shamans impersonate bears; the paw is the equivalent of the mask. It is believed that shamans have power literally to turn into bears,‡ just as bears may divest themselves of their skins and become people.§ Bears and bear shamans, they who "can call the Bear"

---

* Stephen 4:863, n.1. The Cochiti hunter rubs on himself as a strength-giving tonic the root of an unidentified plant called lion medicine (Goldfrank 3:86; Stevenson 2:576). This is used by the Cactus war society of Zuni.

All this is close to the widespread concept of getting power from animals or plants. Plant medicine is a form of power.

† The members of Zuni curing societies are called "animals"; the chiefs are White Bear, Wildcat, Mountain Lion (Benedict 3:I, 64); cf. p. 232.

‡ "One time at Nambé there was a man who did not believe in the Bear men. He thought the Bear man carried what he sucked out in his bear paws. This man became an Outside chief. When they are curing, two Outside chiefs are sent to watch the Bear men, to see where they go, into lake or sky. Two Bears took the Outside chief to the lake. Then the Bears jumped in. They stayed a long time. Then one Bear came out, and told the Outside chief to follow. He went behind the church; the Outside chief followed him. 'My helper is going ahead,' he said to the Outside chief. He went to the middle of the plaza. A real bear came out from the stone shrine and went to the east. (It was the Bear left behind in the lake.) Out from the shrine came the man bear and the real bear, his partner. There were two bears there. The doubting Outside chief now began to believe. 'Perhaps they are really bear,' he said" (Parsons 49:303–4).

Note the characteristically Tewa references to supernatural "helper" or "partner," the same English terms that are used elsewhere for guardian spirit (cf. Ray, 594).

§ A conspicuous belief among the Kwakiutl of the Northwest Coast and in California. This belief in metamorphosis is related to nagualism, the early

(Zuni), carry on their ceremonies jointly, the bears visiting the ceremonies of the societies* and after death the shamans going to live with their bear colleagues. In the Zuni tale of the bear wife, after the bears dig the youth up from his grave and carry him to Shipapolima, the animal society men hold their ceremony, restore him to life, and teach him their song sequences, their prayers, and their medicines. They make him a corn fetish, bidding him join one of the "life-giving" societies on his return to Zuni. When the boy spends the night gambling instead of in a society assemblage, he "really" dies and goes to Shipapolima to stay forever.[58]

Badger is the Hopi curer animal.† He owns herbs and roots which "he is always scratching out."[59] Badger is the curer patron of the Poboshwĭmkya, a society that was lapsing fifty years ago. Badger "came up" at a kachina dance at Oraibi, carrying his medicines and his exorcising buzzard feathers. The kachina said they would become Badger clan people,[60] and ever since it has been considered proper for the medicine chief of the society to be a Badger clansman. A Badger clansman is sent to collect the herbs requisite for the Snake society medicine (Oraibi).

Antelope heads are placed like fetishes on or near the altars of the Antelope society (Oraibi) and of the Agave society (Walpi). Antelope horns are worn on the head by the Horn

---

Mexican theory of the animal double or familiar, and more remotely to the guardian-spirit concept of the Plains tribes.

* In curing sickness, the Isletan Bear doctors have to summon their partners, the real bears. When they stand up to cure, they put a plant into their mouth and become real bears. In their medicine bowl they can see where their partners have gone. Bear chief will look in and say, "Our helper is at Durango or California or up in the sky or underground." On Isletan (and Acoman) ceremonial walls bears are painted with a shaman's rattle in the right forepaw and his two eagle feathers in the left. Initiates are made bear. From under the blanket wrapped around him and his ceremonial mother the initiate appears as a bear. "That is the way they are born, in the form of a bear" (Parsons 52:316; also 447–48; cf. Lummis 2:86).

† In a Laguna tale Badger Old Man appears as doctor to revive a witch-killed girl (Boas 2:58). The Acoma society fetish is the usual corn ear but it is called *ho'nani*, Hopi for badger (*hona'ni*). At Isleta a badger paw called Badger Old Woman is placed on the ground near the parturient woman by her doctor.

society or carried in the hand. Antelope appears to be a medicine animal.

Buzzard feathers are used in exorcism, but Buzzard, the scavenger or cleanser, may work on his own, purifying the town (Laguna)[61] or serving as patron kachina of the Giant society (Cochiti).[62] At Taos the bird may not be killed because it has helped recover slain warriors. Acoma War captains are called Canyon Wren (*shuti*) and Mockingbird and in performing their duties are said to behave like those birds. From Mockingbird the nations get their languages in Hopi myth, and some of the societies their songs.[63]

The animals cause sickness as well as cure it. They frighten people, and fright is a cause of sickness.[64] When the Bear doctor slaps with his bear paw, it is to cure a person from fear of bear,[65] just as Wildcat and others scratched and terrified and then restored the Tewan who was to be known as White Wildcat Man (see p. 250). Possibly the handling of snakes in snake rituals is another expression of this type of cure for a like type of fear sickness. Disease from certain insects is different; they get into a person's body, and in the case of ants at least they have to be brushed out. Ants are vindictive; disturbing their "house," particularly urinating on it, will always anger them and necessitate treatment by Ant doctor or society. Venereal disease is associated by the Hopi with wood lice and with an insect said to be found today only in a fossilized form. These creatures are the patrons of two of the women's societies. Dragonfly is an impersonation in the Shuma'kwe society (Zuni)* which at Hano cures sore eyes.† Beetles (Hopi) and ants (Zuni) are helpful

* Benedict 3:II, 1 n. 1. It is taboo to kill a dragonfly (Zuni; *ibid.*, II, 9) which has supernatural power (San Juan; Parsons 42:10). Dragonfly, also bees, are mentioned as shamanistic creatures in San Juan myth (see p. 250).

† Parsons 40:104. The Hano Shumaikoli impersonation is blind (Stephen 4:343). For Hano and Laguna myth explanation why Shumaikoli is both lame and blind see Parsons 42:254 ff.; Parsons 20:116. The dragonfly Shumaikoli masks of Zuni have small eyes, and, if a Zuni woman looks at one during pregnancy, her child will have sore eyes.

Since Dragonfly is associated with the game animals, possibly he is to be identified with the Hano-Hopi insect kachina Nepokwai'i or Kokopelli, a hunter who seduces girls or makes them bridal moccasins and whose "hump" is really a

creatures in war, covering tracks.* For this reason and others
the Ant society has ritual functions in Zuni Scalp or War dance.
Hopi have locust medicine for wounds, for dreaming true, and
for warm weather,† proprietary medicine of the Flute societies
on whose altar tiles Locust is depicted playing the flute (Walpi).‡
(That "humpbacked flute player" so intriguing to the archeolo-
gist in the Southwest is Locust.)[66] Beetles are brewed in the
medicine of the warlike Snake society. "Beetle is the warrior's
pet," and there is one in the fetish of the War society chief,[67] just
as there is said to be a frog, a rain-caller, in the fetish of a Zuni
Rain chief. A stone frog figures on the altar of the Water-Corn
chieftaincy of Walpi.[68] With the Snake society of Sia the Kapina
society is associated, and Spider is the Kapina patroness or
mother. "Spider is our mother," says the Antelope chief of
Shipaulovi; "she is the mother of all."[69] In Keresan mythology
Sussĭstinnako is the universal mother, and Sussĭstinnako is
Spider.[70] The War Brothers always have a grandmother, and
usually she is Spider Woman. She has her own stone image
(Walpi) and her own shrine, where the Antelope society chief

---

gift-containing sack. His prototype may be represented in the pictographs,
shooting mountain sheep.

* Compare Navaho Hail Chant. Navaho insects protect and warn (Newcomb and Reichard, 65–66).

† In Shipaulovi tale the Locusts keep their kiva warm by playing their
flutes, and in the same way they melt the snow for the Snakes. In winter prayer-
stick-making, priests (? Flute chiefs) will throw pieces of a locust on the fire
"because the smoke and odor bring warm weather" (Voth 5:217 ff.). The
Locusts sing:

> Hao my fathers, hao my mothers!
> Drab Flutes, Blue Flutes [the societies]
> My fathers, beautiful living
> In summer will begin for us.
> In summer blossoms wave, in summer blossoms will sway.

‡ Locust, the unwinking, is accounted a brave man. The Clouds shot their
bolts through him, and he merely continued to play on his flute (Stephen 3: 5–6).
After the Emergence, the people shot Locust with arrows; he died and then
came back to life (Cushing 7:167–68).

asks her to keep away storm and sickness and send rain (Mishongnovi).[71] She is the patroness of the Spider clan and Blue Flute society of Oraibi.[72] Ritually Spider Woman is associated with war* but in all the Pueblo tales where she figures she is a benevolent, helpful old woman who takes care of stray girls (even the Earth Mothers) or bereft husbands or anybody in distress, having ideas or medicines for all emergencies. When the Hopi girl, Cactus Flower, is being tested by the kachina, one of the tests is not to weep at a song they sing about her unhappy experience in leaving home. She does weep, but Spider Grandmother is sitting on her cheek in her familiar role of ear prompter or monitor, and this time swallows the tears as they fall. To another girl Spider Old Woman gives medicine to rub on her hands so that her wafer-bread in baking will increase in size.[73] In a tale about T'aiowa stealing Yellow Cloud Boy's wife, Spider Grandmother gives Yellow Cloud Boy some medicine to spray on T'aiowa, and she herself sprays medicine in front of T'aiowa to make him slow in the race against Yellow Cloud Boy in which the stake is the woman or rather all the women T'aiowa has stolen. Again, after the Eagles have rescued Blue Corn Girl and Yellow Corn Girl who have been changed into coyotes, they summon Grandmother Spider to turn the coyotes back to girls by plunging them into boiling water and twisting off their skins after medicine has been spat into the water by Spider. In the Laguna tale of freeing the kachina from their underground prison, the Gumeyoish are at a loss what to do until they are hailed by Spider Old Woman. "Grandchildren!" she calls, "Come here!" They look all about, but see nobody. She says, "Be careful, grandchildren, do not step on me! I am under this weed." Then she directs them to Badger Old Woman, that is, to the maternal house of the Badger clan. "I am always glad to help people who are in trouble," says Spider Grandmother after feeding the starving Zuni boy from her inexhaustible basket.[74]

Coyote, who introduces death (Hopi), confounds the stars,

---

* She is the patroness of old women (Hopi) whose conduct toward the scalp of the slain enemy is significant (Taos, Zuni, Hopi; pp. 351, 624, 644, 680).

scorches the earth,* and figures in almost all the humoresque animal tales, is not associated with any cult or society in particular; he teaches witchcraft, and in tales he may figure as a witch animal or, as noted, as a hunter; he is offered prayer-sticks by hunters.† To Taos Coyote first brought the buffalo, instituting the Buffalo dance. He warned Taos people of the coming of enemies, and he is a weather prophet. When he calls by day, it means rain; at night, enemies or sickness (Hano). To White House where Keres lived after the Emergence Coyote brought fire, wrapped carefully in his tail by the underground Mother.

Stone and fossil have a place among Pueblo spirits. Fossilized wood is a fetish of the Hopi goddess of game animals, Childbirth Water Woman, and of Jemez war gods and scouts. Ancient stone hoes called Chamahia by Hopi are altar fetishes (Hopi, Acoma). They represent the Stone people (Hopi), "people of the stone when it had speech and life," living in the four corners of the earth; from the four quarters, from the Chiefs of the Directions, the Chamahia are invoked.[75] Unworked conical stones are also called Chamahia and, dressed with feathers and beads, stand on altars, representing mountains (Laguna). Fetishes called Tsamahi'a and Tsamai'ye stand either side of the altar[76] that the Kaʙina society chief places to instal the Acoma War chiefs. The War gods are identified with Chamahia (Acoma, Sia, Santo Domingo). A Santo Domingo who has served four times as War captain representing Oyoyewi, the younger War god brother, bears the honorific title of Tsamahi'a.[77] The War gods of Taos enshrined on the mountainside are referred to as the two Stone Men.‡ Elder Brother stands as a great

* He attempts to carry the sun across the sky (Laguna, Boas 2:31–32): a widely distributed tale which fits well into Pueblo notions about Coyote as one who tries to do everything and fails at everything, a marplot.

† And asked to chase and tire out the deer the night before the hunt (Mishongnovi; Beaglehole 2:6). For Coyote as a hunt patron at Zuni see Cushing 6:401 ff.

‡ In the stone cult of an early coastal culture of northern Peru there were some curious Pueblo parallels. The sacred stones were sons of Sun, who in anger had turned them into stone. Near by were great mounds of small stones or sticks left by worshipers (Means, 61).

rock at the salt deposit in Grand Canyon.[78] The Kaye' of Tewa include not only images of Bear and Lion but shrinelike rocks, selected for form or color, and set on end, in the hills. Prayer-meal is sprinkled on these stones, Stone Old Man or Stone Child or Stone Old Woman (Montezuma's grandmother!)[79] and people ask them for what they want. In Nambé tale the parents and kindred of the Blue Corn Girls are described as lying under the shrine in the court, turned to stone, and the stone on top of the shrine is called Spirit Stone Old Man. The supreme fetish or Mother of the Tewa Town chiefs of the Winter moiety is a "white" stone, their Ice Mother.[80] A Laguna kachina is mentioned as having been turned into stone, when the soft mud world was hardening. A concretion in the dance rock shrine of Walpi is called Hehe'ya kachina.[81] About the concretions or other stones kept in medicine bundles (see p. 329) not much is known, but at Isleta it is said that these stones get power from the animals whose shapes they resemble.

After the Zuni flood, when the mud hardened, the refugees to Corn Mountain found the sacrificial boy and girl turned to stone, two stone pinnacles. Mountains themselves are sacred; they are represented by altar effigies (Laguna, as noted; Isleta, Taos, First Mesa; see p. 330), named for particular mountains (Isleta, Taos). Yet the degree that mountains are personified is not at all clear; they are so closely associated with the kachina or with the Chiefs of the Color-Directions.

The quarry from which Hopi bakeslabs are to be taken is addressed with prayer-feathers, and on the way home, if the party stops to eat, the slabs must be fed also (Oraibi),[82] just as in the house the slab is fed by making on it four longitudinal marks of dampened wafer-bread,[83] and in every baking by throwing the first bit into the fire (Mishongnovi). The quarry has given of itself. There are many tutelary beings who "give themselves." In Sia tale, Utsĕt, Corn Mother, plants bits of her heart to produce corn. The Corn Maidens of Zuni "give their flesh" to the people. To potters, Clay Woman of Corn Mountain "gives her flesh." Zuni prayer-stick-makers refer in prayers to "our mothers" Clay Woman, Black Paint Woman, Cotton Woman.[84]

> With our mother
> Cotton Woman
> Even a roughly spun cotton thread
> Four times encircling them and tying it around,
> With a rain-bringing hair feather,
> We gave them human form.
> With the flesh of our two mothers,
> Black Paint Woman,
> Clay Woman,
> Clothing their plume wands with their flesh
> We gave them human form.

Salt Woman, who now lives at Zuni Salt Lake, gives herself, primarily to the Parrot clan (Acoma, Laguna). One of the War Brothers turns himself into salt and thus gives himself to Hopi travelers to Grand Canyon.[85] White Shell Woman lives in the west, and into her house Sun descends at night;[86] but, wherever among the towns she has bathed, she has left the rubbings from her body, white olivella shells. Ashes Man yields himself to the Sia doctor to make good medicine, ashes being ever prophylaxis against disease or witchcraft. (Ash Boys or Poker Boys figure in many tales of Cochiti, Tewa, Mishongnovi.) Awl Man comes to life in order to befriend the abandoned little boy.[87] Flint Boys of the color-directions are asked to help cut wood for prayer-sticks (Acoma).[88] Poseyemu, himself conceived through a piñon nut, is the sender of piñon.

Trees and plants are asked to give themselves, since they are alive, like the little spruce trees planted in the Hopi dance court and called brother and sister, or like the pine and piñon on which a face is indicated before they are set at the hatch of the chamber of the Zuni Big Firebrand society,[89] or like the two little ones, brother and sister or two brothers who live in datura, Jamestown weed (Zuni) or in *tenatsali* and show to one in trance the whereabouts of lost persons or articles, or why a horse or burro has died suddenly, or, like bear root, the witch who is causing a sickness.[90] There is a special plant in their cactus bed on Corn Mountain which the Zuni Cactus society addresses with a beaded prayer-feather.[91] Cactus Grandmother is brought in from "her town" to the altar of the Tewa Winter Town chieftaincy and passed from hand to hand, demonstrating her power of becoming smaller and finally vanishing as she returns to her town where she is visited at the conclusion of the ceremony and fed corn meal. In spite of all that handling she will appear to be growing as a fresh and beautiful plant.[92] Yucca is impersonated as a kachina, Yucca Old Man, chief of a kiva entered from the heart of the yucca (Hopi).[93]

Game animals are all impersonated by mask or pelt and addressed with prayer-feathers or prayer-sticks, and by hunters animals are asked to reveal themselves or to "send their children." A dead deer is laid on the ground, head to the east, like a dead person; it is covered with an embroidered blanket and a necklace of beads, and sprinkled with meal and smoked (Zuni, Laguna, Isleta, Cochiti [smoked only], Santa Ana, Sia, Jemez).[94] "We are glad you have reached this house," Zuni householders address the deer, "we hope you will come many times."* When a Hopi sets a coyote or fox trap, he puts down a prayer-stick and a shell bead or bit of turquoise and invites the animal in.[95] Coyote may be impersonated in the Hopi Buffalo dance as Buffalo's younger brother.†

The Pueblos are animists. Not only are all the precious yields of nature animated by spirits, but spirit is incorporate in simulacres of a corn ear, in scalp or buckskin taken from the enemy, in shield or drum, in staff or standard, in lightning-riven wood‡ or fire-stick or fossilized wood, in the clay nodule of the kickball race, in bakestone, in crystals or weathered stones, perhaps in anything that seems fantastic or unusual to its finder. To the Zuni "not only are night and day, wind, clouds, and trees pos-

* Benedict 3:I, 94. Salt was treated and addressed in much the same way, and even valuable clothes. "We ask you to tell other garments to come also," say winners of stick-race bets (*ibid.*, 43, 101).

† Stephen 4:127–28. The coyote head is over the head of the impersonator with the pelt down his back. Across his eyes, a narrow line of black, and black spots on his forearm.

‡ Of which a cradle should be made (Zuni, Acoma), also images of the Zuni War gods, also prayer-sticks.

sessed of personality, but even articles of human manufacture, such as houses, pots, and clothing, are alive and sentient."[96] Since Hopi not only address prayer-feathers to beings associated with their clans at the winter solstice ceremony but fasten prayer-feathers to almost everything that they value, to what we consider the most inanimate of things, say a stove or a watch, they may be considered quite as systematic animists as Zuni. "The universe is endowed with the same breath," remarks Ĭn'tiwa, the Powamu society chief, "rocks, trees, grass, earth, all animals, and men."* This ideology probably exists in the East. I am fairly certain it occurs at Taos, although the clues are less substantial.

The Pueblos are also by way of being fetishists, for the spirit is not always present in the sacred object, but comes and goes. A corn-meal "road" is sprinkled from entrance to altar or to fetish on altar, for the Spirit to travel in on. When a mask is removed and waved around the head four times, the Spirit is bidden farewell. "Go home, my friend!" says the impersonator.

Fetishists, animists, animatists, Pueblos are confirmed anthropomorphists. The greatest distinction Zuni can make between a spirit and a man is to call the one a "raw person" and the other a "cooked person," referring to the heated sand bed a human infant is placed on at birth.† All Pueblo Spirits act humanly— Clouds, kachina, and the Dead, cosmic beings, the animals, birds, and insects, indwelling spirits of trees, plants, and stones— all have human tastes and interests, all live under familiar economic or social conditions.

---

* Stephen 4:706. When Ĭn'tiwa's uncle was once passing a cliff, a lizard in a crevice called to him to come in. He found the Lizard people walking about like other people and the Grass people, about as high as his knee, spoke to him in rustling tones. Rattlesnake chief said, "Put your feet on our shoulders and walk across!" Cottonseed Boy is mentioned at Mishongnovi (Nequatewa, 104).

† Keres use these terms but, curiously enough, apply them quite differently. The "cooked" are the initiated, the "raw" are the uninitiated, more particularly when they are serving as if initiated.

Papago refer to the man experienced in war or eagle-killing or salt-collecting as "ripe," and Underhill compares this reference with Keresan usage.

The Spirits are well housed. A ring around Sun (or Moon) is called his house (Mishongnovi),[97] but Sun also has his house in a hill or mesa that may be seen from the town; and in myth Sun was visited in his sky house by his adventurous sons who finally settled down within high commanding places. "To you whose houses are covered with the mountain tops I give shells, to Yellow Ahayuta, Blue Ahayuta, Red Ahayuta, White Ahayuta, Many-colored Ahayuta, Black Ahayuta,"[98] say the warrior impersonators in the Zuni Scalp ceremony. "I think it will be well for you to make your shrine in Sandía Mountain, high above the earth, and not return to the people of the earth," Sun says to the War Brothers of Sia. "All right, my father," answers Maase'we, "we are contented and happy to do as you say."

Maize Mother lives at Shipapu, whence she never emerges. "I will remain in my house below" (to be visited by the dead), she says to her children of Sia. Masauwü is a restless night-walker, but he also has a house below, whither the dead journey. The dead and the kachina are all town- or house-dwellers, underground or underwater. Tewa Cloud kachina live under springs or pools. The place where a projecting kiva ladder has been seen is pointed out to the youth of Taos when the townspeople make their pilgrimage to Blue Lake, under which live those dead who become kachina. Zuni kachina and Zuni dead, or some of them, live in a town under the Lake of Whispering Waters.

Far south of Zuni on the shore of the encircling ocean, stand the white houses of the Uwanami, packed even to the fourth inner room with thick mist, the breath of these Cloud beings.[99] The Hopi Clouds have houses in the cardinal directions, although no one knows just where they are.[100] The Horned Water Serpents are well housed in their springs. After the mother of Water Jar Boy dies and with her son enters the spring of the boy's father, Red Horned Serpent, the boy's aunts say that they are glad their child has come to live in their house.[101] Around the Hopi mesas Wind has several houses, rock fissures which harbor air currents.

Of any fiesta bower it will be said, "They made a house for the Saint." When the Saint's house, the church, is in ruins, as at Pecos or Zuni, she is sheltered in the house of her guardian, the Sun society chief at Jemez or at Zuni a Rain chief where she is fed daily, like other fetishes, and taken out on ceremonial occasion. Images of the war spirits also "live" in the house of their guardians. All fetishes—bundles, befeathered corn ears, stones, and masks—are given shelter or protection in some way —in boxes or jars or bags, often in wall niches or closets. At Zuni certain masks are kept in certain houses, it is said, because, when the respective supernaturals visited Zuni, they picked out those houses to live in, knowing that in them they would be well fed and cared for. Scalps have been well sheltered, being kept in small stone houses or "scalp houses," in kiva niches, or in caves, as are at Zuni the skulls of prey animals.

In the shrines where prayer-sticks are offered, the Spirits do not live, although the shrines may be referred to as their house— Yellow Woman's house (Cochiti), Sun's house or Echo's house (Zuni), Kachina house (Hopi)—and the Spirits visit the shrine "to get their feathers." In Hopi the generic word for shrine is *pahoki*, prayer-stick house. *Pahoki* are often named for the house or abiding place of the supernatural to whom the *pahoki* is dedicated, e.g., the Sun in First Mesa opinion lives at Mucho, a gap in the mesa five miles or more to the northeast, here is "Sun's house," but on First Mesa itself there is a Sun shrine called Mucho. At Oraibi there are proxy houses for Black Mountain and San Francisco Mountains, the homes of many kachina.[102]

Like men, the Spirits are of a migratory habit. Sun makes his diurnal journey, in Keresan tale, to carry his mask or shield across the skies, or, in Isletan tale to make his three daily stations, stopping at the midmost to descend to earth and "meet his sons." And his winter and summer courses vary; he has "to be turned back" to summer or to winter. His rate of travel may vary, in Hopi opinion, for the ceremonies may date according to whether Sun has been traveling fast or slowly. His journey is regulated by foot races (Taos, Picurís, Isleta) or by the pace of the prayer-stick messengers to his "house" (Hopi).

War gods were great travelers. Ma'sewi of Laguna was sent forth by the underground Mothers to the four corners of the world; his travel-worn feet dripped blood.[103] The War Brothers were always going off whither their grandmother told them not to go, but their first distant trip was skyward to visit their father Sun. Later they roamed the country, generally in trouble if not making or curing it.

Sia War gods travel on the rainbow, as in Tewa tale do Cloud Youths when they court Corn Maidens or other maidens. A Cloud Youth may even take his girl with him on his rainbow, after first bidding her close her eyes. "I am tired," the girl will say. "I can't go farther." "Let me carry your load," says Cloud Boy, and takes from her the meal she is carrying to his mother. She goes on again, but again she grows weary. "I can't go any farther." "Well, my house is a long way off. Close your eyes and don't open them until I tell you!" So he puts up his rainbow, and they go on the rainbow until they get to his house, and the girl opens her eyes to look upon a beautiful place of grass and flowers.

Ritual in connection with several kachina consists largely of telling a migration tale. Thus at Zuni the night the "kachina come" migration tales or talks are recited or intoned for hours by Long Horn kachina and by the Shalako. At the initiation ceremony of the Kachina society Kiaklo talks in like vein at all the kivas, and among Hopi at the corresponding ceremony of Powamu so does Müy'ingwa, who is not a kachina but who taught the Hopi, remarked the Town chief of Shipaulovi, "all we know about seeds and vegetation."[104]

Nowadays the kachina travel, if only to leave their homes under lake or spring, on mountain summit or underground to come to town to dance with their human representatives or to get the offerings made them of feathers or beads or food. Zuni kachina stand behind the dancers, each behind his own mask, and when the dancers go to "wide-water" to unmask, the kachina turn to ducks and fly back to Kachina town. Similarly at the close of Shalako all kachina dance masks are taken to the east side of town to Red Bank, whence the "kachina go" to the east, on a trip to Shipapolima (or in forthright Acoma terms they die; see p. 539), not returning to Zuni until four days after the winter solstice ceremony. The *sipapu* exit of the Hopi kiva is opened for the kachina also four days after the winter solstice ceremony; but the Hopi kachina depart in July at the Home-going (Nima'n) kachina ceremony, to stay away almost half the year.

Salt Old Woman is ever a migratory spirit. She takes offense and deserts to a distant place,[105] at Zuni taking Turquoise Boy along. Zuni's Saint was a wanderer. She lived in the west as a Mexican girl who never went out until Sun impregnated her. Then she escaped from the soldiers who were going to kill her, to Kachina town where she lay in and bore twins. Then mother and children became "other sorts of persons"; they became stone. The mother lives today at Acoma, "because she likes their dances." The elder of the twin sisters lives at Zuni; the younger went south where other Zuni people are said to live.[106] Poseyemu or Poshaiyanki of the Montezuma-Jesus cycle of hero tales also disappeared into the south or else traveled through all the pueblos and the world over before he disappeared in the usual way into the earth.[107] As for Ne'wekwe, because he was Sun's child, "he could travel across the whole wide world in one day."[108]

Ceremonials of bringing Water Serpent into town indicate that he, too, is a traveler. Processions are made with his image to springs (Hopi, Jemez). There are somewhat confused reports that he lives in the mountains as well as in valley springs. Possibly it is or was believed, as in Middle America, that Water Serpent has to be brought down from the heights, where he stays part of the year, to the springs or pools where he stays when rain is wanted. Rattlesnake, who hibernates in winter, must also be brought into town.

The Spirits are farmers* and hunters;† like Kwatoko they kill the enemy or they are war leaders like Po'haha, the Tewa girl who was sent to fight by her uncle because she was such a tomboy;[109] or they make war like the Acoma kachina who, enraged at being ridiculed, destroyed almost all the townspeople; or, like the Zuni Ky'anakwe, who captured three kachina from Kachina town before the War Brothers learned that the heart of the giant leader, Chakwena Woman, was in her rattle; and the Spirits run races and play games. The War Twins are such notorious gamesters that their Zuni altars are dressed with miniature gambling implements, and they are invited to be present at games of hidden-ball. Kaina'nyi of Laguna is a gambler kachina.[110] In Hopi and Tewa tales the Cloud Boys are ever quick runners, winning in races because they are Cloud Boys. Wolf Boy is also a successful racer.[111] Since, after death, people continue in their usual interests, deceased stick-racers are addressed in prayer: "My forefathers who were stick-race men (managers), and you who ran in the stick-races in your lives, choose our side and help us win. We are giving you valuable things (wafer-bread and turquoise)."[112]

There is family life among the Spirits, more particularly among Hopi kachina, who may be represented in family groups like the bogey Soyok or Natashka or as Tömash and her boys, the whipper Tungwup kachina. Hahaiyi Woman, mother of the kachina and wet nurse to the Water Serpents, is thought of as the firstborn daughter of Sand Altar Woman, wife of Masau-

---

* Bunzel 6:162. All the kachina from Kachina town come to plant, cultivate, and harvest for the abandoned Zuni children (Benedict 3:II, 3–6). Kachina, likewise Masauwü, come out to plant for a Hopi field party (see p. 866). Nawish kachina (Keres) are expert farmers; and on going out to their fields Acomans ask them to help.

† Any kachina may go ahunting (see p. 283, n.*), but specific kachina huntsmen are, of course, Coyote kachina (Zuni), Kokopölö (Hopi) or Nepokwa'i' (Tewa). In Tewa tale Nepokwa'i', a big black man, comes in with a buckskin from which he will make moccasins for the bride (Parsons 42:206). Chaque (blackfaced Chakwena), great hunter and moccasin-maker, is asked for help by Acoma moccasin-makers (Stirling). The War Brothers are always ahunting.

wü and sister of Müy'ingwa.* Hahaiyi's counterpart at Zuni, Hemokyätsik[i], is great-grandmother of the kachina, Koyemshi Old Woman being their mother. Pa'utiwa, kachina chief, has a son, Cottonhead, and a daughter who marries a Keresan kachina.[113] K'imash[o], chief of Acoma's kachina abode, also has a daughter, White Woman, whom he marries to the son of Sun, the clown or jester[114] called Paiyatemu, the Youth (Ne'wekwe youth), by Keres or Zuni. Zuni kachina at large have children who are impersonated by young boys, the youngest members of the Kachina society.[115]

Moon at Zuni is the younger sister of Sun. In tale Sun begets the War Twins and other twins. Zuni and Hopi impute any twin birth to solar agency. The act of intercourse is supposed to have taken place in the daytime, with one child begot by the man, the other by Sun.† At Taos a male twin is called Sun child. Pa'utiwa, Zuni kachina chief, is another begetter of twins on a human mother. Like causing like, the War Twins themselves beget twins; although of a promiscuous raping habit, they even settle down into matrimony. Knife-Wing also steals girls, and so does Arrowpoint Boy of Santa Clara. Paiyatemu (Laguna, Zuni) and T'aiowa (Hopi) are attractive seducers. Various kachina or Cloud Boys go courting and have marital adventures. There are Kachina or Cloud Girls as well as Kachina or Cloud Boys. Hopi society patrons are generally paired: Snake Youth and Maiden, Antelope Youth and Maiden, Flute Youth and Maiden, Marau Man and Maiden. Wind Old Woman is paired with an old man (Tewa,‡ Taos, Laguna); even Salt Old Woman

* Stephen 4:261. This is consistent with the identification of Sand Altar Woman with Iyatiku, the Keresan Corn Mother, since Iyatiku created the kachina.

† Consistently with the idea of double paternity, one twin is named not by the father's kinswomen but by adoptive clanswomen (Oraibi; Eggan). In some such practice may lie the explanation of why at Zuni the War God Twins are taken into different clans, Bear and Deer. But why do the Acoma Maize Mothers, sisters, but not twins, adopt different clans?

‡ To be or become woman-man is a common Tewa term for the possession of supernatural power (Parsons 49:262–63) as if Power or Spirit were thought of as of dual gender. Compare a like conception of duality in the pantheons of Middle America.

(Sia, Cochiti),* even Spider Old Woman (Walpi) is given a mate. In Tewan tale Morning Star and Evening Star have been earthly mates. She dies, and, "before they send her away," he follows her. In spite of desire, he cannot bring himself to sleep with her and escapes. She pursues. In an arrow, they are shot up into the sky to continue forever flight and pursuit.

In the pantheistic as in the ceremonial organization there is little or no supremacy, no high god, every Spirit controlling his own sphere without interference from others, but there are some ordered relationships. Distinctions prevail between group kachina and kachina chiefs who are in charge of cult groups or special persons, and of whom special performance is expected. Of all the Zuni kachina, Pa'utiwa is chief, with powers of presiding, of appointment, and of instituting customs. "When we have need of anything, Pa'utiwa picks out someone (from the kachina) to do it," says a Zuni, "and that is the way we do it from that time on."[116] Eototo is chief among the kachina who visit First Mesa; and among Keresan and Tewa kachina K'imash° (Acoma), Heruta, and Djeng sendo appear as leaders. The primacy of the north holds among kachina who are grouped by direction-color, as also among the spirit animals of the directions or to whatever plant, tree, or star (Hano) beings, the direction-color order is applied.

The spirit patrons or prototypes of the Clown societies are described as messengers or jesters for Sun or Moon (Keres, Zuni). The Zuni kachina Shulawitsi is called Sun's speaker. Kiaklo is speaker to Pa'utiwa. Long Horn and his followers are war chiefs; the Shalako are war scouts or messengers. The Cloud beings of the Tewa have each his messenger. Through identification with Morning Star, the messenger of Sun, the Tewa war god may be thought of as Sun's war chief. When Badger Old Woman undertakes to free the Laguna kachina from their imprisonment, she asks them who their chief is. Kauk'a'-

---

* Her grandson (Benedict 2:7). Salt Woman is generally associated with the War Brothers unless Spider Grandmother usurps her place. In Hopi tradition the Brothers have themselves encroached upon Salt Woman (Hopi, Titiev 1; cf. Laguna, Boas 2:17–22; Zuni, Parsons 53:37 ff.).

kaya says, "I am chief." Then Antelope picks him up on his horns and tosses him to the sky. He dies and becomes Red Star. Meanwhile his brother grieves for him, pulling out his hair. That is why he is called the Griever and, as a kachina, has but a few strands of hair.

Spirits even die! When Zuni kachina die, they turn into deer. In the Tewa tale of Handmark Boy, the kachina dies because he cannot survive the heat of the sun. On a hot June day his wife sends him out to weed; he feels weak and stops working. When his wife finds him, he is dead, and, later, grass grows where he lay, "his bones become grass"; he was an ice boy and he melted away. Once Shumaikoli, the kachina, was barely saved from death, to go forever limping and blind.[117] There is a San Juan tale of killing a ghost. The youth pulls out the ghost's heart.* "So he died, the second time. Two times he died."[118] The ghost-girl who pursues the War Brothers is repeatedly killed until, after being killed in the right way, she stays killed.

The most interesting and important thing about the Spirits is the way they feel toward human beings. "Sun is a man like us," a Tewa once said to me, "and so he knows what we need," and, Yellow-Mountain might have added, "we know what he needs." In the Zuni Emergence myth Sun feels lonely; there is no one to give him prayer-sticks, and so he sends underground for the people. Sun and all the Spirits are thought of as liking the feathers that adorn and clothe, precious shell or turquoise, food in various forms, and in some cases rabbit sticks, gaming implements, or weapons. To the spirit Snake chief the Sia shaman prays: "I send you prayer-sticks and pay you sticks of office, kick-sticks, hoops, shell mixture, various foods, that you may be pleased and have all things to wear and eat. I pay you these that you will beseech the Cloud chiefs to send their people to water the earth that she may be fruitful and give to all people abundance of all food."[119] Wind is paid with food to stay

---

* This is quite inconsistent with the belief that the dead have no heart. In the exorcising speech made to the deceased at San Juan he is even reminded that he has no heart; and in the San Juan tale of Morning Star and Evening Star the husband star is sometimes overtaken because the wife star, having once died, has no heart and is a faster runner.

at home before a rain dance (Hopi).[120] In Sia tale Mountain Lion gives Coyote food to give to the Spirits, in order to kill a deer. Since Coyote is greedy as usual and eats the food himself, he fails in his hunt. Then Mountain Lion sends out one of his own people to hunt, and when a deer is brought back, Mountain Lion says, "We will pay the Spirits with prayersticks."

After Spider Old Woman has pointed out the road to Badger Old Woman, she is rewarded by the questing kachina with a piece of meat (Laguna). Spider gets feathers from the Tewa hunter and helps him, saying, "We *have* to help you, because you never forget us; because you always take feathers out for us, we help you." Similarly, each of the animals of the six directions who come to the Zuni youth in search of his wife asks him for a downy eagle feather and, on receiving it, says to him, "Since you have given me this feather, I will guard you all night."[121] In the Oraibi ceremony of Powamu when the fields are ceremonially put in order, a dead mouse and corn meal are offered to the Ants that they may not destroy the crops.[122] When Hopi kachina whip clowns or the runners they overtake, "they have to pay back with rain." Cloud chiefs say in a Powamu song, "Let us go, we are indebted," meaning that because of the prayer offerings made to them they must make return by bringing rain.[123] To the Second Mesa youth who is visiting their town the dead say, "You make prayer-offerings for us and we shall provide rain and crops and food for you. *Thus we shall assist each other.*"[124] Exchange of services, mutual aid, the familiar Pueblo way!

The other important method of controlling or directing the Spirits is harder for us, given our own cultural habits of mind, to understand, the method of mimetic magic, setting patterns of behavior, so to speak, which have got to be imitated, compulsive patterns. But from the Pueblo's point of view this is a highly effectual method, which he uses again and again, in rites of running for rainfall or snow or to regulate the course of Sun or Moon, in rites of aspersing or sprinkling water and of smoking to induce rain or make clouds, and, I surmise, in the ritual practices of throwing or giving away things to the on-lookers at a dance.

Identifying a spirit with yourself, your relatives, or your cere-monial group is another much-used mechanism of control. The most conspicuous instance is the adoption of the scalp. The killer who has adopted the scalp as his "son" will not be pursued or harassed.[125] Snakes will not bite their "grandsons," Snake society men.[126] Fire will not burn Fire shamans. Deceased mem-bers of your own society should aid, not harm, you. Kachina initiates will not suffer from kachina-sent hallucinations or rheumatism or sore eyes. It is safe enough for you to imper-sonate your ancestral clan kachina or to have dealings with any beings associated with your clan, whereas it would be highly dangerous for an outsider. The practice of applying kinship terms in general to Spirits or to any "raw people" is a means of getting close to them, an anti-fear mechanism that is far from being confined to the Pueblos. Anthropomorphism itself is such a mechanism of participation.

By rite or concept of participation, by mimetic ritual, and by ritual of gift or compensation the Spirits on the whole are well managed. They may be paid to do harm, as once to kidnap a girl[127] Rainbow was paid; and, since they cure disease, they can also cause it and so are ever potentially dangerous, but there are few Spirits malicious or malevolent by nature. The War Brothers, Lightning, Sandstorm,[128] the Water Serpent sender of flood or landslide, Moon, who "eats" lip or ear of an unborn child[129] or in the dangerous month may kidnap an infant (Hopi),[130] Skeleton (Masauwü) when he helps an envious girl to introduce death,[131] Shumaikoli, the kachina of blindness or deformity, Echo who can make you insane,* Twister, patron of pain in two Hopi societies,† and various disease-causing in-

---

* But only when he is solicited to do so. Then the victims are sent to him, the usual Pueblo reference for ritual execution, and he receives them gladly as wife or godchild (Benedict 3:II, 118–21, 147).

† Wüwüchim and Marau. Twister man or woman enters the body and screws around until reaching the heart (Stephen 4:869, 923, 928), very witchlike con-duct.

TABLE 2

SPIRITS

	Zuni	Hopi

Clouds
Mountains
Chiefs of the
  Directions
Lightning
Rain beings
	uwanami, clouds and all moisture
	Lightning, War gods, deceased War chiefs
	the dead, Scalps
		o'mauwü mongwitü, Cloud chiefs of the color-
		  directions
		sho'tokününgwa (Lightning, Star, Sky)
		the dead

Sun, Sun
  Youths
Dawn
	yätokyä, Sun
	paiyatemu, Youth, or *bitsitsi* or *molaillona*
	  (melon-having), first Ne'wekwe
	Dawn Youths, Dawn Women
		tawa, Sun
		t'aiowa, son of Sun, first Wüwüchimtü
		talatumsi, Dawn Young Woman

Moon	*tsita ya'onan'e*, Mother Moon	*müiyawü*, Moon (male)

Stars	Morning (*moyachunthlana*, Big star) also Liar
	  Evening
	Pleiades (Seed stars, *kupa'kwe*)
	Orion (Row, *ipi'lakä*)
	Galaxy (*yu'piyathlan'e*)
		Morning star (*talashohü*) or Big star (*wuko
		  shohü*)
		Pleiades, *chavau'wütakamü*, clustered ones
		Orion, *wutom'kamü*
		Aldebaran (*wuyok shohü*, Broad star)*
		Galaxy, *songwuka*

Wind	North winds (*suni ashiwanni*) Winds of the Directions Whirlwind (*u'nasinte*)	Wind Woman, *hükyangkwü* Whirlwind, *hala' kabü*
Earth	*a''wi'teli'n tsita*, Earth Mother	*tihküyi wühti*, child-...edicine woman *tüwapongtümsi*, earth altar young woman
Maize	Corn Maidens	*müy'ingwa* (male) *müy'ingwa mana* (maid) Corn Maidens

Salt Woman
White Shell
  Woman
Clay Woman
Turquoise Man
Stones
Fire, Ashes
Echo
	ma'we tsita, Salt Mother
	kohakwa, White Shell
	he'tethl o'kyä, Clay Woman
	thli'akwa, Turquoise
	concretions, small stones (*aklashi*)
	Grandmother Fire
	Echo
		war god Salt Man
		hürü'ingwühti, Hard Being Woman
		chamahia, Stone hoe people; concretions, small
		  stones, petrified wood
		Stone kachina
		masauwü, god of fire
		Ash or Poker Boys

Animals Birds Insects Serpents	Mountain Lion, Bear, Badger, Wolf, Coyote Eagle, Knife-Wing (*ächiyälätopa*) Spider Woman, Dragonfly, Ants Horned Water Serpent (*kolowisi*)	Mountain Lion, Bear, Wildcat, Wolf, Coyote, Badger (*honani*) curer *kwatoko*, giant eagle, Hawk Spider Woman, Beetle, Locust *ka'toya*, rattlesnake patron Water Serpent (*palülükong*)

War gods	*ahayuta achi: matsailema* or *masewa* and
	  uyuyewe
		pü'ükonghoya, little smiter, and *pa'lüngahoya*,
		  also called Echo
		masauwü

Clown patrons	*koyemshi* (kachina), *bitsitsi*	*t'aiowa*
Poshaiyanki	*poshaiyanki*	*pose*
The Dead	old ones (*aklashinawe*) Scalps	the dead Scalps
Kachina	*koko*	kachina

* Prayed to by Pobosh doctor (Stephen 4:860).

TABLE 2 (cont.)

	Keres	Jemez

Clouds
Mountains
Chiefs of the
  Directions
Lightning
Rain beings
	shiwanna, Cloud People
	sha'k'ak'ᵃ, winter, North, Yellow Mountain
	shruitirawana, spring, West Blue Mountain
	maiyochina, summer, South Red Mountain
	shruisimina'wi,† fall, East White Mountain
	putruaishtji, Lightning
	the dead, Scalps
		dyasa, Cloud or Rain People
		hoti dyasa, Lightning
		kopistaya, mountain spirits, yellow, blue, red,
		  black
		the dead

Sun, Sun Youths Dawn	*osha'ch*, Sun *paiyatyamo*, (Sun) Youth	*pedyasatọe*, Sun(?) spirit father *patyabo* (first *tabösh*)
Moon	*tauwach*, Moon (female) (Sia, male)	*padyasatọe*, Moon(?) spirit father
Stars	Stars (*shidyita*) Morning star (*gaiukumushi* in winter, *g'aidyu- we*, in summer) (Laguna) Pleiades (*tsio'k'oish*) (Laguna) Orion (*ts'iashp'sh'*) (Laguna) Galaxy (Acoma)	Morning star (*shobawụhụ*) Pleiades (*söwụhụ*, seven stars) Orion (*wiyish*, rows) Galaxy (*wapahgwahọsh*, sky backbone)
Wind	Feather Man, *shpa'yak'hä'ch'tse* (Laguna) Whirlwind (Laguna)	Whirlwind (?)
Earth	Mother Earth (Acoma, *naiya k'ats'*; Sia, *haarts*)	(3) *hụụ* or *hụnạpeta*, Earth
Maize	Corn Mother, *iyatiku* (Laguna-Acoma), *utshtsiti* (Sia), *uretsete* (Cochiti) and her sister or sisters	*tse'eh*, Mothers (of four directions)
Salt Woman White Shell Woman Clay Woman Turquoise Man Stones Fire, Ashes Echo	Thought (?) Woman (Acoma) Clay Woman (Cochiti, Laguna) Stone "mountains" (*chamahia*, Laguna Stone kachina (Laguna) *hakanᵘi tseeutsa* (fire, oldest), Fire Old Woman (Cochiti) Ashes Man (Sia), Ash Boys, Poker Boys	petrified wood
Animals Birds Insects Serpents	Mountain Lion, *shuhuna* Bear (*ko"haiya*), curer; Badger (Laguna) Giant eagle, Buzzard *sussistinnako*, Spider (creator, S.) *skatowe*, serpent of north, and 5 individually named serpents of the directions (S.) "Water Serpent"	Mountain Lion (*kyamide*, Bear (*köide*) Eagle (?). Spider Grandmother (*kịị olö*) Horned Water Serpent(s) (*wanakyudy'a*)
War gods	*ma'sewi* and *uyuyewi*	*masewi* and *uyuyewe*
Clown patrons	*wikore*, *koetsame* (Cochiti) *wikoli*, *hotokoli* (Laguna)	
Poshaiyanki	*poshaiyänne* (Sia), *pishuni* (Acoma), *p'asha- ya''nᵛ'i* (Laguna)	
The Dead	the dead Scalps	the dead Scalps
Kachina	*k'atsena* *k'oʙishtaiya* (Acoma)	*k'ats'ana* or *dyasa*

† Santo Domingo terms. See White 4:32, n. 69 for dialectical forms in other towns. Given in Stevenson 1:28 as tree terms
also—Spruce, Pine, Oak, Aspen.

TABLE 2 (cont.)

	Tewa	Isleta
Clouds	*oxuwah*, Clouds of the color-directions	*thliwan, wenin*, Chiefs of the Directions, *węide*
Mountains	Lake Old Men of the color-directions	(sing.)
Chiefs of the	Lightning, *tsihguwenu*, stone arrowpoint boy	*thleachi*, rain people
Directions	the dead	Water people
Lightning		Rainbow (*berkwi*)
Rain beings		Lightning (*upinide*)
		Thunder (*koanida*)
		Mountains
Sun, Sun	*t'ąn sendo*, Sun Old Man	(*kika'awei*) *tur(ide)*
Youths	*tamuyowa enu*, Dawn Youths	(our father) Sun
Dawn		
Moon	*p'o sendo*, Moon Old Man	(*kike'ewei*) *p'aide*
		(our mother) Moon
Stars	Morning (Big star, *agoyoso'yu*) or *agoyono-*	(*kimuwei*) *paxöthlan*, (our sons) stars
	hųseh (Dark Star Man), *ponu'chona* (Hano)	Morning star (*puyu paxöthlade*, bright star)
	Evening, *tseqę kwiyo* (yellow-going old woman)	Evening star (*tarape paxöthlade*, prayer star)
	Pleiades *tirini* (*tiging*, in a bunch)‡	Pleiades (*maköchuin*, jumbled)
	Orion, *w'irini* (*qwiri'ing*, in a row)‡	Orion (*piun*, fawns)
	Galaxy, *'opatuk'u*, universe backbone‡	
Wind	*wąkwiyo*, Wind Old Woman (Old Man too)	*wathluthli*, Wind Old Man
Earth	*nang kwiyo*, Earth Old Woman	*namire*,‡ Earth
Maize	*kutsębu kwiyo payakaga*	*iemaparu* (Corn Mothers)
	kutsobukwi oyikaga	
Salt Woman	Salt Old Woman, *anye kwiyo*	Salt Old Woman (*pathlithliu*)
White Shell		Beads Old Woman (*ködithliuu*)
Woman	*kaye'*, small boulders	Clay Old Woman (*namburuthliu*)
Clay Woman	white stone, Ice Mother	stone mountains (*shunai*)
Turquoise Man	*pahpobi kwiyo*, Fire Flower Woman	stones (*ke'chu*) for animals, birds, rain people
Stones	*pahteenu*, Fire (Poker) Boy	Fire Old Woman (*kefethliu*)
Fire, Ashes		
Echo		
Animals	Mountain Lion, Bear (*keh*) curer	Mountain Lion, Bear (curer), Badger
Birds	*awę kwiyo*, Spider Woman	Eagle, Shrike (?)
Insects	Dragonfly (San Juan)	Spider grandmother
Serpents	*avanyo*, Horned Water Serpent	*ikanare* (rattlesnake) or *piruthlade* (big snake)
War gods	*towae' sendo*, little people old man, 6 or 12	
Clown patrons	*payachiamu*	*ka'pe kabede* (name-making chiefs), *ka'an*
		(fathers) *paiunin*
Poshaiyanki	*poseyemu*, dew falls	*puspiyama*
The Dead	the dead	the dead and stillborn
	Scalps	Scalps
Kachina	*oxuwah*	*thliwan*

‡ Harrington.

TABLE 2 (cont.)

	Taos
Clouds Mountains Chiefs of the Directions Lightning Rain beings	*thliwana*, lightning, cloud beings, deceased chiefs *thlatsina*, Clouds of the color-directions Lightning *thlatsi* (Thunder) Mountains
Sun, Sun Youths Dawn	(*kitâmena*) *tul*(*ena*) (our father) Sun
Moon	(*kitâmena*) *pana* (our father) Moon
Stars	*paithlana*, (our fathers) the stars Morning star (*tôba paithlana* or *paxôthlana* Galaxy, universe backbone‡ Falling stars
Wind	*wǫthliu*, Wind Old Woman *wǫthluthli*, Wind Old Man Whirlwind (*thl'aipomoloona*) *kliwǫ*, refuse wind, disease-bringing
Earth	*pǫ'ona*, Earth Mother or *namena*,‡ Earth
Maize	*kuyune* (Corn Mothers)
Salt Woman White Shell Woman Clay Woman Turquoise Man Stones Fire, Ashes Echo	Salt Man (*pathlesöanena*) Dirt (refuse) Boy (*hięu*) Echo (*natunkwanoho*)
Animals Birds Insects Serpents	Red Bear, Coyote, Gopher Woman Spider Grandmother, Spider Man (*paöya tsöanana*) Rattlesnake *pâköathlanna* (Big Water Man or Bear, Frog)
War gods	*hayunu'*, Stone Men, two brothers
Clown patrons	
Poshaiyanki	
The Dead	the dead Scalps
Kachina	*thliwa* *thlatsina*

sects or animals—these are the most uncertain and tricky Spirits, and even they are amenable. There are ghosts who come for the living, but they, too, may be kept satisfied and against them precautionary measures may be taken, such as not burying in the same place two members of the family lest they draw to themselves others in the family (Zuni) or not grinding corn at night in the dangerous moon lest a ghost "do something" (to a girl, First Mesa) or not leaving an infant alone, without a guardian, an ear of corn (Zuni, Cochiti, Tewa), a fire poker (Laguna), a brush (Taos), lest, held by a ghost, the child die, within four days, or be subject for life to ghostly visitation. Having the unamenable, irreconcilable element in life or environment put down to witches, malevolent human beings, rather than to the Spirits,* is a very good thing for the Pueblo or any other pantheon. Bad people may make for good gods.

* As among some neighboring tribes. Havasupai, like Pueblos and many Indian peoples, suck out disease-causing objects; but these noxious things are sent into the body by Spirits, not by witches (Spier 2:277 ff.). Witchcraft is familiar enough among Navaho, in both Pueblo and Mexican terms (Morgan, Valkenburgh), but sickness "is caused by jealous and angry supernaturals, who make demands upon humans, which must be satisfied" (Haile, 12).

CHAPTER III

COSMIC NOTIONS, THE EMERGENCE, AND THE NEXT WORLD

The story of creation is a story of emerging from the under-world. There is no query about how the earth was made* or about the first people, that is, people prior to those who emerged.† The Emergence is a satisfying starting-point, that drama of finding an opening into the sunny upper world and the climb up by tree or reed. Similarly the most precious things the people have today, the "mothers," the "old ones," as well as the societies and their ceremonies, the war gods who are leaders or watchmen, sometimes the kachina, all are accounted for as coming up with the people, all just as they are today. To secure a sense of authenticity or validity for fetish, spirit, or institution, the Pueblo has but to say, "It came up with us."‡

* Except in Acoma myth (see p. 244). In sand-painting the Earth Mother is held in position by the Galaxy arching overhead, and a stick-image of the Mother is called center pole; it holds the four stratified skies and the four stratified earths together, so to speak, a pole of gravity.

† Unless we consider hints of lizard-like or fishlike people that seem to come down from a more ancient mythological stratum. The heads on figures in kiva wall-paintings at Kuaua, a Piro, Pueblo IV, pre-Spanish ruin near Bernalillo appear to represent the bodies of fish (Hawley). Before they emerged, the Ashiwi (Zuni) had tails and webbed fingers and toes, and after they emerged the children lost off their mothers' backs as they crossed the river became water creatures to swim down river to become kachina. The forebears or prototypes of the kiva Water People of Taos swam upstream as fish (Parsons 58:13), which mythical bit explains why Tewa ceremonialists are referred to as Fish people (Parsons 49:141). The myth of trying to cross a river on a bird's tail which gives way, the people dropping into the water and turning into fish, is told by Tewa (Parsons 42:14). Western San Carlos Apache describe pursuers trying to cross on a heron's leg and, on falling into the water, turning into ducks (Goddard 3:70).

‡ Clanship is not validated in this way. The clans get their names, i.e., develop, later, while the people are wandering, after the Emergence. The kachina also usually derive from this later less significant and less esoteric period. To

The world above, before or for a time after the Emergence, may be described as soft, damp, fluescent, to be hardened later into rock, in which are sometimes preserved tracks of the early beings.[1] And it was at this time that some of the Spirits became stone, among others Lightning Man who was traveling south with the Laguna people from White House[2] or those dim Stone people called Chamahia who lie on altars or are invoked in rituals.

"Long ago when the earth was soft" all the relations with the Spirits were more intimate. Everything could talk, animals, plants, even wood or stone.[3] The kachina came in person to dance or, as at Acoma, to fight. Coyote was a well-behaved messenger between the underworld and White House. The War Brothers begotten by Sun or Water not only produced order by finding the directions or making mountains and valleys but led the migrant people or borrowed curing societies or freed people from dangerous personages or from monsters the women had borne in the lower world after they quarreled with the men. Sun became a handsome man to appear on earth to his sons. It was a golden age. Water gushed from rocks (Isleta). Dew Boy made corn grow for the people of Oraibi in a single day, giving the seeds to the Corn clan.[4] The seeds the Keresan Mothers obtained from their skin were planted at sunrise, ripened at noon, and were dry at sunset. It was only after the trouble with P'ashaya·'ny'i that corn had to be planted as it is planted today.* In those days all growth was miraculously rapid. The War Brothers as well as other children begot by the gods grew up overnight or rather in four days. Even human persons were wonderful. The two girls who played hide-and-seek with Ne'wekwe and perched invisible on his hair plumes were able to do this "because the world was still new. When

---

this period, while the Keres lived at White House, the organization of medicine societies may be assigned. Pekwin (Zuni) and Town chiefs (Isleta, San Juan) are post-Emergence.

* By the sweat of the brow (Boas 2:232). In Acoma tradition Poshayanyi or Pishuni is plainly identified with the Serpent in the Garden, tempting not through sex but through promise of offspring!

the world was raw, people used to be like this. They were very wonderful in those days, the old people tell us."⁵

The underworld, the four underground wombs or levels, was dark (Zuni); Sun sent emissaries to the underworld people to bid them come up into the light. Sun wanted company and prayer-sticks and prayer-meal.⁶ In Keresan myth (Acoma excepted) the upper world was dark, the sun was a secondary creation. The "Mothers" send out Ma'sewi to look for the sun and, having found it, to place it properly. Tewa emissaries to the upper world seek for the proper "directions," but they are not aided by Sun. In Tewa, Isleta, and Jemez myth Sun does not figure at all in the Emergence. Hopi make their sun by throwing upward a back tablet or shield covered with buckskin or cotton cloth together with a fox skin and a parrot tail, for the lights of dawn.

Sun's course across the sky is interrupted when he permits his sons to carry his shield (Tewa). In Hopi myth Sun had to be helped to move on across the sky by killing a child, and his transit is still dependent on "somebody dying every day, at morning, noon, and evening,"⁷ also on ritual racing by the town youths. The Tiwan relay race is to help Sun (and Moon) in his seasonal journey. His diurnal progress is promoted, in Isletan myth, by his son's kick-stick play. Sun has two houses for daily use. In the morning he "comes out standing to his sacred place"; in the evening he "goes in to sit down at his other sacred place (Zuni)."⁸ This is the house of the White Shell Mother, Hurü'ing (Hopi) or Kohakwa (Zuni),⁹ in the western ocean. In seasonal or solstitial ceremonial there are other references to Sun's house. The farthest point on the horizon that he reaches at sunrise or sunset, the northernmost point in summer, the southernmost point in winter, is the "house" where he remains four days before "turning back" to winter or to summer.

In no Pueblo myth except one recorded at Oraibi is Sun described as a creator. The creator, as far as there is one, is either the Mother who lives underground (Keres;* among the Hopi,

---

* The sky-dwelling male creator of one Acoma tradition (Forde) is inferably a Christian derivative; the Hopi sky god is not creative, although in

a male being with a female companion) or mountain-dwelling war spirits, specifically the War Brothers, and their creation is rather of institutions than of men. They gave the people their plan of life, notably their societies and ceremonies. However, the Tewa war spirits made mountains and determined the "directions," and the Hopi War Brothers made watercourses,[10] hardened the ground, and undertook to place sun, moon, and with Coyote, unfortunately, the stars.

To Zuni mythologist the stars seem parts of the ancient monsters, for the conqueror cuts up the body and throws head and members into the sky to become stars. Scalps at Hano are called Morning Star, and Scalp women are called Dark Star Man (Northern Tewa). As the Rainbow is the road of the kachina,* the Galaxy is the road of the first Ne'wekwe.† The first Koshare, too, had an arch to play on. Again the steadfast Galaxy is the beam holding up the earth (Acoma); and the sky has four levels like the earth.[11] Or the sky is a "stone cover" (Zuni), solid and resting upon the earth like an inverted bowl.[12] But there are breaks or a passage in the cover; if you pass through, you reach the home of the Eagle people.[13]

Zuni believe that under the circular earth is a system of waterways all connecting ultimately with the oceans, the four encircling oceans. Springs and lakes are the openings to this system.[14] This cosmological complex has not been reported for the other Pueblos, except that at Acoma the lowest of the four underground worlds, the white world (the others are red, blue, and yellow), is all water surrounding a small piece of land,[15] truly an ocean. Then, too, there is the general belief that springs and lakes are openings to the homes of the Clouds or other people: Blue Lake of Taos, Sand Lake of the Tewa, Kishyuba or Shaded Water of the Hopi, and the Shalako springs or the Lake of Whispering Waters of Zuni. This lake, the river that

---

Flute society tradition he suggests to his underworld nephew Müy'ingwa, god of vegetation, how to create the dawn (Stephen 4:798).

* Navaho gods also travel by rainbow (Newcomb and Reichard, 27, 36, 39).

† Bunzel 2:487. Made by a handful of ashes thrown upward by the War Brothers (Benedict 3:I, 38).

feeds it, and the mountains the river flows between were created by Zuni clown kachina.

Flood is caused by Water Serpent and must be checked by human sacrifice. Water Serpent also causes landslide, called earthquake at Zuni, and fissures in the ground. These are terrifying specifically because they may let up "wild animals" from underground (? supernaturals mentioned on p. 226 or perhaps Water Serpent himself), or, in general, because "it must mean something;* earthquake "does not happen for nothing," since rocks are hard and "mountains are valuable."[16] It is implied that mountains or mesas have power; they are the homes of supernaturals, great shrines or sanctuaries, and perhaps they are themselves supernaturals, at least the four sacred mountains of the directions. Mountain effigies on altars testify to such belief.

Besides mountains and mesas, rivers and lakes and springs, there are other places of interest in Pueblo geography, usually places where people stopped or lived during their early migrations. At Hanthlipinkya, where there are many pictographs, the Ashiwi (Zuni tribe) stopped and got their clan names. There is the cave on the road from Paguate to Laguna where Lightning Man sat down and became stone, promising life and strength to anyone who gave him pollen; also a little beyond Oak place there is a rocky terrace or boulder where Yellow Woman, weaver of women's dresses and of baskets, also sat down, because she was tired, promising to impart her skill to those who would visit her.[17] The abandoned cities of Cibola are remembered as once the home of tale hero or heroine, son or daughter of a Rain chief. The ruins of Sikyatki or Awatobi are where suitors became aggrieved or a chief felt outraged. Pueblo history and geography are a series of archeological or topographical legends, al-

---

* Once it meant that Pekwin was going to die. In vain the Rain chiefs made offerings where the rocks gave way in order "to save themselves"; a year later Pekwin died. "Because he was going to die, the rocks fell" (Bunzel 6:54).

Why did the rocks fall at the early Village of the Great Kivas, near Nutria, and demolish houses? (Roberts 1:158). A stone serpent head was found in this ruin. See p. 334.

most as naïve and fanciful about near events* as about remote
or cosmic ones.

The general outline is simple: "We came up, we moved southward (or eastward) and built houses, something happened, a
quarrel or choosing a fateful egg or being stung by mosquitoes,†
we moved again, we kept on seeking the middle place until we
found it here, where we are to live forever." Into this legendary
frame a considerable number of narratives are embroidered and
a few songs,‡ for ritual recitation or for edification. Versions
vary, for there will be stressed or introduced myth bearing upon
the ceremony or organization the particular narrator is connected with. As yet only a few ritual recitals or chants have been
recorded, mostly Zuni. These ritual versions are known only
to those in charge of them; even when recited semipublicly,
like the Shalako and Sayatasha myths, they are not attended
to by outsiders; they are merely part of the ceremony. In this
respect these unique Zuni recitals suggest the all-night song
myths of the Mohave which constitute Mohave ceremony or
the Athapascan song myths which are also part of the ceremony. In general, however, Pueblo mythology and ceremonial
are far more separate than are Navaho-Apache song myths and
ceremonial.

Of the less esoteric and more comprehensive Emergence myth
as told by the older men to the younger, informally or more or
less prescriptively at solstice or other ceremonial season, I will
give in part or in summary what has been recorded among Hopi

* Compare Benedict 3:I, XLIII. "Standard literary versions of battles may
do service in different connections." A true story of Zuni treachery against
Navaho visitors was told by the grandson of the chief actor as an origin of
albinos in Zuni, yet immediately after telling the tale he named albinos born
considerably before the date of the incident. He saw no inconsistency. But
see p. 1158.

† Given by Water-Corn clan people of First Mesa as a reason for leaving
the Little Colorado. Because black ants sting and *kill by witchcraft*, the Navaho move up into the blue world, in their Emergence myth (Goddard 5:127–28).

‡ The song the Zuni Wood society sings when they go off to the eastward
(p. 223); songs by the Acoma Corn Mothers on first seeing the sun, when they
separate from each other, or when Iyatik directs the placing of the first altar; and
probably the "water run song" of the Hano winter solstice ceremony.

and Keres, at Zuni, Jemez, San Juan, and Isleta. The record is often fragmentary, for this myth is too explanatory of the ceremonial life to be told freely to rank outsiders. Being etiological, it reveals organization and may be a key to interpreting ritual or drama, as in Zuni or Acoma kachina or war rituals or as in the Hopi Flute ceremony.

With few exceptions life after death is envisaged as the same as before death; the deceased journeys to a town where he joins a group such as he was associated with in life—racers, hunters, curers, dancers, or rain-makers who may be thought of as clouds or lightning. The major exceptions are Hopi, and they express the idea of punishment after death, in itself exceptional in Pueblo ideology. On the road to the *sipapu* in the west, the place of Emergence where the Hopi dead return, or some of them, an actual spot in the wall of the Grand Canyon (Oraibi), the breath body is met by Tokonaka, an Agave spirit sentinel. If Tokonaka finds the traveler good, he allows him to pass on; otherwise he makes him go up a forking trail to the four fire pits.* From the first pit the breath body may come out purified and be allowed by the Tokonaka in charge to return to the main trail. Otherwise the breath body has to go on to the second fire pit. If good on emerging, it is changed into a beetle; otherwise it goes on to the third pit. If it emerge good, it changes into an ant; otherwise Tokonaka takes it to the fourth pit to be consumed and remain soot (Walpi).[18] Second and Third Mesa tales of the youth who takes a narcotic, "dies," and journeys to Skeleton house express the idea of punishment still more plainly. The youth passes by a very wicked one who "does not want rain in summer" and so offends the Clouds that they run away,† a

---

* This has a Navaho flavor. "If you marry one of your own clan, you will go crazy, and go into the fire," says First Man (Goddard 5:128). Transmigration also sounds more Athapascan than Pueblo.

† Another version of the witch who summons wind to blow away the rain clouds. See the Nambé tale of the man shocked by Lightning after saying that if he were a Cloud Man nothing would keep him from raining. Yellow Cloud Man carries him to the mountaintop to see the rainbow blown to bits and to be hurtled about himself. "If you are man-and-woman (so brave)," say the Clouds, "why

murderer who puts something bad into somebody, and a woman carrying stones in a burden basket, the bowstring which is the tumpline cutting into her forehead.* These witches and sexual offenders are all detained on the trail which after all leads them only to the Agave man and his destructive fire where they become smoke, unhappy, unfed—mere smoke.[19] In another Hopi tale witches are said to become snakes, bull snakes, after burial. Killing the snake liberates the spirit, allowing it to proceed to Skeleton house.[20]

The town of the dead may be underground (Hopi, Keres, Zuni) or underwater (Zuni, Tewa, Taos). Perhaps the underwater town is restricted to those who become kachina, or to the dead who merely visit the kachina dance-house. Then there is Wenima. Wenima is a western resort of the dead, beautifully wooded and watered, not a town. Whether it is above or underground is not quite clear. After going underground to Shipap in the north, Keres dead move on westward to Wenima. This place name, if not the concept, is familiar in the Western towns through songs or prayers.

In the Hopi and Zuni origin or Emergence myths that follow, the first to die, little girls or boys, return in the Keresan way to the world below the place of Emergence. Thus Coyote or the First Witch arranged for death to keep this world from being overcrowded. Any Hopi burial place is called Masauwü's house (*maski*), as is the great house or place of Emergence in Colorado Grand Canyon, but the dead appear not to live with Masauwü or even visit him as deceased Keres visit their Mother in Shipap.

Yet Masauwü is also, like Iyatiku, a sort of vegetation spirit, an owner of crops who performs fertility ritual. Into

---

don't you stop the wind? We have a hard time when bad people do not let us rain." Cured of his unbelief, the man tells the Town chiefs all about it. "That is why the people are afraid of the Cloud People, afraid to say anything against them, even if they do not believe in them" (Parsons 52:301–2). There are more ways than dramatization to compel belief through fear.

* Basket carrying is the punishment for women and men who have broken the rule that only virgins should mate with virgins (Titiev 3). Carrying weights or prickly cacti is the punishment of those who are "bad to the maidens and women" (Voth 5:119)

the Hopi grave, we recall, is thrust a planting-stick, "a ladder to Masauwü," "the dead are planted," seed corn is left where they lay in death, and, very curiously, among the earliest cave sepulchers of this land were circular slab-lined pit granaries, a very early association between death and fertility indeed!

ZUNI*

In this world there was no one at all. Always Sun came up; always he went in. No one in the morning gave him sacred meal; no one gave him prayer-sticks; it was very lonely. He said to his two children, "You will go into the fourth womb. Your fathers, your mothers, *kyäetowe, chu-etowe, mu-etowe, thle-etowe,†* all the society chiefs, society criers, society war chiefs, you will bring out yonder into the light of your Sun father."

Laying their lightning arrow across their rainbow bow, they drew it. Drawing it and shooting down, they entered. Someone was out hunting in the dark. With dry brush and grass and their bow on top they kindled a fire. The man fell down crouching. He had a slimy horn, slimy tail; he was slimy all over, with webbed hands. "Poor thing! Put out the light!" He spat on them. "Why do you do that to us? Do your people do that to each other? We do not like that. Where do your people live?"— "On the north side." There were no houses; they just lived in burrows in the ground. The people said, "Why have you come?" —"Our Father Sun has sent us in for you people to come out into the daylight of your Sun father. Our Father Sun knows everything, but none gives him prayer-sticks or sacred meal or shell."

The War chiefs went north with yellow prayer-sticks to get pine, but the pine tree did not reach out; they went west with blue prayer-sticks to get spruce; they went south with red prayer-sticks to get silver spruce; they went east with white

---

* This "talk concerning the beginning" I have compiled from two versions (Parsons 35 and Bunzel 3), eliminating the repetitious element. For narrative style and formal or ritualistic phraseology see Dr. Bunzel's text translation. For another version and for analysis of all variants see Benedict 3: I, 1–6, 255–61.

† Rain and seed fetishes and the fetishes of the Thle'wekwe winter society.

prayer-sticks to get aspen. At last they planted reed. That reached out.*

In four days the War chiefs went down and said to the people, "Now it is time to come out. Our father has sent us down again." So all the people got ready and took all their *e'leteliwe*.† First they came to soot world. The second world they came to was sulphur-smell-inside world or raw dust world; the third world was fog world; the fourth world was wing inner world because they saw their Sun father's wings. Here, as the Dogwood clan came out, they caught hold of dogwood twigs and so got their name.‡ When all came out, they saw Father Sun, and they shut their eyes because it was so bright.

When they came out at early dawn, they put down their sacred possessions [water and seed bundles] in a row. After they saw the sun, they could not tell which was which of their sacred possessions. Near by an old man of the Dogwood clan lived alone.§ Spider told him to wash his hair. The two War chiefs came to fetch him. Spider clung behind his ear and told him which was which of the water and seed bundles, and he named the months for the people. "Thank you! You shall not be poor, our father. Even though you have no sacred possessions toward which your thoughts bend, whenever Itiwana is revealed to us, because of your thought, the ceremonies of all these shall come around in order." They gave him the sun. "This shall be your sacred possession."

A little way from where they started they lived for four years. Then the earth rumbled, and they said, "Now who is behind?" —"We had better go and see who it is," said the two War chiefs.

* The people send the two War chiefs to get permission from the paramount Rain chiefs. They send out in turn, Eagle, Shokyapiso, Chicken Hawk, Hummingbird; they see nothing. Locust goes up through three worlds, and his strength fails. Reed Youth succeeds and finds the daylight (Bunzel 3:585–89).

† "What we live by," referring to the *eto·we* or fetishes for rain, snow, and seeds.

‡ In the same sort of a way Hopi clans got their names.

§ He is to be the first Pekwin. Pekwin did not come up with the others; Pekwin must be chosen from the Dogwood clan.

So they went back to where they came out, and they saw two witches* sitting down. "Now why did you come out? You ought not to come out. Have you something useful?"—"Yes, we are to be with you people because this world is small. As it becomes crowded, we shall kill some of the people. Besides we have everything of which you people have none—we have yellow corn, blue corn, red corn, white corn, corn of different colors, black corn, and sweet corn, whereas you people just live on different kinds of grass seeds." So they took the two witches to where the people were. "Let me have one of your children, I will try it out with him," said one of the witches.† "The day after he dies, he will be where we came out. That day he will be alive again. If you disbelieve, you may find out tomorrow." So they gave him the daughter of a Rain chief. The little girl died. She went back to where they came out. The next day two of them went back to see her. When they got there, they went into the house where she was. They saw her sitting by the fire, her hair washed.‡ "Have you come?"§ she said. "What have you come for?"—"Well, we did not believe that you were going to live again."—"I am not dead; I am living here, only I cannot go back to where my people are. I shall stay here forever. After they find Itiwana, whoever dies will come here."—"All right, we will tell the people that you are living. We go."

Then, after four years, it was time to start again. They started again to Slime Spring. The two War chiefs made them bathe in the spring. They were all covered with slime. There they cut their tails off and cut their fingers apart.‖ "This is the way you people ought to be; you ought to be like us," said the War chiefs.

* The Mischief-maker (? Coyote) and the Mexicans (Bunzel 3:593).

† The two corn-bringing witches say: "We wish to kill the children (the two they ask for), that the rains may come" (Stevenson 2:30).
In 1803 the Spanish *Alcalde mayor* of Zuni reports on "witchcraft, rain-making superstitions and attempted human sacrifice" (Twitchell II, 430).

‡ As is the head of the dead.

§ The formula of greeting.

‖ They also cut vents: mouth and anus (Benedict 3:I, 4)

They lived there four years. Then they said, "Now it is time to go again." They all started again and went on until they came to Cattail Spring. "Now we will stop here." In succession they stop four years at Standing-wood Spring, at Muddy Spring, at Tapelyan, at Tenatsalin.*

Then they made two leaders for themselves, the girl and boy of a Rain chief, Siwuluhsiwa and Siwuluhsi'etsa. After the two went ahead, they all started. The people of *thle'etone*† (Wood society) went in front. The people who lived by *e'leteliwe* (Rain chieftaincies) were behind. The girl and boy came to a hill. The day was hot. "I am tired; let's wait here till they come!" said the girl. "All right, let me go and see if the people are coming." So he went off a little way. When he saw them coming, he returned. His sister was lying down by a tree asleep. Her legs were uncovered. He copulated with his sister. She awoke; she tried to talk. She talked like Komokyatsiky, Kachina Old Woman.‡ Her brother talked like Koyemshi.§ "*Hawai!*"‖ There they marked the earth with their feet, and they made a river. They made two mountains, and the river flowed between.[21] At last the people came. They saw the two walking on the mountain. "Look at them! Who are they? Why have they changed like that?"—"They did something bad," said the War chiefs.

When they came to the river, the two War chiefs said, "Now go across!" The women carried their babies on their backs and

---

* *Tenatsali* is a plant with narcotic properties, which belongs to the Rain chiefs and to the medicine societies. Massed Cloud Spring, Mist Spring, Standing-wood Spring, and Upuilima are the stopping-places given to Bunzel.

† The snow-bringing bundle belonging to the Thle'wekwe, the Wood society. To them have been assigned two winter moons (January and February), the rest of the year they are poor persons.

‡ For a young woman to wake up as an old woman is a common Pueblo tale incident; even Snake Youth after sleeping with the Woman of Hard Substances finds her a hag in the morning (Voth 3:351, n. 2).

§ The native etymology is *ko(ko)oyemashi*, kachina husband, the reference being to the foregoing incident. The Koyemshi are often referred to as the old ones, *athlashi*, as the dead are referred to.

‖ Exclamation of fatigue much used by Koyemshi.

in their arms. They went into the river, and the children turned into snakes, and their mothers were afraid and let go. All the people of *thle'etone* went across. They lost all their children; the old people were alone. The rest of the people came up. "Now go across! Hold your children tight. Even if they turn into snakes, do not let go! After you have crossed the river, they will be all right." So everybody went into the river. The children turned into snakes and turtles and scratched their mothers, but their mothers held them tight.

They crossed and went on a little way, and there they lived. In the evening the mothers of the lost children would cry, longing for their children. Then they heard singing from the lake which Kachina Old Woman and Koyemshi had made. (They made everything at once for the lost children.)* "We hear singing; perhaps it is our children."—"We believe they are your children. Let us go and see about them!" said the two War chiefs, and they went to the lake.† When they got near, they heard singing and dancing. Through the middle of the lake they saw a road. They walked on that road to the middle of the water. They went down. Inside they were all dancing Kok'ok-shi.‡ "Everybody stop for a while, our fathers are coming. Maybe there is some news. That is why they come." So they all stopped. They said, "Sit down! Now, our fathers, what have you come for? Maybe there is some news. Let us know!" They said, "Our children who have lost their children are crying, longing to see you."—"We are happy here. Our mothers ought not to cry about us. We shall stay here forever. Itiwana is near now, that is why we stop here. To where we began will be too far for the people to go after they find Itiwana. We have stopped here, so in the years when there is little rain at Itiwana you will not have so far to go; you will not have to go to where

* It was they, too, who transformed the children. They wanted their company.

† At the junction of Little Colorado and Zuni rivers (Stevenson 2: Pl. IV).

‡ Good Kachina. The most sacred of the kachina dances and apparently the oldest.

we began. They must not cry for us. After anybody dies, he will stop here instead of going to where we began."*

They all lived there; they made their little houses and stayed there for four years. When it was time to go again, they separated the people. They put a crow's egg and a parrot's egg in a basket. The parrot's egg was not so pretty as the crow's egg. The War chiefs said, "Now which of these eggs are you to belong to? Choose one!" The people of *e'leteliwe* chose the crow's egg. Others got the parrot's egg. "Now we are to go to the south, and you people will go to the east. Wherever you find Itiwana, there you will live forever. And we will go to the south to live somewhere there."†

The *thle'etone* people started out first, to go to Shipapolima. The people staying behind saw them starting out, and the women said:

> Naiya,‡ look, the *thle'etone* is going!
> Naiya, look, the society members are going!

Those on ahead began to sing that song.§ In white stripes of hail they went. The parrot egg people started to the south.‖

After four years all the people with *e'leteliwe* started again. They came to Hanthlipinkya (where they got their clan names).¶ After four years they started again. They came to House Mountain, and the Ky'anakwe were there. The people that came wanted to go through, but the Ky'anakwe would not let them pass. They began to fight. They fought all day. In the evening,

* A rationalized reconciliation of the underwater and underground theories of the future life.

† The migration myth for trips to the headwaters of the Gila and downstream! (Roberts 3:24). See p. 1026. Told too at Acoma (p. 248) and among Papago.

‡ Keresan for mother.

§ It is the song the Koyemshi come with at the initiation into the Kachina society or at Shalako. It is also the song sung when the fetish is carried around the box in the court in the Thle'wekwe ceremonial. See p. 698. On First Mesa the borrowed Koyemsi will sing in Keresan (Stephen 4:435).

‖ "No one knows where they are now, perhaps in Central America!"

¶ In much the same traditional way as Hopi got clan names, from something seen or encountered (Stevenson 2:40).

when they quit, they sent the two War chiefs to their children at Kachina town, Kothluwala, to ask for help. "You children, go and help your old ones tomorrow. Certain people won't let our children pass."—"We shall be there." The next day their children started from Kachina town. They started in a drip of rain. When they got there, they began to fight again. It rained all day. In the afternoon when they quit they went back to Kachina town. They told them to come back again. The next day when they started out, they came with a heavy rain. Their bowstrings were of deer sinew and those of the Ky'anakwe of yucca fiber. The deer sinews of the kachina got wet and broke. When the bowstrings of the Ky'anakwe got wet, they tightened. The Ky'anakwe captured Kothlahma,* Blue Horn, Itsepasha.† When they caught Itsepasha, he began to cry. His mouth looked just as it is now. The big woman of the Ky'anakwe, the Chakwen woman, went in front of them while they fought. They shot at her with their arrows, but she did not die. She had her heart in a gourd rattle.‡

Somewhere near was a big mountain creek. During the heavy rain in the waterfalls there was a lot of foam. There the two Ahayuta and Pa'utiwa§ began. They are the children of rain, rain children.

When they stopped fighting, the two Ahayuta made up like men and went to the people. When the people saw them, they said, "Maybe those two know something. Perhaps they are

* Kachina man-woman.

† One of the ten Koyemshi.

‡ The mask, bandoleer, and rattle of Chakwena woman are tied to the ladder of the Mustard clan kiva at Walpi in the winter solstice ceremony. The Mustard clan at Walpi as at Zuni has Keresan traditions. Were the Ky'anakwe an actual tribe and were they Keres? The songs and prayers of the Ky'anakwe kachina ceremony are in Keresan (Sia) (Stevenson 2:218, 225), and after their fight the Ky'anakwe went on to Acoma. See below, p. 227, n.‡.

§ Chief of Kachina town; but curiously enough in no versions of the Emergence myth is he thus described. In other tales Pa'utiwa welcomes visitors and hears their requests. No kachina may visit Zuni unless Pa'utiwa sends him; Pa'utiwa controls the kachina calendar, but he never refuses requests for kachina; he even supplies new kachina.

brave." So they called them. "Do you know of anything that you can do to those people who will not let us pass."—"No, we are only little fellows, but we will try." Next day they began to fight again in the rain. The two Ahayuta could do nothing. "We can do nothing. Prepare meal and turquoise for us! We are going somewhere; we shall be back soon." So the women gave them meal mixed with turquoise. After they had gone a little way from town, they made a ball of the meal (to throw ahead for their road). They looked up at the sun in the middle of the sky. "That's where we have to go," they said. When they got to where the Sun was sitting, he said, "Have you come? Perhaps there is news."—"Yes," said they. "The people seeking Itiwana are being held back by some other people and the Chakwena big person." Sun said, "You have supernatural power, but you don't know where her heart is?"—"No," said they. "The big Chakwena person has her heart in her gourd. When you go down, hit that gourd, the Ky'anakwe will run away." Sun got his turquoise (rabbit stick)* and gave it to Elder Brother.

They began to fight again. Elder Brother said, "Now, do you want me to try?"—"No, I don't want you to try, let me do it!"—"You will miss it."—"No, I won't, I am your elder brother, I should act because I am the elder."—"I know, but then you will miss Chakwena giantess." Elder Brother walked in front of all the people, and let go his turquoise. He missed, and his turquoise went to the north at Shiprock. A bear was there in hiding. He heard the turquoise coming, and he stood up and waited until it got there. It came swiftly, and it hit him in the belly. He bent down. It almost broke his backbone. Elder Brother followed his turquoise. Bear said, "You hurt me very badly. I am bent double." Ahayuta said, "You are all right. This is the way you always will be. When your back was straight, you did not look good, but now, although you do not

* To inquiry the turquoise was described as a rabbit stick (as in Stevenson 2:38; Bunzel 3:600). Probably it is amulet or charm. Western Apache refer in just the same way to the turquoise of the war gods, a swordlike weapon (Goodwin). Navaho war gods have clubs of precious stones (Reichard). See p. 1109, n.*, for turquoise witch-shot.

seem to be looking at anything, yet you are looking. Therefore everybody will be afraid of you. You look good."

Younger Brother said, "Now I will do it. I told you that you would miss." He went in front of all the people and let go his turquoise. He hit the gourd. Then the giantess fell down, and everybody ran away, into their spring.

The two Ahayuta went to the top of their high rock. They put up stones to sit on, they fixed their pottery drum, they put meal on top, and they called from the fourth inner world Whirlwind, Wool-Rolled-Up, and other raw persons (supernaturals).* So they came out to sit down in the daylight. When all the people got there, Elder Brother said, "Is there any Yellow Corn clan among the coyote?" At last they found him, a Yellow Corn clansman. They made him beat the drum.† Elder Brother said, "Is there any Deer clansman?" At last they found one. "All right. He will be my father [ceremonial father]. I will belong to this clan,"‡ said Elder Brother. Younger Brother said, "Is there any Bear clansman?" They found one. "He will be my father. I will belong to this clan," said Younger Brother. When everything was ready, the coyote Yellow Corn clansman beat the drum. Then the creatures from the bottom of the earth started the songs.§ When the quick songs were over, they began the strong ones. The Big Shell society blew the big shell. At that time they blew all the people that lived around back to the east. Where the people were singing and dancing around, their feet made marks.

* These underground people can cause earthquake. They are punitive. After a sexual debauch, people heard the earth rumbling. The angry War chief said, "The people under the earth don't want you to behave like this"—promiscuously (Benedict 3:I, 13).

† Coyote was going about hunting. He gave them their pottery drum (Bunzel 3:599).

‡ A very curious inconsistency, since you do not belong to the clan of your father, ceremonial or actual.

§ This Shomatowe song series is known only to the War chiefs. They sing them at medicine society assemblages (? at the winter solstice) and in the game of hidden-ball; also at the Scalp ceremony, when Coyote clansmen participate (see p. 636).

The next day the four War chiefs said,* "Now is the time to go again." They came to a town, Heshatoyala.† They went in the houses. "This will be my house," each said, choosing his house. At last they came to a house where there was one little boy and one little girl and their mother's mother. They had been left behind.‡ They were sitting in a room with a jar of urine. They put cotton in their ears. They were smelling the urine to keep from smelling the *koliwa*.§ "These are ghosts," they said. The War chiefs said, "Do not harm them, for they know something. In spite of danger, they are still alive." The two War chiefs went inside. "We have a sacred object," said the old woman. "If your days are the same as theirs, you will not be slaves," said the War chiefs. "It does not matter that he is only a little boy, even so he will be our father. It does not matter that she is a little girl, she will be our mother."²² So the War chiefs took the old woman and the children to where the people were. "Of what clan are you people?"—"We are Yellow Corn."—"Now after this you are not to be Yellow Corn. You will be Black Corn clan because you are black now. Because of the bad smell you have become black."

"Now we are going to do rain-asking tricks,"‖ they said. "You will be the first."—"No, you will be the first." They asked them (the Black Corn people) four times to begin, but they said, "We are not going to be the first." So the people said, "All right,

---

* The first two leaders plus the two Ahayuta. In Bunzel's version, two Ne'-wekwe have been made leaders. They kill two girls washing a woolen dress at the river. They scalp them. "Then they set the days for the enemy," i.e., the Scalp ceremony. Follows the reference to the song cycle by the spirits of the underworld. Also narrative about the hidden-ball game played between the animals of day and of night. Killing the girls and hidden-ball by the animals are Jicarilla Apache.

† Large ruin, half a mile from the river, and southwest of Hawikuh (Spier 1:219–20).

‡ By the Ky'anakwe who went to Acoma (Benedict 3:1, 8, 263, 264).

§ The smell from the big shell that was filling the earth and killing the people.

‖ "Tricks" is the common translation for rites; magic were the proper word.

we will be the first."* So they made their days. Those four days it rained steadily. After the four days it cleared off, and it was the turn of the others to make their days. The little boy went off to get sticks. When he came back with them, his grandmother worked on prayer-sticks with the stone knife. Then they planted their sticks. Those four days it rained. It rained steadily for two days, and the last two days came heavy rains. "Now we are equal. You people will be with us. You shall be the Black Corn clan."†

They lived there for four years again. "Now we are to leave this place and go to another place." They came to Matsakya.‡ "Now we will stop here again." After a few years many children were raised. They had no way to amuse themselves. So the War chiefs went to Kachina town.§ They saw the road into the water. They walked in. Inside all were dancing. "Have you come? Sit down! Now, our fathers, why do you come? Perhaps there is news. If not, you would not come."—"Well, there in Matsakya many children are growing up, and there is no way of amusing them. That is the reason our people met every night. At last they thought about you people, and they sent us. We want your powerful breath (*sauwanikya pinane*). That is why we come."— "All right. Our father Shulawitsi is the one to say." So they called him in. "My fathers, *konaton tewananatea*."—"*Kyetsani-shi*."—"What is it you want to say? Let me know about it." [The two War chiefs repeat their message.] "I cannot say any-thing. I have a grandfather. He is the one to say. Thlimna (Kiaklo)." So they called him in. (All is repeated for the yellow Salimobia who is in the north, on a yellow hill, and for the other

* These interchanges about who is to begin occur in all narratives of com-petition.

† These are the Ky'anakwe rain society in charge of the Ky'anakwe kachina ceremony and affiliated with the Corn clan and Chupawa kiva (Kroeber 2:171; Stevenson 2:44–45; Benedict 3:I, 9–10). Note that their clan name is altered and is contingent on their rain bundle, a good illustration of how clanship is of secondary importance to ceremonial.

‡ A town ruin (see p. 872) about two miles east of Zuni, where Pekwin, the Sun priest, has a shrine and makes solar observations.

§ Here begins the myth of the initiation into the Kachina society.

Salimobia, blue, red, white, speckled, black, also for Anahoho, Wooden Ears, Cotton-hanging, Nawish, Koyemshi, Tsitsikya [little bird],* Kolowisi [Water Serpent], Muluktakya, Blue Horn.) They said, "Are we all in now?"—"Yes."—"Well, when you go back to your houses, fix up six large houses for us, seven, including the house of our grandfathers [Koyemshi], and make days for us. On the first day of eight days let your children make prayer-sticks and put them at Oshokwe ima (head-sitting). We shall get them from there. And when you make prayer-sticks the second time, give them to every direction, and we shall get them. On the same day our grandfathers will be there for an entire night and an entire day." So the War chiefs returned. Next day they worked on the houses. And the day after they had them all ready, they worked on the prayer-sticks and carried them to Oshokwe ima. When they came back, they put them in every direction, and thence they got them at Kachina town. That same morning Kiaklo came on the backs of the Koyemshi and went into the different kivas, all day and all night until morning. Then in eight days he came in the morning for all day. The Koyemshi brought him on their backs. They sang as they came. Before they left, the others said, "We will be there this evening after you have been in every kiva; but if you have not reached the last kiva, you watch, we will make a fire where the road crosses Hawikuh, and Kolowisi,† our grandfather, will call. When you hear him and see the fire, merely send a cigarette to the kiva and come back to Kachina town."

When Kiaklo and the Koyemshi went back, Water Serpent and all the Salimobia came down close to the town, and all the people met them. The Salimobia went each in his own direction, a little way off, and said his prayer. All the people sang for Water Serpent; he cried out, and the ground shook. Little Bird went ahead and peeped in every kiva, and then Water Serpent peeped in, all his grandfathers watching him. The last kiva he

* Identified by Dr. White with *tsĕtsĕk'a* in Keresan which is Sonora yellow warbler (White 3:62; White 4:204).

† When Water Serpent called, the earth would shake. The ground was not very hard yet.

peeped in, he went in. The eldest brother, the yellow Salimobia, went in the house where Water Serpent went in. They danced all night until morning. The people looked toward the south, and they saw Kiaklo coming with the rest, and they all cried out, "This side the rest of them are coming." When Kiaklo said *hashi!* they all said *hashi!* and ran after him. (None might call his own call; they all said *hashi!*) As they came, Tomtsinapa cried out *ikoko!* (his own call). Then it began to storm. "Why did you do it?" they said to Tomtsinapa. "Did they not tell us that not one of us was to give his own cry?"

[Follows a long repetitive passage about each kachina in turn depositing a prayer-stick bundle.] After they had gone out to all the directions, all the brothers Salimobia went to drink, one at a time, at the house of their elder brother, yellow Salimobia, where they prepared a "spring" for them. After they drank, they went out and looked for the people. When they saw anyone walking about, they whipped him. When everyone had drunk, the Ana-hokwe went around the village and threw down pots or anything laid out for them on top of the houses for them to cleanse the town. Shulawitsi burned up the things. Then they gathered to-gether all the children. Ahayuta elder brother was to be initiated with the children. When everything was ready, they all went and initiated the children, Salimobia, Cotton-hanging, Wooden Ears, Nawish, Shulawitsi, and Anahokwe. Then the Blue Horns whipped the children. The first round they whipped them gent-ly, the second round they whipped them severely, the third time they stepped on the backs of the children, the fourth time they also stepped on them. Then they said, "Now look at us care-fully, so whenever it is time to initiate again, you can do it for yourselves. We shall come (with the clouds), but not as we are now." They went back to Kachina town.

The people lived on there. At last the Rain chiefs began to think about moving away. "This place where we now live, we think it is the Middle, but perhaps it is not." They kept on meeting every night to consider about moving away and making another *hepatina** to endure forever. They sent for Hawk. "We

* A shrine indicative of the middle of the world.

want you to find the middle place for all these sacred things, because you know every place in the world."—"I will try," he said.
He went all over the country. When he came back, they asked
him, "Did you find the middle?"—"No," said he, "I could not
find it." Then at night they met again. They called Eagle. [He
fails and so does Crow.] At last the War chiefs thought of the
big water skate. He took them below the place where *hepatina* is
now, and he laid his heart there. From there he lifted himself up
and stretched his arms toward east and west and south and
north. Eastward his arms could not fully stretch out. "This is
not the place. My arms are not fully extended to the east. May
be over there where there is a little hill; may be that is the place."
There he laid himself down. Then his arms stretched out fully.
"This is the place. Now put a stone down where my heart
beats!" So they put a stone under his heart. From Matsakya
all the people started out. They made their town here (old Zuni
on the south side of the river) and made a new *hepatina*. The
two War chiefs left and went to Tealatashinakwe, where they
went in under the earth to live there forever.

The two Ahayuta left this place and went to the west and
explored the world. In some places they would find a girl and
stay with her overnight. The next day they would kill her and
move on to another place. They went to Yutsi.* They saw a
girl. "Your home is far."—"No, I shall be there soon."—"No,
you won't get there." They stayed with her that night. In the
morning before she woke, they killed her. As they went on they
saw a girl (it was the same girl) coming after them. "There is
another one coming." They stayed the night with her. Next
day, when they woke up, the girl was dead and covered with
earth. "This is the one we killed yesterday. She followed us.
Let's take out her heart!" So they took out her heart and
smashed it to pieces. After they had gone a little way, they
looked back and saw her coming. "There she is coming again!
Let's run! She won't catch us." So they ran. They looked back.
She was close behind. "There she is coming. She has died twice,
but if she catches us, she will kill us." They came to Shipapolima

* A Navaho place in the north.

where there was a Stone knife (Flint) society. "Here our people live. They will save us." When they sat down, they gave them to eat. They took the bread and dipped it in the stew and put it in their mouths, four times only. "Do you know any way to save us? Someone is chasing us."—"Yes," they said. To each they gave a bow, the bowstring to be held away from them as in the Thle'wekwe dance. They made them blacken their faces. They sang the songs to save them. At the second song they reversed the bows. They sang the song for them to get angry. As they began, she got there, they heard her step on the roof. She said, "My fathers, have they come, my two sons?"—"Yes, they are here."—"Send them out for me!"—"They are here. Come in and take them out yourself!" She stepped down one step and drew back. "Send them out for me!"—"Come in yourself and get them out!" She stepped down two steps and drew back. "Send them out for me!"—"You come in and get them yourself!" She stepped down three steps, and went up again. "I can't go in. Send them out for me!"—"Come in and get them yourself!" She stepped down four steps and then she fell down inside. She made a noise in her throat like a sheep when you cut its throat. When she stood up, the two went at her with their clubs and knocked her down three times and killed her. "Now go and throw her far off. Don't leave her near by! Here is my knife," said Bear, "with this you take off her scalp!"—"And here is my knife," said Mountain Lion, "with this you take off her scalp!" Then Knife-Wing said, "Here is my knife, with this you take off her scalp!" Then at last White Bear said, "And here is my knife. With this you take off her scalp. When you take her far off, lay her on her face, with the knife we gave you last make marks around her back; and with the knife we first gave you take off her scalp. Throw it up and shout! Pick it up a second time and shout! Pick it up a third time and shout! A fourth time pick it up, throw it up and shout! Then come with the scalp." [After doing all this] they cut down a cedar tree. On the top of the tree they put the scalp. They started back with the scalp, singing.

The people inside (the kiva) told them to cast meal on the

altars. "Now look around carefully; someone may be coming in." They saw tracks, and Elder Brother said, "Somebody is going out." Younger Brother said, "No, someone is coming in." —"No, he is going out."—"No, he is coming in." The people inside said, "Don't worry so much! Look at the altars! Perhaps someone is there." So the two looked, and they saw a chaparral cock sitting behind the altars.* His tail was white at the tip. "Catch him and bring him around!" They caught him and smoothed him down. "Count his tail, see how many feathers he has in his tail!" So the two Ahayuta counted the tail feathers. "There are twelve."—"All right. That many days your *teshkwi*† will last. You have been killing a lot of people, and you have never made any *teshkwi* for the persons you killed; that is the reason she followed you. Now after this when you kill anyone, make twelve days,‡ and you will have no trouble."[23]

They stayed there all night. At midnight they initiated the two Ahayuta. They began the first song for cleansing. Then the *animals* stood and looked at their children, the two Ahayuta. All night they did that. In the morning they repeated the cleansing. Thus they were initiated into the Flint society.[24]

At sunrise, while they were eating, the two Ahayuta said, "These people who came up last brought away everything—all the different kinds of stones, *athlashi* and the stone knife, so we have nothing, although we came up first. How would it be if we introduced the societies?" They returned to the west and found some people to take with them to Shipapolima. All the different kinds of societies were there. They did not sleep for two nights, getting all the songs and all the things they did. In the morning when they began to eat, the society chief said, "Now you will leave this place. On your way do not drink water while you wear your cap or bandoleer, take off everything you have on. Do not

* His track, whether coming or going, is the same.

† Period of taboo.

‡ See pp. 101, 369. Parts of the Scalp dance refer to this myth. Compare the Santo Domingo and Acoma versions (White 4:187–91; Stirling). In Acoma tradition the ghost girl is represented in the dance (*ăshiă*) by the mother of the War Brothers. At Laguna this dancer is called their sister. Compare Hashiya girls in Zuni Scalp Dance.

blow on the water before drinking it.* Otherwise, all of us will take your scalps."—"We will keep these rules. You are our fathers, and these women are our mothers; these boys are our brothers, these girls are our sisters. We belong to your people." The society chief said, "We may not believe you because you boys are naughty. But if you keep to these rules, you will live forever and take care of your people. In the high hills, in the forest, that is where you belong."

When they separated at Kachina town, (the people of) *thle'etone* went north and made their towns on the way to Shipapolima. Then they started back toward the west. They came to Toya (Nutria). They lived there. Their two War chiefs were out hunting. They came to Meoshte (the mountain the other side of Black Rock). They saw the smoke this way, and they said, "We believe some people are living there. Perhaps they are our people, the people we separated from in the beginning." So in a few days they said to the people, "Let's all go now to find that town! We will live there." They came to Narrow-Black-Rocks. There was a hole and their chief put the stick he swallowed down on the rock and went through the hole, back into the fourth world.† The *thle'etone* came to Katikia‡ and joined the people there. They and the people of Katikia arranged for a trial§ to see which would be the head. No one wanted to try it out with them. At last the Rain chiefs who are now called Pathltok Rain chiefs (chieftaincy of the East), said, "We will do it." They asked them (the Pathltok chiefs) to start. They did not want to and asked the *thle'etone* people to start. "All right!" they said. It was during the summer. From the beginning of the first day it snowed. It snowed all day and all night for four days. The snow was so deep (indicating about five feet). Then the Rain chiefs made their days. The first day it began to

* Anything in the water should be swallowed down with the water, to make them strong.

† Just as Keresan shamans revisit Shipap.

‡ Spier 1:234, site 58.

§ Just as on arriving at First Mesa the Water-Corn clan competes with the Snake clan in making rain or snow (Stephen 4:853).

rain. It rained all day and night for four days. After four days, it cleared off the snow, and the sun shone. The people said, "You are the same; only we will give you two moons during the wint because you people are cold. During the other moons you will be just like the poor people."—"All right. When we make our turn during the winter, plenty of snow will be on the ground. So during the spring, while our Earth Mother keeps it wet, during all that summer, our corn, anything we plant, will stay alive."— "During the summer it will be our turn to make the days," said the people here.

For some reason the earth or "ocean" got angry,* and all the little springs became larger, and this land began to fill with water. Then all the people with all the sacred things ran to Corn Mountain. They lived there. The water got higher all the time. All the water animals were there, and Kolowisi was lying on top of the mountain now called Nose-Face. He lay on that point looking toward this side and crying out, and the water almost reached the top of Corn Mountain. The people did not know what to do. At last they looked for a boy who knew nothing about girls and a girl who knew nothing about boys. They were the children of Rain chiefs. All the people made prayer-sticks for them. "Now, our children, you are to go in the water to save your people." So they took them to the north side, and there they gave them a large bundle of prayer-sticks. They sent them down both at the same time. As they went down, the water would lower, each day. Where the suds stopped, the rocks are white, and the marks of the heels of the two children you can see

* Cf. Benedict 3:I, 10–11. A Corn clansman feels outraged about incest within his clan. He appeals to his deceased uncle, is touched by him, dies, visits the kivas, terrifying people, and then turns into Kolowisi, Horned Water Serpent. This Kolowisi floods the valley. Compare the Hopi Water-Corn clan story of the youth who is caused by his father to bury himself alive and, turning into Horned Water Serpent, sends flood which is not checked until a boy and girl are sent into the water, to meet their uncle, Water Serpent (Parsons 42:181–86).

In Acoma myth after the Twins steal from the sleeping Chiefs of the Directions the staffs with which they made snow, hail, lightning, and frost, the chiefs send Water Serpent after them, and the people are flooded. The people take refuge on a mountain. The Twins kill Water Serpent with the arrows of Sun (Stirling). Compare Papago flood myth, p. 1003.

in the rocks. Where the water got very low, there the two were standing. They had turned into the rocks now standing at Corn Mountain. They call them the boy and the girl. The girl stands at the north, the boy at the south.

After the people came down from Corn Mountain, they scattered into the different towns, and that was the time the Mexicans came.*

HOPI[25]

When they were way underneath, they were ants.† Then they came to another place and turned into other creatures. At still another place they became like people but with long tails. They knew they had tails and were ashamed.

They were very crazy;‡ the women would not mind their husbands. They said, "We are not dependent on marriage to live."§ There was a river, and they divided; the men went across the river, and the women stayed where they were, at their village. In springtime the women planted their corn and melons by themselves, and the men planted, too. The men raised lots of crops, and the women, too. But next year the women raised only half of what they raised before. In the third year, the women got very little corn and few melons, but the men got more than before. In the fourth year the women had no crops, but the men

* In another account Mexicans "came up" with Zuni. But the Mexicans wanted to be waited on so much, not to speak of how the priest would whip those who did not go to Mass or put them in the stocks, that the Zuni got tired of the Mexicans, "made a bundle of them and threw them to the south."

† As in White Mountain Apache mythology (Goodwin 3); in Navaho mythology they were insects of different colors (Reichard). For Navaho parallels throughout see Goddard 5:127 ff.; Stephen 3.

‡ They were fools. Youths copulated with the wives of the elder men, and the elder men deflowered virgins. The chief proposes separating the sexes by river (Walpi). They were bad people, smearing the aged with excrement, killing them with bones of porcupine and of the dead (Shumopovi). Their spittle and mucus fall on others because they are so crowded (Oraibi 1).

§ After they separate, sex indulgence is practiced artificially, through a gourd of deer or hare blood or liver or through an eagle feather. Thus the War Twins are born (Walpi 1) or the early monsters (Walpi 2).

Also at this time, inconsistently since it is before the Emergence, the War Twins are born through solar impregnation or raindrops (Walpi 2).

had large crops. "Throw us some corn, some watermelons!" the women called across. "We can't throw anything to you," the men answered.

About that time a flood was coming closer and closer, and the women began to build a tower. They built and built, but they never reached the sky. The women thought they were braver than the men, smarter than the men; but the men thought women could not do much. The tower fell down.

Then the men began to think about it, for the flood kept on coming. They were thinking about what would reach the sky. First they planted pine, it grew and reached the sky, but could not go through. Next they planted reeds, and sang a song to make the reeds grow. They sang and sang, and the reeds grew and grew and reached the sky and went through.

It was Badger they sent up first,* and he stepped on the reeds and went up and up and up. Pretty soon Badger went through and was looking around. But there was not enough light to see. Then Badger went back. "What did you see?" said the men. "Did you find the earth?" Badger said, "I could not see much up there. It was dark."

It was dark where Shrike came out and very cold. He saw a little stick and perched on it. He looked around in search of someone. Soon he saw a fire to the northeast, a very small fire. "I guess someone lives over there," he said to himself. He flew toward the fire and soon reached it. There was a little house and a little field with very high corn in it. The cornfield was a very small place. Someone was watching the fire. He was sitting with his back to the fire, eating green corn. Shrike went by, flying slowly. He was soon close to the man; the man did not hear him. Shrike came up to him, stood there, and asked him: "Who are you living here?" The man turned round suddenly, saw Shrike, and started up to get something. Close by him was a mask which he had taken off and left near him. He stretched out for it but

---

* Spider Woman plants the reed. After Badger, Locust goes up, plays his flute, and is indifferent to the lightning bolts hurled by the Clouds. The Lakon society sends up the dove to look for the *sipapu;* the Agaves send the *mochini* bird (Walpi 2). The scouts are Dove, Sparrow Hawk, Chimney Swallow, and Mochini (Shrike), who goes through and finds Masauwü (Shumopovi).

could not reach it to put it on. "Oh, oh! oh, oh!" he said. "I did
not know anybody was coming." It was Masauwü.

"Where did you come from?"—"From over there."—"All
right; you outsmarted me. I cannot put on my mask. I did not
know you were coming. It is all right; it makes no difference.
Sit down! Sit down!" His mask was a large one with only a little
hair on it and with big eyes. Whenever he hears people, he puts
on his mask and frightens them away, so they do not catch him.
Soon Masauwü gave Shrike something to eat. He had watermelon, muskmelon, pumpkin, and squash. He gave Shrike a lot
to eat. Shrike took his pipe, put in the tobacco, took four puffs
and handed it to Masauwü, saying, "My friend!" Masauwü took
four puffs and gave the pipe back to him, saying, "My friend!"
Masauwü asked, "Whence come you? Perhaps you are looking
for something. I have never heard of you. I live here alone."—
"Yes, I came out of the earth."—"Is that true?"—"Yes, I came
out of the earth."—"Oh! I have heard that people live down in
the earth."—"That is where I came from."—"What has happened there?"—"A great deal of trouble. A great many people,
especially the young people, pay no heed to anyone, they respect
no one. They are continually fighting and killing and causing
sickness. They are always doing medicine man tricks, always
planning how to make someone sick. They get power, they pass
it on to another.* None is concerned for the consequences of
what he does. If a man meets a girl, he will take her off to have
intercourse. There is much sickness, too much trouble. The chief
does not like this state of things. That is why he told us to hunt
for the way out. I found it."—"All right; you outsmarted me.
You saw my mask; I could not reach it. Had I heard you coming, I should have put on my mask, and your people would not
be able to get out. But now when you go down, tell the people
to come out, you have got the better of me. I will give you my
land. When you come out, send me word!"

"Four days from today we go up," said the chief. Then, just
when the flood was close to their village, they went up—they all

---

* "They change into coyotes" (Shumopovi).

went up.* Mockingbird was sitting close to the hole where the people were coming out. He gave them a language. That is how they got their language, Hopi, American, Navaho, Paiute, Shoshone, and all the other Indians.†

There was no light. They talked about it at the hole where they came out. "How can we get a light?" Somebody said, "We will make stars." So they made stars. Coyote was sitting with them (different kinds of animals came out with them), he could understand them, but he could not talk. They said to two boys (inferably the War Brothers), "Go to a certain place and place these stars properly!" Coyote said to himself, "I will go with the two boys." They put the Seven together, the Pleiades, in a good position, and those six, Orion, they put them together, and the biggest one they put toward the east, and another they put on the south side, and another on the west side, and another on the north side. Then they put up the Dipper. Just when they had put all these up, Coyote said to himself, "It is a big job!" He said to the boys, "We shall never finish this work, we shall all die first, why can't we do this?" And he took the stars and threw them in every direction, improperly. So they came back, the boys and Coyote. Next night they were watching and they saw the Big star come out, before daylight. That will be Dawn star. Soon another star came out from the south. Then they said, "We will call that star Ponu'chona." Then two came up, but did not give much light. When they were going down in the west, another big star was going ahead of them. "We will give him a name," they said. "We will call him Tasupi," they said. About that time a north star came out. About that time the Pleiades came out from the east, then the six came out, it began to get

* "I think we are ready to start," said Town chief as he came out and stood in front of them. The War chief was much farther back, watching the bad people in order to keep them from coming out of the earth. The other people now sang the Kwa'kwanda [Agave song], a long song. For four days all of them were acquiring power through this song (Shumopovi).

Spider Woman, the War Twins, and Mockingbird are the first to climb up and out. As the people emerge, Mockingbird sings the songs that are still sung at the Wüwüchim ceremony (Oraibi 2).

† Shumopovi, Oraibi 2. The underworld language was Keresan (Oraibi 2).

cold. They did not give much light. Then they saw stars scattered all over the sky. The people said, "Bad Coyote, you did that?"—"Yes," he said. "If you had not gone with them, all the stars would be well placed. But you are bad Coyote; you scattered them all over the sky."* They were very angry. But Coyote said, "That's all right. It's a lot of work to put them all into good positions, better to scatter them around."

Well, those stars did not give much light, so they thought about what they could do for more light. So somebody said, "We will make Moon." They asked him what they could make it of. "We will make it of a wedding blanket." So they sent for those same boys who put up the stars. They put up the wedding blanket in some way. Then they saw a light coming out, and it was Moon, and they gave it a name. It gave them some light, but not enough, they said. Then they thought about it again. "We will make something else for a better light," somebody said. He gathered a blanket, a buckskin, a white foxskin, and a parrot tail and he sent for the same two boys, brave boys, and they took the things to the east and they put them up in some way, somehow. Well, when the moon came out and went down, about the time daylight would first come, out came the foxskin for daylight, next came the parrot tail, making it yellow.† Then the sun came out, but it could not move. "Something is wrong. Why can it not move?" Then they asked one another, "What can make it go?" At last Coyote said, "Nothing is wrong with it.

* Down in the cave world Coyote had stolen a jar which was very heavy, so heavy that Coyote was weary of carrying it. He therefore decided to leave it, but he was curious to see what it contained. So now that it was light he opened it, whereupon many shining fragments and sparks flew out and upward, singeing his face in their passage. Hence the coyote has a black face to this day. These became the stars (Oraibi 1).

† They make circular shields covered with buckskin, painted with a face, and girt with eagle feathers. The moon's shield is of hickory wood, the sun's shield of raw cotton, one side red, the other side yellow (Shumopovi). Spider spins and makes a white cotton mantle. They make a shield of white unpierced buckskin, painted turquoise. The shield-light they send to the east where it becomes the sun, the mantle-light they send to the west where it becomes the moon (Oraibi 1). The moon-shield is of buffalo hide. The sun-shield is of cotton cloth and like the back tablet worn by the flute players in the Flute ceremony. A person stands on each shield and is thrown up with it (Oraibi 2).

All is fixed as it should be. Nothing is wrong, but if somebody should die right now, then it would move." Just then a girl died, and the sun began to move. When it got to the middle of the sky, it stopped again. "Well, what is the matter?" Coyote said, "Nothing is the matter, nothing is wrong. If somebody die right now, it will move." Then the son of one of the head men died, and that made the sun go again. "It is only by somebody dying every day—morning, noon, and evening—that the sun will move every day,"* said Coyote. Coyote thinks more than anybody. Smart fellow!

First a girl died, then a boy, then a woman. After four days she came back again. "Well, if somebody dies, in four days they will come back again." Then Coyote said, "I don't think that will be right for us. If we die and come back in four days, we won't be afraid to die. I will die and never come back." Then he overate and died, and after four days he did not come back. He never came back. About that time another woman died, and

---

* When the moon was two or three hours above the horizon it stopped, unable to go farther. The chief said, "We will give a child to it in order to make it move." He procured a little child which had never been sick, killed it, and buried it. Soon the moon moved, moved, and finally went down. The child died, and it is now his moon. (His spirit went up to the moon, entered into it and moved it; now it goes down in the same place.) When the sun was up about breakfast time, it stopped. It could not move. The chief said: "We will give you something." They buried a child. Its spirit came up, then the sun moved on. About four o'clock it stopped again, this time in the west, unable to move farther. It was very hot. It could not move; it remained stationary. The chief gave him another child, one which was not sick; he killed and buried the child. Then the sun went on.

But the sun was not high enough in the sky, it was too hot. They first told the wild turkey to try to raise the sun. The turkey made the attempt. His head was burned, and all his feathers came off. That is why the wild turkey's head is red and without feathers. He became tired, his head was too hot, his feathers were gone and he stopped trying. The chief told the buzzard to try. He is cleverer and stronger than the turkey, and he pushed the sun farther up. All his feathers came off, yet he persisted for he is a powerful medicine man. After a while he stopped; he quit and came down. That is why he has no feathers on his head. Next the eagle tried. He burned his head slightly. That is why he is yellow on his neck and head. He told the hawk also. Then all of them flew up, and together they helped to raise it. Now it was high enough and of just the proper warmth (Shumopovi).

they counted four days, but she did not come back because Coyote died and did not come back.

This made the people feel very bad. The husband of the woman was very unhappy, and he went back to the place where they came out; they had put a round cactus over the hole. He pulled away the cactus and looked down into the hole. His wife was way down underneath, she was combing her hair. And Coyote was there too. Hearing something, he raised his head and said, "You know I am dead and your wife died too, but we came back here. And after this, when anybody dies, he will come back here and live forever. So do not feel so bad about your wife!"*

The world was still soft, muddy from the flood; so the Twins shot their lightnings and made canyons for the waters to drain into. The Twins made the mountains and everything that is of stone (Walpi 2).† They hardened the mud into rocks, spraying with medicine from Spider Grandmother (Shumopovi). The chief suggested to all the horned animals to tear the earth into valleys.

KERES‡

The first people live in a dark world, underground, very crowded. They come up in the north at Shipap or from Shipap

---

* Powako, Witch, who has followed the people up the reed, kills the chief's daughter, but after they look down the *sipapu* and see the girl combing her hair and smiling up at her father, Witch promises that in four days the girl will return. However, Coyote throws down a stone which vexes Witch, who says that now she can never come back. That is why the dead do not come back (Walpi 2). The chief's daughter dies suddenly without being sick. To discover the bad man who has killed her, the chief throws up a ball of corn meal. It falls on the head of the chief's nephew. "My nephew, I shall send you back," says the chief, "I do not want that kind of man to live with me here." But the young man shows the chief his daughter playing with the other girls. She has washed her long hair. "Look! she is alive; she is happy" (Shumopovi; Oraibi 2).

The ball of meal falls on the head of a little girl who was jealous of the chief's daughter. The descendants of this death-dealing girl are witches (Oraibi 1).

† First with his wings Vulture fanned the waters away from the mountains (Oraibi 1).

‡ Acoma, White 2:142-56; Forde 1; Laguna, Parsons 20:114-16; Sia, Stevenson 1: 26 ff.; White 5; Cochiti, Dumarest, 212 ff. None of these tales has been recorded in Keresan, and the English translations all seem fragmentary or paraphrased; so I give but brief summaries. Dr. White believes that the Keresan

(A.,* L., S.). Here† lives the Mother, Iyatiku or Uretsete or Utshtsiti (A., L., C., S.). She has one or more sisters (A., L., C., S.). The sisters grow up instructed by Spider, Sussïstinnako, Spider or a voice (ear-prompter) (S., C., A[S].). The Mother has one son, Ma·sewi (L.), or two sons, Ma·sewi and Oyoyewi (A., L.).‡ The Mothers send forth Ma·sewi to find the sun. He finds it in white earth down in one of the four corners. After they try it out in the sky,§ in the north, the west, and the south, they place it in the east. Ma·sewi brings the people up into the light, to White House (L.), or the Mothers send Gopher to dig down for them (A.),‖ or Tsitstinako gives the Mothers a basket of seeds and of images,¶ and they plant four pine seeds, and up on the tree they send Badger and then Locust, each brought to life from his image, to make an exit hole and to plaster it. Then the two sisters, Iyatiku and Nautsiti, go up, sing the creation song, and pray to the Sun. They are blinded by the light. They chose their clans, Sun clan (Nautsiti) and Corn clan (Iyatiku). The

---

origin myth as known to medicine men has never been recorded and that through such esoteric mythology only, Navaho fashion, is much Keresan ritual to be explained.

Since the foregoing was written, Dr. Stirling has kindly made available the origin myth he recorded recently from a renegade Acoma family visiting Washington. I doubt if it is the desired esoteric version, although it contains much new information. The narrator was a Koshairi and so had access to various ceremonials and listened to stories told while preparing for ceremonies. I refer to this Acoma version as A(S) or A(F), Dr. Forde having recorded and published part of it.

* The underground world is called *mauharokai* and Chief kiva is so-called (Stirling).

† In the lowest of the four worlds, yellow, blue, red, and white, inferably in Flint society tradition (Boas 2:9).

‡ As creative (particularly from her own skin) and as mother of the War Brothers, Iyatiku is to be compared with Esdzanadle, Changing Woman of the Navaho (Franciscan Fathers, 356).

§ Compare White Mountain Apache (Goodwin 2).

‖ The horned clowns of the Isletan moieties, Black Eyes and *Gophers*, dig a way up for the people at the Emergence. See pp. 255, 257.

¶ This is their sacred bundle, but note that it is basketry. Compare pp. 324, 988.

sisters are creatures of Ut'siti, creator of the universe who cast away a clot of his own blood to become the earth and in it planted the sisters. Ut'siti lives four skies above. He wishes the Sisters to complete the world under the direction of Tsitstinako. They grow corn, receive fire from the sky, plant tobacco, and are taught how to roll it with cornhusk and the rule, if a man smokes when a request is made of him, he must grant the request (A[S]).

The Sisters create through singing to the seeds or images in their baskets. The first animal image they sing to is field mouse. The Sisters throw stones from their baskets in the directions and make the four sacred mountains. As the Sisters are giving life to fishes and snakes, a snake image falls out of the basket and comes to life on its own, with power—Pishuni (A[F]).

Uretsete and her sister Naotsete quarrel. They try each other out, in a sort of shamanistic competition. Uretsete can name the tracks of turkey; but Naotsete fails to name the tracks of chaparral cock. Uretsete names the track of the serpent, and, when he comes out to her call, she sprinkles his head with prayer-meal. "A witch!" charges Naotsete. The sisters fast for four days and then are to see on whom the sun will shine first. Spider Man sends Magpie to cover the rising sun with its wing in such a way that the first rays will fall on the eagle feather upright on the head of Uretsete. The War captains bind the defeated one, and Uretsete cuts open her chest and tears out her heart. From one half there comes out a squirrel, and from the other, a dove (C.). In the Acoma version this ferocious incident is omitted, but ill feeling between the Sisters is intensified by the Sun and Magpie incident.

Naotsete is the mother of White people; Uretsete, the mother of Indians (C., S., A.).* The two sisters, Iarriko and Utshtsiti, compete in preparing a feast; the meat of buffalo, deer, elk, antelope, and turkey(!) is set against beef and mutton and chickens; corn bread and baked pumpkin, against wheat bread

* Nau'ts 'it^y'i is the Mother, the creator with all the functions and powers of Iyatiku; but Iyatiku (Ich'ts'it^y'i) has become male, the White people's Father, taking orders from the Mother; for example, placing the sun for her, yet in the trial first shone upon by the sun (Laguna, Boas 2:1–9). The Laguna pantheon has become as disordered as the Laguna ceremonial organization.

and cakes. Iarriko's people finish eating Utshtsiti's food when Utshtsiti's people are only half through Iarriko's food.[26] Th sisters compete with gun against bow and arrow. The bullet goe half through the pine tree; the arrow goes clear through. Naustiti with her cannon knocks down the tree; Utshtsiti with her throwing-stick knocks down the trees, the rocks, and the hills, and with her lightning she splits the tree,* "half-witch," as she is. Naustiti departs to go up to Heaven, where she will watch over her people. Utshtsiti returns to Shipap, whence she will help the Indians, with rain and crops. She sends her brother Poshaianyi to take care of the Indians. He cures them of inter-tribal fighting by having Lightning kill and revive them. Again Poshaianyi sends a flood against the bellicose people which de-stroys all but those he inclosed in a hollow pine tree. To the survivors Poshaianyi says, "I am going away to the south. Do not fight one another! Should Americans try to kill you, I will kill them off in half a day, their blood will be ankle deep" (S.).

This Poshaianyi (P'ashaya''n^y'i) is a juggler (S., L.), deceiving the shamans or the War Brothers by bringing two burros, bridles and all, up from his toe, taking pebbles or bits of cloth from his mouth, making water flow from the kiva wall or making a bear come out (L.).[27] He (Pishuni) kills a girl friend of the War Brothers, rubs himself with her blood to impersonate her (be-coming the ghost girl of the Scalp ceremony), and leads the War Brothers an ugly chase (A[S]). Drought and famine follow his teaching until the Mother takes pity and sends Ma'sewi after him in the south to kill him by drowning (L.).

Before this, Pishuni has talked to Nautsiti, the unhappy one, about the happiness of having offspring and tells her to go to Rainbow. On her way, as it rains, Nautsiti lies on her back on a rock, and the rain streaming up from the ground enters her. She bears the Twins. Tsitsinako is angry and abandons them. Nautsiti takes one boy with her to the east, together with the

---

* Compare Isleta, the trial between Dios and Weide (Parsons 52:412-13). At Laguna and Sia, Naustiti will suffer a change of sex and be identified with Dios.

images of the domestic animals and the seeds of wheat and vegetables, none of which her sister wants. Now Iyatiku makes alive from her basket the chiefs of Winter, Spring, Summer, and Fall and sends them as Chiefs of the Directions to the sacred mountains. Next she vivifies the kachina (A[F]).

Longing for something to make her laugh, Iyatiku rubs her skin and covers the ball of epidermis with a blanket. From underneath comes Koshare to make fun and make people forget their troubles. Iyatiku makes an arch for him to climb up and down (L.).

Iyatiku creates the kachina from the dirt left in her basket, first the chief, Tsitsinïts, then all the others, in pairs, male and female. They are to live at Wenimats in the west and rule the summer clouds. From more dirt Iyatiku creates the K'oʙishtaiya, ferocious-looking and so having to live apart, in the east, to rule the clouds of winter. The oldest man in the Antelope clan she makes father of the kachina, to welcome them. He represents Tiămuni, the Twin who remained with Iyatiku and whom she married (!). Iyatiku institutes the Hunt society and all its rules; also she appoints a man of the Sky clan to be Outside chief to whom she gives prayers and the broken prayer-stick that will draw all the people together and give power over them. She also gives Outside chief two helpers, Canyon Wren Boy and Mockingbird Boy. Outside chief is to watch the plants and thus tell the seasons. (Later he was to watch sun, moon, stars. Now Antelope man, Town chief, watches the sun for the solstices.) Iyatiku institutes the kiva, a round house in the ground, like the place where *she* emerged, a place to accommodate the kachina (A[F, S]).

When the people are sickened by Pishuni, Iyatiku tells Outside chief to choose a medicine man. In council with Antelope man and Hunt chief he choses an Oak clansman to be Fire society chief. Iatiku gives him as partners Bear, Eagle, and Weasel. In turn, Fire society chief is to initiate and make altars for Kaʙina society chief (representing Tiămuni), Flint society chief, and Giant society chief. Flint society will cure for sickness from Clouds or Lightning (A[S]).

On their journey southward the people quarrel and are decimated by epidemic. They (Town chief, Chraik'ats[i], War chief [S.]) send Coyote to ask Uretsete for help (for fire [S.]). She gives him meal and tobacco to carry to two men asking them to visit her. To endow her people with her own power, she makes an *iareko*, by winding deerhide thongs around an ear of corn and at the top placing the feathers Turkey sheds for her. Spider tells her to add parrot feathers and at the neck some eagle down. Her two visitors she makes into medicine men, *chaiani*. "This has the same power as I," she says, giving them the *iareko*. "Take it that the sick may recover" (C.).

Ma'sewi of Laguna always obeys his mother, but Ma'sewi and his brother Oyoyowe of Acoma are less patient. Every night they dance before the Mother's altar so that clouds will arise from the altar bowl and spread over the world; but, when Iyatiku becomes indifferent to the nightly ceremonial, the Brothers desert, carrying with them corn collected from the houses. They bury the corn in a deep hole, making Horned Toad the watchman, and Iyatiku sees the water in her bowl and in the town's spring dry up. Despite Iyatiku's appeals to the Rain chiefs of the Directions and to the kachina who come and dance, drought and famine ensue, and the people begin to perish. Not until Iyatiku's bird emissaries find the Brothers, and she sends them something they really like to eat, will they send back seed corn or return from their underground abode at Flower Mound.* After one night on the altar, the seed corn multiplies; it rains four days and four nights; the Brothers visit the fields,† and the crops mature at once. Then the people realize that the Brothers possess great power, and after the harvest they set aside a day to visit them. At Laguna and Cochiti, Iyatiku herself is the one to withdraw and cause famine and drought, "putting away the clouds." The shamans send gifts to her by Hummingbird and Fly, who has been created from epidermis from the knee of a chief's daughter.[28]

---

* Reminiscent of where Masauwü of the Hopi lived, as is the incident of the bird quest. See p. 237.

† Another Hopi reminiscence. See p. 789.

When the people were at Shipap, the kachina from Wenimats[i] in the west* came and danced for them, bringing them bows and arrows, clothing, pottery, and tools. After the people have been led by Ma·sewi to White House, they summon the kachina, and, after the dance, while they are playing hidden-ball, some men burlesque the kachina dancing. One of the kachina reports it, and the angered kachina make an attack on White House, killing most of the people. The kachina scouts, the Gomaiowish, inform the survivors that they will never again see the kachina; they can only impersonate them (A.). This is the myth of the Kachina Attack dramatization.

The kachina hide away or are lost on their way back to Wenimatse. Their Gomaiowish scouts and Antelope clan men search for them. They inquire of Spider, who directs them to Salt Woman, who directs them to Badger Old Woman. The Gomaiowish dig a little with their stone knives, then the Antelope man digs with his crook, then Badger digs the rest of the way, and Antelope breaks open the door with his horns. Kimash°, the Kachina chief, agrees to come out and make rain and bring fruit, but first he must return to Wenima while the Gomaiowish and the Antelope man go back to Shipap. For four days it rains, and then the people plant. Kimash° says the Antelope man is to be cacique (Town chief) and father of the kachina because he was the one who brought them back (A., L.).[29] (Thus etiologically are explained the domination of Antelope clan and, at Laguna, Badger clan in the Kachina cult.)

The people are not agreed about impersonating the kachina (after the dramatization against skepticism when men were actually killed [Stirling]), so small bands scatter southward, stopping at various places. At Aco they have to choose between the two eggs their leader Ma·sewi presents, a blue egg and a white egg, a crow's egg and a parrot egg. Those who chose the blue crow egg remain at Acoma, those who chose the white parrot egg go on southward (A.).

* The Zuni origin myth of the kachina is known at Laguna (Parsons 8:190): how the children fall into the water, becoming snakes and frogs and going to Wenimatse to become kachina; and how the Kumeyoish originate from the incestuous acts of two *brothers*.

TEWA*

There was a big lake, Ohange pokwinge, Sand Lake. The people underneath the water were talking about how to go up from the water, how to get ready to go up. And so our Mother was born, White corn summer mother. After four days our winter mother, White corn ice mother, was born.† Then those people said they would get a man and woman. They said to somebody, "You are a man and woman."‡ That man said, "I am not a man and woman." Then they asked him again if he would not be a man and woman. And he repeated he was not a man and woman. They asked him three times. The fourth time they said, "You have to be a man and woman." So he said, "All right. Yes, I will be a man and woman for all the people who are in here."§

At that time, while they were under the water, they did not know where the north was or the west or the south or the east or the zenith or the nadir.‖ So they told this man he was to go up. "Are you going to meet with good fortune, we wonder. If you find anything good, you must come back and tell us." Then he went up to the north. He came back ragged and brown. "What did you see where you were?" He said he did not see anything except big hills. "You must think like a man and woman. Now you must go westward." He went and came back. He had seen nothing but bare ground. Now he was to go southward. He went and came back. He was to go eastward. They asked him again what he had seen, and he said again nothing but the bare ground. "You have to be a man and woman, now you are going up above." He went up and came back. They said to him, "You did not see anything when you went, now you belong to White

---

* San Juan version.

† The Mothers are the corn fetishes of the Town chiefs. The Corn Mothers of Isleta are also "just born" (Parsons 52:277).

‡ This puzzling and ever recurrent phrase appears to be synonymous in Tewa usage for ceremonial potency, also for personal courage and adequacy. There is no implication of hermaphroditism.

§ Note the characteristic Pueblo implication of the compulsive nature of the fourth request.

‖ Note the characteristic Pueblo circuit.

Wildcat Man. You have to go out from here. Will anybody love you, we wonder." So he went out and came to a large court. He was in an upper story with somebody. Below them were different kinds of animals—mountain lion, bear, wolf, fox, wildcat, dragonflies, also bees, the big and the little ones. He was frightened. They said, "We are your friends." They jumped up on him and scratched him. They had power. Then he recovered.* Then they sat him down. They gave him arrowpoints and buckskin to hang over the right shoulder (a bandoleer), red feathers for his hair, moccasins, and buckskin leggings, and shirt. "These are what you are to use," they said. They painted his face with black. They put downy feathers all over his hair. They told him to take his bow and arrows. "Now you are ready. We love you," they said. So he went out from there. He went back to the lake. As he came near the lake he began to dance and sing and call "U——u!" They heard it, they said, "That's good! That's good! Maybe somebody loves us." He came in, and they saw him. He was White Wildcat Man Yellow-Bird Circle Boy. He was the first one (the prototype of the War or so-called Hunt chief of San Juan).

Those Corn Mothers were still in the same place where they were born. Then White Wildcat Man said, "I need a woman." He *laid hold* on a man and stood him up, and he got our White corn summer mother and gave it to the man he caught. He said, "Now you are Water Run chief, Summer chief. You have to care for all these people in the summer time. You are their father and mother. Should any man or woman or child talk against you, do not get angry with them; they are your children. You must treat them well, even if they speak against you." Then White Wildcat Man looked for another mother and laid hold on a man. He gave him our White corn ice mother and said, "You are the father and you are the mother. If any man or woman speak against you, do not get angry! You have to treat your children well" (as Winter chief). So those were the old ones, Pat'owa sendo, Fish people old men. "Now we have found a mother and a father, we have to go up from here," they

* An initiation is being described.

said. So they turned to the north. "This is not the place!" They turned to the west. "This is not the place!" They turned to the south. "This is not the place!" They turned to the east. "This is not the place!" They were singing *poęka*, the song of running water.* From the north they came out.

While they were under the lake, they had made two T'owa'e,† two little people. They told them to go up and go to north, west, south, east, and bring back a true account of what they saw. "Try it, *tiupare!*"‡ So he took out his arrows. Then he said, "If I shoot this way, and the arrow does not come back, this way is the north." He shot and the arrow did not come back. "Now we know where the north is." [In this way they name the six directions. After the war gods return under the lake and report, they say to them:] "Now you have to get them all together, two by two, blue, yellow, red, white, dark and variegated, twelve T'owa'e." (They are to guard the people. They belong to the Outside chiefs of Taos, Picurís, San Juan, Santa Clara, San Ildefonso, Nambé, Cochiti.) They said, "Now you have to think like a woman. You have to place the mountains." So they took a little mud and threw it in the directions, and there were the mountains. Then they said, "When we work *pinan* (magic power), the sky will get dark, there will be white ones like a flower (clouds), a rainbow, lightning, the sound of falling rain, and fog."

They came out from the lake. They could not walk. Summer chief kicked a ball,§ and it did not move. So he said, "Winter chief, now you try, *tiupare!* He threw it. It ran, making a noise. Where it stopped lay hoarfrost. It hardened the ground.

As they went along, some got headache, and some got stomachache. They said they still needed something. "Maybe

* It is sung to ask the Mother "to give good times," in the seasonal transfer ceremonies of Winter chief and Summer chief. It is sung at the winter solstice ceremony of Hano.

† The little war gods.

‡ Younger elder (brother or sister). This compound term is applied to a ceremonial colleague.

§ Compare the Laguna account of how they come up from the underworld playing kick-stick (Boas 2:1).

the Mothers we are carrying are not good Mothers." So they went back. Then White Wildcat Man said, "Whatever does she need, Summer mother?" He opened her stomach, and she had pointed things and stones in her stomach. He took all these bad things out and put in good things.* Then they moved on again. They still had headache and stomachache. They still needed something. So they came back. They needed Pu'fona, doctors. They made four Pu'fona, and went out again. The Pu'fona gave them medicine.

They came to a big river. Magpie stuck his tail across the river, and on it the T'owa'e passed over. The two old ones, the caciques (Summer chief and Winter chief), were still on the other side. Then Magpie lowered his tail in the middle of the river, and some people fell into the water. Those old Mothers (caciques) said, "You have to turn into fish. Who is not lazy will catch fish and eat them." Now some were on one side of the river and some on the other side. They called across to one another. They threw sticks and stones. Then those on this side said, "You will be Navaho, Ute, Apache, Kaiowa, Comanche. You will have different languages." The caciques said, "You do not need to build houses. You can make houses of deer hide and buffalo hide. When you have babies, you will have to use deer meat. If you fight with our people, it will run blood." That is why when the Comanche and Kaiowa fought with our people only one or two of our men were killed. (So much for historical accuracy against national conceit!)

The Outside chiefs were walking along, sorrowfully. "We need something," they said, so they went back again, those older ones, into the Lake. Then they brought with them the Kossa. The Kossa made fun, and the people began to laugh and grow glad.

The Summer Mother got the western hills and the Winter Mother got the eastern hills. So the Winter Mother comes up in

---

* Presumably seeds. Elsewhere corn-ear fetishes are hollowed and seed-filled. In a Santa Clara tale where Arrowpoint Wind Boy is subjected to similar treatment, the good things are pink quartz and turquoise, the bad things are cactus spines.

the east with her Oxuwah (Clouds, kachina) and the Summer Mother comes up in the west with her Oxuwah. Their children traveled along in the hills. When they were going to have a kachina dance, Posew'a* would call from hill to hill. Then they came together in Tekeowinge. That is how they came up from that lake. *Hu'*!

JEMEZ[30]

At Wawanatutu (Shipap) they were living. Here is where everything was settled; here is where we got medicines, the "mothers," everything. Fotease (chief of the War society) was the man who planned it all. While they were still in Wawanatutu, Fotease said, "Let us see, my people, if our customs and medicines are going to be good, are going to have power. If they have power, we shall live when we come out into the world, we will bring rain and crops and good health. Let us observe our ceremonies!" They began. The day they began it was cloudy and raining; there were lightning and thunder; the Shiwanna were making noises; the turtle rattles were sounding and the shell rattles were sounding. Fresh corn was found, and melons, apples, fruit, everything we have now. They were very glad. "Thank you, my people," said Fotease. "This is very good. This pleases everybody. With these ceremonies we shall live, and have good crops and rain, and bring happiness to all the people in the world. So, my dear children, keep these secrets to yourselves, scrupulously." So all the summer customs they observed as we observe them now.

Then everything was ripe, everything was harvested, and they said, "Let us see about the sun and moon and stars!" Then took place what was called *pesa*, when they dress the Sun. When they give the Sun shirt, stockings, and shoes, all that is necessary. They said, "Let us see if we can make the days cold and freezing, to change the year!" So the morning they started it was very cloudy, windy, and stormy. The winds whistled; it was very cold. They said, "Again let us try, let us bring forth spring and summer!" Those were called Batash; they break up the frozen ground and bring to life everything that has been frozen.

* The Tewa folk-tale name for Coyote.

And so they did. There were flowers, and the birds of summer began to sing, cheerfully. So they had the power for that, too.

Then they made four mountains on which to set up their feathers for the Fathers or Spirits or Kopistaya: Yellow-Flint Mountain, Blue-Flint Mountain, Red-Flint Mountain, Black-Flint Mountain. All was done just as they wanted it, perfectly.

Fotease said, "Now I will go ahead; I will lead you all, and Daiasoma (his second) will go behind." Then they walked out with all their medicines. Then Fotease said, "Let us look around now to see the direction we will take! The direction I choose is toward the south." After they went a little way, he said, "Let us stop here and camp! Here let us see if our power will work in the same way out in the world as in Wawanatutu." Then just as in Wawanatutu they began to observe their ceremonies. The first ceremony was done just right. It was cloudy and rainy, it lightened and thundered. They completed all their ceremonies, just as in Wawanatutu. And they said, "It is all right now. We will go on farther." Then Fotease made a road of micaceous hematite, made an eagle-tail road, made a red-tail hawk road, made a chicken-hawk road. They went along until they came to another place. There they camped again and went through the same ceremonies. From there they moved again, in the same way, Fotease making the road. Finally they got to the place we now call North side. There they built houses, little houses. There they observed all the ways that they had observed in Wawanatutu.

In the place called Hokingtselekwa (white place?) they quarreled, consequently the Eagle society and the Arrow society went away, to the other side of Sandía Mountains. After a while they turned back and went up on Dyapuʻoyu (mesa to the east), and there they saw the smoke made by the people they had left. Then they got together again.*

Then they wanted to move again, and they reached here where the pueblo is now. "This will be the place for us forever; from here we are not going to move the pueblo to any other

* Is the split to Pecos here adumbrated?

place." They put down red-stained eagle feathers to be the roots of the town.

(When this narrative is finished, all who have "mothers" say, "This is the way we came up from Wawanatutu, my friends, my children, my leaders." Each one holding his "mother" in both hands goes around to bless, and those without a "mother" breathe from the "mother.")

ISLETA[31]

I

They were living under the earth at Wimdaa and following the customs. Elder Sister (chief of Town Fathers) and Younger Sister (chief of Laguna Fathers) were together, but each had a separate ceremony. In some way Wẹide had to send us up into this world. For four days they were getting ready. Black Eyes chief and Shure' (Gophers) chief had to come out first. They had those K'apio. They were the ones to dig up the earth with their horns. (That is why today they wear their hair in a horn.) When they made a gap up to the earth, all had to come up with their own ceremonies. In some way they separated when they were going up: Black Eye K'apio came out from Shipapunai, and Shure' K'apio came out from Kaithliripeai.

The Mother* thought that nobody would remember her after they had come up into this world. So Wẹide had Witch chief born with us, come up with us, through whom we would remember the Mother.† That is why there are witches, we believe; from getting sick through witches, people will remember the Mother and Wẹide.

They were already up in this world when they fell sick and had to ask the Mother for power to cure the sick. They were living on a mountain. They could not find the way to begin it (the curing ceremony). They had a meeting to find out how to ask for power: Kumpa and Kabew'iride and Withlaweri (all

---

* Iemaparu, the corn-ear fetish, the Corn Mother.

† Keresan.

War chiefs) the White Corn Mother and all the other Corn Mothers (chiefs of the Corn groups).

They were thinking it over, thinking it over. There was a youth* the others did not like, and in order to harm him they told Withlaweri, the War chief, he could tell them what they needed. So Withlaweri called him in and gave him a seat and asked him if he knew how to ask the Mother for her power. "Yes," he said. (She was helping him.) "For this power you need the head of the world; you need T'aikabede (people chief, i.e., Town chief)." They did not know who T'aikabede was. The youth said, "For you to have me tell you, you must ask me properly, you must give me mist (a smoke)." So Kumpa rolled a cigarette and offered it to him. He did not take it. He said, "This is not the right kind.† You need mist tobacco. If you have faith that I am the one to get you out of this trouble, keep your mind on your ceremony, on one road, and I will get you this mist tobacco." A young girl was sitting there. He went up to her and said to her not to mind what he did, and he kissed her. That was the first Mother.‡ That is the way the Mother came out. Now he was holding a big piece of the mist tobacco which he had got with his power when he kissed that girl. He knew she was powerful like himself. He gave the mist tobacco to Kumpa, who rolled a cigarette and gave it to him, and he smoked. Before he finished smoking, clouds were all around. Lightning and thunder began to come and rain fell. Then he had to say that he would be their head man (T'aikabede),§ and the girl would be their Mother. That is how they learned to make their ceremony. When they were underground maybe they were asleep and did not pay attention. That is why they did not bring their ceremonies up with them. So they started their ceremonies as they do them now.

* Big Head (Tousle Head).   † Compare Laguna, Boas 2:10, 12.

‡ Possibly referring to the Mafornin (see p. 926).

§ In another version Big Head goes to Tsipapuna to fetch Town chief who had stayed below because he had two hearts, i.e., was a witch.

The Hunt chief is similarly procured for the people by the hated little boy, conceived through a piñon nut. Compare Tewa, Parsons 42:106 ff., 108 ff.

When our father Węide decided we were going to come out from the bottom of the earth, all joined their thought into one thought. They thought over how we should come out, and they asked the Town chief what should be done. He called his Pą'i-withlawen and Withlawen and talked it over. The "little captains" suggested they put in some Kyapiunin to have charge over the people, to guide them. The Town chief and Pą'iwithlawe thought that was good. Long willows were given to the Kyapiunin to punish people who did not obey. Then he separated the people into Black Eyes and Shure' (Gophers). The Black Eyes were to go ahead. The Shure' were to come out second. So Withlawere was told by Town chief to pick six men from each moiety. So he took six from the Black Eyes and six from the Shure'. These clowns were fixed just as they were to be in the world. The hair of the Black Eyes was tied on each side, that of the Shure', on top of the head. They told the Black Eyes to dig up in order to go out. They tried to dig with their heads, day after day, but they failed. They told their younger brothers to try to dig. When the first one tried, some dirt came down, a little bit; the second tried and made a larger hole, then the third and fourth and fifth and sixth all tried. The sixth dug it almost out, but not quite. Then the head one tried again, and on his second try he made a gap for the people to go out.

But first the Kyapiunin had to go to a pole in the middle of the house, where there were turtle shells and clothing of all kinds. The Black Eyes were so anxious to start they took only the turtle shells. The Shure' took the drum and buckskin and whatever was left. The Black Eyes got out first. The Shure' stayed behind until all the people got out. Then they came out last. From there they all came, from the north.

One thing they did not have, an eagle feather. A woman on the way had a little baby who cried and cried. They forgot this woman and left her behind. While the baby was crying he saw an eagle. The eagle flew lower and took out a feather, letting it fall on the baby's chest. When they found out that the woman was missing, the Kyapiunin had to go back to look for her. She told

them how they were left behind and how the eagle threw down
its feather. So they named the baby Eagle person.* Finally they
caught up with the party ahead when they were close to Shiawi-
ba (Isleta). Right there the old people decided for them all
to live there always and not to move hither and yon like other
peoples.

III[33]

After they came up, the War chief was planning to feed the
people. He summoned the men, and they sang hunting songs.
The next morning they went hunting—men, women, and children. After they had made their first surround, one girl lingered
behind, and as she passed by the spring she heard a voice singing.
She wondered who was in the pool. "I wish I could see him and
talk to him." A youth came out of the pool. He told her he did
not live in this world but in Wimda. The War chief looked for
the girl, and, when he found her, he asked her why she stayed
behind; he whipped her and ordered her to overtake the others.
After the third surround the War chief asked the girl again why
she had stayed behind. She told him about the boy.

After the people went home, the War chief called all the chiefs
to the kiva, and the War chief brought in the girl. After all had
come in, they removed the ladder. They had to learn why the
girl stayed behind in the hunt. They asked her about it. She
said she stayed behind to talk to the young man. Elder Sister
(chief of Town Fathers) and Younger Sister (chief of Laguna
Fathers) talked together and went out to gather their things.
They kept the girl there, and she cried. Elder Sister and Younger Sister brought in their Mothers and laid down their altar and
began to make their ceremony, placing the girl near the altar.
They used their crystal and with power from the Mother they
said the girl was not expected to live in this world; she belonged
in Wimda. The youth she talked to was from Wimda. He was a
powerful man. They were calling to her from Wimda to come to
them. The town had to prepare what she was to take to Weide.

---

* Prototype of the Eagle Corn group. Inferably this is the origin story of that
group.

Town chief preached to the people about what they were to prepare for the girl, and how they had to take her where she belonged.

They went out and took the girl with them and fed her, not letting her go home but keeping her in the Town chief's house. The Town chief, and the chiefs of the medicine societies and the War chief were the ones to clothe her, all in cotton clothes. That night all, including the chiefs of the Corn groups, went back to the kiva, where the War chief talked to them. They were to fast for four days.

The first day they began to work at the clothes, at the manta and belt of cotton, and at the moccasins. The girl was there, crying all the time because they were going to send her away. They made wẹmi (large bunch of prayer-feathers, feathers of all kinds tied together) and a cigarette; also painted feathers for her hair. On each of the four days in the morning the War chief called out that everybody was to vomit.

People went to the chiefs of their Corn groups to ask for prayer-feathers to give her to take down with her. On the fourth morning the War chief called out that everybody who wished might come to the ceremony in kiva. They had to come barefoot. So they took their feathers into the chiefs of the medicine societies. After all the people came in, they began their ceremony, with the girl in front of the altar. First they cleaned up with their feathers. Then they told the people how the girl belonged in Wimda. Then they arrayed her, and gave her the prayer-feathers. She had to say goodbye to them all. The people were crying because she was going away.

First went Elder Sister, then the Town chief, the girl, Kumpa, the War chief. So they went, about noon, to the spring. When Elder Sister stepped on the log near the spring it began to sink; he had to use his power to go in close to the spring.

He told them he was bringing the girl to offer to them. Then a tree rose up, and on the tip of it was sitting the young man. He shone so that he blinded them, all but Elder Sister who was gazing with his power. Then they threw meal toward him and told him what had happened to the girl and how they were ready now to offer her to him. The young man said all that was true. She had been born into this world *to go back alive into the other world.* After twelve days she would return to this world to live. She would belong to the Town chief. She would be his Mother.

Then they placed a flat stone from the bank to the tip of the tree and, holding the prayer-feathers, she walked on it to the young man. The men on the bank were crying. They returned to the kiva. After sprinkling meal in the directions and to the Mother, they told the people of everything that had happened. The people were crying. They said, "At the end of twelve days this girl will be back again." These twelve days all the chiefs had to fast, and all those who were present might also fast if they wished to help.

At the close of the twelve days, they made their ceremony again, before noon, and then they who had taken her went after her. At noon the same tree came up again, and both the young man and the girl were sitting on the tip. She was dressed even more handsomely than before, and she was shining enough to blind them. In her arms she carried the Mother. The young man laid down the stone, and she stepped back to where the men stood giving thanks that she was back with power. They thanked the young man. He said goodbye and went down.

They returned to the kiva. The girl was shining so the people could not look at her. They gave her a seat in the line of the Fathers. The chief took the Mother from her and showed it to the people. They had a newborn Mother to be used by the Town chief. Besides the Mother, she brought up with her the three things the Town chief uses: his hair feathers, his buckskin moccasins, and his buckskin pouch.

IV[34]

Long ago Nashönuchu was the son of Sun. He lived in a cave toward the sunset (in the west). He had a kick-stick with zigzag marks of all colors on it. He would come out in the morning and throw some pollen toward the sun as the sun was rising. With his toes he threw his kick-stick toward the sun. The kick-stick flew to the east, and when it hit the ground at the place of sunrise lightning came out, and Sun knew his own son was working for him. The sun would rise, and Nashönuchu would come singing from the west. When he got to the east, it would be about noontime. He got his kick-stick again, he poured out some pollen again toward the sun, and again he threw his kick-stick, and where it struck lightning came out. Then Sun came down at noontime and talked to Nashönuchu and thanked him for the work he was doing for him. That's why people say Sun always stops a while at noontime and comes down and meets all his sons.

Nashönuchu had some prayer-feathers for Sun. (They are what we clothe Sun with.) Nashönuchu sprinkled some pollen and got his kick-stick, while Sun started to the west. Nashönuchu threw his kick-stick to the west, and the kick-stick and Sun met again, at the place of sunset. So there Sun and his son met again. Nashönuchu gave thanks to his father for all the good works he did for all the world, and for long life. Then the sun set, and he, Nashönuchu, stayed in his cave-house.

Then Sun met Blue Corn Girl and Yellow Corn Girl. (They lived where the sun set.) They told Sun they had heard some singing that had made their hearts happy; it must be a nice young boy who was singing. The girls said, "We wish we might see each other in the other world." Sun said to them, "No, dear children, do not think such thoughts!" So they went back to their place. But all night they were wishing to see the young man in the other world, and they hoped that next morning Nashönuchu would repeat his song. In the morning Nashönuchu kicked his stick, but because of the wishes and hopes of the girls the kick-stick did not reach the place of sunrise; it reached only the noontime place. Blue Corn Girl and Yellow Corn Girl opened the gate of the world, and the kick-stick came down to earth where the two girls were. When Nashönuchu found that his kick-stick was down there, he stopped at the gate and said, "Oh my! Blue Corn Girl and Yellow Corn Girl!" He found out their thoughts at once; he knew they wanted to marry him. So he said, "Nobody can marry me." The two girls laughed and said, "Shame! shame!" and bowed their heads over their grinding-stones. One was grinding corn and one was grinding wheat.

Blue Corn Girl was feeding Sun with corn meal. Yellow Corn Girl was feeding the people of the world with wheat flour.

Their grandmother was sitting by the fire. She said, "Do not think such thoughts! You are not supposed to marry Nashönuchu." Nashönuchu was standing at the gate, listening, and he asked the girls to give him the kick-stick, that he was working for his father, Sun, and for all the world, so the people would have a good life and a long life. Now his father would be missing the kick-stick and would be late. He asked the girls three times. They said they were not going to give him back the kick-stick unless he promised to marry one of them. He answered that he could not marry. He said, "I am going. I am late meeting my father." So he started to the place of sunset. When he got there, he was late; his father was gone already. Then he turned back, sorry, worrying about his kick-stick.

At sunrise he stopped again at the gate. "Akuwam' (greeting)!" The old woman answered, "Akuwam', grandchild!" He asked again for his kick-stick. After he had left, the girls went up on top of the gate with the kick-stick and sang:

> Nashönuchu
> He is thinking of us.

They threw corn meal to the north. They flew out and shook their wings. That made wind blow on the world, that was what made the wind. They descended on top of the mountain Narpyenai'. They threw their corn meal east, north, west, and south, and they sang the same song again. They were drawing Nashönuchu with this song. Then, expecting to die, they cast themselves off the mesa.

Cliff Swallow saw them coming and flew out from the rocks and caught them and carried them gently down to the ground. When they got down, the girls thanked the little bird. Swallow told them to be good children and not think bad thoughts.

The girls flew down to a cave where Witch Old Woman lived alone. The old woman heard their song. She said, "E——e, grandchild! Blue Corn Girl, Yellow Corn Girl, come in! Come in!" They went into her house. The old woman asked, "Why are you around in this world? You are not supposed to go around

in this world. You are from another world." She gave them
seats. The old woman asked them what they were worrying
about. The girls answered that they were worrying because they
had stolen Nashönuchu's kick-stick, and he might come after
them, and they were afraid he might kill them. The old woman
laughed and said, "E——e, grandchild, do not worry! That is
nothing. I will help you. He won't do anything to you. If he
comes here, tell him you are going to pay him for the kick-
stick."—"But what are we to pay him with? We have nothing
to pay with." The old woman said, "Don't you know how to
work?"—"No, we do not know how to work; we are not supposed to work." She said, "I will show you how to work so you
can pay back Nashönuchu for his kick-stick. You the elder,
Yellow Corn Girl, I will show how to make a basket for him; and
you, Blue Corn Girl, you the younger, I will show how to make
a belt for him." The girls thanked the old woman and were
pleased and began to work, one making the basket and the other
the belt.

Nashönuchu was following the girls, sprinkling pollen toward
the north, on their trail, and singing:

> Yellow Corn Girl,
> Blue Corn Girl,
> They make me think of them.

He flew out and dropped on the mountain where the girls had
dropped. Like the girls he thought he might be going to die
there. He repeated his song. The girls and Witch Old Woman
heard it, and Witch Old Woman said to the girls, "Grandchildren, Nashönuchu is singing." They listened. They were
afraid. They asked the old woman what to do. She said to keep
still and go on with their work.

When Nashönuchu threw himself down, Cliff Swallow caught
him and brought him gently down to the ground. Swallow asked
him where he was going, and he said he was trailing those girls.
How long before had the girls passed there? "Six days," the
little bird answered. They had passed in the morning, and he
came in the afternoon, but by their power they had made of it
six days.

When Nashönuchu arrived at the entrance of the cave, he said, "Greetings!" The old woman answered, "Greeting, grandchild!" She asked him why he was around there and not working for his father and the whole world. He said, "I am after my kick-stick that Yellow Corn Girl and Blue Corn Girl took from where I was working for all my sons in the world to have a good life and a long life. But the girls got my kick-stick, and I am after it. I trailed them for six days, and now I find them here and what I want is just my kick-stick." So the girls spoke, "Yes, we have your kick-stick, but we will give it back to you, as we told you before, only if you marry one of us." He said, "No, I cannot marry you." The girls said, "All right, thank you. We will pay you now for taking the kick-stick." He answered, "No, I want no pay. I just want my kick-stick." The girls said, "Yes, but we are going to pay you." Yellow Corn Girl said, "I pay you with my basket." Blue Corn Girl said, "I pay you with my belt." And they gave him back the kick-stick. They told him the day would come when he would remember them. He said, "I am going back again, goodbye." So he went back again. He threw his pollen to the south and sang his song:

> Yellow Corn Girl,
> Blue Corn Girl,
> I am going back.

He flew up; Cliff Swallow caught him and carried him up to the top of the mountain. He thanked his friend, the little bird. He threw the pollen to the south and sang the same song. He flew away toward the south. He did not reach the cave where they took away his kick-stick. He fell on top of the mountain Taköapien. He dropped the basket and fell right on top of it, and he turned into a snake (the belt was a token),* into Ikaina're (the cave-dwelling, hissing serpent patron of Kumpa, War chief or Scalp chief).

---

* Nachuru'chu, Blue Light of Dawn (Nashöröchi, colors of abalone shell) turns his enemy into a rattler by having him seize the belt he unrolls (Lummis 3:34 ff., 53, 241). The prototype of Kumpa whose function it is to shoot witches (*ibid.* 80), himself acts the witch!

V³⁵

Long ago, when the world was new, they came with the Town chief and Moiety Kyapiunin and Scalp chief Pą'ide and War chief. They were not very happy because they had no dances, nothing to make the days pass happily. So the little captains (Withla-weun) went to Pą'ide (Kumpa) and told their thought and asked if they could have a dance to make their people feel happy. Pą'iwithlawe thought they should go to the Town chief and tell him about it. Town chief said he could not decide, even if he was a chief, until he gathered up all the men into a big council. At the council the old men said that, when they were coming out from the beginning, the Fathers were instituted, so if there is anything in the world they cannot find out, they are to ask the Fathers whose power was given them by Węide. They themselves were blind; they could not see which way to do. Pą'ide, the one to go to the Fathers, went to Elder Sister and told him he was sent by the Town chief and all his children to find out how they could live happily by dancing, and Elder Sister asked for four days in which to do his work. After four days, at night, they met again, and Elder Sister told them he had gone to the east, toward the sun. There he found Day people; then he went to the north and found Poplar people; to the west he found Earth people; to the south he found two brothers, the elder, Water-Bubbler, blowing water through his cane pipe, the younger killing little rats for his senior to eat. (That is why they are called Shichu, "rats.") He went on; he came to the middle of the world. He found Eagle people, Magpies, Corn people, also Black Eyes chief and Shure' chief, and he asked their advice and asked for a dance for his children.

Black Eyes chief said his dance was Spruce dance, in summer; he could not give it, because it was winter. So he went to Shure' chief, and Shure' chief told him he had to go to White Eagle Mountain, where there was a lot of snow, and ask in all directions for the winter Spruce dance. With Węide's power somebody would come out and show him how it was to be.

They had to divide their people up before the dance. They put leaders, three men to each side, to divide the people. They told them they would be governed by Town chief first, then by Pą'ide.

While in the east they heard a song and followed it. They found a man all dressed up, just as the dancers were to be. So Elder Sister and Pa'iwithlawe asked the man if he could come with them and show the people how to dress and dance. They brought him home with their power. They gave him to All-the-Directions people. So everybody received him. From that man from Węide they learned the winter dance.

Summer came. As before, they went to Elder Sister and Pą'iwithlawe and asked how they could get their summer dance. Elder Sister told them to go back and wait four days while he was doing his work. Then he went to Black Eyes chief and asked if he could send a man dressed properly and with songs. He told him to go again to White Eagle Mountain. They went and heard a song. They followed it and found a man dancing. He was dressed entirely different. Clowns (both kinds) were with him, with watermelons. They brought them home and had their meeting and gave them to the people, and from them they learned their summer Spruce dance (for crops).

Thus we learned our dances.

CHAPTER IV

RITUAL

Pueblo ritual is kaleidoscopic. There are many ritual patterns or rites, and, almost as accommodating as tale incidents, they combine in many ways. Thus ritual is both fixed and mobile. Mobilized into a comparatively constant combination, a group of rites may form a ceremony, sometimes with, sometimes without, a dramatic idea. These ceremonies we shall consider in a following chapter, taking up now each rite or ritual element in itself, as a separable element or unit, in an order partly logical, partly suggested by the extent the rite is used, more particularly in the West; opportunity for observation in the East has been limited.

In logical order we may consider the ritual of making offerings or giving pay to the Spirits; the fetishes and representations of the Spirits, those images or effigies which the Spirits invest when properly invoked, and which convey power or title;* the assemblage of fetishes and other sacrosanct things to form an altar; mimetic weather or crops ritual, including running and dancing and throwing gifts, rites which express with peculiar vividness the feeling or ideation of mimetic magic, of performing in little or representatively as a form of compulsive magic† what is desired on a large scale; and finally purificatory ritual to prepare for or to conclude ceremonial, cleansing for or after contact with sacrosanct and dangerous things.

It is more difficult to classify medicine which is used in many ways and for different ends, or that part of ritual which is ever the most precious and secret—prayer and song. Is the feather deposit a gift of hair feathers or clothing or a message, "like a letter" or a passport? Flagellation by kachina I had always thought of as a purificatory rite, in view of Zuni explanation, until Crow-Wing wrote that in the kachina races on First Mesa the more runners the kachina overtook and whipped, the more rain the kachina would have to send in compensation, implying an entirely different theory of ritual flagellation. Interpretation by the observer must be open to revision, and he must realize that just as "that's why" varies for the same tale, so varying explanations are given or held, within narrower limits, for rites; contemporaneously or from period to period. Interpretation of

* Pauwatiwa tells Stephen that all the domestic animals, even those in the hands of other peoples, are virtually his because he holds their Mother (a wooden star effigy). All these animals came through the Hopi and through this Mother. Hence it is very wrong of Navaho to steal Hopi animals. (We wonder how the Hopi War chief himself came to be connected with domestic animals unless by raids.)

† As Bunzel has admirably pointed out, the magical mechanistic techniques of the Pueblos belong to Pueblo religion, since they require a special setting to be effective. They must be performed by special persons at stated times and places, in the presence of certain powerful fetishes and to the accompaniment of set prayers, songs, and other ritual acts (Bunzel 2:492).

ritual by the performer is quite as a posteriori as is myth to ceremonial. Reinterpretation is an important mechanism of change.

OFFERINGS

1. Prayer-Stick*

There is no ceremonial, as far as I know, outside of Tiwan and Tewan towns in which, in some connection, prayer-sticks are not offered or used.[1] Indeed, it can be said that Pueblo ceremonial consists of prayer-stick-making and offering together with prayer and other ritual. Buried in field or riverbank or riverbed; cast under shrub or tree or into pits; sunk in water, in springs, pools, lakes, river, or irrigation ditch; carried long distances to mountaintops; immured in house or kiva wall or closed-up niche; set under the floor or in the rafters, in cave or boulder or rock-built shrine; placed on altar or around image or corn fetish, as in the case of the War Brother images of Zuni or of the Walpi image of Dawn Woman or of the corn fetish of Sia; held in hand during ceremonial or cherished at home for a stated period or for life, prayer-sticks are used by members of all ceremonial groups, and in the West by "poor persons," even by children.

At Zuni, "poor persons" offer or "plant" prayer-sticks to the dead, after a death in the family, at Shalako and at the solstices when women plant to the Moon, and men to the Sun and kachina, all these solstice sticks being placed in the middle of one's cornfield. At Shalako, all the men "plant" to the kachina. In certain house walls and in the houses where they are entertained, the kachina themselves enshrine prayer-sticks. In every ceremony kachina impersonators plant to those beings they impersonate, and four days before a dance the kiva chief sends prayer-sticks to the kachina chief asking him to dispatch the kachina.[2] Society members "plant" at the solstices and periodically throughout the year to deceased members, to their fetishes and patrons, to the War Brothers, the Ants, Rattlesnake, Spider, or the prey animals. "We will cut prayer-sticks for our father, Yel-

---

* Zuni, *telikyanane;* Hopi, *paho;* Keresan, *hadjamuni, hächamoni, hachaminyi;* Tewa (First Mesa), *odupeh;* Northern Tewa, *peh;* Isleta, *to'ai* or *shii';* Jemez, *wotaki;* no prayer-sticks at Taos.

low Wolf," says the boy in the tale of the abandoned children. "It won't do to have him living near us here. We shall have to send him away." So he cuts prayer-sticks, and takes them to Wolf's house. One prayer-stick he gives to father Wolf, one to mother Wolf, one to the Wolf sons, one to the Wolf daughters. Father Wolf he bids go to the north, mother Wolf to the west, the boys to the south, "their two little sisters," to the east. "That is why today the wolves are in the hills in every direction."[3]

About to take a journey of importance, a Zuni might offer prayer-sticks, or they would be offered for him. When Lina Zuni's father started for the east to sell his little Navaho slave, "it was the same as when someone dies, the whole house went out to plant prayer-sticks."[4] A crook stick or cane is offered for an Acoma traveler.[5] It is "because they are going away" that prayer-sticks are given to the dead or to kachina departing to their underlake town.[6] "If you meet anybody," say the father and uncle of the Hopi youth who was to go boating down the river and meet the Snake people, "give them these prayer-sticks," as a letter of introduction, so to speak. Hopi call the prayer-stick placed with a corpse his letter, and thereby, say the Keres, in the underground world the Mother will recognize the deceased. Even Cristo would have a deceased Indian bring him a prayer-stick as his "license," prayer-stick rather than Crucifix or New Testament.[7]

For four years after death, at the winter solstice ceremony, Hopi offer prayer-sticks to the deceased (not offering, like Zuni, to the dead at large). At this time, likewise before planting, a man buries a prayer-stick in the middle of his cornfield, perhaps for Müy'ingwa, the farmer's god who barters his plants for prayer-sticks,[8] or perhaps for the Cloud Chiefs of the Directions. In all ceremonies sticks are placed in arroyos or springs or other places associated with the Cloud chiefs, and after every dance sticks are given the kachina, to be placed in shrine or in field. Masauwü is given prayer-sticks at most ceremonies. Monthly offerings by impersonators or society members are not made— there are no yearlong Shalako impersonators and no curing societies. At the winter solstice the War chief makes prayer-sticks to be placed in the rafters of all the houses to make the house strong,* just as on building a new house to make it strong prayer-sticks are placed under the cornerstones, and prayer-feathers in the rafters (Mishongnovi).⁹ Powamu chief buries four prayer-sticks close to the foundations of a house, in each of the four edges of town (Oraibi). These prayer-sticks are called the roots of the town† or house.¹⁰

Similarly, as town "roots," prayer-sticks are buried in court or "middle" at Laguna and Jemez. At the Laguna solstice ceremonials all the adult males are supposed to make prayer-stick offerings to the Sun. Only women society members have ever offered sticks. Laguna secular officers offer special sticks. A large number and variety of sticks are offered at Acoma.

At Sia, prayer-sticks are given to the Sun and, in the fields, to the Cloud People to pay them for their services.¹¹ After a hunt, prayer-sticks are given to Mountain Lion. A stick given to the deceased on the fourth day after death is made, as are sticks for the deceased at Laguna and at Jemez (Fig. 1b), by the society chief asked to take charge of the death rites.¹² At San Felipe and Jemez a flat lightning stick is made.

At Isleta, in most Keresan towns,‡ and in Jemez, none but society members "tie feathers," i.e., attach feathers to sticks.§ From the societies Jemez men obtain the prayer-sticks which at the solstices they deposit in the center of their field, to the Clouds. In kachina dances each impersonator carries a stick

* These sticks are pointed at the tip; stick and string are painted red (Stephen 4: Figs. 59, 66). This stick is pictured at Acoma; it is used, inferably, at the winter solstice, and pointed not only at the tip but, unlike Acoma sticks and like Hopi sticks, at the butt (double-ended "arrow" for War god) (White). The paint is said to come from Hopi (Stirling).

† The Town chief of Zuni refers to the town as "rooted" (Benedict 3:I, 27). Compare the sticks inspected at Shalako and Winter Solstice (pp. 517, 529, 578) and the permanent cavity for prayer-sticks in the chief dance court (p. 309).

‡ At Acoma any kachina initiate may make prayer-sticks. Women make only prayer-feather bunches (White 7; White 2:127).

§ Although Zuni "poor men" may make sticks for themselves on stated occasions, for personal occasions they might apply to a chief.

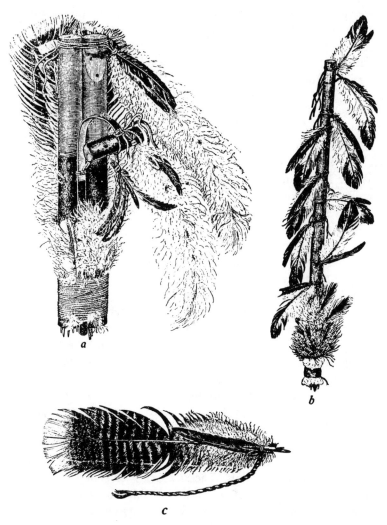

FIG. 1.—Jemez prayer-sticks and prayer-feathers

a, For the kachina (black and blue sticks, yellow "face")
b, For the Dead (blue stick, eagle, and bluebird feathers)
c, For the Dead (turkey, eagle, bluebird, and yellow warbler feathers)

which after the dance he throws into the river for the kachina (Fig. 1a). Sticks for the War gods are put down by newly appointed War captains. After their rain retreats the societies offer sticks to the Clouds. To check storm winds, the War chief offers a stick. Hunters offer sticks.

At Isleta at the solstice ceremonials the Corn "Mothers" make prayer-sticks to be taken to the fields, called corn glume prayer-sticks, together with crook prayer-sticks. The Town chief and the moiety chiefs also make prayer-sticks, and presumably the chiefs of the medicine societies. Prayer-sticks are given to the Water People in the river, to the spirits of the stillborn, and to the kachina-like spirits from the mountains. In English the Isletan uses the term "prayer-stick" or "prayer-feather" indiscriminately so that the recorded information is not exact, but one gets the impression that prayer-feathers are preferred to prayer-sticks which are of a simple form.

At Taos there are no prayer-sticks, only prayer-feathers (pp. 290–91), and among Tewa the prayer-stick is used only in drought when sticks are made by all the chiefs to be deposited on top of Mount Tsikomo (and probably on other peaks). Shrines near town have yielded no prayer-sticks, although in a wash just north of San Juan a few much weathered prayer-sticks were found of the type of those offered elsewhere to the kachina.

The wood most commonly used for prayer-sticks is willow; oak is used (Zuni, Acoma, Laguna) and cottonwood, spruce, and pine and probably other woods. At Isleta a jointed reed or cane is used. One moiety uses red willow; the other moiety, yellow willow. Willow is associated with the water or rain cult, and oak and pine, with the war cult. The Fire society chief of Acoma uses lightning-riven wood.[13] Sticks are sometimes for unknown reasons left in the bark ("blue willow needs no paint" [Walpi]),[14] but mostly they are decorticated and painted.

Pigments are fragments of blue or green malachite or copper ore mixed with white bean meal and water (Hopi) for turquoise or blue-green, yellow or brown ocher for yellow, carbon or shale

(Hopi) or an oxide of manganese (Zuni)* for black, kaolin for white, specular iron (Walpi) or iron-stained sandstone (Shipaulovi) rubbed down in water or red hematite[15] rubbed on dry, for red, and purple cornhusk or cactus flower for purple (Zuni). Turquoise is associated with maleness and yellow with femaleness; black is associated with the dead and the kachina, carmine or purple with war—"blood is red" (Acoma). At Jemez turquoise and yellow are used for various types of sticks in summer; in winter, red and white.

Pigments are mixed with sacred spring water and with flowers: the Rocky Mountain bee-plant, in black pigment (Zuni);[16] any flowers," in Big Firebrand society pigment, or yellow flowers for the yellow ocher pigment used by any Zuni society;[17] larkspur and yellow tulip, in blue and yellow pigments (Walpi). Honey is sprayed on (Hopi, Jemez).

The feathers most commonly used are turkey, duck, hawk, and eagle, turkey[18] being associated with the dead, turkey and duck with the rain cult, and hawk and eagle with war or leadership. Generally used likewise are feathers of flicker, jay, bluebird, oriole, towhee, yellow warbler, and McGillivray's warbler. At Zuni, where birds are associated through color with the six directions, in some cases feathers from these directional birds are used together. There is a specialized use of feathers in different groups, the use in some cases based on fancied resemblances between the bird and the functions of the group. The summer promoters at Isleta, the Shure', use the bluebird feather. At Zuni the call of the *tsutsua* is taken as a sign of rain; therefore the Rain societies use its feathers. The chaparral jay is a bird that flocks chattering in purposeless flights; therefore Zuni War chiefs would bury its stick-mounted feather near the enemy to rob them of their wits. Dove feathers are used by the Little Firebrand society, and sparrow-hawk feathers by the Shi'wanakwe (by the Kwirena of Laguna, Santo Domingo, and Santa

---

* Bunzel 5:859. To this ordinary black paint, carbonized corncobs found in ruins or a bit of the sacred black paint brought from the underworld and belonging to the Rain chiefs should be added in order to make the Rain chief's prayer-stick "finished," to give it worth (Bunzel 4:645, n. 6).

Ana as well, and by the Black Eyes of Isleta and the Ts'un'ta-tabö'sh of Jemez). The flicker is associated with war. A cowbird (*tokotska*) feather is used on the Hopi Powamu stick. In the spring when this bird appears, Oraibi people will say, "The *tokotska* has come, it is time to plant," and at once they begin to plant the earlier varieties of corn.[19]

There is also a selection of feathers from special parts of the bird. Wing feathers are accounted strong and suitable for war sticks (Zuni, Hopi). The curving tail feather of the duck is used reversed to the other feathers in sticks for the kachina (Zuni, Laguna). Reversed feathers are on the Cochiti prayer-stick for the dead.[20] At Laguna the feathers of sticks for the prey animals are cut across the tip.[21] Downy or breast feathers are bound into the sticks for the Cloud spirits of Jemez and into Rain chief sticks at Zuni.[22] Downy feathers are associated with the Pekwin and are used in all Zuni sticks to Sun or Moon.[23]

Sprigs or cuttings from plants or trees are fastened to the sticks: cattail by Ne'wekwe and Shi'wanakwe; an unidentified grass, by Ne'wekwe and Shuma'kwe (Zuni);[24] and for the Acoman mountain Chiefs of the Directions spruce (north), water reeds (west), cattail (south), corn leaves (east).[25] Sage brush is used in the stick for the Sun, and sunflower* in Rain society sticks (Zuni).† Sage and other plants are used on First Mesa as well as pine needles. In one type of Jemez stick the feathers are fastened to a spruce twig, and twigs as well as sticks are found among Tewa mountain offerings. For sticks to Jemez Cloud spirits a high grass growing about springs is cut the length of the stick and bound in. An unidentified blue flower is bound to the clown Tabö'sh society stick; and artemisia, to the sticks of the Women's societies. Native-grown cotton is used as pendant or tie-string by Hopi and at Isleta, and, unspun, as a wrapping around the butts at Jemez or in a War god stick at Sia. But

---

* "What they most worship is water," reported Castañeda, "to which they offer painted sticks and plumes, or bunches of yellow flowers, and this they do commonly at the springs." They also offered turquoise (Bandelier 2:47).

† Salt bush, for rabbits; sumac, by the Wood society for their fetishes (Stevenson 3:88, 97).

commercial cotton is being generally used.* At Zuni milkweed fiber was also used.[26] Yucca serves as a tie (Zuni, Laguna, Jemez, San Juan). Cornhusk is a common wrapping (Zuni, Laguna, Hopi). In certain Hopi sticks hairs from the turkey's beard or tassel are bound in as "heart hairs."[27]

Rings an inch or two in diameter or even larger are mounted on a stick (Zuni, Laguna) or unmounted (Zuni, Ne'wekwe; Hopi, Sia). By Hopi they are placed near springs or washes as a prayer for water.[28] These rings may represent ring rests for water gourds, if not implements of a game (see p. 981). Rings framing a net of cotton (Zuni, Acoma, Laguna, San Felipe) or of yucca leaf fiber (Hopi) are mounted on stick or eagle-wing feather in the war cult.

Beads of turquoise, white and red shell, and abalone may be strung on the pendant string (Zuni). They are referred to as for "the heart."[29] At Isleta the prayer-feather for the Moon has a red bead. On the bowstring of the miniature red bow put down for rabbits at Jemez is strung an olivella shell.†

A man collecting wood for his sticks will sprinkle meal on a neighboring tree or bush of the same species, and say a prayer.

> Yonder on all sides our fathers,
> Priests of the mossy mountains,
> All those whose sacred places are round about,
> Creatures of the open spaces,
> You of the wooded places,
> We have passed you on your roads.
> This day,
> Prayer-meal,
> Shell,
> Corn pollen,
> We offer to you, my fathers,
> You of the forest,
> You of the brush,
> All you who in divine wisdom
> Stand here quietly [Zuni].‡

* Cotton is no longer (1929) grown in Hopiland (Forde 3:394).

† Bowstring with olivella shell appears in Navaho sand-paintings (Newcomb and Reichard, 50); also the netted shield (Reichard).

‡ Bunzel 4:643–44. Said by a Rain chief on collecting willow sticks.

At Zuni the sticks may be made up at home or in ceremonial assemblage. In the latter case organizations usually meet to make their sticks the day before they are to offer the sticks, although in long ceremonials the chiefs may be engaged in stick-making for several days. Many pictures of Hopi prayer-stick-making are given by Voth and Stephen. The following account of the chief of Powamu society and two other men making and dressing their sticks is characteristic.

They first make prayer-stick stems (legs), length from center of palm to tip of middle finger, and paint them green copper carbonate. Next they make the prayer-feather: hawk breast feather and four turns of string around fingers of left hand, not held very close. They make the food packet in twisted strip of corn husk, a pinch of prayer-meal and a drop of honey, these twisted up in strip and fastened to the end of the prayer-feather string. The prayer-stick stems being now dry, two are laid side by side and a turkey tail feather laid below them, butt of quill toward butt of prayer-stick; the food packet is then laid on the prayer-stick stems and a small sprig of *bamnavi* and sprig of sage laid below the turkey feather. The whole is now wrapped with many turns of cotton string, about an inch or two from the butt of the prayer-stick, the food packet always pointed tip up.[30]

In the process of making, the sticks may be kept lying upward in a basket, and the placing of completed sticks in a basket may be regulated according to the several destinations of the offerings, those laid on the north side being destined for a shrine to the north, those on the west side, for one in the west, and so on.[31] Completed sticks also may be laid across two long willow wands (Walpi). At Zuni when prayer-sticks are taken home, they are placed indifferently in the house until they are offered. Feathers for the sticks are kept sorted between paper in oblong wooden boxes (Zuni). Such boxes may be seen today among Hopi; but they do not occupy a conspicuous place on the wall as at Zuni, and most people keep their feathers in paper boxes. Jemez ritualists wrap theirs in a buckskin bundle pouch, Navaho fashion (Reichard).

Women members of ceremonial groups mix pigments or paint the sticks (Zuni, Sia, Isleta), and in the Hopi Nima'n kachina ceremony women assemble the parts of the sticks they give to the kachina.[32] In Hopi Women's ceremonies the women chiefs may make the entire prayer-stick; nevertheless, most of the prayer-sticks are made by the men chiefs or assistants. Isletan women offer sticks to the water spirits on filling their ritual water jars. Lay women (Zuni, Hopi) have no part at all in making the sticks they offer. At Acoma and in the East, Isleta apart, no women offer sticks.

Prayer-sticks are measured on finger, hand, or arm, the shortest being a finger-joint long and the longest a fathom, the length of the outstretched arms. Standard length is from wrist to tip of middle finger (Zuni, Acoma), or from center of palm to tip of middle finger (Hopi).[33] The ordinary long stick is measured on the forearm, from inside elbow to tip of middle finger.

At Zuni, and in some cases at Sia and Acoma, the sticks are flat at the base, and at Zuni whittled down a little for about an inch above. Among Hopi and at Laguna the base or butt end is rounded off to a point or (Laguna) cut in four facets to a point, or roughly whittled off (Acoma), not cut off sharp. The distal end is pointed or terraced or ringed around or faceted in many ways. The facet may be given three black dots for eyes and mouth, and referred to as a face (Zuni, Hopi, Acoma, Jemez). The faces may be painted turquoise (male) or yellow (female) or with the colors of the directions (Acoma). When the male stick is without a facet, it is because he has turned his back, "so you don't see his face" (Jemez). A knob tip represents a water jar (Jemez, Acoma); a pointed tip, a mountain (Acoma). Sticks may be split, i.e., the back rounded and the front flat (Zuni, Acoma).* In several Hopi ceremonies slabs of wood are used,† and Jemez War captain Lightning sticks are cut from a shingle. (Compare a like stick from San Felipe.)[34] The handsome red-painted pine stick offered to Lightning kachina at Jemez has the arrow of lightning cut into the bark (on War chief sticks at

---

* Represents a trail, and is laid on the trail, a trail prayer-stick (White 2:127; Stirling).

† In the Oraibi Oaqöl ceremony the slab stick which the women place in their field or corn store is elaborately painted with corn-ear design surmounted by the rounded cloud glyph (Voth 4: Pl. XI).

Acoma). Crook sticks are common at Zuni, Acoma, Laguna, Sia, and Jemez, with a string tied bowlike across the crook[35] or with the wood making a complete circle. They are explained, at Zuni, as canes or tokens of longevity, or, the closed circle, as something for the Spirits to come down on,[36] in Jemez terms "to pull down the rain." At Laguna a cross-stick together with sticks to the Sun are offered after the annual election to office by the secular officers. The cross is tied with red yarn. At the winter solstice ceremony a cross-stick is also made by Hopi for sheep and cattle. It is called a Laguna prayer-stick. There is no cross-stick at Zuni; there the stick made at the winter solstice for the domestic animals (and other property) is of the same type as the hunter stick, a short stick, measured on the little finger. A distinctive winter solstice stick is made at Hano, a "sun ladder," notched on both sides.[37]

Sticks are bound together in pairs—sometimes when the Spirits to whom they are offered are thought of in pairs*—or in small or large bundles (Zuni, Hopi), or sticks are offered singly or in unbound lots. In the paired sticks of more than one color the colors frequently alternate, e.g., where there is blue on one stick, on the other stick there will be yellow.

The erect feathers may be referred to as the dress of the stick (Zuni, Acoma, Oraibi)[38] or the mantle or blanket (Hopi, Jemez, Laguna);† and the hanging feathers (Zuni, *lashowane*), as the feathers for the hair. Frequently (Zuni) there is one less feather in the pendant than in the erect set, perhaps because the turkey feather is omitted from the pendant. As a rule turkey feathers are not worn in the hair. A single turkey feather is placed between sticks bound in pairs at Laguna and by Hopi, and a somewhat similar arrangement is found in the Ne'wekwe sticks of Zuni,‡ and in Jemez sticks. The pendent feathers are tied on one of the two pendent strings (Zuni) or on both (Laguna). Cer-

---

* Compare Navaho, Matthews 3:42; Matthews 4:6, 37, 53, 67, 92, 93. When the pair are male and female, the male stick is to the right of the female.

† A reference reminiscent of the turkey-feather blanket formerly worn (Luxán, 85) or used from the earliest period (Bartlett 1:46).

‡ Likewise in Navaho sticks.

tain sticks (notably sticks to the Snakes and to the Ants) have only pendent feathers (Zuni). Again feather pendants may be spaced evenly down the length of the stick (Hopi, Laguna, Jemez). The two black spots on each string (Zuni) or the black rings or spirals on the cotton girdle (Hopi) are said to represent rain (Zuni) or a ladder (Hopi). The butts or "legs" of the Hopi Agave society sticks are always black to represent the black clouds of the nadir.

Not only have different groups characteristic sticks but subdivisions or positions within the group may be associated with different sticks (Zuni). The stick may indicate rank or societal classification. The stick is also thought of as representing the Spirit to whom it is offered. Sticks with "faces," for example, are said to be offered to the Spirits who have faces, so that they know their sticks when they come for them (but see below). The coloring of sticks is determined by the sex of the supernatural, or in the case of warrior sticks by their function.

Dead wood may never be used for Acoma prayer-sticks, since the prayer-sticks themselves are considered to be animate.[39] "I have made my prayer-sticks into living beings," says the Zuni shaman. He prays:

> With the massed cloud robe of our grandfather,
> Male turkey,
> With eagle's mist garment,
> With the striped cloud wings
> And massed cloud tails
> Of all the birds of summer,
> With these four times wrapping our plume wands,
> We shall give them human form.
> With the one who is our mother,
> Cotton Woman,
> Even a roughly spun cotton thread,
> A soiled cotton thread,
> With this four times encircling them and tying it around,
> With hanging rain feather,
> We shall give our plume wands human form.[40]

The meaning of the use of feathers on the sticks is obscure. The feathers are intended, as already suggested, as an offering of something the Spirit likes to have, like beads or hair feathers or feathers representing raiment—"with feathers we clothe the Sun," says the Isletan; again the feathers may be thought of as conveying a message (Zuni, Hopi, Keres), the prayer that is said when the stick is offered. Birds are messengers to the supernaturals.*

In a San Juan folk tale this latter aspect comes out very strikingly in connection with prayer-feathers. Mountain Lion Man wants to send a message to Lightning, so in his hand he holds turkey feathers and talks over them, then Lightning hears and from a distance answers.† In another San Juan tale, on the other hand, the feathers are mentioned directly as clothes: Spider Grandmother tells the hunter she will help him because he takes out feathers for her, which are clothes. Before the Bear shamans at Shipapolima send the Zuni youth home, they say to him: "The clothing that someone gave us long ago is now full of holes. We wear feathers in our hair. When you reach your own country, for as many of us as are here you will make hair feathers. Hair feathers and prayer-meal, shell, corn pollen, sparkling paint, you will prepare. You will take them down to your field. At the eastern end of your field [Shipapolima being eastward] you will give them to us. When, with our supernatural power, we have clothed ourselves‡ with the hair feathers, the

* The generic term for them at Zuni fits into this conception—*wotsanna*, little servant.

† Parsons 42:55. When Benavides sent a peace embassy of Santa Clara Indians to the marauding Navaho, the old men gave the head war captain "an arrow with a feather of colors in place of the flint [a feather-stick!] and a reed full of tobacco (already) begun to be smoked [see p. 297]; with another feather, which showed on it that which they (Tewa) had smoked (unfortunately obscure). For the arrow was in order that, arriving in sight of the ranchería and coming nigh, he should shoot that tame arrow in signal of peace; and the reed (was) that he should invite them to smoke, and that he should run this word and peace into the 'interior'" (Memorial, 45–48). It is hinted that the Navaho captain felt *compelled* to agree to the request for peace.

‡ In connection with prayer-sticks there is considerable use of the word play or *double entendre* Zuni are given to. Zuni for "I here hand you these prayer-sticks" means also "I clothe you with these prayer-sticks." Again, "I tie the cotton about it," is the same as "I belt him with a cotton belt" (Bunzel 2:619). Through these ambiguities "the image of the making of the prayer-

prayer-meal, the pollen, the shell, the sparkling paint, then with our long life, our old age, we shall bless you."[41]

The meaning of prayer-feather or prayer-stick as a whole, indeed, is far from clear. In what measure is it offering or pay, in what measure prayer or summons? The makers themselves may not know the answers, or ever ask themselves the questions. It is clear, however, that the Spirits come for their sticks or know when they are to be sent to them.* Sticks for the Snakes are made in the society room, not at home (Zuni), and offered the same day they are made (Zuni, Hopi),[42] so that the Snakes will not come to the house for them, overnight. When the snakes are carried away from the town at the conclusion of the Snake ceremony, prayer-sticks are carried with them so that the snakes will not return.[43] Sticks or feathers that are sucked down when offered in a spring are being taken by the Spirits who live there.[44]

There are hints, too, that prayer-sticks or feathers have in themselves some magical potency. When Cloud Youth wants to make time with the runaway Zuni girl he takes her on his back, and by means of his prayer-sticks and his downy feathers he makes a wind on the strength of which they rise into the air.[45] The feathers pendent on the face of the deceased Hopi are to make him light, that he may travel quickly to the *sipapu* of the dead. Ritual couriers wear downy feathers to make travel easy. Obviously all this magical technique was conceived of through analogy.

Feather-sticks called *tethlawe* (Zuni) which in the usual way are sprinkled with meal and breathed from are used as insignia of kachina impersonation or of such position as host to kachina

---

stick . . . . is built up linguistically. It is very difficult to tell how much is word play, how much metaphor, and how much is actual personification." Since the same personification exists among other Pueblos, it is probably not merely verbal play. Of course, there is the hypothesis that the concept started as verbal play at Zuni and spread thence as actual personification.

* "The kachina always know when they will get their prayer-sticks, just as we know when to expect our pay checks (a government employee is speaking) and on these days they do not go out hunting, but stay at home" (Bunzel 5:1040).

impersonators (Zuni). They are retained by impersonator or host until the role is played out, and then, like other sticks, they are buried. In certain Keresan prayer-sticks is included the stick of authority* of the Spirit to whom the stick bundle is offered. Befeathered crooks are set on the altar of Bent Prayer-Stick, the Acoma Town chief. Permanent prayer-sticks are also set up on Hopi altars to represent deceased society members or the "strong" dead, and others are attached to the masks of the clan ancients. Rods called chief's stick are bundled with the lightning sticks on the Nimán altar.[46] Some of the supreme fetishes or "mothers" of the Marau society and the Zuni Shuma'kwe fetish are bundled prayer-sticks. Prayer-sticks are bundled around Zuni War god images. The feather-bundled image of Mother Iyatiku kept by the Acoma War chief as the prop of the universe is a great prayer-stick, or vice versa. Possibly prayer-sticks developed as images of the Spirits.

After they are finished, prayer-sticks are "smoked" and prayed over (Hopi, Sia,[47] Zuni); before final deposit, they are breathed from[48] and a prayer said. They are sprinkled with meal[49] upon deposit (Zuni), or meal has been inclosed in the cornhusk wrapping (Laguna) or raw-cotton wrapping (Jemez), or together with pollen and honey (sometimes with sand or in war sticks with specular iron) in a small appended packet of cornhusk (Hopi). The packet is referred to as "food." Honey may also be spurted over the offering (Hopi, Jemez) or held in the mouth while the string is drawn through (Hopi).

When deposited, in shrines or in the earth, the sticks are commonly faced to the east (Zuni, Hopi), sometimes to the town (Hopi, Isleta). The cross-stick offered by the secular officers of Laguna faces the Catholic church, a significant reference to the connection between these officers and the Spanish institution.

On offering, sticks may be "planted" in more or less symmetrical rows (Zuni), or they may be left in the clay stand, "prayer-stick field," in which they stood on the altar (Hopi).[50] At Zuni, where the quantity of sticks offered is very large and

---

* Acoma-Laguna (White 2:129), Sia (Stevenson 1:76, Pl. XI*b*, *c*, *d*). See pp. 325–27.

shrines fill up quickly, the old sticks are uprooted and heaped back of the shrine. Laguna sticks and many Cochiti and Jemez sticks are placed under clumps of cedar, sometimes weighted down with stones. To bury a prayer-stick is said at Isleta to bring misfortune, but at Santo Domingo sticks are always buried. Hopi sticks, also Zuni Molawia sticks, may be placed nearer town each successive day or other period of deposit, indicating that the Spirits are drawing nearer, and the sticks may diminish in length (Oraibi Flute ceremony).[51]

The condition of prayer-sticks after deposit, in fact their behavior, is diagnostic of the character or condition of their offerer. The Hopi messenger-depositor will withdraw after putting down his prayer-sticks and then return to observe conditions. If a stick has fallen down, it means that the man while making it had a bad thought[52] and his offering has been rejected. (A characteristic expression of what we would call the sense of sin.) After Water Coyote has been dispatched by the chief and has planted prayer-sticks at the edge of the water, he finds that while remaining erect they have become wet through, a promise of rain. "Then he knows that the chief is honest"; and says, "That chief is a good man; he does not lie."[53]

2. PRAYER-FEATHER*

Feathers, loose or tied together but unattached to stick, are offered with prayer to the Spirits by all the Pueblos, and they are also worn in the hair to express a wish or prayer. Hopi may give prayer-feathers instead of prayer-sticks to kachina impersonators. Hopi and Acoma[54] tie prayer-feathers to fetishes on the altar. At Zuni the prayer-feather or feather-string is usually not offered independently, but attached to some sacrosanct object, for example, to ceremonial gourd bottles or baskets, to the skirt of the Shalako kachina or to the flowing hair of several kachina, notably Shalako and Good Kachina. The kachina impersonator[55] and the curing society member (Zuni) wear a

---

* Zuni, *uk'yahana;* Hopi, *nakwakwosi* (*nakwakwa,* want, wish); Keresan, *waponyi, waˑʙanᵛⁱ;* Tewa (F M), *pehlehchidi;* Tewa (N), *pe;* Isleta, *nashie';* Taos, (?) *pe'ana.*

prayer-feather (*lashowane*) in the forelock. A prayer-feather is fastened to the hair of initiates (Zuni, Hopi) and of prayer-stick couriers or depositors (Hopi). The Town chief of Isleta wears in his hair prayer-feathers (*thlawashie'*, fringe, feathers) painted in the colors of the directions.

A prayer-feather is tied to the forelock of a deceased Zuni, and prayer-feathers are hung over the face of a deceased Hopi for him to wear in the other world. In tale the dead complain to a visitor from this world that the prayer-feathers before their faces are old and worn and that no prayer-feathers are placed in shrines for them to come and get.[56] Actually Marau society women make such prayer-feathers for their own dead relatives,[57] naming each one, an unusual particularization. A Zuni girl tells us she was initiated into a curing society because her dead kindred had appeared and asked her for feathers.* In cleaning the Frog clan spring at Black Rock, prayer-feathers were offered to deceased Rain chiefs.[58] Downy prayer-feathers are attached to the tips of stiff feathers† in the prayer-sticks for a deceased curing society member, wing feathers from his broken-up corn-ear fetish.

The downy eagle feather worn by society members at Zuni is reddened, a sign of medicine.[59] By his red feather Coyote reveals his identity as a medicine being‡ to the Zuni hunter in Cushing's charming tale.[60] Once in dancing Good Kachina an impersonator wore in his hair a bluejay feather, the Rain chief feather, and there was talk of whipping him for betraying his identity.[61] By Hopi the reddened feather is called *omawnakwa*, cloud wish or prayer, the uncolored feather, *nakwa*, wish or prayer.§ At Isleta

* Bunzel 2:482. Possibly prayer-sticks are meant, since prayer-sticks are the regular offering to the dead.

† Possibly these downy feathers were hair feathers. The hair feathers of War society chiefs are also tied to prayer-stick feathers (Stevenson 2:596). Tying feathers to the tips of feathers was done on the Northwest Coast, by the Aztecs, by the Tupinamba of Brazil, and inferably by many other tribes.

‡ Feathers (and string) for the Ants (Zuni), also on the Jemez Lightning stick are stained red.

§ Voth 3:286, 295. As worn in the hair by every participant in ceremony it is called *nahwaita* (Voth 2:91, n.). This is reddened in the Snake-Antelope ceremony (Dorsey and Voth 2:179).

solstice ceremonials the midribs of prayer-feathers are colored black or red, the pigments being ground and put on to song.

Animals that are caught and then let go will have a prayer-feather fastened to them (Zuni). Similarly, in snaring eagles Hopi in letting loose one of the captives would tie a prayer-feather to its leg, and prayer-feathers are tied to the wings and legs of captive eagles after they are killed, that they may not be angry, that they may hatch young ones[62]—conservation measures. In First Mesa tale Owl Boy and Deer Boy have prayer-feathers fastened to them. To Owl Boy his father fastens two prayer-feathers to each leg and one around his neck. "Now you may go back to your people," he says. "You are no longer our son; you are an owl. If an enemy approaches, come and tell us! If sickness comes, tell us!" Owl nods his head, encircles the house four times, and flies away. For Deer Boy everybody makes prayer-feathers and brings them together with meal to his house. His grandfather leads him by the horn, and the people tie their prayer-feathers[63] to both horns.* In Zuni tale the chief of the Little Firebrand society summons the animals of the six directions and to each he fastens a reddened eagle feather, bidding the animal intercede with the rain spirits for rain.[64] In another tale the animals of the six directions come to the man in search of his wife and each asks him for a reddened eagle feather. The man puts a feather on the middle of the animal's back. "Because you have given me this feather," says the animal, "I will guard you all night; nobody will hurt you." Bear Girl puts the feather her Zuni husband gives her on her back,[65] just as to the hunter's fetish animal a feather is fastened. In tale the Coyotes fasten the feathers the youth brings them to their turn-skins, over the heart.[66] To the heart of Antelope or Wildcat painted on a kiva wall Hopi will attach a prayer-feather.[67] An Isletan deer-hunter offers prayer-feathers which he gets from the Hunt chief. At Jemez prayer-feathers are put down in the hills for the domestic animals.

* To the horns of the Buffalo headdress and to the horns of masks prayer-feathers are always tied. They may be seen tied to deer horns on Sia housetops (White). They are tied to the horns of the serpents in the sand-painting of the Hopi Antelope society.

Prayer-feathers may be attached by Hopi and Hano Tewa to whatever is the object of a wish, more particularly during the winter solstice ceremonial. At this time every man makes a quantity of these feather-strings, to present to all his relatives, to address to beings associated with his clan, and to attach to property: peach trees, a stove, a clock. They are tied to ladders to prevent accident, placed in the cattle and sheep corrals, and in the chicken-houses "that the hens may lay eggs," and tied to horses' tails and to the necks of dogs, goats, and sheep, "for increase."[68] The prayer-feather of the short-wing feather of eagle or hawk, instead of the usual solstice downy eagle feather, a race prayer-feather (Tewa, *salapehle*), given to offspring and to sheep, cattle, and horses, is a prayer that "they grow up quickly." The feather-strings received from relatives are attached to willow twigs, i.e., made up into a prayer-stick, and offered in the tutelary shrines of First Mesa. At Oraibi similar prayer-sticks are planted in the ground, for the dead. During the solstice ceremonials of Isleta prayer-feathers are attached to the fetish of the Sun.

When plants for medicine or dance or for other ceremonial use are collected, a prayer-feather is attached to some of the species left behind. For example, in getting spruce to wear in the dance for anklets, armbands, or mask collars, Laguna kachina impersonators will hang "four" prayer-feathers, a feather bunch, to a near-by spruce tree. Each impersonator also fastens a prayer-feather to the tree that has been cut and brought in to town. Analogous practices occur at Sia,[69] probably among all Keres, at Zuni, Isleta, Hano,* and among Hopi. Into the holes made by digging up the two little spruce trees, the "brother" and "sister," that are to be replanted in the dance court, the Hopi spruce-gatherers place prayer-feathers as "pay," and still other prayer-feathers are deposited at the base of a standing tree as pay for the spruce that has been collected for kachina collars or costuming.[70]

---

* Tewa fasten to a small spruce bough the prayer-feathers that are to be deposited at a spring (Stephen 4:376), or, probably, elsewhere. Some such practice may have been a factor in the development of the prayer-stick.

In fetching sand for the sand-painting or the sand ridge of an altar, a Hopi will take with him some meal and two feather-strings. Arriving at the sand hill, he holds the feather-strings and meal to his lips, whispers a prayer, deposits feather-strings and meal on the sand hill, and then fills his blanket with sand. His "prayer" is: "This I have made for you; you will have this, but I shall take your sand along."[71]

In several if not all Hopi ceremonies prayer-feathers (and meal) are cast into the kiva fire. The fire-tender may say: "This I have made for you; very brightly you will burn."[72] In making the fire offering of the Wüwüchim ceremony, Masauwü, god of Fire, is mentioned. Prayer-feathers are laid in the hunt fire (Hopi).[73] During Home-going kachina on First Mesa the chief has his messenger deposit prayer-feathers for Spider Grandmother in behalf of the old women, and prayer-feathers for the War spirits in behalf of the old men and warriors.[74] Characteristic of Hopi rain ceremonials is depositing prayer-feathers (or sticks) for the Chiefs of the Directions, the Cloud Chiefs, in ever narrowing circuits, the distribution on the final day being very close. Each day the clouds are supposed to draw nearer town or altar, on the last day arriving overhead to pour down rain.*

A long feathered string† is used by the Hopi as a prayerful expression, in particular for propitious journeying. It is laid by travelers on the trails to the salt deposits. It is laid on trails over which the Spirits are expected to travel into town or out, as, for example, on the trail to a spring from which water has been fetched for ritual purpose. Ordinary prayer-feathers will first be placed at the side of the spring and then the "road-marker" will be laid on the trail a little way from the spring. On or leading to Hopi altars there is a road-marker for the Spirit to enter by and

---

* Stephen 4:780, 835. This pattern of narrowing circuit or lessening distance occurs also in the Zuni Molawia ceremony and on the arrival of Pa'utiwa in the winter solstice ceremony.

† Hopi, *pühtabi*, "road placed," i.e., road-marker (Dorsey and Voth 1:19); Hano, *p'olo*. There is also a short feathered string, *pühu*, road, with one twisted string and one single string; the *nakwakwosi* has only the twisted string (Voth 9:108).

take possession of corn-ear fetish or of image. The string extends out from the fetish or is attached to a crook stick in a clay pedestal.

A road prayer-feather consisting of a downy eagle feather and two cotton strings is laid at the Oraibi grave on the fourth day after death. It is placed to the west of the grave, the longer string pointing westward, as the deceased journeys westward. From the string westward prayer-meal is sprinkled, continuing the road. The road for an uninitiated child is made toward his mother's house, since his spirit abides there.[75] The *pühtabi* placed on the corpse, from heart to mouth, is called "breath-leg."[76]

A road-marker is placed by the Tewa of First Mesa, in the winter solstice ceremonial, under the meal road from ladder to altar. At Jemez the long feathered string is also found; but here, spaced with downy eagle and turkey feathers, it is said to be used to encircle prayer-sticks in the making and called "arrow line." I have seen long feathered strings on deposit with a prayer-stick to the dead and to Lightning. On a journey a man might put down, particularly at a divide, a short feathered string.

At Jemez prayer-feathers are made for the deceased by all the men in the family (Fig. 1c). The Isleta chiefs of the matrilineal Corn groups make prayer-feathers for the dead to be taken out with the food offering on the fourth day after the death. The Oraibi Marau women who make turkey prayer-feathers for their dead cast them together with corn meal and cooked food from the kiva supper in a ritual circuit around town.[77] At Cochiti, at Jemez, and at Taos turkey feathers are put down on All Souls' Night for the dead; at Cochiti the feathers are bundled and buried,[78] at Jemez loose untied feathers are placed toward the north, under shrub or tree.

The feather offerings of Taos are, with few exceptions, untied, loose feathers. For the dead, turkey feathers are put out,* on the north or northeast edge of town, under a stone with a little corn

---

* In the corners of a ruined house of Picurís where the Scalps were kept I observed loose turkey feathers.

meal, that is, first the corn meal is put on the ground, then the feathers, then the stone. Turkey feathers are also offered at the sacred lake, thrown into the water to float away, or left on the bank. These are offered by all who go to Blue Lake, women as well as men. Downy eagle feathers are fastened to trees at the lake or on other occasions put down for Sun and Moon. Eagle and woodpecker feathers are painted red, tied and bundled, and put down anywhere in the mountains for the war spirits. To Lightning, Cloud spirits or kachina, tied turkey feathers are offered, in springs, in river, in lake, on the mountain.

The feather offerings of Tewa are also tied feathers (for the Clouds),[79] little bundles of downy feathers or single feathers. Only medicine men make prayer-sticks at Santo Domingo and Santa Ana and probably among all eastern Keres, but any man may tie prayer-feather bunches.[80] San Felipe spruce-gatherers not only tie feathers to a high branch "to bring the Shiwanna from the mountains," but on the trail back now and again they place a turkey feather pointing toward town, the simplest of road-markers.[81]

Like the prayer-stick, the prayer-feather is either "pay" or conveys a request. It may be also a peculiar expression of sympathetic magic;* itself light, it renders the wearer light. That is why downy feathers are placed over the face of the dead (Hopi) or, possibly, on the crown of the head (Zuni), and why a downy feather is tied to the scalp lock of a Hopi depositor of prayer-sticks and, I suggest, to the hair or "beard" of kachina dancers. That is why the Uwanami rain beings of Zuni carry downy feathers when they would ascend from the springs to the clouds.[82] Here may be a clue to the requirement that the hair feathers of kachina impersonators be from live birds (Hopi),† the power of conveying lightness would be greater from live birds.

---

* As when the feathers of the bird of courage, the chaparral cock, are worn in moccasins or hair by Zuni scalp-kicker in order to gain courage (Stevenson 2:584). Again, the feathers may serve against pursuit. See pp. 156, 233.

† They are supposed to be dropped for the kachina by eagles in flight; but, as these donations are scarce, captive birds are plucked.

3. Meal: Pollen: Shell Mixture: Tobacco: Pigments

Corn meal is even more associated with prayer than prayer-stick or feather. Usually the meal is held in the hand to the mouth and prayed on and breathed on,[83] before it is sprinkled. Over prayer-sticks in the making or set out on the altar or offered in shrine or buried, prayer-meal* is sprinkled as well as in the hole for the offering.

Meal may be offered and buried without prayer-stick, or sprinkled on shrine or ground to any Spirit that is being addressed but especially to Sun, who "wants it." Says the Zuni, "We want *tekohana* [light, i.e., welfare] from Sun, therefore we sprinkle meal for him." Meal is sprinkled toward the east at dawn by all Zuni ceremonialists and in all Zuni and Hopi ceremonies.† The Oraibi ceremonialist will pray: "Sun, my father! O make it rain, and we shall drink." After their return from the springs, throughout the year, Acoma War chiefs walk through town calling to the people, even to the little children, to come out to sprinkle meal to Sun.[84] In many towns, Zuni, Isleta, San Juan, Hano, and probably elsewhere, any person may perform this rite, unprompted, at dawn. "Eat!" says the Tewa sprinkler, as he prays for life.[85]

Meal is sprinkled over the heads or shoulders of kachina in the dance or on domiciliary or kiva visits. At Cochiti, as the kachina are about to leave, onlookers throw meal toward them, saying, "Eat, eat that you may give us life, health, melons!" When Espejo and his little party visited Walpi in 1583, the townspeople came out to meet them, and, writes the chronicler, "each one carried his bag and jicara (gourd bowl) of *pinole* (corn meal), scattering some of it on the road and some over us and on the horses and servants."[86]

Meal is sprinkled over kachina masks when set out on the

---

* Hopi, *homñumni*; Zuni, *k̇awaiawe*; Keres, *pĕ'tana*; Jemez, *dahbö*, coarse meal; Tewa, *k'ẹbowa*.

† Voth 4:28; Dorsey and Voth 1:23, 51. "Go to behold" [dawn, sun] Voth 4:17. Probably also at Taos and in other pueblos.

altar,* over the Corn Mothers and other fetishes. It is sprinkled on the Hopi Snake whip or on the clay nodule used in the kick race, with a prayer to the nodule to keep its course, away from cactus or yucca, not to lose itself in brush or rat hole.[87] The first steam locomotive seen by Acoma people was sprinkled with meal.[88]

Meal is sprinkled on the corpse or rubbed on the face, or dropped into the mouth (Cochiti). In the grave of man or of eagle, meal is sprinkled before the body is lowered. Meal is sprinkled on a deer after it has been killed and when it is brought home and laid out like a deceased person (Zuni, Acoma, Laguna, Santa Ana, Sia, Isleta, pollen too). In the kachina rabbit hunt (Zuni) and in the Hopi Snake-Antelope ceremony[89] meal is sprinkled on the rabbits taken. On Second Mesa a rabbit is laid with its head pointing in the direction of the hunting-ground and sprinkled with meal (or wafer-bread crumbs), the woman praying that the rabbit will be satisfied and allow its children to be caught.[90] When a rabbit is given to a Hano woman, she sprinkles it "to feed it."[91] At Taos meal (and pollen) is sprinkled on dead deer and rabbits, and on the animal heads used in the Deer and Buffalo dances meal is *rubbed* as well as on Deer impersonators.[92] In San Juan tale meal is given to the Snakes and the Ants.

When wood or plants are gathered, meal is sprinkled on a plant or tree of the same species which is growing near by and not taken (Zuni, Laguna), and spruce brought into kiva is sprinkled (Isleta). Analogously, clay-gatherers will sprinkle meal (Isleta, Taos, Hano).[93] Meal or pollen is sprinkled into springs and into the "spring" bowl of water on the altar, presumably for the Clouds. Meal balls are cast down the kiva hatchway in Hopi or Zuni ceremonies. "Now he (the kachina chief) has brought in to us the warm breath of summer, so that we may have good crops," says the Zuni kiva manager who receives the meal ball the kachina has cast down the hatchway. This meal will be used to pray with by kachina personators if they are afraid of early frosts in summer.[94]

---

* Acomans passing a kiva at night will cast meal into the opening near the ground, inferably for the kachina masks within (White 2:31).

A cornhusk packet of meal will be given to men chosen to impersonate kachina (Zuni) or to present to the kachina (Cochiti), to a society officer invited to attend the meeting of another society, to a doctor whose attendance is thereby requested,* or to the man chosen to become one's ceremonial father in joining a society. In all these cases the packet is presented and received with prayer,[95] and the meal will be offered in turn to the Spirits.

After hair-washing in naming ritual, meal is rubbed on the face and chest (Hopi, Hano). "They wash your old name and life away; with the meal they give you new life; you start afresh." Ceremonialists who have been sprinkling meal may "wash" their hands with it; and in this way they wash their hands before handling the more sacred fetishes (Zuni, Hopi) or a tray of prayer-sticks (Oraibi). Wüwüchim society men rub meal on their face.† Pekwin rubs meal on the foreheads of the Koyemshi.[96] In these practices the meal represents life, vitality, I take it, rather than actual food.

Again meal, a meal line or cross or circle, is used to mark sacrosanct places or positions, where a mask or corn fetish is to be placed or a standard set (Hopi) or where a kachina or ceremonialist is to stand or sit. At the close of the Oraibi Snake ceremony a circle of meal with lines for the directions is made by the Snake chief, and into it all the women of the Snake clan throw meal, "a bed" for the snakes.[97] In the installation of the Zuni War chief he and the installing Town chief stand on a meal-painting made by Pekwin.[98] Like Pekwin's cloud terrace design or the six convergent meal lines of the Hopi altar of the directions, meal-paintings may be part of the ground altar design or the whole design may be of meal (Zuni, Sia, Isleta, Santo Domingo, Santa Ana).

Two or four parallel lines of meal may be laid on each wall of a

* A loose handful may be carried to the doctor, "if you are in a hurry" (Hano).

† Possibly to beautify themselves, T'aiowa, their patron spirit, being a handsome man. Hopi women will rub meal on their face for looks (Stephen 4:143, 840, 901); Zuni women too.

house and on roof and floor, as in Shalako (Zuni) or in Hopi ceremonies* or as ritual for a newborn infant. These Zuni marks are made by Shalako elder brother and then switched with yucca by Shalako younger brother "to make the house strong," it is said, or "to send down roots for the house,"† so many people are coming into the house that among them may be witches, i.e., the rite is of an exorcising nature. The lines made by kachina on the kiva hatch have been interpreted as a tally (Zuni); each day of reckoning (or every fourth day after Hopi childbirth) a line is rubbed off. Tally, exorcism, invocation—not unusual, such interpretative plurality.

White corn is almost always used for ceremonial meal.‡ The meal is coarse, since it is ground but once.§ In the West women may hold grinding-parties and sing or invite men to sing or make music,[99] but prayer-meal may be ground at any time by any woman, preferably by an innocent girl (Hopi).[100]

The meal to be sprinkled may be carried in a bowl as by the dance leader at Zuni, or in a pouch fastened to a bandoleer (Zuni, Hopi, Keres, Isleta), or in a small sack (Hopi), or it may be wrapped in a cornhusk packet and tucked in the belt. A bowl of

---

* Stephen 4:172, 173, 842, 845, 872, 878, 894, 917. The marks are called *kihu*, house. They appear in the sand-painting of the "house of the Sun" in the Powamu ceremony (Voth 2:76 n.). Voth heard these wall marks called "houses of the Clouds" (Voth 7:49), and they are to summon the Clouds to sit over these places. The marks are made at recurrent words of the altar song, the "house song" (Voth 4:14; Voth 8:70-71, Pls. V, XIV).

† Hopi houses are said to have imaginary blossoms and roots (Voth 2:76 n.). Among the corner deposits for a new house there are pieces of cactus "to give the house roots so that it will stand solid and strong" (Beaglehole 3:58).

‡ The meal in the Oraibi Powalawu ceremony is made of corn and of the seeds of watermelon, muskmelon, squash, cotton, etc. (Voth 2:78). The priest at Santa Ana in charge of the irrigation ditch makes his meal of a small white bean, *Phaseolus vulgaris* (found in pre-Spanish sites) (it might possibly be *Phaseolus acutifolius*). While the ditch is in use he prays with this meal, to the Horned Snake and perhaps other Spirits (White). For bean meal as Tewa medicine for neuralgia see Robbins, Harrington, Freire-Marreco, 100.

§ An exception is the meal thrown down the kiva hatch. This must be very fine, to cohere, like the meal the girls in Zuni tale have to grind and throw at an abalone shell as a courtship test (Benedict 3:I, 317, 337).

prayer-meal is generally available on the mantel or other convenient place in the house* or on any altar.

Corn pollen† may be used to sprinkle with or a shell mixture—commonly white shell and turquoise, to which may be added coral, red shell, abalone, or micaceous hematite—may be mixed with meal or offered without meal (Laguna, where meal may also be first sprinkled, then pollen, and then the shell mixture).[101] The Santo Domingo shaman is invited or summoned with the shell, turquoise, and meal mixture.[102]

Between corn pollen and corn meal there appears to be little discrimination in usage‡ except that pollen is favored for offerings to the animals, particularly snakes. In San Juan tale pollen is offered to Parrot chief, and pollen is sprinkled on the heads of snakes (Hopi, Laguna, Sia). "Put the pollen on the top of my head that I may eat it," says Rattlesnake to Coyote in the Sia version of bungling host. Hopi mix corn pollen with pollen from other plants, from larkspur and yellow tulip, and with petals. The chief of the Zuni Big Firebrand society sprinkles with flower pollen.

A particular way of offering pollen occurs at Taos; it is blown into the air,§ up to the Sun, by racers. In Taos tale when Sun's sons start to fly to Sun each on a wing of Hawk, their uncles blow pollen to give them strength to reach Sun.[103]

At Zuni shell mixture‖ is used for Rain chief prayer-sticks, to deposit under a new house, to sprinkle and "save yourself" if you break a continence rule, or as an offering for deer or for eagle. It is sprinkled below the eagle nest "if the hunter wants the birds very much and wants them to let him catch them easily"; and again, when an eagle is plucked, shell mixture is

* Noted at Santa Clara, San Ildefonso, Picurís, Laguna, Acoma, San Felipe, Jemez and other towns (Bourke 1:508).

† Zuni, o'nean'e; Hopi, tala'si; Sia, hatawe; Isleta, papthur; Taos, mawiena.

‡ Pollen may be sprinkled on the dead (Sia); but it appears never to be sprinkled on the kachina.

§ Pollen is blown out of the hand in prayer to a supernatural by the Western Apache (Goodwin). It is thought of as reaching or hitting the Spirit because it is blown. Compare Bourke 1:501, 503.

‖ KI'o'o, hard; Laguna, tsatyni (shkati˙na), Sia, i'ʰsatien.

sprinkled on the ground that the new feathers may come in white. "Tell your people that whenever they want our feathers, they have to give us shell mixture," the Eagles say to the Zuni boy they have rescued from bewitchment into a coyote. Where the deer is killed, shell mixture (with pollen instead of meal) is put into a hole, and the deer is laid over it, "to get deer again easily" (Zuni).[104] The Laguna hunter puts shells and precious stones in the deer tracks he sees; shell mixture is cast into the rabbit hunt fire. Hopi cut out the deer's penis and sprinkle it with turquoise and pollen. Similarly the Acoma hunter took out the stomach of the deer or antelope, and in it placed the vulva or the penis and testicles of the animal and sprinkled pollen.[105]

Half-burned reed or cane cigarettes have been found with prayer-sticks or prayer-feathers (Zuni, Jemez, Tewa). These are cigarettes, probably of wild tobacco, which have been puffed in the directions;[106] but, since they are deposited with prayer-sticks or feathers, they are also in the nature of an offering or request* in themselves. This is true also of the reed cigarettes bound in with prayer-sticks around the images of the Zuni War gods, and offered besides in War god shrines. At Acoma cigarettes are added to the food given to the war fetishes on the altar of the KaBina society. I found no cigarette offerings at Laguna; but in folk tale they are given to the supernaturals.[107] Reed cigarettes stoppered with cotton and yellow bird or bluebird feathers are offered with lightning War god sticks at Jemez;† and feather-stoppered blue-painted‡ cane cigarettes are used on First Mesa.[108] Reed or cane cigarettes are among the offerings to the Spirits at Isleta where requests for ceremonial, for example, for the service of a shaman, are made with the presentation of a cigarette.

---

* We recall the half-smoked reed cigarette sent on the Santa Clara peace embassy to the Navaho (p. 282).

† Similarly stoppered reeds offered by the Oraibi War chief contain specular iron; the feathers are blown through kiva hatchway as a wish for warm weather when the summer birds come (Voth 2:78). This may be the meaning of the feather stoppers elsewhere.

‡ Cane cigarettes are painted black at Zuni (Cushing 6:162) or the colors of the directions (see pp. 623-24).

Quite generally a cigarette should accompany a ceremonial request. When the Isletans are examining the little boy about the office of Town chieftaincy, he says, "For you to ask me properly and have me tell you, you must give me a smoke,"[109] and he insists on getting native tobacco. At Zuni a kachina dance group will be invited to dance with a cigarette, and native tobacco and reed must be used. Recruits for temporary clowns are made through offering a smoke (Santo Domingo, Acoma). If a man accepts the shaman's cigarette, he must come out as Kashale.[110] If an Acoman give the Fire society chief a cigarette, the chief has to initiate him. The Kashale themselves made a long cane cigarette with a little honey in the mouth end (Fire society cigarette similar), and anyone who smoked it was bound to do what the Kashale wished.* The cigarette, even more than other offerings, is compulsive (see pp. 80, 486).

Pinches of tobacco are offered to Masauwü on First Mesa,[111] to Buzzard in Laguna tale,† and to the Ants in curing at Isleta. Tobacco is sprinkled not uncommonly over food offerings (Hopi).

Iridescent black pigment‡ and red pigment are offered with other things in Zuni War god shrines.

> Now this night,
> My prayer-meal,
> My shell,
> My corn pollen,
> My sparkling paint,
> My red paint,
> My water roll (cigarette)
> You have taken.[112]

Red pigment and sticks of black pigment may be carried at Zuni as amulets.[113] The black and red ritual pigments of Isleta are

---

* Stirling. Compare Isleta, Parsons 52: Figs. 21, 22. During the Acoma Scalp ceremony nobody could smoke any but Kashale cigarettes (these four days Kashale were in charge) on pain of being killed in battle or of being haunted as were the War gods.

† Boas 2:12–13. Caterpillar wipes his hands off on cornhusks, and tobacco comes off.

‡ *Tsuhapa*, a kind of plumbago bartered from Havasupai or found in mines toward the west (Cushing 1:35), identified as fine grains of quartz sphalerite and galena, a ground concentrate of zinc ore (Bunzel 5:861).

given to the Sun, flipped up between thumb and index finger, at irrigation ceremonial.[114] Specular iron powder is blown through the kiva hatchway by the Oraibi War chief.[115] Pigments, inferably black and red, belonged to the Kapina society of Laguna;[116] and red pigment together with white mica, beads, meal, and pollen are offered to Mountain Lion by the Laguna hunter Arrow Youth.[117] The skulls and bones of antelope and deer were painted with red on Second Mesa.[118] Red pigment is offered to the Stars and to the Scalps at Taos, and scalps were painted red inside. Among Tewa, a "black dirt" (*poshu̜*), found after rainfall, is an offering to Lightning and to Water Serpent.

4. BEADS

Beads of shell, coral, or turquoise may be strung on the pendants of prayer-sticks, particularly when something specific is prayed for (Zuni). For example, white shell beads are strung on prayer-sticks for offspring in the shrine on Corn Mesa; and "when he has been sick," i.e., in connection with a cure, a person's prayer-stick may have a bead.* Beads are put down with the food offering to the kachina which is deposited at the river at the summer solstice ceremony.[119] A turquoise bead may be laid under the kick-stick of the race,[120] one may be fastened to the paint pot of a Rain chief,[121] or to the back of an animal fetish.† The bead pay made a Zuni chief or doctor—the standard string is long enough to encircle his thumb—is hung around his fetish.

Strings of beads may be hung around any fetish. The corn fetish always has one. When the Zuni corn fetish is broken up at death and the feathers made into prayer-sticks to be buried near the river, the string of beads is broken and the beads strung on feather pendants. Beads are included in the offerings to the dead

* At a Chakwena dance at Laguna for a sick woman, prayer-sticks were given to the kachina and four beads "to represent the woman"; but I have never seen a Laguna prayer-stick with a bead. Beads found in ruins are given to the War captains (Boas 2:286). What for? Hunting?

† Amulet usage. Sometimes the turquoise is inlaid (Sia, White). At Taos a turquoise bead is worn in the belt against witches. See p. 180 for turquoise used as charm.

at Cochiti.[122] From ancient times bead necklaces, bracelets, or earrings have been buried with the dead.

A red bead, a woman's bead, is attached to the Isletan prayer-feather for the Moon,[123] and red beads and turquoise beads are put down by deer hunters.* A bead necklace is hung temporarily around the neck of a laid-out deer (Zuni, Acoma [Stirling], Laguna).

Turquoise has power to make attractive and desirable.[124] It was offered to the War gods before going to war (Zuni). It is placed under the foundation of a kiva (Acoma [Stirling]) or of any Zuni house. Among other wonders Fray Marcos was told of turquoise in connection with the houses of Cibola (Zuni Valley) —"in the door-sills and lintels (!) of the principal houses (!) [are] many figures of turquoise stones"[125]—and turquoise was buried in or near Casa Grande, records Father Velarde (1716),† a clue to Pueblo occupancy long overlooked.

Olivella shells, the wampum of the Pacific Coast, are used in the war cults, strung around War god images (Oraibi, Zuni)‡ or on the string of a miniature bow (Jemez) or used on wrist guards (Jemez) and dance bandoleers. The hero of Tewa tales is called Olivella Flower. With early Pueblos and the Basket Makers olivella beads had great vogue. Strings were placed in graves, or loose shells in the mouth (Basket Makers).[126]

5. Food

Corn meal and pollen are the staple food offerings. Honey, too. In the Cochiti tale of Montezuma his food is that of the Spirits—corn pollen and wild honey mixed. Honey, we recall, is

---

* Compare Mishongnovi, p. 197.

† Pima and Mexicans prized turquoise, mainly because of its valuable quality of restraining the flow of blood in men and women (Velarde, 127). Was this belief ever entertained by Pueblos? It would account for offering turquoise in war. Possibly it is merely a posteriori belief among Pima and Mexicans.

‡ Voth 3:287; Stevenson 2: Pl. CXXXVIII. An abalone shell gorget must also be hung to the annually made War god images of Zuni. This kind of gorget also appears on War god images at Oraibi (Voth 2: Pl. XXXVIII). Such gorgets or pendants were found on skeletons in the Pueblo I pit houses at Kiatuthlanna, forty miles southwest of Zuni (Roberts 1:160, Pl. 42).

part of the food package on Hopi prayer-sticks, and honey is spurted on the sticks.[127] After Powamu chief deposits prayer-sticks and prayer-feathers and meal in a certain kachina shrine, he takes a little honey into his mouth to spurt to the cardinal points, which is called "feeding the clouds."[128] Honey is dropped on the whizzer for calling the clouds (Hopi). Frequently honey is put on the tongue of prayer-stick or feather depositors, and before smoking the cloud-producing pipe, honey may be taken into the mouth.[129] Honey, we recall, is in the Acoman Kashale's cigarette. Hopi rub honey on the spruce from which they cut branches for ritual use.

Food is offered in other forms, uncooked and cooked.* Rabbit meat is taken to the fields as an offering at planting and harvesting, "to feed the corn" (Cochiti).[130] Mishongnovi farmers throw a bit of food from their noon lunch onto the field they are planting.[131] Deer meat and bread crumbs with meal and pollen are placed by a Laguna man in the middle of his field when he starts to plant it with wheat. This is food for the Spirits—Storm Clouds, Earth Mother, and Kopishtaya; in gratitude they will send rain and further the crops.[132] After his kill the Isletan hunter cuts off the tip of one of the deer's ears for the Dead, besides throwing aside a piece of meat for the People of the Directions and burying a piece for Earth to eat. In the Oraibi Powamu ceremony four food balls made of dough which is prepared from various kinds of cooked food are deposited outside town for the Cloud people.[133] At the kiva supper the night before a Hopi kachina dance an offering of bits of food is made to Wind Woman by the head of the dance, just as at any festive household meal a child will be sent out to drop bits from each dish for Sun (Mishongnovi).[134] When a spring is cleansed, a bowl of food will be deposited at the bottom (Mishongnovi),[135] presumably for the kachina. Zuni kachina impersonators or chiefs of the Kachina society take food nightly[136] as well as from a feast to where the river widens, the express station to the kachina (and

---

* At Zuni, meal was sometimes toasted before being offered (Stevenson 2:177; Cushing 5:22). The corn meal offered to the Ants in the Oraibi Powamu ceremony is from an ear slightly toasted (Voth 2:79). At Isleta anyone at any time may sprinkle crumbs of food to the Ants.

the dead); the women of the house will throw scraps on the fire. At special kachina shrines food may be deposited, for example, a Cochiti youth may offer grains of corn to Yellow Woman in her "house" to ask for the favor of his girl.[137] The kachina bring or throw away food gifts to the people on endless occasions, and are also recipients on their domiciliary rounds* or at dances. In connection with the entertainment of Zuni Shalako every household contributes food. The woman who withheld food would fall or in some other way hurt herself. "The kachina are dangerous."[138]

Food for ghosts or for the dead should be cooked;† the odor only is absorbed.[139] "Whenever one puts anything into the fire, when it burns the ghosts eat it (Zuni)."[140] And so wafer-bread is thrown into the hunt fire for deceased hunters, the hunters saying, "Here, grandfathers, eat! And whoever had good luck in hunting lend me your hand and your thoughts!"[141] Formerly a bit of food was cast into the fire by everybody before eating or muttering this grace: "Receive, grandfathers, and eat! Resuscitate, by means of your wondrous knowledge, your hearts; return unto us of yours the water we need, of yours the seeds of earth, of yours the means of attaining great age."‡ Formerly at Mishongnovi and Laguna at every meal a bit of food was crumbled on the ground for the Spirits, as done today at Acoma (into the fire) and by the Rain chiefs of Zuni.[142] The modern Mishongnovi woman says, "For the first year, when you think of him (the deceased), you throw aside a little food, but after that you don't think about it any more."[143] At Isleta, food from the meal is dropped for Weide (kachina) from the right hand, for the Dead,

---

* At Zuni the kachina visit the houses singly or in couples. They give their call and take dance steps, but do not sing. Maskless impersonators of the San Juan Turtle dance sing and dance on their Christmas Eve rounds, just as do men or children at Acoma and Taos on evening rounds in connection with the installation of the secular officers.

Serenading and food-distributing are Navaho traits (Haile, 65, 227) which are found also among northern Athapascans, among Northwest Coast tribes, and elsewhere.

† As among the Kwakiutl of the Northwest Coast and probably elsewhere.

‡ This is the first prayer taught a child, and, until he knows some of it, he is not regularly weaned (Cushing 6: 574, 575).

from the left hand, offerings which are made in the same way on many ritual occasions on the ash piles and other places.

On Grandmother's Day or All Souls' Day at Zuni all the men take food to the river, the women as usual throwing their offerings into the house fire. Men go from house to house to sing and receive food. On this day in the East large quantities of corn, wheat, beans, peas, watermelons, wafer-bread, boiled meat, as much as twenty wagonfuls, wrote Father Dumarest, of Cochiti, are taken to the church or churchyard (Santa Clara).[144] At home, too, food is set out in bowls for the Dead, and from Cochiti kivas or rooms where the men assemble, food is cut up into small pieces and thrown out for the Dead. Isletan women bake meal in the form of rabbits, horses, etc., for their deceased children.

Isletans send food offerings (and small prayer-sticks with hummingbird feathers) to the cliff of the stillborn (possibly all unbaptized infants) at the winter solstice ceremony.[145] At the Walpi Hümis kachina dance in May, 1893, when the women brought the kachina their feast of wafer-bread, corn pudding, and stew of corn, beans, and flesh, a kachina maiden impersonator took a small pinch from each woman of each item of food and laid the handful at the foot of the ledge of the children's burial ground in the cliffs.[146]

Scalps are well fed. Food is thrown to them on the pole (Taos), and after the dance, when they are deposited in their house, food is deposited (Zuni, Sia).[147] (At Zuni during the nights of dancing around the pole men visit the ceremonial houses, sing, and are given food; the last night they may visit all the houses.) Food is crumbled at the foot of the niches in Isletan roundhouse kivas where the Scalps are kept. Every Sunday the Town chief of San Felipe feeds boiled rabbit to the Scalps[148] and to his stone fetishes. (Note Catholic day count.)

The fetishes are carefully nourished. At Zuni, bits of all the food served are taken after every meal by a society member and offered to his corn fetish and sacrosanct stones. Masks are fed, crusts being thrown into the closet or back room. The woman member of the Rain chieftaincy feeds daily their cane-filled fetish. In any house where fetishes are kept the woman of the house will make an offering in the fire before serving a meal,[149] the sometime general practice surviving as a more restricted rite.

Among Hopi, all fetishes are fed daily: masks, corn-ear fetishes (*tiponi*), and the animal figurines which guard each house. In the Snake-Antelope ceremony, after the men eat their breakfast in kiva, each is expected to place a morsel before the fetishes on the altar.[150] Wafer-bread and *pigumi* pudding are taken to Masauwü's shrine in the Home-going kachina ceremony,[151] as "Masauwü his food." The Hano War Brother images are fed. The corn fetishes of Laguna and the kachina masks are fed, a function too important to be intrusted to Americanized women, commented one of them, lest they "starve them." Dumarest describes an invalid holding an image of the Sun to his breast and saying, "Cure me or I will give you nothing more to eat."

The mountain-lion image which is kept at hand in the Zuni household when a man goes deer-hunting is fed each day, and on the hunter's return the blood of the quarry is smeared on the muzzle. Zuni or Keresan hunter will plunge his coyote or mountain-lion fetish in the heart or blood of the deer.[152] The animal figurines of a San Juan family are fed at the meal for the dead on the fourth night.

The Laguna-Isleta hunter brings back grasses the deer like to feed on to be offered to the dead deer as it lies under its ceremonial blanket. The offering at Zuni is an ear of corn, a double ear, placed between the forelegs of the laid-out quarry, deer or rabbit. In Zuni tale the rabbits instruct a boy to lay them heads to the east, to place an ear of corn between their paws, and to sprinkle them with meal. "But we have no corn," says the boy. "Look for a squash seed, then, and after you lay us on the coals and we begin to puff up and sizzle, throw in the seed; that will be our lunch. We shall go back to where we came from; we shall not die." Actually, except in the kachina rabbit hunt,[153] rabbits are not laid out, but in cooking them a grain of corn is thrown on the fire, "their lunch." In the hunt fire bits of brush are thrown in as a food offering to the rabbits (Hopi).

6. Implements

Miniature weapons—bow and arrow or netted shield—are given Sun at the winter solstice ceremony (Santo Domingo, Cochiti, Laguna, Acoma)* or at a springtide ceremony (San Felipe). Rabbit sticks or clubs are also a Keresan (Sia,[154] also Jemez) offering to Sun. In the pit or crater shrine used by Laguna and (?) Acoma at the winter solstice have been found not only miniature bows and arrows but full-size rabbit sticks of a type not in use today.†

At the winter solstice miniature bows are offered by Hopi War chiefs, probably to the War gods.[155] Miniature bows and arrows figure in the offerings of Jemez War captains and Hunt society, and they have been found at Cochiti. Jemez War chief and Oraibi and Isleta chiefs put down a netted ring (Hopi, Jemez, "sandstorm shutter") to keep devastating wind- or sandstorms from the fields.[156] Along with the ring, Isletans deposit miniature bow and arrow, in ceremonial which corresponds in ground-cleansing functions to the Hopi Powamu. At Zuni, netted ring or shield‡ and miniature bow, arrow, and club are fastened to very long sticks or staffs and stuck upright into the hilltop cairn shrines of the War Brothers;§ at the winter solstice all the

* "Shield of oak ring and cotton string, given to all the K'oʙishtaiya (Stirling; White 2: Pl. 15).

† Parsons 13:384–85. Their four grooves identify them as of Basket Maker type.

‡ This magic shield of the War Brothers is empowered to turn back any weapon. Spun out of clouds [cotton], like clouds this water shield will carry its possessor through the air and will send down water (Cushing 4:1).

§ Parsons 13: Fig. 47, see also Stevenson 2: Pl. CXXXVIII. On Corn Mountain arrows are shot into a rocky crevice (Stevenson 2:439), as was done in Tano country on the San Christobal–Pecos trail (Nelson, 43, n. 1), and in a house shrine or god house north of Oraibi reed arrows with wooden points are offered to the War god images (Voth 8: Pl. XXXII). In the Laguna crater shrine in the "southeast corner," arrows were offered.

Bows and arrows, full size and miniature, were found in the great ceremonial cave of Blue River, the Mogollon-Pueblo region far south of Zuni (Hough 1:51).

At the peace of Santa Clara made between Tewa and Navaho in 1629 the Santa Clara war chief presented his bow and arrows to be placed on the church

miniature weapons fastened to a prayer-stick are set out on the
mesa-top altars of the War Brothers together with miniature
gaming implements.[157]

In San Juan tale shinny sticks and arrows have to be offered
to the War Brothers who have rejected an offering of meal,
downy feathers, and tobacco, saying, "We do not use these; they
do not belong to us; we can do nothing." Similarly in Hano
tale[158] the War Brothers are to be given sticks and balls by the
kiva chief who comes to ask their aid against the witch kiva in
a kick-ball game. The chief finds the little boys so absorbed playing ball that they have to be beaten over the head by their
grandmother to make them stop and pay attention to their
visitor.

Miniature kick-sticks* are included in the Cochiti offering to
Sun, otherwise kick-sticks are associated with the Clouds, since
"the Shiwanna come playing kick-stick"; the mud balls or concretions found on the riverbank after a flood are what they have
been kicking (Laguna). "If you watch the water coming down
off a mesa during a rain, you will see that it does not flow evenly;
it comes in spurts," says an Acoman. "That is because the
katsina (kachina or shiwanna) are running along, kicking their
kick-stick."[159]

A like interpretation is given by the Hopi. Their two-inch
stick† is painted black, the ends green. To the middle is tied an
eagle prayer-feather. This stick represents the small clay balls
which are formed by water in the washes and expresses a prayer
that the washes may rise and flood the fields.‡ Like billets are

---

altar. The Navaho presented an arrow with a *white* point, and the Spanish captain, his sword, and both were placed on the altar (Benavides, 49, 50–51).

* Acoma, *achawai'yi*. There are four sizes, the largest is called "over all,"
Da·wa·k'ª· (White 7); this term (*tauwaka*) is the general term at Laguna.

† *Ǫ̈önqötki, qöonga*, clay ball of arroyo, *tūki*, cut (from a stick) (Voth 3:314,
n. 2), *küñütkya* (Stephen 4: Glossary). Zuni-Keresan provenience may be inferred from this term for ritual kick-stick, since actually in racing Hopi use a
kick-ball.

‡ Voth 3:314. But clay kick-balls themselves are offered by Hopi, to the
Wind spirit. See p. 394, n.*

found with Jemez and Zuni prayer-stick offerings, together with miniature rings (Zuni).* Billet (kick-stick) and annulet may represent a game played for rain by Koyemshi clowns.† Little billets are given directly to the kachina at the Hopi Home-going kachina ceremony, also the disks, goal posts, and paddle of a rain-making game.

Crook prayer-sticks are often referred to as canes of longevity, but the crooks‡ or canes of Acoma are offered on the eve of taking a long trip and needing strength.§ The straight cane of office is also represented in Acoma (and Laguna) prayer-sticks.

7. Shrines: Sipapu‖

Shrines range from a mere boulder shelter or rocky ledge or cave to a ring or cairn of stones, from a miniature stone-slab house to an elaborately carved and painted tabernacle (Zuni Shalako roof box), from the great crater pit in Laguna's "southeast corner" or at Zuni Salt Lake[160] to the small depression near the Taos house door devoted to Filth Boy. In fact, any place which is visited habitually to pray and make offerings may be considered a shrine: a tree, a spring or pool, a housetop (Oraibi).

In planting prayer-sticks, boulders serve as a protection against wind or water and in themselves are not sacrosanct (Zuni, Hopi) unless as among Tewa they are selected for form or color and grouped together to be sprinkled with prayer-meal.[161] At boulder shrines, prayer-sticks from different societies are found, sometimes not far apart.[162] A Hopi will plant his field

---

* As in one of the offerings of the Oraibi Snake ceremony where the ring or wheel is called "rain wheel" (Voth 3:332), and as in the Acoma offering (White 2:127, Pl. XV). The water runs down the "road" which is a flat stick, and, says the Acoman, washes the kick-stick into the annulet which then carries the stick into the fields. This keeps the fields moist all summer.

† Stevenson 2:346. In this game as once played by the people men kicked the stick against women playing pole and ring.

Miniature pole and ring are among the prayer-sticks deposited by Long Horn at Shalako (Stevenson 2:243).

‡ G'onash (White 2:127).

§ We are reminded of the ritual or fetish canes of Aztec traders.

‖ Hano, *nansipo;* Isleta, *kŏkauu.*

prayer-sticks and spruce twigs got from a kachina at the foot of a small boulder, or will pile up some stones in the middle of his field.[163] Field shrines appear to be Kachina shrines.

Any available cave or near-cave like a rock shelf will be used as a shrine. There are several cave shrines in Corn Mountain, the large detached mesa three miles east of Zuni. The one I visited was devoted to the heads of prey animals* deposited by the Hunters society and to Paiyatemu, the musical patron of the Little Firebrand society. A shelf shrine very interesting for the pecked and painted pictures on the wall and the stone figurines on the ledge is a Shalako shrine about five miles south of Zuni, at the head of a canyon and a few paces above a spring.[164] Nearer the spring are planted in the ground the handsome Shalako prayer-sticks, a large mass. On a similar rocky ledge west of the church at Laguna kachina prayer-sticks are laid.

At Laguna (formerly) and other Keresan towns and at Jemez† a ring of stones opening toward the town if not toward the Spirit addressed is the most common type of shrine. Such shrines on mountaintops may have miniature trails running out from them in the directions of the towns of their pilgrim visitors.[165] On mountain, mesa, or hill the War gods, as guards or watchmen of the town, will have their shrines, usually rough stone piles, but on Corn Mesa (Zuni) an elaborate ground altar is laid with images, prayer-sticks, and miniature implements, and out of Oraibi there is a roofed chamber which may be like those "small prayer-houses" reported of Hawikuh where they spoke to the devil and offered him prayer-meal.[166] Another such shrine is on a hillock near the Tano ruin of Pueblo Largo. It contains a large sandstone slab on which is ground in a kachina-like figure with two points on top of the head, possibly a mask, possibly merely a peaked headdress.[167]

---

* Compare the Jemez shrine where the heads of mountain lions and bears are placed, also miniature bows, arrows, and clubs (Parsons 41:62). On Second Mesa deer and mountain-sheep skulls or bones were placed in a shrine (Mishongnovi, Beaglehole 2:11).

† Here a shrine is called "petrified wood place" from the amulet placed in it. Petrified wood is found in many Hopi shrines, but the Hopi shrine is called "house."

Kachina have general shrines, as at Laguna or on First Mesa, but chiefly kachina may have a private shrine, so to speak, like Chakwena Woman of Zuni and First Mesa.[168] A low slab-built shrine stands in the court, the Middle, in most Hopi towns,[169] and such a shrine stands at the site of old Zuni, the "middle place" called Hepatina. (Any ruined site to which migration legend attaches will contain a shrine.) Hepatina contains a jar into which water is poured ritually, so Hepatina may be a *sipapu* like the water-jar *sipapu* placed in Hopi fields.[170]

The Pueblo court also contains a *sipapu* or pit shrine which is theoretically the most sacred of all spots, for to it the people are "tied." It may be represented as the place of Emergence or place of connection with the lower world.* At Walpi there are three such pits or *sipapu* belonging to clans, Bear, Snake, and Patki clans. In the main court of Zuni a permanent hole for prayer-feathers is associated with Nakee, the patron of the Big Fire-brand society, since at this place he went down into the earth[171] as the chief's son at Palatkwabi went down† and as in the Isleta plaza the medicine chief and Town chief are believed to go down,[172] or as into the "midmost sand navel" or the shrine of "magic roots" the Bears in Nambé tale went down.

There are like pits in kivas where offerings are made‡ to the Below[173] or where images and other sacred things are kept such as sacrosanct stones (Isleta)§ or kick-balls (Hopi) or even an altar

---

* In Acoma tradition, in cleansing a new site of "diseases," the shamans buried in the center a basket of prayer-sticks and an arrowpoint for protection.

† This concept of inhumation may throw light on the well-like constructions, three feet in diameter and about eight feet deep, lined with stone, found in the courts of ruins on Blue River (southeastern Arizona) (Hough 1 : 18).

‡ Prayer-sticks or feathers deposited in the kiva *sipapu* (or in outer-wall cavities) are gathered up by the War captains and deposited in the outlying shrines of the Directions, where hunters also deposit their prayer-sticks (Acoma, White 7). Note the impress of stick (2 feet) and feathers in blow sand in kiva niche in the Village of the Great Kivas (1000–1030) (Roberts 1: Pl. 12*b*). In the *sipapu* which was covered with a circular slate disk (Pl. XII*a*) were found small stone beads and two bits of turquoise.

§ In the Basket Maker pit houses excavated at Kiatuthlanna in the Zuni Valley, small plastered pits were found in floors near fireplace or ladder. These were sometimes filled with clean sand, and imbedded in the sand of one was a

(Acoma). These kiva pits or *sipapu* are covered over with a perforated plank or stone, the opening being over the pit and covered by a removable plug of wood or stone which is withdrawn during ceremonial involving contacts with the beings of the lower world (Hopi). Stomping or dancing may take place on the plank (see pp. 382–83).

The *sipapu* is represented in a sand-painting on one of the Oraibi Powamu altars, a small square set in concentric squares, yellow, blue, red, and white, the lower worlds. From the *sipapu* runs to the southeast, to the rising sun the road taken at the Emergence which every Hopi still travels through life. On it are designed the four crooks of longevity from the tallest to the shortest used in very bent-over old age. Between the crooks are footprints on the road, a feature in Aztec codices.[174]

In Acoma myth* the kiva as a whole represents Shipap,† the place of Emergence, also parts of the universe. The roof beams are of wood from the four kinds of trees planted to emerge by, and the beams represent the Galaxy which is called Beam-above-the-Earth. The walls represent the sky, and the kiva is (was) round because the sky looks like a circle. The ladder is the rainbow (compare the ladder-like mask decoration called rainbow).‡ Under the ladder is the fireplace called bear (?). Alongside is the planked-over resonance pit called "another altar placed under"

---

smooth, slim, cylindrical stone which Zuni workmen declared to be a "kiva stone" (Roberts 1:52), a statement more informative perhaps about contemporary than about ancient practice.

The kiva *sipapu* may well have been derived from such pits which may be also compared with the refuse pit near the door (ladder base) of a modern Taos house. Dirt Boy lives in this pit, and he is prayed to by the housewife whose husband is off hunting. No need of looking to Emergence myth, Dr. Roberts, to interpret Basket Maker floor pits! Myths are such young things.

* Stirling. Possibly Chief kiva only is referred to. This is the only kiva with the resonance pit. See p. 382.

† Compare the concept that in retreat medicine men go to Shipap or that Wüwüchim novices in Hopi kivas are in the underworld (Stephen 4:973).

‡ So-called because the Mothers did not know where their tree ladders touched, just as none knows where the rainbow touches.

because at the bottom is an altar like the one Iyatiku first made.*
On the north side is another pit, representing the door to the
sacred Mountains, North, East, and West, to Sun and Moon;
and people pray into this doorway (with corn meal, dropping it
into an outer vent as they pass by the kiva at night). Around
the entire base of the kiva is a bench called fog seat, and the
Spirits are invited to sit here. (Very Navaho-like imagery, all
this! To what extent it may occur among other Pueblos is not
known.)

Places or caches for sacrosanct objects have a shrine-like
character. The Black Eye clown masks of Taos and the Scalps of
Laguna are or were kept in a cave; the snake jars of the Hopi
Snake society and the stone cloud-depicted tiles of the Flute
ceremony are kept "in the cliffs."[175] In some cases such sacrosanct things may be thought of as too dangerous or potent to be
kept at home, even if their "house," their shrine, is sealed or
luted down with clay. Shrines themselves are dangerous places,
taboo to all but the ceremonialists charged with visiting them
(Zuni).†

8. PRAYER

All offerings, in fact, almost all rites, are accompanied by
prayer or petition. Pueblo prayer is petition, "asking for this or
that" in the right (i.e., formal) way. The Cochiti morning prayer
to Sun is: "Sun Youth, take the corn meal that I and my children may flourish and have clothes, beads, food, fruits; that I
[Tseiatsa, a woman of the Sage clan] may have life, that is what
I ask."[176] When the Hano farmer puts down prayer-feathers in
his field, he says, "My field, you will be good all the time," or,
addressing flood waters, he says, "You will not go just in the
wash, you will flow everywhere."[177] A Mishongnovi farmer prays
to Müy'ingwa for rain and a crop unspoilt by worms or rab-

* This concept of altar in the *sipapu* is not expressed by Hopi, but sacrosanct
objects like kick-balls are left in the *sipapu* just as they might be left on an altar.

† Bunzel 2:502; Stevenson 2:356, 358. But townsmen vary in their hardi-
hood, some taking the risk others would not take.

bits.[178] The Zuni woman offering food on the house fire mumbles: "Eat! May our roads be fulfilled!" or "May we be blessed with life!"[179] When a Zuni hunter finds deer tracks and puts down prayer-meal and shell, he prays: "This day, my fathers, my mothers, in some little hollow, in some little thicket, you will reveal yourselves to me."[180] A Cochiti deer-hunter in offering meal to Fire Old Woman says, "Here, Fire the oldest, today let us have deer, all animals!"[181] The Governor of Laguna tells the people to ask San José "for good health and that the stock will be well and that our property will be plentiful and that we shall have a good winter and that the new year shall be good."[182] Putting down prayer-sticks and praying to all the spirits excepting the Animals, Ko·t'e of Laguna says: "I wish for good life and crops and clothing and beads and game and for your rain storms. This I wish, father and mother. I whose name is Ko·t'e."[183]

These are personal prayers: the prayers of chiefs or of society members have the same theme of petition, but far more elaborately expressed, particularly at Zuni, where there is remarkable formulaic phraseology,* and prayer is one with that art of oratory† which prevails throughout the Southwest and Indian Mexico. Over his winter solstice prayer-sticks for the War Brothers the War chief prays:

* Prayer texts from shaman or chief have not been recorded elsewhere, Hopi excepted. In Tewa oratory the use of "hard words, long words," is greatly admired, so there is inferably a ritual vocabulary, as among Keres. The War Brothers of Acoma "being great chiefs spoke a language that differed somewhat from the language of the common people," saying, e.g., four days when they meant four years (White 2:152)—esoteric verbiage recited again and again in Pueblo mythology, also in Navaho.

In arranging a hunt, to deceive the game Hopi will speak of mice or rats instead of mentioning deer or antelope (Beaglehole 2:5, 10); and animals are often given tale names (marked in Taos tales).

† Were Zuni chiefs or impersonators to be put through a catechism as were Mayan chiefs (see Parsons 61), they might be asked: What is the meaning of: Water roll? (Cigarette.) He took his grandmother by the hand and made her sit down in the doorway? (A coal of fire held to the end of a cigarette [Bunzel 4:713].) Calling for the cedar bark torch to light his cigarette, a man would say, "Hither with the *root* or the *blossom* (flame)!" (Cushing 6:136), in modern Mayan phrase, "sweet speech" (Redfield).

To my children
Long life,
Old age,
All good fortune whatsoever,
You will grant;
So that I may raise corn,
So that I may raise beans,
So that I may raise wheat,
So that I may raise squash,
So that with all good fortune I may be blessed.[184]

The prayer of the impersonator of Long Horn, the warrior kachina, is similar:

I asked for light [life] for you,
That you may finish your roads,
That you may grow old,
That you may have corn,
That you may have beans,
That you may have squash,
That you may have wheat,
That you may kill game,
That you may be blessed with riches,
For all this I asked.[185]

These prayers, like all Zuni prayers, conclude with petition or request; the preceding parts of any prayer state the occasion (the acts leading up to the prayer) and describe the offering,[186] the pay for what is asked for. "Zuni do not humble themselves before the supernatural; they bargain with it."[187]

Hopi prayer is less bargaining. It is concerned with people's state of mind, and it includes an appeal to pity.[188] Over their completed prayer-sticks at their smoke talk Oraibi chiefs pray as follows:

Now we have for these different chiefs (the Cloud spirits), our fathers, prepared these prayers (offerings). Therefore, being provided with these, do not delay anywhere, but quickly have pity on us with rain. Therefore, sixteen days after tomorrow these Snakes and Antelopes, if they have a good heart, will celebrate or will agree on this (ceremony). Hence from now on we must not live at variance with each other (troubling others). May some chief with dropping rain have pity on us! Now, therefore, being happy, being strong, we shall live.*

Crier chief's announcement or prayer from the housetop the following morning is as follows:

You who live to the north, loom up, please! Who live west, loom up, please! Who live south, loom up, please! Who live east, loom up, please!† Now, then, after this, in sixteen days, these Snakes, Antelopes, if they preserve a good heart, will conclude this. Hence that many days may we live, not having any trouble with each other. Thus some chief may pity us with some dropping rain. On that we shall subsist. May all the people live happily, strongly, or encouraged.[189]

The prayer of the Antelope society messenger to the sacred spring is:

Now, then, these prayer-sticks I have brought for you. With these I have come to fetch you. Hence, being arrayed in these,‡ rain on our crop. Then will the corn stalks grow up; when they mature, we shall here in the light,§ being nurtured, be happy. When you thus beautiful grasses will provide bountifully, we shall be glad over them. Then our animals, when they eat, will also be happy. Then all living things will be in good condition. Therefore do we go to the trouble of thus going in (retreat). Therefore have pity on us! Now let us go! We shall all go. Let no one keep anyone back. You all (the Spirits) follow me![190]

The narrative part of Zuni prayer may be compared with the use of narrative in oratory[191] or with such reports as are required of any prayer-stick depositor or ritual messenger (Hopi). Long Horn's long prayer-chant at Shalako reports all the activities of the Long Horn group during the year, including an enumeration of the shrines where they offered prayer-sticks.[192] Other prayer-chants during Shalako narrate what the ancestors did after the

Emergence. Emergence or origin narratives are themselves
"prayer-talks" which explains why even in secularized versions
they are given reluctantly.

Prayers are precious. They must be paid for. The ceremonial
father who teaches his child prayers for making and depositing
prayer-sticks will be paid a shirt or a headband or a few pieces of
turquoise.[193] "My husband may not teach me his prayers," a
woman said to Dr. Bunzel. "I would have to go to my 'father'
and give him a present for teaching me."[194] Unless a prayer is
learned from someone who has a right to teach it, and is paid for,
"maybe you can say it but it won't mean anything, or maybe
you'll forget it when the time comes to say it."[195] At the close of
their service, Shalako kachina impersonators who have spent
many nights learning their prayers give them back to their
teacher. On the night after the ceremony they recite the prayers
to the Shalako manager who breathes in, and they do not, and
so he takes from them the prayers[196] which are both precious and
dangerous.

Prayers are potent in themselves, and they impart power. It
is dangerous to lose or impair them. Nick fell sick during the
time he was dictating prayers to Dr. Bunzel, and, in telling her
of a dream that portended death, he said he expected to die,
since he had given away his prayers and had nothing to protect
himself with.[197]

9. PRAYER-IMAGES: KACHINA DOLLS

Prayer-sticks and feathers may be wordless petitions. "I
never learned any prayer for the prayer-sticks," said a Zuni
woman, "and so I just put them down and sprinkle corn meal
without saying anything."* There are still other ways of appealing without words. At the Nima'n or Home-going kachina ceremony Hopi brides of the preceding winter are expected to don
their wedding blanket and attend the final performance "to
show the clouds they want rain."† Again, when the men plant

* Bunzel 2:493. A miniature longevity cane or a corn-planter (digging stick)
in Zuni prayer-sticks are prayer-images (Parsons 19:284).

† A historical explanation occurs to me. It is customary at Santo Domingo
(Twitchell I, 473) as among many Spanish-Indian communities to celebrate

they go barefoot because the Clouds will say, "Let us make rain, to cool their feet." Cloud and rain designs in meal or paint are pictorial prayer, quasi-written prayer, a sort of glyph (see p. 359). Prayer-feather designs on pottery (Zuni) are this sort of prayer.[198] Building or decorating a kiva is a prayer for rain or crops.* Plastering or muddying anything, kiva or, as the clowns do, a human being, is a prayer for mud-making rain.† In the Mishongnovi Antelope race a Cloud clansman not only makes the cloud-and-rain glyph on the trail but daubs mud from the sacred spring on the sole of each runner as a prayer to Cloud.[199] When Üüwa had been daubed all over at the mock fight of his son's wedding and went to the kiva with the mud still on, Stephen asked him why he did not remove it. "No," said the old man, "it is a very effective rain prayer."[200]

Images of what is wanted convey prayer, like the Hopi prayer-stick modeled or painted as a corn ear‡ or cornstalk.[201] In firing a large water jar, a miniature jar is cast into the fire to insure even burning (Mishongnovi).[202] Squash blossoms of dyed rabbit fur or yarn over twigs, a common arrangement at the ears of a mask, are "for plenty of melons and squashes."[203] Hopi deposit squash effigies in their fields.[204] Before a hunt the Chraik'ats[i] of Acoma in charge of the game supply would make cornhusk images of deer, rabbits, or quail and early in the morning of the hunt scatter them outside the town. "That would make lots of game for the hunters,"[205] just as game and other creatures, we note, were created by Iyatiku from images in her basket, and as images of corn, squash, and beans are left overnight on the altar

---

weddings on the patron saint's day, often the only time the padre is at hand. Possibly the appearance of Hopi girls in wedding array is a faint echo from the time the padres of Walpi tried to introduce the marriage sacrament, Nima'n taking the place of a saint's day.

* Stephen 4:198, 211; Beaglehole 3:14. A clue here for the refacing of the Mexican pyramid.

† The girl plasterers want the rain to turn the sand in the valley into the same sandy wash that they use on the walls (Stephen 4:198).

‡ Made in the Oaqöl ceremony to be placed in the granary (Oraibi), also in the winter solstice ceremony (Walpi) (Stephen 4: Figs. 36, 55).

used by the Town chief in the fertility Auwĕ dance and then "planted."[206] The wooden eagle eggs deposited by Hopi at the winter solstice ceremony are inferably prayer-images. Hopi figurines of domestic animals made for the increase of the animals are set out on winter solstice altars together with seed corn and meal images of peaches and melons. On the corresponding night at Zuni, which is also the night before the Saint lies in, the animal figurines are set around the Saint or, in a Rain chief's house, set on the altar. At Laguna on Christmas Eve the figurines are taken to the church, and at Acoma on the Saint's day, they are set on the altar erected outdoors, and after the altar ritual they are buried or immured in the sheep, cattle, or horse corral. The Zuni figurines* of the Rain society altar are placed in an underground shrine in the chief's house. Inferably the animal figurines, many with punctuate designs, found at Hawikuh, in the Canyon de Chelly, and at Pecos, were prayer-images.†

Dough images of the domestic animals are made at Jemez at Christmas and buried in corrals. Near the church ruin dough crosses are buried in a hole that is first sprinkled with corn meal.[207]

As animal figurines are made for increase,‡ so are human figurines or dolls, "babies."§ A clay "baby" may be placed upon a Zuni Rain chief's winter solstice altar by a woman desirous of

---

* Among them are bits of clay representing money. Hopi potters leave miniature clay vessels at their clay pits (Bartlett 1:53), and in early Hopi sites are found clay miniatures of vessels. A miniature water jar was found near Cochiti; for Zuni, see miniature jar on altar (Stevenson 2: Pl. XXXV). At Gallo springs, southwestern New Mexico, hundreds of miniature vessels were found (Hough 1:19). In the shrines at springs, in caves, in mountaintops throughout the head waters of the Gila, the territory of the Mogollon-Pueblo culture, miniature pottery vessels abound, also, as noted, miniature bows and arrows, also cane cigarettes. Pottery types from this region (Tulerosa) are found in Zuni country (Kidder 1:96).

† Parsons 19: Figs. 38, 40. These were found in both pre-Spanish and post-Spanish sites. Compare the herd of clay animals found by Cushing in southern Arizona.

‡ Zuni, *itsumawe*, increase by magic; *santu itsumawe* or *shiwanni itsumawe*, saint increase or Rain chief increase.

§ Zuni, *wiha*; Keresan, *uwak (oaka)*; Hopi, *tihu*; Tewa, *holong'e*; Jemez, *k'ats'ana ki*, kachina child.

offspring. More commonly the "baby" is made of wood and dressed like a kachina. During a dance a woman who has suffered miscarriage may be given one of these kachina dolls by a kachina dancer. The kachina says to the woman, "Here I increase (by magic) children to you." The woman inhales, sprinkles the kachina dancer with meal, and gives him bread. As Flora and I were talking of this matter, a little boy came into the room, and Flora related that before the birth of this boy his grandmother had given an old doll to Father Koyemshi to dress as the kachina Hututu and give to her daughter, an expectant mother who had lost several children through syphilis. Then I was shown the doll. It was being kept carefully as "the heart" of the child. Were anything to happen to the doll or were they to sell it, "the child it brought would not live."

At the Hopi Powamu ceremony appear masks representing old women* who carry doll babies† partly hidden in spruce twigs. Childless women throw corn meal to these dolls, throwing to the male doll if a boy is desired, to the female doll, if a girl.²⁰⁸ Possibly these dolls are given to the women. On First Mesa, Butterfly-Wing showed me the boy doll she acquired before the birth of her little boy. It was a large figure, dressed in shirt and overalls. At Laguna, Cochiti, and Jemez, "babies" are or were given women by the kachina. During her pregnancy a Cochiti or Jemez woman would carry the "baby" on its miniature cradle board and talk to it. Were she to die, the "baby" would be buried with her or put away, probably in a cave.‡ These

* ? Tihküyi, Child Medicine Woman who sends infants inside women (Eggan).

† Compare the "conjuring" dolls of Plains medicine women used in curing sick children (Kurz, 315), but probably Hopi dolls represent deceased infants who are to be reincarnated (see below). Possibly kachina dolls in general derived from doll babies. We recall that in Zuni mythology the kachina began as infants. Resemblances with Yuman funerary images are dimly suggested.

‡ Such a cradle board was collected by Cushing in a cave near Tucson, Arizona. A typical parti-colored mask was painted on the stick in the cradle, the first archeological evidence, by the way, for pre-Conquest use of masks or, cautiously speaking, of mask decoration. The cave contents are dated 1300–1450 by Haury; they were left by sojourning Pueblos who before they came into the Gila Valley lived on the Little Colorado.

"babies" represent the spirits of deceased children (Cochiti), probably those who are to be reincarnated (see p. 71).

Kachina dolls are given little girls by the kachina in the dance court. The doll may have been made by a relative of the child and given to the impersonator to pass on to the child and have her think that it comes from the kachina (Zuni, Hopi, Laguna). Dolls are also "traded" by Hopi Barter kachina[209] or by Zuni kachina who pay domiciliary visits, bringing dolls for girls, and bows and arrows for boys, and in return getting bread and meat. The dolls will be called Kachina Old Woman's babies. Children are told to drop smooth pieces of wood into the river when it is full, before the winter solstice; for the wood will float down into Kachina Lake and into the mouth of Kachina Old Woman and turn into a baby.[210]

Dolls may be carved at home, even in the presence of children, but they are painted and decorated privately, mostly in kiva. Until painted and decorated they have no significance (Hopi).[211] In the West the "dolls" are very elaborate, beautifully carved from river-borne cottonwood root, and meticulously costumed. Among Keres and at Jemez there is much less elaboration, a board or cylinder is painted and given a head feather. There are no kachina dolls among Tewa, or at Isleta, except those made for Isletans by their Laguna immigrants.

FETISHES

10. CORN FETISH

Among different types of fetish, stones, wooden or stone images of the Spirits, or masks, the ear of corn is pre-eminently sacred or precious—*teshkwi* (Zuni) or *tsatyiu* (Keresan).

Two kinds of ears are sacrosanct: the ear which flattens out at the tip* and which is thought of as mother and child and placed, at Zuni, in the middle of the corn store† or left alongside

---

* Zuni, *mikyapane*, corn, flat; Hopi, *gwahihikpi*. By Hopi the flattened ear is used to give water to captive eagles; at Laguna it is fed to cattle, probably for increase.

† At Cochiti and Laguna four unhusked ears of corn or four cornstalks are placed after harvesting in the four corners of the corn storeroom and called the

a woman in confinement, and the ear completely kerneled,* which is placed also in the middle of the granary (Zuni,† Isleta) to song (Isleta), or in the sweet-corn oven (Mishongnovi).[212] Six perfect ears are sung to by the head of the Zuni household during the winter solstice ceremony that the corn may not feel neglected when so many other beings are receiving attention.[213] The perfect ear is thought of as male. It is left alongside a male infant,‡ and it is used in the society fetish.

The fetishistic importance of the full kerneling is well brought out in the Cochiti tale of the perfect ear which intrusts itself to the abandoned children. "Handle me with great care," says Perfect Ear, "because if you let me fall and a grain comes out of me, I shall not be able to speak any more." After the accident of dropping Perfect Ear, the weeping child says, "We have lost a grain of our mother Perfect Ear; we have killed her; she no longer speaks." On the restoration of the missing grain, by Shrew, Perfect Ear again speaks.[214] Sings the Hopi Powamu society chief,

> A perfect corn ear,
> My clan mother.[215]

The corn ear figures in death ritual. An ear is placed near the deceased and referred to as his heart (Cochiti).[216] At Zuni a perfect ear is laid between the legs of the deer that is laid

---

Mothers (Goldfrank 3:92). There is a similar practice among the Zapoteca of Mexico, who will refer to the cornstalks as the shepherds, *los pastores.*

* Zuni, *yapota;* Keresan, *kotona* (Acoma, *tsatchikotsch*); Hopi, *chochomingwu* (*chochimingwa*) (Voth 2:130, n. 1; Stephen 4: Glossary); Jemez, *pöhde;* Tewa (First Mesa, *pochtsele;* eastern Tewa, *kukaye^e*; Isleta, *iekaᴾ,* corn tip, or *kaimu,* corn in husk cover.

† Formerly in the Zuni corn store was also placed an ear of corn that had been dipped ritually in the Salt Lake (Cushing 6:168). Today, Mishongnovi salt-gatherers carry with them a Mother corn ear and place it in a small hollow in the salt bed as a protector. Later this is hung in the house (Beaglehole 3:54).

‡ At any time it has something of a protective or beneficent character. Once Lusteti found a black corn *yapota* lying on the road; thereafter he used to take it with him when he carried out the refuse at the winter solstice ceremony. I don't know whether this innovation or invention was ever copied, but in this way an invention might start. See p. 1119.

out.[217] Among Hopi, we recall, an ear of red corn lies as surrogate for the deceased, for four days.[218]

In Keresan towns, as at Zuni, the corn ear is a guardian of infants. A perfect ear* is placed alongside the infant (Cochiti), the same ear that has been used against witchcraft before the birth. At Sia a corn ear is breathed on and passed down the body of a woman in labor, four times, to hasten labor. On the fourth morning after the birth during the ritual of presenting the child to the Sun, this ear, which has meanwhile lain alongside the infant,† and one other ear are carried by the woman doctor and the mother. Subsequently, the two ears are wrapped together and laid under the cradle to stay there until the next corn-planting, when the grains are planted,‡ apart from the main field, to produce a crop to be eaten by the child. Planted also are the two ears of perfect corn used in the San Juan naming ritual and left as guardians for the infant. Sacrosanct corn quite generally ends by being planted as seed corn. Corn given away by the Zuni Koyemshi clowns is always the first seed corn to be planted.

In all name-giving ritual, not alone in infant-naming, a perfect ear of white corn is used and given to the initiate. Thus the initiate into the kachina cult everywhere receives an ear to be his "mother." This is unadorned, but the ear§ given the initiate

---

* Such ears are especially potent when obtained through the Women's society from the Town chief's crop of blue corn (Goldfrank 3:46, 67, 76).

† Jemez: When labor begins, a corn ear is hung from the wall. This ear is laced alongside the cradle board. The first woman who arrives takes out the ear, points it in the directions, breathes on it, and names the infant (Harper). See p. 1050 for the fetishistic character of the cradle itself (Laguna). The Acoma cradle board is made of wood from a lightning-struck tree. During the solstices cradle boards are taken to the curing societies to be cleansed and charged with power (White 2:135). Let us keep cradle-board ritual in mind when we reconstruct the history of the early head-deforming Pueblos.

‡ Compare Acoma, White 2:134. Kernels from the ears of seed corn are hung in a little bag to the cradle board.

§ Zuni, mi'li; Hopi, tiponi; Keresan, iärreko (Sia) iareko (Cochiti) or iyatik'ᵘ (Laguna) or ho'nani (Acoma); Tewa (First Mesa), pochtsele, popular term, kulung', corn dressed; Eastern Tewa, kutsubukwipayokaga (the Summer mother), kutsubukwioyikaga (the Winter mother); Isleta, iamaparu'; Jemez, tse'e, "mother"; Taos, ? itemayakie.

into the society or medicine order of a society is elaborately
dressed with feathers and beads. The butt of the corn fetish is
set into a buckskin-covered piece of cottonwood root and the
lower part wound with cotton and at Zuni covered with a piece
of fine wicker. Seeds of various kinds are contained in the hol-
lowed-out cob (Zuni, Laguna), or honey (Acoma [Stirling]).
The corn-ear fetish of the Snake clan and Crier chief of Walpi is
described as a small symmetrical white ear impaled on a small
wooden spike in a wooden cup containing a cotton wad, corn
kernels, beans, piñon, and other seeds. Four corn ears of the
sequential colors are painted on the outside of the cup, and the
glyph of the directions, a cross, is painted in black on the whitened base.[219] The corn fetishes of the Oraibi Agave society chiefs
have a small replica attached.[220] Sia, Santa Ana, and Santo
Domingo fetishes are surrounded with sticks (? prayer-sticks) or
wrapped with a mat of canes bound together with cotton
string.[221]

In society ceremonials these corn-ear fetishes are set out in line
at the rear of the altar (Pl. IV); Hopi chiefs and Zuni society members will carry their corn fetishes in procession (Pl. II), and a Hopi
(also Hano) chief exhibits his corn fetish, after the people have
planted for him, for them to pray to and sprinkle with meal.[222]

At Zuni the corn fetish *mi'li* of which every member of a
medicine order is possessed* is thought of as personal property.
When a society person cuts his monthly prayer-sticks, he takes
his *mi'li* down from the wall and sprinkles it with meal, to
prayer. A *mi'li* is never borrowed or passed on to another.† At
the owner's death it is broken up by his ceremonial father or
society chief, the corn being given to a kinsman of the deceased
to plant, and the feathers, beads, and basket base made into a
prayer-stick bundle and buried in the river bank. The life of the

---

* Also every member of the Hunters' society, and every Shuma'kwe society
member whose septum is pierced for the feather. The Wood society, like Hopi
societies, has but one corn-ear fetish (Stevenson 2:416, 417).

† Except by the Shi'wan'akwe society. At death it is passed on to a man's
son if he wishes to join the society (Stevenson 2:418). For *mi'li*-making see
ibid. 419–20.

PLATE IV

ALTAR OF THLE'WEKWE (WOOD SOCIETY), ZUNI (STEVENSON 2: PL. CVIII)

owner is closely connected with his fetish: "He lives as long as his *mi'li* wants him to live."

At the death of its owner the Cochiti fetish is also broken up by the Town chief, the kernels to be given to the people present at the burial, to be planted later on, and the feathers, beads, and yarn to be buried by the Town chief in the field of the deceased.[223] Acoma[224] and Laguna corn fetishes are preserved in the family and loaned out. The San Felipe fetish is returned to the society chief who made it.[225] The Isletan fetish is kept by the widow until she remarries, when the society chief takes it from her and "sends it back" whence it came. To the Isletan layman the Mother is "born," not made.

The corn-fetish *tiponi* of the Hopi society is the property of the chief, or rather the chief is trustee for the *tiponi* which is "handed" within the maternal family possessed of the ceremony. Jemez chiefs have charge of society Corn Mothers; members have each his own corn fetish. Tewa Town chiefs have charge of the Corn Mothers, Summer Mother and Winter Mother.[226] The Town chief of Isleta has a Mother that is "head of them all." At Cochiti, Goldfrank heard of only one group or society Mother, that of the Women's society. Some precious things are wrapped up and handed down by the Town chiefs of Taos, from father to son, but the bundle contents are not known.

11. Seed-filled Cane

The corn ear in the two fetishes of the Zuni War society as well as the corn ear in the fetish of the Great Shell society are surrounded by reeds, six reeds colored for the directions and filled with grains of corn of the six colors and with other seeds, the other reeds filled with tobacco. Corn ear and reeds are encircled with eagle-wing feathers dropped in flight, and the base is covered with cotton cloth and cord and strung with beads.[227] The *tiponi* fetishes of the Hopi Wüwüchim and Singers societies consist of an ear of corn and a hollow cane. With the *tiponi(s)* of the women's Marau society are prayer-sticks bundled in a rough basket.[228] The fetish of the Zuni Shuma'kwe society consists not of the regulation ear of corn but of bundled prayer-sticks.[229]

On the Hopi altar of the Directions next to each ear of corn radiating from the central bowl lies a hollow stick, with feathers tied to one end, and wound entirely with cotton twine. These sticks or prayer receptacles (*nakwa mokiata*)[230] are called the husbands of the corn ears. At Zuni such a receptacle or container, *eto·ne* (pl., *eto·we*), is the supreme fetish of the Rain societies, a bundle of four seed-filled* or water-filled canes wound with cotton. The chiefs "brought them up" bundled in a mat of straw in a rough basket.[231] Each Rain society has one bundle or more. Most of the clans and the societies are said to have *eto·we*,† but in these cases what the fetishistic objects are which are called *eto·we* is obscure. The image of the Saint may be referred to as an *eto·ne*. All the *eto·we*, except the Saint and the bundle of the Water Serpent Rain chieftaincy from Hawikuh, "came up" with the people (see p. 219): "That is why we think so much of our *eto·we*."

An *eto·ne* is kept in a jar, very privately and secretly, and never disturbed or exposed except to be placed on an altar or when wearing out to be repaired. (In general, fetishes are moved reluctantly and with great care, carried only by their trustee or guarded by War chief or captain. Exposed casually, something might happen to the fetish—loss of power?) Food is offered daily to the bundle by a woman of the house where it is kept. The bundle is a dangerous object: if anyone except a Rain chief saw it, he would be struck by lightning;‡ were it not cared for properly, properly fed and the proper songs, prayers, and prayersticks[232] made for it, the family in the house would die off. There was an *eto·ne* in Nick's maternal house, and Nick once observed to me that a great many of his family had died. He was advising with Waihu'siwa, Rain chief of the East: should they bury the *eto·ne*, the usual disposition of whatever is too dangerous to

---

* Note the pouch of seeds in the early Pueblo medicine kit from a cave in the San Francisco Mountains (Bartlett 1: Fig. 30).

† Kroeber 2:169-73. Badger clan has two *eto·we*. People with *eto·ne* are called *elleteliwa*.

‡ Once a cat knocked over a sacred object on the altar of the Rain chief of the South. The son of the woman responsible for the cat was struck by lightning.

keep? A young man whose bundle-holding family had died off had asked Waihu'siwa to take the bundle, but Waihu'siwa refused.

12. STICK OF OFFICE: SOCIETY STANDARD

In the Keresan prayer-stick offering we noted the stick of office, and at Zuni the prayer-stick that is kept during the period of kachina impersonation or of playing host to the kachina. There are prayer-sticks or sticks of office of a more permanent character; for example, the two large crooks with ear of corn and feathers attached midway which are carried at Zuni by kachina dance announcers in the winter dance series. These crooks belong to the high Rain chiefs. A similar crook with corn ear and feathers is carried by the Water-Corn clan kachina at the Walpi winter solstice and by the Hopi Powamu chief when he impersonates the Maize god in preaching to the children who are to be whipped.[233] To be noted, too, in this connection is the stick called *rupsi* carried by Aholi kachina in the same ceremony, and belonging to the Town chief. It is about four feet long with six aspergills attached to the distal end.[234] A crook of office is insignia of the Keresan Town chief,[235] and in Keresan tales the Town chief is generally referred to as Hachamun'i kaiuk, prayer-stick bent or holding,* a reference to his stick of office.

A chief stick (*mongkoho*) is used or made for the Hopi Town chief, for various kachina, Aholi, Aototo (Oraibi), and Auhalani (Walpi), and for every member of the Agave and Horn societies. This stick, carried horizontally by a cord and carved with terrace cloud or, for Walpi Agaves, with Water Serpent,† is very sacred; it is buried with its Agave or Horn owner.[236] Besides, for the Agaves, at the first winter solstice after a youth's initiation into the society his sponsor has to make him the crook feather-stick he is to keep for life (Walpi).

* *K'ayo·'k'ᵃ*, bent; *k'ayo·'k'ᵃⁱ*, holding (Boas 2:288). At Acoma and Sia the translation given is "bent" (White 5). I think there has been confusion in the use of these terms both by recorders and by informants, particularly at Acoma where one term and one type of prayer-stick are referred to the Town chief, and another term and prayer-stick type to the War chief.

† Associated with Water-Corn clan to whom the Agave chieftaincy belongs.

Each member of the clown societies of Cochiti is possessed of a crook painted in the cardinal colors and with a pendant of feathers.[237] The painted stick[238] belonging to the Zuni Ne'wekwe may represent a flute.

A stick of office with a pendant of twelve stone points belongs to the Oraibi War chief,[239] and to the Zuni War chiefs belongs an arrow-tipped stick or staff which is held in alternate years by Elder Brother and Younger Brother, the transfer taking place at the War society–Wood society ceremony. The War captains of Acoma have each two sticks of office (Keresan, *ya·ʙi;* Zuni, *tethlan·e*). The one handed on at election is a three-foot staff with feather pendant, the other is smaller and is kept permanently in a lionskin quiver;* both have "power."[240] The War chief of Cochiti had a little black staff[241] with downy eagle feathers. The annual War chief or captain of Isleta is referred to as Cane war chief; his "cane prayer-stick black old man"† lies on the altar in general curing ceremonial. The Town chief of Isleta del Sur has a black cane, forearm length.

To the Zuni War chief particularly in charge of witchcraft cases belongs a cane which is probably of Spanish make. Each of the three War captains of Laguna has a cane which in ceremonies may lie on the altar; during the saint's-day Mass at Sant' Ana I noted three official canes propped against the altar in the church (Pl. XXIV). The little war captains or herders of Santo Domingo and San Felipe have sticks of office reminding us of those of the errand-men *topiles* of Mexico.[242]

To all the pueblos but the Hopi, President Lincoln presented a silver-topped cane of office for the Governor. The Governor's staff of officers acquire each for himself or through his predecessor a cane of office.‡ In the East (Cochiti, Isleta, Jemez) these

---

* Similar staffs are to be seen in Zuni War god shrines (Parsons 13:404, Fig. 47; Stevenson 2: Pl. CXIII).

† Impersonation of prototype is implied since Black Cane Old Man, writes an Isletan, "first gave us the bow and arrow." Black Cane Old Man is a personage in Taos folk tales.

‡ Spanish, *vara, vareta;* Acoma, Laguna, *ya·ʙi (iapi, yapi),* Sia, *hĕr'rotuma;* Zuni, *tame;* Tewa, *tuyo pe,* chief stick; Isleta, *tu* (?); Taos, *t'aabuthlane* or *thlauwatohne,* chief stick.

canes are blessed on the Day of the Kings (January 6) by the Catholic priest and sprinkled with holy water. Isletan canes are also sprinkled from the medicine bowl of the Town chief. The canes of the Zuni officers have clearly enough a fetishistic character; possession of the cane is vital to office-holding; without it, authority would lack. Were a caneless officer to give a man an order, the man would ask, "Where is your cane?" and, if he chose, disregard the order. Similarly, men who retain their canes, in theory remain officers. There is actually a set of such theoretical officers in Zuni. The chief rite of installation of Governor and officers is passing on the cane, and, at Zuni, breathing from or on it. Zuni folk etymology for the widespread term for governor, *tapup*, is "he who breathes on the cane."

As a group variant of the individual stick of office may be considered the society standard* which is placed outside the kiva, at the hatchway, when ceremonial is in progress,† or which is carried in dance or on parade (Hopi), or given to the War chief to hold (Sia).[243] Although it may consist of other objects, the standard is commonly a stick or sticks with feather attached. For example, the Powamu standard consists of four sticks about twenty inches long to each of which four eagle feather-strings are fastened at different places with three or four eagle feathers to the upper end.

The Hopi make most use of the kiva standards, no doubt because Hopi kivas are used by various groups. The standard is a notice of pre-emption, also a notice or summons to members or to the Spirits. Like a flag, the standard is raised at sunrise (with a cast of prayer-meal) and taken down at sunset, without ritual.

Standards are carried in the East and at Acoma in saint's-day dancing, either at the head of the dance line or shaken by the bearer over the midline dancer. While the dance set is within the kiva, the standard is left projecting from the hatchway.[244]

The characteristic Eastern standard is made of a wooden ball

---

* Hopi, *natsi;* Hano, *pe'i,* trap, excepting the standard of the winter solstice ceremony which is called *enu,* youth, and which the children sprinkle with meal.

† The stick of office of the War chief of Oraibi is actually so placed while he is conducting his war ceremony the fourth night of the winter solstice ceremony.

painted turquoise with a black-and-white block pattern, surmounted by parrot and eagle feathers, and running down the
long pole is a belt or a strip of embroidered cloth to which eagle
feathers are fastened. At Acoma a foxskin is attached; the pole
is "dressed just like a dancer" and is called Sun Youth.[245]

Kiva standards in the West sometimes consist of objects used
in the ceremony like the Walpi War chief's standard of bow in
bow case, arrows in quiver, bandoleers, "hail" headdress, beaded
or netted skullcaps,[246] or are representative also of some ceremonial feature as, for example, the cactus standard of the Zuni
Cactus society or the bow standards of the Snake and Antelope
societies, sometime war societies, or the coyote pelt and red-hair
standard of the Flute society which appears to refer to the creation of the sun. These coyote and bow standards are set up on
the fourth day of the ceremony, replacing the standard first used.
Replacing the standard is a practice in other Hopi ceremonies.

At the winter solstice the Mustard-Chakwena clan of Walpi
fastens the mask of their clan "grandmother," Chakwena Woman, around the north pole of their kiva ladder, also her rattle,
bandoleer, and queue-dressing frame.*

The standard of the Singers society of Oraibi is a crook, and
early one morning during the Wüwüchim ceremony all the
townspeople file past Singers kiva and touch the crook as a
prayer for a long and prosperous life.[247] A similar crook stick of
longevity is held by a chief and touched by returning racers in
connection with several Hopi ceremonies.

All the Wüwüchim societies carry a feathered rod in their
dance processionals, a kind of standard or flag. Dance sticks are
quite generally used, particularly by women dancers: the Buffalo girl dancers carry a feathered notched stick, "Cloud ladder";[248] Zuni Thla'hewe girls and Hopi Marau women carry
elaborately painted sticks with grasses and feathers;[249] the
women in the Acoma war dance and the Taos Mothers of Game
carry a feather piece. Then there is the trident stick of the
Matachina dancers.

* Stephen 4: Figs. 29, 78. This is used ritually also at Acoma (Stirling).
See p. 396, n. 11.

13. STONES: SHELLS: STONE POINTS AND HOES

At Zuni and elsewhere there are certain sacrosanct stones*
believed to have come up with the people.† A society member
may have two, three, or four; a chief will have more. The chief's
pebbles or concretions are set out on the altar in front; the members set theirs, during a ceremonial, in the rear of the altar.
Ordinarily they keep them at home, where they can offer them
food. Were the stones not fed, "they would disappear." These
stones may be laid upon the corn ears on the altar (Hopi) or
dropped into the medicine bowl (Zuni, Hopi, Sia, Isleta), and by
Hopi they are called "medicine water stones." As the Zuni shaman (Big Firebrand society) drops them into the medicine bowl,
he prays:

> Yonder in the north
> On all the mossy mountains,
> On the tops of the mountains,
> And along their slopes
> Where the ravines open out,
> You hold the world in your keeping;
> Ancient yellow stone,
> You will make your road come hither
> Where lies my white shell bowl,
> Four times making your road come in,
> You will sit down quietly.
> Then with your living waters
> Our young ones will nourish themselves;
> Reaching to Dawn Lake,
> Their roads will be fulfilled.‡

The Isletan stones are kept by the medicine men in the bag
with their corn fetish or bundled in a buffalo-skin bag. Some are
said to look like and to represent birds and the animals; others
represent the mountains where bird or animal stones are found.

* *A'thlashi*, ancient stone (Bunzel).

† No doubt these sacrosanct stones are of very early usage. Note the black
pebble in the medicine kit of the early Pueblo cave in the San Francisco Mountains (Bartlett 1: Fig. 30) and a concretion found in the eleventh-century ruin
sixteen miles northeast of Zuni, the "Village of the Great Kivas" (Roberts 1:
Pl. 56d).

‡ Bunzel 4:784. This is repeated for each color-direction.

The "mountains" are set along the "road" of the altar, each stone being named for a particular mountain.[250] Mountain effigy stones are also used at Laguna[251] (among Hopi, mountain effigies for the altar are made in meal, clay, or wood),[252] and they were found in the Village of the Great Kivas near Nutria, Zuni's farming colony.[253] The "Mothers" of Tewa Winter chiefs are crystals or white stones to represent ice—their "ice mothers" (Nambé, Tesuque, Hano).

Spiral and various concretionary stones, also small boulders, are kept in shrines where prayer-sticks or prayer-meal are offered and identified with Sun, Cloud, or other supernatural (Hopi, Hano);[254] in some shrines there are pieces of petrified wood, which are fetishes of Childbirth Water Woman, goddess of game. Petrified wood is found in many Jemez shrines and, dressed with feathers and beads, is set on the altars of the Men's societies to represent kachina chiefs or warriors; it is kachina or War god fetish. At Zuni petrified wood has also been associated with the War gods,* and pieces are fastened to the belt fringes of the Oraibi Snake war society. A Taos mountain shrine is referred to as the Stone Men, i.e., the War Brothers. San Juan shrines consist of tall, narrow boulders referred to as Stone Old Man or Stone Child. At Santa Clara and at Cochiti[255] similar stones have been found within the circular shrines.

Very important in ritual is a crystal-like stone which is peered into for second sight in finding lost objects or in diagnosing disease or in witch-finding. Such stones enable the doctor to see in the body objects sent in by witches.† Hopi chiefs use a crystal to refract a ray of sunlight onto their altar, when completed. On the altar of the Oraibi Marau society is a crystal set into the tip of a wooden cone or "mountain," and such is the chief fetish on the winter solstice altar.[256] (Note crystal in mortuary bowl of a Piedra Pueblo I chief [Roberts].)

Shells, more particularly abalone and olivella, are largely used

* Benedict 3: I, 83. A petrified stump marks the spot where Pekwin makes solar observations (Stevenson, Bunzel).

† This function is attributed to all the "ancient stones" at Zuni. See "Clairvoyance," p. 450.

in Pueblo ritual. "Big shell" (it was blown on, [?] a conch) is a Zuni fetish with its own Rain chieftaincy. The fetish is associated with the War Brothers and borrowed by the War society. And some such association may have been made on First Mesa because Wĕhĕ of Hano, a chief in charge of War god images, begged his generous friend Fewkes to send him eight small conchs.[257] We noted the use of white shell fragments in Zuni offerings both of meal and of beads, likewise the practice of attaching shell beads to fetishes. Around the necks of the War Brother images of Zuni, Oraibi, and Jemez an abalone shell should be hung, and abalone-shell pendants are necessary to the costuming of the Zuni Mahedinasha kachina. White shell and abalone are inlaid in the Walpi War chief's wooden fetish.[258] Olivella and scallop shells are fastened to the Hopi Snake society bandoleer; they are the warrior's token (see p. 665). Olivella shells figure on the Zuni War chief bandoleer,[259] and olivella shells may have been filled with war medicine that was to be spurted by mouth (Zuni).[260] At Jemez, kachina bandoleers and wrist guards are studded with small olivella shells.* The olivella wrist guards given the Acoma War gods were never to be taken off; they were their hearts.

In the bowl of water from which a San Juan infant is washed a large olivella shell or a cowrie may be placed, and an abalone shell may be used as a dipper. These shells descend among the women of the family.[261]

Very generally medicine water is dipped or given out from a shell. Sometimes medicine water is dropped or aspersed from a stone point.

Arrowpoints or spear points are kept in the bowl of meal for sprinkling (Jemez) or fastened to fetishes or placed on altars, often at the end of a line of fetishes, as a guard. Alongside each corn ear on one of the Oraibi Powamu altars lies a stone point.[262] When fastened to the Zuni corn fetish, points are said "to keep off witch sickness." Arrowpoints are usually fastened to the fetish images of the prey animals. In Tewa tale a boy is told by

* See White 4: Pl. 7c for an olivella bandoleer from Santo Domingo.

his corn "mother" to place an arrowpoint in the basket with Awl,* who is going to make him clothes overnight.

A stone point is very generally used in personal protection as charm or amulet. The arrowpoint that has been fastened to the Acoma infant's cradle board is hung around his neck when he leaves his cradle of lightning-riven wood.[263] A Laguna War captain wears an arrowpoint in a buckskin bag under his shirt.[264] This arrowpoint he will slash through the air as he stands on guard at door or window during ceremonial. In folk tale Star gives a man arrowpoints to kill the witches.[265] At Isleta a stone point is passed over walls and door in the house of the dead; with a point a line is drawn around the grave to keep away witches (Taos practice too), and the witch bundle in medicine ceremonial is cut open with a stone point (Pl. IX). Scalp-takers of Sia and Zuni put an arrowpoint in the mouth, as does the Isletan racer. The Zuni racer has one in his hair.[266] A Laguna man or woman who goes out at night may carry an arrowpoint in the mouth, and women may wear an arrowpoint all the time in their belt (Taos practice also). Dzaidyuwi of Laguna undid her belt and showed me an arrowpoint her husband's brother had picked up in a ruin; she had worn it for seven years. A San Juan woman told me her mother would urge her to keep her arrowpoint or "lightning stone" securely, "so she would live a long time."

Stone points are generally called lightning stones or associated with lightning. They are dropped from the fingers of Lightning (Hopi) and, when discovered, should be picked up by Lightning's

---

* Compare the personification of Awl suggested by the face incised on a bone awl found at Hawikuh (Hodge 2: Fig. 21) and referred to by Hodge as a Shuma'kwe mask. Did his Zuni workmen thus describe it because they associated the society's Dragonfly mask Shumaikoli with awl and moccasin-making? Just as Kokopelli or Nepokwai'i (Tewa), an insect and phallic kachina, is thus associated on First Mesa? The Zuni Shumaikoli came from Hawikuh, and we recall the incontinence of the Shumaikoli impersonator whose mask stuck to his face.

Again, is there any relationship between Kokopelli and the phallic Zuni kachina Ololo who has been identified with Water Serpent (see p. 780, n. †), perhaps questionably? The similar dramatization at Laguna opens the hunting season (Parsons 33:223, n. 4). For dramatization at Walpi without mention of phallic personage see Fewkes 12:93–94, Pl. XXXII.

At Laguna, Awl Man is patron of the Kapina society.

representative, the Flute society chief (Walpi).[267] At Isleta points are believed to be found after seven years near trees which have been lightning-struck (points are also coughed up by the deer* the Hunt chief "draws in" through his ceremony). How points are possessed of Lightning's power is illustrated in the Zuni tale of the two Beetle Boys who kill the horned water serpents in the western ocean. Elder brother Water Serpent says to his younger brother, "Should anyone show against me a yellow arrowpoint, I would die," and younger brother says, "Should anyone show against me a blue arrowpoint, I would die." And when the Beetle Boys look in the ruins for arrowpoints and expose the serpents to the points, the serpents die forthwith.[268]

In the ruins of the San Juan drainage and nowhere else, except at Awatobi, have been found the blades of yellow hornstone or black slate that were used as hoes.[269] Such *chamahia* are placed on the Powamu altar (Oraibi)[270] and on Antelope altars (Walpi, Second Mesa),[271] and I notice one figured on a Zuni Rain chief's altar.[272] The stones in the Mishongnovi and Oraibi Antelope society's *tiponi* fetishes appear to be *chamahia*. The base of the Mishongnovi fetish is wrapped with coils of buckskin strips stained red. Within the projecting eagle-tail feathers to which red-stained, downy feathers are attached, is concealed "a handsome and finely polished jasper celt, yellow in color, and about ten inches in length."[273] To Hopi, *chamahia*† represents "rain knives" dropped from above by the Chiefs of the Directions; and the term is also applied to ancient Stone people,‡ but whether to the stone when it was alive or to users of the implement is not always clear, although the Chamahiya are described as snake-swallower prototypes of stick-swallowers.[274]

* Apparently confused with bezoars.

† Mountain effigy stones of Laguna (cf. Pl. IV) are also called *chamahia*, human beings who when the earth settled became stone (Boas 2:39), inferably mountain spirits. Between mountain effigies of all kinds and the Mountain Chiefs of the Directions I surmise some ancient association. Were the so-called nipple effigies of early Pueblos mountain effigies?

‡ It is applied to fetishes on the Acoma Kaвina altar, but these are corn, not stone, fetishes (White; Stirling).

14. Images or Effigies in Stone, Clay, Wood

The mountain fetish stones of western Keres have been noted. Similar natural formations but with bits of turquoise set in for eyes and mouth have been collected among Tewa.[275] Natural formations more or less carved have been collected at Cochiti, and the Town chief is guardian of a stone image referred to as Mother.[276] The Town chief of San Felipe also has a stone Mother, a circular stone* eighteen inches in diameter and four inches thick, with a "green face."† He has anthropomorphic stones called Paiyatyamo, patron of the Koshare[277] and, at San Felipe, of other societies. Tewa Kossa have a stone Payachiamu.[278] San Felipe societies have an image of Ma'sewi.[279] The Zuni Shi'wanakwe society has a small female image, ten inches high, "their mother."[280]

Near one of the Zuni Shalako springs, set out on a ledge under an overhang of cliff,[281] is a large number of small stone images of kachina or Bear or Mountain Lion, some quite elaborately carved, others merely natural formations slightly shaped. Remarkable Pueblo sculpture are the life-size (?) stone heads of snake, deer (?), and frog, found in the Village of the Great Kivas,[282] and the two pairs of mountain lions on the Cochiti potreros,‡ life-size crouching figures cut into the rock in high relief, each pair inclosed in a circular walled shrine from which leads a stone lane or trail.[283]

* From Isleta I have just received the drawing of a round stone fetish (*haka batö*) belonging to the White Corn group and associated with the east. To the back of the knobby head are attached five plumes tipped with downy feathers, and around the neck hang bead necklaces with turquoise and abalone-shell pendants. Compare the "White Mountain" image of the Taos Day or Sun people (Parsons 58:75, Fig. 3).

† See Dumarest, Fig. 30, for wooden painted disk fetish of Cochiti, and Parsons 52:414 for leather-covered, painted disk fetish at Laguna. Between the disk fetish and the Aztec ritual shield is there possibly a relationship?

‡ One pair is near the Painted Cave in which is a large serpent pictograph. We recall that the sand-painting of the Hopi Snake society (Keresan-like society) is a mountain lion, formerly a pair of lions.

Animal images* are used in the hunt[284] and by warriors (Zuni), also they serve as altar or house guardians. They are efficacious in childbirth when placed under the pillow of the parturient women (Sia); and a doctor would leave an animal image to look after his patient who places it under his clothes (Cochiti).[285] A death in the household is announced at San Juan to the family's animal guardian, and this image may be placed in the bath of the newborn infant. At Laguna the animal images were said to have been kept by the clan chiefs, but those I saw were being kept by an old woman who would not sell them without the consent of her brother-in-law who lived with her and "might need them hunting." My Hopi hostess also kept an animal household guardian which she inherited from her mother.

A little altar is made by the hunter for his fetish animal, i.e., he sets it out on the ground and sprinkles meal (Zuni, Laguna). At Zuni he also offers a prayer-stick and withdraws a little distance to sing a hunt song; on his return, if he finds tracks about the altar, the omen is good. After the kill, the fetish animal is rubbed generally with a bit of the deer's heart. Images are kept by the keeper of the Deer fetish and borrowed from him (Zuni), or individuals finding stones shaped like the prey animals will take them to the Hunt society, together with arrowpoints and beads, to make up into a fetish, i.e., to consecrate.[286] To "make alive" such fetish the Acoma Hunt chief would sing:

> It comes alive
> It comes alive, alive, alive
> In the North Mountain
> Lion comes alive
> In the North Mountain comes alive.
> With this the meat-eating animal
> Will have power to attract deer
> Will have power to attract antelope
> Will have power to be lucky (succeed).†

* Zuni, *wema*, animals (curing society members are also referred to by this term) and for birds, *wo'le tsanna*, little servant; Laguna, *shuhuna* (a term for a specific animal which has not been identified (Parsons 20:127). See p. 187, n. §.

† Repeated for Wolf (West), *shŭhō'n'a* (South), Wildcat (East) (Stirling).

An arrowpoint is kept tied around the animal fetish, and sometimes beads and a prayer-feather. A tiny buckskin bag of corn pollen may be tied around the neck of the image, "its food" (Laguna).

Animal fetishes are thought of as having once been real animals which were changed to stone (Zuni,[287] Hopi). We recall that in tale Mountain Lion, the hunter par excellence, has the power to change into a living animal and actually run down the quarry. At Taos the mountain-lion fetish is said to have come from the stomach of a "medicine deer." (The bezoar is familiar also at Nambé.)*

Jemez animal fetishes are made of clay, and such clay images there are also at Zuni. The image of Water Serpent on the Hano winter solstice altar is of clay. Clay or wooden images of birds are used on Cochiti[288] or Hopi altars, and of frogs on Hopi altars.† On his winter solstice altar the War chief of Walpi places wooden images of the domestic animals, of Big Snake, their guard, and of course their starry Mother, his wooden shell-inlaid effigy.[289]

Keresan townspeople are represented collectively by clay images. The Town chief takes care of his people by looking after their figurines, "his children" (San Felipe, Santo Domingo),[290] just as the Mother whom he represents looked after the images in her basket. When the chief of Awatobi invited the Oraibi chief to destroy Awatobi, he displayed two clay figurines, representing one, the townsmen, the other, the townswomen. "Here I have brought you my people," calmly he said. The legend, as incredible as the report of a Soviet conspiracy trial, goes on to say that according to his choice the Oraibi chief was to get the men or the women of Awatobi.[291]

---

* Another Spanish-Pueblo enigma of provenience! From Pimería it is reported in 1716 there are "many deer that . . . . raise the highly prized *vezuales* stones that are in such demand in Mexico and in various other parties as remedies and are even sent to Spain, the Spanish valuing them so much that the Pimas now prize them too, and do not sell them as cheaply as before, especially in these latter years, when so many have died of rabies" (Velarde, 129). In Europe bezoars were touchstones for poison.

† See p. 317 for prayer-images of the domestic animals in clay.

Zuni War Brother images which are made annually* at the War ceremony at the winter solstice, and set out after the night ritual on the mesa-top altars of the War Brothers, are of wood, elaborately painted and befeathered. The wood must be from a lightning-riven tree. Prayer-sticks encircle the base of the image, likewise a cotton fringe (*hakwin*) made by women and representing a garment.† From the neck hangs an abalone-shell gorget or a piece of abalone (Fig. 2).

On the altar of the Oraibi Snake society figures a somewhat similar war spirit image. It is made of cottonwood root, partly covered with rawhide. Around the body is a belt of wampum and a string of red horsehair, also a string of prayer-feathers‡ added to in Acoma style at each ceremony. On the back is a netted shield; the cap is of buckskin or elkskin to which is fastened a warrior's *hurunkwa* (see p. 398). Prayer-sticks encircle the breast. The lower part of the image is merely a block of wood to which feet are fastened. The face is well carved and realistic, not, like the Zuni image, conventionalized.[292] The War god images and the image of Chowilawu on the Oraibi Powamu altar have fringe kilts of red-stained horsehair[293]—horsehair instead of cotton. Other Oraibi War Brother images[294] and the images of First Mesa,[295] Laguna, Cochiti,[296] Sia, and Jemez are in stone. The head of the Jemez image is painted red;§ the body, black, with the characteristic parallel marks. The head of the Hano image is black, the body red.[297]

---

* A unique trait in Pueblo image-making, suggesting an annual installation, or, genetically, an annual prayer-stick.

† On Blue River in southwest New Mexico the ancient costume consisted of front and back fringed skirts of cords, and this garment in miniature was deposited as an offering in the great Bear Creek ceremonial cave (Hough 1:20). Cord skirts date back to Pueblo II; so do leather skullcaps (see below). Basket maker women used string aprons (Amsden).

‡ Noted also on Flute Boy and Girl figurines (Oraibi) (Fewkes 6: Pl. I). Compare the wooden Marau images (Voth 8: Pls. XIII, XIV, XXXIII). For wooden images at Walpi see Stephen 4: Figs. 163, 421–23, 461–63, 484.

§ Compare the Hopi clan name, Red-headed Men, for the Masauwü-Fire Cedarwood-Coyote clan, a warrior-like clan.

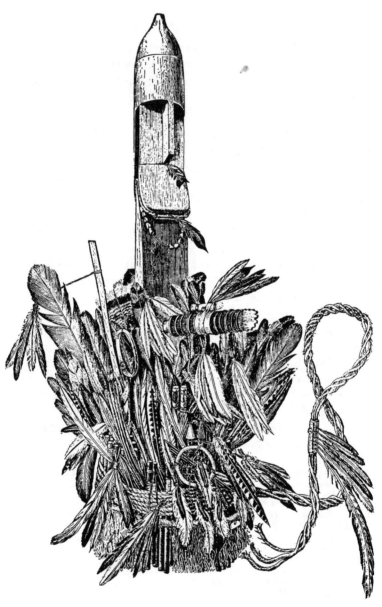

Fɪɢ. 2.—Zuni War god image and prayer-sticks. From altar-shrine on Corn Mountain (Parsons 13:394–402).

15. MASK: MASK-IMAGE

Masks are of two types, the false face* and the cylinder which covers face and head.† The latter, the "head," is the common type of the forty-six masks listed for San Felipe, thirty-four are "heads," as are thirty-seven out of forty-six masks at Santo Domingo,²⁹⁸ and I think this is about the ratio elsewhere. At Zuni all but two of the permanent or chiefly masks are cylindrical.²⁹⁹ "Heads" are generally flat on top with a superstructure of feathers, unspun cotton, sheepwool for hair, flowers, horns, and wooden slab or tablet, or with side or back slabs or feathers. Ears, gourd or wooden snouts, a tongue flap, bulging eyeballs of buckskin stuffed with cotton, wool, and seeds may be attached. There will be a large collar or ruff of fur or feathers or spruce. The spruce may be tipped with popcorn (Keres, Zuni), sometimes to represent stars (Zuni).³⁰⁰ The false face has beard instead of ruff, a long beard, usually of black horsehair, sometimes of yucca fiber dyed red or of leather (San Felipe, Santo Domingo), which is spotted with white-eagle down (San Felipe, Santo Domingo, Zuni‡) or along which hang feathered strings or bunched feathers. There may be a hair bang, made sometimes from the hair of the owner§ or a bang of close-bound willow twigs. Black triangular or rectangular or circular "eyes" and white "teeth" may be painted on, sometimes a nose; a projecting nose is usually a feature only of burlesque false faces. A ring of braided cornhusk may surround eyes or mouth.

Masks are generally made of leather,‖ deerskin or elkskin or

* Zuni, *pachin; shoyan'e,* face (Bunzel 5:857). Compare an Isletan clown term, *pachu'un.*

† Zuni, *ulin'e > ule,* from within a deep receptacle; Hopi, *küïtü,* head; Laguna, *nashkainia,* head; at Taos "head" is also the reference to mask.

‡ Chakwena, a Keresan mask, and Hainawi, the beheader (Bunzel 5:867, Pl. 32*b*). The down is stuck on with yucca syrup.

§ Not at Zuni, where human hair or the hair of a live horse should not be used on a mask, lest person or horse die (Bunzel 5:845). Human hair might not be used on the kachina mask borrowed from the Pueblos by Havasupai (Spier 2:267).

‖ Bought in the store today (Zuni) (Bunzel 5:849, 856); compare Stevenson 2:243, n. *a.*

buffalo hide or cowhide;* a few of gourd or wicker, none of wood; ears or horn may be of wood. Snouts, also horns, may be of gourd neck or ox horn heated and flattened out and reshaped. The horns of the fierce whipper kachina represent buffalo horns (Stirling, Acoma, possibly elsewhere). Koyemshi clown masks are of native cotton cloth (stained pink with "kachina clay"),† except at Acoma where they are leather. These masks have balls on top which give them their name,‡ knobs filled with soil from the footprints of townspeople (Zuni) or with seeds (Hopi, Laguna, also turquoise and shell), and to these potent or sinister knobs prayer-feathers are tied.

Seeds of all kinds are chewed by the Zuni mask-maker and sprayed over the mask. "Now I have given you life," he says. "I have made you with seeds and given you life. Bless us with your strong spirit, and whenever our day [dance day] may come, call the rains for us as long as you live. I have made you into a person."[301]

Now he puts on the first coat of white clay.§ Many masks are elaborately painted with the formal designs of Pueblo art, with the butterfly which allures to the dance, with corn, cloud, rainbow, Galaxy,‖ or lightning designs. Ground-down copper ore is

---

* Masauwü's mask is unique, fresh rabbit skins are molded over head and face, fitting so tight that they do not look like a mask. The face is painted like a skull, with big eye-holes, big mouth, no nose (Forde 3:397 quoting Freire-Marreco). But see p. 789.

† This very sacred pigment is also used on the bodies of the Koyemshi, the Good Kachina, and a few of the more sacred kachina. It is kaolinite brought from the shore of the Sacred Lake by the kiva chiefs on their summer pilgrimage (Bunzel 5:860–61).

‡ Zuni, Molanhakto; Hopi, Tachükti; Tewa, Huntamehle; Koyemshi is a nickname (Bunzel) meaning kachina husband, but it spread to Hopi (Koyimsi) and to Keres and Jemez (Gomaiowïsh, Acoma; Gumeyoish, Laguna, Jemez).

§ At Zuni this is bartered from Acoma.

‖ White band (Hano, Parsons 40: Fig. 23) or band of little alternating black-and-white squares (Zuni, Bunzel). But other designs may be called Milky Way "just to please Milky Way" just as something may be painted on the mask to please the earth or the sky (Bunzel 5:862). The Galaxy in Acoma sand-painting is a ladder-like figure (Stirling).

used for turquoise, the favored mask colors;* hematite mixed
with clay, for pink (Zuni); charcoal or shale, for black (Hopi) or
at Zuni black stone† or burnt corn from ruins‡ or corn fungus;
and for yellow, yellow ocher from Kachina Lake, and so belonging to the Kachina society head men who grind and mix it with
dried petals of yellow flowers and Paiyatamu medicine from the
societies, Paiyatamu flower meal (Zuni).[302] (Compare the yellow
body pigment of the Hopi Wüwüchim society whose patron is
Paiyatamu or T'aiowa.) Shale is ground with saliva generated
from chewing muskmelon seeds. Gloss or shine is got from piñon
gum or white of egg (Hopi, Zuni) or from corn fungus or pollen
mixed with yucca syrup (Zuni). Pigments are sprayed on or
brushed on with a charcoal strip of yucca. The mask is ren-
ovated each time it is to be worn, even the permanent mask
(Zuni). In repainting, water is first sprayed on and the old pigments are scraped off, and these scrapings are deposited in a
kachina shrine (Hopi). The pigments are what make the mask
sacred, "valuable," what "makes it into a living person."[303]

But only now and again is there any personal mark or interpretation in the painted decoration. Kachina Old Woman has a
red mark on her face because, when her brother lay with her,
begetting the Koyemshi, she was menstruating. Up around her
face is a dance kilt; "she wants to hide her face because she is
ashamed."[304] The masks (and bodies) of the punitive Behead-
ers—Hainawi, Homachi, Temtemchi—are painted or spotted red
with blood, from their victim or victims. A bear paw is painted
on Ahu·te's mask because Ahu·te is a warrior.[305] There are two
red stripes across the face of Ne'paiyatamu, the kachina Ne'wekwe, "to make him see well,"[306] because his Ne'wekwe prototype
Bitsitsi is so marked and was sharp-sighted in finding the hidden
Corn Maidens.

* This "blue stone" mixed with piñon gum is traded from Santo Domingo by
Zuni for feathers (Bunzel 5:861).

† Pyrolurite, mined at Corn Mountain by society people, mainly for prayer-
stick pigment (Bunzel 5:859).

‡ Ground with prayer "shell." For this pigment, for black stone, and for
yellow ocher pigment, grinding-parties with girls are given by the society, men
singing (Bunzel 5:859–60; Stevenson 2:532).

Masks are always made, painted, or repainted by chiefs or kiva managers or special persons.* Inferably only a few persons in any town understand the art, which restriction is somewhat significant in standardizing local patterns or in borrowing patterns. In the East masks are kept in a plastered-up niche in kiva† or in a ceremonial chamber, and there is no individual ownership or custody; but in the West dance masks (not kachina chief masks) may be personal property (Zuni, Hopi, Laguna). At Zuni, as soon as a man can afford the expense of the ritual, he will have a mask made for himself,‡ and his mask is buried§ for him when he dies. (This interment also at Laguna,‖ Jemez.) Among Hopi some masks are personal property—a man may own one, two, or even three masks;¶ but masks are inherited by kinsmen, by a son, brother, or nephew.[307] Masks are kept at home as are Zuni masks which are fed daily** by a woman of the household and which bring a blessing to the house. The woman prays: "My fathers, you sit here still. Eat! Let us reach the end of our road. Our father, make the road long and let us go to the

* For example, at Laguna the lightning sticks on the Hemish mask or headpiece had to be made by the Storm Cloud shaman. In Acoma tradition the shamans animate the masks just as the Hunt chief animates the stone animals.

† In Hopi kivas some masks are kept similarly in the "kachina house" or shrine.

‡ By the kiva chiefs during the *teshkwi* period before a kachina dance (Bunzel 5:850). Before wearing the mask its owner must be whipped by the Badger clan members of his kiva (Parsons 20:222, n. 1), or by the four head men of the kiva (Bunzel 5:852).

§ At the river, with prayer-sticks made by a kinsman for Sun, the dead, and the kachina (Bunzel 5:856).

‖ The personal mask is buried in the river only when there is no son to inherit. A would-be mask-owner has to feast all members of the Kachina society (Parsons 20:221–22).

¶ Also at Zuni. A man likes to have masks of different form types so that whatever dance his kiva presents he may dance in his own mask (Bunzel 5:848). Apart from restrictions imposed by its form, any mask, excepting Chakwena, may represent any dance kachina (Bunzel 5:858). Not only were the shiny black pigment of the Chakwena mask difficult to remove but this is a particularly dangerous kachina, a war kachina.

** Neglected, a mask would send mice to eat the corn or would himself eat around the edges in the storeroom (Bunzel 5:854).

end."[308] A poor man, one without ceremonial connections, is especially desirous of having his own mask in order "to save his life, to make him valuable." Through his mask he may return to Zuni after he dies. His household is glad to contribute to the cost of acquiring a mask "because they want something valuable in the house to pray for (by)."[309]

Besides personal or kiva dance masks there are clan or society masks. Most, if not all, Hopi clans are possessed of a mask which they call their *wöye*,* old man, as their senior clansman is called; "our oldest uncle" is the English rendering. This kachina is believed to have come up with his clan, i.e., on the first migration from Below he was encountered by the clan wanderers and invited to join them. A clan mask is kept in a maternal family within the clan; like the *tiponi*, it is passed on within this family. If the family is possessed of a ceremony, during its performance the mask will be set out on the altar or worn, often by a "child of the clan."

At Zuni certain kachina chiefs are impersonated by certain clansmen, and the individualized masks of kachina chiefs are kept permanently in certain houses,† much as among Hopi; but at Zuni it said that these kachina merely elected, when they first came to town, to live in these houses, because in them they knew they would be well cared for; they would be given boiled venison; they would not starve. However, had the mask to be moved, the lineage dying off, the removal would be made to a family within the same clan. In a few cases mask and the function of impersonating are within the same clan or lineage. Several permanent masks have understudies, so to speak—imitations that can be worn with less responsibility or danger. But if a man does not want to have an understudy made up for him, he will borrow the permanent mask, paying its keeper and planting prayer-sticks.[310]

At Acoma and Laguna the Shuracha (Shonata) kachina has

---

* This term is never applied to a mask by Stephen. Possibly it was my Hano informant's rendering for *sena*, old man, the usual Tewa term for chief.

† Sixty-seven permanent masks, including society masks, and twenty-two houses have been listed (Parsons 55:83–85; Bunzel 5:881–85).

been in some measure associated with the Corn clan, and with a family within that clan; otherwise there is no association between masks and clans. There is no association in other Keresan towns or among Tewa.

How the masks of kachina chiefs are cared for in Zuni is well described by a woman member of the maternal family in charge of one of the kiva masks.

The Shalako mask for He'iwa kiva* is in our house. Four days before Shalako comes, the two Shalako managers in He'iwa kiva and the two personators of Shalako will come for it in the evening. Everyone who belongs to the mask will come, and everyone will bring something for the mask. Anyone who has been in the house when they sprinkle corn meal on the mask will belong to it after that. One time my mother-in-law sent my husband's little sister over to mind the baby while we had our ceremony of bringing out the mask. We did not know any better; and, when the girl came, we did not want to send her back, so she stayed. And when they brought the mask, she sprinkled corn meal on it. Then they told her, "Now you have joined in this ceremony and each year you must come back, and each year you will bring something for the mask." So she has always to come back since then. If she should quarrel with us, she would not have to come for the ceremony of bringing out the mask, but then on the following day she would have to take a bowl of food to the house where the Shalako people have gone in. This is to pay the mask so that she won't have trouble because she stayed away from the ceremony of bringing it out.

All these people come in the daytime, the women bringing flour for the wafer-bread they are going to cook. They stay all day, and at night, when Shulawitsi lights the fire on Grease Hill, the two Shalako kiva chiefs and the two Shalako personators will come. While they are sitting down, my uncles will go to the back room and take the mask out [from its jar† in the closet] with a prayer. The Shalako kiva chiefs and my mother's brothers‡ have charge of the mask. They spread out a cere-

* There are six Shalako masks, each associated with one of the six kivas.

† All the old masks (masks of kachina chiefs) and "dangerous ones" are kept in jars. An ordinary mask may be wrapped in buckskin or cloth and hung from the roof (Bunzel 5:853).

‡ Rain chiefs of the South. He'iwa kiva is generally described as the kiva of the North. If there were any fixed connection between the Rain chiefs and the Shalako masks, the He'iwa Shalako mask would be kept in the house of the Town chief, Rain chief of the North.

monial blanket in the front room and set the mask down* and cover it with a buckskin so the children won't see what it is. Then the people of the house and all the people who have come to help will take off their shoes and sprinkle corn meal on the mask and say, "Now your time has come and you have been taken from the inner room where you have been sitting praying for us." Then the four men who have come for the mask get up and do the same thing.

Then the people of the household take one bowl of meat and one basket of wafer-bread and one basket of peaches or melons or anything else they have and give it to the men who have come for the mask. This is to pay them because they have worked for the household during the summer. (In the spring the Shalako personators come to the house where the mask is kept and say, "We have come to ask when we shall work for our father." The head of the house answers, "We shall let you know when we have a feast ready for you." Then when the people are ready they let the Shalako personators know, and the Shalako personators tell all the men of the kiva to go and work for them. Then they hoe or cut wheat or do anything that is asked for one day and go to eat at the house where the mask is kept.)

Then the two personators of Shalako take the food, and the two kiva chiefs take the mask and the things that belong with it, and they go out. They take the mask to the house of the personator of elder brother Shalako where they are going to go in (i.e., in retreat).

The ceremony may be different in the six Shalako houses. They keep the Shalako mask of Muhewa kiva in Andelesi's house. They are afraid to touch the mask, and so my father, who is Shalako manager of Muhewa, has to go into the room and bring it out himself. When the Andelesis moved from their old house, my father had to go and get the mask and take it to the new house because none of the people in the house would touch it.† In our house my uncles are Rain chiefs and so they are not afraid.

When masks are taken out from their permanent quarters, they are placed on the altar or in themselves constitute, so to speak, an altar. They are sprinkled with meal or "given a smoke," i.e., incensed (Zuni, Hopi, San Felipe).[311]

* Presenting it to the six directions, they set it down on a cross of meal (Bunzel 5:971). The Bunzel and Parsons accounts are quite similar, since they were obtained from the same informant.
The Kiaklo mask and probably other permanent masks are brought out and called for in much the same way (Bunzel 5:981-82), as are Water Serpent images on First Mesa (Parsons 40:56-57).

† From this it is plain that the permanent masks are not kept necessarily in sacerdotal houses.

Several societies, Keresan and Zuni, are possessed of masks which appear at initiation or curing ceremonial and, at Zuni, at winter solstice ceremonial (Big Firebrand kachina). The Giant society of Cochiti has a mask of Buzzard, and the Hunters society of Santo Domingo, a mask of Rohona (Shuhuna), the unidentified ritual animal[312] that may be jaguar (p. 187, n. §). All the Jemez societies are possessed of masks. At Sia all the kachina masks were once in charge of the Querranna society chief,[313] and there is some evidence that this was formerly the case at Laguna, before the introduction there of the Zuni kachina system. The only masks of Isleta or of Taos are (were) worn by the clown (moiety) societies. Both the Zuni clown groups are mask-wearers or mask-holders; the permanent masks of the Koyemshi kept by a major Rain society and renewed by Big Firebrand society and Ne'wekwe society are peculiarly sacred, but there is a Koyemshi mask (Hatashuku) borrowed from Laguna which is pseudo-sacred.* Sets of burlesque masks (Hewa-hewa) in the keeping of the Ne'wekwe are less dangerous than ordinary masks. The Hopi Singers society keep burlesque masks. The clown societies of Santo Domingo are in charge of the Gowawaima masks of which some are burlesque or bogey and none is truly sacrosanct.

A mask is put on and taken off with the left hand (Zuni, Hopi) and then waved in exorcism around the head (Hopi). If you try on a mask casually, without being engaged in ceremonial, you will die (Zuni).[314]

A change of being appears to be effected by the mask. Wolf, Rabbit, or Locust takes off his mask and becomes a man; Beetle Boys are said to be insects because of the masks they wear. Po'haha, the Hano warrior maid, was seen by the men fighting with her to be wearing a mask, parti-colored blue and yellow

---

* Anybody who wants a hastily improvised mask will take a piece of buckskin or canvas to any older man to make it up for him. The sacred pink clay is used and the maker assures the kachina that he will be as valuable as others. "Do not think yourself cheap, but have a strong soul like the others and bring my people good luck!" Nevertheless, the wearer does not have to be whipped, "because it is not a real mask." One of these masks, Hatashuku, makes jokes about people, in Keresan (Bunzel 5:1023–24, Pl. 40*b*).

with long teeth. On her return, after killing all the enemies in one day, she took off her mask and hung it on the wall and said, "After I die I will still be with you, the mask is I."

Again, the mask appears merely to unite the wearer with the being who is his "father." Before putting on the mask, the Zuni impersonator prays: "Now we shall live together, having one another as father. Do not be vindictive against me. . . . . Now you stand before me. Ask for long life for me."[315] A common way for a mask to be "vindictive" is to stick to the face, causing death. This may happen when an impersonator has broken a rule, like the incontinent Shumaikoli impersonator of Hawikuh.

Masks, the old masks, are always fearful* or "dangerous" whether as warriors† or in accordance with the general Pueblo theory that whatever has power for good has power to harm. The recent history of the mask of Chakwena Woman is in striking illustration. In 1905 the guardian and impersonator died under his mask while making the domiciliary rounds to bless the houses with infants. The following twenty years there was much sickness at Zuni, particularly among infants. Every year, at the winter solstice ceremonial Chakwena Woman made her rounds. In 1925 the War chief decided that a new mask should be made. The old mask to which the dead man's skin had stuck was destroying, not bringing, life.[316]

Between mask and image there is a type of effigy which may be called mask-image, such as the Horned Water Serpent[317] image,‡ the bird images of Zuni[318] and First Mesa,[319] the deer, antelope, and buffalo heads of Cochiti and probably of other towns, the Pecos bull at Jemez,[320] the Santiago Horse Saint of Cochiti, Santo Domingo, and Acoma.[321] All these have special

---

* When Masauwü put on his mask, he frightened people away from catching him, he frightened them to death (see p. 238, compare Wallis 2:6). Similarly, clown police masks may be dangerous to others, but protection to the wearers who engage in offensive duties.

† For example, the mask of Hainawi, the Beheader who is painted with blood, is so dangerous that no young man would dare to wear it, only the kiva chief (Bunzel 5:1003).

‡ The paps of Walpi's mother serpent are stuffed, masklike, with seeds (Stephen 4:300).

guardians, like masks, and are similarly fed, and on their public dramatic appearance they are treated like kachina and strewn with meal.

Of interest as possible prototypes of masks are the hair bang worn to the tip of the nose by Zuni-Hopi women performers (p. 831) and the spruce twig pendants masking the face of kachina dancers in the home-Shalako presentation of Second Mesa. This spruce veil hangs from an elaborate headdress, tall and conical for males, like a hat with low crown for females.

16. Impersonation without Mask

In the Hopi ceremony of preparing for the crops, Powamu ceremony, the chief represents Müy'ingwa, the Corn god or spirit of germination. Corn god and Seed goddess are impersonated at the initiation of the Oaqöl society (Oraibi). The Zuni Corn Maidens are impersonated in the Thla'hewe ceremony and in the Molawia celebration at the close of Shalako.

Again in war cults impersonation is prominent. The War Brothers are impersonated by the Hopi War society in their ceremony after the winter solstice, by the Zuni scalp-taker and his "father," and by Zuni and Keresan War chiefs or captains who are called regularly Elder and Younger Brother, Ma sewi and Oyoyewi. In Keresan war dances the Brothers are also represented with their "sister," the murdered girl who pursued them until they scalped her with proper ritual. In actual war, Hopi impersonated Masauwü.

Bitsitsi, the first Ne'wekwe, appears in Molawia as one of the most impressive of Zuni characterizations. Of his Hopi homologue, T'aiowa, the handsome patron spirit of the Wüwüchim society, Crow-Wing writes: "While they are dancing, he is with them, making them good-looking." This suggests impersonation, let alone the fact that Wüwüchim men powder their faces with corn meal, as girls do, which "wonderfully brightens the complexion, lending to the old grizzled faces the smoothness and dainty soft glow of a maiden." Of the four Men's societies the Wüwüchim is most admired by the women.[322] The interest aroused not only by the Wüwüchimtü and Bitsitsi but by the clowning societies in general suggests that clowns without mask are or were thought of as spirit impersonations, like clowns in mask.

In kachina dances it is not uncommon for some or all of the dancers to appear without mask, nevertheless, in some measure as impersonations. Thlịwale of Isleta is an out-and-out kachina impersonation, without mask. And so is the figure of Ice in the Hopi winter solstice dramatization. In this also appear impersonations of Sun, Cloud, Hail, Poshiadta, T'aiowa, Antelope, Eagle, Hawk Youth and Hawk Maiden.[323] In Hopi summer ceremonies appear Snake Youth and Snake Maiden and Flute Youth and Flute Maiden who have been described, perhaps dubiously, as impersonations of clan forebears. The first denizen of Hopiland, Masauwü, ordinarily god of fire and death, is impersonated as a god of fertility in planting and harvesting ritual, and his impersonator, as noted, would come out before an actual fight.[324] He wears bloddy rabbit pelts, and skin molded masklike on his face.

Keresan society members in their winter solstice ceremonies are said "to act like Shiwanna" or rain spirits,[325] a concept which approximates impersonation. Similarly, Hopi Antelope society chiefs represent the Chiefs of the Directions. Some degree of union, if not actual impersonation, between the Rain chiefs of Zuni and the Uwanami, Cloud chiefs of the Directions, is suggested in ritual, organization, and exigencies of personal conduct.

Bear is impersonated through claws or paws or hide in the Keresan-Isletan curing society, also together with Mountain Lion in the initiation ritual of the Hopi Snake society. Impersonators behave like the animals, growling or clawing somebody. Invoking the curer Animals of the Directions, the Zuni doctor declares, "When you sit down quietly, we shall be one person" (see p. 416); the actual impersonations of the Beast Gods are of a very exciting and violent character. In the war dance of San Felipe the War chief is called Mountain Lion, as is the Hunt chief of San Juan who brings in the Deer dancers as an impersonation of White Mountain Lion Man of the Emergence. In the animal dances of Taos, Tesuque, and San Felipe, Deer or

Game Mother is an impersonation, as of course are the animals themselves, also Eagle, in any of the animal or eagle dances. When Powamu chief gives notice to kiva members that they are to plant their ceremonial beans, he is considered to be representing the cowbird that arrives with the spring, a harbinger for planting.[326] When Kumpa, Pouch War chief and Snake society chief of Isleta, takes his powder from his pouch, rubs it on his eyelids, and twists and turns and hisses like a snake, he appears to be impersonating the snake, almost, we might say, to be possessed. Between possession, transformation, and impersonation, lines of demarcation may be psychologically well marked but ritually rather fine!

17. Scalps and Heads

The dead enemy is supposed to invest his scalp, or at least return to it, and so, after a measure of abuse and insult, the scalp is adopted and considered a beneficent fetish. Like other fetishes, it must be well housed and well fed. Formerly at Acoma the Scalp-takers fed the Scalps wafer-bread and stew of rabbit or deer meat, and gave them water.* Had the Scalps become hungry or thirsty, sickness or grasshopper plague would have devastated the town.[327] At Santo Domingo the Scalps are fed daily and given a smoke in a house in charge of a Flint society man.[328] The San Felipe Town chief feeds the Scalps in his ceremonial house.[329] The Nambé Scalps are kept in the house of the chief of the Winter People, but the San Juan Scalps are kept in the house of the woman war chief, whence they are brought out at an initiation into her society. At Hano, too, scalps were probably kept in the War chief's house, his maternal house.[330] At Oraibi the Scalp-taker kept the Scalp in his own house;[331] it was his child. (The Scalps are also called children at Santo Domingo. "My niece" the Zuni Scalp chief calls the Scalp.) At Walpi the Scalps are kept in a cliff crevice, like the Hopi dead.[332] Laguna Scalps were similarly kept, in a cave. Isletan and Taos Scalps

---

* When the Opi organization lapsed, the Scalps were buried. The Scalps of Sia were disposed of in similar circumstances and probably in the same way (White 5).

are kept in kiva, and offered pollen, meal, and red pigment, and Taos Scalps are painted red inside. A painted skull was found at Hawikuh.* Two Hopi skulls marking the Hopi-Navaho boundary were daubed with red by passing Hopi or Navaho.† A cairn of stones on the northwest side of town is the Zuni Scalp house, and here in the Zuni Scalp ceremony baskets of wafer-bread are carried. The Sia Scalp house was like that of Zuni.[333]

It is believed in Isleta that their Navaho Scalps talk and cry, sometimes very noisily. Thus Taos Scalps give warning of an approaching enemy. Tewa Scalps are called Mist or Light Rain and foretell precipitation. People say, "We are going to have a little rain, the Scalps are crying."[334] Zuni Scalps also foretell through omens "how the world will be, how the days will be"; they are "water and seed beings," bestowing waters, seeds, wealth, longevity, power, and strong spirit.[335] First Mesa Scalps were also water beings, since, in welcoming the returning war party, the cloud and rain sign was made on the trail by the Town chief and on it the women cast the scalps, all this three times before the final cast down the hatchway of Chief kiva.[336]

In Isleta for toothache the Scalps may be "fed"; you scatter meal below their kiva niche;‡ and the water the Scalps are washed in is given as medicine against worry or longing.§ Similar Scalp wash is given young men at Santo Domingo to make them strong and brave.[337] The water from the Zuni Scalp

* Deer skulls and skulls of the larger game or prey animals are painted (Acoma). A deer skull is painted to look like deer, a black line down the nose and white under the jaw. Balls of cotton are stuffed in the eye sockets and the centers painted black (Stirling). Deer and antelope skulls were painted red at Mishongnovi, on eye-sockets, jaws, and nose, and other bones were streaked red (Beaglehole 2:8). Deer and antelope bones painted red or black were found at Hawikuh (Hodge 2:141–42).

† Nequatewa, 108. A boundary stone between Shumopovi and Oraibi was carved as a head of Masauwü, Skeleton god (Stephen 4:390, n. 1, Fig. 220).

‡ Compare Lummis 3:235 n. 1. After dark you carry food to the round kiva in your left hand and drop it after making a threefold circuit.

§ Parsons 52:241, 327. Also for similar medicine the two women called Mafornin, "mothers" for Kumpa, the Scalp chief, bite pieces from the Scalps which they spit into a bowl, mix with mud, and envelop in cornhusks. These women carried the Scalps on their back in the Scalp ceremony.

wash is carefully run off, yet the Scalp is emotionally cathartic. Says the Scalp chief:

> To cleanse the thoughts
> Of whoever has angry thoughts
> For this you will stand up here.[338]

After the hide-and-seek playing girls of Corn Mountain kill Ne'wekwe Youth and place his head in a jar, he continues to amuse them and "talk funny."[339] Throughout Pueblo tales or myths *heads*, not scalps, are referred to in killing or fighting episodes. Inferably scalp-taking is a later trait, an overlay on head-taking.* The putative trait of talkativeness and practices of enshrining animal skulls or using them, apparently, as war fetishes (Walpi)† may hold over from head-taking times.

18. Sacrosanct Supplies

Together with spring water for the altar medicine bowl, plants growing in or around the spring are usually collected for various ritual uses, likewise mud or clay for pigment, as in the case of the Zuni Ne'wekwe who are daubed over with the mud from their particular spring, in which their supernatural patron lives. Shulawitsi, the Fire kachina, must have clay from the Sacred Lake for his fire drill. Yellow and pink clays are brought from the Sacred Lake for painting prayer-sticks, masks, and the bodies of kachina impersonators (Zuni). These pigments belong to the kiva chiefs.

Ritual pigments are largely proprietary. The mineral black pigment used on Zuni prayer-sticks and occasionally on masks and the charred corncob pigment used on masks and occasionally on prayer-sticks are fetched by curing societies from the ore bed on Corn Mountain or from the ruins. Just as there are grinding-parties for the preparation of prayer-meal, so the societies hold

---

* Practiced in northern Mexico (Beals, 191) as well as by Aztecs, also in California and the Northwest (Spier 2:259). Skulls without bodies have been found in two Pueblo I sites (Roberts 1:169).

† Stephen 4:41, 46, 70, Fig. 26. Three antelope skulls are prayer-befeathered and kept in kiva by the Agaves, and in Chief kiva near the War god images during the winter solstice ceremony. All were permanently cached in Snake shrines. A mountain-sheep horn helmet was used as a guard on Chief kiva hatch.

parties to grind pigments. They invite outside girls as well as girls who are society members. The girls dance after they finish grinding, and each receives a handful of the pigment which was hard work to grind, precious beads having to be ground in. Women members contribute food to a repast.

Near mountain springs, the homes of kachina, grows spruce, and spruce is peculiarly associated with the kachina. Twigs are used in almost every kachina dance, whether carried in the hand or fastened into armlets, anklets, or belts. Onlookers will take pieces of spruce from the dancers, to impart virtue in field shrines, in the corn store, or to kachina dolls on the walls. In the East spruce will be fastened to crosses or church pictures. For church feasts spruces are set either side of the altar, at Taos quite sizable trees until the priest asked for small ones.*

Spruce is gathered with ritual (see p. 288). Small spruce trees are set out in the Middle, except at Zuni, for kachina dances, and clowns will rub against them, exclaiming, "It is my home" (First Mesa).[340] Prayer-feathers are attached, and at the close of ceremonial the trees are given to the kachina "father" who plants them in his field (Hopi), as do Zuni chiefs who get the spruce trees used in society ceremonials. At Isleta people will ask the moiety chiefs for the trees, asking for them ritually with a cigarette; they want the trees for house ladders. Elsewhere the ritual trees may be cast into the river. After ritual use spruce twigs also may be cast into the river or near a shrine.

19. ALTAR:† SAND-PAINTINGS: GLYPHS

The Pueblo altar consists of fetishes or of representations of the Spirits, of their guards, and of sacrosanct supplies to be used in ritual such as medicine bowl and aspergills, prayer-meal bowl, rattles, or bear paws, including objects which are to be given to

* By edict of 1716 the Indians are compelled to decorate with branches of trees on the fiesta of Corpus Christi (Twitchell II, 180–81). At this season cottonwoods would probably be used. Cottonwood, not spruce, is used for the kachina from the "south" at Santo Domingo.

† Zuni, *teshkwine;* Hopi, *pongya;* Keres, *yaBaishĭnĭ,* meal altar, *aichĭn* (house), frame altar; Tewa, *sente′, nansipu, owi* (town); Hano, *owing;* Jemez, *wagi;* Isleta, *nake′e, nakitụ* (town); Taos, *howitsöne.*

the Spirits or to those participating in the ritual. Thus the altar is an assemblage of the things upon which the attention will be concentrated or by means of which ritual will be performed.

At the head of the altar will be set the paramount or presiding fetish or fetishes, usually the corn-ear fetishes or a particular image. Near by will be an animal guardian figurine or a stone weapon. These may be placed on top of a picture or "mosaic" of meal or of colored sands representing a spirit (Sun, Moon, Stars or Galaxy, Earth, Mountain Lion, Snake, or kachina) or something associated with the Spirits, perhaps the cloud designs or ideograms, or the "house" of the Sun[341] or of the kachina.[342] The cloud and rain design or ideogram is made in meal on the trail in Hopi ceremonies, and the *tiponi* is put down (Flute ceremony).* On the Hopi Flute society altar, a cornfield is represented by blue and yellow corn kernels (Oraibi) or by pollen and blue flower petals (Walpi, Fig. 3). On this altar artificial flowers are set in front of the figurines,[343] and the image of Flute Youth has a necklace of artificial flowers (Mishongnovi).[344] Pulverized blue-flower petals, and pulverized green leaves, pollen, and colored sands or ochers are used in the very simple ground-altar designs of Taos: designs of lake, corn plant, or lightning. Like designs in pollen or meal are made on Tewan and Isletan altars, all of very simple structure.

In the West, among Keres, and at Jemez, a reredos is in use consisting of painted cloth (Hopi), of painted wooden slabs, and of sticks or other paraphernalia† set upright. These upright sticks on Zuni altars are brought forward in square formation (Pl. VI). Surmounting the reredos may be carvings of birds or

* Stephen 4:797, 806 ff., 815-19, Figs. 431, 440, 443. Compare the cloud design made by Zuni Rain chiefs at the Emergence, Pekwin's meal altar. The birds of the directions alit on the altar as on the Flute altar. These birds were to be Pekwin's *e'tone* (Stevenson 2:26 ff.).

† Among them, on two Hopi altars, Antelope and Flute, are painted stone or clay tiles. Butterfly, Locust, and Cloud are represented (Stephen 4:617, 684, 784, 797-98, Figs. 338, 339, 433, Pls. XXI, XXII; Fewkes 14:586, Fig. 61). These tiles are glyphs of a kind, portable glyphs, just as the altar as a whole is a kind of migratory shrine.

A Walpi transvestite, deceased in 1891, is mentioned as a tile-painter (Fewkes 4:11 n.).

FIG. 3.—Walpi Flute society altar. *1–11*, *tiponi* ridge; *a–d*, bird images

images of Knife-Wing or of tutelary spirits. The upright sticks
are painted with the animals of the directions or carved in the
form of snake or lightning. Acoma uprights represent the War
Brothers on guard at either side, and the Mothers. On some
Hopi and Hano altars deceased members are represented by
upright sticks. The eight uprights on the Acoma Town chief's
altar are befeathered crooks. Crossed sticks representing the sky
may hang horizontally over the altar (Hopi, Zuni, Pl. VI)*
to be aspersed[345] or given a twirl which is called *awethlua ishemea*,
clouds calling (Zuni). Sticks, slabs, or fetishes are often set in a
sand ridge at the rear or single feathers are set thus. Wall-
paintings are made, mostly pictures of the Spirits, animal,
cosmic, or kachina (Zuni, Acoma,† Laguna, Isleta, Jemez, Hopi,
including Awatobi) (Pls. IV, VI). At Tesuque tracks of the
chaparral cock are painted on the walls. At Nambé Kossa clowns
are painted on the central post of the kiva.

In front of the fetishes spreads the sand-painting (Pl. IV);
it may be over or around the *sipapu* (Hopi). A parallelogram of
brown sand is first sifted from a basket sieve and on top white or
colored sands are sifted or poured from finger and thumb by
the chief or his helpers (Hopi, Zuni).[346] Seldom does a woman
work on the sand-painting, although the chief of the women's
Lakon society is reported[347] as making their elaborate sand-
painting with very considerable skill; she poured the line and
body colors out between finger and thumb steady and straight,
completing the mosaic in about an hour and a half.

In addition to sand-painting and elaborate frame altar, Hopi
will lay down in the same ceremony a small meal altar, generally
referred to as the altar of the directions. Meal lines, "roads," are
sprinkled from the six directions and at their intersection, on a
sand bed,‡ is placed the medicine bowl. The meal lines are set

* Crossed sticks are also tipped with feathers and carried by kachina associated with the sky (Bunzel 5:1026).

† On all but the south wall.

‡ Called sand center or middle and representing the earth (Voth 4:27, n. 3).
Compare Acoma's earth altar, p. 406. Etymologically and from their encircling
lines, Tanoan altars appear to represent the pueblo.

with corn ears of the colors associated with the directions. With the ears lie seed-filled canes, the "husbands" of the ears, sacrosanct stones, and in some cases birdskins. A meal altar of more elaborate design, usually of cloud design, may be combined with the frame altar (Hopi, Acoma) or may merely extend from a rear line of fetishes (Hano, Zuni Pekwin). At Isleta altar paraphernalia may be set out on a buckskin. Pollen "roads" and a sandpainting are made on a buckskin* at the installation of the Zuni Pekwin.[348]

The prayer-sticks or prayer-feathers that are to be offered to the Spirits, together with the meal or pollen that is to be sprinkled, the gourd jug† of water or the plants which may have been collected from a place of pilgrimage in connection with the ceremony, all of which are to go to those in charge of the ceremony, are also placed in basket or bowl on or near the altar, for distribution at the close. On the Hopi winter solstice altar seed corn is left overnight and models of melons and peaches and of the domestic animals, for which increase is asked. The corn ears stacked back of the Flute society altar (Walpi) are probably seed corn. Under or near the corn store, sand from the altar cloud-painting will be placed (Oraibi Oaqöl ceremony).

With the exception of the Hopi Snake society altar which is assembled at night,[349] altars are set up during the day, in the hours preceding the night ceremonial. Frequently the fourth day is the time for setting the altar. The major fetish is in the care of the chief but other paraphernalia—aspergills, water gourds, or painted slabs—are contributed by assistants (Hopi).[350] The setting-up or laying-down of the altar is done very reverently and frequently is in itself a ritual conducted with prayer or chant.

---

* Painted deerskin was not unfamiliar. A Sia messenger sent up First Mesa by Governor Martinez during his extraordinary negotiations in 1716 reported that on a strip of deerskin were shown fifty-four figures of potential tribal allies to whom the apostates had sent for aid (Bloom, 207–8). In the Heye Museum is a deerskin from Oraibi painted with masks and other Pueblo designs.

† Called chief's jug by Hopi. To its net envelop a prayer-feather will be fastened, sometimes a small ear of corn (Voth 4: Pl. VII*c*). Various persons are owners of the gourd bottles set down on altars, possibly as having clan interests in the springs the bottles are carried to.

On entering the kiva and approaching the altar, people generally cast a pinch of prayer-meal on it or toward it. Initiates are brought formally into contact with the altar, led over the meal road or made to step on crosses of yucca or feathers.[351] The Isletan initiate stands on the head of the altar snake design and steps along the coils of the snake.[352] Where a sand-painting is made for initiates into the kachina organization, initiates are stood upon it to be whipped (Pl. VII).

Before dismantling the altar or rather the first motion toward dismantling is laying the fetishes down on their side, inferably because the Spirits have left them.* It is prescriptive that an altar having served its purpose should be at once removed and paintings effaced, sand-painting or even such elaborate wall-paintings[353] as are made for the Powamu ceremony at Walpi.[354] This rule which is stringent also among Navaho may be part of the ideology about isolating supernatural power when it is not under rigorous ritual control.†

For designs painted or pecked in caves, on rock walls or on boulders, another point of view must prevail, these being permanent.‡ Pictographs and petroglyphs are a conspicuous feature of the Southwest, made by Pueblos, by their Basket Maker predecessors, and by Navaho and Apache. There are geometric and naturalistic or seminaturalistic designs, and among the latter supernatural beings are well represented: Sun, Moon, and Stars, Clouds,[355] Kachina,[356] and mythical fauna like the monster eagle Kwatoko[357] or the Horned Water Serpent or Locust, the

---

* See p. 635. In Kiva A of the Village of the Great Kivas two conical stone fetishes ["mountains"] were found on their sides (Roberts 1:61), and the Zuni workmen insisted, without explaining, that they should lie so (when not invested by the Spirits).

† Possibly there was once the idea that the design might be used in black magic. The Havasupai rubs out any drawing made in the sand for fear someone will use it to make the draftsman sick (Spier 2:288). A Zapoteca mediciner erased at once and carefully the Indian ritual design he drew on the ground for me.

‡ Geometric designs are incised on the plaster of a Chaco Canyon kiva (850–1000) (Brand, Hawley, Hibben, Pl. X) and intended to be permanent, at least until the next plastering, as are some painted designs on Hopi kivas and possibly all the designs on Acoma and Isleta kivas. See p. 493.

flute-player. Between Locust and Mountain Sheep there is a conspicuous association[358] which intrigues us because of contemporary association on First Mesa between the Flute ceremony in which Locust figures and the Horn clan.

Clan glyphs are made not only on rocky wall or boulder[359] but on boundary stones (Hopi, Zuni),[360] on kick-sticks (Zuni),[361] on the backs of racers (Hopi, Zuni),[362] and on house walls when salt is to be distributed (Acoma).[363] Clan glyphs commemorative of events are mentioned in Hopi tales. When Eagle clansmen are dispatched as a search party, men with eagle wings are pictured on the rock, and a Wolf clan visitor is drawn by one of the chiefs as a wolf with tail fastened to a trail leading straight south, "showing that the Wolf clan still belonged to us although the Wolf man had departed." The picture of an eagle and deer drinking together at the same spring testifies in Aztec mode to the relationship of two fusing settlements.[364] Then there are the land titles on stone, given by Masauwü and cherished by the Town chiefs of Oraibi and Shumopovi.[365]

Glyphs of the directions, four or six lines crossed within a circle, and of the clouds, terraced or stepped and half-circles or triangles with falling rain, are used in many ways: the directional signs, on Salimobia masks, on meal in the basket effigy in the Zuni Wood society ceremony,[366] on the wall of the sacred waterfall cave of Taos, on a Powamu sand-painting (Oraibi),[367] as "bed" for the snakes in the Hopi Snake-Antelope ceremony; the terrace cloud or, as Acoma calls it, field, as kiva fire screens, as kiva or church wall, painted on wall,[368] on pottery,[369] clay tiles, and as an altar meal-painting, notably as the Zuni Pekwin's altar; the falling rain cloud, on pottery and tiles, as a meal-painting on trails (Hopi) and altars,[370] on kiva or shrine walls (Hopi),[371] on masks or, particularly significant, over an ear of corn painted on a prayer-stick (Hopi, Oaqöl).* An effigy of rawcotton clouds with pendent prayer-feathers for rain lines hangs over the winter solstice altar of the Walpi War chief.[372] Interlocking half-circles, "friendship mark," and the double triangle

---

* Voth 4: Pl. XI. Note the Keresan character of this glyph.

are painted on kachina (Zuni, Hopi) and on rock walls (Hopi). In Hopi tale[373] it is suggested that concentric circles or spiral, a widespread rock design, is a record of years. Near a First Mesa trail is a historic record, a rock-rubbing, of Ute and of Apache fights. The Ute design is of moon and friendship marks and cross on a Ute shield which is read: "When the moon was full, with our friends we slew the Ute." With the Apache shield is a decimal tally of Apache slain and a sign of an indefinite number of Apache women (? captives).[374] On a Zuni calendar stick Cushing observed a little socket, a fire socket, for the first month in which new fire is made, and this he called a glyph.[375] The signs of the cosmic beings painted on wooden disks (altar pieces) seen by Father Dumarest at Cochiti* might be called glyphs—glyphs "of those things in the universe which most inspire veneration in the Indian because of their utility," remarks the caustic friar.[376]

20. ROAD-MAKING: ROAD-CLOSING

From the chief fetish on the altar (Hopi) or from the altar design of cloud or town (Zuni, Isleta) is usually sprinkled a line of meal toward the ladder or door; it is called explicitly the road† for the Spirit or Spirits to travel in by, "the road for them,"‡ as Crow-Wing speaks of the line of meal leading ladderward from the images of the War Brothers and Spider Grandmother on the Hano winter solstice altar. "Prayer-meal becomes a road" (Zuni).[377]§ (See Pls. IV, VI.)

The "spring" bowl of the altar is placed at the junction of meal roads from the directions (Hopi), and meal is sprinkled into

---

* Compare the painted cottonwood disk from Chaco Canyon (Brand, Hawley, Hibben [Frontispiece]), a more naturalistic design.

† *Onane* (Zuni); *hi'anyi* (Keresan); *p'çide* (Isletan). Compare Zuni, *oneathlanna*, pollen road; Tewa, *kegi po'*, *pochashu po'*, *kastipi po'*, corn-meal road, black-dirt road, pollen road; Hano, *polong;* Hopi, *homnumni pühü*, prayer-meal road. The Hopi War chief also sprinkles a road of specular iron. See p. 559.

‡ Cf. Robbins, Harrington, Freire-Marreco, 88. "Their road lies for them."

§ Compare Papago. Curiously enough the only other parallel I find is from the early Chimu people of northern coastal Peru: the dust of sea shells was scattered by a special official upon the ground where the chief was to tread (Means, 51, citing Father Miguel Cabello, 1576–1586).

PLATE V

KACHINA MOTHER MAKING THE ROAD FOR KACHINA CHIEF, NAMBÉ

the bowl from the directions: all roads for the Clouds, the rain-maker chiefs. As he pours in the water, the Zuni shaman (Big Firebrand society) prays:

> Yonder from the north
> The rain-maker priests (chiefs),
> Bringing their waters,
> Will make their roads come hither.
> Where lies my white shell bowl,
> Four times they will make their roads come in.*

Casting meal on the altar Hopi call road-marking.[378] When meal, pollen, or shell is sprinkled outdoors to the Clouds, a Laguna man raises his hand, lowering it while sprinkling with sweeping gesture as if making the road from sky to earth. Laguna Governor and officers in putting down prayer-sticks will sprinkle meal with a gesture toward the church, a road for the Saints. When Sun is named in song at a race, the Isletan Town chief sprinkles meal for him in a line from east to south, which is "like calling him," i.e., making a road for him. In kachina dances the leader often sprinkles meal during the song, and I surmise he is making a road for the kachina when the singers name them. In leading kachina into a house, meal is sprinkled from the door to the altar by the man of the house, "to open the road," *althtiya*, he opens. And, in leading the kachina from place to place, their leader habitually sprinkles meal in front (Zuni, Hopi, Tewa), "to make the road" (Pl. V). The kachina-like impersonation of the Isletan mountain spirit Thlįwale has a road sprinkled for him when he is led into town; and a meal road is laid from the house door to the corpse in the Isletan death ceremony, by which the deceased may be both summoned and dismissed.

Human participants in ceremony may also approach the altar by the meal road.[379] A meal road is sprinkled for the War chiefs of Acoma when they come into their house from the sacred springs,[380] and meal is laid in the trail for returning wood-gatherers in the Hopi Wüwüchim ceremony.[381] Meal is sprinkled before kick-stick racers and racers in the Molawia ceremony

---

* Bunzel 4:783. Repeated for each direction.

(Zuni). In Hopi and Hano tales, when the bride is arrayed and sent back to her home, meal is sprinkled in front of her; "it is a road for her." In several Zuni and Hopi ceremonies before descending the kiva ladder each participant throws a handful of meal, a ball of meal, in front down the hatchway.[382] In tale, a Zuni about to take a journey may sprinkle meal in front of himself, with prayer, as does the youth who in search of his wife throws a ball of meal ahead each morning that Sun may open or disclose to him his road. In Hano tale after Pour-Water Woman raises her head out of the lake to invite the runaway girl into her underwater kiva, she takes a ball of meal out of her placque basket and throws it across the lake; the water divides (like the Red Sea!), leaving a road for the girl. A ladder even rises up from the lake in the rendering of the incident at San Juan. Possibly the throwers of a ball of meal down the kiva hatch are dramatizing some such mythical situation or concept, a descent into the lower world.

While a Zuni deer-hunter is absent, every morning his wife may bring out a mountain-lion fetish and from the image sprinkle a line of meal in the direction taken by the hunter, and on the hunter's return with a deer a meal road will be sprinkled from the house door* to the middle of the floor, *below the Shalako roof shrine*. After the kill, a road of pollen is sprinkled from the deer toward the town (Laguna),[383] and "road-markers" are put down by hunters for the animals to travel by (Laguna, Hano).[384] An Ant society man will lay a trail of meal away from an ant hill, for the ants to leave by (Zuni). Just so the final rite of the Hopi Wüwüchim ceremony is laying meal on shrine trails in order to make a return road to their "houses" for attendant Spirits.

The altar "road" in eastern pueblos may have laid on it crossed pieces of yucca as stepping-marks.[385] They represent, it is said, tracks of the chaparral cock. As these tracks do not indicate direction, they preclude witch pursuit.† Four feathers are spaced along the "road" of Hano winter solstice altars.[386] Step-

---

* To the house door, at Santa Ana (White).

† Compare the use of the chaparral cock feather in the toe of the moccasin of the Zuni scalp-kicker.

ping-marks at Zuni are cross-lines in meal which are said to represent the four worlds of the Emergence. We may recall the "road" laid at the Emergence for the people of Jemez.[387] On one of the Oraibi Powamu altars[388] is laid a line of pollen to represent the road traveled by the people on emerging from Shipapu. On other Hopi altars this line is set with longevity crooks.* The line is drawn to the southeast, to the rising sun, the road everybody still travels through life, and which is put down ritualistically for all the people by the chiefs in several Hopi ceremonies, usually with a feathered string "road-marker."[389] The chief will bury a "road-marker" from twelve to fifteen feet long on the east side of the mesa pointing toward the east, and sometimes all the society members will walk slowly along this line as a prayer that the people may walk on the good road or lead a straight, upright life (Oraibi).[390] On First Mesa a "road" is put down for the people at dawn after the announcement of any major ceremony. After his corn has been harvested by the people, the Walpi Town chief puts down a "road" for them; and for four mornings they are expected to go out to this "road" and with meal pray to the Sun "to have a long life."

The meal line from fetish to ladder is not only a road for the Spirits but, as it may not be crossed, it "closes" the chamber against intrusion.[391] A meal line may be drawn across a trail to indicate that it is closed (Hopi, Hano) or "cut."[392] During the Wüwüchim initiation the trails to First Mesa are closed in this way. Formerly, any stranger venturing across the line would have been killed by the Horn society guards, just as Estevan was killed at Hawikuh when he crossed the line drawn on the trail against him by the warriors.†

Hopi draw four black parallels with cedar charcoal, in four places on the trail between the house and the grave, to close the door against Masauwü, the god of death.[393] When the K'oʙish-

---

* Graduated from tall to short. Prays the Hopi: "On that (age-mark) you must be resting as you go along (through life), over there at the last one, the shortest one standing, may you fall asleep as old women, old men! (Voth 3:311).

† Hodge 3:41. A like line of closure was drawn against Captain Alvarado in 1540 by men of Acoma (Winship, 491).

taiya of Acoma unmask, the impersonator draws with an arrow-point four lines on the ground between his mask and himself, to keep the Spirit from returning to town.[394] The Isletan grave is marked around with an arrowpoint to keep off witches, it was said, but it is probably also to keep the deceased from wandering, just as square or circle is traced around the unbeliever (Keres)[395] or as in ritual juggling a rabbit will be "tied" in a circle made by an arrowpoint "so it cannot move away."[396]

Marking the burial road at San Juan may be also setting a boundary for the ghost, but as the foot is drawn four times along this "mountain" the survivor may be conceived of as crossing mountains away from the ghost, as in the elaborate trail exorcism of Acoma. The doctors make a sand-painting of four mountains, triangles in the colors of the directions, for the people to step on, halfway up, on top, and in the valley. After this "journey" by glyph we might say, they are brushed off by the doctor; they spit their "sadness" into yucca plants; they step into a rec-tangular yucca frame which the doctors swing backward four times, spilling out the sickness; and finally they brush them-selves with anything they pick up from the ground, speaking to it to take away sickness and sorrow. Everything is buried by the doctors who, after performing all the ritual on themselves, make four lines on the ground with their arrowpoint to bar their trail to disease.*

The practice of sprinkling a line or half-circle or full circle of ashes or meal around the kiva or in front of the house or chamber where ceremonial is going on is also an act of closure, although it may be described merely as a form of "trapping." For example, at the Acoma Fire society's solstice ceremony, when people were eager to get in first to get the good seats, they had to wait on the roof of the chamber until the society sang their welcoming song

---

* Stirling. Given as an incident during an early migration caused by epi-demic; it is the usual society exorcism in concluding ceremonial. Compare the Zuni Shuma'kwe manipulation of a yucca square over the invalid, to song (Stevenson 2:530). Such a yucca object hung on the wall of my room in the house of the Fire shaman of Jemez; but at that time I had no clue whatsoever to its use, although it is pictured at Sia (Stevenson 1: Pl. XV).

and a member came up and scraped away the line of ashes with his arrowpoint.[397]

21. ORIENTATION: CIRCUIT:* PROCESSION

The ritual directions are six—North, West, South, East, Above, and Below†—or, combining Above and Below and Middle as do the Isletans, or concluding as well as beginning in the East as do they of Taos, five.‡ And in passing from one direction to the other the order as given for the cardinal points is followed, so that the ceremonial circuit is sinistral or anti-sunwise. Associated with the directions are colors, clouds, lightning and rain, the prey animals, birds, ants, corn and other plants, trees, stones or shells,§ and many of the Spirits. With the North, yellow (Tewa, Taos, blue; Isleta and Picurís, black), mountain lion, and oriole are associated; with the West, blue (Tewa, Taos, Isleta and Picurís, yellow), bear and bluebird (Zuni), *rohona* (Acoma) or weasel (Laguna);[398] with the South, red (Isleta and Picurís, blue; Taos, [?] buff), badger (Zuni), wildcat (Hopi, Acoma, Laguna),[398] and parrot (Hopi); with the East, white, gray wolf, and magpie; for the Zenith, all colors (Zuni, Tewa) or black (Hopi, Hano, Laguna), eagle, and hepatic tanager (Hopi); for the Nadir, black (Zuni, Tewa) or all colors (Hopi, Hano), mole, and *toposhkwa* (Hopi). At Zuni, where the associations of color-directions are most thoroughgoing, each animal species may in turn be subdivided by color and direction.

* Zuni, *lesite kwintakya*, toward directions.

† Among Hopi other points are usually observed: northwest, southwest, southeast, northeast; for zenith, the north, for nadir, the south. When the cardinal points are observed, the zenith is identified with the northeast, the nadir, with the southwest, except in the Agave society at Oraibi when the zenith is identified with the northwest (Voth 9:116), a very curious variation.

Among Hopi the directions are determined by sunrise and sunset, and this is probably so elsewhere.

‡ A neat bit of evidence for the theory that cardinal directions are influenced by favored numerals.

§ The feeling for color-direction associations in shells is plainly indicated, but the particular associations are inadequately recorded. See Voth 8:70–71; Voth 2:133, n. 5.

(Noted at Hano.) At Taos color-direction associations appear to be only with the kachina.

In sprinkling meal, pollen, or other offerings, or aspersing fluids, the directions are observed, the sprinkling being outward toward the different points or inward from the points to the prayer-stick tray, medicine bowl, etc. The waving of ashes or cedar bark, of mask or swallowing-stick in a circle is conceptually a matter of waving in the directions. The directions are observed in smoking ritual; the smoke is puffed out in the directions, with a final whirl, at Zuni and Jemez (also in aspersing), to signify the circuit or all directions.* At Zuni, after a man presents a ceremonial cigarette or meal package, he moves the clasped hands of the recipient in the directions. Holding the newly delivered infant in his hands, the Isletan doctor points its head over lines of the directions made on the ground. Zuni kachina impersonators or other dancers are frequently turned by a leader or motioned in the cardinal directions. For Zenith and Nadir the head may be carried forward and back.[399] When the Pekwin is installed, he is held by the back and turned in the four directions. *Pekwin onanyat'enapkya*, hold by the back, is the term for the installation.† The moving or directing of persons or objects to the directions is called in Zuni *lesite kwintakyana ukia*, toward directions give [to the old ones, *athlashinawe*]. From behind, with your hands on his shoulders, moving him in the directions and making him sit down on a cross of meal is the ritual way of seating a person.

In dance or ceremonial or in kiva the turn is ever to the left, i.e., on an arc of the ritual circuit.

Kachina impersonators are frequently grouped according to the six directions as indicated by color, e.g., Zuni Ky'anakwe who are Corn People, on entering town proceed by color, first yellow, then blue, red, white, variegated, black. Certain warrior kachina are classified by color-direction, and so are the Cloud beings to whom offerings are made in circuit, generally in succes-

* By Cushing this is interpreted to mean the center or a seventh direction.

† The buckskin Pekwin stands on is quartered by lines of pollen (Stevenson 2:169).

sive directions on successive days. Each day the circuit may be narrowed to show that the clouds are approaching.

At Zuni the six paramount Rain chiefs represent each a direction; they are referred to collectively as *atemplakyakwe* (of all the directions). As the four chiefs of the Hopi Antelope society represent the Chiefs of the Directions, their positions around the altar and in the ritual are determined by direction. The Walpi War god altar is placed in the north corner of the ceremonial chamber ("from the north the wind brings icy cold") and in Hopi kivas the chief of the ceremony ordinarily occupies the northwest corner.[400] The Acoma altar is on the north side of the kiva (Stirling). In placing the altar in a Zuni room, a principle other than that of the compass comes into play: the altar is placed on the side away from the door, "the valuable place."[401]

Zuni kivas are referred to as representing directions: He'iwa, the north; Muhewa, the west; Chupawa, the south; Ohewa, the east; Uptsannawa, the zenith; Hekiapawa, the nadir. He'iwa is chief kiva, since it represents the north, which has ceremonial primacy and with which all-powerful Lightning is associated.

The north has primacy when the other points or a circuit are involved, otherwise the east is the favored direction, the direction associated with the Sun. The Tiwa ritual circuit, in fact, starts in the east, and at Taos any ritual road is made to the east. Prayer is said ordinarily facing the east. Shrines ordinarily open to the east, and altars are often set facing eastward.

Just as the dead are buried head eastward, a dead deer or rabbit is laid out head eastward (Zuni, Acoma, Laguna, San Juan, Taos). At Isleta the head of the quarry is pointed toward the sun, eastward or westward; but just after the kill the head is pointed toward the town. By Hopi the head was pointed in the direction of the kill, the better for the animal spirit to return home. For like reason the heads of eagles buried in the middle of a cornfield were pointed toward their home buttes.[402]

At Zuni and Santo Domingo men are buried to the right of the great central cross in the cemetery, facing out from the altar (Zuni, south; Santo Domingo, north), and women to the left (Zuni, north; Santo Domingo, south). These are the positions

taken by the sexes in church, also in accordance with sex position in relation to the native altar or in prayer-sticks, the female
to the left of the male.

Dance-processions occur in war, kachina, and saint's dances,
and there are processions with images or other fetishes, including
the spruce-set corn baskets carried by the clan mothers of Walpi
at Powamu. The Shalako come into town in procession (Zuni,
Hopi of First Mesa), performing their running ritual en route;
kachina impersonators from another town, probably all ceremonial visitors, are met by their hosts and convoyed into town.
Mishongnovi salt-gatherers are met on the edge of mesa by the
chiefs and the "aunts" to whom they bring salt. The chiefs
sprinkle meal before the men; each aunt steps forward, shakes
hands with her man, thanks him, and sprinkles him with meal.
Then a procession is formed; first the chiefs, then Bear clan
woman of the Town chieftaincy, then Coyote clan woman and
the other women, each with her nephew behind her, the bag of
salt on his shoulder. After the nephew has been bathed and his
salt paid for with meal and food, another procession forms to
escort him to his house, as a bride is escorted.[403] Hopi do seem
fond of processions!

22. FAVORED NUMERALS AND FOURFOLD FEINT

Several psychological or social roles of favorite numbers
among the Pueblos have been noted (pp. 100–101): how four and
its multiples, or among Tanoans five, give a sense of compulsion
or achievement or certainty. The familiar numeral carries conviction; there are no skeptics of primitive statistics. If the number
was not *four*, let us say, it should have been *four*. A three-part
arrangement is requisite for certain designs on Zuni bowls, yet
the potter always expresses in words a preference for four
parts.[404] "Why the use of four?" I once asked Tsatiselu. "The
Americans do not always speak the truth," he said; "they will
give any number. But we Zuni speak the truth and so we give
the true number, the number *four*." To disprove information in
a book about Taos, it is said there to have been contributed by
three persons.

Anything repeated four times is done properly, is right and respectable, is pledge or fulfilment. Feinting an act three times and completing it the fourth time is a dramatization of this idea. This feint pattern which has a widespread distribution occurs in several Pueblo rituals: most conspicuously in offering prayer-sticks to kachina in the Walpi Home-going ceremony (p. 774). At Zuni before knocking on a door with his murderous knife Atoshle kachina will dash up to it and retreat three times, a spectacular approach. Spectacular or elaborate was the farewell to a warrior made by his wife if she were a woman who "knew something." "When he stepped on the first rung, his wife would pull him in. Then again he would go out. When he stepped on the second rung, again she would pull him in. Again he would go out. When he stepped on the third rung, again she would pull him in. Then again he would go out. When he stepped on the fourth rung, again she would pull him in. Then he would go out and go." At the house of the Great Shell this feinting was repeated and again at the house of the Navaho fetish.[405]

In general, repetition emphasizes any rite, and repetition is regulated by the conventional number: there will be four strokes of the yucca whip; prayer-sticks are bundled in fours; anything waved around the head in exorcism is waved four times; songs are sung in stanzas of four; at a ritual meal four mouthfuls are eaten; ceremonial or taboo days are counted by four. After killing an enemy, Zuni warriors were under taboo for four days; the slayer, for eight days: four for the slain, four for himself; and the War chief, for twelve days: four for the slain, four for Elder Brother War god, and four for himself.

Apart from appearing as a multiple of four, twelve is a favored numeral, particularly in connection with war and particularly among Tiwa.[406]

Ten is a conspicuous numeral in Shalako. The tally cord is counted decimally, and ten shrines are visited in the yearlong ceremonial. There are ten Koyemshi clowns. In Acoma kachina ceremonial there is also a decimal count and tally, and in Acoma tradition counting was taught on the fingers, beginning with the little finger of the left hand (Zuni way also), by the Mother,

Iyatik, to the War chief so that he might know how many K'oʙishtaiya kachina were coming.[407]

23. Smoking: Bonfires

The initial meeting to arrange for a ceremony is popularly referred to as smoke assemblage or talk (Hopi)—"they are going to have their smoke" (Zuni); and no ceremony is conducted without intervals of smoking, which is a matter of personal relaxation and enjoyment, but which is also associated with the ritual idea of increase to the clouds, in Zuni ritual terms, with smoke "he adds to their hearts,"* or in vernacular comment "smoke makes the mist and the clouds; you feed them with smoke, you give more flesh to them." The ritual term for smoke is "mist." Isletans also refer to ritual smoking as "mist-giving." On First Mesa, ritual smoking is always referred to as "drinking" (rain water). Crow-Wing will write, for example, for offering a man a smoke, "The kiva chief gives him a drink."

Crow-Wing expresses again and again the relationship between smoking and rain or snow. After telling how the spruce-gatherers for the dance on January 22 are given a smoke by the kiva chief and then asked to describe their journey, Crow-Wing adds: "Everybody listens and of course everybody smokes to bring rain and snow." Nevertheless, it has been a dry year, so on May 10 Hano men are summoned to one of their kivas to spend the evening smoking. "Four nights we have to go there and smoke. It is something like praying for rain. We have had a poor year, so we are trying very hard to get rain." August 10, the day after the Snake ceremony is announced, the Snake clan people meet and smoke "because they want to have some rain so that it will not be very hot the days they hunt snakes, also to have good crops and lots of grass so that the stock will have good feed and get fat."

Commonly the smoking interval is initiated by each smoker

---

* The usual reference to offerings of smoke or food (Bunzel 4:713).

puffing the smoke in the six directions, with a final whirl of the
cigarette (Zuni, Jemez) for all the directions.

> Four times inhaling
> Into my body
> I made this mist pass through.
> Then with the mist
> I add to the hearts of my fathers of all the directions.[408]

At Isleta smoke is puffed in the direction of any Spirit that is
being addressed as, for example, toward the river for the Water
People—"he thanks the Water People with smoke"—or upward
toward the sun when Sun is being asked to help in the race.
Isletan and Laguna[409] hunters puff in the directions.

Various sacrosanct objects are "smoked," as it is said at Zuni:
masks on the altar and other altar-set fetishes, water in gourd
bottles or in medicine bowl, prayer-sticks or feathers; and smoke
is blown on kachina impersonators* or into the water that will be
sprinkled on them (San Juan). In Zuni tale, after a deer is laid
out head to east, it is not only meal sprinkled but "smoked" and
so are rabbits brought into kiva after the Hopi snake hunt.[410]
Smoke is puffed up the nostrils of the dead deer at Cochiti[411] and
on to the Scalps at Isleta. All these are the recipients of prayer
or associated with prayer, so it may well be that smoking is
thought of as conveying prayer; smoking is "to make everything
meet and connect" (Acoma). Possibly the compulsive power of
tobacco is or was once implicated.

The cigarette or, among Hopi and in the East, the pipe may
be passed from one smoker to the other. It is given and received
with a term of relationship: my father or grandfather, my son or
grandson, says the giver, the recipient responding with the
reciprocal term. "Younger-brother-elder-brother," the term
used between ceremonial colleagues, is said by Tewa. "Yes," rejoins the recipient. The Zuni way is to wait until after smoking†
and then to rehearse all the kinship terms in a kind of litany.[412]

* For a far-flung parallel see picture of Tupinamba shamans blowing smoke
on dancers, given by Métraux (first plate, but unnumbered).

† Ordinarily, in asking anyone for a light, kinship terms are exchanged
(Zuni); and they are exchanged on giving and receiving sacrosanct things in
general, e.g., prayer-sticks of office or medicine water (Zuni, Hopi).

Hopi smoke clay pipes with reed stems, and they have a cone or pear-shaped clay pipe or cloud-blower used in puffing large volumes of smoke over altar or into medicine bowl.[413] The tubular clay pipes of Pecos are incised with cloud designs.

The following account from Oraibi Powamu ceremonial shows how smoking combines with other rites: The members stand in a semicircle before the altar, Powamu chief on the extreme west side and next to him Kachina chief. The pipe-lighter hands the "cloud-producer" pipe to Powamu chief, who blows large clouds of smoke from it over the altar and into the medicine bowl, and then asperses, handing back the cloud-producer to the pipe-lighter. All take a little corn meal in their right hand, Powamu chief takes an aspergill, Kachina chief, a rattle, the next men also a rattle, and each of the others an eagle-wing feather. All these are waved up and down in time with the singing. Follow thirteen songs. During the first four Powamu chief asperses. With the fifth song he takes from a cornhusk a pinch of corn pollen, drops it from the north side into the medicine bowl, blows with an eagle-wing bone whistle into the medicine bowl, and asperses. This is repeated from the other cardinal points, from the northeast (for zenith) and from the southwest (for nadir). Eight songs follow; at the end Powamu chief says, "Thanks!" All lay down their rattles or feathers, sprinkling them with the meal in their hand.

The pipe-lighter, having lit the pipe and smoked a few puffs, hands it to Powamu chief, exchanging with him terms of relationship. Powamu chief smokes a few minutes, blowing the smoke toward the altar, and especially toward the corn fetish (*tiponi*) and medicine bowl, hands the pipe to Kachina chief who smokes it, and then all the others smoke it, all in turn exchanging terms of relationship. In exchanging these terms, the one who has received the pipe always smokes a little while and then speaks, addressing the giver who at once replies. When all have smoked, the pipe is handed back from one to the other, each again smoking a few puffs. Powamu chief who smokes last calls to the pipe-lighter, "Come get it!" The pipe-lighter gets it, cleans it, and places it on the floor near the fireplace. Each chief utters a short prayer to which all respond *anchaa* (so be it, all right), whereupon all hold a little meal to their lips and sprinkle it from the six directions toward and on the altar, dropping the last pinch on the rattles or feathers they used in beating time.[414]

In connection with Shalako at Zuni, bonfires are built by Shulawitsi, the Fire-Corn kachina; the smoke appears to have the same significance of cloud-making as pipe or cigarette smoke. Yet the Hopi would not build bonfires when in summer they perform their Shalako—"it would dry up the ground," and at Acoma the ritual bonfires of Shuracha are "to heat Mother Earth to make her more fertile."[415] These Acoma fires are also signal fires and probably the Zuni fires derived, too, from signal fires, such as are made by returning salt-gatherers (Zuni, Mishongnovi) or warriors (Mishongnovi) or by many Indian peoples. A signal fire is built on Corn Mountain at the winter solstice ceremony.

Fires are made for Masauwü, Hopi god of fire, and offerings are cast into the flames. Christmas bonfires are made in the East and formerly at Zuni, where meal was sprinkled on the fire.[416]

During Isletan exorcising or witch-finding ceremonial, fires may not be lit outdoors, since the smoke would blind the medicine men in their pursuit of witches, just as deer or rabbits are blinded or bewildered by the ritual smoking of the Hunt chief of Isleta or by hunt bonfires elsewhere. No explanation has been given for the taboo on outdoor fires during the winter solstice ceremony of Zuni and the period of "staying still" at Taos.

24. Aspersing*

Water or fluid is sprinkled from the medicine bowl (set on altar or carried in hand [Pl. II]) with eagle feathers bound together with cotton (Hopi) or with two loose eagle-wing feathers (Zuni, Sia). One feather after dipping may be tapped from below with the other feather or both feathers tapped with the gourd rattle. At Isleta duck feathers are in use as aspergills. In a tale of how Dove makes rain, Dove takes a feather out from each wing and

* Zuni, *akyathlalu*, all, water, sprinkle.

with them, from the pool he has made, he sprinkles in all directions (Zuni). As he sprinkles and sings, the clouds begin to gather.

The sprinkling is to the directions or upon the altar or upon kachina impersonators. When a single Zuni kachina comes into the dance room, first of all he dances up in front of the society medicine chief (*akwamosi*) sitting alongside the altar, in order to be aspersed. During the group dance, the medicine chief will leave his seat and pass along the line of dancers to asperse them one by one. Sometimes he carries his bowl with him; sometimes, after sprinkling three or four dancers, he goes back to the bowl on the altar to redip his feathers. "This sprinkling is just like rain dropping on you. It makes you strong and lively."

Among Hopi, as dance groups pass by co-operating kivas, a society member, theoretically a Badger clansman, since Badger is medicine chief par excellence, comes out on the roof of the kiva with bowl and aspergill first to sprinkle the passing dancers and then to sprinkle to the directions. This concluding aspersing I have seen performed so quickly or perfunctorily that it looks like a merely circular wave of the aspergill. During the Oraibi Snake dance the Antelope medicine chief or sprinkler asperses the dancers at short intervals (Pl. II).[417]

The Turtle dancers of San Juan, maskless kachina dancers, are aspersed by the Town chiefs. All present at the Cochiti ceremony for general curing are aspersed from the medicine bowl, as well as given a drink. Members of the Kachina society are given a drink of the water they have fetched from the spring, and the water is also sprinkled on the ground, as the chief promises rain.[418]

Aspersing the corpse before it is taken from the house is a common practice. At San Juan and probably in any pueblo where the Catholic priest attends in house or at grave, he asperses the corpse from his silver aspergill.

The padre may asperse the canes of the secular officers. Isletan canes are also aspersed by Town chief, Scalp or Snake chief, and War chief of the Cane.

25. Water-pouring: Drenching

Water is fetched from a sacred spring in many Pueblo ceremonials. Arriving at the spring, the Hopi messenger whirls his
rhombus and blows four times on his eagle-bone whistle. He
prays and deposits prayer-feathers or prayer-sticks. Then he
sprinkles meal into the spring from the six directions. He dips
water into his netted gourd bottle from the six directions with
buzzard feather or corn ear, or he dips a little water with the
gourd, six times, pouring it on the ground near the spring in order
to induce the clouds to bring more water. Then he fills the
gourd. Coming up from the spring, he places his "road-marker"
on the trail and sprinkles a line of meal from the spring over the
feathered string toward the town, so that rain when coming to
the spring may also go to the town. He must be careful not to
let his gourd of water rest anywhere on the ground until it is
deposited on the altar, lest it rain over that spot; the rain is
wanted over the altar (Hopi).[419]

The gourd may be left on the altar to be poured from later on
his field by the chief[420] or by some special person like the winner
in the Hopi Antelope race.[421] Or water may be poured from
gourd into medicine bowl which is sometimes called the spring,
poured from the directions, often to song,[422] or it may be poured
upon ears of corn placed in the bowl.[423] At the conclusion of a
ceremony the contents of the bowl may be poured into the court
shrine[424] or *sipapu*.[425]

Three kachina who come out in the Oraibi Powamu ceremony
perform water-pouring rites. The night before their appearance,
a small pit has been dug by a Bow clansman who has placed in it
a prayer-stick and some meal. At this pit which is called "well,"
Āototo kachina sprinkles a line of meal from the north side
toward and into the opening, and then from the same side pours
from his gourd bottle a little water. This he repeats from the
west, south, east, northeast, and southwest. Aholi kachina repeats the ritual. Both kachina go on to Badger kiva where, after
rubbing some meal on the north side of the hatchway, Āototo
pours water into a bowl held by a man standing on the ladder.

Āototo repeats for the three other sides of the kiva. Aholi repeats the ritual.[426]

After corn is planted in kiva in the Hopi Water Serpent celebration, water is poured, explicitly as a mimetic rite; "thus we hope rain will come copiously after our corn is planted in the fields."[427] The Hopi Antelope race is started by dashing to the ground a gourd filled with water from five springs. "Thus may the rain fall!" prays the starter.[428] At Acoma the War chiefs fetch water from sacred springs to pour into the reservoirs of the mesa summit that they may not fail.*

Water or urine (perhaps in burlesque, perhaps because urine is clown medicine) is poured on the clowns or clowning groups in all the western pueblos by women or by the kachina. "The Koyemshi represent the rain, therefore we throw water on them."[429] It is a rain prayer, just as any sort of daubing with mud was considered.

At Oraibi, Hahai-i, called in Tewa Pour-Water Woman, appears with the procession of girls led into town by Powamu chief; she gives corn-mush packets to the children whom she besprinkles or drenches with water.[430] Yucca kachina pours water down the throats of the clowns to hasten the rain, thus demonstrating to the Clouds that the clowns are thirsty (Hano).[431]

26. SUDS: CLOUD BOWL OR "SPRING"

Sud-making to imitate clouds occurs in rain ceremonial (Keres, Zuni). The suds are stirred in the altar bowl, the cloud bowl (Sia, Zuni), and then thrown to the cardinal points or on to the altar (Zuni, Shuma'kwe) or rubbed on themselves by those present (Zuni), or put on the head, to represent clouds (Cochiti). The women who do this for the Cochiti Giant society† are called Shiwanna, thunder clouds. The little Zuni tale of the burrowing owls who dance for pleasure and the good of the town with bowls of suds on their heads connotes this sud-making rite.[432]

---

* White 2:45, 47. Compare the Mexican practice of pouring into wells water that has been blessed on Holy Saturday (Parsons 62:276).

† Women members make suds for the Quirena society of Sia (White 5). For San Felipe see Parsons 31:487.

The altar or medicine water bowl from which aspersing is done and into which meal roads of the directions are sprinkled is thought of generally as a spring or pool. "Our spring children," says a Zuni shaman referring to society members who have drunk from the medicine bowl.[433] The bowl is commonly filled with water from a spring, "that the springs may always be full (Zuni)";[434] and bowl ritual at the altar may be quite similar to ritual performed at a spring, with whistling or singing to "call in" the spirits, with meal-sprinkling, i.e., road-making, and with water-pouring from the directions (Hopi, Zuni, Isleta). And just as spring water is used generally for ritual pigments, so at Isleta water is dripped ritually from the altar bowl on to the stone of the woman who is grinding ritual pigment.

27. RHOMBUS:* THUNDER STONES:† LIGHTNING FRAME:‡
ROOF HOLE AND REFRACTION: SUN SHIELD

The rhombus (bull-roarer or whizzer)[435] is swung to make wind, since wind brings storm clouds (Zuni), or to arouse Thunder, since it makes a noise like thunder, and to produce storm (Laguna, § Hopi). "The thunder prayer-stick calls to Cloud to listen and send rain." It calls for the good lightning which causes fertility and drives away bad lightning and bad clouds (Hopi).[436]

The whizzer is used in pilgrimage to springs (Zuni, Hopi), or in any procession, by the warrior in the van. At the summer rain dances of Zuni it is swung by the attendant Koyemshi clowns. Hopi Koyemshi swing it, as do Hopi Cloud or Lightning kachina, in the Water Serpent celebration. In the Flute and Snake-Ante-

* Zuni, *numnunanne;* Keres, *oyamamuts;* Hopi, *ümükpi* (Stephen), *towo'king-piata* (Voth).

† Zuni, *kululunawe,* perhaps the reference is to the game, Tewa, *kotįti* (Parsons 42:146); Acoma, *toki^amoti,* see p. 981.

‡ Hopi, *talawipi kihu,* lightning-house; Keres, *pŭtruïst.*

§ The whizzer has not been noted among other Keres, or in recent years any-where in the East, but Bourke states that he saw it in Rio Grande pueblos (Bourke 1:477). Isletans say they do not need it (or the lightning frame) since Thunder (and Lightning) come of themselves in their rain ceremony, i.e., they have another way of calling them.

lope ceremonies it is swung in kiva, at the hatch, on the trail. It is swung at Zuni altars[437] and is seen on Hano altars. It is used to stir suds in rain ceremonial (Laguna), and serves as an aspergill. It is anointed with honey (Hopi).

The Hopi whizzer is painted for one or another of the color-directions. At one end it is carved into a cloud terrace from which is painted a lightning design.[438]

In Zuni Rain chief ritual two stone balls are hit together or rolled along in front of the meal altar[439] "to call the thunder"; they make a noise like thunder. (Compare the kachina game of Acoma and Walpi, pp. 510, 981.) Such a ball is mentioned at Isleta as belonging to the Town chief. It was used to send thunder and lightning against the enemy. Santa Clara societies use two stone points to make thunder noise.

The "lightning-house" or frame is the familiar European set of sticks which fold up or extend into a series of lozenges. It lies in front of the War god images (Walpi)[440] and is used by kachina (Hopi, Zuni, Cochiti), by Buffalo dancers (First Mesa), in the Acoma Flint society, and in the Hopi Snake society. Snake men shoot lightning frames toward the east or the sun in making ritual circuits, or within kiva they shoot the frame, four times, toward the hatchway, swinging the rhombus also, to represent lightning and thunder.[441] Flint doctors who cure Lightning-sent disease strike initiates over the heart and on the back with this frame made from lightning-blasted pine or spruce, in order to impart the power of Lightning.[442]

In the ceremonial chambers of Zuni Rain chiefs a roof hole is made so that the sun's ray can fall upon the altar,* and Hopi refract a ray by crystal through the kiva hatchway. At Isleta, Sun and Moon, Lightning and Thunder, are said to be brought down into the ceremonial chamber through a roof hole.

A back shield,† a tablet or disk on which Sun's face is conventionally depicted, is worn in various dances or ceremonies, in

---

* Hearsay; there is no specific description, but I have seen such an opening.

† Back shields were worn by Jalisco warriors as represented in the Lienza of Tlaxcala, warriors who were painted with a black line under the eyes, kachina impersonator style.

the Hopi and San Felipe[443] Buffalo dance by the girl dancers, in the Oraibi Flute ceremony,[444] in a Mishongnovi girl's dance called Rain-drink Maidens,[445] and in a Tewa Sun (or Moon, with Moon's face) dance. A rectangular back tablet with red-stained horsehair and eagle feathers is worn at Zuni by the Eagle kachina, a Hopi-derived kachina, in the Kings' Day dance by the Laguna colonists at Isleta, and in a "Laguna kachina" dance on First Mesa.[446] Blue Eagle, a maskless impersonation in the Walpi winter solstice ceremony, wears a back tablet, as do certain Agaves in initiation ceremonial.[447] The Marau woman chief at Oraibi wears a square back tablet ("copious rains or rain water") on which a human-headed eagle is painted.[448]

In Tewa myth Sun's shield is carried across the sky, and the shield dance in Walpi winter solstice ceremonial is said to dramatize a like mythical incident.[449]

28. WHISTLE: FLUTE: DRUMS: NOTCHED-STICK RASP: RATTLES

Whistling is a mimetic call or summons to the birds or animals or to the Spirits. In the Oraibi Powalawu ceremony after the War chief ascends the kiva ladder and blows yellow oriole feathers and corn pollen from a yellow-colored reed tube toward the north, he blows a few short, sharp notes on his whistle of eagle-wing bone. Within the kiva he repeats the rite on the west, south, and east sides of the altar. He is summoning or imitating one of the birds of warm weather.[450] When Powamu chief whistles into the medicine bowl, the song is directed to the birds of the six directions—oriole, bluebird, parrot, magpie, asya, road-runner—who are supposed to be asking the Chiefs of the Zenith for rain clouds (Nima'n, Walpi). The Antelope society messenger to the spring blows four times on his eagle-bone whistle to announce himself or call the Water spirits: Clouds or Water Serpent. In Isletan tale, as the people are starting forth on the hunt, the little boy who is to be their Hunt chief blows his whistle, and the clouds come out. "It was dark, dark, and the people were glad; they had not seen those clouds for many years. 'Maybe the Hunt chief has been born (installed),' they said, 'maybe we are going to have rain.'" The second time the boy whistled, it began to thunder and lightning. The third time he whistled, it began to rain, and it rained all day long.

Keresan shamans wear eagle-wing-bone whistles to blow on when they sally forth to fight witches. An Isletan shaman has only to whistle like an eagle, calling it, to get the power of flight (see p. 719), which in the tales of all the Southwestern peoples is a desired and convenient power. In the Zuni Molawia ceremony Bitsitsi of the Ne'wekwe whistles as he stalks through the dance court after scouting for the lost Corn Maidens. The whistle carried in his mouth is referred to as "rabbit tongue." Small bone "bird-calls," perforated on the side, were found at Hawikuh.*

The flute of bone or reed is played at the altar of the Hopi Flute society to a song series; at the altar of the Zuni curing society, played by the medicine chief;† and at the altar of Jemez societies who with it call the Spirits.[451] With few exceptions all such invocatory rites are excellent illustrations of the preference among Pueblos for the mimetic rituals of sympathetic magic as against direct transmission of spirit powers, the shamanistic principle.

In the early world T'aiowa or Paiyatemu, the Sun Youth, played his flute as the young men sang and the Corn Maidens ground. The songs were prayers for the return of warmth and vegetation.[452] Musical grinding-parties were observed among southern Tiwa by Coronado, and they are held today‡ in the western pueblos.§ At Acoma and Santo Domingo the flute is played, but a pottery drum or a hide bundle is beaten at Walpi, Laguna, Isleta del Sur, and Zuni. Zuni songs are from the Corn dance (Thla'hewe) which, though sung to a drum, are called Flute songs[453] because formerly a long flute-trumpet also was

* Hodge 2:128. Compare the whistle set out on the Walpi Lakon altar (Stephen 4: Fig. 457). Whistles date from Basket Maker times. Eagle-bone whistles are used by Plains tribes.

† Flutes of turkey bone six or seven inches long were found at Hawikuh (Hodge 2:126 ff.).

‡ The music of grinding songs recorded in Laguna and Zuni is Piman in character (Herzog, 311).

§ And until recently in Taos and in Isleta del Sur (Fewkes 10:71).

PLATE VI

ALTAR OF LITTLE FIREBRAND SOCIETY, ZUNI
(STEVENSON 2: PL. CXXVII)

played, as we learn from Cushing's charming account of a grinding-party at which the girls danced.[454]

A kachina dramatization of the musical grinding-party is called at Zuni Ololowishkya.[455] It is asked for by Pekwin. Two women grind with the clownish Heheya kachina to wait on them, Red Paint kachina dance and sing, and the musicians of Little Firebrand society or of Bedbug society play their flute-trumpet, a long reed with a bell-shaped gourd at the tip (Pl. VI). Possibly Ololo, who is represented with an immense gourd penis, is an impersonation of Paiyatemu,* as the flutist may be also in the Flute ceremony of Jemez which is presented by the two Women's societies. Prayer-meal is sprinkled on the Jemez flutist and on his trumpet-flute. Prayer-meal is sprinkled on the penis of Ololo who cures for venereal disease.

The flute was used in war. Ma·sewi, the elder War Brother, blew it, we noted, at Laguna, Ma·sewi's flute; and during Governor Martinez' campaign in 1716 a war party of Hopi and Tano (Hano) descended the mesa uttering loud yells, throwing earth (? meal or pollen) into the air, and playing a flute.[456] Locust, the flutist, is war medicine. Zuni warrior kachina, the Shalako, are led from town by society flute players.

The pottery drum is used in the Zuni curing societies, also in the Scalp ceremony for the Coyote clan Shomatowe songs. Zuni pottery drums may be painted with the animals associated with the societies.[457] The Shomatowe drummer prays to his drum and sprinkles it with meal.

The Zuni society drummer is conductor, holding the sequence of the songs.[458]

---

* At Laguna the flute is associated with Ma·sewi, the elder War Brother, as it is among Western Apache, Slayer-of-Monsters playing it in courtship (Goodwin). Among Wind River Shoshoni men known as "does-not-know-anything" carried a long flute as their only weapon. Such a warrior would try to hit an enemy over the head with his flute. If he killed the enemy, he became a war chief and threw the flute away (Lowie).

Among Hopi the flute is associated with Locust. This "hump-backed flute player" is pictured on the cliff walls near the Village of the Great Kivas in Red Paint Canyon (Zuni). Here the term Al'lolowish'keh was applied to spiral designs (?) (Roberts 1:150, 151). Flute player (Chu'lu'laneh), Red Paint Canyon, Al'lolowish'keh! Had we but the key!

Zuni Koyemshi use the barrel drum which is used throughout the East. Butterflies are imprisoned within the drum[459] to allure the sex that in Pueblo lore run after butterflies. Inside the Acoma drum are corn kernels or seeds for its heart, and the head is painted like a shield with star or Galaxy or horned kachina design and in blue sky and yellow earth colors. The drum invokes the clouds. The drummer is a specialist (Acoma) who observes continence four days before a celebration, and emesis as soon as song-making begins. Without a good heart the drummer's arm would grow numb or paralyzed.[460] At Santa Ana a drummer serves for life. Drums have "voices"; they are given personal names; they are alive (White).

A bundle is beaten for certain Zuni kachina, the home Chakwena and the home Mixed dance. The bundle consists of different kinds of clothing or cloth and of jewelry wrapped very tight in a buckskin or today in a canvas wagon cover.* Because of the valuable clothing and beads, people will come running to hear this bundle drum; at least this is what the Kachina chief says to all the things when he makes a bundle of them.[461]

A plank resonator, the so-called foot drum, is used by Pueblos,† in kiva or court. At Acoma it is the rectangular board-covered pit in Chief kiva with altar beneath,‡ a sort of sunken altar. The board is danced on by medicine men only, to get power.§ At Walpi a pit about a foot square in the kiva floor is covered with a wooden slab five or six feet long perforated over the pit, the opening closed by a plug. Performers in the winter solstice dance posture or stamp on the slab and the slab is tapped with the plug in the Home-going kachina ceremony.[462] A plank

---

* Sheepskin bundle drum at Isleta del Sur (Fewkes 10:71).

† Also by the northern Maidu of California, by Californian tribes with the Kuksu spirit impersonation cult, and by the Seri of Tiburon Island, Sonora (Lowie, *American Anthropologist*, XL [1938], 174).

‡ *Tsiwaimityim* (White 2:31; Stirling). Roberts suggests that the kiva floor vault and *sipapu* in the Village of the Great Kivas (Pl. 11) is a like "built-in drum."

§ In Sun's sky kiva this place is filled with hot coals from which Sun gets his heat, and into this place the War Brothers are thrown when they are being tested (Stirling), just as Fire society initiates are treated.

is stamped on over a cavity before the court bower in the Snake dance.[463] Temporary boards are placed over two excavations in the court of Zuni in the Scalp ceremony, for the Shake girls to dance on. The excavations should be made very early by the Scalp chief, when nobody is around. Meal and shell are sprinkled in the excavations.[464] This foot drum and dance are to communicate with the spirits in the underworld. It "draws" them. They are enemy dead,* and they are terrified. The Snake stamper on the plank which he sprinkles with meal is also trying to communicate with his supernatural patrons for whom under the plank in the cavity have been placed prayer-sticks (Oraibi).[465]

Notched sticks stand on the Walpi War society altar; the leg bones of a bear† are scraped on them.[466] Otherwise the musical rasp or notched rattle[467] or fiddle is restricted to kachina dancing and almost to one dance, the widespread "Jemez kachina" dance (Zuni, Hemishikwe; Hopi, Hümis or Sio [Zuni] Hümis; Jemez and Cochiti, "Hopi dance"; Laguna and Acoma, Hemish; Santo Domingo, Tsaidyadyuwitsa; Tewa, Pogon share;‡ Isleta, Kompör). The fiddle is also used at Zuni in Muluktakya and on First Mesa in Cochiti-Añakchina, Hehe'ya, or by Marau society women burlesquing Hehe'ya.[468]

This "kachina gourd fiddle" is played by women or by men or boys§ impersonating women, for it is associated conceptually with grinding. The sticks are propped on a gourd resonator which is painted white and decorated with cloud design (Hopi). The sticks are scraped with a deer or sheep shoulder blade. Each player places the resonator in front of her and on it rests one end of the notched stick, the other end held in her left hand about as high as the breast, and, with the edge of the scapula held in her right hand, she scrapes downward on the sloping notched stick,

* Built-in drum, and stomping dance, pit or *sipapu*, underworld enemy spirits and sinking-in to become a supernatural (see pp. 309, 631): have we here a complex of human sacrifice by inhumation?

† Shin bone of a Navaho (Oraibi, Kennard).

‡ Robbins, Harrington, Freire-Marreco, 42–43. Described at Santa Clara on October 21, 1912, and on January 13, 1926 (Parsons 49:186).

§ Little boys without masks (Parsons 6:210).

producing with quick strokes a succession of abrupt, hollow, rasping sounds, in time with the measure of the song. At certain cadences of the song, the downward stroke of the scapula is interrupted by drawing it back more slowly and upward upon the notched stick.[469]

The gourd rattle is used in almost every dance (except by female dancers—probably because they never sing) to mark rhythm or in kachina dances to express response or appreciation. A bunch of deer or antelope scapulas or elk or ox hoofs is used as rattle by certain kachina, by Hopi race announcer, and by Hopi Men's societies. Other societies (Hopi, Flute, Marau; Keres, Kurena) use a cluster of olivella shells tied to a crook. The rattle of Hopi Antelopes is a wooden ring over which is stretched an antelope scrotum skin which is gathered on the lower side around a stick about three inches long.[470] Inside are corn kernels.* Small pieces of petrified wood are fastened for rattles to the fringes of the Snakes' buckskin belts (Oraibi).[471] (Hopi Agaves use cowbells for rattles on their night patrols against the dead or, a European practice, against witches. Bells are often fastened around the legs or waist or at the girdle of dancers or runners [Taos, Hopi].)

A turtle shell with deer or sheep hoofs is worn behind the right knee† of members of Hopi Men's societies and Snake society and of most kachina dancers everywhere. This rattle "makes the thunder come" (Zuni).[472] The turtles are secured at the Zuni sacred lake on the summer solstice pilgrimage, or, by Hopi, from the Little Colorado,‡ or from the Rio Grande, particularly near

* In Acoma tradition the rattle of the first shaman, the Fire society chief, was made of the scrotum of elk, filled with agave seeds (Stirling). Scrotum rattles are familiar at Mishongnovi (Beaglehole 2:9).

† Zuni Ky'anakwe kachina dancers who wear a long dress (such as was rumored to be the dress for men as well as women in Cibola [Hodge 3:14] and as seen in pictographs) carry this rattle in their hands.

Acoma clowns will wear turtle shells over the knees instead of behind them (Stirling).

‡ If not from White friends. At Crow-Wing's request I once sent him some turtle shells. He found them unsatisfactory because the meat had been boiled out and the shell rendered friable. First Mesa way is to expose the turtle to ants. Zuni throw the meat into the river.

Isleta, where turtles abound. Isletans distinguish between land turtles, which they associate with the Shure' moiety, and water turtles associated with the Black Eye moiety. One of the maskless kachina dances is called Land Turtle dance. Permission to catch turtles must be got from the moiety "grandfathers" or clowns.

There is "power" in rattles (as in drums). Chakwena Woman's rattle hangs with her mask and bandoleer as a kiva standard at Walpi,[473] and when she fought against Zuni with the Ky'anakwe or White Kachina her heart was in her rattle (see p. 224). Witches use rattles to travel on (Mishongnovi).[474] When Estevan of the Barbary Coast sent forward his gourd with a few strings of rattles, a white feather and a red feather, together with a message that he was coming to cure the sick, the Hawikuh (Zuni tribe) chief threw down the gourd angrily, saying, "I know these people, for their rattles are not of the make of our own." Estevan and his large Indian escort were refused admission to the town, and within a day or two Estevan was killed,* undoubtedly as a witch. He may have asked for turquoise and women, according to another report, but I surmise the rattle was at the bottom of it. (Perhaps Estevan, *el negro*, was Chakwena Woman, the black-face warrior whose heart was in her rattle!)

29. Dancing and Dance Patterns

Pueblo dancing is to honor somebody—chief or Spirit—in entertainment, or it is a form of compulsive mimetic magic, setting an example to rain-maker or crop-bringing or curing Spirits; or, as noted (p. 383), it conveys a message to beings underground, as in the Oraibi Oaqöl ceremony to the gods of growth.[475]

Quite generally the houses of chiefs or annual officers or persons conspicuous in ceremony are danced in or before. At Jemez

* Hodge 3:20, 21. Hodge suggests that Estevan may have got his shaman's rattle in Texas on the Cabeza de Vaca expedition. The Indians brought the explorers gourd rattles used in dancing and curing. These rattles had virtue (power), said the Indians, and nobody but the owner dared touch them. Afterward, among the tribes, the Spaniards and Estevan used these rattles as insignia of rank with good effect.

they dance in front of houses having fetishes, Mothers. In Girls' dances at Zuni the company may go to dance inside the house of the saint—"they dance for her because they like her." This might be said of dancing before the saint's bower at any saint's-day celebration or before the image carried in procession at San Juan or Taos. The Christmastide dancing of Cochiti and Sia are referred to as "going to Jesus" or "for Jesus";[476] Zuni dance for the new Scalp. Says the Scalp chief after giving food to the Scalp:

> In the corn priests' rain-filled court,
> All the children of the corn priests
> Will be dancing for you.[477]

During a kachina dance that lasted for several days a group of "little dancers," boy impersonators, came one night to dance in the kiva "because the dancers could not go home to their wives, and were lonely. The little dancers danced for them so that they should not be sad."[478]

The kachina may dance to entertain, but kachina[479] dancing is primarily a rain-making function. When the rain-makers dance or when their impersonators dance, it rains. The dancing itself compels the rain. When the little Tewa boy uncovered the bowl where the kachina masks were kept, out came the kachina and began to dance. *Then it began to rain.* When the Hopi beetles were suffering from drought, their chief said, "Let us have a dance and perhaps if we dance, it will rain." So he made a song for them, and they practiced the song and dance in the evening. Early in the morning their chief deposited four prayer-feathers west of their town and spoke to the clouds in the San Francisco Mountains, saying, "We are thirsty here, so you come quickly this way and bring us some water that we may drink and not die!" Then they formed in line and one of them acted as leader. They sang, and, as they sang, the clouds came nearer, and it began to rain and thunder.

Kachina dancing is in line, one line or, when there are female impersonations, as in the Good Kachina of Zuni, two lines. The dance chief or director stands in the middle of the line. At the head or tail of the line stand the conspicuous impersonations or, after the dance begins, out in front of the line, as "side dancers" (Jemez). The line dancers remain on the same spot, the step being merely a lift of the feet, the right foot beating the rhythm. The beat of the "female" is considerably less emphasized than that of the male. At the beginning or close of a song the dancers may make a half- or quarter-turn, and the males dance with their backs to the audience, face to face with the "females." In turning, always to the left, the right arm, the rattle hand, may be swept over the head.

Outdoor kachina dancing, likewise saint's-day dancing (in line with both feet stomping), is performed in set places in a regular sequence, in Zuni there are four dance stations, and a dextral or sunwise circuit is followed, the dancers walking single file from station to station. Theoretically, the circuit is made four times in the morning, then, after the midday meal which is eaten in kiva, the dancing is confined to the main dance station or court. In the intervals between dances the dance group withdraws to a house corner on the north edge of town, while in the court the clowns may come out to play.

Repetitions may be asked for in the afternoon dancing, and at the close an extension of the whole dance may be called for the following day. Such requests are generally made by Rain chiefs or society officials (Zuni).

A society member leads the dance line, sprinkling meal ahead as the line defiles to or from the dance place, or sprinkling meal between songs (Zuni). This leader is without mask, a band of yucca encircles his head, and in his forelock is a downy red-stained eagle feather; a line of black paint crosses his cheekbones. He may wear a buckskin over back and right shoulder or a be-ribboned velveteen shirt. In his left hand he carries his corn-ear fetish and in his right, a bowl of meal. Among Keres and at Jemez the leader is from one of the two Clown societies or is the Ma·sewi War captain followed by a society man (Santo Domingo, Santa Ana). Among Hopi the leader or "kachina father" represents Powamu (kachina) society chief.

In indoor night dancing, dance sets follow one another from dance house to dance house (Zuni, Hopi). Similar to this visiting pattern is the exchange of visits by ceremonial groups holding synchronous meetings, as the Cochiti societies do on All Souls' Night or the Cochiti and Jemez societies on the night of the winter solstice ceremony.

Apart from this highly systematized group dancing there is what is called "going around town" by the kachina (Zuni, Hopi, Acoma); single figures or small groups make town circuits and in their progress, as they encircle the kiva, they may dance (Hopi). They dance, too, after they enter the kiva.

The Kachina cult is par excellence the dance cult, but dancing is also a character of curing and war cults. The Kapina society of Laguna danced, outdoors, on the four sides of a square,[480] and the Keresan and Tewan Clown societies have their own dances. Hopi Snakes and Antelopes, Wüwüchimtü and Singers, and the Women's societies all dance outdoors, Snakes and Antelopes in line, the others in oval or circle. Wüwüchimtü dance holding hands,* fingers interlocking. At indoor initiations and curing ceremonies the shamans dance singly or in small groups, often in imitation of animals or birds.

Circle dancing is practiced in society indoor dancing,[481] in Women's society outdoor dances (Hopi, Jemez), in a Keresan spring dance for crops,[482] in many of the borrowed tribal dances, and in the dance by men and women around the scalp pole at Zuni, Isleta, and Taos or at Taos as a popular secular dance. Circle dancing is definitely associated with war in contrast to the dance in line by kachina and saint's-day dancers.†

In war dances and, at Isleta, in dances presented by the moieties, two groups alternate, each coming out from its headquarters as the other withdraws. This kind of dance alternation is practiced among Keres and at Zuni in the Saint's dance and at Jemez by the Men's societies, also in the Tablita and Buffalo dances. In the Hopi so-called Girls' dances which include Buf-

---

* As seen on a Post Basket Maker bowl design of a large circle dance (Morris, Fig. 22). For modern distribution see Spier 2:269–70; also Papago (Underhill 4).

† Is there any causal relation between dance formation and shape of kiva? If so the circle dance predates the line dance, and a light would be thrown on the archeological puzzle of the change from round kiva to square kiva.

falo and Tablita dances and in Women's society dances, in the Jemez Flute dance, and commonly in the saint's-day or Tablita dancing of the East, as in the many maskless dances which go by the name of another tribe, the same kiva or house may be used, but one dance set follows the other with time only to transfer from set to set the dance paraphernalia—headdresses or hand pieces.

What we may call the cumulative idea or feeling shows in many cases in conducting ritual. Whenever a rite is repeated by members of a group, the least distinguished members, perhaps the youngest, begin, and the most distinguished, the chief, the master of ceremony, concludes. This order is notable in dance program, where there is increasing participation in the dance as the ceremony goes on, more and more individuals taking part in any dance set, and more and more dance sets "coming out." In Girls' dances of two days or more, juniors, sometimes quite small children, as in the Hopi Buffalo dance, will dance the first day, to be followed the next day by the senior participants. Similarly in races, the first of a series will be for the children.

The practice of throw-away or tossing presents to lookers-on may be noticed here as a dance pattern, since it occurs notably in the final dances of the Hopi Women's societies, when basket-trays and other things are tossed, and in certain kachina dances, particularly at Zuni, when toward the conclusion of the dance kachina may toss to the spectators ears of corn, melons, other fruits or vegetables, calico, as well as miscellaneous merchandise. As might be supposed, these throw-away dances are popular, and the throw-away arouses great excitement which I have seen reach a peak when the dancer takes off something, say his shirt, and throws it.[483] In Acoma tradition the kachina are supposed to throw away everything they have on, except of course their masks. Whether throwing corn or raiment, the dancers are acting as they wish the beings they impersonate to act, and as the *real* kachina when they came to dance did act.*

---

* For a Hopi kachina myth highly expressive of this mimetic behavior see Stephen 2:66. For resemblances between these Yehohota kachina and the K'oʙishtaiya kachina of Acoma see p. 538, n. §.

Kachina dancers also make a more formal presentation of gifts not only, as noted,[484] to children but to adults. Cochiti kachina will bring presents to adults who are particularly industrious—green corn and melons in autumn or in winter dried corn and meat, arrows to the men, large stirring-sticks to the women.[485] Dr. White saw an Oraibi kachina make a food present to a visitor from San Felipe. Chiefs, clanswomen, or persons connected in one way or another with the celebration are often given ears of corn by the kachina. The presents brought in on their backs by the Zuni Ky'anakwe for the high chiefs who have not contributed anything specific to the ceremony suggest a sort of tribute.

On saint's days food may be thrown from the housetops to troops of visitors. Usually the houses visited are those of persons named for the saint whose day is being observed, e.g., all the Juans and Juanas will be visited on St. John's Day. I suppose they do not feel they are personating the saint.

Presents or "pay" to those who have danced for you is a familiar and a widespread practice. When Coyote gets hungry, he makes a big sack and goes to town and into a house and begins to dance. He carries his tail in the air, as he spins around, and the San Juan people laugh and give him bread. On their domiciliary visits the clowns are always given food, also the kachina and other dancers. In kiva or court, women will give food or packages or baskets of meal to favored dancers (Tewa,[486] Isleta) or to clowns who sometimes share with spectators (Isleta, Walpi).[487] In war or scalp dances food and other things are thrown to the Scalps or to the dancers by relatives (Zuni, Acoma, Cochiti).[488] At Cochiti after a society initiation, bread is thrown to the dancers by all the townspeople.[489] Dancers entertain but they also bring a blessing that must be paid for.

30. Gesture and Posture

There is considerable dance gesture, a sort of gesture language, used by dancers, by choir, and particularly by clowns. The Tewa Kossa peers from under his hand to indicate that he sees the kachina or the clouds approaching.[490] Bending his arms at the

elbows and turning his palms downward, he shoots them repeatedly forward: "The clouds are coming here to the fields."
By a zigzag motion of hand and arm above his head he indicates
lightning. Holding his hand horizontal, palm down, he lowers
it by a succession of jerks: "Rain falls." Other gestures express
the growth of corn.[491] The choir at the Laguna saint's-day dance
gesture for rain or rising clouds, for corn, for deer.[492] The falling-
rain gesture is the same as that of San Ildefonso. Kachina dancers use similar gestures (Zuni), and they express assent or response by shaking their rattles (Hopi, Jemez).[493] "Navaho kachina" begin their dance by bending over to the right, giving
a brisk shake of the rattle quite close to the ground, then swinging the rattle hand high overhead and turning quickly around
from right to left. Hehe'ya kachina at certain strains lift their
hands and bring them down, pointing in a darting motion toward
the earth.[494] In their Wüwüchim dancing when they sing about
the women, Hopi Singers use derisive gestures in connection with
the vulva sticks they carry. The most characteristic gesture or
posture of the Keresan woman dancer is an up-and-down alternating arm motion, the upper arms at right angles, and the lower
arms parallel, to the body, and bent upward, as may be seen on
a Post Basket Maker bowl from a grave of La Plata Valley.[495]
Flower kachina and his Maid each lifts an ear of yellow corn in
the left hand to the forehead, turning left to peer under it, and
then does the same with the blue corn in the right hand.[496]
Buffalo Youth dancers also hold their rattle or lightning-stick
over their eyes, and one of their dance songs is:

> Buffalo Youth
> Dance gladly, we desire,
> Dance gesturing.[497]

Initiates are carried on the backs of their "fathers" or sponsors (Zuni and Acoma kachina initiation, Zuni Little Firebrand
society, Hopi Wüwüchim) or led into the ceremonial chamber by
the tips of the eagle feathers their "father" holds backward over
his shoulders (Acoma, Sia, Isleta, Zuni).[498] In prayer the sponsor

will place his hands under those of his "child" (Acoma,* Zuni). In passing on canes of office or prayer-stick bundles, officers or kachina dancers kneel on one knee (Zuni), probably a Catholic derived posture, although this was formerly the conventional posture in eating (Hopi, Laguna).⁴⁹⁹ Sitting up straight with folded arms is the posture of ritual concentration (Zuni), of "sitting still."⁵⁰⁰ Sitting with bowed head means acquiescence, "thinking about having a good heart" (Isleta).† The familiar squat on the heels is a common posture not only at any time but also in prayer. The ritual way of carrying a mask (Zuni) or corn fetish (Hopi), probably anything sacrosanct, is in the crook of the left arm.⁵⁰¹

Motioning or pointing an object in the directions is a general practice (Jemez, see p. 321, n.†; Isleta,⁵⁰² Zuni), for example, to receive anything ritually, say a package of prayer-meal, you first move it in the hands of the donor in the six directions (Zuni), or again, to seat a person ritually, standing behind with your hands on his shoulders, you first turn him in the directions (Zuni). For zenith and nadir the head is bent forward and back.⁵⁰³

Circling something—ashes, cedar bark—around the head, four times, and throwing it away is the common gesture of exorcism. Passing the right palm rapidly across the left palm, at right angles, means done, finished, gone, as in the same European gesture. Making this pass with feathers is a gesture of exorcism.‡

There is a summoning gesture, a sweeping motion like our own, which is made in prayer to Sun or the kachina (Laguna, Acoma, Oraibi:Marau, Oaqöl), four times to cover the four lengths of the trail Iyatiku made for the kachina (Acoma, Stirling).

Sacrosanct objects are circled or waved up and down in front of a person, four times, in blessing (see p. 672). To the rhythm

---

* Is this what in 1540 Castañeda refers to? "To make the most secure peace they put their hands across each other" (Winship, 490–91).

† Parsons 52:301, 376. Noted among Navaho (Reichard), and as a respectful attitude among Papago (Underhill).

‡ *Epofere* (San Juan); thus the rain cleans the air of dust.

of ritual song sacrosanct objects are dandled or pounded with, as when the corn is "danced" at Zuni[504] or when in the Marau ceremony time is beaten with an altar stick representing a defunct member, in order to announce to the others in the lower world that their ceremony is in progress.[505] Hand-clapping by the choir to drumbeat occurs in the Taos saint's-day dance, and it was noted in a kachina-like dance at Isleta del Sur, the Tiwa settlement after the Reconquest.[506]

31. Running: Wrangling

Running occurs in many ceremonials and in several forms, but always as an expression of mimetic magic, to assist the movement of Sun and Moon, to speed up the Clouds, or to hasten the growth of crops. Tiwan and Tewan relay race by moiety is to help or control the progress of Sun and Moon, Morning star and Evening star. Sing the Summer People:

> Sun Old Man,
> Stand ready at dawn
> On Cactus Ridge!
> Moon Old Man,
> Stand ready at dawn
> On Cactus Ridge!
>
> Stand ready at dawn,
> Thence for San Juan
> Stand ready at dawn
> For Eagle-Tail-Rain-Standing Road!

Sing the Winter People:

> Little people white men*
> From Stone Man Mountain
> Stand ready at dawn!
>
> Dark Star Man,
> Stand ready at dawn
> Thence for San Juan![507]

Did not the Hopi prayer-stick courier to "Sun house" at the summer solstice slow down his pace on his return, the Sun would

* War god white men. Are the war god Stone Men on Taos Mountain being referred to?

travel too fast, and it would freeze too early. When prayer-feathers are deposited for the Cloud chiefs, the Chiefs of the Directions, the bearer "runs swiftly, that the clouds may come swiftly, that his prayers may be quickly answered (Hopi)."[508] Says the Hopi Flute society chief of his prayer-stick depositor:

He runs swiftly, that the clouds may come swiftly. His hair is flowing, for thus the Cloud chiefs carry the rain clouds. He makes a far circuit on the first day, because the Cloud chiefs live far away. He goes to all the cardinal directions to call the attention of all the Cloud chiefs. On each succeeding day he travels a shorter radius. Thus we want the rain clouds to come, nearer and nearer, until on the concluding day of the ceremony they shall have come overhead and poured down their heavy rains.[509]

Prayer-feathers to be deposited in the spring at the conclusion of the Water Serpent ceremony are taken down by the fastest available runner. "He has to go down quickly and come back quickly so rain will come quickly."[510] The Keresan shaman and his guard run all the way to and back from the spring where they deposit prayer-feathers summoning rain-bringing kachina.[511] Kick races represent the Cloud spirits flooding the arroyos,* and the prayers of a fast runner have special potency; the Clouds will have seen him and will be glad to listen to him.[512] To hasten the crops, Hopi farmers will race together after planting corn.[513] The sunrise race of Antelope, Snake, Flute, and Lakon societies is to hasten vegetation, as was the midnight running of the Masauwü prayer-stick depositor who made decreasing circuits the four nights of his retreat in order to bring the rain clouds nearer (Mishongnovi).[514]

After the Hopi, Hano, or Jemez summer ceremonies (dance or race), women, young or old, will chase the clowns or other men to grab from them the garlands they are wearing or whatever crops they are carrying, corn or melons, also baskets or pottery.

---

* Since kick-balls are offered to the Hopi spirit of high winds and sandstorms and the Oraibi race circuits are connected with the places where these offerings are made (Voth 2:81), it is possible that the races are associated in some way with the Wind spirit. Still another association with kick-ball is suggested in the San Juan origin myth where winter Town chief plays kick-ball and the ground hardens with hoarfrost. See p. 251.

Among Hopi this wrangling (*nyöliwa*) goes on for four days, in court or in the fields. It is "great fun," writes Crow-Wing. "The meaning of it is to hurry the watermelons and the corn to ripen, also to hurry the clouds to bring rain. When it rains and there is lots of water, the animals will be happy and run around. If a girl gets lots of melons and corn and baskets and pottery, her father will have lots of crops in the fall."[515]

32. RITUAL PIGMENTATION AND ARRAY

The color marks of Walpi kivas, in kick-ball races, are: Chief kiva, white stars on face, breast, arms, thighs, calves; Wikwalobi, yellow over breast and forearm, three parallels on upper arm and on ribs, on leg from ankle to knee, and a band above knee; Nashabki, blue-green over entire body; Horn kiva, broad white stripes on body and limbs; Goat kiva, red ocher over entire body.[516] Isleta racers are dabbed on the cheek with red or with white, and in the irrigation ceremony people are similarly dabbed, according to moiety, with black or with red. The legs and chest of Taos runners are painted white, and down is dabbed on. The knees of Zuni stick-racers (and of certain kachina dancers) are painted red, for speed. Hunters use red face paint. Formerly Hopi deer-hunters painted yellow; the remains of sunflower blossoms used as face pigment by the Lakon society women were taken by the men after the dance and rubbed on throwing-sticks and behind ears and on the face.[517] Rabbit hunters painted white stripes over red, the face striped red, with a red line under each eye. Laguna hunters paint themselves on the hunting-ground, they dip the right index finger into the paint, raise it toward the sun, breathe on it, and ask for the painting of the War Brothers, the sons of Sun: face lines or bands of black, red, black, red.

The Clowns are commonly striped black and white or, at Zuni, smeared all over with pink (Koyemshi) or gray (Ne'wekwe). Ne'wekwe, like their Koshare counterparts in the East, have circular facial marks in black, such as are said at Laguna to represent the whirlpool whence the Clowns emerged.[518] Kachina impersonators have a black line across nose and under eyes; the medicine men of Isleta have a red line, with a dab of red on each cheek.* Initiates into the medicine order (? "third degree") of Sia societies and into the Hopi Agave society are painted on face and body. The body and limbs of kachina dancers are painted in a variety of ways. Hands or feet of female impersonators may be painted white or yellow (as are those of war or saint's-day dancers).† The covered parts of male impersonators are painted white (Zuni). Double lines of yellow dots may run from the waist to the shoulders and down the arms, front and back, representing raindrops (Zuni).[519] The maskless kachina dancers of Taos and Antelope Youth of Oraibi are similarly dotted.[520]

On Hopi Snake or Antelope society dancers, from shoulder to waist, in front and behind, also on upper arms and thighs are white zigzag lines called lightning marks.‡ Similar marking was laid on the body of the warrior by the War chief. (The stone that was pulverized as pigment is called "War god vomisis.")[521] Keresan and Isletan shamans are painted with similar zigzags. Also Isletan and, inferably, other Eastern shamans§ are painted with black hand marks or outlines, representing bear hands (Isleta, chief only). The queue or double triangle design is a mark of the War Brothers and of warrior kachina like Chakwena or Bear.‖ The bow design is also used, and short parallel lines are a warrior mark. The pink spots painted hand size on Hopi

* Recently received pictures show a red line across the bridge of the nose and below a broken line of black and a broken line of red. The Shikani society of Laguna painted four lines of red across the face (Parsons 20:119).

† The Keresan tale heroine or dancer is Yellow Woman.

‡ For Sia Snake shaman compare Stevenson 1: Pl. X*c*.

§ The Tewa youth who makes up as a witch puts black hand prints over each shoulder (Parsons 49:125) and the Cochiti witch doll is spotted with what may be hand marks (Dumarest, Pl. VII, Fig. 1). Handmark Boy is a Hano-Hopi kachina.

‖ On First Mesa it represents the way the hair is dressed on one side of the head of Chakwena Grandmother (Stephen 4:117, 120, 122) and, in Navaho mythology, the wide queue of Changing Woman about to give birth to the Brothers (Haile, 179). Also this mark may represent the double bandoleer of the Brothers, explained by the myth of the blood-filled guts which fool the monster eagles (Dumarest, 220, n. 2).

Snake society members are war medicine and are referred to as "strong or hard body painting." Snakes and Antelopes and Buffalo youths have blackened faces, and Zuni warriors have blackened chins. The chins of the Maid and Youth in the Snake-Antelope and Flute ceremonies are painted "water blue,"* i.e., black, to represent black rain clouds. It is a prayer for rain. Black paint on the chin, hands, and feet of the Lakon society woman is a like prayer.[522] Corn smut as a body pigment used by the Snake society (also by Hano clowns) is a similar form of prayer, a chromatic prayer for rain:[523] corn smut abounds when rain abounds. White pigment on the body is for the Sun (Zuni) or shows Cloud that white rain clouds are wanted.[524] The rite of smearing white pigment on face or body during ceremonial[525] is also presumably a chromatic rain prayer. Smearing the Chakwena kachina of Zuni or the Masauwü impersonator of First Mesa with blood may be a fertility prayer,† unless it is merely a means of identifying the impersonator with the supernatural.‡ Until the paint of a kachina dancer is washed off, he is holy or identified with his patron.§ Conversely, until a kachina doll is painted it is not a sacrosanct object.

The hair-parting is sometimes smeared red (Hopi, Laguna, Isleta, Tewa, Taos). A downy eagle feather is commonly tied in the scalp lock of kachina impersonators or society members, and for the latter painted red (Zuni and Isleta). Kachina with society affiliations also wear the red feather. The hair feathers of

* "Water-blue" is slime from a spring (Stephen 4:713; Voth 3:306, n. 1).

† In his prolonged search for the sun, Ma'sewi's feet began to bleed and from this blood sprang the flowers of the Rocky Mountain bee plant, taboo to the Kurena of Laguna and Santa Ana and the Shi'wanakwe of Zuni (Parsons 9:333). Where the head of Sun's Ne'wekwe jester and son was cut off and his blood soaked the ground, flowers blossomed and the blood trail became a trail of flowers (Bunzel 6:258), "fructifying the land" as was said figuratively of the blood of the martyred Franciscans (Benavides, 6 n.).

‡ As when Pishuni of Acoma painted himself with the blood of the girl he had bewitched to death *in order to look like her*, in the eyes of the War gods (Stirling).

§ Yet Hopi do not wash off body paint, as do Zuni (also Navaho), theoretically rain should come and wash it off (Stephen 4:371, 488).

the Isletan Town chief are painted. Downy feathers are sometimes fastened to the tips of stiff hair feathers.*

In personal array, as in prayer-sticks, certain feathers have
more or less fixed associations. Parrot feathers are appropriate
to the kachina; turkey feathers to the Koyemshi and Kashale
(Acoma)[526] and to the dead. Sparrowhawk feather is worn by
the Shi'wanakwe society of Zuni, by Keresan Kurena, and by
Ts'un'tatabö'sh of Jemez.

Cotton or bird down may be used on the hair to represent
clouds. (The body too may be spotted with cotton or down.) A
headband of yucca blade is commonly worn by kachina impersonators and society members. There are other more elaborate
headdresses such as the cap of the Zuni War society or of the
Hopi War chief or of the Hopi Agave society which represents
the helmet of the sky war god,† or such as the hollow medi-
cine-filled stick or cane, begirt with feathers and closed at the
ends with buckskin taken theoretically from the clothes of slain
enemies, which is worn by Zuni warriors‡ and by Hopi Snake
society members.[527] The behorned§ caps or helmets of the Hopi
Agave and Horn societies were worn in fighting.[528] At Hano in
the victory war dance by two men and the two maids who had
gone out to meet the war party, an elaborately carved extensive

---

* This feather arrangement is used on Snake "whips" which are just like
prayer-sticks, but it is not used on prayer-sticks. The arrangement is familiar
among Navaho, on the Northwest Coast, and elsewhere.

† Stephen 4:975, 1307. Stuck onto it is eagle down to represent snow.

‡ This is the warrior's "great feather" (Zuni, *lashowanthlane;* Hopi, *herunkwa*),
eagle-wing feathers with downy feathers and duck feathers fastened to small
reeds. The "great feather" may be borrowed by a warrior kachina. If the tips of
the feathers point backward, the kachina come peaceably; if the tips point forward, he comes for violence, for in this way the "great feather" was worn on the
warpath (Bunzel 5:864). The same distinction is observed by the kachina in
carrying their yucca switches. See Hano's whipper kachina with switches and
"man feather" (Parsons 40: Fig. 23).

Zuni's warrior's "badge" is also described as a feather-covered lightning-
stick (Stevenson 2:206).

§ In Navaho opinion horns give power, so in sand-paintings the globes representing Sun and Moon may be given horns. Whipping kachina or powerful
kachina like the Shalako have horns, so the same concept may occur among the
Pueblos.

wooden headdress was worn by the maids,[529] possibly the prototype of the tablet worn everywhere in the East in the saint's-day dance.

Because of prescriptual headdress, haircut or hairdressing is ever important to the Pueblo. There should be a scalp lock or a well-covered crown for the feather of initiate or courier, or for the warrior's "great feather" worn on the top of the head if not in queue. Clowns wear their hair bunched on the side, girl fashion (Hopi, Tiwa), or hanging in side bunches representing clouds (Acoma) and tied with up-pointing cornhusk (Acoma, San Felipe),[530] or hornlike on top (Zuni, Isleta) since with this hair poke their prototypes opened an exit at the Emergence (Isleta). Long hair is necessary to impersonate long-haired gods, and hair must be worn loose or flowing because thus the Cloud chiefs wear their hair (Hopi). The Acoma boy may not let his hair grow long until after his kachina initiation (which is a reason why boys want to be initiated early). The part between bang and long hair is identified with the Galaxy (see p. 1083, n. ‡); therefore in ritual it may not be covered by a hat.[531] The bangs of Zuni women are let fall to the end of the nose to form a sort of mask, in certain dances. Hopi women who have no bangs have to make false ones for their Buffalo dance and for the Chatumaka impersonation in the Marau ceremony.

Hair may be associated with the ritual of personal crises, with adolescence, marriage, or death. In adolescent ritual the Walpi girl's hair was arranged in great whorls or "wheels" or "squash blossoms"* which at marriage were to be taken down by her prospective mother-in-law, her hair dressed in clay-incased twists. Kachina female impersonations wear their hair in whorls over a permanent frame (Hopi, Zuni).† At death the long hair of the Acoma man is cut off, and he is given a Dutch cut "to look

* Formerly this headdress was worn by Zuni girls. It is a very ancient style, a Basket Maker fashion, as we can infer from petroglyphs and from Post Basket Maker pottery design (Morris, Figs. 22, 31a). But the hair of buried Basket Maker females is cut short (Amsden).

† Introduced (? with the earliest kachina dance, Zuni, Kok'okshi, Hopi, Aña kachina) by Patki clan people from the Little Colorado (Fewkes 12:93–94).

like Iyatiku,"* the great Mother of the underworld he is about to visit.

Hopi women are or were buried in their great cotton wedding mantle,[532] and obtaining burial raiment is alleged as a reason for having a wedding. If a boy dies, he will be buried in the kilt given him at his kachina initiation. A white cotton yarn-embroidered kilt is worn with cotton or yarn-brocaded belts and pendent foxskin in both masked and maskless dances. Society men wear a dark-blue woolen loincloth, the ends embroidered (Zuni).[533] Isletan dancers wear a piece of white embroidered Hopi cloth as a breechclout. Society women or women dancers wear the native woolen dress which at Santo Domingo even on-lookers at a dance are required to wear. Hopi mantles are much used in dance or ceremony, the white woolen blanket with red and black or dark-blue border and the elaborately yarn-embroidered white cotton blanket. To these blankets, when worn by Shalako or Ky'anakwe kachina, feathers are sewed. Feathers are also sewed to the horn of the serpent design on the kilt of the Jemez Buffalo dancer.[534]

One or two eagle-wing feathers may be carried in the hand or hands of kachina or of shamans. They may be stuck into the belt behind or into the bear paw worn over the left hand (Isleta). Zuni Koyemshi carry eagle feathers. Bitsitsi of the Ne'wekwe carries them in the Molawia ceremony and motions with them. They are called "hands" at Zuni; they suggest the eagle-wing "fans" of Plains tribes. During an indoor dance at Zuni the medicine chief will arise from his seat at the south side of his society's altar and with his "hands" asperse the line of dancers.[535] As single dancers enter, they will pass in front of the medicine chief who without even dipping into the medicine bowl will tap together his "hands" in front of the dancer. "Hands" are used for aspersing or for cleansing.

In general, archaic apparel or ornament is chosen for cere-monial array, such as netted leggings (Pueblo II) or the inlaid

---

* This haircut at death is inconsistent with kachina ideology; for the kachina dance with flowing hair, and, if the dead are to become kachina, their hair should be left long.

turquoise earrings of Antelope maid[536] or the Hopi fringed "rain belt," or the high or fringed moccasins worn by many kachina and by the Town chief of Isleta. Analogously, as archaic practice, more particularly in indoor altar ritual, men's clothes will be discarded save for breechcloth, also moccasins or shoes, and hair will be left flowing or bands and hats removed. One Shalako night at Zuni, when I was accompanying the Governor from house to house, he made a point of knocking off the hats of all the pushing Navaho visitors he encountered, greatly to their surprise. Moccasins are taken off on entering the corn storeroom (Zuni, Cochiti)[537]; or at least one moccasin (Zuni). On summoning a doctor with a package of meal, one should go barefoot (Zuni). Voth says he never saw a man wearing moccasins during a ceremony. (Women were less scrupulous in this as in other ritual particulars.) Bare feet may be an ancient mark of respect.*

In dances there is always a great display of necklaces consisting of white shell, turquoise, coral, abalone shells, silver, or blue yarn. Necklaces are worn close to the throat by society members (Zuni).[538] At indoor ceremonial, society men wear a necklace of bear claws (Keres, Isleta). Anklets, armlets, wristlets, or wrist guards are generally worn in dances. Painted wooden pins for women's blankets were used by Acoma Koshare and deposited as prayer offering.[539] Bandoleer and pouch are worn by the Scalp chief of Isleta and by warrior kachina who may borrow the warrior's bandoleer of buckskin decorated with fringes under the left arm and with four shells for each scalp taken, hair from each scalp being sewed into the fringed portion (Zuni).† Arrowheads were sewed into the Acoma War chief's pouch in which some ant-hill gravel was kept; pouch and bandoleer were made from an enemy's outfit.[540] Every enemy slain afforded the Hopi warrior a new bandoleer (made from breechcloth or shirt) which was added to the old, so that a famous war-

---

* Compare Inca usage (Means, 369–70). Moccasins are removed during smoking ritual by Northern Shoshone (Lowie, personal communication).

† Bunzel 5:871. Compare p. 331. Navaho and Apache used warrior bandoleers (Haile, 65, 315; Bourke 1:550 ff.).

rior had a bandoleer as thick as his arm. Some had two bandoleers worn cross-belt fashion. (Compare War god impersonators.) The ends of the bandoleer were loosely wrapped, a snare
to the foe who would grip the bandoleer and fall over backward
to be finished off with an ax. This crafty device together with
medicines in the bandoleer (see p. 416) kept a warrior from having any fear of an enemy.

Arraying the impersonator of a kachina chief is an important
function, vested in a lineage (Hopi) or in a cult society (Zuni),
just as painting body or mask is, as we have seen, a specially
vested function.

33. Song

Now and again a woman will sing lullaby or grinding-song, but
men are the singers, and they sing not only to dance or to altar
ceremonial but when they work in the field, singing "shouting
songs" (Tewa),[541] or when they herd sheep or drive the horses to
water or travel from town to town or as grandfathers take care of
the baby. Yet singing is primarily a ritual art. Songs are as significant and valuable as the prayers with which in altar ceremonial they more or less alternate. Song words, like prayer
words, have in themselves the magical or compulsive character
general in Indian ritual singing.

Songs have to be carefully taught. When the Snake people
instruct their Hopi visitor in their Snake ceremonial, they are
described as teaching him "all about it; they sing him the
songs."* It is his songs which distinguish the Zuni doctor.[542]
Such songs are naturally esoteric. Certain songs a Pueblo might
refuse to communicate, just as the song of White Shell Woman
creating by epidermis was withheld from Goddard. "Not
this song," said his Navaho singer, "I live by means of it."†

---

* Parsons 42:189 (compare Apache statement about the myth going with
the songs, p. 1060). A suggestion here that the myth is built up around the songs,
as in many Indian circles. Actually there is no narrative content in the Snake
society songs. Nor is there much if any song content in Pueblo myths. In the
Acoma origin myth there are some songs and some Taos tales are near-ballads.

† Goddard 5:168. Compare the Chemehuevi Paiute who says when his songs
and "power" pass to another, even in the family, that now he has "nothing to
live for" (Kelly, 130).

Frequently songs are sung too low for those present to overhear, as when the Town chief of Hano sets up his winter solstice altar to four songs which the other chiefs present may not hear,[543] or when Walpi winter solstice chiefs whistle their songs.[544] Anyone overhearing Zuni Rain chief songs will die—the familiar and convenient automatic sanction.

Songs have a magically coercive character. When Coyote, the witch, seduces Blue Corn Girl and Yellow Corn Girl, "he sings a song to make them become his wives."[545] In Zuni and Hopi war ceremonial there are songs for snow or "to make the ground freeze"; and kachina songs which are songs of fertility may not be sung at this time, for they would cancel songs for freezing.[546] Sometimes even during the singing the desired consummation is expected to occur. In such incantation there will be, as a rule, four songs to be sung during which the result is achieved, the fire kindled, the spruce fetched,[547] or, in tale, the tree grown. When the underground Hopi planted reeds to ascend by, they "sang a song to make the reeds grow. They sang and sang, and they grew and grew."[548] Dew Boy sings in order that the corn which was forgotten underground and recovered by Swallow should grow and ripen within a single day,[549] just as the corn on the Hano winter solstice altar is matured overnight, thanks, I infer, to the songs.[550]

Particular songs attach to particular rites,* as songs for grinding pigments or painting and tying prayer-feathers (Isleta) or prayer-sticks (Hopi),[551] for painting the scalp (Taos), for painting the person in kachina or warrior dance (Zuni), for aspersing and meal-casting, for marking the walls with meal (Hopi), for blowing smoke, for pouring out water (Hopi),[552] for exorcising with buzzard feather (Hopi). In laying down the Zuni society† altar at sunset the sequence of eight songs is called "For

---

* Characteristic too of the Navaho (Haile, 197, 231: red ocher songs, emetic songs, etc.) and of other Indian peoples.

† The following information was given Dr. Bunzel for the Big Firebrand society (Bunzel 4:782), but she states that the procedure is about the same for all the societies. Compare Stevenson 2:463.

Acoma society songs are recorded for setting the altar, for fetching (? pouring) water, for making the sand-painting, for giving medicine (Stirling).

Pouring in the Water." At the beginning of the fourth song two men go out to offer food in the river; and the society *pekwin* makes the meal-painting and sets up the corn fetishes. At the fifth song the chief takes the bowl for the medicine water; at the sixth, he mixes the medicine, putting in the plants associated with the animals that he invokes; at the seventh song he puts in the sacred colored pebbles; during the eighth, he smokes the altar. There are specific songs of invocation, "calling songs." There are initiatory head-washing songs.[553] The Hopi Antelope society sing their series of sixteen songs to meal-casting, blowing smoke, beating time with prayer-stick or tapping with the *chamahia* stone hoe, and whizzing the rhombus.[554]

When reference is made in ritual song to an act or object of ritual, the rite is performed, just as formal gesture is made to song reference—dramatization begins. For example, when the meal road is referred to, meal will be sprinkled on the "road."[555] When the word "cleanse" or "discharm" occurs in song, the exorciser will cast the ashes from his buzzard feather.[556] In a song to the birds of the directions, when each in turn is told to whistle, the whistle is blown (Hopi).[557] As the Isleta Hunt chief sings, the hunter moves his offerings in the directions, prayer-feather, cigarette, meal and pollen, turquoise, and a red bead. Hunt songs are very important to the Pueblo hunter.*

In the society songs that have been recorded, Acoma, Sia, and Hopi songs, the most familiar trait of Indian song, repetitiousness or "parallel phrasing,"[558] is very marked, the same stanza will be repeated for each of the six color-directions, for its corn, cloud, rain, or lightning, or for each bird or animal or tree or stone-and-shell of the directions. In songs of sequence, in fact in any ritual song, accuracy is important, theoretically an unfollowed sequence or a misplaced word will impair the efficacy of the performance. Repetitiousness with the change of a key word, such as cloud or fog, is also characteristic of dance songs.

Dance songs may be old and traditional like some of the Zuni Good Kachina songs or the Santo Domingo Tsaiyadyuwitsa, or

---

* And throughout the Southwest. Without knowing hunt songs, a Navaho would not go hunting; he would be afraid (Goddard 5:163).

they may be newly composed, particularly in the Kachina cult, entirely new, or new words set to old rhythms. There are episodic rhythms, for coming in or going out, the initial or less vigorous song, and then the "strong songs." Old or new, kachina songs should not be sung promiscuously about town; they are to be sung when a man is away in the fields or out with his horses or sheep or in kiva practice by night or at those Hopi spinning-parties called "kachina spinning" from the all-day singing of kachina songs to familiarize all, but especially the younger men, with words and tunes, the elders or other experts correcting errors in words, refrain, or time.[559]

New songs are composed for war and saint's-day dances. Eight days before the Zuni saint's dance the sacristan (Sakisti) calls out to make songs; so the young men, composers and singers, meet in all the kivas and then four days later rehearse their songs with the dancers for four evenings, the fourth night staying all night in kiva.[560] The distinction between new songs for the popular dance (among which the saint's-day dance is included) and old songs derived from the Spirits (from the birds, Hopi would say) is mentioned at Acoma[561] but almost certainly not observed, and here as elsewhere there is little if any distinction between kachina and saint's-day songs.

Obsolete words are used in song as in prayer, and whole songs may be in another tongue which is not understood.* It is obvious how this may happen. A visitor who understands or partially understands the language of his hosts learns a song and on his return home teaches it to his own people. Again songs of immigrant groups may be retained after the descendants have lost their language. Even the song in current language may be unintelligible or ambiguous, like poetry elsewhere, so incoherent its words, and so full of short cuts, its expression. Besides, familiar words may be altered to suit the rhythm, as in the case given

---

* This is notable in Hopi songs, in which there are only a few words, the lines being filled out by repeating or dragging out certain syllables or ejaculations (Voth 8:69; 2:126; compare Bunzel 2:495).

Even in newly composed Hopi songs, special facts are referred to in such loosely connected phrases that only the composer really knows the meaning (Voth 3:311, n. 1).

by Stevenson where in a rain song of the Sia Giant society the word for badger, *tuo'pi*, is changed to *tupina*, to make the stanza more rhythmical.[562]

In making the sand-painting of the Earth given by Mother Iyatiku, the Acoman society sing:

> Earth plant
> Earth plant
> Toward the north
> Your arm lies spread out,
> Toward the west
> Your legs lie spread out,
> Toward the south
> Your arm lies spread out,
> Toward the east
> Your head lies spread out.
> Midway
> You are centered.*
> From the middle up
> The plants grow
> From the middle down
> The people stretch (lie spread out)
> From the middle outward
> Breath is breathed.
> Earth plant
> Lies spread out.†

Before giving the final drink of medicine to kachina or to people present at a ceremony, Antelope clansmen or curing society sing as follows:

> Yonder in the north,
> Snow Mountain,
> To your yellow-colored pool
> To your medicine pool
> With sacred vessel
> I am going for a drink.

* Here at the heart the medicine bowl is placed.

† Stirling. This was sung at the setting-up of the first altar, at Shipap. Any medicine man may use this song in making an Earth-painting, and in making any painting the song is sung, to different words.

Yonder in the west,
Turkey Mountain,
To your blue-colored pool
To your medicine pool
With a sacred vessel
I am going for a drink.

Yonder in the south,
Enchanted Mountain,
To your red-colored pool
With sacred vessel
I am going for a drink.

Yonder in the east,
Standing Mountain,
To your white-colored pool
To your medicine pool
With sacred turquoise vessel
I am going for a drink.[563]

The following hunt song is sung at the altar and out hunting
to get power from the prey animals of Acoma:

On the northern edge
Lion hunt chief has come out.
With glittering paint
With yellow head feather tip waving
He has gone.
Bravely will I go
To get spruce
Acquiring blessings.

On the western edge
Rohono the hunter has come out.
With glittering paint
With blue head feather tip waving
He has gone.
Bravely will I go
To get spruce
Acquiring blessings.

On the southern edge
Wildcat the hunter has come out.
With glittering paint
With red head feather tip waving
He has gone.
Bravely will I go
To get spruce
Acquiring blessings.

On the eastern edge
Wolf the hunter has come out.
With glittering paint
With white head feather tip waving
He has gone.
Bravely will I go
To get spruce
Acquiring blessings.

Here are songs from the Oraibi women's Oaqöl ceremony, on
aspersing, in addressing corn ears on the altar, at daybreak
around the altar or casting prayer meal outside, and on discharming:

There!
There!
Beautiful white rising has dawned.
Beautiful yellow rising has dawned.
There!
There!
Go, the day has dawned.
Go, the day has dawned.
Figured butterfly maiden,
White butterfly maiden, hao!
Everything (and anything) bring,
Figured butterfly maiden,
White butterfly maiden, hao, hao![564]

Hao! my mother,
Yellow corn ear, my mother,
We together
Go to Tū'wanashave.*

* Voth 4:27. Tū'wanashave is earth or sand center, center of sand on which
stands the medicine bowl, the "center of the world."

The day has risen!
The day has risen!
Go I to behold it.
The Mu'yingwa chiefs
With shelled corn busy themselves.
He is croaking
The water frog,
About big corn ears.[565]

The white dawn has risen.
The yellow dawn has risen.
That I shall light embrace.[566]

Discharm!
Discharm!
From the north,
Yellow buzzard,*
With the wing![567]

The fullest group of Hopi songs recorded is for the Powamu ceremony at Oraibi. The following stanza is from one of the color-direction sequences:

Ha-o, my mother!
Ha-o, my mother!
Due north, yellow corn ear, my mother!
Due southward, blooming *hashi*,
Decorate our faces,
Bless us with flowers!
Thus being face decorated,
Being blessed with flowers,
We shall be delighted, we shall be delighted,
Ha-o, my mother.[568]

Kachina songs are legion, for they are being constantly composed; the music has been recorded, but the words of comparatively few songs are known. The following are typical songs of the Good Kachina of Zuni:

---

* Repeated for all the color-directions. This song will be sung by the society chief not only at the close of ceremony but over anyone afflicted by the society sickness, a swelling on top of the head.

"Guess, younger brother,
Whose fine tracks go all about here?
All over my water-filled field
He has walked about.
Can you not guess?"
Thus he said to his younger brother,
"The child of the rain-makers,
The water frog,
Goes about hurrying his fathers, the rain-makers."

In the west at Flower Mountain
A rain priest sits
His head feathered with cumulus clouds
His words are of clouding over Itiwana.
"Come let us arise now!"
Thus along the shores of the encircling ocean
The rain-makers say to one another.[569]

The following Keresan songs are the first two from Santo
Domingo,[570] the others from Acoma:

At G'o·'wawaima*
In a tree
Sits (long) tail parrot
Clouds cover him.
Today from the north
It will rain.
From west, south, east
It will rain.
Sprouting with two shoots
With four shoots
The plants will ripen.†

Now Sha·k'ak'a shiwana‡ is lonesome
Because the people believe in him no longer.
No longer early in the morning
Do they go outside
And pray with pollen
To Sun Youth.

* In the south whence come the Spanish-like kachina, but the word is Hopi
(see p. 771; cf. Stephen 4, glossary, Kowa'waimovi).

† Sung by Tsaiyadyuwitsa kachina.

‡ Storm cloud or chief of the North; he appears also as a kachina.

Now Sha·k'ak'a shiwana is lonesome
Because the people believe in him no longer.
No longer early in the morning
At their grinding-stones
Do they pray with corn meal
To Yellow Woman.

Already this morning
The Shiwana have come out
With cloud they come
Already this morning
The Shiwana have come out.
With fog they come
Rainbow, Lightning
From Snow Mountain
From Turkey Mountain
Thence their road
With rain, corn crops
They make for us.
With clouds
With fog
From Enchanted Mountain
From Standing Mountain
Thence their road
With thunder, vine crops
They make for us.[571]

Look there in Shipap
Somewhere below
The kachina are painting up.
Their cloud moccasins putting on
Their kilts and pretty belts
Ready to return.

Look there in Shipap
Somewhere below
The kachina are painting up.
Their fog moccasins putting on
Their kilts and pretty belts
Ready to return.[572]

This last Acoma song is sung at the saint's-day dance. Here is another saint's-day dance-song, a magic rain song, from San Juan:

Ready we stand in San Juan town,
Our Corn Maidens and our Corn Youths!
Our Corn Mothers and our Corn Fathers!
Now we bring you misty water
And throw it different ways,
To the north, the west, the south, the east
To heaven above and the drinking earth below!
Then likewise throw you misty water
Toward San Juan!
Many that you are, pour water
Over our Corn Maidens' ears!
On our Wheat Maidens
Thence throw you misty water,
All around about us here!
On Green Earth Woman's back
Now thrive our flesh and breath,
Now grows our strength of arm and leg,
Now takes form our children's food![573]

The Good Kachina of Zuni, Mahedinasha, and particularly home-Chakwena may all sing satire against individuals. For example, Good Kachina once sang: "Our two daylight fathers journeyed to the east to visit the Sun and the Moon. When they returned, their children questioned them, 'What did the Sun say to you?' But they had not seen the Sun." This refers to a visit to Washington by two Rain chiefs, to lay grievances before the Commissioner of Indian Affairs. They returned without having seen him, and the people felt they had bungled things badly.[574] Mahedinasha made a song about a jilted Bear clan girl who dragged her rival from the dance and beat her up: "The Raw People are dangerous. They are wise. But even the Raw People are afraid of the Bear girl. When she showed her claws in the plaza, even the Raw People ran away." Home-Chakwena will twit Koyemshi for the infidelity of their wives while the Koyemshi are in their long retreat. If a man is trying to marry a woman who does not want him, home-Chakwena "talks right out about it." For the children, home-Chakwena will sing against precocious intercourse or against disobedience. They will mention ritual errors. For example, they sang: "They were putting a child into the Shi'wanakwe society. Then my mothers of the

Dogwood clan gave their child a drink." During the initiation ceremonial a "child" should not eat or drink.[575]

Hatashuku, a kachina borrowed from Laguna, also "jokes about people,"[576] so we may infer that kachina satires are current also at Laguna. They are current in the maskless kachina cult of Isleta. I surmise they are common everywhere in the kachina cult, serving as potent sanctions for standardized behavior.

Hopi Men's societies, Singers and Wüwüchim, sing satirical songs against the Women's societies, the women reciprocating at the time of their own ceremonies. This "song-tying" or song-binding obliges the person sung against to make a food present to the singer's society. These songs greatly amuse the audience.*

Pueblo music, more particularly the music of the western pueblos, is said by Herzog to be the most complex music of North American Indians, showing a great variety of distinct patterns and stylistic features. Stylistic complexity, greater elaboration and formalization, increases toward the West, and between West (Hopi, Zuni, Keres) and East (Tanoan) there is considerable differentiation, obscured, to be sure, by parallels between songs having the same function, such as animal dance songs. Kachina dance music of the West is the most complex music of all. In general, Pueblo style, in spite of its great formalization, is exceedingly exuberant and ready to assimilate suggestions from the outside, and Pueblo music, as described by Dr. Herzog, is consistent with Pueblo style and with the other ritual arts of the Pueblos.

34. MEDICINE†

Home remedies, herbal medicines for the most part, are used everywhere,‡ and medicine may be given by doctors with little

---

* Stephen 4:905; Beaglehole 3:79–80; Voth 8:32, 56–57. Beaglehole translates song-teasing which is also the reference in English to the equivalent practice at Isleta by the Black Eye or Red Eye spruce-gatherers who are given cigarettes to close their mouths (Parsons 52:321–22).

† Zuni, a'kwa; Hopi, nahu' (nata, rub on); Keresan, wawa; Isleta, wah; Tewa, wo'le; Taos, waapahona ("life-water").

‡ See the ethnobotanies of Zuni and the Tewa towns (Stevenson 2; Robbins, Harrington, Freire-Marreco); unpublished botanical notes from Hopi and Keres

or no ritual (Zuni).[577] Isletans and Zuni,[578] probably other Pueblos, will carry medicinal roots around with them in belt or pocket. At Zuni, societies have proprietary rights in certain plants. Used in one way the plant may be free to all, used in another way it belongs exclusively to a given society. Societies everywhere have a special medicine which is aspersed or administered by shell from their altar bowl to all who have been present at ceremonial.* This "charm medicine" or "discharming medicine" is believed to give immunity to the disease controlled by the society (Hopi).

Medicine may be a diagnostic for the doctor. At Zuni, datura, Jamestown weed, is used as a narcotic† in ritual derived from Navaho, for finding strayed or hidden persons or animals or things lost or stolen.‡ A plant called *tenatsali* which has never been identified is similarly used by Rain chiefs. "Bear medicine," used by all curing societies, induces a trancelike state in the doctor during which he can see the witch causing the sickness.[579] The bear root of First Mesa has been identified as aster root (*ericæ folius* Rothrock).[580]

Hano clowns have a medicine which enables them to eat anything, and possibly their public exhibitions with voidings are to

---

indicate like medicinal usage. For the picture of an excellent botanist and herb doctor, the best doctor in Oraibi, also assistant chief of Oaqöltü, see Voth 4: Pl. V.

* The white, saltless wafer-bread eaten in Chief kiva during the Walpi winter solstice ceremony is given out after the ceremony as medicine, "it makes the flesh good" (Stephen 4:36, 51). If ever the Indians saw the friar taking the Host, they must have considered it medicine.

† Used, but not ritually, at Oraibi (Stephen 4:557, n. 3), also by Papago and Havasupai who warn against it (Spier 2:269). For other Yumans and for Tarahumara and Huicholes see pp. 990, 1009.

‡ Parsons 4:169. Compare Stevenson 2:385 ff. According to Stevenson, datura is used also as anesthetic; she saw Naiuchi, who in addition to his other functions was a doctor in the Little Firebrand society, operate on a breast abscess in a woman completely anesthetized by datura. Datura is a proprietary medicine of the Rain chiefs and of the Little Firebrand and Bedbug societies (Stevenson). I saw Tsatiselu, a Ne'wekwe doctor who used datura for recovering lost things, operate on an abscess in the neck without using datura. His patient who was his own daughter whimpered or cried throughout.

prove this.* At any rate ordure is considered good medicine (Zuni, Hopi, Laguna, also Navaho). A medicine of snake droppings was given by the Kaʙina society to Acoma War captains (see p. 595). At Taos a fainting or unconscious person will be fumigated in a smoke from buzzard droppings (cf. p. 191). Droppings from Rainbow cure chest complaints and give strength against a rival (Mishongnovi).[581] At Zuni the lightning-shocked are bathed in urine,† and urine is poured on hot stones in (?) steaming for twisting (cramps, ? rheumatism).[582] When "Ololo comes" his "urine" is mixed with the corn meal ground by the kachina maidens and distributed to spectators.‡ The fat and the sexual organs of a badger are medicine for impotent men.[583]

Not uncommonly the medicinal plant or mineral has some feature it is desired to impart to the patient. Corn pollen is this kind of medicine (First Mesa, Isleta, Taos), and so probably are corn meal rubbed on the face "for a long life,"[584] and honey rubbed on at prayer-stick making or depositing (Hopi).[585] The War society of Zuni used the fat or oil of the rattlesnake to rub

---

* Stephen 4:557. Compare, for Zuni, Stevenson 2:430, 435. A link is supplied by Tarahumara and Jicarilla Apache beliefs. Ashes from dog droppings are Tarahumara stomach medicine, and human feces will be rubbed on gums for toothache (Bennett and Zingg, 264). Jicarilla believe vomiting is caused by touching human or animal feces, against which the clowns have a medicine of excrement of child and of dog mixed with white clay and a plant (Opler 6:184, 206). Here is a clue why the clowning Black Eyes of Taos are called upon to cure infants.

Jicarilla clowns wear a bandoleer of breads. The clown will put some of this bread into his own mouth and then into the mouth of a patient, curing him. Clown medicine sharpens sight; the clowns can see at a great distance (Opler). Here are clues for the bread bandoleers worn by San Juan Kossa and for the ability of San Juan and Hano clowns to see the kachina approaching from far off.

This trait as well as several other Pueblo clown traits is remarkably paralleled in the Blue Jay characters of the interior Salish who acted as sentries and as sheriffs for proper behavior, talked backward, or with people not at all, observed long fasts, specialized in finding lost articles and in curing, taking foreign bodies out of the stomach, although differentiated from shamans, painted black and wore little clothing (Ray).

† Urine, applied internally or externally, was also a favorite early European remedy.

‡ We recall the Aztec rite of eating the dough image of the war god.

on the face that the enemy might fear the anointed one as he feared the snakes.[586]

A plant medicine may be associated with an animal or insect, probably by a kind of substitution, for, as Tsatiselu of Zuni told me, "They can't always get the creature, so they take the root (of the same name)." For example, the name of the root medicine of the Hopi Snake society is derived from that of a black beetle which is also a snake antidote.* Into the composition of the Walpi warrior's bandoleer went powdered herbs or roots called bee, wasp, and beetle, mountain lion, and bear.[587] At childbirth a weasel skin is passed down the body of the woman to hasten labor—the weasel moves quickly—but, if the skin is unavailable, a weasel plant medicine (*linum rigidum* Purch) is used (Oraibi).† Bear root is named, of course, for Bear, the curer. As the Zuni shaman (Big Firebrand society) drops his pulverized roots into the medicine bowl, he prays:

> Yonder in the north
> You who are my father,
> Mountain lion,
> You are life-giving society chief;
> Bringing your medicine
> You will make your road come hither.
> Where lies my white shell bowl,
> Four times making your road come in,
> Watch over my spring.
> When you sit down quietly,
> *We shall be one person.*‡

Spring water is efficacious for medicine. At Laguna the knobby clay balls which are left on the riverbank after a flood and which are thought of as the kick-balls or sticks of the Cloud

---

* Voth 3:286–87; Stephen 4:715. I am wondering if this medicine was known to Tsatiselu, who was a Ne'wekwe doctor, and the Ne'wekwe had plant medicine to cure rattlesnake bite (Stevenson 2:392).

† Voth 7:51; Dorsey and Voth 3:34 n. The weasel medicine is one of the two herbs used in the Oraibi Snake medicine or antidote (Voth 3:354).

‡ Bunzel 4:783–84. Repeated for the other animals of the directions: Bear (West), Badger (South), Wolf (East), Knife-Wing (Zenith), Gopher (Nadir). For "animal" root medicines of the Little Firebrand society see Stevenson 2: 552–53. Possession?

spirits are used as medicine. Cochiti kick-stick runners are given medicine to drink after their race, by the Giant society,[588] and I surmise that river clay is used. To those sick from worry the Town chief or Scalp chief of Isleta will give "Navaho mud," from the washings of the Navaho scalps or consisting of bits of scalps chewed* and mixed with mud and put up in a cornhusk like a Mexican *tamale*. Scalp wash is today a regular Sunday tonic at Santo Domingo.[589] Medicine clay is fetched from the Catholic sanctuary of Chimayo† by Tewa and Keres and even by sons of Taos.‡

Scrapings from a penis-shaped stone are drunk by Zuni women who want a male child, and a little stone from the Boy rock or Girl rock at Corn Mountain will be ground and drunk in water as conception medicine for male or female infant.[590] Sand or meal or pollen from the altar picture is often rubbed on the person by those engaged in the ceremony or taken home to rub on kindred. Altar sand is placed under or near the corn store (Walpi, winter solstice ceremony; Oraibi, Oaqöl).[591] In Oraibi war ritual those present help themselves to a pinch of the clay with which the impersonator of the War god has been marked and, returning home, moisten the clay with the medicine water they have kept in the mouth, and rub a little on the breast, back, arms, and legs of each member of the household.[592] In corresponding war ritual on First Mesa, the representatives of the War gods rush past the houses with a bowl of medicine, and the man of the house chases them to get some medicine as a drink for the males of the house and as an unguent for the females. Before going to war, Hopi

* See p. 625 for biting into the scalp at Zuni. Acoma and Laguna scalpers and War captains chewed scalp (White 2:96; Boas 2:290).

† From a pit in the sacristy of the church of San Esquipula. The medicine pit, like Zuni Salt Lake, fills up again, it is believed, and the pilgrimage to Chimayo, which is about fifteen miles east of Santa Clara, can be made in magically short time. Indian ideas, perhaps, but the "medicine" was introduced by the Franciscans. At Esquipulas in eastern Guatemala kaolin cakes from a mold of the Virgin were blessed by the priest and traded as medicine throughout Chorti Indian territory (Wisdom).

‡ Isletans also visit Chimayo, and my *guess* is that the clay they fetch as medicine for rheumatism and for "being sad" is that used in making the scalp *tamales*.

would be spotted with a pulverized stone called the vomit of
Pöökong, the War god, which made their flesh tough and arrow-
proof. Today Snake society men are painted in the same way.[593]
In the Zuni tale of the Beetle Boys who kill the Horned Water
Serpents, the boys rub themselves with the vomit of the serpents
and straightway become very handsome fellows. In a San Juan
tale women warriors get medicine to rub on their bows and arrows and on their persons and to spit all around, from Spider
Grandmother, ever a purveyor of self-protective medicine in
emergencies of all kinds.

Spitting, spurting, or spraying medicine is one of the most
common ways of applying it; it is a common Indian way of applying water or any liquid, in washing the person and in sprinkling the ground or anything else. The tongue is pushed between
the lips, then quickly withdrawn and the material on the tongue
(honey, pieces of roots or herbs, i.e., "medicine") is then forcibly
blown out. Thus in the Powalawu ceremony of Oraibi the War
chief, having licked some honey from the spear points on the
altar, ejects it to the cardinal points.[594] In the rain ceremonial of
the Querränna society of Sia the chief sprays the society medicine
of water mixed with a powder of plants and ground-up shell and
turquoise into which a fetish has been dipped, to the cardinal
points that the Cloud People may gather and send rain.[595] The
performers in the Oraibi Snake ceremony spray their discharming medicine on whatever has been in contact with them, on
vessels and clothing and into springs from which they have
drunk during the snake hunts.[596] Just before Zuni kachina
dancers leave the kiva, in order to make them beautiful and
attractive the kiva chief will spray each with Paiyatamu medicine made of flower petals by the curing societies.[597]

In Tewa tale Spider Grandmother usually carries with her a
bundle of medicine which she applies by spraying. Thus, when
Cactus Flower Girl is given ice to grind, Spider spits medicine
onto the ice to make it melt. Again she spits medicine to make
T'aiowa, the seducer, lose his race. She tells a hunter to spit the
medicine she gives him into the tracks of the animals sent to do
him in. In tale a Taos warrior spits medicine against approach-

ing enemies, and medicine is sprayed in order to lower river waters or to open a way through the waters of the sacred lake.[598] In the Zuni tale of White Bison, the bird which sleeps by day spits medicine upon Mockingbird and then upon the Bison youths to put them all to sleep. After the kachina Shitsukia frees the game from their stone corral, he spits medicine on their wardens, turning them into ravens.[599] In the early days dogs gossiped about women "stealing husbands," so the War Brothers spat medicine into their muzzles. "From now on you shall not be able to talk," they said. "You can hear and see and taste, but not talk."[600] Analogously at Zuni the beak of a plucked eagle is spat into, with corn and kaolin; just as corn grows up, the feathers will grow out and, like kaolin, be white.[601]

Medicine—a bit of cedar, roots liquified or chewed—is often sprayed or spat on the hands which are then rubbed or passed over body or face. External application, anointing, is indeed a commoner way of taking medicine than taking it internally. Discharming or exorcising medicine as well as ashes or gum are rubbed on (see pp. 106, 464). Sprinkling from the tips of feathers is another way of applying medicine.

35. Breath Rites

There are two, perhaps three, breath rites: breathing from* or breathing on,† in order to receive or impart, let us say, influence or life (see below)—the two rites being conceptually closely associated and practically confused (where you would expect inhalation, your informant may describe exhalation and vice versa, and direct observation is of course difficult, if not impossible); and a third rite which is a forcible expulsion of breath and is properly a rite of exorcism.

* Zuni, *yechu*, which is the general term for both rites, or *pinananaha*, breath goes in, for the rite of breathing from; Hopi, *hüh'tü* (Stephen 4:1222, 1271); Laguna, *tsuputsana* or *kuityia;* Isleta, *ishuchi wa'shihan', washi,* give long life, *han > haniwe,* breath; Tewa (F.M.) *hatsiperi* (*ha,* heart; *tsiperi,* blow); among eastern Tewa this term refers to breathing on; breathing from is *ihakonde* (pl.) *ha,* heart, *ko,* take it.

† Laguna, *chishatsa* or *g'oputs;* Jemez, *refuse,* breath blow out; Isleta, *ham'-bewe.*

Before prayer meal is offered, it is breathed *on* whether it is to be strewn for Sun, on altar fetish or kachina, or sent in a packet, let us say, to a doctor. A recipient would breathe in.[602] In a Chakwena dance held for the benefit of a sick woman of Laguna, the kachina visited the woman, bringing her a present of corn, melons, and chili; and the woman breathed on the present. When I showed to Juanita of Jemez the ear of corn I had been named with on First Mesa, my "mother," she breathed on it, very reverently; similarly her husband breathed on the blossoms Juanita had snatched off a clown in the wrangle after a dance. After a dance when the Zuni kachina impersonator removes his turtle-shell rattle, he breathes from it. In the Laguna tale of José Crito the ox in the stable breathes on the infant, and in another Spanish Laguna tale fluid from the bodies of old persons who are being baked for rejuvenation is breathed on.

Prayer-sticks are breathed from by Hopi—to inhale the essence, Stephen calls it. Thus Sun inhales from prayer-sticks and feathers. When a Zuni is preparing his prayer-sticks, from time to time he will breathe on the feathers, and in Laguna tale offerings of prayer-sticks, pollen, and beads are breathed on.[603] In Acoma myth Iyatiku, in making the first corn fetish, breathed on it.[604] "Thus from her breath we shall receive the health she is herself possessed of," says the Town chief of Cochiti.[605] A Zuni never takes his corn fetish out of its bag without breathing from it. A corn ear held in the hand by a dancer will be breathed from (Zuni).[606] The prayer-stick which each Shalako host keeps for the year may be brought out to be breathed from by connections of the household. "I breathe from your feathers, so make me strong like you," says a man in Zuni tale in praying to Eagle.[607] The eagle feathers of Isletan shamans are breathed from. When Zuni prayer-sticks of office are presented, they are breathed from.[608] Similarly all those at the installation of the Town chief of Sia breathe from his crook stick of office.* In Zuni initiations the corn fetish is breathed from by the recipient[609] and breathed

---

* Oraibi Oaqöl women wave a crook, and sing to Morning Star or Sun, "I shall light inhale" (I breathe from the Sun) (Voth 4:40). Possibly this is a consecration of their crooks which in turn will be breathed from.

on by the giver. On being installed into office, Zuni Governor and Lieutenant-Governor each breathes from the cane of office which first his predecessor and then the Town chief passes four times in front of his face.*

On the installation of the Zuni War chief, he breathes from the hand of the Town chief;[610] and, when Pekwin is installed, everyone present breathes from his hand. Breathing from the hand of another is at Zuni a not uncommon form of the breath rite, applied to any distinguished person or person you would distinguish. It is proper whenever a Rain chief comes to your house to clasp his right hand in yours and raise it to your mouth to breathe from. In return the chief raises your hand still clasped in his to his mouth, when he breathes on his own hand. When members of another society are invited to an initiation, they are greeted with this breath rite. The first man Cushing met on his memorable walk into Zuni took his hand and breathed *on* it and *from* his own,† just as did old Chasra of Walpi when he met Zuni visitors on the trail.[611] Flora Zuni told me that when she was married about twenty years ago, by American license, all her people performed the rite of *yechu* with her hand, each party breathing from the hand of the other. In greeting old José of Laguna, Storm cloud shaman, I would breathe from his hand and he always completed the rite by raising my hand toward his lips. At Isleta, after a society member has completed his ritual and is taking leave, you breathe from his hand. And so at Cochiti a sick person will breathe from the clasped hands of the doctor.[612]

Breathing from or on may be done not in approximation with the sacrosanct object or personage but, in substitution, with one's own clasped hand or rather thumbs, the thumbs lying side by side and the fingers imbricated (Zuni, Hopi, Isleta, Laguna, Sia).[613] Among Tewa the animal fetish itself is not breathed

* Acoman shamans blow (breathe) four times on the canes they hand on (Stirling).

† Cushing 2:191, 193; see 199 for another occasion when Governor and officers breathed from the hands of their Washington visitors. Compare Cushing 6:114, 122.

from, but the hand after it has been passed over the fetish. After sprinkling meal (Zuni, Cochiti)[614] or offering prayer-sticks (Zuni), after any prayer or chant (Zuni),* the thumbs are breathed from. In Laguna terms, after praying you "take back breath."

In the spruce dance or maskless kachina dance of Isleta when the dancers enter the kiva, all present breathe from their own clasped hands. After winning a stick-race, the Zuni winner as he reaches the plaza and the piled-up stakes breathes on his thumbs,[615] and in the Shalako running rite the onlookers breathe on their thumbs after each run. On visiting, a Shalako impersonator will say, "I give you the breath of Shalako"; and those present will breathe from their thumbs. At a Hopi deer-kill each hunter, as he comes up, jumps on the deer and grabs a horn, then breathes on his thumbs, saying, "I want to catch a deer like you." Zuni and Cochiti deer-hunter would touch the deer and breathe in,[616] as would anyone in Isleta on encountering the deer or coming to look at it. The Zuni hunter breathing in the breath of the deer is supposed to say: "Thanks, my father, this day have I drunken your sacred wind of life."[617] When a pregnant woman has asked to have the *santu* brought out, she breathes from her thumbs (*santu yechu*), four times, and the girls who carry the image in the saint's dance do likewise.

The Zuni prayer that regularly accompanies the breath rite is:

lena ho tek'ohanna anichiatu
thus I light (life) wish much.

Similarly the Isletan will refer to the rite as "to have more life."

In the preceding rite the breath passes through the lips puckered up; in the rite of forcible expulsion the mouth is open and the expulsion is from the throat.† Thus the snake-bitten has to breathe on the sore navel of an infant (Zuni, Laguna) or

---

* Bunzel 2:481; 5:1025. After listening to prayer or song, Western Apache may breathe in, inhaling the power of the prayer or song (Goodwin).

† Jemez, *hehuba;* Taos, *ihathliameho.*

a Hopi doctor* on his patient.† On giving the infant a name, the San Juan godmother, holding some medicine water in her mouth, breathes in from the fetish corn ear, ejects the water into the mouth of the infant, and then breathes out on the infant. The Hopi antelope- or deer-hunter exorcised the "odor" of women and babies, disliked by the animals, by drawing the hands over all parts of the body in turn, each time breathing out.‡ After the hunt he blew away the "odor" of the animals in the same way to keep them from troubling the village.

36. HEART

In Pueblo ideology the heart is the life, and considerable attention is directed ritually and in tales to the heart: "heart" is given to ritual objects or persons or "heart" is renewed, cleansed, or replaced. Witches steal the "heart." Medicine may be made from heart. Just before going out to dance the Zuni kachina takes out from his belt his package of seeds, spits on it, and says, "Now you shall be my heart. You shall make me into a raw person (spirit). You will bring good luck, for me and for all my

---

* The Havasupai doctor sends his "familiar" into the patient by mouth. The familiar retrieves the object injected by another spirit or "familiar" (Spier 2:279, 280). It is possible that western Pueblos borrowed the practice from Yuman culture, without borrowing the spirit familiar, or with only an obscure hint that the doctor is sending the animal helpers whom he addresses into the patient's body (Stevenson 2:415; pp. 716, 717).

The Western Apache doctor blows on the afflicted part (whether from lips or throat is not stated) to drive out sickness or pain. This is done directly after the doctor has called the names of powerful supernaturals or objects, and it is as if the doctor breathed the power from such sources right onto the sick person. Again, the doctor may apply to the body some object with power to draw out the sickness and then he will blow on the object in order to blow away the clinging sickness (Goodwin).

† Stephen 4:149, 862; see p. 717. The ear of an infant with earache would be blown into, four times, by someone once lightning-shocked, and any sick infant would be blown upon. The blower is not a doctor, but the infant is "given" to him and will join his ceremonial groups (Parsons 55:12, 15).

‡ Compare the Havasupai rite on dreaming of the dead. On awaking, a man will say: "I am not dead: I only saw you dead people. . . . . It is bad to dream of the dead; . . . . so go away." Then he *blows into his hands* and brushes them down face and body. "So I brush the dream away into the night" (Spier 2:334, also 285).

people, so that our corn may grow."[618] Here, as usual, good luck is synonymous for "blessing."

In the sand mosaic of Sun on the Hopi Powamu altar a small quartz crystal is placed in the center and called heart* of the Sun,[619] and in every image of Water Serpent is fastened a quartz crystal "heart."[620] At Zuni a piece of turquoise is set into the cradle board, near where the heart of the infant will be, "to give heart (a good heart) to the cradle that it may not hurt the child."

In Tewa tale the people are suffering because their fetish Mothers have pointed things and stones in their "stomachs" (hearts). The Mothers are cut open and refilled with good things, probably seeds. Similarly Arrowpoint Boy is given literally a change of heart by replacing the cactus spines inside him with pink quartz and turquoise.[621] After the Sia Corn Mother was killed by her sister, her heart was found to be full of cactus. Once the red Horned Water Serpent was sending sickness to Sia and had to be caught by the doctors and killed in order to have his heart cleansed of cactus spines.[622] The Isletan boys who are seeking their Sun father are warned by Spider Grandmother that Sun is "mean" because he has a heart of rock. After finding Sun, the older boy cuts open his chest and restores his rightful heart, the younger boy sewing him up.

To his Acoma twins Sun gives wrist guards of buffalo leather which the boys are never to take off as their hearts are in them (Stirling). Chakwena Woman's heart was in her rattle. Your heart may be inside your body, in any part of it, or outside.

Scalps and heads were taken in war habitually by Pueblos, but they might also cut open the chest and take out the heart. A solitary cedar to the north of the wagon road between First Mesa and Second Mesa was pointed out to me as the place where the heart of a Navaho chief was buried, to insure against Navaho attack. In a fight by Oraibi against Navaho and Walpi men disguised as Navaho, some Walpi men capture a particularly brave

---

* A "road-marker" prayer-feather is attached, just as prayer-feather is attached near the heart of animal figurine or fresco (see p. 287). Animals are often pictured with a line, a red line, from heart to mouth.

Oraibi man, cut open his breast, and tear out his heart.[623] In Hano tales the heart of the enemy is commonly cut out. For example, Yellow Cloud Boy, after defeating T'aiowa in a race, cuts open his chest and takes out his heart to cut it up into small pieces and mix with sand and throw in every direction. When the War Brothers kill Giantess, they also cut open her chest and take out her heart which was an abalone shell. Bear tears out a man's heart, in a Hopi tale, the heart of Gambler.[624] A Cochiti youth is advised not to pursue the bears when they eat in his cornfield, since he will be first to be captured by the Bears. "We will open your chest," say the Bears, "and tear out your heart. *Then you will remain here and live with us always.*" To be taken into any Witch society the initiate must produce the heart of a relative,[625] and, in curing, a doctor has to recover from predatory witches his patient's heart.[626]

The War gods of Sia preserve the hearts of the monsters they kill, Mountain Lion, Wolf, and Bear, and, when the gods are organizing the Mountain Lion, Bear, and Giant societies, they give them for medicine bits of the hearts. In Oraibi war ceremonial a powder made of hearts taken from slain enemies is put into the medicine bowl.[627]

37. RITES OF CONTACT OR CONTAGION

Casual physical contacts appear to be much less common among Pueblos or other Indian peoples than among ourselves, and physical contact when it does occur has more significance, just as breathing in from anybody means more than kissing. A person must be a benefactor or a source of power for you to pass your hands down his body or arms,[628] or to rub your back on his picture.*

Belief in the efficacy of contact or in contagion is expressed variously as when ritual corn, beans, or spruce are placed in granary or field shrine, or when Acoma warriors when they first saw horses rubbed their sweat on themselves[629] just as an Acoma or Santa Ana person today would touch a laid-out deer and then

---

* As an Acoman shaman may do today before sucking out disease (Stirling).

pass her or his hand over face or body,* or when the Hopi crook
of longevity is touched by racers or others, or when an ear of
corn is passed down the body of a woman in labor to hasten
delivery (Sia), or when at the conclusion of war ritual in the
Oraibi winter solstice ceremony those present either sip the
medicine water from shell or cupped hand or, sucking it from a
stone, hold the stone to their heart in order "to make their heart
strong."[630]

Similarly, various sacrosanct objects may be pressed or drawn
against successive parts of the body: feet, knees, shoulders, face,
top of head, or in reversed direction. (Ritual whipping or sprinkling may also follow this successive pattern.) Again the corn
ear or ritual stick may be applied lightly to the body or merely
motioned toward it. At the Zuni winter solstice ceremony sponsors who give their godchildren not yet initiated two prayer-
sticks and four ears of corn, with the corn touch the shoulders,
forehead, and heart of the novice—making the sign of the cross, a
Catholic would say. In Hopi naming ritual the corn-ear dipper
is circled up and down in front of the godchild on conferring the
name. At the initiation into the Antelope society the chief waves
the *tiponi* toward each initiate, first toward the head, then
toward the lower part of the face, then somewhat lower, then
toward the heart, saying, "Long will you preserve your life and
you will grow up to be an old man."[631]

At Isleta, probably elsewhere, a circuit that is made with the
sacrosanct eagle feathers or with the clasped hands seems to have
the meaning of gathering in some influence either for one's self
or to bestow it on others, as when the chief waves his feathers
toward the Mother on the altar and then waves them toward the
audience, or when, after breathing on his clasped hands, he
moves them in circuit and says, "The Water People are sending
you all long life and health." The Isletan runner will make a like
gesture, as he asks for help from the Scalps or from the Sun. At
Laguna, in addressing the cosmic K'oвishtaiya, the arms are outstretched, palms upward, and drawn back with a circular mo-

* "Because the deer is pretty and not lazy" (Stirling), or to get a "blessing"
for hunting (White). Taos people will stroke the deer, saying, "Thank you!"

tion, four times. When the doctor addresses the Sun in presenting an infant, he makes this gesture;[632] light is life, and the
gesture is for longevity. As used by the San Ildefonso clown it is
a gesture of drawing down the clouds.[633] The Jemez kachina
who is to present a "doll" to a would-be mother raises or points
the "doll" in each direction and from the direction he motions it
to the recipient.[634]

As contact or touch may be efficacious it may likewise be
injurious. During the first four days of the Zuni Scalp ceremonial, were anyone to touch the initiate, his "elder brother," or
the women scalp-kickers, or were he to give them food directly,
he would risk death.[635] The Scalp itself is dangerous. "Should
anyone by mistake touch you, may no evil consequences befall
him," prays the Scalp chief.[636] The widowed is dangerous and
should not be touched, for four days. When Lina Zuni became
a widow, her grandfather said to her, "You must stay alone, in
the corner; only your little boy may hold you. No one must
touch you. It is very dangerous."[637] At kachina dances onlookers shrink away from contact with impersonators; they are
dangerous. People have been turned into Echo kachina merely
through contact with Echo man's baton or with his cuticle.[638]

Witches have the power to kill merely through touch (Zuni),[639]
just as broken bones may be mended by the touch of the lightning-shocked.[640] Oraibi Snake society dancers must swallow
their own sputum during their dance with the snakes, for should
they spit it out and anyone step on it or come in contact with it,
he would swell up and, if not discharmed, burst.[641] (In Zuni tale
a baby becomes a snake through contact with snake skin.)[642]

All sacrosanct objects are dangerous, unless properly handled,
by those who know about them. Places where they are kept,
such as back rooms or shrines, are taboo to outsiders; trespass
may call for initiation into the group to overcome the danger; if
initiation is not possible, the trespasser may be ritually whipped
and ritually fined, making a present to his "father" (Zuni).[643]
Sometimes masks or other fetishes have to be moved into another house. This is usually done during the performance in
which the object is being used, in order that the proper handler

serve as mover. When none knows the proper ritual for fetish or other dangerous object, it is buried, "put away in the hills."

38. Continence: Fasting

During periods of special ceremonial activity continence is exacted, whether the performer continues to live at home or retreats to kiva or ceremonial room. Fasting may or may not accompany continence; but continence, at Zuni and probably elsewhere, is essential to being *teshkwi*, sacred.[*]

Zuni Rain chiefs observe continence during their four- or eight-day retreats, i.e., when they "make their days." Similarly, Hopi chiefs and their helpers are continent for four or eight days during ceremonial, and in some cases for four days after its close. Pekwin must also observe continence after his announcement of winter or summer solstice and on many other occasions. In fact, after a man had served as Pekwin for a year or so, unbroken chastity was expected of him.[†] After their monthly prayer-stick-planting, all Zuni society members and all kachina depositors are continent four days. During Shalako all impersonators are continent, the Koyemshi for sixteen days. During their eight-day retreat at the Kachina initiation the twelve Salimobia impersonators not only observe continence but are supposed not even to mention a woman. When they go out to fetch wood, they go before daybreak and return after nightfall (a Koyemshi rule also) to avoid seeing women.

Kachina impersonators are always expected to observe continence while their paint is on and usually for four days before (Hopi, Keres) or after (Zuni)[‡] their dance. Acoma impersonators of the K'oBishtaiya kachina are continent for eighteen days afterward, and medicine men engaged in the ceremony, for four

---

[*] Keresan, *gaoɒyash* (White 4:188, n. 13) or *Kauchü'* (Parsons 20:113); Hopi, *kyakyauna* or *kyala* (Stephen 4: Glossary).

[†] This attitude has changed. Stevenson (2:169, n. *b*) and I were both told about it; but Bunzel found no evidence for it (Bunzel 2:505).

[‡] Summer kachina impersonators, excepting chiefs, do not plant prayer-sticks and so do not observe continence after their dance (Bunzel 2:507). In some kivas impersonators are *teshkwi* two days *before* a dance (Bunzel 5:850).

days. In the maskless kachina Spruce dance of Isleta the K'apio clown impersonators are continent for six days.

During their four-day treatment and for four days afterward Acoma doctors observe continence.[644] Sia doctors are continent for four days; and continence is expected of the patient and his family.[645] During the Cochiti novitiate into a curing society, a period of four years (are not days or months being called years [see pp. 73, 312, n. *), continence is required.[646] Continence during ceremonial is required of Isletan shamans and Corn groups. Every Zuni is continent during solstice ceremonies and every Hopi at the winter solstice, since all the men "go in" from one night to four nights.

Continence was required of an Acoman war party, on their return home, for thirty days; likewise, at Zuni, it was required of all members of the War society. For the first four days all the Zuni war party were *teshkwi* for themselves, planting prayer-sticks at the end of the period. During a second four days, the scalp-takers were *teshkwi* for their victims, and the prayer-sticks planted at the close were for them. Members of the War society were *teshkwi* during the first four days for the victim, during the second four days for themselves, and during a third four days for the War gods, their patrons. Besides, scalp-takers had to remain continent for a year, and then, before having intercourse with his wife, the scalper had to copulate with another woman, even if he were an elderly man.

Continence is observed four days before a communal hunt (Sia).[647] Four days before an antelope hunt at Isleta the war captains observed continence, and, at Mishongnovi, all participants.[648] Mishongnovi men observe continence four days before going on a salt-gathering trip, always a dangerous venture, and in the old days Zuni was not visited en route lest the gatherers see women and they or their burros break out in sores.[649]

Falls on the part of Zuni Shalako or Koyemshi impersonators are imputed to incontinence, which made them ritualistically weak. Did not the stick-swallowers of the Wood society remain continent the night before performing their rite, their throat would become sore. Were not the two girls and the man in the

Muwaiye ceremony to remain continent four nights before, their headpieces would drop off or the paint on their face would run. At Laguna, if the weather is unpropitious during a dance, if there is windstorm instead of rainstorm, it is suspected that some dancer may have violated the rule of continence before or during the performance. There was a violent windstorm during the performance of the Yakohanna dance in February, 1919, and after the dance "their father" called a meeting to discover the offender. During the dance it had been observed that from one headdress in particular the feathers had been blown off and the turquoise paint had run.* The wearer of this headdress had been seen to visit the house of a woman with whom he was known to be intimate, ostensibly to take a dance doll to the woman's daughter. The case was closed, the offender was dipped through an ice hole in the river.

It is related at Zuni that once the Shumaikoli mask stuck to the face of the impersonator who had broken his continence taboo, and there are like Hopi, Tewa, and Jemez stories or beliefs. During a First Mesa performance of the long form of Powamu ceremony in which a girl and two men impersonate kachina, the girl and one of the men "tried at being sweethearts" on their way up from the kachina shrine. When they returned to the shrine to unmask, they could not remove their masks. So now they tell the young people not to think of love-making at this time lest their masks stick to them. The Tewa tale runs that the impersonator of the kachina chief asked his sweetheart to meet him in a corner of a ruined house during the dance so he could lift his mask and show her that he was indeed the kachina chief. The vigilant clowns saw the girl and caught the dancer. They tried to take off his mask, but "because he talked with the girl" his mask stuck.

Other accidents may be due to incontinence. At Zuni accidents through horses may follow incontinence after prayer-stick-planting. We recall the Isletan tale about the horse who threw the incontinent War captain.[650] Were the Hopi kachina imper-

* The same consequences occur from incontinence during four days before a kachina dance on First Mesa or at Cochiti (Goldfrank 3:104).

sonator incontinent before his dance, he would be very sick, he might die,[651] no doubt of one of the diseases sent by the kachina, possibly rheumatism. The rheumatic who is treated during the Powamu ceremony must observe the kachina impersonator's taboos: continence and fasting from meat and salt.[652]

Ritual fasting is not as a rule thoroughgoing, certain articles of food merely, such as salt, meat, or grease, being taboo, or meals are restricted to one a day as in the four-day fasts preliminary to dancing kachina or as in the fasts of the Rain chiefs of Zuni, of Hopi chiefs or Acoma doctors, of the Zuni scalp-taker or initiate into the War society,* of the widowed[653] Zuni or of the Hopi woman during her twenty-day confinement.[654] Taos boy initiates may eat only native food, and the initiate into Isletan medicine societies fasts from wheaten dishes. Sia shamans in retreat eat no Mexican or American food, and like Keresan shamans generally in retreat they fast from salt and grease.[655] During Isletan and Jemez fasts round cakes of blue corn meal are supplied, also mush made from a wild water-plant. Corn cakes with yeast are made for the fasting Rain chiefs of Zuni whose fast from grease as well as from meat and salt is so strictly observed that they must have their own water jar and gourd dipper lest some one with greasy mouth contaminate jar or dipper.[656] In Tewa tale only rain water may be drunk at rain retreats.[657] In the Zuni summer solstice ceremony kachina including Koyemshi may not drink the night they come in nor until noon the following day; but, if it rains, they may drink.[658]

The fast of Koyemshi before and during the Molawia ceremony, a day and night, is complete, from food or drink. They begin to fast after a formal midnight meal, four times "their father" dips his bread into the stew set before them. He may dip fast or slowly, but at the fourth dip they must stop eating (like Hopi guests at ritualized working-parties or in fact like mannerly Hopi guests at any time or like sometime Zuni guests).

---

* In his ten-day fast from flesh and salt all his food had to be served cold, hot food taken at this time would make him corpulent (Stevenson 2:587). Hot food is taboo for one year. This taboo applies to mourners, particularly to the widowed, for four days (Bunzel 2:502).

The following midnight "their father" gives each a drink which means *teshkwi* is over. Were their fast to be violated, grasshopper and coyote pests would come and eat in the gardens and fields. This mimetic notion or rite covers other persons, for none may eat in the dance court or at Red Bank during the performance of Molawia, lest "they come and eat." Flora told me that once when she was among the girls to race at Red Bank, a War chief "got after" her because she put some snow in her mouth.

Here is an interpretation of fasting as a rite of sympathetic magic. There are other like instances. The Zuni Wood society abstain from duck eggs. The Wood society are stick-swallowers, and duck eggs are bad for the throat, "ducks have a weak voice!"* At the winter solstice the Hunters' or Coyote society do not join in the fast from meat because Coyote is a meat-eater. Again, fasting may attract the attention of the Spirits and arouse pity or interest,† a notion very familiar among Apache‡ or Plains tribes.

But fasting as well as continence or other forms of abstinence is primarily compulsive or will magic. Pekwin in his summer retreat for rain does not fetch spring water like the other Zuni Rain chiefs; he sets the bowl outside when it rains; until it rains he has no medicine water. Pekwin is in retreat "in order to try himself."659 The abstinent are trying themselves, that is, trying their power, not altogether over themselves in our sense, but over

---

* To a conspicuous instance of food abstinence at Zuni (and Laguna) no key of interpretation has yet been found: the abstinence of the Shi'wanakwe society of Zuni and the Kurena of Laguna and Cochiti from jackrabbit (see p. 22) and from the Rocky Mountain bee plant eaten as greens (Parsons 15:333; Bunzel 2:502). Jackrabbit is a Mescalero Apache taboo (Opler 3:25).

Abstinence from salt is a very widespread practice associated no doubt with different ideas among different peoples. Possibly one conceptual factor in the Southwest was identification with nonsalt-eating animals. See pp. 189, 515, and Parsons 53:38 ff.

† Compare the effect upon the Spirits of going barefoot. Hopi farmers plant barefoot, "to make the clouds come out." The Clouds say, "Let's make rain, to cool their feet" (Parsons 40:91).

‡ Compare the Mescalero Apache rule for hunters to set forth on an empty stomach in order that the deer take pity on them (Opler 3:18). Laguna hunters fast (Boas 2:297).

nature,* over the gods or through the gods. "We shall be strong! We shall be firm!" is a Hopi response to prayer.[660]

Secondarily, the continent may be separating themselves or others, their mates, from their "power" or from contacts with the supernatural which is always dangerous. This might explain the continence taboo on scalpers or the widowed[661] or on the Hopi Lakon society woman who wins the race and must remain continent for four days "because she has carried the society standard."

39. SILENCE: SECRETIVENESS

Speech is restricted or taboo in certain ritual circumstances. While being purified for four days after her husband's death, the Zuni widow "should not speak."[662] Salt-gatherers had to preserve silence or soberness while getting out the salt (Mishongnovi, Acoma, Cochiti),[663] as did the Zuni quarry party while tempering the slabs for baking wafer-bread.† The Hopi antelope-hunter might not joke or laugh (Second Mesa).[664] Hopi snake-hunters talk not at all or in whispers,[665] and this is sometimes the rule in Hopi kiva ceremonials. Masked impersonations often have a call, but they may not speak; nor may maskless impersonations, except formally. After the Isletan Corn chief has swallowed his root medicine and performed his dance, for some time he remains silent, because "his power is still in him." Silence is part of the concentration that compels results. Quite literally is demonstrated the power of silence.

"Our ways would lose their power if they were known," says the Taos townsman. "People have learned about the ways of the other pueblos, and those pueblos have lost their power." Here is a profound conviction about the reasonableness of secretiveness plus a little Pueblo conceit. The same attitude is found elsewhere. The witch who confesses loses his power. In a Tewa witch assemblage the witches are unable to transform as usual

---

* If a Zuni is continent for four years, he qualifies for power to cause an "earthquake" (Benedict 3: II, 82).

† Cushing 6:329; Stevenson 2:362. A spoken word or any excitement would impair or blight the stone. Compare Mishongnovi, Beaglehole 3:59.

into animals, because somebody is spying.[666] Ordinary society exclusiveness may be explained in part from this point of view. Any Zuni "who gives away" his prayers loses some of the power they impart. "I have given you all my religion," said Nick to Dr. Bunzel, "and I have no way to protect myself." Nick was sick and he was relating a dream which he believed portended death; within two days he died. "He gave away his religion as if it were of no value," commented a Zuni chief, "and now he is dead."[667]

In English, Zuni and other Pueblos will refer to being secretive as being *stingy*; like Navaho[668] or many Indian peoples they feel they are losing something by communicating it; you will actually draw it from them. Once Dr. Bunzel sprinkled meal on a mask. It was reported to the Kachina society chief who became very indignant. "One doesn't give corn meal away for nothing, one always asks for something in one's thoughts, and the people are afraid you will take all their good luck (blessings) with you when you go, because of your corn meal."[669]

The secretiveness of the Pueblo about religion is developed in various ways, by various sanctions: being talked about, confiscation of property, imprisonment,* death or threat of death; but in last analysis secretiveness is founded on the concept or feeling that power communicated is power lost.

This conviction may be associated, of course, with the more generalized attitude that reticence precludes attack: your critic or enemy does not suppress or purloin what he knows nothing about. The peculiar secretiveness about the kachina is due to opposition from the Church which was once influenced perhaps by Spanish anti-mask laws, and possibly to the fact that dance groups were once warrior groups which are always secretive

---

* Place in a circle traced about his feet the prisoner is forbidden to move from a standing or sitting position on pain of being shot by the War captains (Dumarest, 197, n. 3, 201; White 4:23). Dumarest writes that penalties against betraying secret matters or against disbelief were rigorous at San Felipe and Santo Domingo, but of little weight at Jemez; yet recently a Jemez man writes me he was deprived of his water rights for a year because he was suspected (quite mistakenly) of giving information.

about war magic* or organization and exclude not only aliens from ceremonial but their own children and women. On First Mesa women may not look out upon the Wüwüchim night patrols by the war societies, and my window was covered over, just as it was in Jemez to preclude seeing the kachina as they passed by. Walpi windows are covered so townspeople will not see certain kachina preparations the last day of Powamu.[670] In Acoma tradition it was planned that only "grandmothers" were to know that kachina were merely impersonators.[671] San Felipe kachina dancers go to a mesa ten miles away for rehearsal so that the women and children will not know what they are up to. Finally it must be remembered that the gifts or blessings of the kachina are for the Pueblos only, not for outsiders, so why should outsiders be admitted to their dances?

40. VIGIL

At Zuni during Shalako night everybody present in the dance houses is expected to stay awake—"to help with their prayers," or rather with a prayerful state of mind, much as we expect of churchgoers not to sleep in church. But at Zuni anyone dropping off runs the risk of being whipped, lightly, if any kachina with a yucca switch happens to be present.† Once at this all-night ceremonial there sat next to me an old man and a little boy; whenever the child began to nod, the old man would give him a gentle jerk. At the rain ceremony of the Sia Knife society, a boy member who falls asleep will be awakened by having his face tickled with a feather.[672] With the bill of his stuffed wild duck Kiaklo will peck anyone in kiva falling asleep over the long narrative prayer.[673]

The night at Zuni before the "kachina go" the Koyemshi are required to stay awake in return for the gifts they are to receive the following day from their father's clan. One year the Koyem-

---

* Note that at noon the day the snakes are washed in kiva an Oraibi Snake man announces that all the townspeople are to withdraw indoors, an injunction less promptly and scrupulously heeded today, remarks Voth, than formerly (Voth 3:339).

† This rule also holds for First Mesa in its borrowed Shalako celebration (Stephen 4:437, n. 1).

shi grumbled over the exaction, and were sharply criticized; they were to get so much the next day, they should work for it. Similarly Pekwin tells the people who are to dance around the scalp pole:

> Even though you ache from singing,
> Even though you fain would sleep,
> In order to win the enemy's waters,
> His seeds,
> His wealth,
> His power,
> His strong spirit,
> To win these,
> Throughout the nights,
> Throughout the days,
> Tirelessly, unwearied
> You shall live.[674]

In the case of society members falling asleep at Shalako, it is said that they who fall asleep will lose their property to those who stay awake. Such magical penalty likewise befalls sleepers on the last night of taboo of the winter solstice ceremony. After the Shitsukya kachina has passed the house, the ten-day accumulation of refuse and ashes is to be carried out. The first person to leave the house will get the things of those asleep in the house. The second person to go out will get half the things; the next person, a quarter of the things, and so on. A Tewa folk tale relates how certain townspeople lost their kachina masks to two naughty little boys who took them from where they were hanging, while the people slept. "You people, when you slept, you did not take care of those Oxuwah." On the recovery of the masks the people were adjured, "Watch them well, you had a hard droughty summer because you did not take care of them."

One night during the Hopi Powamu ceremonial every man has to go to kiva, otherwise he will be fetched by kachina, and in the kiva he has to sit up all night. Were he to lie down and sleep, he would be whipped. "This night we must be very careful of the plants," i.e., the beans which are an omen for the year's fertility. A person sleeping at a Hopi ceremony is likely to retard the growth of beans or corn. The sleepy ones make the corn sleepy.[675]

Probably some such idea of sympathetic magic runs through other Pueblo rules about not sleeping on ritual occasions, this idea and a feeling of compelling results by staying awake. After Ne'wekwe has found the fleeing Corn Maidens, he returns to the council of the chiefs and says, "I cannot bring them back alone. I need your help. Go into retreat, do not stir, do not urinate, do not drink water, do not eat, do not smoke, do not speak to each other, do not sleep!" Says the Town chief, "No matter how sleepy we are, we must not let our minds wander. We must think of nothing else." And so for four days the chiefs do not eat or drink or speak or sleep, and the Corn Maidens return.[676]

41. RETREAT

Being inside or going in* is the usual way of referring to the withdrawal into kiva or ceremonial room that ethnologists have called retreat. It is not only a period of continence and fasting from certain foods but of sleeping and eating† in the ceremonial place. Once you go in, you may not come out, except temporarily, until the period concludes.

The usual period of "making or counting their days" is four days or eight days, the chief or chiefs going in sooner or staying longer than mere members. The minor Rain chieftaincies of Zuni go in for four days, the major Rain chieftaincies, for eight days. At Shalako the Koyemshi clowns who are referred to as Kachina Town chiefs are in for sixteen days, the longest of all retreats.

Retreat provides good practical conditions for the performance of time-consuming ritual, for ritual "work"; altar rituals, prayer-stick-making or preparing paraphernalia in general. It is also a time for telling tales or myths and for learning by watching or assisting one's seniors. But, together with other forms of abstinence, retreat may be considered primarily as a condition for concentration on the "work," a form of withdrawal to exert religious compulsion.[677]

* Zuni, *u'pe*, to be inside; Hopi, *yungwa*, to go in; Keres (Santo Domingo) *ᵥyinyimĕ*; Jemez, *peyup*, fast, or *peyuhtsote* (*tsote*, go in). Isletans say, "Our Fathers are inside."

† This rule is variable. At Zuni, curing society members in retreat may eat at home (Bunzel 2:505).

However, not all the time of a ceremony is spent in grave concentration between rituals; there is easy conversation on any
subject, and during dance rehearsal there may even be a certain
amount of skylarking, particularly by Hopi and particularly in
women's ceremonies. Voth describes a kiva supper party during
the first evening of Oaqöl as "seasoned and flavored by a lively
conversation, by jokes and laughter, of which Hopi are very
fond."[678] Even Hopi snake-hunters, silent and grave while making or consecrating their prayer-feathers, in getting ready to
hunt talk freely and joke and laugh as usual (Mishongnovi).[679]

42. Burlesque, Caricature, Satire: Gluttony and Filth-eating: Obscenity: Speaking Backward

Burlesque, caricature, and satire are characteristic of the
Clown societies and of Women's societies, but kachina and others
also employ these methods of public amusement or castigation.
The subjects of caricature are other peoples—Indian, Mexican,
American—and their ways, likewise ceremonial organization at
home.[680] Sacred personages and respected sacerdotalists are not
immune. The Koyemshi of Zuni and the Hopi clowns dance
alongside the kachina, mimicking them. At the fiesta of San
José at Laguna in 1921 the two masked clowns who used whip
or lariat against crowding lookers-on and led the way in and
out of the plaza would try to whip up the dancers with their
lariat or would imitate their steps.[681] At Jemez I saw a burlesque
of the society that had just been holding a rain ceremony, at the
dance after the close of the ceremony. During the Turtle dance
at San Juan in 1925 the Grandfather masks performed a mock
Catholic wedding to the unbounded enjoyment of both Indian
and Mexican onlookers.

Gluttony or mock gluttony and the eating or drinking of voidings are also traits of the behavior of the clowns. Also sexual
display. This type of behavior might be interpreted as phallic,
as, for example, the realistic vulva effigies carried by the Singers
society in the Hopi Wüwüchim ceremony; but the copulatory

burlesques of First Mesa[682] or Koyemshi references to bestiality*
must be described as obscene in quite the same sense as we conceive of such sexual expressions when designed for amusement.

Possibly ritual obscenity and gluttony are related psychologically with inverse speech, as departure from normal behavior.†
Again, drenching with urine or smearing with ordure may be
thought of as curative practices. There is no direct Pueblo evidence; but the indirect evidence that may be drawn from Jicarilla Apache practice (see p. 415, n. *) is strong. Also in evidence is
the fact that the gluttons or Ne'wekwe of Zuni cure all diseases of
the stomach.[683] They eat anything‡ to prove that they have
medicine to cure anything.

Speaking backward or saying the opposite of what you mean
is characteristic of the Ne'wekwe of Zuni, the Koshare of Santa
Ana, the Black Eyes moiety of Isleta, and the Ts'un'tatabo'sh of
Jemez. When Paiyatuma, the original Ne'we, is summoned by
the War chiefs, he sits down on a refuse heap, saying he is about
to make a breakfast of it. "Why and wherefore do you two
cowards come not after me?" he asks. "I will not go with you,"
and straightway he follows them to the dance court.[684] Just so
the Isletan Black Eye chief will say to his Red Eye colleague,
"I do not need you at my place," to summon him to his ceremonial chamber. Kumpa, the Scalp chief of Isleta and shooter

---

* Bunzel 5:952. "Our daylight fathers, our daylight mothers, after so many
days, eight days, on the ninth day you will copulate with rams." In characteristic vein the clowns are picturing the most sacred ceremonialists doing the most
monstrous thing imaginable.

† The Jicarilla Apache who have borrowed the Black Eyes or Kossa from the
Pueblos make this interpretation. "See the Chashjini!" a parent will say to a
child, "he is doing a shameful thing (mock copulation, for example) which you
should not do" (Opler). A living warning! This fits in with Pueblo ideology; as
sheriffs or disciplinary enforcers of propriety, the clowns may be violators of
propriety.

‡ "I have seen one of them gather about him his melons, green and ripe, raw
peppers, bits of stick and refuse, unmentionable water, live puppies—or dead,
no matter—peaches, stones and all, in fact everything soft enough or small
enough to be forced down his gullet, including wood-ashes and pebbles, and,
with the greatest apparent gusto, consume them all at a single sitting" (Cushing
6:621).

of witches, talks "corners way," instead of naming the cardinal points he names the points between, or for the fifth direction instead of saying up, down, and middle, he says middle, down, and up. He mentions the sunset before the sunrise.* In the emergence myth of the Shuma'kwe society of Zuni, the society warriors also use inverted speech,[685] as does the Koyemshi warrior.

43. Jugglery: Tricks with Fire and Boiling Water: Stick-swallowing

These ritual feats are characteristic of certain societies: Big and Little Firebrand and Wood societies of Zuni; Keresan and Jemez Fire and Flint societies, Tubahi society of Cochiti and Jemez; Yayatü and Nasosotan or Nakyawimpkya stick-swallowers of Hopi; and Laguna Fathers of Isleta. The performances are in order more particularly at initiations.

Some of the tricks are making corn or wheat plants grow under your eyes, drawing grain from wall pictures or from corn-ear fetishes, getting spruce from a distant mountain within a few minutes, producing a live animal (rabbit or deer), making feathers or other objects levitate, tarnishing silver, or shriveling leather. Sia shamans, reports a townsman, "can make a bowl dance on the floor, with nobody near it. They can call clouds and make it rain in their room. If they ask Boshaianyi for corn, it will fall from the ceiling. They can call in different kinds of animals, and their fur will fall from the ceiling."[686] Yayatü could parachute off a cliff in a basket, transform inanimate things into living creatures, and once after eating a rabbit stew they laid the bones together, covered them over, and changed them into four rabbits which ran up the ladder and jumped across the kiva hatch and off to the valley. Another time the Yayatü terrified a visitor from Isleta who wore a black hat and fancy garters. They covered the hat and garters with a white blanket, and soon

---

* Cliff bird, Canyon wren (Keresan, Shuti, assistant War chief or Koshare) and the Kumpa War chief of the Chiefs of the Directions direct the Pecos survivor about to enter into a trial with witches to say, "We are down in the mountain, at the bottom," when actually they are at the top (Lummis 3:140 ff.). This inversing formula appears to give power, and suggests an interpretation for backward speech in general.

something was seen to move under it, and, when it was removed, the hat was found transformed into a raven and the garters into a snake.* They called to the Isletan to come and get his hat and garters, but he ran off afraid, crying he did not want them.[687]

Fire tricks were among the feats of the Yayatü society. They once took a Walpi man below the mesa and trussed him up by hands and feet in a squat posture. They dug a hole in the sand large enough to hold him, and in it they made a big fire, and, after it was reduced to embers, they put the man in this hot pit and covered him with embers and with an airtight covering of sandy clay. The victim's brother came among the Yayatü, lashing at them with a rope and clamoring for his brother. They disclaimed all knowledge of him and told him to look in the pit and see for himself, which he did but found nothing in it but embers. The man went on to Walpi where the Yayatü were dancing and found his brother dancing with them.† His brother was not entirely unharmed for he showed marks of roasting on shoulders and hips, and his queue was burned off.[688]

Zuni and Keresan societies, more particularly the Fire (Firebrand) and Flint societies, perform fire and hot-water tricks, also sword-swallowing, at initiations. At Zuni, in 1884, Stevenson saw coals taken into the mouth for periods of from thirty to sixty seconds, also burning cornhusks.[689] Again she describes a wild scene of pelting with burning cornhusks at an initiation of the Shuma'kwe society, inferably into their Fire order, at which both men and women were "too crazed with excitement to be conscious of physical pain."[690] Sia Fire shamans walk on live coals or eat them, and in their dance the following day they swallow long sharp sticks.[691] Cochiti Fire shamans take burning straw, put out the flame, and put the ashes into their mouth.[692] After a four-day retreat Acoma Fire shamans dig a shallow pit in front of their house. Around pit and house is drawn a line of ashes and, if anyone trespass, he has to be initiated. A fire is built in the pit, the War captains having ordered the townspeople

* Isleta's mythical serpent was produced from a garter. See p. 264.

† Perhaps it was something of this kind that Zuni shamans had in mind in telling Bourke that they could kill and then restore to life (Bourke 1:471).

to contribute wood. Women members bring out four pots of water and build fires under them. From their baskets they throw meal into the boiling water, stirring it with their bare hands. They take out the mush and throw balls to the people on the housetops. All the members dance in anti-sunwise circuit around the pit, while they sing four songs. The chief stirs the live coals and ashes with his hands, then he and the other men jump into the pit. A woman member throws a basket of shelled corn into the pit, and on top of all the men throw the novice. After he is taken out, the chief scatters the ashes and embers and the corn kernels, and the onlookers pick up the parched kernels.

This fire performance is followed at Acoma as at Sia by an exhibition of stick-swallowing.[693] Some of the "sticks" are saplings whittled down with the foliage left at the top, others are flat, painted boards. (Both types are used by Zuni and Hopi. The Zuni stick is somewhat curved and is surmounted with feathers.)[694] Women accompany men in their stick-swallowing dance, but do not swallow sticks. At Zuni women formerly did swallow sticks. The initiates have to go through with it, sometimes with difficulty (Zuni, Acoma). It is reported that death has resulted from stick-swallowing. Like kachina dancers, the stick-swallowers come and go, dancing four times in the morning and four times in the afternoon (Acoma, Zuni).

Stick-swallowing is practiced at Jemez by subdivisions or orders of the Arrowhead (Flint) and Fire societies;[695] and at Zuni by orders of the Big Firebrand and Wood societies,[696] the Wood society conducting its exhibition jointly with the War society. Hopi stick-swallowers are an order or affiliation of the War society.

Stick-swallowing and most of the other feats are reported or interpreted, when interpreted at all, as convincing manifestation of power, as, for example, in Isleta Shunad ceremonial: The chief begins to dance to the singing of his assistants, and presently a rabbit is seen in his hand, there through his power. He gives the rabbit to the Hunt chief, who says, "Thanks! thanks! thanks!" and in turn gives it to the War chief who stands out in the middle of the room showing the rabbit to the people and saying, "What power our Fathers have, to bring in a live rabbit! Believe in them!"[697] (Rabbit from hat and yet how different!)

Similar manifestations of power are referred to in myth or tale. "Let us see who has more power!" says Węide to Dios. So God shoots at a tree with a gun; but Kachina chief shatters the tree with a bolt of lightning.[698] Again and again the War Brothers display their power; and in tale immigrant chiefs show off by making rain as a kind of passport.[699] On their way to Zuni the starving people are led by two Walpi chiefs who, possessed of power over space, "gather the earth together" to shorten the journey.[700] Such power is frequently imputed to shamans (Keres, Isleta) or to supernaturals (compare Apache); but all are outdone by the Spanish nun, María de Jesús who in 1620 began to make trips from Spain to New Mexico, sometimes doing twenty thousand miles a day.[701]

44. OMEN*

Trustees of masks deduce omens from the appearance or condition of their mask (Zuni). One year the buckskin of a Shalako mask was torn, and the kiva Shalako manager told the people of the house where the mask was kept that it meant misfortune for their house or his. "Right after Shalako the aunt who helped us cook for Shalako died, and we knew that this was what he meant."[702] The Saint also "tells what will happen." If it looks dry about her bower when she is set out in her dance, there will be drought. "Last year at the Santu dance," related David, "the first day when I looked at the Santu her eyes were all right, but the second day they were rolling, like the dead. That winter my cousin died alone in a sheep camp, and for three days the sheep were by themselves." One year spots of blood appeared on the Saint, and, in the dance that followed, two men were accidentally shot. During a performance of the Owinahaiye war dance two girls were similarly wounded, one dying. The day before a basket of prayer-feathers in the War chief's house was

* Zuni, *teliuna;* Hopi, *toauta;* Tewa, *piyepoʻ.*

seen to rise in the air,* and the War chief had a warning called out to the people.[703] Indeed any self-movement by sacrosanct objects, like an arrowpoint on an altar[704] or the ball that is to be used in the game of hidden-ball, "means something."

In visiting shrines, particularly the more distant houses of the Spirits, omens are looked for. When the Mishongnovi salt-gatherer deposits his prayer-stick under Zuni Salt Lake and withdraws his hand, if a bit of cornhusk is sticking to it, it is a good sign; a hair is a bad sign.[705] Ko‘t‘ye of Laguna told me that on both his trips for salt to the Zuni Salt Lake where lives Salt Woman, the War gods, and the Gumeyoish, he saw growing corn and wheat pictured in the water, as we would say, a favorable omen. An unfavorable omen would have been a recumbent figure, an omen of death. There is a small pit on the summit of San Mateo (Mount Taylor), from which the Clouds emerge. Here, too, corn and wheat may be seen growing when the year is to be good.† The shamans of Sia claimed they saw melons and corn, on looking down into the crater house of the War gods in Sandía mountains,‡ (? the shrine in the "southeast corner").

At shrines or elsewhere the position or condition of prayer-sticks may be a matter of omen. At the Zuni winter solstice ceremony and at Shalako, prayer-sticks are placed in certain house walls, for the six directions. These prayer-sticks are inspected later by the kachina, Pa'utiwa or Shulawitsi. If the sticks have fallen down, there will be sickness. In pilgrimage to Black Mountain, to the spring Kishyuba, one of the headquarters of Hopi kachina, after the prayer-sticks are deposited, the bearers withdraw out of sight. On returning, if they find a stick fallen, it is a bad sign; if moisture has accumulated on the offerings or on

* See below, also p. 448, for the position of feathers as omen. Feather levitation is familiar in Navaho jugglery.

† When I looked into it, I saw only some electric light bulbs discarded by the American surveyors camping near by and unaware of the sanctity of their dump pit.

‡ Stevenson 1:57. Only the "good of heart" were said to be able to see such things, according to Stevenson. Rather was the sight accounted an omen, I surmise.

the ground, it is a good sign.[706] At sweet-corn roasts if the pray-er-sticks which are bundled with sacrosanct ears of corn for the oven come out unscorched, it is a good sign; damaged sticks mean poor crops or sickness in the family (Oraibi).[707] Analogous-ly on First Mesa "road-markers" may yield omen. First Mesa fetchers of spruce may deposit on their way to the forest the "road-marker" or feathered string the chief has made for them, and on it they put a stone so the wind will not blow it away. On their return journey if they find the "road" still there, it is good; if its position has changed, it is bad; for if anything happens to the "road," something else will surely happen. At Isleta the prayer-feathers deposited in a certain spring are said to be whirled about five times, then, if it is to be a good sign, they are drawn into the water.

Small footprints are a good sign to Hopi prayer-stick de-positors and also in the cave visited by the Eagle hunt society of Jemez.* At Laguna on the eve of a deer hunt, meal or dough images were offered to "animals" (mountain lion?) and, if the images disappeared, it meant that deer would be killed. At Zuni a small sand mound was raised and covered with meal, meal being also sprinkled round about. If deer tracks were found over-night in the meal, it betokened a successful hunt. Like mounds are one of the hunt features of Shalako. Tracks or droppings of sheep near by are a good sign; a crack in the meal lying thick over the mound is a bad sign.† In the ceremony of 1915 cracks were found in the mound; disaster was foretold. It proved to be disaster, according to town talk, for the visiting Navaho, for the whiskey they had brought with them to trade was con-fiscated by the American Farmer and the Governor.

Gamesters and stick-racers (Zuni), hunters and warriors (Zuni, Hopi), would listen for omens. In gathering medicine plants for an initiation into the Zuni Cactus society, a war society, the party leader will deposit an offering a little distance

* Dumarest, 193. Presumably the footprints are those of the diminutive War gods. Compare, for Sia, Stevenson 1:57.

† Possibly because landslide and fissures in the ground are ominous of mis-fortune. See p. 214.

from the camp and then sit still, waiting for omen.[708] On the eve
of a raid, a Zuni warrior would go to the riverbank at night, plant
prayer-sticks to the dead and bury wafer-bread, and listen for
signs. He would take four steps back from the river, sit down
and listen, doing this four times. Thus, without looking back,*
he would go directly to the house of the War chief. After a ritual
smoke he would be asked what he had heard. Hoofbeats or river
sounds or owl hoots or the sound of lips smacking were all good
signs. To hear nothing was a bad sign. Another account: The
war party has started and camped for the night; the two leaders
go off a little ways and "make the world" (a meal ground altar ?).
Sitting down they sing male (war) songs. They deposit an offering of wafer-bread, cigarettes, and prayer-sticks. A little way off
they sit down and listen. If they hear nothing, they sit down
again a little farther on. Then a branch breaks or there is a
thump or the footfalls of an animal. If they find the ground
trampled, it is revealed that they will encounter people with
animals, and they will go on to the enemy's country. Bear tracks
are not good, and the War chiefs will have the party return to
town for the night.[709]

There are omens or signs of an approaching enemy. At Taos
the owl was said to hoot in warning; and in Hopi-Tewa tale Owl
Boy is directed, "If an enemy approach, come and tell the
people." When Coyote called out once and once only at night,
it meant to the San Juan War chief that the Navaho were on top
of them.[710] A rabbit and a certain little brown bird "talking"
together was another warning of Navaho.[711] The Navaho scalps
themselves give warning at Taos, by making a noise and falling
down.

The Hopi hunt leader or chief would have his men sit in concentric circles, he and a few other men making the innermost
circle, which was kept open to the east, the chief sitting to the
right of the opening. All smoked. Two men appointed by the

* This is a recurrent admonition in omen-getting or other ritual, particularly
at Zuni. The only recorded interpretation is in connection with Hopi salt-
gatherers. As they leave the lake, if one looks back, his spirit will never leave the
lake, and he will soon be near unto death (Beaglehole 3:54).

chief and given prayer-feathers would leave camp to deposit the prayer-feathers. On putting them down, together with their mountain-lion fetishes, the men would withdraw a little distance and listen. On their return to camp the chief would give them a smoke and then ask what they had heard. The best signs are sounds of coyote* or crow because after the kill coyotes and crows come for the leavings, or of wolf, because it means that very night a wolf is chasing the deer that will be tired the next day and easy to kill. Another good sign is the ringing of a bell.† The sound of a man is a bad sign. Dream omens are believed in by Hopi, Cochiti, and Taos hunters.

"Our dreams will tell us," says the stick-race manager in a Zuni tale[712] after the team heard a crow when they were listening for omens. (It was a bad omen, but they did not know it.) Good omen would have been the sounds of owl or hummingbird or of water in the stream or of a bank caving in. Should a water bird be heard flying northward at night prior to the Home-going kachina ceremony, it means a heavy rain before the kachina leave (Mishongnovi).[713]

In his account of how he conducted the Hopi Water Serpent performances Crow-Wing mentions listening for omens. "When we got down to the spring I had to listen to what I might hear. I heard a water-bird singing, and we were very glad for it. Just then the rain started to fall. It was raining when we came up." At the spring visited in the Flute ceremony they listen for the sounds of frogs and of flowing water.[714] The messengers to Black Mountain to gather spruce for the Home-going kachina report one year that at the kachina spring, when they put down their prayer-sticks, they heard a big storm. "The people are very glad about it." On their return from a spring, members of the Kachina society of Cochiti will tell of what they encountered on the way. Rabbit, deer, or snake are good omens; a crow is bad.[715]

At the beginning of the Snake-Antelope ceremony the Antelope chief catches a rattlesnake and, after bathing it and attach-

---

* At Taos Coyote calls out to predict deer.

† A bad sign on Second Mesa (Beaglehole 2:6).

ing a prayer-feather around its neck, the chief places the snake in a circle of meal. The direction in which the snake moves out of the circle will be the direction from which will come the rain spirits to be induced by the ceremony.[716]

Ritual ejection of fluid is observed as an omen, as when the Cochiti image of Water Serpent ejects water,* or fluid is ejected from the gourd penis of Ololo kachina of Zuni. If it flows evenly, it is a sign of well-being to the people; if jerkily, a sign of sickness. At San Felipe should the basket upset in which the Town chief keeps his stone fetishes or any of the figures fall out, the Town chief would know that "something was going to happen," some misfortune.[717]

At Cochiti, when people want to know the outcome of a project, they may send for a shaman who, after fasting, will draw a line of meal from the door to the opposite wall where the fetishes are set out. While the shaman sings, his corn-ear fetish will advance from its position on the meal line toward the door providing the outcome is to be favorable, otherwise it remains immobile. At other times the corn-ear fetish will be placed in a bowl behind which a large piece of cloth is stretched. If the outcome is to be favorable, the fetish will slowly rise up during the singing and move in the air from east to west.[718]

At Isleta, feathers are said to levitate, in curing ritual. The doctor encircles the patient five times with the feather; then the feather flies upward. When it drops, if it falls within the circle drawn about the patient, the patient will recover; if without the circle, he will die. If the kernel of corn which represents the witch-stolen heart of the patient is seared or mouldy (San Felipe) or, at Laguna, if one of the four representative kernels is missing, the patient will die.[719] After the Zuni Shuma'kwe doctor exorcises the patient through his yucca square which is tied at the corners, he rubs the corners between his palms, and, unless the knots come undone, the patient will die.[720] On the west side

* The note is fragmentary. I surmise that it is the way in which the water is ejected that is observed, not merely the fact of ejection. Also I surmise that at Zuni the way Water Serpent ejects water and seeds is also observed as a matter of omen.

of Laguna may still be seen part of the ruts in the flat rock where
the doctor pushed along a pebble under his foot to see whether or
not his patient would live; if the pebble slipped out from the line
or its loops, it forecasted death. There is a rocky grooved floor in
the mesa north of Zuni* where runners did the same thing to
gain assurance about betting on their race.[721]

In smoking their ritual pipe, Hopi say that if a large cloud is
made it is an omen of copious rain; if a thin cloud, of little or no
rain.[722] In new fire-making, both on First Mesa and at Zuni,
where the fire drill is used, the time taken to ignite is an omen.
The society in charge have four songs to sing. If fire is made during the first song, it is an excellent sign; if all four songs have to
be sung or even resung, it is a sign of misfortune, of a poor year.

On First Mesa, bean-planting, at Powamu, is pregnant with
omen. If the beans grow high, the year's crops will be good. If
they break before the evening of the night they are to be cut, it
is bad, and kiva members will be whipped by the inspector, the
whipper kachina (Oraibi).[723] Since it is said that "bean-planting
(in February) is for the sake of the summer's planting," this rite
of bean-planting may also be a rite of compulsive magic. I surmise that the bundles of sample crops used in Isletan ceremonial
are fraught with omen.[724] When the Isletan chief calls or repro-
duces lightning and thunder in the kiva, if the thunder crashes
several times it is a sign that the year will be good with rain; if
only twice or thrice, the year will be bad, without rain.

In ritual shinny on First Mesa the bursting of the ball which
is stuffed with seeds is taken as an omen. If the ball does not
tear apart in four days of play, "they say it is not well," i.e., they
will not have good crops that year. In 1921 the ball burst on the

---

* At the foot of Corn Mountain another grooved rock is reported in connection with pebble-pushing to get rid of fatigue (Benedict 3: I, 117); and at Acoma
pebble-pushing in the grooved line looped in four places is also described as an
exorcising rite, to cease from yearning for the dead or absent or to keep them
from appearing in dreams. The pebble is kept under the *left* foot and at the end
thrown over the shoulder. This "forgetting" ritual is performed four days after
death (Stirling). In Acoma migration tradition the ritual was performed on the
site of what was to be Laguna, which means that the marked rock at Laguna
was known to Acoma narrators.

second day. "It was very good," wrote Crow-Wing. "We all feel good and happy about it."

45. CLAIRVOYANCE: DREAMING

Clairvoyance or second sight is practiced through crystal-gazing and through peering into the medicine bowl. When Giwire, chief of the Shikani society of Laguna, was looking for his patient's heart, stolen by witches, the "great light" or crystal was held up to him by his assistant,* just as at Acoma the chief holds up the crystal for the others to gaze into, saying, "Look! Look!" They are to look for an invalid in need of treatment or for the witch who may be lurking outside the ceremonial chamber.[725] After María of Taos was brushed and sucked for "itching all over," her doctor looked into his crystal and saw that what he had sucked out had been sent in by the doctor of Cochiti whom she had been visiting. Zuni and Hopi doctors locate ailment or what the witch has "shot" into the body, by holding a crystal in the light, before the patient.[726] The Isletan chief will see in his crystal the helper engaged in capturing the witch bundle or how the War captain is protecting him. "Somebody is near him, perhaps a Mexican," the chief will announce through his Crystal Intelligence Service. In the Isletan crystal may be seen whence wind or rain will come and on what day, what general sickness threatens, how long it will last, how to get rid of it, where the Grasshopper chief may be found and carried away so that his people may follow him.[727]

The crystal is worn as a pendant underneath the bear-claw necklace (Isleta),[728] it may be dipped in medicine water and rubbed on the eyes, giving them second sight (Acoma).

When the Isletan initiate gazes into the medicine bowl, he may see pictures of the dead or of witch machinations.[729] A picture of witch-finding through the mirror bowl is given in the following San Juan tale[730] of the witch doll.

A young man was married to the daughter of Pu'fona sendo (curing society old man or chief). This curing chief had power to catch witches; but the youth did not believe it. The youth was a fast runner; nobody

---

* Parsons 20:119. The same term, "great light," is used at San Felipe.

could beat him. The curing chief *stayed in* four nights, and after four days everybody would go into the big kiva, men and women, and the doctors would give them medicine. The Outside chief would go around to every house to call them. About this time, in the middle of the afternoon, the youth's head was being washed by his wife, and he was thinking, "I am going to see if they have power, if it is true or untrue." As she was brushing his hair, he thought, "I am going to make a doll,[731] and I wonder if they can catch me."

He got a rag and shook it well and put it under his blanket. He got another and put it under his blanket and he got another and put it under his blanket. "This is enough, I can make a big doll." He went to the river, and sat down and began to make the doll. He made ears and eyes and mouth, and he held it out and looked at it. "I think it is good," he said. He made arms, too. "I am going to lay it here, and after supper I will come after it." He laid it down and covered it with earth. As he left, he looked back, and there was the doll running after him. "*Hewemboharihq'!*[*] It lives!" he said. He caught it and laid it down and covered it. This time it did not run after him again. He came home. His wife and father and mother were bathing and washing their heads to get ready. "Where were you so long?" said his wife. "Just taking a walk," he said. It was growing dark. They said, "We will go first, so the women can get good seats. When you come, lock the house!"

"I am going to get ready now to go *chuge* (witch)," he said to himself. He took off his shirt and trousers and tied his hair way up on his head and put white clay all over his head. He had a looking-glass. "I need something yet." He got a ragged old dress, and tied it on. He put black hand prints over each shoulder.[†] "If they catch me, they have power. If they do not catch me, they have no power." As he was getting ready, in came the doll. "*Hewemboharihq'!* This is alive!" He caught it and went out.

Those doctors were at work now. The Outside chiefs were up on a roof looking around. The young man picked up a little stone and threw it at the Outside chief. Nobody saw him, the witch helped him. Then they looked into their medicine bowl and saw what the man was doing. The doctors got mad and threw out their arms, and that hit him outside. So he ran away back to his father's house, the doll under his arm. He hid in the upper story, behind the corn store. The doctors went in and took him down. He was struggling. There were lots of people in the kiva, and they took him in with his doll. They did not know who it was. They sat him down where the doctors were sitting. That curing chief! It was his son-in-law.

* Usual Tewa exclamation of surprise and dismay.

† The Isletan curing society chief is painted thus, all over, but the print represents a bear paw.

Then the chief said, "Here we are all together. You believe in what our Mother is working here for us. But my own son does not believe it. Now he will see it." And he gave him medicine. The young man looked into the water in the altar bowl and he saw himself in there. "My wife is combing my hair." He thought of how he was shaking out the rags. He saw himself shaking one rag, then another. He thought of how he went to the river and made a doll. "There I am hiding the doll. Then I went along with the doll running after me. I caught it again and hid it again. And I came in my house and my wife gave me something to eat, and my wife went to the kiva with my mother and sister. And I was painting with white, and putting on black hand prints, and tying an old dress on my arms and legs. Then the doll came and I took it." He was talking of all he had done.* "I came out and threw a stone at the Outside chief, and, when the doctors shook their arms at me, I nearly fell down, and I ran away and hid up in the stack. They followed me, caught me, and brought me into the kiva." All this he saw in the bowl. So now he believed, and he became a doctor.†

Dreaming does not figure in ritual as much as you would expect from the importance attaching in daily life to dreams; nor is dreaming a regular function of the Pueblo ceremonialist, as it is of shamans throughout the Southwest, but dreaming sometimes affects the ceremonial life. Were not Laguna scalpers continent for four days, the War Brothers' "sister" (see p. 233, n.‡) would appear to them in their dreams, *with large teeth*.[732] The locust medicine of the Hopi Flute society gives power to dream coming events, as does snake feces medicine to the Acoma war chief.‡ There is a remarkable reference in a Second Mesa tale to the ability of chiefs to diagnose the cause of drought by dreaming.§ Societies may be joined now and again as the result of a dream. A Sia man joined the Snake society because, while he was sick of smallpox caused by ants, he dreamed of snakes and felt he would die did he not join.[733] Kaaihiĕ of Laguna

* Suggesting confession.

† Initiated through a kind of trespass.

‡ At Zuni certain persons, not necessarily ceremonialists, are believed to dream true (Bunzel 1:481). Cf. Taos, Parsons 58:68.

§ Wallis 1:20 ff. And in this tale Water Coyote remarks to the chief who visits him, "I do not know how I can help you; I do not know how to cause dreams."

dreamed that her deceased grandfather whose corn fetish was in her house came and bade her become a shaman as he had been; she did so.[734] If you dream of the Koshairi, you should join them (San Felipe),* consistently with the general belief that, if you dream of the dead, you are going to join them. Dreams of the dead or hallucinations which are accounted bad dreams (Zuni) and omens of death are good reasons for joining a society or for being whipped by a kachina. The most common hallucinations are the apparent movement of sacrosanct things on an altar, especially masks (Zuni).† We recall the ominous rolling of her eyes by the Zuni saint.

PURIFICATORY RITES‡

46. BATH OR WASH: PURIFICATORY AND BAPTISMAL

Bathing before engaging in ritual or, in particular, before handling sacrosanct things, and bathing in concluding ritual are general Pueblo practices carried out more commonly in the East by washing the body and, in the West, by washing the head.

A ritual bath is taken by the Winter Town chiefs of San Juan in connection with their seasonal transfer ceremony "because they have left summer behind." The Town chief of Taos "washes away" the time of "staying still," i.e., he concludes the winter ceremonies by a bath in the river, and he is followed by all the townspeople. Sia shamans take a river bath before their retreat, as do Zuni Wood society men during their ceremony.[735] Kachina dancers will bathe in the river (San Ildefonso, Sia, Jemez) or have their sacrosanct and "dangerous" paint washed off in the house of wife or "aunt" or Shalako hostess (Zuni). Scalp-takers (Zuni) and salt-gatherers (Zuni, Mishongnovi) are bathed by their "aunts."

The sweat bath is used at Isleta and Taos, water being thrown

* White 3:18. This comes very close to typical shamanistic dreaming among other Southwestern peoples.

† Bunzel 2:482. Possibly there is more than a fortuitous connection between dreaming and the kachina cult. See p. 1096.

‡ Zuni, *shuwaha*, "wiping off," "cleaning"; Hopi, *navohchiwa*; Hano, *ma'pedi*; Jemez, *nowho'*; Isleta, *thlua*; Keresan, *kukats*.

on hot stones. It is a ritual practice, but the details are not known.* Acoma kick-stick racers sweat-bathe.[736]

Head-washing for the deceased, for burial attendants, and for the household has been noted (pp. 70, 72). The dawn of the day the Hopi bride and groom are to sleep together, the bride's head is washed by the groom's mother and kinswomen, and now or later the groom's head is washed by the bride's people. Head-washing with naming is a part of any initiation† or introduction into any social organization: curing society, dance society, or clan.

Head-washing invariably accompanies naming ritual but it may be observed without name-giving, in making a friend (kihe') at Zuni, for scalps (Zuni,‡ Sia), for a bear (Zuni, Jemez), for a captive eagle (Jemez; Hopi eagles are named as well as head-washed),[737] for snakes in the Hopi Snake-Antelope ceremony, for human participants in that ceremony at its conclusion, or for prospective participants everywhere in all kinds of ceremonies. As the people began to emerge from underground, Spider sprinkled water on the hand and head of the first man out, *so that he would belong to her* (Shumopovi).[738]

Before cutting prayer-sticks at Zuni, or in the case of women —women never cutting prayer-sticks—before planting them, a person's head will be "washed."§ So head-washing is preliminary to all Zuni retreats, at which prayer-stick-making is ever the chief function. The rule holds for Sia retreats.[739] At Isleta

* The practice is probably borrowed from the Apache where it is a curing practice conducted by a shaman and followed by continence for twelve days. A steam bath is a curative society practice at Laguna (Parsons 20:108, n. 2) and is used by Hopi women during their twenty-day confinement, every four days.

† A person given to a Zuni society may wait for years before being initiated; so every year at the winter solstice he is "washed" at the house of his doctor or prospective sponsor.

‡ See p. 626. The Sia scalp was washed by every member of the Knife society at dawn. "You are now no longer our enemy," said the chief, "your scalp is here; you will no more destroy my people" (Stevenson 1:121, 122). The old scalps are washed at Isleta and Santo Domingo (White 4:60, n. 56), but for medicine.

§ This rule does not hold in the monthly prayer-stick-plantings of Zuni society members.

head-washing is part of winter solstice altar ritual. There are
several occasions at Zuni when everybody or every male cuts or
plants prayer-sticks, at the solstices and at Shalako, so that
these are also times for general head-washing.* Also before a
kachina dance, head-washing may be general (Zuni, Hopi).[740]
While the hair hangs loosely to dry, a person will go about his
affairs and walk through town if need be. In fact, one of the
surest indications for a stranger that a dance is in prospect is the
number of persons he sees abroad with flowing, wet hair.

The washing is in suds from yucca root. The roots are broken
up, pounded, and placed in a bowl; water is poured on, and,
after a swinging movement of the hand in the water, the suds
form. These are dipped on to the head with hand or corn ear
four times, which formality may or may not be followed by a
thorough wash and rinsing. Usually women wash the hair of
both men and women; but men may wash their own hair. Any
woman of the household may serve, but in many cases it is the
express duty of the "aunt," a kinswoman of actual or ceremonial
father. The "aunt" will meet the initiate or dancer or clown in
the court or fetch him from kiva, escorting him to her house and
sometimes after the wash regaling him with refreshments
(Zuni).[741] To an initiate godparents will give presents, usually
of clothes, a dance kilt or moccasins (Hopi), receiving the customary return or acknowledgment in food (Mishongnovi).[742]

Head-washing seems to be primarily a purificatory rite, a
cleansing before coming into contact with the supernatural.
How did it come to be associated with naming or renaming?
Was a name also a means of receiving power or of dispelling a
dangerous influence? Or were head-washing and naming associated merely through the Catholic rite of baptism and, like
it, thought of as a rite of allegiance, as Spider put it, of belonging
to someone.

47. EMESIS

Vomiting is associated with retreat or is a sort of alternative.
On First Mesa in the morning about eight o'clock a man in

* General at Hano also at the winter solstice.

retreat will go to his house, drink water, and lying down on the roof with his head over the edge thrust his fingers down his throat and force himself to vomit.[743] A similar society practice prevails among Keres and at Jemez, although the four-day period of emesis generally precedes the four-day period of retreat; but kachina impersonators in their preliminary retreat take a morning emetic.[744] For four mornings at sunrise Zuni initiates into the War society take an emetic, a gallon of greenish-yellow medicine water.[745] (Cushing, poor man, did not find the provocative turkey feather necessary!) Before stick-swallowing, at Zuni, and probably elsewhere, an emetic is taken, and it is taken by Zuni stick-racers before and after racing,[746] and by Jemez racers four mornings in advance. Acoma racers vomit.[747] Vomiting is practiced by participants in winter solstice ceremonials (Isleta, Santo Domingo, Laguna, Hopi). Before the summer solstice ceremony of 1920 a Laguna shaman of my acquaintance was very insistent that he was not going to participate, but he gave himself away by not keeping out of sight the cedar brew for his morning rite.

"After you start to vomit, you breathe differently from other people" (Santo Domingo). "After you vomit for four days, you're different."* This is purification or getting power for what is to come or happen; purification for what has happened is also common. If the Laguna continence taboo of twelve days after childbirth is violated, the woman would "dry up" and die unless an emetic were administered by the shaman.† The emetic prescribed for Acoma hunters who have failed to get game seems to express an analogous point of view—cleansing from a deleterious condition. This is certainly the proper interpretation for vomiting after a death at Laguna[748] or as prescribed at Zuni for the widow of a man killed in fighting. "You must drink medicine and vomit," said her grandfather to Lina, the widow. "It is very dangerous." Even making an offering to the dead may seem

---

* White 4:164. Vomiting may be practiced, ordinarily, as a tonic, or, at Jemez, for physical prowess (Harper).

† For violating any continence taboo Western Apache will hold curing ritual (Goodwin).

dangerous; after making the balls of food that are to be distributed to the dead, the chief of the Hopi Marau society and her assistant purify by vomiting.[749]

Vomiting as a means of separating one's self from dangerous spirits is practiced by the Hopi messenger on his return from Kishyuba, the home of the kachina, and at the conclusion of the Snake-Antelope ceremony by the Snake men. When Tsashji of Laguna was lightning-shocked in 1920, he was segregated in an empty house for four days and each morning given an emetic by his doctor, a man who had also gone through the experience of lightning shock.* There appear to be two methods of treatment for lightning shock at Zuni: the patient is washed with urine and given black beetle in wafer-bread and greasy meat, or he is given rain water, segregated for four days, and each day made to vomit. Without this "cleansing," sickness might result at any time, even years later, from lightning-caused tadpoles in the stomach. At Laguna stomach cramps and swellings are caused by merely smelling "the smoke" from lightning. The Lightning doctors of Acoma treat "bad smells in the stomach."[750]

48. Waving in a Circle and Discarding

The motion is made around the head, from right to left, with something held in the hand, the motion or circuit (anti-clockwise) repeated four times. A bit of cedar bark or some ashes may be used or a pebble or something picked up from the ground. The rite is performed on a trail before casting stone or twig onto a pile to rid one's self of fatigue;[751] it is done in the Zuni war dance "to take away the bad killing influence."† In the Hopi Buffalo dance whatever is picked up and waved is thrown after the departing "buffalo" who are to take away with them "any sickness of the people." Below the mesa, when the Buffalo youths remove their headdress, they wave it round their head,

* Parsons 33:275. At Zuni in 1917, Justito, Rain chief of the South, was summoned to doctor his own son for lightning shock, he himself having experienced lightning shock. He had to refuse, however, as he was about to set out to fetch water from the spring associated with his Rain chieftaincy for their retreat.

† *Awek shuwaha*, ground-cleansing, the rite is called, and probably the reference is to self-cleansing by casting on the ground.

four times, saying to Buffalo, "You may go home!" Similarly, on unmasking, the Hopi kachina impersonator waves his mask around his head. After this he also waves around his head a pinch of ashes, so as not to get sores on his body, bad eyes, or grievous illness,[752] or "so as not to dream about it."

At Zuni, too, the rite is "to get rid of bad dreams" or bad effects. Before the corpse is carried out of the house, those there will take a pinch of meal from the bowl from which the corpse has been sprinkled, and wave the meal, four times, around their head, and sprinkle it on the corpse. When the widowed wish to remarry, they will throw away some possession in the road early in the morning, and whoever would appropriate the object should first kick it with the left foot, four times, and then wave a piece of cedar bark around the head, four times, with the left hand.[753] To preclude having twins, a woman who has unwittingly eaten of the wafer-bread her husband may have brought back from a deer hunt, bread intended to be an offering to the game, should wave the bread, four times, around her house ladder. The sometime snake-bitten man who has been called in to breathe upon an infant's sore navel also has to wave some ashes about the infant's head.

Waving with ashes is a very common rite in concluding a Hopi ceremony; it is *navochiwa*, cleansing, a discharming rite, Voth has called it. The following account at the close of the Oraibi Snake-Antelope ceremony is characteristic: All participants stand around the kiva fireplace in a half-circle, first taking off their moccasins. The chief takes a long buzzard feather in his left hand, a pinch of ashes in his right hand, and all the others some ashes in their right hand. All then hum the *nawuhchi tawi* or discharming song, waving their hands slightly up and down to the time of the singing. Between their left thumb and forefinger the men hold a pinch of ashes, which they have taken from their right hand. This they circle from right to left four times at a certain point of the song and then throw it toward the hatchway, the chief doing the same with the feather and wiping the ashes from the feather toward the hatchway. He sprinkles another pinch of ashes on the feather, the others take a new pinch from the right hand, and the performance is repeated five times, corresponding to the number of verses in the song. After the last stanza all beat off the ashes from their hands and then rub their bodies and limbs.[754]

A similar cleansing may be made with prayer-meal. During prayer-stick-making for Sun at the winter solstice in Walpi, while the other chiefs are praying, Sikyaustiwa is described as sprinkling a pinch of meal on the wing feather of a buzzard, praying under his breath, beating time with the feather, sweeping the air over the prayer-stick tray and along the meal road on the altar, and then tossing the meal off the feather up the hatchway, seven times. On making the final exorcism with ashes, Sikyaustiwa, praying inaudibly, sprinkles ashes off the buzzard feather onto the feet of all present, and each waves a pinch of ashes in his left hand around his head and casts toward the trap door; then Sikyaustiwa makes successive rounds to draw the feather across knees, breasts, mouths, and heads. Each gathers up what is left of his little mound of ashes, mounts the trap door, casts away the ashes, and spits violently.[755] Marau chiefs at Oraibi cast their ashes away to song and then spit, casting and spurting for each of the four directions.[756]

The Sia shaman casts ashes off his eagle plumes, to the directions, it is said,[757] but this may be merely a circular waving motion; these motions are similar and possibly related. At San Juan a broom is waved around the head in infant-naming ritual, and then the poker the woman holds is cast away.

A gesture of discarding without waving has been noted—the widespread gesture of passing the right palm rapidly over the left palm and onward.* This familiar Pueblo gesture† indicates as usual something finished or done with and is used also ritualistically as an exorcising gesture, with the palms of the hands or with the "hand" feathers (Keres, Isleta) or even with a broom (San Juan). In San Juan naming ritual it is referred to as blow-

---

* Havasupai, "all gone, all washed away" (Spier 2:329); Plains tribes, also Idaho Shoshone (Lowie, personal communication); Zapoteca (Parsons 62:488, n. 18).

† Keresan, *tsauwakats.*

ing away as the wind blows;[758] at Acoma it is called "whipping the disease away."[759]

49. Spitting

We saw Hopi ritualists spitting after casting away their purificatory ash. After the Yayatü doctor exorcised with ashes off eagle feathers, all present spat violently.[760] Spitting may also precede casting away, as in the Zuni war dances[761] where cedar bark is waved and spat on.* At the close of the Laguna war dance the Kashale clowns shoot arrows in the direction the Scalp comes from, the people first spitting into the quivers; the Kashale are shooting away whatever fear or scare may have been caused by the Scalp. In Zuni myth Paiyatuma, the Ne'wekwe (Kashale) patron, directs the people to spit and, as we would say, cleanse themselves of their misconduct toward the Corn Maidens.[762] On unmasking, the Hopi Nima'n kachina impersonator spits upon his mask before waving it around his head, and, as the kachina are leaving the court, the onlookers spit after them.[763] "The kachina are taking away everything bad."[764]

Below the mesa north of Zuni where racers got omens stands a big cairn. A pebble was waved around the head in the left hand and then before it was cast on the pile it was spat upon so that the runner might be rid of his tired breath and start his race with fresh new breath.[765] On many a mesa pass such a pile of stones may be seen, made, it has been generally said, to get rid of fatigue or ailment. There must be such a pile on the road up to Paguate from Laguna, for the medicine-carrying shaman who became stone on that road said that after offering food a man was to spit four times on a stone and cleanse his body by passing the stone down front, back, and sides,† and, he added, "on my head the stone he shall throw; then in one day by means of my magical power I shall cause to go away whatever hurts his body to Tau't⁷umi" (a mountain in Mexico).[766]

At the close of the Zuni Thle'wekwe ceremony the onlookers pass both hands down their sides and then spit "to clear them-

---

* *Ichukotenapka*, spitting in exorcism.

† Compare Acoma, p. 364.

selves of trouble" (*ishuwanankya*, cleanse one's self). The jars that are thrown down from the housetops* in the kachina ceremony of whipping the children are first spat into. Old Luisantsita† told her little granddaughter to spit in a certain jar, a cracked one, adding, "You can go down with it."‡ After spitting, the girl waved a pinch of meal four times around her head and dropped it on the spittle. In the ceremonies of the Isletan curing societies there is a jar on the altar into or toward which everyone present will spit. Fleeing from epidemic, the early Acomans spat into yucca plants (see p. 364).

At Laguna the food that is put on the house fire for the deceased is spat upon by every member of the household. Giwire had been snake-bitten, so when he visited his newborn greatnephew, lest the navel become sore, Giwire had to spit. The Chakwena kachina§ dance held in October, 1918, was for the benefit of a sick woman who during the dance approached one of the kachina, sprinkled him with meal, and spat on his yucca switch, as did the spectators of the performance. This spitting by the people (*gayaishupsdia hano*) "takes away bad sickness."

50. LEFT

We noted the use of left hand and left foot when a Zuni remarries, and of the left foot in scalp-kicking. After the Zuni widow has completed her four-day fast, before dawn, far from town, she carries black prayer-meal in her left hand to pass it over her head four times and sprinkle, inferably as an offering to

* Throwing something down hard (as here or after waving around the head) might be considered a distinctive exorcising rite, as Dr. Reichard has pointed out for the Navaho.

† Luis, his mother: teknonymous usage. Zuni still "evade inquiry" about personal names as did old Pedro Pino, former Governor and father of the then Governor, when Bourke inquired in 1881 (Bourke 2:191).

‡ In this house-cleansing (*kyaken shuwaha*) the spitter as well as the house is purified. "He spits out his troubles." On making peace, Comanche and Lipan Apache spat into the same hole, "burying their troubles" (Opler). On settling among Hopi the Tewa spat into a hole, burying their language from their hosts, they *now* say.

§ According to a Laguna story, the Chakwena when first introduced were spat against as witches.

the dead, although it is spoken of as a cleansing.[767] The San Juan
youth who pulls out the heart of the ghost uses his left hand and
holds the heart fast until his hand is opened in kiva.[768] Meal or
shell mixture for the dead is held in the left hand (Sia), and food
offerings to the dead are dropped from the left hand at Isleta,
where the left is ever associated with death and with witchcraft.[769]

At Cochiti some of the food offered to the deceased is placed
under his arm, his left arm. It is said at Cochiti that, when your
left eyelid quivers, all your family will fall sick or die.[770]

A mask is put on and taken off with the left hand, and prayer-
sticks or feathers and prayer-meal given to the impersonator are
put into the left hand.* In discharming rites the left hand is used
(Hopi),[771] and in the Powamu discharming rite with ashes the
left moccasin is taken off.[772] A conceptual relationship between
kachina and the dead is suggested. Masauwü, god of death,
behaves contrariwise.

Inferably the use of left foot or hand is a case of contrary
behavior which among Pueblos and elsewhere is associated with
the dead. In support of this interpretation it should be noted
that at Zuni eating is done as much as possible with the right
hand; formerly a mannerly person would even keep his left hand
pressed to his stomach, out of action.[773] Hopi observed the same
rule, and the right hand was called "the food hand," the hand
not sacred.[774]

51. Ashes and Embers: Gum

Ashes, we noted in the Hopi discharming rite, may be used to
wave with and discard. Zuni also exorcise with ashes, placing
the ashes on top of a feather and, as in aspersing, tapping the
under side with another feather.[775] During the Hopi Marau ceremony the woman chief was observed to lay some peaches beside
the fireplace and sprinkle around them with ashes. She wanted
to give the peaches to children who had never seen the altar. If
they ate peaches which had been in kiva and not discharmed,
their hands and bodies would become distorted or twisted, like

---

* Compare pictures of Maya gods (Stephen 4:371, n. 2).

Twister, the spiral fetish of the society,[776] causer and curer of what is inferably arthritis. When Crow-Wing finished his drawing of the Tewa winter solstice altar, he took a pinch of ashes from our stove and waved it four times in anti-sunwise circuit about his head, remarking that this was the first time the altar had been drawn and it was "dangerous."

The Mishongnovi hunter of mountain sheep would wave and cast away ashes to purify from the smell of woman which is disliked by game (and by snakes),[777] and in breaking camp again he purified himself, casting the ashes in the direction away from town. The hunter's wife in her turn would rub ashes on her head behind the ears, and any Hopi going out at night during the dangerous moon (December) would smear his forehead with ashes, since "witches are around everywhere."[778] Before leaving the house, on presenting her infant to the Sun, the Sia mother rubs ashes over herself. Ashes are waved three (?) times around the head of an infant by visitors before leaving and then thrown away outside (Zuni),[779] and ashes are rubbed on the infant, if not as a depilatory (Zuni), as prophylaxis against witchcraft (Laguna). One morning I asked Juana of Laguna if her two-week-old baby had been rubbed yet with ashes. "No, but mother has been thinking about it," she answered, and the following morning I noticed that the child's forehead was ash-besmeared.* Sometimes the ashes are rubbed on in the form of a cross, on forehead, chin, and legs. When an older child is to go out at night, a cross in ashes may be rubbed on his forehead. At Zuni, the first time a baby is taken out at night dampened embers are rubbed over his heart that he may not be afraid in the dark; a child waking up in a fright would be similarly treated, and given a drink of water mixed with embers.†

The Sia mother has put into her mouth a bit of charcoal that cold winds (winds of sickness, *mal aire*, let Mexicanists note!) may not enter her body. Ash or ember from the mouth of a Fire society man is medicine. There is a taboo at Zuni on feeding

* Navaho practice also, against malice of the dead (Franciscan Fathers, 445).

† At Laguna, a remedy for spider bite.

corn to horses until four days after the winter solstice ceremony; but, if this rule has to be broken, the corn will first be sprinkled with dampened embers. Whenever corn or wheat is to be taken out of the house, it will be similarly sprinkled in order that all the store of grain may not follow.

At the close of the winter solstice ceremony of Zuni, the women of the household pass embers along the house walls (*kyakwena shuwaha*, house-cleansing), beginning with the eastern wall, and throw out these embers after the Chakwena kachina has passed by the house. Chakwena "is taking troubles away." When the blanketed Kwelele pass by the house, embers are thrown on them, also for "cleansing."

The use of ashes is distinctively antiwitch prophylaxis (Laguna and eastern pueblos). Doctors engaged in witch pursuit are rubbed with ashes, as are patients afflicted by witches. Women have demonstrated to me how they would cast a pinch of ashes against the window of their house or drop ashes at the threshold whenever they feared a lurking witch (Paguate, Isleta). In Tewa tale ashes are thrown into boiling piñon gum to make the jars crack and spill out the bad medicine the witches are making.

Witches themselves use ashes. Any ash-besmeared person would be taken for a witch. Witchcraft is often imputed to the clown societies, Ne'wekwe or Koshare, and they use ashes to make the line or "house" which, if strayed across or into, necessitates initiation.[780]

During the dangerous December moon, not ashes but gum, piñon gum, is rubbed on the forehead and chest of a Hopi infant, so that Moon Old Man will not carry it off.[781] Gum or, speaking in Middle American terms, copal is incense in exorcism (Hano, Zuni; see p. 69).

52. BRUSHING*

Brushing out or away whatever is injurious is a common rite of exorcism. The shaman uses a buzzard feather or his two eagle-

---

* Keresan, *kukats;* Isleta, *nathlöa pöare*, witch bundle brush.

wing feathers.* For ant-sent skin disease, brushing is the usual treatment (Zuni, Keres, Isleta, Tewa). Ants or other things which have penetrated the body—pebbles, bits of cloth, cactus points—are seen to fall from the eagle feathers. The motion was described by a Laguna-Isleta Fire society member as "sweeping in, like catching a fly, and then shaking down." A woman in labor may be brushed down (Sia).[782] The walls of a death-tainted room are brushed down (Cochiti).[783]

In a night war ritual the Oraibi Town chief brushes stick-mounted hawk feathers over the feet of the singers, then over their knees, shoulder, faces, and heads.[784] When Antelope Maid and Youth are discharmed in the Snake-Antelope ceremony, the eagle-wing feather on which ashes will be placed is first waved along the front part of the body to the knees,[785] as if something were being removed. The Kurena of Laguna made exorcising passes with feathers.

The Kurena society of Cochiti carry leafy wands, referred to as whips, with which they brush people starting out on a rabbit drive,[786] and Isletan clowns carry whips of willow or yucca. Passes with a bear paw which Keresan or Isletan shaman draws on as a mitten is another form of brushing exorcism.

Persons undergoing stress in initiation or in witch-hunting may be massaged (Hopi,[787] Laguna), perhaps for merely physical relief, perhaps for relief from exposure to the supernatural.

53. Sucking Out Sickness

Things sent into the body† by a witch will be sucked out by the sufferer's doctor. The things are described as thorns, cactus spines, sharp stones, anything sharp, a thread or bit of cloth, bone from a corpse, little snakes, lizards, or insects; but the only object that has been seen by any outsider and at that

---

* Zuni, *asiwe*, hands; Keresan, *hashami*. Feather "hands" are used also to motion with, as by Bitsitsi in the Zuni Molawia ceremony. Brushing away may be done actually with the hands.

† Jemez, *wa'thlowa*; Isleta, *nathalö*; Spanish, *chizo* > *hechizado*, bewitched.

only glimpsed at (Zuni, Hopi)[788] looks like a "headless centipede."*

At a general curing assemblage the doctors will go about
among those present and suck out things (Zuni, Isleta,[789] Keres,
see pp. 532, 539, 728). In Taos tale a dead girl is revived by
each witch sucking from her body what he sent into it. "This
is the place I shot her," he said, and he sucked that place.
When porcupine quills were sucked from her heart, she came to.

54. Fumigation

Fumigation by burning piñon gum (Zuni) or a certain unidentified root† is prophylactic against witchcraft (Zuni, Keres,
Tewa, Isleta, Taos) and is practiced in the sickroom, at death
(Taos), or at confinement (Laguna,‡ Cochiti). At Cochiti the
root is placed around and inside the grave.[790]

Fumigation may be practiced in the house after the corpse
has been carried out (Zuni, Laguna, San Juan), "because the
dead do not like the smell of piñon gum" (Zuni).[791] The practice
of burning some of the hair of the deceased for the relatives to be
smoked in is quite general, although it is reserved in some towns
for one who has harassing memories or dreams of the deceased.
The harassed Tewa (F.M.) would use piñon gum or cedar.[792]

The Hopi big-game hunter smoked himself on his return over
a bowl of burning juniper (cedar).[793] All members of a Mishongnovi spring-cleaning party hold their hands over a sprig of
smoking juniper (cedar) before they enter a house, lest those

---

* Near the Village of the Great Kivas are petroglyphs of centipedes and
other poisonous insects which Zuni workmen said represented the War
chiefs sent through song against Navaho enemies (Roberts 1 : 150, Pl. 61a); compare the centipede warriors of the Peruvian Chimu (Means, Fig. 14). But let us
read between the lines. Young Zuni would have little if any knowledge of esoteric War society songs, while they would know all about bewitchment through
centipede. Loath to talk about this to their White employer, they produced
something like it as a war practice, from their point of view a very credible
invention. I have very little doubt they believed this petroglyphic spot was a
place for witch assemblage.

† San Juan, hunka'; Cochiti, katshrana (Dumarest, 153, 154); Laguna,
kachurna (kshurna); Isleta, pakunthli; Taos, taulu.

‡ At birth of twins (Goldfrank 1 : 387).

within suffer from swellings or sores.[794] This is also done in the final exorcism of the women's Marau ceremony at Walpi.

At Taos anyone in a faint might be smoked with buzzard droppings. Buffalo skull is burned for a smoke against drought or high winds or severe cold. Smoke from cedar is fanned on a Peyote patient or on anyone returning to the assemblage after going out.

55. WHIPPING

At Acoma the annual War chiefs are whipped at their installation* and at their retirement from office. Anyone may ask to be whipped by the shamans at this time; the rite strengthens and gives luck [power] in hunting, racing, and gambling.[795] The warlike Cactus societies of Zuni and Jemez whip with cacti. At the initiation into the Hunt society of Sia a shaman impersonating the animal called *rohona* whips the candidate. All the society members are whipped and in his turn Rohona.[796] One of the kachinas of the curing society of San Juan whips at an initiation,[797] as do the kachinas of the societies of Cochiti and Sia[798] and the kachina of the Zuni Ne'wekwe clown society.[799]

In the West the kachina whip the children and adults who ask to be whipped, in the early spring ceremony of general exorcism, Powamu among the Hopi and at Zuni a very complicated quadrennial or sporadic ceremony referred to as the whipping of the children. The Zuni godfather covers the little boy with several blankets and takes him on his back. They pass by the line of kachina, each of the eleven kachina striking the boy four times. The godfather takes the boy down into kiva and transfers a prayer-feather lying at the head of the kachina in the sand-painting to the boy's head. The medicine chief of the Big Fire-brand society gives the boy a drink from the medicine bowl, and the boy stands on the sand-painting while the sand is rubbed on

* Benavides reports (1630) but without mentioning Acoma: "To make one a captain, they used to come together in a plaza and tie him naked to a pillar [perhaps Benavides is thinking of the Spanish whipping-post]; and with some cruel thistles they all [?] flogged him, and they afterward entertained him with farces and jestings. And if to all he was very unruffled and did not weep nor make grimaces at the one, or laugh at the other [cf. First Mesa, p: 923; Parsons 30:170], they confirmed him for a very valiant captain" (Memorial, 31–32).

his body. Now the whipping rite in the court is repeated, the boy kneeling and being stripped of his blankets. The fierce Blue Horns whip, and the boys "cry terribly." For four days the boy fasts from meat. Then in his godfather's house the boy's hair feather is removed and his head washed.[800] This "second whipping" has been described as if occurring outdoors, in the court. I surmise that it occurs in kiva, either following upon the outdoor ritual or during a subsequent Shalako ceremony, years later. At this kiva whipping the Blue Horn kachina removes his mask, and the boy puts it on and in turn whips the kachina. When still later in life a man has a personal kachina mask made for him, he is whipped before he first wears the mask.[801]

The First Mesa Hopi godfather or godmother gives an ear of corn with prayer-stick to the little boy or girl his or her mother has brought to the court, also some prayer-meal which the child is told to cast on the whipper kachina. The kachina plies his yucca switch on the boy's bared back, the little girl keeps on her slip. The children scream from pain and fright; but the whipper exercises discretion. Over one particularly terrified little girl, Stephen observed, he merely swirled his whip and then motioned her away. The godfather, not the godmother, is also whipped, casting meal toward the kachina and holding out his arms and legs. After the whipping, the godparent ties a prayer-feather in the child's hair. For four days the child fasts from meat and salt and each morning deposits a feather from his prayer-stick and casts meal to the Sun.[802] Now the children may look upon sacrosanct objects and upon "kachina in kiva" (kachina preparations?).

This court ritual is followed by a kiva ritual which has been described for Third Mesa as follows:*

The children with their godparents (each boy or girl has a godfather and a godmother) enter the Marau kiva which is the women's kiva, and after listening to a talk from the Maize Spirit Müy'ingwa, who is impersonated by the Powamu society chief,

---

* Stephen was informed of the kiva ritual that was to follow in a year or two, but he did not see it (Stephen 4:203, 208); Voth says nothing about an outdoor ritual on Third Mesa.

PLATE VII

WHIPPING A CHILD AT POWAMU, ORAIBI

"Father" and child stand on the sand-painting; Hahai-i kachina holds the yucca switches for her "son," Ho kachina (Voth 2: LXIII).

they await the whipping kachina. Presently a loud grunting noise, a rattling of turtle-shell rattles, and a jingling of bells are heard outside. The two whippers and Hahai-i, their kachina mother, have arrived. They first run rapidly around the kiva, four times, then dance on each side a little while, beating the roof with whips, jumping and howling. Descending, the two whippers stand on the east and west side of the large sand mosaic; their "mother" stands at the southeast corner, holding a supply of whips. The children tremble, and some begin to cry and scream. A godfather places a boy on the sand mosaic, holds his hands upward and one of the kachina whips the boy, four times, quite severely. The girls have on their usual dress; the boys are nude (Pl. VII.) Some of the children take it with set teeth and without flinching, others squirm, try to jump away and scream. Occasionally a godfather, pitying the child, presents his own hip, snatching the child away, and receives part of the whipping. Then the whipping is very severe. After all have been whipped, Haahi-i steps on the sand mosaic, bends forward, raises "her" blanket and is severely whipped by her sons who then whip each other. The kachina are given prayer-sticks and prayer-meal and leave the kiva. Now the children may know about the kachina and impersonate them.*

The whipping of the children at Sia is of a piece with the western ritual. As soon as a boy or girl reaches the time when "they have a good head," ten or twelve years of age, his or her father suggests to the chief of the Querränna society that he would like his son or daughter to know the kachina. He also speaks to the Town chief. Then, the next time the kachina come, the Querränna chief makes a meal-painting in his ceremonial room. Father and child and, if the child belongs to a society, his society chief, go to the house of Querränna chief, the child carrying his corn-ear fetish, if he belongs to a society. Town chief and War chief are present. Two kachina stomp about the room. Querränna chief leads the child before the meal-painting, where he receives two strokes across the back with the yucca switch

---

* Voth 2:98–105. Children initiated into the Powamu or Kachina society do not undergo this whipping, nor are they whipped at their own initiation.

of each kachina, unless as a society member he is exempt. (Compare Hopi.) One of the kachina places his mask on the child, the other kachina mask is placed on the meal-painting. The kachina rubs meal from the painting upon the child, and the others present rub themselves with the meal. The child is instructed not to speak of what he has learned. The child deposits a prayer-stick given him by Querränna chief at the shrine of the Querränna, to the west, saying, "I now know you, kachina, and I pay you this prayer-stick." Querränna chief deposits a prayer-stick for each member of the society.*

At Acoma† boys and girls are whipped in kiva in a sporadic kachina ritual very much like that of Oraibi; later, boys are taken by their uncle to an open-air assemblage of kachina and Antelope clansmen to be talked to by the Town chief and to see the impersonators seated with their masks lying on the ground in front.[803] At Santo Domingo boys only are whipped. The curing societies are in charge, Shikame for Squash kiva, Flint for Turquoise. The society's altar is laid down, and the chief in mask is the whipper.‡ There is no whipping ritual before dancing kachina at San Felipe or among Tewa.

The kachina are dangerous beings; they send nightmare and disease, and some of them cause accidents of all kinds. Even knowledge about them may be dangerous. As they cause troubles, they alone can remove or preclude them, hence they are called upon to whip. Boys are whipped, as Zuni say, "to save their lives."§ This is the general theory of the whipping of the children, I think, as well as of whipping before dancing kachina. But the theory is not held or applied consistently in the general interpueblo cult. Girls are no more exposed to the kachina among Hopi or western Keres than at Zuni and yet they are

---

* Stevenson 1:117–18. This ritual has lapsed (White).

† And, formerly, at Laguna (Parsons 33:264–65).

‡ White 4:101–4. At Cochiti boys only are whipped (Goldfrank 3:55).

§ In one instance this did not mean to save merely from exposure to the supernatural but from being actually killed. "Don't cut off his head! Just cleanse him, whip him with yucca!" urges Koyemshi Father (Bunzel 6:86). Flagellation as a substitute for ritual killing!

whipped whereas Zuni girls as a rule are not whipped. (Only Zuni girls who have actually suffered at the hands of the kachina, through hallucinations, are taken into the Kachina society "to save their lives," and are therefore whipped.)[804] And why is there no "second whipping" at Acoma, where the kachina cult is flourishing?

The Blue Horns of Zuni whip for ceremonial lapses or mistakes. Were a Shalako impersonator to fall in his ritual running, a sign of incontinence, he would be whipped the next day by a Blue Horn. Meanwhile the Salimobia who had been "out" with the Shalako would whip everyone he met in the town. Anyone falling asleep in a ceremonial house the night the "kachina come" is liable to be whipped by the Shalako "brother" who is at the time "naked," i.e., maskless. Salimobia on the kachina rabbit hunt whip those who fail in an attempt to catch an animal; and, if a Salimobia himself fail, he, too, will be whipped. Unauthorized persons visiting the lake under which live the kachina and the dead are whipped.[805] Any trespasser during a ceremony is subject to whipping by anyone present, a sort of alternative to initiation for trespass. Persons suffering from "bad dreams" or from sickness, if too poor economically to join a curing society, or if dreading its continence taboos, will be whipped instead by a kachina, by any kachina who carries habitually a yucca switch.* During the whipping of the children persons may stand forth in the court and ask to be whipped, and anyone abroad during the ceremony may be whipped unless he or she carry some corn or water. Similarly at Hopi Powamu during the public whipping of the children men ask to be whipped, against rheumatism, and during the Hopi Shalako and the kachina races the kachina whip to impart vigor,† just as kachina may switch one another during an interval in the dance.[806] In Keresan towns the kachina will visit the house of an

---

* E.g., at a Ky'anakwe ceremony two Chupawa kiva members were whipped (switched across arms and ankles) for "bad dreams" by the warrior kachina (Stevenson 2:220).

† During American military campaigns Apache scouts were observed to sit down and lash their legs with thistles to expel fatigue (Bourke 1:471).

invalid (one who has been sick a long time) to whip or rather stroke him with their yucca blades. At Zuni a collective whipping takes place on the final night of the winter solstice ceremonial when men and women who seek cleansing from nightmare or from bad luck (*hanasima*) go to the kiva to be whipped by the Blue Horns.

On the last night (March 5) of the Zuni winter series of kachina dances in 1918 this rite of whipping was performed in each of the six dance houses by the Blue Horns. I was present in one of the houses. The four Blue Horns entered, led in by the Kopekwin and followed by the Komosona and the Kopithlashiwanni (the four officers of the Kachina society, crier, chief, and warriors). The Blue Horns came in hooting and stood in a row against the wall. Thereupon all the men in the room, beginning with the choir, and, after the men, all the women, passed one by one down the line of Blue Horns. Each man paused in front of each Blue Horn to receive four strokes from the yucca switch, each man holding out rigidly at right angles to the body first his right arm, then his left, and, raised straight in front of the body, first his right leg, then his left. After delivering the four strokes the Blue Horn held his yucca switch to the man's mouth for him to spit on. The spitting was in some cases actual, in others, merely indicated. As the women passed along the line, each, with her blanket drawn well over her head, stooped in front of each Blue Horn and received four strokes across her shoulders. After the strokes, the Blue Horn waved his switch twice in circuit from right to left over the stooping woman. Several women held a child in front in order, it was plain, to include the child in the rite. After the whipping, each person, the men first, passed again down the line of Blue Horns, sprinkling meal on head and switch of each figure, and, as he or she sprinkled, saying a prayer and, after the last sprinkling, breathing with prayer from their own clasped hands. Then the Blue Horns, after making four times a circular gesture with their arms as if drawing something toward themselves, left the house to continue the rounds of the other dance houses. As they waved, the Blue Horns said in their hearts:

toshu anikchiatu
seeds wish much (fortunate)*

utenanna anikchiatu
property wish much

teapkonan anikchiatu
offspring wish much

kwahothltempla anikchiatu
all whatsoever wish much

I heard that had the War chief of the Kachina society led in
the Blue Horns the whipping would have been severer. As it
was, only the Blue Horn first to whip put any muscle whatsoever
into the strokes. The whipping of the women was even more
perfunctory than the whipping of the men. Nevertheless, the
rite as a whole was impressive, extremely impressive. Everybody looked grave or resolute. Everybody present was supposed
to undergo this cleansing. The spitting, like the whipping, was
"to get rid of bad habits [mishaps]." The women were said to be
whipped because, although uninitiated in the Kachina society,
they had been present during the winter series of kachina
dances. It was also said that during one of the dances of the
series, when a dancer was engaged in throwing things to the
people, the snout of his mask fell off, therefore all the people had
to undergo the cleansing.

A Cochiti dancer who "loses his ornaments" will be whipped
by the whipper kachinas, in the belief that the dancer has broken
taboos. If a mask slips in a Jemez dance, in the same belief the
"side dancer" will whip. One version of the destruction of Awatobi begins with an account of the clowns pulling the mask off
an ugly kachina. All the spectators and the clowns too had to
be whipped. This made the clown impersonators angry and
started the feud. When it was reported to the chief of the Zuni
Kachina society that a man had sold a mask to the trader, the
Blue Horns came out at a summer rain dance, visited the kivas,

* "May you be blessed, translates Dr. Bunzel, *to' towashonan anikshiat'u*,
may you be blessed with seeds. This is the formula for any kachina whipping
(Bunzel 2:518).

and went around town, whipping all they met, "to take away the bad luck."[807] Similarly, after a man had threatened to shoot the kachina if they beheaded his little son for talking impiously, in the midst of the great excitement the kachina went through the town whipping all they met. "The people ran into their houses. There was no one about."[808]

In certain Hopi kachina dances the kachina whip the clowns, and this might well be thought of as exorcism for the perverse behavior characteristic of clowns; but it is not. The kachina say to the clowns, "You are our fathers, now we must whip you that rain may come." Sending rain was said to be compensation for whipping.[809] In the opinion of others it might be a way of imparting power, a sort of inoculative magic. The silent prayer of the Zuni kachina when they whip suggests a similar line of thought, and so possibly does the Hopi practice of hitting a young boy hunter with the first jackrabbit he kills (p. 602) or the Isletan practice of hitting a scalper with the scalp (p. 642).

The meal marks which are put on the house walls the night "the kachina come" at Zuni are switched, elder brother Shalako makes the marks and he is followed by younger brother Shalako who switches. Presumably it is a rite of house-cleansing—in fact, I was told that it was prophylaxis against witches who might happen to be in the large assemblage gathered in the house for the night.

Whipping by the Blue Horns or by the disciplinary or bogey kachina of Zuni, of Cochiti, or of Tewa may take on a punitive character. Had not the man who sold the mask escaped to the American Agency, the Blue Horns, *it was said*, would have whipped him to death. The knife or whip of Atoshle is an instrument of punishment. Children and big girls do not ask Atoshle to whip them; they run from him in terror, hiding in corrals or doorways. The Zuni scene as I saw it is complemented very prettily by a San Juan account in a tale about Tsabiyu, bogey Grandfather.

The Governor said, "Everybody has to go and get onions." So everybody went, except two Yellow Corn girls, down at Achuga. They said, "We will go afterward and bring the onions." In the evening they went, when the others were coming back. "Let's run!" they said. They ran and ran and ran far away, where the onions were. They pulled up just a few. "Let's go," they said, "the sun is going." The younger said, "Somebody is singing." The elder said, "Nobody is coming; they all went home."—"Somebody is singing."—"No," said the elder, "I am singing through my nose." The younger said, "Let's wait!" Then one of those Tsabiyu old men came with long yucca blades. He came and said, "You do not mind the chiefs!" The girls said, "We will go with you."—"No, I did not come to bring you home." Then he drew out his whip and whipped one and then the other. They ran and cried, and he ran after them and whipped them, and they ran and he after them. And the laces of their moccasins broke, and their leggings fell off, and they left them there and ran; and their belts came off, and they left them there and kept on running. He was after them and whipped them. And they threw off their shawls and dropped their onions. And he ran and he whipped. Their underbelt came off and dropped. He used up all his blades. Then he said, "Yellow Corn girls, next time you won't do this. When people go out, they should all go together. This is what happens to girls who do not obey their chiefs. Now go home!" They went home, without onions, without their moccasins or belts or shawls.

At Cochiti the whipper kachina are told in advance whom they are to whip—disobedient children or adults who have broken the *costumbres*.[810] A Cochiti woman told Mrs. Goldfrank that as she no longer participated in the dances she did not dare attend them from fear of being whipped. Recently a Jemez man breaking the rule against cultivating by machine was ordered from his field and whipped (White). In a San Juan tale of a trial of supernatural power, when the rain- and hail-bringing kachina use their yucca switches on the people, including the Town chiefs, the Town chiefs weep and say, "We have done bad things! We will not do them again!"[811] The Isletan Town chief who breaks his rules by chopping wood and going rabbit-hunting is whipped by the invisible hand of his deceased predecessor.[812] The willows carried by the moiety clowns of Isleta, the K'apio, are to punish the disobedient. Lucinda of Isleta, widow of a Laguna immigrant, told me that, if she betrayed Laguna customs, after she died she might find her husband waiting for her with a whip. I heard whipping referred to as a "penance" by an Isletan who was a devout Catholic. When the Fiscal of Sandía was installed, he was given a whip (White). "God's whip" used to hang or still hangs in certain Keresan churches for the Fiscales or Alguazil to use against persons late to church or on sinners asking to be whipped after confession.[813] At Acoma a nonattendant was tied to the whipping-post and whipped until he or she "said yes."[814] Were the Acoma shamans copying padre or Spanish governor* when they had their Governor whip the first Americanized "schoolboys"? From twenty to thirty youths were made to kneel down in the middle of the kiva while the Governor lashed their bare backs with a Mexican horsewhip. For that "madness" the Governor spent ten years in an American jail.[815]

Punishment, expiation, cleansing from nightmare or sickness, freeing from danger from ritual infraction, or from danger from knowledge of the supernatural, inducement to the gods to send compensatory blessings, imparting power—a wide range of motivation for a single rite.

RITUAL COMPLEX AND RITUAL IN RELATION TO WAY OF LIFE

How do rites from this list of more than fifty-five ritual elements combine into a ceremony? Typically as follows: After

---

* Whipping was also a secular punishment for White and Indian, under Spanish administration. During his Hopi campaign, upon any Indian in his all-Pueblo army leaving camp without permission Governor Martinez imposed a penalty of 100 lashes (and being driven through camp on a burro) (Bloom, 201). In 1775 a Taos Indian was tried for "bestiality" and sentenced to twelve lashes for eight consecutive days (Twitchell II, 256). Whipping is practiced today in Taos by the Lieutenant-Governor, and inferably at Santo Domingo. The Governor of Santo Domingo put a stop to stealing railroad ties by whipping two thieves at a post in front of the kiva. Don't send them to jail, he told the American authorities; "they like that" (Twitchell I, 472).

Tarahumara officers whip in punishment, and anyone might be whipped for doctrinal ignorance (Bennett and Zingg, 207, 321). Among Papago, from eight stripes delivered by the Alcalde for absence from Mass or for drunkenness (1618) whipping became a sanction against murder, adultery (both offenders whipped at the post and the woman sent back to her husband, just as formerly at Taos), marital quarrel, *disobedience in children*, and slander—all offenses in the eyes of the Church; also against failure to perform a daughter's puberty ceremony, this a notable bit of acculturation (Underhill 3). As Papago, like Pueblos, did not whip children in punishment, were averse to physical contacts or to violent behavior, and held the family rather than the individual responsible for crime, their story of flagellation as a Spanish institution is strong circumstantial evidence that flagellation followed a like course among Pueblos, including ritualistic whipping which was reinterpreted.

spring water has been fetched or sand, wood for prayer-sticks, or other sacrosanct supplies,* the chief and his assistants "go in" to kiva or ceremonial chamber "to count their days." They are to remain continent and to fast, generally from salt and meat, concentrating upon their "work." They raise the standard and lay the altar, making the meal- or sand-painting, setting up the screen or slabs, placing the fetishes and all the paraphernalia of medicine-water bowl, meal basket, whizzers, whatever is to be used, and sprinkling a meal road or placing a prayer-feather road, to the principal fetish for the Spirit to travel. Songs, prayers, aspersings with prayer-meal or with water, and ritual smok-. ing are in order to invoke or summon the Spirits to the altar or induct them into the medicine bowl. Now follows prayer-stick-making and prayer-feather-making, sometimes to a song se-quence, and generally concluding with saying a prayer and blow-ing smoke over the offerings which at once or later are deposited in shrine or spring by couriers or by the society in procession, or which are attached to fetishes, or given to impersonators of the Spirits. Other work may be done, repairing or repainting fe-tishes, the corn-ear "mothers," figurines or masks, and prayer and song sequences are repeated. At all meals and at the final feast food offerings will be made to various supernaturals, and prayer-meal is sprinkled at dawn to Sun. Whenever rites lend them-selves to repetition by being performed in the directions, notably aspersing or blowing smoke, they are accordingly repeated. Furthermore, repetitiousness is increased by having participants perform a rite successively, not together, just as usually men march single file, not in lines or in clusters. Initiation ritual (ex-posure to the supernatural power of the society, aspersing the altar, vigil, prayer-feather-depositing, head-washing and nam-ing) will be performed in the course of the general ceremony. Shavings, dottle, spruce—whatever is not to be preserved is dis-posed of with care, sometimes sprinkled with meal. In conclu-sion, on dismantling the altar, exorcising or discharming ritual will be observed; participants must be separated from the super-

* This may be fetched after the retreat starts (Hopi), depending presumably on the messenger service.

naturals they have represented or from power which is ever dangerous unless carefully regulated.

The altar or esoteric ceremony is usually followed by a public dramatization or processional or dance or race, sometimes by the society itself, sometimes by another group which frequently is a kachina dance group. This general arrangement of ceremony, from esoteric ritual by a small group to general or public dance or celebration, is widespread, as we know, among Indians.

In kachina or war celebrations, gifts are made in house-to-house visits or are thrown to spectators. Exorcism is observed at the close of the dance or when scalp or mask is finally removed.

Dramatization lends itself to greater variation than does kachina dance or altar ritual, yet there are certain stereotype features in the highly stylized drama complex: procession and parade of the fetishes; visitation of spring, lake, or mountain summit as the home of the supernaturals addressed; omen-seeking; closing or opening or making the "road"; adoption or birth into the ceremonial group; finally, all those mimetic rites which consist in acting as you would have the Spirits act. In some cases the performance is actually dramatization in that it enacts a myth; in other cases there is no myth, at least none remembered or recorded. In all cases the acting is highly conventionalized, consisting merely of a series of rites which have more or less of a mythical reference; it is no more naturalistic in our sense than are cloud designs naturalistic pictures of clouds.

And so rites combine and recombine, the rite itself fixed or conventional but the combination less rigid; indeed the elasticity of Pueblo ritual is ever marvelous. And yet ritual rarely appears loose-ended, probably because it is so well integrated with social life at large, expressing or directing it. The following is but a partial and meager survey of such relations.

House.—We recall the marking of house walls with parallel lines of meal which are called "house" (Hopi) as a rite presumably to strengthen the house, also the rite of purifying the house with embers, and the placing of prayer-sticks in the rafters to make the house strong, or in the four corners of a new house, or at the base of certain house walls or in the Middle, this to give roots to the town. At Acoma, before performing the Fight with the kachina, the War chiefs go from house to house to fortify the walls by pressing their bow and flint against the house corners. At Zuni, turquoise is placed in the four corners of a new house. A major fetish protects the house where it is kept; "it gives you something to pray for and makes the house valuable."[816]

New houses or new rooms in which to entertain the kachina are built at Zuni every year in advance of the Shalako ceremonial. This is a considerable factor in the growth of the town. Also it is a factor in the calendar. Frequently the ceremonial is postponed for ten or even twenty days because the houses are not ready. During Powamu, Hopi girls mud-wash kiva walls, as a rain prayer,[817] and the youths redecorate with ritual designs. In the East the eve of a fiesta is always an occasion for plastering or white-washing house walls and for general house-cleaning.

The making of shrines is house-building, so to speak, for the Spirits (a shrine is called house by Hopi and Zuni),[818] and so is altar-making, since the Spirits are supposed to dwell within their altar-set fetishes. Indeed altar-making songs may be called house songs (Walpi).[819] At Jemez the altar frame is called society house and Hopi and Keres refer to the frame or slat altar as a whole as "house." The Hopi Water Serpent's elaborately painted screen is his "house." The house figures explicitly in altar pictures. On the Powamu altar around the sand-painting of the "face" and "heart" of the Sun are four circles in the colors of the cardinal points, which are called "house of the Sun."[820] (In the solstice prayer-sticks for Sun is a circle stick called Sun house.)[821] At Powamu initiation, a square altar sand-painting is made and called "house," each side a "plank."[822] Like design and like terminology occur in the sand-painting of the Antelope society.[823] The meal circle around the Tewa altar is called "town," as is the terrace or step design in meal on the Isleta altar. At Zuni the meal step design as on the Pekwin's altar at the Scalp ceremony is called house of the Clouds, "my father's massed cloud house."[824] The step design is called field at Acoma, but generally it is thought of as a cloud design.

Meal altars, indeed all altars, are transitory affairs, but the places where the fetishes are kept constantly are disturbed as little as possible; kiva or chamber sanctuaries are sometimes sealed, by the ancient way of luting down with clay, and except at the proper ceremonial time there is always the greatest reluctance to remove a fetish, which is sometimes left behind, but looked after, in an otherwise abandoned house. Analogously, when a sacred spring goes dry, prayer-feathers are still deposited there, and the water for the altar fetched from the nearest running spring (Hopi).[825]

When a fetish has to be removed, say the mask of a kachina chief, the people of the house wait for the regular ceremonial occasion for taking out the fetish and then at the conclusion of ceremony or dance it will be taken to its new quarters.

Skeleton house (*maski*) is the name given by the Hopi to that place in the west where the dead travel. Cemeteries are also "skeleton houses." In cliff-side cemetery, in refuse heap, or in churchyard, corpse lies barely separated from corpse—much as the living sleep. Skulls of the prey animals are kept at Zuni in the same cave shrine with offerings to Paiyatemu, the Sun Youth, as, in general, prayer-sticks to various Spirits are often deposited together, or as images or fetishes of various Spirits will be set together on the same altar. At Zuni and probably elsewhere the Scalps are housed apart; they are so very dangerous; otherwise shelter is not an exclusive affair.

Travel.—To altar bowl or fetishes lead lines of meal, and on trails from or to shrines or springs meal is sprinkled—all for the Spirits to travel over. Casting meal on the altar is making a road for the Spirits. Similarly kachina dancers have the road opened to them, as they move outdoors from place to place or as they come indoors. One type of prayer-feather or feather-string used a great deal by Hopi indicates the road for the Spirits to travel by; among Zuni prayer-sticks a crook stick, representing presumably the rainbow, is for the Cloud people to come down on.

Prayer-sticks or prayer-feathers may be put down before or on a journey, and for this reason they are given to the dead, and, at times, to the kachina. Kachina depart to their lake or mountain-top whence for a long period they will not journey into town.

Ritual chant by Zuni kachina chiefs or by the Hopi Maize god is a narrative of migration, as is the origin story of almost every group, whether clan or society. People traveled carrying their sacred things on their backs, and this nomadism is still suggested by the very temporary character of the altar or guest house to which the Spirits are summoned.

Farming.—In those early days pollen from wild plants may have been given the Spirits, but the offering of corn pollen or meal implies a more settled way of life. The use of sacred meal is pay or tribute to the Spirits from an agricultural people. Analogously, there is the pay or gift of corn, seed-corn, to those in charge of ceremonial profitable to the people. Seed-corn figures on altars in a rite for increase, and seed corn is given away to people by the kachina, the bringers of crops, or by medicine men after juggling out grains from wall picture or Corn Mother. Since growth is associated with the crops, meal or pollen represents growth or new life and so figures in all rites where new life or rebirth or renewal is in mind. Corn-bearing stalks are also tokens of growth. The corn ear to which attention is peculiarly drawn because of some comparatively rare feature—the double ear or the perfectly kerneled ear—lends itself as a fetish for the Corn or Earth spirit. To increase supply in grinding meal or as protection for the corn store or for pregnant women, the new-born, or the novice, the perfect corn ear appears as part fetish, part charm, indistinguishably. Certain wild plants formerly used for food are used today only in ritual, and tobacco and cotton are cultivated today only for ritual use.

Weather and season, always of paramount interest to the farmer, may be expected to figure in his ritual. Probably no Pueblo ceremony is without song or prayer for moisture. Prayer-stick-making is in large part for moisture, and certain prayer-sticks are prayer-images for rain, the miniature kick-stick which is deposited in arroyo or irrigation ditch, or the miniature ring which represents the clay balls cast up by the arroyo or wash in flood. Around springs much ritual centers—prayer-sticks or prayer-feathers are offered in or near them, and water is fetched from them to be used in altar ritual or to be poured out, as possessing peculiar virtue, upon the fields. Prayer-sticks or prayer-feathers are offered also in irrigation ditches. Precipitation is sufficiently erratic and localized to make tenable the idea that the individual may be either favored or discriminated against by the Spirits; consequently, drought becomes a sanction for the proper performance of ceremony. "Rain will not fall on your field" if you are remiss in ritual observance. Ritual dancing and running are primarily for rainfall or snowfall.

Food.—Food is ever the chief form of return for service. You feed those who work for you. And so with food offerings you feed the Spirits whose aid you call upon, or whose "flesh" you desire, sprinkling meal or pollen in your summons as a kind of preliminary act of hospitality. As the dead are expected to serve you, you give them food, too, whether enemy dead or your own dead. As you feed all members of your household, so all fetishes in your care must be fed, day by day. To the Spirits, in general, a bit of food may be crumbled at mealtime or crumbs may be thrown on the fire. Certain dishes are associated with certain ritual occasions, as *pigumi*, the baked corn pudding made by the Hopi in connection with every ceremony, or as wafer-bread, which in some eastern towns is made only on ritual occasions, or as wheaten bread contributed to the altar on the patron saint's day (Santo Domingo).* In the East, rabbit is virtually a ritual food, and communal rabbit hunts are directed largely to provide food for ceremonialists and their fetishes. It is very dangerous to withhold food, particularly from kachina impersonators.

Hunting.—When hunting fetishes are engaged in working for you, they must receive particular attentions in the matter of food. The blood of the quarry is smeared on them. Game animals themselves must be rendered well disposed. Dead deer or rabbits are given corn kernels or sprinkled with meal or pollen. Grass for the rabbits who are to suffer themselves to be caught is put on the rabbit-hunt fire. There is grass in the Tewa's

---

* Twitchell I, 473. Probably this is pay to the padre for the marriages he has performed.

feather offerings to Buffalo. In Hopi prayer-sticks for the domestic animals is included the kind of grass the animals like.

Domestication.—Prayer-images are made of the domestic animals and, by Hopi, prayer-images of the egg of their quasi-domesticated bird, the eagle. Prayer-feathers may be attached to all animals, wild or domestic, since all in one way or another are valuable. Wild turkey was domesticated for its feathers which are the most generally used feathers in offerings.

War.—Prayer-stick offerings made by War chiefs include miniature weapons—bow and arrow and war club. The fetish "mother" of Red Bow Youth, the woman war chief of Tewa, is a small bow and arrow. Arrow points or spear points are attached to the sticks of office of Hopi and Zuni War chiefs. Stone points are used as protective fetishes in many ways—on altars, fastened to fetishes whether of corn or stone, in medicine or prayer-meal bowls. As defensive charms, they are carried on the person; and they are used in making passes against witches. War god images are made annually at Zuni; everywhere war gods are impersonated. Enemy scalps are cared for as fetishes for rain or for public health and safety. Objects taken from the fallen enemy were placed in the headdress or bandoleer of War chiefs or members of warlike societies.

Dress.—The feathers on prayer-sticks are thought of as raiment, and the single turkey feather in Hopi and Laguna sticks in particular as a mantle or blanket. The husk of a corn ear is called its dress (Hopi),[826] but corn-ear fetishes are "dressed" in feathers. They are adorned with beads. A cotton fringe on the Zuni war god image or around the neck of a mountain-lion fetish represents kilt or blanket. Annually Keres dress the Sun with miniature clothes. The ceremonial array of chief, society man, or dancer consists in many particulars of archaic forms of dress or headdress into which a special meaning is sometimes read, as when Tewa of Hano say that letting the hair flow loose at prayer-stick-making is a token of falling rain.[827] Impersonation requires meticulous array, long hair to impersonate long-haired gods, and face or body must be painted just as is the person of the god; if the god carries staff or stick of office, shield or tablet, so must his impersonator. Ceremonial moccasins are worn or impersonators must go barefoot. As the dead are going to join special groups, their raiment is important; a little boy is buried in the black cotton breechcloth he receives prior to his kachina initiation. A young man is buried in his kachina dance kilt; an older man in a blue breechcloth kilt. A woman is buried in her bridal robe. To possess burial raiment is said to be one of the compelling motives for getting married.[828]

Sex.—In so far as prayer-stick feathers or beads are thought of as offerings of feather or blanket or beads to the Spirits, prayer-stick-making is consistently in the hands of men,[829] the suppliers of clothes and adornments. Besides, bead, feather, wood, and, among Hopi, weaving techniques have probably long been in the hands of the men. (The offering of cotton fringes by women at Zuni indicates that weaving was in the hands of women, as it was.) In the prayer-stick itself sex is frequently represented. The faceted, "face" prayer-stick is commonly female, and the female stick is always placed to the left of the male, which is the position at the altar, in bed,* and in the graveyard. The yellow stick is female; the blue-green, male. Other color associations with sex, if any, are obscure. The terrace or angular cloud design, whether on prayer-stick or kachina doll cradle or headdress, is thought of as female, possibly because it is a house, the cloud house. Lightning designs on a Hano winter solstice altar (Corner kiva) are thought of as male (north and south) and female (east and west).† The cylindrical kachina doll of Keres is male; the flat doll, female. Sex distinctions are always imputed to Kachina impersonations. Why men impersonate female kachinas or why in some towns women are or were kept ignorant about masked impersonations are aspects of the kachina cult unwarranted by anything in the general culture.

Sex organs are represented on ritual sticks or painted conventionally as a sex glyph on the body or on rocks. Gourd models may be attached to the body. The act of coition is repre-

---

* Benedict 3: I, 125. Implying a turn to the left, anti-sunwise, in coition.

† Fewkes 8:269, n. 2. Perhaps a Navaho touch.

sented in various ritual ways, particularly by the clowns. Binding the penis of the Koyemshi clown kachina is a negative sex rite, as is ritual continence in general. Thus in various particulars sexuality is expressed in Pueblo ceremonialism, although sex as a classificatory device is not greatly used, and, as Bunzel has well pointed out for Zuni, the concept of sexuality of the universe as the source of life is curiously lacking.*

Relationship.—The exchange of kinship terms in smoking ritual or on giving or receiving something special is presumably to affirm a bond of good will, as is generally the purport of extending kinship terms as courtesy terms. Similarly, initiation into any ceremonial group is thought of as a courtesy birth involving naming ritual and adoptive kinship. Conventional assignment of particular rites to particular kindred, such as headwashing to the father's sister or prayer-stick-depositing to a "child of the clan," her brother's son, is an integrating factor of great importance throughout the social organization.

Manners.—The formal behavior we call manners is much more conspicuous in Pueblo ritual than in everyday life. For example, thanks are said by Hopi for all individual contributions to ceremonial as when a messenger brings back water from a spring or collects plants or sand, or when somebody gives you prayer-feathers or sticks or ceremonial food, whereas in the household acts of passing something to another or performing other slight service it is not customary to say thanks. Again, prayer or ceremonial speechifying will be listened to with reiterated expressions of agreement, *anchaa*, amen, say the Hopi audience, over and over, whereas in ordinary talk interruption and failure to listen are not at all uncommon. Taking only four mouthfuls from any dish or exchanging kinship terms in giving or receiving anything (Zuni) are ritual rather than ordinary manners. Breathing from the hand, the Spanish hand kiss, was practiced at Zuni and Laguna, in greeting chiefs, not in ordinary intercourse. Verbal greetings or formulary beginnings of con-

---

* Bunzel 2:488. For this reason the much-quoted discussion by Haeberlin on "the idea of fertilization in the culture of the Pueblo Indians" has always seemed to me misleading.

versation are very much elaborated in ceremonial circles. The messenger says, "My fathers, my mothers, my children, how have you lived these days?"—"Happily! Come in! Be seated!" —"Now this day here you have passed us on our road." To the usual goodbye, "I am going," you add, "After a good day may you come to evening." The Hopi kiva greetings are: "Am I welcome?"—"Very good, thanks!"[830]

Compulsion through gift.—All offerings made to the Spirits, if accepted, are compulsive. Prayer-sticks when planted may fall down, which is an unfavorable sign and indicates that the offering has not been accepted. Tobacco is the most compulsive of all offerings or presents.* If you accept the cigarette, you must perform the ritual service asked of you. Complementarily, if you do not pay up, you will not get what you ask for, like Lihkila of Zuni who did not get her baby because she made no "presents" to the Rain chieftancy of the South after leaving her baby image on their winter solstice altar.

Vow.—This is included in ritual in the more comprehensive attitude or belief that whatever you undertake you must see through. If you go into a ceremonial assemblage or attend a curing treatment, you must stay to the close. If you undertake an office, you must fill it for the stated term or for life. If the winter solstice dancer of Santo Domingo dropped his role, "he would die. He's got to do it all his life."[831] Obviously this doctrine and feeling give a great deal of stability to the social structure.

Concentration.—Most ritual taboos, whether restriction or abstinence, appear to be directed toward insuring concentration on the object of the ceremony. Various distractions are precluded by continence, fasting, peaceableness, silence, secretiveness, vigil, staying in town, retreat.

---

* Spanish administrators were informed on this. When Governor Martinez sent emissaries from all the pueblos to Hopiland, he gave them the blessed Cross and some handfuls of tobacco to give in his name to the chiefs (Bloom, 193). To this day any request made by a White person is facilitated by tobacco. Once the manager of Ohewa kiva in Zuni was willing to send out the bogey kachina because I asked for him with Bull Durham.

Sympathetic magic.—A very large part of ritual is based on it, particularly on the concept that like causes like. On the prayer-stick buried by the Zuni War chief near the camp of the enemy was a feather of the chaparral jay in order to make the enemy behave like the bird which flies at dawn every which way, as if in panic. A stick-racer might carry an owl feather to overcome his competitors with owl sleepiness.* In general, the selection of feathers and woods for prayer-sticks is determined by comparable ideas, likewise the use of plants in prayer-sticks. Plants used in windbreaks are placed on the Oraibi Powalawu altar as a mimetic prayer for the protection of crops against the sand-storms for which windbreaks are made.[832] The Hopi prayer-stick messenger to Sun's house at the summer solstice gathers flowers to give to the Winter solstice chief to use in pigment for his prayer-sticks at his ceremony "so there will be more flowers" the following summer.[833] Oraibi kick-race balls are made of pitch and horsehair, the hair of swift horses. Sometimes rabbit hair is added and a few of the hairs that grow over men's big toes, the hairs of specially good runners.[834] (I am wondering if Taos shinny balls are not stuffed with deer hair for like reason.) The Acoman[835] who undertakes to impersonate Santiago, the horse saint, has to visit several pueblos to collect horse and sheep dung to distribute during the fiesta and make the townspeople rich in animals.† Masks which are always "dangerous" are peculiarly so in pregnancy lest some feature be reproduced in the child, like the small eyes of Shumaikoli (Zuni). The cure for any abnormality in a child caused by a mask is for the father to put on the mask and dance before the child (Zuni), just as anyone sick from fright or anyone who is to be hardened against fear must be brought into contact with the fearsome object.‡ During the

* Benedict 3: I, 98–99. This in tale, whether it is ever actually done, we don't know. I guess it is.

† He also collects and distributes seeds, a ritualistic "agricultural explorer"!

‡ "When a man runs at night (ritually) and sees something moving in front, he must go up to the thing whatever it turns out to be, bush, tree, or stone, and rub some of the stuff of which the thing is made over his body. This will make him brave and strong and no longer afraid" (Mishongnovi, Beaglehole 3:46).

Walpi War chief's ceremony to make the ground freeze it is called out that men are not to sing kachina songs or women to grind, pursuits associated with soft and rain-soaked ground, and therefore hurtful to the efficacy of freezing ritual.[836] Walpi children are invited to go and eat at the houses where the summer solstice ceremony is being conducted. "This eating means to have lots of corn and watermelons."[837] In the Powamu ceremony Ahul kachina rises gradually from a prone position until at sunrise he is erect. Then he lowers his head to the ground and bends backward very slowly, four times facing the east, four times facing the west, "to make the summer long and the sun move slowly."[838]

Like may be seen to be causing like in other forms of dramatic prayer which is largely setting an example, so to speak, to the spirits. Ritual running is a conspicuous example, especially the kick-race, since the clouds are to fill the watercourse with water rushing as swiftly as the runners and, like them, kicking clay nodules, which are formed in watercourses during rain freshets.[839] The plasterers of Hopi kivas want the rain to come and make the sand in the valley like the sandy wash they use. When people touch the longevity crooks set in First Mesa shrines at the winter solstice, they say to the shortest crooks, representing heads bowed to the ground, "I want to be like you, very old."[840] Cornstalks are carried in the Hopi Antelope dance that young people may grow straight and vigorous like the stalks.[841] Ears or grains of black corn are carried by anyone in hiding (see p. 637), to make his road dark. Again, prayer-images are an expression of like compelling like, as, too, may be corn or rain models or pictures. For many Indians there is power in paint; for example, when a Navaho patient is painted with the sun or with the stripes of color that represent Sun's house, he is impersonating Sun or visiting him and getting power or strength.[842] Rules about body- or mask-painting among Pueblos all point to a like conception, although it has not been verbally expressed. But, when War chiefs paint to look like the War gods, they are surely getting power from them. In fact, this concept is probably implicit in all impersonation or transformation, whether by paint or mask, or by animal pelt, paws, or claws. If you look like one with power, also if you act like him, you get his power.

Related to these ways of sympathetic magic is the ritual practice of substitution or representation, of substituting part of a thing or the image or representation, for the thing itself. Ordinarily, in accounts of Pueblo culture this is referred to as symbolizing, a misleading term; for, unless by symbol merely sign is meant, we connote a larger measure of abstraction than is characteristic of Pueblo mentality. Pueblos think in concrete, specific terms. They are forever asking for what we or Navaho would call blessings, but for these the only general words are white day or light (Zuni, *tek'ohanna*) or road (Keresan, *hi'anyi*) —the road by which the Spirits travel. Nor do Pueblos have to protect their religion by metaphysical vagueness or ambiguity, not being troubled as yet by inroads of science; and never is a Pueblo like the White man a seeker after symbols as secret answers to queries about the Unknown. (Somehow the White man associates Pueblo secretiveness with this kind of esotericism unaware that complete Pueblo explanations would no more satisfy him or even arrest his attention than in his own culture does laboratory knowledge of life or death.)

Yet to the Pueblo a large number of ceremonial objects are representative, e.g., the lightning-stick; cotton used on masks or on the face of the dead as clouds; the single duck or turkey feather for the whole bird or plumage; altar image or sand-painting of bird, star, rainbow, etc. Such representations are in varying degree forms of compulsive magic insuring the presence or imparting the power of the thing represented, and they are referred to by the very name of the thing represented—lightning, clouds, rainbow, star. Similarly, shrines which represent the more distant houses of the Spirits are called by the same name as these houses, just as when rooms in dwelling-houses are used, as at Zuni, for kivas or, as among Keres, for the underworld, they are referred to by kiva or underworld name.

In ritual hair-washing occurs a form of substitution through abbreviation: instead of washing the whole head, you may dip suds to the crown with an ear of corn, or as in the Hopi funerary hairwash, you dip two fingers (of your left hand) in the bowl of suds and pass the lock on your forehead through these fingers, four times, brushing with two or three twigs. The hand kiss or, in Pueblo expression, breathing from or on the hand, is abbreviated or curtailed, the clasped hand being withdrawn before it reaches the mouth. Paying a deer for the buckskin she expects, a woman places her ceremonial blanket and her string of beads over the laid-out animal, but only for a short time.

Orientation and color.—A feeling for the middle place, the center, is expressed in the ritual of smoking or aspersing, in "rooting" the town by prayer-stick, in the "earth center" sand on which rests the medicine bowl and from which extend the meal lines of the directions (Hopi), and in the seating of persons or placing of objects at the center of a meal cross of the directions (Zuni, Hopi). Ritual performance is strung, as it were, on the thread of orientation; for repetition is ruled by the cardinal directions. Persons are presented to the directions, and offerings of all kinds are deposited in the directions; the routes of hunts, races, or processions may be similarly determined. Dances will be repeated in the different directions, and altar rites of all kinds: smoking, aspersing, pouring water, exorcising. The basing of prayer, of song sequences or ritual narrative on the directions becomes a sort of mnemonic device, establishing an order not easy to stray from, an important matter where error invalidates ritual. In sand-paintings, in masks or various ritual objects, the color-direction scheme is very important. Where the scheme is ignored or little emphasized, as seems to be the case among Tiwa, particularly at Taos, we may infer that a large part of Pueblo ritualism is lacking.

Repetitiousness.—The repetition of a fixed formula which has been well called formulistic magic[843] characterizes not only speeches, prayer, and song but many altar rites as well as court or shrine performances. The sense of order or of achievement through order is involved here too, as it is in the fixed sequences or numerical preconceptions of the Pueblos which tend to arrest or preclude observation but which are very satisfying. There is no denial, I presume, that order gives assurance, or that ritualism in general is reassuring.* "Since we perform this rightly, we must certainly attain its objects," says in his prayer the Hopi Antelope chief.[844] The Acoman shaman who is wearing his hair "cornerwise" in accordance with the perfect number (Stirling) undoubtedly could say with the lady of fashion, "I feel as well as my hair looks."

Separation from danger.—Supernatural power is always thought of as dangerous. It must be used with circumspection; persons using it must be more or less segregated; and, after using it, you must return it to the bestower or separate yourself from it. This is the theory of almost all cleansing or exorcising rites at the conclusion of ceremonial or in exercising precaution toward nonmembers during a ceremony. Possibly one explanation of ceremonial continence can be made in these terms.

Co-operation.—Pueblo ritual involves so much co-operation it is difficult to select special aspects. We may note the performance of ritual by particular clans or lineages, by societies, or by cult or kiva groups for the good of the whole community; the contribution of more or less personal bundles or properties to the joint altar, and the great amount of loaning of dance properties and costume; also the planning of public dance or race after esoteric altar ceremonial or retreat, at which distribution of

* Why such reassurance or sense of security is needed or secured in one culture more or less than in another is the question. If you lean with Radin to the theory that fear from economic insecurity is the basis of religion, you can find plenty of supporting evidence among Pueblos. The psychologist suggests that ritual is a group catharsis for the traumata produced by the socialization of the child (or of life in narrow quarters). But, as Dr. Du Bois points out, "the diffusion of rituals makes such an idea more difficult than the mere statement implies." Moreover, the Pueblo child is socialized largely through imitative processes, and the infant is comparatively untrained in those matters the psychoanalyst dwells upon.

Nevertheless, the field psychologist *who has mastered Pueblo ritual* would find the Pueblos a profitable study could he deal with their technique of secretiveness. How make an analysis of what ritualistic participation signifies for a person when that person will refer in no way to ritual and there is little or no opportunity of seeing him or her engaged in ritual. Seldom if ever will the observer be as fortunate as was Voth, when at dawn, after watching old Tangakweima take up her Marau standard, very reverently, wave it from the directions, sprinkle it with meal, and set it into the kiva hatchway, he heard her say: "Now it is going to rain; I asked the rain to come"—participation and assurance, an act of faith indeed.

presents to onlookers by kachina or clown is frequent; and, finally, all the communal hunting, farming, grinding, and cooking that serve ritual ends: rabbit drives held to feed the fetishes of the Town chief; crops raised to supply the kachina with corn to give away or to supply food to impersonators, food that townswomen are called upon to grind or cook. In one way or another, directly or indirectly, through service or through paying for service, everybody co-operates in the ceremonial life—everybody is a ritualist.

CHAPTER V

CALENDAR*

The ceremonial calendar is or was based on solar and lunar observation together with the principle of one ceremony following another in fixed order, and on a general adaptation to the economic round or seasons for farming, weaving, war, hunting, and even building. Hopi building goes on after rain- or snowfall, to facilitate mud plaster-making; or when the little mesa-top reservoirs are full as in early summer or late winter.[1] During the February ceremony of Powamu, kivas are plastered† inside by the girls, and lightning and cloud designs made on the beams.[2] At Zuni, house-building or repair is carried on in early spring or late autumn in the weeks before Shalako, for at this time the kachina have to be received in new or newly repaired houses, and there is a definite demand for eight sizable houses. Moreover, guests for this ceremonial are expected from other towns or tribes. If the houses are not ready in time, the ceremony may be postponed for ten days or even twenty.

At the departure of the Shalako kachina, there is hunt ritual; and a deer hunt is or was made in advance to secure pelts for ritual use. Rabbit hunts are held regularly in the autumn (First Mesa) or in early summer when the fields must be protected from depredation and when captive eagles must be fed (Mishongnovi), but a drive may be held at any time of the year (*not* in December by Hopi)‡ in connection with ceremonies to secure food for the chiefs or their fetishes or for celebrants in general.

---

* I suggest that after reading the preliminary general discussion the reader pass on to chap. vi on ceremonies before taking up the detailed calendrical records of the several towns.

† Kiva plastering was noted at San Juan in the middle of November (Parsons 49:104). Throughout the East, houses are replastered in anticipation of Christmas or of the saint's day.

‡ See p. 505.

A rabbit drive is generally held in connection with a saint's day celebration. The animal dances of the East, Buffalo, Deer, or Eagle dances, are usually performed at Christmas or on January 6, Kings' Day.

Scalp dances are held sporadically at Zuni, Isleta, and San Felipe, perhaps elsewhere; at Zuni as an initiation into the War society, at Isleta in connection with springtime racing, at San Felipe at Chrismastide at the behest of the kiva chiefs. The last scalp dance of Acoma was held the end of October.[3] Autumn, after the harvest was in, having been the favorite time for raiding, was and is associated with war dances such as Owinahaiye or Howina. Other war ceremonies or rituals are held in the winter or early spring; there is a functional relation between them and weather control, control of snowfall or of high winds. In the war ritual during the Hopi winter solstice ceremony prayer-sticks are distributed to strengthen the houses. The houses of Acoma are strengthened by the War chief before the Fight with the Kachina; perhaps house-strengthening by Hopi was also against enemies.

At Zuni the winter games are associated with the War gods. Gaming is assigned by Hopi to early winter, to the Play moon. Weaving is an indoor winter occupation, and, as it plays a big part in Hopi marriage ritual, marriages are celebrated in the winter, also the so-called Girls' dances which in a general way lead to marriage. Ritual shinny and kick-races are in the nature of fertility or rain magic, and belong to the spring and early summer.

Irrigating, planting, and harvesting are all activities associated with ceremonial. Throughout the East there is ritual on "opening the ditch" and, at Isleta, an elaborate ceremony. Before planting, the Eastern societies perform cleansing ritual for the fields, and there is analogous ritual in the Hopi Powamu ceremony. On First Mesa in May the Sun-watcher "has to watch the sun very carefully for the people to plant." Certain chiefly families plant in turn at intervals of five or six days as the sun reaches particular points on the horizon at sunrise, which points give their names to the planting times.[4] The day before, the

Sun-watcher informs the rain chief whose turn it is; others are glad to plant at the same time; it is a favorable moment; "they join together so to bring rain." There is no planting series on Second Mesa, but the watermelon-planting by all for themselves, the first corn-planting by all for the Town chief, and, sometimes, another planting for the Crier chief are all timed on a horizon calendar. For his corn-planting the Town chief watches the sun, and the Crier announces four days in advance.[5] Formerly at Zuni Pekwin announced dates for planting. "Some fine morning in May, the voice, low, mournful, yet strangely penetrating and tuneful of the Sun Priest is heard from the housetops," wrote Cushing,[6] and our friend Nick remembered Pekwin's calls to plant corn or beans.

Kachina dancing to promote rainfall or snowfall occurs almost throughout the year at Zuni and among Keres; but in Hopiland the kachina "go away" in July at the Nima'n ceremony, and subsequent weather ritual is performed by the Snake-Antelope or Flute societies, the dates of the ceremonies being determined by the state of the crops. Crop-destroying thunderstorms occur in midsummer so the ceremonies which are associated with Lightning may be a check on devastation. The banishment of the rain-bringing kachina in July may be similarly motivated, since corn plants are uprooted by flood in the washes.[7]

Zuni Rain societies and throughout the East almost all societies conduct retreats for rain during the farming season, and more especially in time of drought conduct pilgrimages to distant kachina shrines. At Zuni and Taos these pilgrimages are fixed at the summer solstice or toward the end of August, irrespective of weather conditions. Society retreats for rain among Keres and at Jemez are always followed by kachina dances, for the shamans are supposed to visit Shipap and to bring the kachina back with them. (Probably that is why at Zuni a society member will lead the kachina, even if Kachina town is in the west and Shipapolima is in the east.) In general a public dance, a dance for the enjoyment or profit of everybody, follows an esoteric and specialized ceremony.

As kachina are conspicuously the patrons of the crops, the

oldest and most significant kachina come out in the agricultural season. No chances should be taken at such times. Novel and therefore less important kachina appear in winter dances; winter is for amusement or play.

Women's society ceremonies or dances, when they occur, are associated with war, fertility, or harvest. The three Hopi women's ceremonies are celebrated in the autumn. Some time after the harvest the seasonal transfer ceremony or ritual of the Tewa Winter Town chief takes place. The Summer Town chief has his transfer ceremony at the start of the farming season. The moiety chiefs of Isleta also have transfer seasonal ritual.

In the West, sunset and sunrise are noted on a horizon calendar, and solstice ceremonial, more especially winter solstice ceremonial and more especially at Zuni, becomes the backbone or, in Zuni terms, the center, of the calendar. At the Zuni winter solstice, Sun chief (Pekwin) and paramount Rain chiefs and the chief of the Kachina society count their days, and engage in prayer-stick-making and other "work"; the annual appointments of kachina impersonators are made and their sticks of office are presented; kachina chiefs appear, Pa'utiwa performing scalp ritual suggestive of human sacrifice; in connection with Pa'utiwa two or three clans are prominent; synchronous meetings are held by the curing societies, first for weather and later for curing; there is new-fire ritual; all persons observe certain taboos and perform ritual of exorcism and of prayer. At this season the Hopi expect every man to be present in the kiva associated with his clan. The clan kachina of the Winter solstice chieftaincy appear; and various kachina celebrations are planned ahead for the year. There is war ceremonial. A dramatization of the Sun's progress may be held in which various societies take part. In some of the Eastern towns the Town chief makes solar observations and the societies conduct a four-day ceremony, but only in Isleta and Taos does there appear to be anything like the ceremonial concentration of the West.

At the Hopi winter solstice there is no general fire taboo or new-fire ritual; new-fire ritual is associated with the preceding ceremony of Wüwüchim. This November ceremony affects the rest of the Hopi calendar. When the Wüwüchim is celebrated with initiations, in its long form, some of the other ceremonies are lengthened. Only Wüwüchim initiates may take part in winter solstice kiva ceremonial or may dance kachina. With all this in mind the Wüwüchim ceremony is thought of quite properly by Hopi as the beginning of the ceremonial period or year.

Summer solstice ritual among Hopi (First Mesa) is merely to honor the Sun, incidentally to slow up his journey back to winter; but the horizon observation dates a series of ceremonies, Home-going kachina ceremony, Snake-Antelope or Flute ceremony and Women's ceremonies, the smoke assemblage for the next ceremony being held "four days" after the conclusion of the last ceremony (Mishongnovi[8] and, in part, Walpi). At Zuni and elsewhere the summer solstice observation initiates rain retreats and kachina dances. This calendrical co-ordination is slighter in the East, where comparatively little interest attaches to the summer solstice.

The moons* are named† and are a factor in regulating the succession of ceremonies, particularly among Hopi, where each ceremony is associated with a particular moon. At Zuni two winter moons are assigned to the Wood and Big Firebrand societies, and throughout the year the moon is observed for monthly prayer-stick offerings by the curing societies and by impersonators of Sun Youth and of the kachina chiefs of the Shalako groups. The phase of the moon is considered in timing a ceremony which includes initiation, as a waxing moon is favorable to the rebirth which is initiation. Initiations, also installations, are usually made in connection with the annual ceremony.

Whenever ceremonies occur in a series, as in the rain retreats made by societies in succession, the days are counted, i.e., the

---

* Names refer to seasonal or agricultural conditions or to ceremony (Zuni, Cushing 6:154–56; Stevenson 2:108; Hopi, Stephen 4:1037–39; Parsons 55:58–61; Beaglehole 3:23–25; Tewa, Parsons 49:168, n. 337; Isleta, Parsons 52:288; Taos, Parsons 58:83).

† An unexplained peculiarity of the Zuni-Hopi moon-naming is a tendency for the summer-autumn moons to be nameless (Zuni) or to be given the winter-spring moon names (Hopi). According to Cushing, the six nameless Zuni moons are given in ritualistic language the color names of the directions.

societies "go in" in a fixed order, and one or more days are allowed to elapse between the successive four-day ceremonies. Even when there is no series and societies do not repeat approximately the same ceremony, the principle of succession in determining the calendar is important. After the conclusion of any given ceremony people look forward to or prepare for the next in order. The chief of the concluding ceremony may notify the chief of the coming ceremony that it is now his turn to watch the sun (Hopi,[9] Taos).

The priority dating of ceremonies is a kind of ranking, as when the White Corn group of Isleta "goes in" one day ahead of the other Corn groups or the Zuni Rain chieftaincy of the North starts the series of summer rain retreats. At the summer solstice, members of the Zuni curing societies plant their prayer-sticks two days before other people. At the winter solstice, Walpi Town chief goes in in the forenoon; Hano Town chief, in the afternoon.

The Hopi apart, all the towns observe the feasts or fasts of the Catholic Church—Christmastide and Eastertide and All Soul's Day, and each town observes its patron saint's day. Other saint's days may be also observed with dance or race, with rooster pull or food-throwing: Guadalupe Day (December 12), St. Anthony's Day (June 13), St. John's Day (June 24), Peter's and Paul's Day (June 29), St. James' Day (July 25), St. Ann's Day (July 26). In some cases the observance of a saint's day has been shifted to another date in the calendar, e.g., St. Joseph's Day at Laguna has been changed from March 19 to September 19, "because there were so many good things to eat then."[10] Possibly the winter solstice ceremonies of the East were found to conflict with Christmastide and so came to be held at the end of November or early in December and were dated by the church calendar instead of by solar observation. The Zuni ceremony of Melons Come (Molawia) is celebrated some time after melon harvest, because of calendrical convenience, I suggest, the adjustment being the more easy because the ceremony, it appears, was borrowed.

The school year has at times upset the native calendar.

Formerly Acoma held the kachina initiation of the children at the winter solstice, now the initiation is held in summer.[11] Everywhere absence of children at school has led to minor changes in dance dates, as for example holding the Buffalo dance on First Mesa on a Saturday and Sunday in order that the children might be present.[12]

The cultivation of wheat has affected the Isletan calendar, necessitating an early performance of the ceremony of general exorcism, wheat being planted two months earlier than corn.

With the major Catholic observances, kachina dances are not infrequently associated, as at Cochiti and Jemez at Eastertide, or as at San Juan and Taos at Christmas when Turtle dance, a maskless kachina dance, is danced in the plaza. Taos dates its relay races for Sun and Moon by the church calendar, holding them on May 3, Holy Cross Day, and on September 30, San Gerónimo Day.

In the northeastern towns Matachina, the Mexican dance of Montezuma, is a common Christmas dance. In these towns the Mexican custom of Las Posados, the nine nights of hospitality from Guadalupe Day to Christmas Eve, *Noche Buena*, is observed by building little bonfires of crisscross fat pine throughout the town, *los luminarios*, to give light to the Virgin on her journey. Formerly a bonfire was also lit on the mesa top north of San Juan,* possibly by Mexicans.

Native calendars must have suffered some readjustment irrespective of the Church, whenever a new cult or even a new society or celebration was introduced, whether imitated from another town or brought in by immigrants. Such calendrical arrangements may be analyzed out of Zuni or Hopi systems. When the Keresan curing societies were introduced to Ashiwi we may suppose that at some point in what was probably a long history the society ceremonials were confined to the autumn-winter season when they would not clash with the agricultural-weather program of Rain chieftaincies. In tradition *the two winter moons*

---

* Compare the building of beacon fires on the hills near El Paso and Juarez by the Pueblo settlers to guide Moctezuma across the Rio Grande (Fewkes 10:74).

of the Wood society were deliberately assigned to the society. The restriction of Hopi kachina to that half of the year when they will
not interfere with the major ceremonies suggests another de-
liberate calendrical arrangement. So does the holding of ceremonies "every four years" at Zuni. Rendering a ceremony quadrennial, virtually sporadic, helps greatly to lighten an overbur-
dened calendar. Possibly the Hopi device of alternating ceremonies, the Snake-Antelope and the Flute, and at Oraibi the
Marau and Lakon with the Oaqöl, was an arrangement to relieve
the calendar on introducing a ceremony. As Oaqöl is known to
have been introduced from Awatobi the possibility becomes a
probability. The three Hopi women's societies or ceremonies,
Marau, Lakon, Oaqöl, are so much alike that it seems probable
that they were once variants of the same society or ceremony in
different towns. Calendrical repetitiousness and calendrical complexity both may be explained, as indeed they are explained in
the traditions, through the adoption of the ceremonies of immigrant groups. The extreme complexity of Zuni ceremonies in
particular are to be explained along this line. Take, for example,
the double appearance and double clan impersonation of Pa'utiwa, the Kachina chief, at the winter solstice ceremony, or at this
ceremony the intrusion of the Big Firebrand society into a kiva
new-fire ceremony conducted by the Badger clan, or the appearance of the Chakwena kachina who is associated with the
Ky'anakwe ceremony and the Corn people's kiva, traditionally a
consolidated group. The third impersonation of Pa'utiwa by a
third clan in the Molawia ceremony and the insertion of that
whole ceremony as an afterthought in Shalako is another case of
complexity from borrowing. And so, I think, is the Shomatowe
ritual at the conclusion of the Zuni Scalp ceremony. Again, consider the introduction of the Porcingula fiesta by the Pecos descendants, at Jemez, or the Kings' Day dance by Laguna colonists at Isleta or better still analyze the ceremony of communal
exorcism or purification at Isleta which appears to be a combination of the Tanoan conclusion of the winter ceremonies with the
early spring exorcism by Keresan curing societies.

Ceremonies last over periods of one day or four days or eight days; or, in Western terms, night or nights. At Zuni in computing the dates of ceremonies only nights are counted. Taboo periods begin at sundown and continue through four nights ending the fourth morning at dawn.[13] We may infer from Hopi terminology that the Hopi count was similar, the duration being four or eight nights: go in or assembly day not counted, "not anything,"* the third night, *komototokya*, wood-carrying sleeps, the fourth night, *totokya*, sleeps. The days before the third and fourth nights bear their names. The day after the fourth night is dance day, feast day.†

Tally cords are used in one ceremony (Shalako, Zuni, see p. 747, n.‡), and tally sticks are mentioned (Zuni, Laguna).[14] The four parallel lines of meal made in some ceremonies on the kiva hatch (Zuni, Hopi) are said to be rubbed off day by day as tally.

HOPI

In First Mesa opinion the Hopi year starts with the Wüwü-chim ceremony or, as Voth translates, the Adults' ceremony, in Hawk or Initiate moon, the November moon.§ "With this initiate moon everything is changed." The ceremony is annual, but initiations into the four constituent societies, Singers, Wüwü-chim, Agaves, and Horns, occur irregularly, when there are youths enough or at the pleasure of the chief of the Singers society who on First Mesa is chief of the ceremony. Singers chief watches the sun, at sunset, to announce to Wüwüchim chief the time to call the smoke assemblage, always held the evening before the announcement of a ceremony in order to smoke over the

---

* Hopi explain not counting the first day on the ground that it is the last day of the count between announcement and beginning of ceremony (Voth 8:17).

† Compare the Spanish Catholic count: *antevisperas, visperas, fiesta;* but time-reckoning by nights is widespread among Indians.

‡ The tally cord was used more generally in early days. In 1630 it was a mnemonic device among Pueblos who had sins to be confessed (Benavides, 32); the Great Rebellion was timed by a tally cord.

§ In September the Agaves of Oraibi held what appears to be a preliminary prayer-stick-making called "making the year" (Voth 9:113).

prayer-sticks or feathers made earlier in the day.* At daybreak from the top of his maternal house Crier chief announces the ceremony,† sixteen days in advance of the conclusion of the ceremony when there is to be initiation, eight days, the year without initiation. Then Crier chief deposits at the Break, where the mesa narrows into Walpi, the prayer-feathers smoked over the night before. (For summaries of Wüwüchim see pp. 606 ff., 867.)

Follows Soyal, "they come out," which is primarily for the Sun and, as it occurs at the winter solstice, is always referred to in the literature as the winter solstice ceremony, although a war ceremony is performed and the return of the kachina is celebrated. Auhulani, a turquoise-faced kachina with long horn, and his corn-carrying sisters, kachina of the Water-Corn clan, in charge of Soyala at Walpi, visit the kivas at night and do a song to slow pacing, which is repeated outdoors in the afternoon. At Oraibi some clowning kachina come out, and later a kachina dance group of male and female impersonations.‡ From now on the kachina will visit until the Farewell or Home-going kachina ceremony in July.

For Soyala on First Mesa, Sun chief (Water-Corn clan) has watched the sunset and informed Soyala chief (Water-Corn) about the proper time, which is announced as usual the dawn following the smoke assemblage, announced sixteen days before its conclusion when there has been initiation at Wüwüchim, otherwise eight days. At Mishongnovi, where there is no office of Sun chief or watcher, Soyala (also Wüwüchim and [?] Powamu) are dated by solar observation (by Town chief or chief of cere-

---

* This on First Mesa; at Oraibi the characteristic preliminary is called prayer-stick-making; it is held in the maternal house the morning before the announcement; in the evening there may be a smoke assemblage (Dorsey and Voth 1:14). Perhaps only a verbal difference.

† At Oraibi, announcement is always from the roof of the maternal house of the Sparrow-Hawk clan where there is a shrine. Crier chief does not belong to this clan.

‡ What kachina may appear on Second Mesa is not known. In fact, there is no account at all of the winter solstice on Second Mesa. The whole ceremonial story should be recorded for Second Mesa towns.

mony).* At Oraibi solar observation for Soyala is not indicated. The initial day, which is the day of the announcement, appears to be sixteen days after the appearance of the Soyal kachina who the day after the conclusion of the Wüwüchim ceremony sets up the Soyal standard at the kiva hatchway.

From four days to a day or two before Soyala every adult townsman (Wüwüchim initiated) is expected to go into the kiva associated with his clan. *This is the only time any strict relationship between clanship and kiva membership is observed.* The men make prayer-sticks or feathers for relatives and for whatever they wish to pray for. Long feathered strings are carried from house to house to be breathed on, against respiratory disease. Early in the morning of Soyala people deposit the prayer-sticks in shrine (Walpi) or field (Oraibi) or attach the prayer-feathers to the object of their prayer-wish.

In the long form of Soyala at Walpi the War chief's altar is laid in Goat kiva, and there is a ceremony probably for increase of the domestic animals; in Chief kiva there is a very elaborate night ceremony at which the effigy of the patron of the Water-Corn clan in charge, Horned Water Serpent, is addressed and roars back; and various supernaturals are impersonated, Cloud, Hail, Ice, Antelope, Tungwup the Whipper kachina, and others, and the placing of the sun or its diurnal progress is dramatized. Recent Wüwüchim initiates are conspicuous, dance-gesturing and chanting. The slow circle dance called Owĕ among Keres is performed; also a variant of the Hawk dance of Oraibi.[15] A variant of the sun-shield dramatization, War chief ritual, and the Hawk dance are all presented in the Oraibi winter solstice ceremony, in its short form.†

On First Mesa, four days after Soyala, occurs "Sun prayer-stick-making" in the maternal family house of the Water-Corn

---

* Beaglehole 3:23. The summer solstice is observed by Crier chief from a shrine on the west edge of town.

† See pp. 560 ff. Without further records of winter solstice ceremonials, on Second Mesa, in Walpi for the long form (Stephen describes only the final day and night), for Third Mesa in Hotavila, no close comparisons or interpretations can be made.

clan, when "they turn the Sun back to summer." A "child" of the Water-Corn clan whose chief is chief of the ceremony* takes the prayer-sticks to Sun's house, about five miles to the eastward.

Four days after Sun prayer-stick-making, the War chief's ceremony is performed, to freeze the ground, according to Crow-Wing, to make the houses stand fast, and against sickness (prayer-feathers addressed to Masauwü) and evil winds (prayer-feathers to Wind Old Woman), according to Stephen. At sunrise the standard is placed over the doorway of the maternal family house of the chief of the ceremony, a Reed-Sun house. Prayer-stick-making by the assembled society of twenty-one members (1893), and the simple altar of War god images and corn-ear fetish is placed for the night ceremony of which there is no account except that Sho'tokününgwa, the Sky-Star-Lightning god, is invoked in song (Stephen), and four young men in couples are arrayed as War gods, each couple carrying a medicine bowl and an aspergill of olivella shells and the claws of lion, wolf, and wildcat (Parsons). Women who want a son may contribute food. At daylight people open their house doors on a crack. The War god couples run very fast from house to house, pushing the doors open to sprinkle medicine. This was the night when in kiva the Nasosotan society of stick-swallowers performed. The following day in 1893, the first time in thirty years, there was a circle war dance of men and women in the court, to a squatting choir of three or four old men and a drummer. War society members escorted or gathered up the dancers, but did not dance.[16]

These ceremonies and Soyala occur during "the dangerous moon," the moon "they have got to mind." Women do not grind at night, and people are quiet, not visiting around at night. A night wayfarer would dust ashes on his cheeks, to be safe from witches; on a child's head piñon gum might be smeared. During

---

* At Oraibi, Soyala chief was in charge of the Sun from summer to winter solstice, and the other half-year, from winter to summer solstice, the Flute societies were in charge. In June the Flutes held a one-day ceremony of prayer-stick-making for the Sun (Voth 9:129-36). The Flute societies, we may recall, are associated with warm weather.

this moon rabbits are not hunted lest they weep (Walpi),* nor are they dug from their holes (Mishongnovi) for the earth is considered to be too thin at this time† to dig for any animal.

In January, "play moon," the gaming season begins, the special game being hidden-ball. Men may play this game against women; otherwise there is no play of special group against group; anybody may organize the game. Spider Grandmother is called upon to help to victory; otherwise, the game, unlike the corresponding Zuni game, has no ceremonial features. Shinny is played by kiva, as a kind of fertility magic.

At this season Girls' dances, Buffalo dance or Butterfly dance, or kachina dances may be performed. They have been arranged for probably during winter solstice gatherings when the year's program is considered by the chiefs. The Snake-Antelope societies or the Flutes hold a one-day (Walpi)‡ prayer-stick-making ceremonial and raise their standard, invoking the Chiefs of the Directions to the prospective ceremony. The Women's societies likewise make prayer-sticks, in successive moons. At night there may be a kachina dance.

Powamu chief, who at Walpi is Kachina clan chief, watches the moon, and at the full of the December-January moon he plants beans, secretly, in Chief kiva, and the Kachina clan mother has some corn planted for her in her own house (Walpi). The morning after sighting the new moon, the February moon, Crier chief visits the kivas and announces that Powamu§ ceremony has begun. In Chief kiva Powamu chief and the impersonator of Ahül kachina who is associated with the Kachina clan make prayer-sticks. There is night dancing in Chief kiva, by

* Stephen 4:387. No taboos at Oraibi (see p. 570).

† Beaglehole 2:12. Compare the Taos taboo on digging within the town walls during the period of "staying still." Is it in order not to injure "our tender prostrate Earth mother" (Parsons 58:108)?

‡ At Oraibi the year of the summer ceremony the winter ceremony is lengthened to the usual nine days. There are no initiations in winter; no snakes are brought in; instead, a kachina dance.

§ *Powatani* means to put in order, the fields are to be insured against sandstorms, ants, all pests (Voth 2:71 n.).

dance groups from the other kivas, kachina or burlesques or clowns.

Follows before daybreak a society ceremony in which Ahül kachina is arrayed. At daybreak Ahül and Powamu chief deposit prayer-sticks and feathers at Kachina clan springs and visit the kivas and the houses with ceremonial associations, distributing Powamu chief's bean and corn plants and marking the entrances with meal, thereby appealing to the Cloud chiefs to sit over these places. Afternoon outdoor performances by kachina and kachina clowns. Seed corn is distributed from the Kachina clan mother which over a period of four days is to be planted by all the men in the kivas they frequent, together with their beans. If the beans grow high, the crops will be good. Powamu chief understands these omens.

Eight days after the announcement the Powamu society members "go in." That same night three sets of the Natashka or Suyuku bogey kachina come in and go into their kiva in Walpi or Sichomovi or Hano. The next day these kachina make the rounds of houses and kivas, telling the boys to hunt for them, and the girls to grind sweet corn. Four days later the little boys and girls* are whipped in the court by the two Tüngwüp kachina who also whip men for rheumatism. For four days the children will fast from salt and flesh and daily deposit a prayer-feather.

Three nights later kachina dance in kiva, and at daybreak "they cut their beans." The kachina distribute presents to the children; moccasins, bows and arrows, and tortoise-shell rattles to the boys, and moccasins, dolls, and bean plants to the girls. The bogey kachina return. Early in the morning below the mesa they have built a fire, and they say they have emerged from it. The bogeys visit the houses and the kivas, and after farcical play get food and prayer-feathers. Powamu chief places his altar for the usual altar ritual, and there is the ritual of prayer-stick-depositing. This afternoon there is dancing in the court and all night from kiva to kiva. The dance is without masks, and men impersonate female dancers. For the first time the children who

---

* In 1893 there were five children, aged eight to ten.

have been whipped look upon maskless kachina. Women desirous of offspring are given "dolls."

The year of initiation into the Wüwüchim societies Powamu ceremonial is prolonged by one day, in which at an outdoor kachina shrine the meal altar of the directions is laid by Powamu chief and visited by kachina chiefs, and the clan mothers and Wüwüchim initiates carry in procession elaborate basket trays of corn and spruce.

Now into March there is a series of kachina dances in charge of the kiva that is to be in charge of the final kachina dance of the year, in the Home-going ceremony. Dance sets replace each other in the kivas where the same audience of women and children will sit out the night. A repetition by the most favored dance set is given in the court throughout the following day, the dancers having spent the night in kiva. At this season there is also a series of kickball races or runs by kiva (First Mesa).* Besides, at dawn, youths singly or in groups will run down to Sun spring, bathe and cast meal, praying for strength and vigor.

In the March moon, anyone in any kiva may ask for the Water Serpent celebration[17] in which the images of Water Serpent are brought out from the houses in which they are kept, taken down in procession to Sun spring and then carried from kiva to kiva, for a night dramatization. Hahaiyi, the mother of the kachina, appears to suckle the serpents as they emerge through sun-disk openings in their screen "house." A little field of cornstalks is set out, the corn, like the beans of Powamu, having been forced in kiva. The serpents knock down the stalks. Koyemsi sing. Various kachina dance sets or personages come out the night of the drama and in court the next day. Corn plants, also some bean plants, are given away. Prayer-sticks are deposited in fields. The celebration is half "dance," half "ceremony." Like Powamu, it is announced from kiva to kiva, by Koyemshi, Crier chief among them, but there are no fetishes

* See pp. 817–21. Oraibi's kick-ball races are run off "shortly after Powamu," at which ceremony race balls are among the offerings. The race circuit lies outside the points of deposit, a larger circuit for each race, so that the final race covers from eight to ten miles (Voth 2:81, Pl. XLV*a*). No information about race organization.

apart from the Water Serpents and some Shalako girl puppets or marionettes. There is only a meal altar with cloud signs, and there is no permanent chieftaincy. The dance proposer and kiva mates in charge of the six Water Serpent images observe a retreat with continence and fasting. It is fertility ceremonial, Water Serpent is being asked to intercede with Cloud, but curing is also indicated, possibly for venereal disease in men.

On April 15 begins a regulated series of plantings of cornfields and of bean and melon patches which continues until June 16, four days before the summer solstice. The first planting which is of sweet corn is "for the kachina," i.e., it is to supply the corn which kachina are to give to the children in the Home-going kachina ceremony. The Town chief has watched the sun and notifies the women of the Town chieftaincy to shell the seed-corn ears; then he distributes the seed to the men, telling them that the Town chief women say they are to plant the day following. The corn is planted in warm, secluded nooks where the children will not see it growing. The planting continues for four days.

During the planting season there are kachina races. If the whipping kachina whip many youths, the kachina have to compensate with rain. In case of drought now or later there may be special prayer-stick-making and pilgrimage by the clan chiefs, the War chief accompanying the pilgrims to the mountain. The spring rainfall is scant, and June, the season rain is most needed for the crops, is the driest month of the year.[18] In 1893, on July 31, a pilgrimage to the eastern range was made by the chiefs of Singers and Wüwüchim societies.

In May or October, sporadically at Walpi, the year of Wüwüchim initiations at Oraibi (Titiev), in a wild-plant or seed-gathering ceremonial Masauwü is impersonated and ritually killed. The impersonators are said to be men cured of a swelling in the neck, cured by the Masauwü cult group.[19]

In June "they turn the sun back to winter"; it is Sun prayer-stick-making, at Walpi by a Water-Corn lineage, at Oraibi by the two Flute societies who also conduct a one-day Sun prayer-stick-making ceremony in January some time after Soyala. At

Oraibi as now and again in the East one queries whether the big time in winter was primarily a solstice celebration.

In July before the Home-going kachina ceremony on First Mesa there may be, if proposed by anyone, a celebration of Sio (Zuni) Shalako kachina, at Sichomovi. Temporary shrines are made outside of Water-Corn, Mustard, and Lizard clan houses (outside of Badger clan house there is a permanent shrine) where the Shalako will be received; but first the masks of the four Shalako and of the Ancients (the four in Sayatasha's party) also of the Father and Mother of the Kachina are set out in the Badger house where they are permanently housed. There is a kachina procession from the valley spring, with a large number of Koyemsi kachina in attendance, which is followed by the running ritual in the court and the depositing of prayer-sticks in the shrines. There is kiva night dancing; in the morning the ritual running and prayer-stick-depositing are repeated and in the usual way the kachina unmask. Follows a day of dancing in the court by the Mixed Kachina.*

After the summer solstice prayer-stick-making, Powamu society chief watches the sunrise and in about twenty-five days informs Crier chief when it is time to announce the Home-going or Nima'n ceremony, sixteen days in advance. Powamu chief and Crier chief smoke together, and the following morning Crier chief announces. For two months or more the kiva impersonators of the kachina who are to dance have practiced their songs.

Eight days after the announcement Powamu society chief goes into Chief kiva to make prayer-sticks, set up the altar, and perform altar ritual. Later, other members, including women, come in, to make prayer-sticks or feathers. In the kiva whose turn it is to conduct the kachina dance on the ninth day, masks are prepared and there is dance practice at night. On the ninth day, before dawn, they dance, without masks, in the plaza. Later, they mask and return to the plaza, to dance all day.

* There are many variations from the Zuni performance: No fire kachina or bonfires; four instead of six Shalako kachina; instead of ten an indefinite number of Koyemshi; no night recitals or chants of migration myth by chiefs or impersonators; no tally cords; no retreats of impersonators or yearlong impersonations with a series of monthly offerings. See p. 973.

The following morning seven Hümis kachina and Eototo, father of the kachina, assemble near Chief kiva to perform rites in connection with the Powamu society, the most distinctive being the throwing of a plant down the kiva hatch, ritual which was entirely uninterpreted until it was recognized as part of a game associated at Acoma with rain-making (see p. 981). As the kachina start to go home, the lookers-on spit, the kachina "are taking away everything bad." The kachina will not return until December.

The morning after Nima'n is the appointed time to kill the eagles and hawks that were taken from their nests in the spring. The number of birds taken from the clan preserves by the hunt parties varies considerably. One year in Oraibi there were thirty-five birds; in 1893 on First Mesa there were only four or five. With the plucked carcasses are deposited a small tray, a small flat doll and a few rolls of blue wafer-bread (Oraibi) or for the little boy and girl eagles miniature bows and arrows and dolls (Walpi).[20]

At the close of his ceremony (Nima'n), Powamu chief tells Snake chief to watch the sun. Then four days after Nima'n, theoretically, the Snake-Antelope ceremony will be observed, but the condition of the crops is taken into consideration. If the crops are suffering from drought the ceremony is hastened.[21] Inferably the ceremony is also to control thunderstorms destructive to the crops. It was also reported from First Mesa that "if they danced too soon it would freeze too early."[22]

The Snake-Antelope ceremony and the Flute ceremony are given in alternate years: on First Mesa and Mishongnovi, the Snake-Antelope, on the odd year; the Flute, on the even year. For the other towns of Second Mesa and for Third Mesa the arrangement is reversed.

Snake-Antelope ceremony: The announcement is as usual eight days in advance, after a day of prayer-stick- or feather-making in the maternal house of Spider Woman clan (? lineage) (Oraibi). The evening smoke assemblage is held traditionally at Oraibi in the Town chief's house.[23] The morning after (Walpi) or the same morning (Oraibi) the chiefs go into kiva, the Snake men start snake-hunting, going to the north. On this and the three subsequent hunts they may not drink rain water, only spring water (Walpi). Were anybody present when they caught a snake, they would initiate him, "so people don't go in the direction of the hunt."* On the fourth day when they hunt in the fourth direction, to the east, all members, excepting one man left in kiva, have to take part.

The Snake altar is set up in part the evening† of the first day (Oraibi). The Antelope altar of the directions, set up the first day, for a daily morning ritual figures only at Walpi. On the fifth day new standards, the bow standards, are set up, also the large sand-painting Antelope altar at which song ritual is observed of mornings and in the late afternoon or evening by the two societies for four days (Oraibi, Walpi). At these ceremonials Antelope Youth and Snake Maid, keeping step to the singing, walk up and down behind the altar. The Maid carries a pot containing prayer-sticks, corn, melon, squash, and bean vines, and the Youth, a *tiponi* and a snake (Oraibi).

On the eighth day occur the early-morning Antelope race and the late-afternoon Antelope dance. For the race at Oraibi[24] water is taken from a sacred spring, by a Water-Corn clansman who starts ahead on the course and surrenders his water bottle and prayer-stick to the first to overtake him. The race winner will pour out the water in his field and plant prayer-sticks to be given him later in kiva. Prayer-sticks, prayer-feathers, and prayer-meal were deposited at shrines along the route. Snakes and Antelopes do not race, but they join the racers, and the Snake warriors twirl their whizzers and shoot their lightning frames. At the foot of the mesa the racers are given cornstalks, and on top Snake men sprinkle them with meal as they run by. Now the men and boys who have fetched cornstalks and squash blossoms are mobbed by the women and children who will place the trophies of this wrangling in their corn stores.[25]

Later in the day Snake men erect the booth of cottonwood

* This is probably the reason why even men who have been allowed into the kiva ceremonials have been urged vehemently not to go on the snake hunt.

† The only recorded instance of placing an altar in the evening (Voth 3:287).

from which the snakes will be passed out to the dancers, and in front of it is dug a small pit covered by a plank resonator making a sort of foot drum. Out come first the Antelopes and then the Snakes, each group to circle the booth four times and each dancer to stamp on and besprinkle the plank (Pl. VIII).[26] Antelopes and Snakes line up vis-à-vis, the Snakes imbricating fingers, bending over, and waving their Snake whips as they hum a song. Follow louder songs by both lines and stomping dance step. Then both lines dance forward and back, forward and back, while the asperser (Antelope Medicine chief) without his bowl dances down between the lines followed by Snake chief who with his whip strokes the back of Medicine chief [as he would a snake. I take it Medicine chief is impersonating a snake]. From the bower Medicine chief gets a bunch of vines, melon, bean, cotton, and a young cornstalk and holding these in his mouth as Snake men will hold their snakes, again followed by Snake chief, he dances between the lines. He drops the vines, and a Snake man picks them up in the way snakes are picked up. More circuits and then withdrawal single file into kiva.

On the ninth day, Snake race and Snake dance. In the afternoon after the washing of the snakes in kiva and head-washing of the initiates in the houses of their godmothers, Snakes and Antelopes come out as before to encircle the court, four times to stamp on the plank, and to dance and sing in opposite lines. Then pair by pair the Snakes dance up to the bower; one man kneels and is given a snake from inside the bower. With it in his mouth and grasping its body with both hands, he is followed by his mate stroking his back with the Snake whip. They dance in anti-sunwise oval between the lines. Every dancer drops his snake after a few minutes and gets another. The dropped snakes are picked up by another set of men who throw a pinch of meal toward the snake. The gatherers may hold a bunch of four or five snakes, in their left hand. The Antelopes are dancing forward and back in line and singing. When the last snake has been picked up, the gatherers hand all the snakes to the Antelopes who will cast them into a ring of meal inclosing the six lines of the directions made by the Snake chief. Into this ring Snake

PLATE VIII

Snake-Antelope Ceremony

Stamping on the *sipapu* plank (Voth 3: Pl. CLXXXIII)

clanswomen (not necessarily society members) have dumped meal from their baskets, a "bed" for the snakes. Now the Snake men gather up the snakes, each taking as many as he can carry, and take them down to the Snake shrine, below the mesa (Walpi), or to places in the cardinal directions (Oraibi). They hasten down and they hasten up. Outside the kiva they take the emetic prepared in the house of Snake Maiden (Oraibi). After vomiting, they enter the kiva and are finally exorcised by the chief with ashes and buzzard feather. Follows a feast supplied by the women of their households. All day the Snakes have fasted from food and drink, nor have they talked.

Flute ceremony: Horn clan chief who for the past half-century or more has held the office of Town chief (Walpi) tells his "partners," as the Hopi say in English, Bear clan chief, a child of Bear clan who happens to be Reed clan chief,* Water-Corn clan chief and Crier chief, to go in the evening to "their house," the maternal clan house, for the smoke talk. Announcement of the ceremony is made as usual the following dawn by Crier chief. (For a summary of the ceremony see pp. 703–8.)

Four days after the Flute or Snake-Antelope ceremony or, if the "Sun goes slowly," eight days, upon notification by Sun chief, who is a Water-Corn chief, Lakon chief, a Water-Corn clanswoman, tells her "uncles," the seniors of her maternal family, who may or may not be members of the ceremony, to come to her house, for the smoke talk. She also summons the other women chiefs and Crier chief. Follows the ceremony in eight days.

Lakon and Marau were performed in September of even years at Oraibi, alternating with Oaqöl performed in late October or early November. The year Marau was not performed in September there was a nine-day ceremony early in February which was like the alternating September ceremony except that there was no initiation, and on the eighth night kachina danced in all

---

* This man was for several years regent for the Bear clan chief, and he may continue to take part in the Flute ceremony because of his early association. The role he plays today as war scout was formerly played by a Mustard clan chief.

the kivas, with a dance outdoors the following day. We recall that the one-day winter prayer-stick-making of Marau and other Walpi ceremonies is followed by kachina dancing. Lakon and Marau are no longer performed at Oraibi, and Oaqöl, it is said, may be performed at any time. On First Mesa Oaqöl has been performed at uncertain intervals, in 1892, for example, for the first time in twenty years. Marau is no longer performed on First Mesa. Formerly it was celebrated annually, late in September. (For summary see pp. 675–80.)

During November before Wüwüchim, so-called girls' dances, such as Buffalo dance or Howina, may be performed. This too has become the Hopi tourist season; men visit Zuni for the Shalako or go on trips to the Rio Grande.

ZUNI

The following calendar is compiled from records kept in Zuni in 1915–16, also in 1919 by Margaret Lewis, and checked and amplified by footnotes or notes in brackets from Stevenson and Bunzel.

DEC. 6. Pekwin, Crier chief, having observed the sunrise for the winter solstice ceremony, for eight days becomes *teshkwi*.

DEC. 15. According to the old rule, on this day the announcement of the winter solstice ceremony in ten days is due; but the preceding Pekwin increased the period between solar observation and announcement from eight to sixteen days. The newly chosen Pekwin has been bidden by the War chief to observe the longer period.

DEC. 16. Nevertheless, having learned that War chief younger brother and the major Rain chiefs will support him, Pekwin announces the winter solstice ceremony.*

DEC. 23. Members of all the curing societies, excepting Wood society, snow and wind-makers, go into their ceremonial rooms for four days.

DEC. 24. All persons make prayer-sticks or have them made. At night, members of the Ne'wekwe society, referred to as

---

* For this dispute in the hierarchy see Parsons 6:298. Even earlier, December 19, was the very old rule for general prayer-stick-planting; see below (Cushing 6:154).

Kwilaina (from Keresan Kurena) go singing about town. In Chief kiva (He'iwa), the ceremonial fire is lit,[27] and an all-night War god ceremony is held. (Sun has ever warlike traits.)

DEC. 25. All plant their prayer-sticks, the *teshkwi* of ten days begins. No meat or grease may be eaten or touched for four days, excepting by members of Shi'wanakwe society and of Hunters' society. No trading. No ashes or refuse may be taken outdoors, and no light made outdoors.

DEC. 29. All the men make prayer-sticks. The major Rain chiefs make prayer-sticks in He'iwa kiva to offer in a spring.[28] At night, the ceremony of "animals in (until) tomorrow," a curing ceremony in every curing society room for any who come.*

DEC. 30. Every curing society member plants prayer-sticks to the prey animals (beast gods) and to the kachina. The major Rain chiefs and chiefs of the Kachina society meet in the house of the wife of the chief of the Kachina society and make prayer-sticks for Pa'utiwa, chief of the kachina. Corn clan and the children of the clan meet to choose the clan imper-sonator of Pa'utiwa in his role of kachina witch and to make prayer-sticks for him. The clan chief presents meal in corn-husk to the chosen impersonator. With the impersonator Sun clansmen and Corn clansmen deposit the Pa'utiwa prayer-sticks at the river.[29]

JAN. 1. At midnight Pa'utiwa as "kachina witch" visits each kiva, rubbing four lines of meal down the hatchway.

JAN. 4–5. The foremost kachina personators for the year are chosen by the major Rain chiefs—"their father" Koyemshi,†

* Formerly men would go to the house of the Deer fetish, and all the animal hunt figurines would be set out and addressed (Cushing 1:32).

† Father Koyemshi appoints the impersonators of his nine sons from his society (Big Firebrand, Ne'wekwe, Cactus) or nowadays from his kiva or gambling crowd (Parsons 6:183–84; Bunzel 5:949–50). Impersonators should be children of the more sizable clans so they may be well paid by their clan for their year's work. There are several groups of impersonators (four, 1915–27) who serve repeatedly. Should the group whose turn it is to serve have provoked the disapproval of the Rain chiefs, it will be passed over in favor of a new group, perhaps one of the more or less permanent groups that borrow the masks and impersonate during the winter dance series—the appointive or real Koyemshi do not have to come out before the summer series. But they may come out after the first prayer-stick-planting for Shalako (Bunzel 5:950).

Long Horn (Sayatasha) and his warrior, and Melon-Bringer, the representative of the Ne'wekwe society. Ne'wekwe sit up all night, awaiting the choice of Melon-Bringer. The Corn Maiden personators are chosen by the kiva officers. Long Horn and "their father" Koyemshi are given prayer-sticks of office in the house of Pekwin. Pa'utiwa, Kachina chief, having come in, likewise Shitsukya and Kwelele, kachina of the Big Firebrand society,* all stay overnight [with the high Rain chiefs, Kachina society chiefs, impersonators of Pa'utiwa and Sayathlia or Blue Horns who dance and exorcise, members of Pa'utiwa cult, Sun men who take care of Pa'utiwa and choirs] in He'iwa kiva. Here the chief of Big Firebrand society and a Badger clansman who is a member of the Fire order of the society make a fire by fire drill for Kwelele. It is a test; the sticks are damp; if they ignite during the first song, the year will be good; but all four songs may have to be sung or even repeated before ignition takes place—an omen of a poor year. Kwelele takes his fire and the kiva fire-maker (*tsupala ilona*, blood-pudding keeper) the fire he has been tending in the kiva for ten days, never letting it go out as in the case of a blood-pudding fire, out to a field to the east side of town, where they sprinkle the embers with meal. Kwelele goes around town, the women of each house passing embers along the house walls to throw on him as he passes. Then each household takes out the refuse it has accumulated for the ten days, *poche panikya*, refuse or trash take down, which is the vernacular term for the whole ten-day ceremonial. The man of the house takes out the refuse and stacks it on the ground as he would the corn he brings in from the harvest. The refuse represents corn. The woman of the house carries out the ashes and, as she would sprinkle meal at the harvest, sprinkles the ashes on the ground before the refuse is stacked, and then onto the stack. Little boys carry firebrands, like Shulawitsi, the boy

---

* Impersonated by members of Big Kachina order of Big Firebrand society, in whose house their masks are kept. This night they dance in kiva. Anyone dozing is whipped by Shitsukya. These kachina live at Shipapolima, but Shitsukya married the daughter of Pa'utiwa (Bunzel 3:924 ff.).

Corn-Fire kachina. Everybody sprinkles meal and prays to the Sun, asking him to overlook possible violations of *teshkwi*. [Shitsukya and Kwelele dance on the kiva roof, throwing gifts to the people; Pa'utiwa comes into town immuring prayer-sticks and on the roof of He'iwa kiva where he makes four meal lines performing "scalp" ritual. Here and at all the other kivas he leaves the Shalako crook of appointment.]

JAN. 5. Salimobia and Chakwena Woman go past every house. The women of the house pass embers along the walls of the house and, after Chakwena Woman has passed by, throw the embers outdoors. This "house-cleansing" is to cleanse from trouble and witchcraft.*

JAN. 6, 7, 8. Salimobia and Thlelele go around town. Thlelele are without mask, with a pelt or wagon cover over the head. As they pass by the houses, the inmates throw embers at them.

JAN. 8. The Wood society announce that in eight days they will dance. This announcement was due theoretically on January 5, at the close of the winter solstice ceremony. Before this date no dance may be held, i.e., no dance until four days after "trash down." Pa'utiwa has specified during the winter solstice ceremony what dances are to take place between this time and the winter series of kiva dances. These dances are referred to as for "ground-cleansing." Each kiva should present a group or a single dancer, like Atoshle or Natashku.† (See Jan. 20, 21, 23, 29 ff.)

JAN. 9. The Saint's crier announces that "the Saint's childbed" will be held in four days.

JAN. 11. Wood society and Big Firebrand society plant their prayer-sticks and "go in." [Two moons, January and February, are assigned Wood society for snow ceremonial.]

---

* Compare p. 461. No explanation is available for cleansing by embers, although it approximates cleansing by ashes. Chakwena is a war or enemy kachina and at Laguna was once associated with witchcraft. As a witch she may be curing witchcraft.

† Cf. Bunzel 5:974; cf. Hopi Powamu ceremony.

JAN. 13. Saint's childbed.* For four days her image remains set out or rather laid down in the house where she lives, for visitation. Clay figurines of the domestic animals and of other property, jewelry and money, are set about her, a rite for their increase.

JAN. 15. Dance of Wood society and of Big Firebrand society, the latter dancing "Navaho." Each group comes out to dance four times. In between there is a dance circle of men and women holding prayer-sticks. Also the Muwaiye, a dance by two girls and a man, with a kiva choir. All the dancers stay all night in the house of Wood society.

JAN. 19. Little Firebrand society "go in." They fast from sweets (peaches) and beans, otherwise in the fire dance they would get burned.

[Shalako personators, etc., plant prayer-sticks.] Every full moon (theoretically), after their appointment at the winter solstice, the Shalako personators, "their father" Koyemshi, and the representative of the Ne'wekwe, "Melon-Bringer," offer prayer-sticks at a fixed series of shrines, at springs a considerable distance from town. There should be ten of these pilgrimages. When the counting of days to the "kachina come" or Shalako ceremonial begins, there is a planting every ten days, four plantings. After every planting, it is said, rain or snow is likely to fall. (I was in Zuni the day of the first planting in 1917, January 20. It was a rainy day "because they had planted.")

JAN. 20. Atoshle† couple go around. Ant society "go in," for an initiation. [The four major Rain chieftaincies "go in" for four days. They "go in" at full moon again in February and

---

* *La Navidad*, Christmas.

† Obsolete reciprocal for grandfather-grandchild. Old man and old woman kachina bogeys, frightening and haranguing little children when they go into their house (see p. 51) and acting as sergeant-at-arms for men late to kiva. "Nobody would refuse Atoshle." Black mask with white spots; ball eyes; shock of hair falling over face. The old man carries a large knife, the old woman a basket to carry off a child, to devour. Atoshle will pretend to bite an adult on the neck. They give Atoshle or Su'ukyi meat so he won't carry away the child. These domiciliary rounds are more formalized by the Soyok kachina in the Hopi Powamu ceremony (Parsons 2; Bunzel 5:936–41, Pl. 22c, d).

in March;* according to other authorities they "go in" throughout the year at the new moon. The Warrior society "go in" for two moons, February–April.]

Jan. 21. Atoshle go around and enter several houses (to discipline the children).

Jan. 22. Wood is brought in for Little Firebrand society by men chosen for their good looks. Girls relieve them of their load.

Jan. 23. Natashku† goes around, and in house-to-house visits is given much food. Initiation dance of Little Firebrand society. A pit fire is made in the court and sprinkled with meal, and the novice is pushed into the fire.

Jan. 24. Ant society initiate, at Little Grease Hill where the initiate has been kept nude for day and night, exposed to ants, which are then brushed off.

Jan. 29. Hilili‡ is danced by Muhewa kiva. A repetition for the following day is requested by a Rain chief.

Jan. 30. Hilili. Repetition requested by chief of Shuma'kwe society.

---

* One-night retreat by all the Rain chieftaincies (Bunzel 2:514).

† Another bogey kachina, the "starving god." Long-snouted burro-like mask. Carries bow and arrow and wears warrior head feathers. Ponderous tread. Visits house with children and asks for meat (Bunzel 5:935–36, Pl. 22b; Parsons 6: 173). Belongs in Hopi Soyok-Natashka Powamu group.

‡ Said to have been introduced about 1892 from Laguna or Acoma (Parsons 6:224–25). In 1893 at Walpi called a Laguna mask (Stephen 4:192, Fig. 114). A stone knife lies on the top of the mask. Now the kachina initiator of the Laguna Flint society was Heleleka (Parsons 20:116, n. 5). It may have been only coincidence but the society leader of the Hilili performance I saw at Zuni in 1917 was from the Ant (Knife or Flint) society. Compare San Felipe and Santo Domingo Hililik'a who carries a flint knife from which hangs human hair (White 3:Fig. 8; White 4:111, 176–77, Fig. 23). Hel^{y}alika of Cochiti cuts off the bang of anyone not dancing (Goldfrank 3:111). Obviously, Hilili is a Keresan war or scalper kachina. Popular at Zuni and danced by all the kivas. Face particolored turquoise and white, with beard. Snake painted over each eye, and snake image alongside mask or around neck; warrior bandoleer and bag, "scalp bag"; cartridges, formerly arrowpoints, fastened to bandoleer representing scalps taken (Bunzel 5:1067 ff., Pl. 48b). It is a throw-away dance.

With the Hilili group come two Eagle kachina. Cylindrical turquoise mask. Eagle wings on arms. Back tablet or shield, blue with red hair fringe and eagle and hawk feathers. Bells in the hands. They behave like eagles, as do some of the Hilili at the close of the dance. These Eagles were introduced by a Hopi visitor about 1910 (Parsons 6:222–23; Bunzel 5:1067, Pl. 48a).

JAN. 31. Hilili. Repetition requested by War chief.

FEB. 1. Hilili. Repetition requested by Rain chief of the South.

FEB. 2. Hilili. Repetition requested.

FEB. 3. Hilili. Repetition requested by a Rain chief.

FEB. 4. Hilili; the dancers preclude request for repetition* by scattering at the close of the dance.

Afternoon announcement of Upikyaiupona by Hekiapawa kiva. Two kachina of the dance group visit each kiva, or house substituting for kiva. Each carries a crook stick with corn ear fastened to it, which is waved in circuit before each door. Prayer and dancing by the kachina within each house. In the first house visited, the one which is to present the next dance, a cigarette of invitation is presented by the visiting kachina. The date announced has to be after the first prayer-stick-planting by Shalako personators, Melon-Bringer, and the personator of "their father" Koyemshi, because at the dance Koyemshi figure, and they may not "come out" until after the first planting.

FEB. 8. Upikyaiupona† as a night dance from house to house. (During the next few weeks, each kiva will present a rain dance, the other kivas sending out or not, as each may wish, a group of dancers or a single mask. As the series of dances progresses, an increasing number of kivas participate fully until in the final dance of the series it is usual for all the kivas to present groups of dancers. The kiva in charge plants the prayer-sticks all the kivas contribute.)

FEB. 9. Regularly the night dancers or one set of them are requested to dance the following afternoon outdoors; but for some reason on this occasion they are asked to dance at a later date. (See Mar. 2.)

FEB. 11. Announcement of Kok'okshi by Uptsanna kiva. Be-

---

* For the popularity of Hilili see pp. 104, 1106.

† "Downy feathers hanging." Three feathers hang from the bottom of the mask which is painted "green" (turquoise) like Kok'okshi "for the green world." The strip of different colors at bottom of mask, the mouth, is for different kinds of flowers. Body black with yellow breast and shoulders for the oriole because he comes early in the spring. Yellow on arms for yellow flowers and corn pollen (Bunzel 5:1016, Pl. 37a).

cause this is the year of initiation into the Kachina society, the dance series are crowded together. Other years an interval of two weeks or so might elapse between dances.

FEB. 13. The Wood society plant prayer-sticks and "go in."

FEB. 15. Good Kachina (Kok'okshi) and a burlesque of Navaho Kachina by Chupawa kiva.

FEB. 16. Dance, Good Kachina or more probably Navaho, in court.

FEB. 17. Dance by Wood society and Big Firebrand society.

FEB. 18. Announcement of Good Kachina by Ohewa kiva.

FEB. 19. Shalako personators and others plant prayer-sticks.

FEB. 22. Good Kachina. "Silver Belts," a Hopi dance, by Chupawa kiva. Hilili by He'iwa kiva. Ne'wekwe roles by Uptsanna kiva and Hekiapawa kiva, i.e., the Ne'wekwe caps and songs have been borrowed.

FEB. 23. In afternoon "Silver Belts" and Hilili alternately. Repetition requested by War society member.

FEB. 24. Announcement of Good Kachina by Muhewa kiva.

FEB. 29. Good Kachina. "Open Sleeve,"* by Ohewa kiva. "Buckskin people" (a buckskin is worn over the shoulder of the dancer) by Uptsanna kiva. Hilili burlesque.

MAR. 2. Upikyaiupona by Hekiapawa kiva. Repetition requested by one of the Governor's officers.

MAR. 3. Upikyaiupona. No repetition requested because of the death of the father of one of the dancers. Announcement of Good Kachina by Chupawa kiva.

MAR. 7. Good Kachina. Apache dance† by He'iwa kiva.

MAR. 8. Announcement of Upikyaiupona by He'iwa kiva.

---

* Pasikyapa. Shirts with sleeves slit from elbow. Ribbons. Hopi dance (Bunzel 5:1071, Pl. 49a).

† Wilatsukwe. Face mask with straight profile or with projecting nose. Hair flowing with twists of yarn or fur across forehead and hanging sidewise like braids. At sides ribbon rosettes, artificial flowers, feather bunches. Shoulder cape garishly decorated. Long calico breechcloth; buckskin kilt. At back, flat basket, spurs, quoit. Rope or Navaho silver belt. Carries bow and arrow. "Copied from a picture." Songs in Zuni but hard to sing because shouted like Apache songs (Parsons 29:177-78; Bunzel 5:1073-74, Pl. 51c).

MAR. 9. Opening the ceremonial of the whipping of the children*
by the Kachina society, Kiaklo comes in (from near White
Rocks at sunrise), carried by Koyemshi.† He visits Corn kiva
and then the other kivas, to recite in each his "talk of the first
beginning" or migration myth.[30]

MAR. 10. Kiaklo leaves (at sunrise). The personators of the
Salimobia and other kachina are appointed by kiva officials.
They will plant prayer-sticks and "go in" for eight days.

MAR. 11. Upikyaiupona. Wotemthla‡ or Mixed Kachina by
Ohewa kiva. Navaho§ by Uptsanna kiva.

MAR. 14. Salimobia personators and managers, Tsitsikya‖ personator and manager, and Koyemshi personators plant
prayer-sticks. Tsitsikya and Koyemshi personators go around
getting the names of the children to be whipped, each Koyemshi taking a few names to remember, Tsitsikya memorizing
all. The Koyemshi appoint those who are to cook beans of
various colors for the kachina.

MAR. 17. Kiaklo comes in at sunrise and enters each kiva, recit-
ing an abbreviated version of his chant. At the roar of Water
Serpent he runs away to the hills. Water Serpent¶ and the

---

* Not observed in 1919 (Parsons 55:62).

† Kiaklo's mask was brought out during the night in the house of Kachina
society pekwin where it is kept. It is handled by Corn clansmen, the same men
who look after the Ky'anakwe masks which it resembles, and Corn clansmen wash
the head of the impersonator at the close of the second and final appearance.
The impersonator is one of four men who know the chant, a cult group (Bunzel
5:980–85).

‡ Servants or animals, all kinds. An omnibus, catch-all group for any borrowed single kachina. "From San Felipe or Hopi" (Parsons 6:214; Parsons 29:
185, 206; Bunzel 5:906–7, 1025–26).

§ Pakoko or Yebichai. Turquoise-colored mask surrounded by red hair (Bunzel 5:1082, Pls. 56, 57).

‖ Sonora yellow warbler? See p. 229. A bird messenger. Compare Acoma
and Papago.

¶ The head of the five-foot effigy projects through a wooden screen, a spruce
tree is carried on either side, and a shell is blown (Stevenson 2:94–95, Pls.
XIII, XIV).

others come in and go into Hekiapa'wa kiva. Salimobia*
dance in their kivas all night.

MAR. 18. *Hashiate:* two Muluktakwe kachina carry in a spruce
tree, and other kachina run at them crying, *hashiate*, shake!
This performance in each of the four courts. (Ahe'a or
He'mokyätsik[i], the great grandmother of the kachina, suckles
Kolowisi projecting from the kiva wall.)† (Big Firebrand society sets an altar with kachina sand paintings in He'iwa
kiva.) The yellow Salimobia visits the war shrine on the north
edge of town and deposits prayer-sticks. All the Salimobia go
to He'iwa kiva to drink medicine to qualify to whip. All day
they whip, together with the two Wooden Ears,‡ Shulawitsi,§

---

* Twelve masks, two for each color-direction. These permanent masks are
taken out only for the kachina initiation. But masks made up as Salimobia come
out on different occasions in winter, never in summer; they bring wind.

Cylindrical mask, warrior feather badge on top, long snout, dumbbell eye
design. Huge crow feather collar, to frighten the children, since crows bring bad
luck. Right-hand yucca switch carried points forward, left-hand switch points
backward; his seeds fastened to the left-hand yucca; special white embroidered
kilt; blue leather belt; bare feet with spruce anklets.

Running or dancing step. Go down kiva ladder head foremost. Well-set-up
young men appointed to impersonate. To my mind handsomest and most attractive of all kachina impersonations. (Bunzel 5:968-69, 988-90, Pl. 30; Parsons 29:173-74.) Note that head foremost Santa Ana Koshare enter their
kiva (Pl. XXIV).

† She has a projecting chin and nose and elsewhere would be considered a
grotesque impersonation; at Zuni although "she is always funny" she is also
taken seriously since, being so old, she brings long life, and "no one wants to die
young." On her way to the initiation she kept saying, "Oh dear, oh dear! Ahe'a,
Ahe'a! I am the one to bring long life to my people. They shall live to take care of
their great grandchildren as I am doing now." She was going to look after
Water Serpent.

When He'mokyätsik[i] dances out of step, the kachina she has accompanied
may get angry and knock her down, but she never gets angry, and if anyone gets
angry easily people say, "Ahe'a never gets angry the way you do" (Bunzel
5:986).

‡ Their ears are painted red and yellow for beautiful vegetation. In each a
downy feather, so that he may hear well. Just as the feather moves in the slight-
est wind so he can hear the smallest sound. His seeds are in his willow whip
(Bunzel 5:990, Pl. 28c).

§ The mask is not the Shalako Shulawitsi mask. But this impersonation likewise has a ceremonial father, although the impersonation is of an adult. The
actual ceremonial father of the impersonator officiates. He calls upon his clans-

the two Cotton Heads,* and the four Blue Horns. Persons
wishing to be whipped stand out in the court, holding meal.
After being whipped they wave the meal four times around
their head and throw it on the ground. Persons not wishing to be
whipped will carry an ear of corn or a cup of water. The two
Anahokwe† throw jars or baskets off the housetops. A member of the household will have spat on the object and waved
meal four times around the head, dropping it on the spittle.‡
Shulawitsi burns the baskets.§ All the houses are not covered,
so the performance continues to its conclusion the following
day.

MAR. 19. In the afternoon the two Nawisho‖ time by shadow¶
to summon the Whipper kachina, and in the court the children
are whipped. [Then they go in turn into He'iwa kiva, and

---

men to paint Shulawitsi, five men each for one of the five pigments. "If anyone
does not believe in the kachinas, the color will not stay on if he tries to paint
Shulawitsi" (Bunzel 5:994–95).

* He is the son of Pa'utiwa. The personator is chosen by He'iwa kiva manager
from the kiva membership. He repeats the calls of the other kachina, gently, just
like an echo (Bunzel 5:996–98).

† Anahoho brings and takes away bad luck, wearing a collar of crow feathers,
ominous of bad luck. Once the Anahokwe came like crows to warn that the
Navaho were coming. In the fight Elder Brother Anahoho dipped his right hand
in the blood of the Navaho and put it on his face, and Younger Brother did the
same, using his left hand. From this you can distinguish their masks. Impersonators must be appointed by the dance director of Ohewa kiva. The only
person who knows Anahoho's secret prayers for "taking away the bad luck" is
an albino woman with no ceremonial connection (Bunzel 5:993–94, Pl. 29*b*), an
instance of the aberrant forms even the most formalized system is capable of.

‡ Over the jar or basket Anahoho prays: "You are the one to take away the
bad luck from this house. If anyone is sick, you will die instead of him" (Bunzel
5:995–96).

§ A curious suggestion here of Yuman mourning ceremonial. Does this exorcism throw back to the time when the Zuni cremated?

‖ Little lines running out from eyes, for the Clouds of all directions; nose
zigzag for lightning; arms and legs painted with corn pollen, to make the corn
happy. Wears Salimobia kilt and goes down kiva ladder head first, like Salimobia. Represents sweet corn; the seeds in his willow whip are sweet corn (Bunzel
5:991–92, Pl. 29*a*).

¶ Church shadow. Zuni time-keeping is habitually by shadow. Shadow places
were marked for morning and evening meals (Bunzel 5:992, n. 8*b*).

each boy has fastened to his hair the feather his godfather had fastened to the boy's particular kachina painting. Sand from the painting is rubbed on the boy. The boys return to the court and are whipped again severely by the Blue Horns, one on each side of the boy. "The little boys cry terribly." The boys are whipped in the order that the beans have been cooked in their houses, the boy with the yellow beans is whipped first and so on in the color sequence. The boys are taken into Corn kiva or into Ohewa kiva where the image of Water Serpent vomits water and seed corn.]

The Shalako personators, etc., plant prayer-sticks.

MAR. 20. Meat becomes taboo to the children for four days, while they wear their downy eagle feather in their hair.

MAR. 24. The children fasten their hair prayer-feathers to a bush at Red Bank. [The boy's head is washed in the house of his godfather.] The boys and their ceremonial parents exchange bowls of stew.

MAR. 31. Apache kachina by He'iwa kiva, the Koyemshi in attendance. This dance and the following are said to have no particular ceremonial import. "They are to put the children into a good humor after their whipping." (But there is always a spring series of dances. In 1919 the last of the winter series was danced on March 23. On March 26 the spring series began and lasted to April 15.)

APR. 1. Apache dance by He'iwa kiva.

APR. 2. Apache dance by He'iwa kiva; Mixed Kachina by Ohewa kiva, Ne'wekwe in attendance.

APR. 3. Apache dance. Mixed Kachina.

APR. 4. Mixed Kachina: the last dance of the spring kachina season.

APR. 16(?). War society night ceremony.*

APR. 17. The Shalako personators, etc., plant prayer-sticks.

---

* Parsons 55:62; Bunzel 2:527. Shomatowe songs are sung, but the ceremony has never been described. It occurs at the full of the March moon and four days before the first (?) kick-stick race of the season, after which it is safe to plant corn (Bunzel).

APR. 20. [Race by kivas.]

[Race by clan.]

MAY 4. [Race open to all.]

MAY 11. [Race open to all.]

MAY 17. Shalako personators, etc., plant prayer-sticks.

MAY 23. The crier or speaker of the Kachina society and the managers of the Salimobia appoint personators for the Salimobia, the Blue Horns and the Chakwena Woman in the hunt, and men to take care of the Chakwena Woman in her confinement.

MAY 24. Rabbit hunt with kachina.[31] Chakwena Woman has had her legs smeared with rabbit blood,* and she has to take a straight course in the hunt so that the blood will be rubbed off her legs by the vegetation she goes through, and rabbits will be plentiful.† Salimobia younger brother and Chakwena Woman go about town. Chakwena Woman lies in, not according to custom in Hekiapawa kiva because next door a man is ill, but in Chupawa kiva. In the hunt she has worn two ears of corn in her belt, and these she gives to a would-be mother to wear, too, in the belt. The would-be mother gives Chakwena Woman a dress and leggings, and dresses her hair in whorls. The mother of Chakwena personator attends the would-be mother when in due course she is confined and the personator thereby becomes the godfather of the infant, if a male. The Salimobia dance at night in the house of the Hunters' society.

MAY 25. In the evening Chakwena Woman and Salimobia elder brother go around town. The legs of Chakwena Woman are painted red to represent the lochial discharge in childbirth. The Salimobia dance in the house of the Hunters' society.

MAY 26. In the evening Chakwena Woman and Salimobia younger brother go around town. The Salimobia dance in the house of the Hunters' society.

* The first rabbit killed; "so that Zuni women may have their babies easily, like rabbits" (Bunzel 5:935).

† Men will bring miniature clay animals to the house of her lying-in, prayer-images for increase (Bunzel 5:935).

MAY 27. In the evening Chakwena Woman and Salimobia older brother go around town. The Salimobia dance in the house of the Hunters' society.

MAY 28. Chakwena Woman, her manager, the chief and speaker of the Kachina society, Blue Horns and Salimobia and two War chiefs go from house to house to receive gifts of bread and meat, Salimobia getting what is received in the morning, the others the receipts of the afternoon. Salimobia dance in the house of the Hunters' society.

MAY 29. Rounds of houses completed. All deposit prayer-sticks at the river, where the kachina unmask. Rabbit hunt without kachina.

JUNE 5. [The Crier chief calls out for the summer solstice.]

JUNE 15. Shalako personators, etc., plant prayer-sticks.

JUNE 17. All society members make prayer-sticks for the summer solstice.

JUNE 19. Everyone makes prayer-sticks or has them made.

JUNE 20. Everyone plants prayer-sticks. [Taboo for four days on trade.] The Town chiefs "go in" for eight days to call the rain.

JUNE 22. [All Shalako impersonators, the chiefs of societies, Badger clanspeople, and children of the Badger clan, all make prayer-sticks for the kachina.] [Koyemshi come in unmasked, their hair falling over their face. Women drench them from the housetops. Called Tumichimchi from first word of their song.][32]

JUNE 23. The chief of the Kachina society and its crier, the impersonators of the Kok'okshi, the Good Kachina, the Koyemshi, the Shalako and the Sayatasha-Shulawitsi group, all go to the Tohseluna spring at Ojo Caliente about fifteen miles to the west. In the afternoon the chief of the Kachina society leads in the Good Kachina, the Kachina society crier leading in the Koyemshi. The other impersonators follow, swinging bull-roarers. They make the dance circuit and withdraw into Upts'ana kiva to dance all night, the Ne'wekwe society singing. The Koyemshi are in the house of the Kachina society crier.

JUNE 24. Good Kachina by Upts'ana kiva. Ne'wekwe society sing in the house of the Kachina society crier.

JUNE 29. [East or Pathltokwe Rain chiefs go into retreat.]

JULY 5. Good Kachina by He'iwa kiva.

JULY 6. [South or Onawa Rain chiefs go into retreat.]

JULY 13. [West or Koyemshi Rain chiefs go into retreat.]

JULY 14. Shalako personators, etc., plant prayer-sticks.

JULY 21. [Pekwin goes into retreat for four days.]

JULY 23. Good Kachina by Chupawa kiva.

JULY 25. [War chiefs go into retreat for four days.]

JULY 28. The personator of "their father" Koyemshi dies. One of the Koyemshi takes the place, his place filled by the Koyemshi manager. One Appe becomes manager.

JULY 29. [Eagle clan people go into retreat.]

AUG. 3. [Upts'ana go into retreat.]

AUG. 6. Good Kachina by Muhewa kiva.

AUG. 7. [Corn clan people go into retreat.]

AUG. 11. [Water Serpent Rain chiefs go into retreat.]

AUG. 17. Upikyaiupona by Hekiapawa kiva. Shuma'kwe society goes into retreat.

AUG. 18. Upikyaiupona.

AUG. 19. Upikyaiupona.

AUG. 20. Upikyaiupona.

AUG. 21. Upikyaiupona. [Sun clan people go into retreat.]

AUG. 22. Upikyaiupona.*

AUG. 25. Corn clan Rain chiefs or Ky'anakwe go into retreat.

SEPT. 1. Mixed Kachina by Ohewa kiva.

SEPT. 2. Mixed Kachina.

SEPT. 3. Mixed Kachina.

SEPT. 4. Mixed Kachina.

SEPT. 5. Mixed Kachina. This is the last kachina dance of the season. [Usually in September there is the Saint's dance, held after she has been laid down for four days, and set up for four days. Then she is brought out into the plaza, into a bower. She is carried by girls in procession. Her crier calls out for

---

* Six successive days of dancing! And forty years or so ago they might not dance more than one day (Stevenson 2:64).

young men to come down off the housetops to serve as soldiers. Two volunteers at a time. Each is given a Spanish gun to hold. They go up to the altar and say the Mexican prayer. Around the altar sit Rain chiefs and the Governor and his officers. Inside her house the girls dance for her. The big dance outdoors has not been described.]

SEPT. 12. Shalako personators, etc., plant prayer-sticks.

OCT. 12. Shalako personators, etc., plant prayer-sticks.

OCT. 14. Saint's crier summons to bring in wood and announces in four days.

OCT. 17. All Souls' Day (*ahoppa awan tewa*, the grandmothers their day). Men carry food offerings to the river, women throw them on the house fire. At night groups of boys go about town crying, "Tsalemo!" and paying house-to-house visits. They say the "Mexican" prayer at the threshold, and the inmates give them presents of food.

OCT. 22. Shalako personators, etc., plant prayer-sticks.

Nov. 1. Shalako personators, etc., plant prayer-sticks.

Nov. 11. Shalako personators, etc., plant prayer-sticks.

Nov. 21. Shalako personators, etc., plant prayer-sticks. Koyemshi personators "go in." [In 1918 this was the date of the Ky'anakwe ceremonial. Koyemshi went in Nov. 28.]

Nov. 25. Long Horn and Shulawitsi personators "go in."

Nov. 29. All men make prayer-sticks. The "kachina come," Long Horn and Shulawitsi, Shulawitsi inspecting prayer-sticks about town, and the Shalako. All-night ceremonial in eight houses. Navaho Kachina by He'iwa kiva.*

* Navaho (Pakachina) is not a kiva dance, the kiva chief has nothing to do with it, they dance without prayers; but the dance set is named from the kiva of its leader. Any young man who has a good voice may be leader. Ne'wekwe may attend.

About eighty years ago visiting Navaho, it was said, danced kachina at Zuni to take away a bad swelling sickness. They danced at night in the court, by firelight. As they left the people spat and said, "Now you will take away with you this sickness."

The Navaho were given lots of wafer-bread and other things as pay, and later they wanted to dance again, but the Zuni were afraid they would bring back the sickness. So now the Zuni dance Navaho themselves "and it doesn't cost them anything" (Bunzel 5:1083–84). Mask, design, curing by kachina, and probably the high-pitched songs are all indeed Navaho-like but that the loan was made as

Nov. 30. Long Horn and Shulawitsi and the Shalako leave, after a running ritual across the river. Koyemshi go from housetop to housetop, singing. Navaho Kachina in the afternoon. Muluktakya* in evening by Chupawa kiva.

Dec. 1. At night, Towa Chakwena, home-Chakwena† by He'iwa kiva; Mixed Kachina by Ohewa kiva; Chakwena by Uptsanna kiva.

Dec. 3. At night, the same three dances.

Dec. 4. At night, the same dances, plus the Apache dance by a part of He'iwa kiva.

Dec. 5.‡ Outdoor dancing by all the foregoing dance groups,

---

stated seems questionable, a typical Zuni fiction. Zuni visitors at the Navaho Night Chant probably learned the songs. Perhaps old Tsatiselu, the Ne'wekwe doctor, who in youth was married to a Navaho, introduced the dance to Zuni. At the Shalako of 1916 his son took me into the Navaho dancers' green room.

Note that the esoteric part of the Night Chant is not borrowed, only the outside dance.

* Turquoise mask with long curved snout; top and back black with butterfly design, right side two eagle-tail feathers and one parrot-tail feather. Popcorn on spruce collar because he "plants the sweet corn to make the people's skin strong so that it wont crack in the cold weather." Bandoleer of black and white corn kernels. Body pigment from black cornstalk, "for black earth when it is wet from rain." Very deep necklace of coral with loops of turquoise and pendent on back, an abalone shell. Carries nine-foot staff, tipped with tail feather of eagle for clouds, hawk feather for rain, and feathers of all the little birds that sing after the rain, also pendent downy feather arranged in prayer-stick pattern (Bunzel 5:1065, Pl. 47d; Parsons 6:213–14).

† So called because Chakwena proper, "short-haired Chakwena," is from Laguna. As both are warrior kachina, masks and bodies are painted black, and the hourglass war sign, called "bow" is painted in yellow on chest and back. Yellow on shoulders for fine days with sunshine and rain and no wind. The right-angle eye with points down represents the new moon with horns down, pouring water. Buckskin kilt, for he is a good hunter; warrior's buckskin bandoleer. Bow and arrow in left hand, and warrior's "big feather" badge on top of head; also a red downy feather "since he is a society member" (not explained) (home-Chakwena), or duck's head (Chakwena). Home-Chakwena sings "funny things," i.e., moral precepts and personal satires (Bunzel 5:1018–23, Pls. 38a, 40a), quite in accordance with his warrior character. Chakwena is a throw-away dance, again in accordance with war dance character.

‡ Four days later any Shalako house host may ask to have any dance repeated, and they may keep it up until Pekwin starts to plant prayer-sticks for the winter solstice (Bunzel 5:855).

who run away to Red Bank (Earth), the "kachina go."* "Melons come" (Molawia) ceremonial.

KERES

Winter solstice ceremonies are performed, generally several weeks before the actual solstice, by the Town chief and by the societies who hold independent synchronous meetings or retreats, with an open assemblage on the last night. There is a late winter or early spring ceremonial of general exorcism by the societies. Before planting, a slow circle dance (*auwĕ, owe', süwe'e*) by men and women is held in kiva for good crops (Acoma, Cochiti, Santa Ana, Jemez, Isleta, [?] Taos, Hopi at winter solstice [?]). Then come spring or summer rain retreats by the societies, followed by kachina dances, except at Acoma. Kachina dances are performed throughout the year, but kachina dramatization occurs only at Acoma. There are ritual rabbit hunts before kachina performances, before the solstices, before the installation of a Town chief. Each town has its own patron Saint's-Day dance; other saint's days are celebrated. During Christmastide and Eastertide there is much dancing, animal dances (particularly on Kings' Day) and Plains dances predominating outside with kachina dances in kiva at night. All Souls' Day is observed impressively. There are winter war dances, sporadically a scalp dance, in which men are "made" Opi or scalpers. At initiations it is customary for the society to invite the corresponding society in another Keresan pueblo to assist.[33]

As indicated, Acoma presents several anomalies. The societies do not go into retreat in succession, with a kachina dance in con-

---

* On a visit to the East, to Shipapolima. Not only the dance kachina impersonated during Shalako make this visit, but all the other dance kachina. The day before every possessor of a dance mask makes a prayer-stick for his mask (when he is also making a prayer-stick for the Koyemshi). At "Kachina go" he takes his mask to the house entertaining his kiva Shalako. Here he puts his mask on the top of his head (compare Yaqui) and is water-besprinkled by the women of the house who give him wafer-bread and corn meal. Pa'utiwa (in mask) is sitting on the east edge of town, facing the east. Here all the men, dancers and others, set down their masks, sprinkling a "road" to the east. The wafer-bread and prayer-sticks are buried in six holes, one for each kiva (Bunzel 5:854–56).

clusion; there is but one summer rain ceremony. There are kachina dramatizations, and a sort of seasonal kachina dichotomy,
Tewa-like, with the kachina exhibiting at the solstice celebrations. The War captains or chiefs are installed with much ceremonial; with their three stewards they live apart and continent,
throughout their year of office performing rain ritual.

SAN FELIPE[34]

Winter solstice ceremony (H'a·'nik'o) in late November or
early December, by the societies, with their slab altars, and by
the kachina dance groups meeting in Squash kiva, with a mock
combat between the two kiva groups, a dance by two unmasked
dancers called Shpi'nyinyi, or a kachina dance. At the summer
solstice there may be a kachina dance with Koshare but no other
ritual is reported. In April–May the societies conduct ceremonies also called H'a·'nik'o. Miniature bows and arrows are
deposited (? for the Sun). (Possibly this is the seasonal transfer
ceremony of the Tewa.)

Christmastide dancing: Ahe·'na war dance with "O'pi," Buffalo dance or ceremonial with Buffalo, Elk, Deer, and Antelope
represented and the Game Mother chosen by the Buffalo impersonators. Hunt society place their altar and sing; the War
captains participate.[35] There is also a Buffalo dance of the western type.[36] Sporadically, the Scalp dance.

January 1 in Squash kiva the Town chief gives the canes to
the secular officers he has appointed. They go to church to pray
and then return to the kiva to receive instructions and admoni-
tions by the Town chief.

In February–March, communal synchronous cure by the societies to drive out witches, date being set by the War captain.
The shamans use a crystal, suck pernicious witch-sent objects
from those attending, and retrieve the communal heart, a grain
of corn in a rag doll, from the witches they fight with outside.

Good Friday, sometimes a mask dance. A spring dance called
H'ah'abo by women and men, the men wearing a spider-web,
feather-trimmed shield on their back, the leader carrying a
basket which contains a parrot or kachina doll, and seeds which

at the close are thrown to the spectators. Another maskless kachina dance with notched stick playing, May 1, the Saint's-day dance; and the end of the month begin the Giant, Flint-Koshare, Shikame-Quirena society rain retreats, which are followed by kachina dances. The retreats may be repeated. Formerly they were repeated four times. Several kachina dances in September before the harvest, sometimes the Spruce or Turtle maskless kachina dance, the men wearing *tablita*.

All Souls' Day: house-to-house visitation with song. November 2, rabbit hunt with girls.

COCHITI

For the winter solstice ceremonial, observations of the sun in relation to Nipple Mountain are taken by the Town chief. During the night ceremony the societies exchange dance visits. The Kachina society may dance in their own house. Fetishes and masks are repainted, and the societies deposit miniature kick-sticks, miniature wheels of cattail, miniature bows and netted rings, and rabbit-sticks, all for the Sun.

At Christmastide there is or was kachina dancing, and Comanche, Apache, and Hopi (Motsi) dances are given. On Kings' Day, January 6, the Town chief organizes a burlesque by the Koshare. "Buffalo" is danced by sets alternating from the two kivas, or the kivas present alternately Deer dance and Antelope dance. Also Eagle dance. The preceding night the Shikame society who are in charge of the animal dance heads hold a ceremony for hunters.[37] The canes of the newly elected officers are aspersed in the church. Notice is given by the War captains that in four days, at night, there will be a curing ceremonial for all, in the three rooms of the societies, the Flint, Giant, and Shikame. At this ceremonial, shell and meal are sprinkled on the canes. There is a spitting rite.

There are winter kachina dances called by the War captain, at night, in Squash kiva. There is a night war dance, Aiahenats, in Turquoise kiva.

In February the newly elected officers ask the society chiefs to appoint a night for a general cure. All go into the two society rooms (Flint society combines with Giant society), where all are treated with medicine water and aspersing, and noxious things are withdrawn from the body.

Just before Ash Wednesday the War captain orders a dance, Owe', in the two kivas. It is a circle dance, the women forming the inner circle, the men, the outer. This dance is for the crops and, if we may infer from Acoma tradition, prayer-images of corn, squash, and beans are "planted" after the dance.

During Eastertide there is a kachina dance in Squash kiva. On Easter Sunday and the three days following there is a Saint's-day dance in which the women wear tablets. In the morning after the church service the men run kick-stick races by kiva. Formerly they ran by clan. Each day they run in one of the four directions—north, west, south, east. They run for rain. The night of the first race there is a kachina dance.[38] After these races they clean the ditches.

Before planting for the Town chief there is a rabbit hunt. There are rabbit hunts before and after harvesting, and in connection with All Souls' Day—"the grandfathers bring lots of rabbits."

After the summer solstice there is a series of fasts and retreats by the societies, Flint, Giant, Shikame, and formerly Kwirana and War society. The first four days members live at home, but take a daily emetic, the second four days they stay in the society room and fast. While the Flint society, i.e., the Town chief is in retreat, the Giant society members are purging, while the Giant society members are in retreat, the Shikame are purging. For the night after the close of the retreats, if by night, or four days after, if by day, the War captain may plan a kachina dance. Surni (Zuni) kachina may be danced in summer. In summer drought there are or were special retreats and rain ceremonials by the societies.

Early in October occurs the ceremony of harvesting for the Town chief.[39]

On November 2, All Souls' Day, referred to as "Their Grandfathers arrive from the West" or Dead Feast, every family deposits in the church for their dead a large quantity of wheat, corn, beans, peas, watermelons, *tortillas*, wafer-bread, wheat-root bread (*panocha*), or boiled meat. Everybody fasts and remains indoors. Bowls of food are set out for the dead in the house and all the wealth of the household in blankets is hung on the walls. The stock are shut up in the corrals, and no one may ride horseback.[40] The dead, they say, are pleased to see in visiting their kindred that they are prosperous. The house door is left open for them. Society members including members of the Warrior society assemble in their own places, and the members of the two kivas assemble, all in a night ceremonial. The War society members used to go from house to house to dance for the dead. In each assemblage food for the dead is contributed, cut up into small pieces and thrown outside. Turkey feathers, loose or tied together, are put out. This mainly from Father Dumarest. Goldfrank adds that a candle is lit and some Mexican tobacco, the only kind the dead smoke, is put in a cornhusk and set outside the door.

Formerly the war dance A'hena was danced on killing a bear. There were a scalp dance and a Tanoan war dance, none of these ceremonies having any fixed place in the calendar.

Initiation into the kachina occurs every two or three years on the eve of the first kachina dance boys are to take part in.

LAGUNA

Formerly solar observations were made for the solstices; but today December 5 and June 5 are taken, theoretically, as the dates to celebrate the last night of the ceremonials. (In 1919 the summer solstice night ceremony was celebrated on June 14.) There appears to be no retreat, but for four days, early in the morning, the participants take an emetic of cedar brew. They are supposed to fast from salt, to have their bread and water kept separate, and to remain continent. On the third day there is a rabbit hunt, and on the following morning the rabbits are collected from house to house by the War captains to be given to the society members. Theoretically, on this day all the men make prayer-sticks. The ceremony is held at night.

After the great split in the eighties, when the Town chief who

was associated with the Flint society left Laguna together with
the Kashare and the Fire societies, for many years the winter
solstice ceremony was conducted by the chief of the Shikani and
Kurena societies and the Shiwanna society chief (also a Kurena
and formerly a member of the Hunt society), the only surviving
society chiefs of Laguna, each in charge in alternate years.
Ashes and embers were carried around the openings of the room
loaned for the occasion, "because there might be somebody
around not thinking good thoughts and spoiling the ceremony."
The night chanting by the chiefs was in large part a recital of
how Ma'sewi was sent out by his mother from Shipap to find the
Sun and of the wanderings of the people from the place of
emergence. In this ceremonial the clan heads assisted the society
chiefs in making prayer-sticks for Sun and for property.

The summer solstice ceremony of 1919 was held in two different houses, the three Kashare in charge in a Water clan house
where their masks were customarily kept although the men
themselves lived at Mesita, and the Shiwanna chief in charge in
another loan house. In each house several pseudo-shamans, so-
called *shuts* (raw, uninitiated) *cheani*, assisted at the night ceremonial. The War captains and some of the Governor's officers
were on guard. The head War captain or Outside chief, Navaho
by descent, impressing us by his handsome face and his red
blanket but unimpressed by us or by our plea to attend the
assemblages open to all the townspeople, locked Dr. Boas and
me in our house, after borrowing our lamp.

Formerly, after the summer solstice, there was a series of
retreats for rain. The order of going in by the societies was given
by some informants as Flint, Shahaiye (? Hunt society), Fire,
Kurena, Shiwanna, Kashare; by other informants, as Shikani
and Fire, Shahaiye and Saiyap, Kashare. Kuashiwannatyia,
they act like Shiwanna, cloud or storm beings, is the term of
reference for this ceremonial. The Kapina society members who
could allay high winds were in retreat two days and then danced.
Presumably theirs was a winter or spring ceremony.

Throughout winter and autumn there are kachina dances by
three dance groups of which one only dances Chakwena.

Shturuka kachina is or was a dramatization taken from that of the Ky'anakwe of Zuni. Kohashtoch'e corresponds to the advent of Ololowishkya at Zuni, and opens the deer-hunting season. Yakohana (Corn people?) is danced in masks in the autumn; at other times without mask.

Talawaiye, a maskless, head-tablet dance, is danced for four days at Christmas, the first dance, in the morning, inside the church, the rest of the day in the plaza. Comanche is also danced.

The war dance, Ahina, to dance which permission had to be had from the Kurena society chief, was formerly held in April or November; it is held nowadays after the election of the Governor and officers, in January, or on San José's Day, September 19. Two groups dance, one from the east, one from the west. One dancer represents the War god, Ma·sewi. His face is blackened; he wears a bracelet of olivella shells, and carries a bow and arrows. In and out through the choir a woman dances, to represent the "sister" of Ma·sewi. Formerly there were two women. The women dancers are assembled by the War captains. The paternal kinswomen of the War captains throw presents to the dancers. A War captain blows the flute of Ma·sewi. Formerly there were men dancers, in line. The men were painted with a black streak across the eyelids, a yellow streak below the eyes, black on the edges of the lips, and a red spot on each cheek. In each hand the male dancer carried two eagle-tail feathers and a parrot feather fastened to a piece of wood covered with red cloth, red and green yarn and around all, bells. The dance lasts two days. At the close the two groups come together. Kashare society members stand aiming arrows supposedly in the direction the scalp has come from, while the onlookers spit into the quivers of the Kashare, then the Kashare release their arrows, shooting away whatever fear or scare may have been scalp-caused.

ACOMA

The Town chief watches the sunrise for the winter solstice. For four days an emetic is taken by everybody, and on the fifth day everybody makes prayer-sticks (or has them made). From this day to the close nobody may eat salt or meat or have sexual intercourse. In Chief kiva the Antelope altar is set by the Kaвina society chief,* and the societies set their altars in their rooms. Men bury their prayer-sticks in their field; women throw theirs off the mesa edge. On the final day at sunrise kachina who are referred to as K'oвishtaiya come in to make a circuit about town.† They carry "brave" or war prayer-sticks and sing war songs. They search for the little boys who are impersonating rabbits in the rock fissures. The K'oвishtaiya will throw down cattail fuzz, draw up the naked boy, and release a live rabbit. It is beneficial to sickly boys to engage in this, but all boys have to do it four times before dancing kachina. Sick persons approach the K'oвishtaiya to be touched with their lightning-stick, and for manliness men rub up against the cactus carried by some of the K'oвishtaiya (Stirling). The K'oвishtaiya give people seeds. They stay four days. Their masks‡ are fed and given a cigarette three times a day. At night K'oвishtaiya go to Chief kiva and the rooms of the societies to dance and sometimes they dance by day outdoors, the Mixed Kachina. They leave town with exorcising ritual. For eighteen days impersonators must observe continence. The morning the K'oвishtaiya came, the Town chief offered a suit of miniature clothes to the Sun. He was accompanied to Sun's house by the society chiefs.§

For the summer solstice there is also a general prayer-stick-making, and two men and two women are appointed to offer all the sticks at the east edge of the mesa to Sun and K'oвishtaiya. Sometimes there is a kachina dance with K'ashale (Koshare).

After the annual appointment to office, the War chiefs make

* The only survivor of the society. He was assisted by a Flint society man who took his place when not long ago he died.

† They are the kachina of the East, but they are not thought of as kachina or as dancers. Representing strong, hardy beings, they come barefoot and impart strength (Stirling).

‡ Masks are depicted lying on the Town chief's altar which consists of large crook prayer-sticks and painted slabs (White, Stirling).

§ Compare First Mesa, Parrot clan myth of the Yehohota kachina who come from the East and from the Sun, with gifts of corn and kachina guards carrying cactus-topped sticks (Stephen 2:66). Compare also the impersonations who visit Walpi at the winter solstice.

their circuits to the sacred springs and are installed very cere-moniously. Some time later there is a two-day war dance (see pp. 649–54). The War chiefs keep up their circuits to the springs throughout the year.

Before the people leave old Acoma for their fields the Town chief may decide to have a communal curing ceremony. Through the War chiefs he sends word to the Fire and Flint societies who go into a four-day retreat and on the last night hold an open ceremonial, the people going to the ceremonial rooms. Two "cloud men" make and supply cigarettes. Two doctors dance like eagles and, dipping their eagle plumes in ashes, go about the chamber whipping disease away or with their plumes extracting an object from a person's body. In their medicine bowl they see witches, and two by two they go about rubbing or sucking things out of the people. The chief holds his crystal to the eyes of the other doctors or rubs their eyes with the crystal dipped into the medicine water. They may seize a person and take him up to the altar and rub him with their bear paw.

Kick-sticks are deposited as offerings in the early spring by the War chief,[41] so presumably this is as elsewhere the time for running kick-stick races. They are run by kiva and conducted by the War chief and the chief of the Flint society,[42] a shaman of Clouds and Lightning.

The sporadic dramatization of the Fight with the Kachina was also held before the springtime departure of the people to the valley. It was a ceremony for fertility, since the blood of the kachina fertilized the soil, and in the tradition men were actually killed in the first dramatization of the Fight. It is believed that yearly at the time the kachina were killed they die off again for thirty days, so on the twenty-eighth day a two-day ceremony or dance is held by the Antelope clan to revive the kachina.* Curiously Aztec-like! Curiously Christian!

The people must return to the mesa top for the annual summer rain dance and the sporadic kachina dramatization by the Corn

* Stirling. Compare the Zuni departure of the kachina to the East, to Shipa-polima (Ko'anne, Kachina Go) at the close of Shalako, "the saddest day of the year." Is a ritual death suggested?

clan at the close of July. The summer rain dance is performed by two kiva groups, one dancing the first two days, the other the last two days. During the eight preparatory days the men practice; but they do not sleep in kiva until the night before the dance. They come out to dance at sunrise, at eight places in a definite circuit. Before eating dinner they take an emetic. They dance again in circuit. In the third and last circuit they bring presents to the Town chief and to all the people, a throw-away. The War chief goes through the streets telling the women to bring food to the dancers in Chief kiva. At the conclusion of the second dance day for each group, the Town chief gives the prayer-sticks the impersonators have made to the kachina chief. The group withdraws to some distance from town, each impersonator reclaims his prayer-stick and prays with it. For eight days the impersonators must remain continent and fast from salt and meat.

Corn clanspeople are helped in their ceremony by the boys they have sponsored at kachina initiation. At midnight of the seventh day of preparation a couple goes to each of the four sacred mountains to build fires on top and on the route back. Seven kachina, including Shuracha, a young boy, and a female* impersonation who clanks a rattle of deer bones to her slow and heavy tread, come into town from a spring to the westward where they, too, build a fire. Shuracha carries a firebrand of cedar bark and brings in a water jar, a stick of charcoal, and a string of rabbits. He sets fire to the pile of wood in front of the Corn clan house and to the piles at the dance stations. To each house a few drops of his water are distributed and a bit from his charcoal. Fire and water are never to fail the household.

The rabbit hunt preliminary to this kachina dramatization of the Corn clan is conducted by Corn clansmen; other hunts before ceremonials, by the War chief who builds the fire, having drawn a line of meal around his pile of sticks, grass, and rabbit dung and made a cross in meal on top. He prays to Sun, the great hunter who strikes a rabbit and takes away its wits. The hunters sprinkle prayer-meal on the fire and, during the hunt, to Earth Mother so as not to be blamed for killing her animals, and suffer

* Transvestite (Stirling).

hurt. When prayer-meal and pollen are placed under the legs of dead rabbits, thanks are given to Earth Mother.[43] At the close of the hunt the War chief goes from house to house asking for rabbits. To an unsuccessful hunter the War chief will say, "You must vomit!"

Initiation into the kachina organization is held at intervals of five or six years, formerly at the winter solstice, now during summer.* The War chief keeps track of the children to be initiated, boys and girls. The father of the child usually chooses a fellow-clansman to be sponsor, giving him prayer-feathers, prayer-meal, and a cigarette which has been lighted and extinguished. The sponsor takes half the meal and feathers to his brother or uncle who will be the one to tie the turkey prayer-feathers to the hair of the novice, and give him a name. The initiation is in Chief kiva to which the sponsor carries the child on his back. Facing the altar the sponsor puts prayer-feathers in the child's hands, and, holding his own hands under the child's hands, he prays. He throws the prayer-feathers on the altar. Arrive the Whipper kachina and the clowns on top of the kiva where they stamp and holler, to frighten the novices. They remove the buffalo hide from the hatch and throw down gifts of nuts or fruit. The child is placed in the center of the altar to be whipped. The sponsor is whipped too. All night, groups from the other kivas come in to dance. The novice wears the prayer-feather for four days. It is removed by the wife of the sponsor who washes the head of the novice in her house. She gives him (or her) breakfast and new clothes, also fruit, nuts, and corn from the kachina. The corn the novice has to carry home himself and plant. For these four days the household of the novice must observe continence and fast from salt and meat. Most of the other households observe these taboos also. Sometime after the whipping, his uncle (maternal) takes the child back of the church where the Town chief, some Antelope clansmen, and some kachina impersonators are sitting. The masks are on the ground. The Town chief talks and

* According to Stirling, a short time after the Fight with the Kachina in early April. This ceremony is held every five years and the initiation every ten years.

prays and places the child's hands under the hands of the head kachina who is holding prayer-sticks.

The saint's day is September 2, the day of San Estevan. The drum is beaten at the church portal, and the Saint is carried out to the bower made by the War chief. After Mass the priest may perform marriages; this is the only time of the year he visits the mesa. The dance standard which is dressed like a dancer is called Sun Youth. Two kiva dance groups alternate. The women wear head tablets in this Paashko (Sp., *pascua*) dance which according to tradition was planned not by the friars but by Koshare, that wayward fellow who, like Coyote, always knew it all.* As in the Scalp dance, at the request of the War chief, Koshare got the people out, he showed them how to paint and how to put on their kachina kilts. Without permission he took the medicine drum and rattle, and placed the dancers in line, women behind men, joking and talking backward as he did so, and he showed them the step and a conclusive arm motion of pushing aside (*kawis-păts*).†

After the harvest there is a kachina dance, and there is Christmastide dancing—Buffalo, Eagle, Comanche.

JEMEZ[44]

Although the Town chief is said to determine the dates of solstice ceremonies by observing the sun, December 1 and June 1 are the arbitrary dates, as in several eastern pueblos. All the societies observe a synchronous eight-day ceremony (see p. 907).

About December 10 or 12 the Tabö'sh clowns observe a one-night ceremony which is followed by a one-night ceremony of the Women's societies. In spring, in connection with the planting, clowns and women will again hold successive ceremonies for a day and a night, with a preliminary fast of four days.

A few days before Christmas, the year of an eagle hunt the two hunt societies will go into retreat, washing the live eagles.

---

* Stirling. This is the first "explanation" of why Koshare appear in Keresan saint's-day dances.

† Attention! whoever is next to observe a Keresan saint's-day dance.

On coming out the Pecos Eagle society may hold the Pecos eagle dance called Dalöh.

Four days dancing at Christmas; Christmas night Bow dance inside the church. Dough images of the domestic animals, prayer-images, are buried in the corrals. Dancing on New Year's day, the installation of the annual officers having been transferred to December 29 to leave January 1 free for the dance. On Kings' Day, January 6, Buffalo and Deer dance* and Matachina dance. The officers' canes are aspersed in church. During Holy Week, Frog feast, there are kachina dances and on Easter Sunday the *tablita* Saint's-day dance. There are two saint's-day celebrations, on August 2, the Pecos fiesta of Porcingula, and on November 12, the fiesta of San Diego (Santiago), patron of Jemez.

In January one of the two Men's societies, Eagle society, is in retreat for four days, in Turquoise kiva. The War chief's fetish is on the altar. The day they come out they dance kachina and race with the clowns. A maskless personage who overtakes a runner smears him with black paint for good luck in hunting. The other Men's society, Arrow society, conducts its ceremony in the autumn, in Turquoise kiva.

In February, before and after work begins on the ditches, there is a series of kick-stick races, by kiva. Two are followed by a circle dance, in honor of the Governor who superintends the main ditch by the river and of the Fiscales who superintend the main interior ditch. Before the water is run in, one of the societies is asked to deposit prayer-sticks.

In March the two societies, Morning Star and Cactus (? Paste-together society), hold a joint ceremony against cold, to further the spring thaw.

Immediately after the summer solstice ceremony begins the first of the two series of retreats or fasts by the six major societies in the following order: Underchiefs or War society, Ts'un'ta-

---

* Of the San Felipe, Cochiti, Tesuque type: One Buffalo woman, two Buffalo men and two boy Antelope come in from the eastern hills at dawn; they are followed by a separate group of six Deer, six Antelope, and two Mountain Sheep. Choir and drummers (6). Buffalo woman with a Buffalo man on either side dance in center between two lines (King, B. M., citing R. A. Keech).

tabö'sh clown society, Tabö'sh clown society, Arrowhead society, Fire society, Eagle-watchers or Flute society. After a lapse of two weeks the series is repeated. In the second or autumn series the succeeding set go in the night of the day following the day the preceding set come out, but in the summer series there is a "four-day" interval between retreats, "they want to make the summer longer." The Snake society holds a summer retreat.

Each of the six major societies is possessed of a Water Serpent image, which is brought in from its spring to the society's altar on the first day of the retreat, when the altar is laid. In the autumn series a public dance is held after each retreat or a two-day dance at the conclusion of the series. This program is planned by the Council, but the society in retreat actually invites the group that is to dance. Hopi dance, which is a maskless kachina dance, is always the second dance in the series, for there is always a morning race and, not being a mask dance involving kiva retreat, Hopi dance does not interfere with the race.

About the middle of October the Town chief's corn crop is harvested. That morning the Women's societies deposit the prayer-sticks they made the preceding day.

On All Souls' Night feathers and food are given to the Dead. Four days after the saint's-day celebration on November 12, Arrow society holds its retreat for four days in Turquoise kiva, concluding with a kachina dance. Follows a retreat in Squash kiva by Ts'un'tatabö'sh clown society.

ISLETA[45]

The winter solstice is referred to as "North our Father goes," but there is no solar observation; December 4 and June 4 are set for the beginning of the solstice ceremonies which may continue until the twentieth. These four-day ceremonies by the Corn groups and the curing societies consist of rites of emesis, fasting, continence, and hair-washing, of making prayer-feathers and prayer-sticks, singing and taking dance steps, of drawing down the Sun, throwing prayer-meal to Sun, Moon, and Stars, and to the Water people, emersing stone fetishes in medicine water, smoking, sprinkling water from corn ears or feathers, spraying root medicine over the meal altar, etc. On the last day all the group members attend to contribute food and to get a medicine drink and some meal from the altar-painting. Infants are brought in "to get their (corn) name." In conclusion a prayer-stick is taken to the shrine of the Stillborn.

On December 12, "Guadalupe Day," young boys dance from house to house for the Virgin of Guadalupe, the inmates giving them bread and doughnuts or a meal at table. During Christmas week this domiciliary dancing will be repeated at night by boys and girls, dancing Navaho dance or a bird dance.

About December 15, after advising with the Town chief, Kumpawithlawe, War chief and Snake chief, holds his cere-mony of bringing in the Horned Serpent, Rattlesnake, from the mountain cave where he lives. All the ceremonialists are present, but no women or youths. On a buckskin, lightning designs are made with "powders" and on top of meal are set fetishes, arrow-point, pollen bag, and prayer-meal basket. Kumpa brings in Lightning and then the Serpent, his "father," who sucks in the pollen and meal offered him. The Serpent hisses to exorcise the town. Nobody is out that night, and the women close their doors and windows.

December 25–28, several kinds of "Christmas dances," by moiety, men and women dancing together, in alternating sets, Black Eyes and Red Eyes. Comanche may be danced by men. Christmas night the dancing is inside the church; by day in the churchyard or in front of the houses of the chiefs. Presents are thrown to the dancers. The War captains are in charge.

January 6, Kings' Day, the canes of the new annual officers are sprinkled with holy water in the church by the priest. The Laguna colonists may dance Nareipöa, Kings' dance, at vespers, January 5, in the church, and for five days in the churchyard, before the houses of the newly installed officers and in their kachina dance place near the race track. The men bear back tablets of Sun and Moon and carry spruce. The women wear head plumes. Six Isletan Black Eyes and six Red Eyes appointed by the War captain join the Laguna dancers. The night of the concluding day of the dance by the Laguna neighbors, January

10, the Town chief summons all the chiefs and the War captains to his ceremonial house for a night ceremony with sunrise ritual; an order is sent to the curing societies to hold their ceremony of communal exorcism. Now the Town Fathers and the Laguna Fathers go in for four days, fasting completely from food and drink. The War captains call out forbidding outside fires, digging the ground, going out to work; but the town itself is literally cleaned up, and a rabbit hunt is managed by the War chief and his captains. In the final ceremony the society chiefs send out two members with a War captain to notify the Chiefs of the Directions to attend, and if necessary to fight the witch chief with his bundle of all the pests of the fields. Members go out "to clean with their feathers" all the ceremonial houses, the plaza, the corrals into which all the horses have been brought, and the river. The chief chews his narcotic root and goes into a trancelike state, sending his "heart" around the world. After crystal-gazing to find the sick, witch-sent objects will be pressed out of them. Follow jugglery with a rabbit, with sprouting corn and wheat (the advance crops), with drawing kernels from wall pictures, and a conclusive drink of medicine to all present.

With the permission of the Town chief a kachina basket dance may be given any time during the winter. The man who asks for the dance beats on a bundled sheep pelt. He wears little deer horns, and, as he is called *thliwa* (Isleta for kachina), he is presumably a kachina impersonation. Four male dancers, in buckskin mantle with a headdress of turkey-tail feathers; bow and arrow in left hand, gourd rattle in right. Three female impersonators carry an arrow in the right hand, a basket in the left. The dance is in a borrowed house. The Land Turtle dance in February is also a kachina dance, with the moiety chiefs as managers. Alternate sets of dancers, the moiety masks in attendance. These, the Grandfathers, have given permission to catch the turtles which belong to the Winter moiety. Shichu chief presents a dance in the evening "to call" the snow or rain, members of his Corn group being the dancers. At this time infants may be given to the group.

When work starts on the big ditch the Town chief, Kumpa,

the War chief, and the moiety chiefs begin to fast.* On the fourth morning before running the water, all these chiefs throw prayer-feathers into the river to pay the Water People, also bits from the bundles of sample crops carried by the moiety chiefs. By moiety, men make offerings of black or red pigment to the Sun. The procession back to town is met by the women who throw prayer-meal on the moiety bundles, which in the plaza are exposed to view. Ritual follows in the house of the Town chief, and then the moiety chiefs give people permission to dance the round dance, each moiety making its own circle of men and women.

Dark kachina is a spring dance for the crops. Men go to White Eagle Mountain where the kachina live for spruce for the dancers and on returning sing satiric songs. The moiety masks come out with the dance sets. A rabbit hunt concludes the four-day ceremony.

In the spring occur the races of the Town chief who "clothes the Sun and helps him run—that is why they run east and west." At midnight offerings are buried in the middle of the race track, and the next morning anyone may get a drink of medicine water at the house of the Town chief. On the four posts of the Black Eyes round kiva and in the *sipapu* medicine is sprinkled by the Town chief and Shichu chief; the Town chief makes a meal road for the Sun, and as the sun shines through the roof hole the Town chief sprinkles the sunspot with pollen. The runners are chosen for speed, not by moiety. Kinswomen of the winner carry baskets of groceries to the kiva for the chiefs, Town chief, Kumpa, and War chief, for the *loser* to share with all the runners and for Kumpa to sprinkle in bits below the wall niche of the Scalps. The race of the fourth Sunday is run by Corn groups or by the suburbs, with no ritual and more betting. On Easter Sunday there is a race by the little boys painted on the back with a chicken-hawk or rabbit or turtle. The year of the Scalp ceremony the racers ask help of the Scalps as well as of the Sun.

When the Town chief decides upon holding the Scalp ceremony, after a four-day fast the Scalp-takers and young men

* For suggested interpretation see p. 1083, n.*.

carry the Scalps out of town to an overnight camp. The chiefs meet them on their return, the War chief making the meal road A Scalp is carried on a lance; formerly the woman custodian carried the Scalps on her back. A dance in the plaza, the Scalp-takers singing in Navaho. Next day the race by Corn group. At night the dance around the Scalp.

June 16 or 17, "saint go around day," Little St. Agustin's Day. Gifts in wheat or money are made to the priest to say Mass for the saint. Four women carry the saint, from farm to farm, for rain and crops, and against grasshoppers. Late in the after-noon a dance in which the saint is carried all about the town.

Saint John's Day, June 24, men visit the houses where live persons named for the saint, Juan or Juana, who give a cock or a large round cake also called "cock." The first cock or cake received is carried to the church. Rooster pull. Mexican dancing at night.

St. Peter's Day, June 29. Two sets of men carry the banners of St. Peter and St. Paul through the fields. They pull up sprouting corn. When the sets meet, they whip at each other with big whips, the banner bearers running off to the houses where live persons named for the saints, who give sweet bread to be left with the corn sprouts in the church.

The twelve-day summer rain ceremony is in the house of the Town chief. His corn fetish and those of the chiefs of the curing societies are on the altar. The medicine chiefs go forth by their "power" to clean the springs. The last night is open to all; but women rarely attend as they fear the ritual display of thunder and lightning. In the plaza the Town chief and the chief of the Town Fathers "sink into the ground" to ask Węide for rain.

St. Agustin's Day, August 28. The church is whitewashed; the churchyard walls are plastered. In the corners of the plaza bowers are built and under them altars set out, two for Mexicans, four for Isleta and her colonies. Children in veils follow the priest, and the people in two lines throw flowers.

The night of September 25, Chakabede makes a meal road for the kachina from Welima, Zuni Mountain, a maskless imper-sonation who dances and hollers and receives prayer-sticks from

Chakabede. This appearance is followed by a four-day retreat in kivas by the dancers Chakabede has asked of the moiety chiefs. Spruce is fetched with ritual. From each kiva there are six K'apio as dance managers. The Black Eye K'apio are striped black and white with hair whitened and worn in whorls at the side like a girl. The Red Eye K'apio are painted in solid colors, red, yellow or white, their hair in a poke on top of head. The K'apio make a "house" on the ground to which their "aunts" bring food, and where they perform a marriage farce. Chakabede and his assistant lead in the two dance lines. The dancers wear a collar and armlets and leglets of spruce and spruce pendents from their belt. Flowing hair and a *tablita*. Three men play the notched-bone rasps. The K'apio stay all night in kiva and come out at sunrise to dance on the roofs. A rabbit hunt is in order conducted by the K'apio and the Hunt chief. The game the K'apio get they pay to their "aunts."

Sporadically in the autumn Salt Woman is "brought in" to the Black Eyes' round house. "They clean her veins." It is a dangerous ceremony for at it anybody with bad thoughts is subject to be turned into an animal. After the harvest, late in October, the Hunt chief holds his ceremony to draw in deer or rabbits for the Town chief. Hunt chief calls like wolf or mountain lion and the game animals walk into his house into his circle of pollen, through its gap on the east side. Hunt chief closes the gap and kills the animal with his ritual club.

November 1, All Saints. November 2, "Dead day." People take food to the graveyard and light a candle on the graves of their dead. Subsequently all these offerings go to the priest who sells them to the Mexicans.